Praise for Psalms Through the Centuries: Volume One

"A most impressive piece of work ... The coverage is truly encyclopaedic in scope and nothing seems to have escaped Gillingham's attention."
Journal for the Study of the Old Testament

"Gillingham meticulously masters the diverse reception history of the psalms ... Every page is bursting with solid research and influential insight. An invaluable addition to the field."
Religious Studies Review

"This wonderful book whets the appetite both for its second volume, and for more volumes of this valuable series ... [A] highly innovative and promising project."
International Review of Biblical Studies

"This book is a breakthrough in our understanding of the reception history of the Psalter. It will appeal to scholars and students of the Psalms and also to everyone who uses and prays them. The scope is extraordinarily wide and covers both Jewish and Christian use of the Psalms over nearly three thousand years."
John Barton, University of Oxford

"As liturgical and devotional texts the Psalms occupy a unique place in Jewish and Christian tradition. In this impressively wide ranging study, Sue Gillingham explores how over the centuries the Psalms have inspired, been prayed, analyzed, interpreted and spoken with an extraordinary resonance to many kinds of human need. Musicians, liturgists and students of literature as well as theologians, clergy and Christian and Jewish teachers, will find fresh perspectives and new insights in this magisterial survey. We await with anticipation the second volume in which against this background the interpretation of individual psalms will be considered."
The Rt Revd Dr Geoffrey Rowell, Diocese of Europe

Blackwell Bible Commentaries

Series Editors: John Sawyer, Christopher Rowland, Judith Kovacs, David M. Gunn

John Through the Centuries
Mark Edwards

Revelation Through the Centuries
Judith Kovacs & Christopher Rowland

Judges Through the Centuries
David M. Gunn

Exodus Through the Centuries
Scott M. Langston

Ecclesiastes Through the Centuries
Eric S. Christianson

Esther Through the Centuries
Jo Carruthers

Psalms Through the Centuries: Volume I
Susan Gillingham

Galatians Through the Centuries
John Riches

Pastoral Epistles Through the Centuries
Jay Twomey

1 & 2 Thessalonians Through the Centuries
Anthony C. Thiselton

Six Minor Prophets Through the Centuries
By Richard Coggins and Jin H. Han

Forthcoming:

1 & 2 Samuel Through the Centuries
David M. Gunn

1 & 2 Kings Through the Centuries
Martin O'Kane

Psalms Through the Centuries: Volume II
Susan Gillingham

Song of Songs Through the Centuries
Fiona Black

Isaiah Through the Centuries
John F. A. Sawyer

Jeremiah Through the Centuries
Mary Chilton Callaway

Lamentations Through the Centuries
Paul M. Joyce and Diane Lipton

Ezekiel Through the Centuries
Andrew Mein

Jonah Through the Centuries
Yvonne Sherwood

Mark Through the Centuries
Christine Joynes

The Acts of the Apostles Through the Centuries
By Mikeal C. Parsons and Heidi J. Hornik

Romans Through the Centuries
Paul Fiddes

1 Corinthians Through the Centuries
Jorunn Okland

Hebrews Through the Centuries
John Lyons

James Through the Centuries
David Gowler

Genesis 1-21 Through the Centuries
Christopher Heard

Genesis 22-50 Through the Centuries
Christopher Heard

Deuteronomy Through the Centuries
Jonathan Campbell

Daniel Through the Centuries
Dennis Tucker

Psalms Through the Centuries

Volume One

Susan Gillingham

WILEY-BLACKWELL
A John Wiley & Sons, Ltd., Publication

This paperback edition first published 2012
© 2012 Susan Gillingham

Edition History: Blackwell Publishing Ltd (hardback, 2008)

Blackwell Publishing was acquired by John Wiley & Sons in February 2007. Blackwell's publishing program has been merged with Wiley's global Scientific, Technical, and Medical business to form Wiley-Blackwell.

Registered Office
John Wiley & Sons Ltd, The Atrium, Southern Gate, Chichester, West Sussex, PO19 8SQ, UK

Editorial Offices
350 Main Street, Malden, MA 02148-5020, USA
9600 Garsington Road, Oxford, OX4 2DQ, UK
The Atrium, Southern Gate, Chichester, West Sussex, PO19 8SQ, UK

For details of our global editorial offices, for customer services, and for information about how to apply for permission to reuse the copyright material in this book please see our website at www.wiley.com/wiley-blackwell.

The right of Susan Gillingham to be identified as the author of this work has been asserted in accordance with the UK Copyright, Designs and Patents Act 1988.

All rights reserved. No part of this publication may be reproduced, stored in a retrieval system, or transmitted, in any form or by any means, electronic, mechanical, photocopying, recording or otherwise, except as permitted by the UK Copyright, Designs and Patents Act 1988, without the prior permission of the publisher.

Wiley also publishes its books in a variety of electronic formats. Some content that appears in print may not be available in electronic books.

Designations used by companies to distinguish their products are often claimed as trademarks. All brand names and product names used in this book are trade names, service marks, trademarks or registered trademarks of their respective owners. The publisher is not associated with any product or vendor mentioned in this book. This publication is designed to provide accurate and authoritative information in regard to the subject matter covered. It is sold on the understanding that the publisher is not engaged in rendering professional services. If professional advice or other expert assistance is required, the services of a competent professional should be sought.

Library of Congress Cataloging-in-Publication Data

Gillingham, S. E. (Susan E.)
  Psalms through the centuries / Susan Gillingham.
      p.   cm.—(Blackwell Bible commentaries)
  Includes bibliographical references and index.
  ISBN 978-0-631-21855-5 (hardcover : alk. paper) ISBN 978-0-470-67490-1 (paperback: alk.paper)
  1. Bible. O.T. Psalms—Commentaries.   I. Title.
  BS1430.53.G55 2007
  223'.207—dc22
                                                  2007013646

A catalogue record for this title is available from the British Library.

Set in 10/12pt Minion by SPi Publisher Services, Pondicherry, India
Printed in Malaysia by Ho Printing (M) Sdn Bhd

1   2012

For Dick
driver, cook, fiercest critic, closest friend
Little by little, one travels far.
(J.R.R. Tolkien)

BS
1430.53
.G55
2008
v.1

List of Illustrations	xi
Series Editors' Preface	xiii
Preface	xv
Preface to the Paperback Edition	xvii
Works Cited	xix
Introduction: Towards a Reception-History Commentary on the Psalms	1

1 **The Eleventh Century BCE to the Fifth Century CE: Translation, Exposition, Instruction, Liturgy and the Prophetic Bias**   5
    Jewish Reception   5
        From Composition to Compilation to Translation   5

	Exposition: The Prophetic Bias	9
	Instruction through Imitations of Psalms	11
	Christian Reception	13
	The Psalms as Prophecies in the New Testament	14
	The Psalms as Prophecies in the Church Fathers	24
	Alexandrian Commentators	28
	Liturgical Adaptations of the Psalms	40
	Christian Liturgy	40
	Jewish Liturgy	43
	Concluding Observations	46
2	**The Fifth to Eleventh Centuries: Liturgy, Exposition, Artistic Representation**	**47**
	Christian Reception	47
	Liturgy	47
	Exposition, Homily, Translation	55
	Artistic Representation	62
	Jewish Reception	68
	Liturgy	68
	Translation, Exposition, Homily	71
	Artistic Representation	75
	Concluding Observations	75
3	**The Eleventh to Fifteenth Centuries: Learning and Discerning**	**77**
	Jewish and Christian Controversies through Exegetical Works	77
	Preliminary Considerations	77
	Jewish Commentators	82
	Christian Commentators	87
	Christian and Jewish Artists	95
	Christian Illumination	95
	Jewish Illumination	104
	Christian and Jewish Didactic Works	113
	Christian Writers	113
	Jewish Writers	117
	Christian and Jewish Liturgy	120
	Christian Adaptations	120
	Jewish Adaptations	123
	Translation in Christian Tradition	123
	Concluding Observations	130
4	**The Fifteenth to Seventeenth Centuries: Democratization and Dissemination**	**131**

	Reception as Translation: Christian Responses	131
	Commentary, Liturgy, Homily and Translation on the Continent	131
	Liturgy, Homily and Translation in England and Scotland	146
	Reception as Aesthetic Representation: Jewish and Christian Responses	163
	Jewish Reception through Art and Music	163
	Christian Reception through Art, Literary Imitation and Music	166
	Concluding Observations	190
5	**The Eighteenth and Nineteenth Centuries: Secularization and Revitalization**	**192**
	Christian Responses	194
	Exegetical Works	194
	Devotional Works	203
	Musical Reception	220
	Reception through Liturgy	228
	Translations of Psalmody	230
	Jewish Responses	234
	Reception as Translation and Liturgy	234
	Reception as Homily and Exegesis	237
	Aesthetic Responses	239
	Concluding Observations	240
6	**The Twentieth to Twenty-First Centuries: Pluralism and Ecumenism**	**242**
	Christian and Jewish Translations of Psalmody	246
	Liturgy and Psalmody in Christian and Jewish Traditions	254
	Exegetical Studies, Christian and Jewish	266
	Devotional Works, Christian and Jewish	282
	Aesthetic Responses, Christian and Jewish	290
	Concluding Observations	307
	Conclusion: From Introduction to Commentary	309
	Glossary	313
	References	322
	Index of Psalms	351
	Index of Names	361
	Subject Index	368

Illustrations

Figures

Colour plates fall between pp. 4 and 5.

0.1	Psalm 1 from the *Utrecht Psalter*.	
0.2	Psalm 150 in Chichester Cathedral by Marc Chagall.	
3.1	*St Albans Psalter*, Psalm 72.	100
3.2	*Luttrell Psalter*: a Christian illustration of Psalm 137.	106
3.3	*Parma Psalter*: a Jewish illustration of Psalm 137.	107

3.4	Jewish psalms and Arabic art in El Tránsito synagogue, Toledo.	110
3.5	Illustration of Psalms 113 and 114 in the Prato Haggadah.	112
5.1	Illustration of Psalm 2 in the Pictorial Sunday book.	232
5.2	Illustration of Psalm 3 in the Pictorial Sunday book.	232
5.3	Illustration of Psalm 8 in the Pictorial Sunday book.	233
5.4	Illustration of Psalm 12 in the Pictorial Sunday book.	233
6.1	Psalm 142 by Arthur Wragg.	294
6.2	Psalm 22 by Arthur Wragg.	295
6.3	Psalm 148 by Michael Jessing.	296
6.4	Psalm 42 by Roger Wagner.	297

Maps

1.1	Jerusalem: the centre of psalmody for early Jewish and Christian communities.	6
2.1	Rome: a centre of psalmody in the early Middle Ages.	48
3.1	France: a centre of psalmody in the later Middle Ages.	78
4.1	From England, Scotland and western Europe to the New World: centres of psalmody during Reformation and Commonwealth times.	132
5.1	Great Britain, Europe and America: the spread of psalmody during the Enlightenment period.	193
6.1	Great Britain and the English-speaking world: the spread of psalmody within the twentieth century.	243

Series Editors' Preface

The Blackwell Bible Commentaries series, the first to be devoted primarily to the reception history of the Bible, is based on the premise that how people have interpreted, and been influenced by, a sacred text like the Bible is often as interesting and historically important as what it originally meant. The series emphasizes the influence of the Bible on literature, art, music, and film, its role in the evolution of religious beliefs and practices, and its impact on social and political developments. Drawing on work in a variety of disciplines, it is designed to provide a convenient and scholarly means of access to material until now hard to find, and a much-needed resource for all those interested in the influence of the Bible on western culture.

Until quite recently this whole dimension was for the most part neglected by biblical scholars. The goal of a commentary was primarily if not exclusively to get behind the centuries of accumulated Christian and Jewish tradition to one single meaning, normally identified with the author's original intention.

The most important and distinctive feature of the Blackwell Commentaries is that they will present readers with many different interpretations of each text, in such a way as to heighten their awareness of what a text, especially a sacred text, can mean and what it can do, what it has meant and what it has done, in the many contexts in which it operates.

The Blackwell Bible Commentaries will consider patristic, rabbinic (where relevant), and medieval exegesis as well as insights from various types of modern criticism, acquainting readers with a wide variety of interpretative techniques. As part of the history of interpretation, questions of source, date, authorship, and other historical-critical and archaeological issues will be discussed, but since these are covered extensively in existing commentaries, such references will be brief, serving to point readers in the direction of readily accessible literature where they can be followed up.

Original to this series is the consideration of the reception history of specific biblical books arranged in commentary format. The chapter-by-chapter arrangement ensures that the biblical text is always central to the discussion. Given the wide influence of the Bible and the richly varied appropriation of each biblical book, it is a difficult question which interpretations to include. While each volume will have its own distinctive point of view, the guiding principle for the series as a whole is that readers should be given a representative sampling of material from different ages, with emphasis on interpretations that have been especially influential or historically significant. Though commentators will have their preferences among the different interpretations, the material will be presented in such a way that readers can make up their own minds on the value, morality, and validity of particular interpretations.

The series encourages readers to consider how the biblical text has been interpreted down the ages and seeks to open their eyes to different uses of the Bible in contemporary culture. The aim is to write a series of scholarly commentaries that draw on all the insights of modern research to illustrate the rich interpretative potential of each biblical book.

John Sawyer
Christopher Rowland
Judith Kovacs
David M. Gunn

Preface

This, the first volume of two on the Psalms in this series, has itself undergone some reception history, albeit over only ten years. I am most grateful to the Theology Faculty at Oxford University for constantly providing me with funding for research assistants, without whom this book would not have emerged. From 1997 to 2002 graduates from Worcester College – Andrew Hudson, Sharon Moughtin-Mumby, Chessie Stavrakapoulou and Helenann Hartley – spent tracts of time, usually for one year each, and between them they set this project in motion. Then between 2002 and 2004, first Abbie and then Esther Gillingham built upon their foundation, searching out and cataloguing copies of countless books, papers and websites, and setting up an effective database from which I could work on this volume and the next. I am indebted to all of them for their different ways in keeping me going when the task seemed too great (the bibliography in this book and on the website represent only a third of the resources used).

When research turned into writing, and I needed space away from the administrative pressures of Oxford, I used parts of two sabbatical summers at a wonderful hideaway in Nassau, a setting close to paradise, through the gracious invitation of Rubie and Kendal Nottage. There I wrote most of the first chapter, and later, much of the fourth. The Diocese of the Bahamas has become inextricably linked with the project, and I am profoundly grateful for their affirmation and hospitality. More close to home, Burford Priory, near Oxford, has been a constant spiritual resource and I am similarly grateful to Abbot Stuart OSB and the whole community for their encouragement and prayerful support.

Between 2004 and 2007 other students have given a good deal of time to this project, of whom Hannah Cleugh and Sheenagh Nixon deserve especial mention. My deepest debt is to Natasha O'Hear, who has worked with me throughout most of this period, and because her own research overlaps with mine, her intuition and organizational skills have been invaluable.

My Oxford colleagues have been most supportive. Christopher Rowland, as one of the editors of the series, has been a wise counsellor from the outset. John Barton went far beyond the call of duty and read the entire manuscript: I am constantly indebted to his shrewd suggestions and his unassuming encouragement. Within my Faculty, other colleagues, too numerous to mention, have offered their expertise in matters of church history, liturgy, literature, art and music, and this volume would have been much impoverished without their advice. Further afield, Geoffrey Rowell has been singularly generous, despite his intense schedule travelling within and beyond Europe, in finding the time to read the manuscript in full and to make constructive and perceptive suggestions. John Sawyer, another editor of the series with responsibility for the Old Testament, has also been unstinting with his time and in reading the manuscript he has been an unfailing source of advice, information and enthusiasm.

The team at Blackwell Publishing has been most helpful, particularly in the last stages. Andrew Humphries, the commissioning editor, Bridget Jennings, the senior publishing coordinator, Karen Wilson, the editorial controller, Helen Nash, the picture researcher, Caroline Milton, the senior production controller, and Annette Abel, my copy editor, have been firm and affirming in equal measure. I tested their patience in several ways – not least in issues of the word limit – but they have enabled me to produce a more polished work whose deficiencies can now only be my own responsibility.

Throughout this period I have made life difficult not only for Abbie and Esther, by being constantly distracted even in apparently free time, but also for my husband, Richard Smethurst. I owe each of them a huge debt. He in particular has unfailingly believed in this project, and although he has been partly compensated by our research travels in Europe and America, he has borne the brunt of late-night and long-weekend working – without too many complaints. Further, as a 'non-theologian', he has read and corrected the manuscript with terrifying attention to detail and historical sense. It is most appropriate that this work, which he has both loved and loathed, should be dedicated to him.

Preface to the Paperback Edition

In the four years since the publication of this volume in hardback, several relevant works have appeared. Some have started with a particular psalm and looked at its influence in just one cultural context; others have begun with a particular interpreter and looked at the use of relevant psalms within a defined period; whilst others are edited works of experts writing on the reception history of just one psalm, of which *Psalm 29 through Time and Tradition* (ed. L Handy: Eugenem Ore.: Pickwick, 2009) is a good example. Dictionaries and encyclopaedias on reception history are also beginning to appear. First, de Gruyter's thirty-volume project, *The Encyclopedia of the Bible and its Reception* had its initial publication in 2010: it is a survey of what is currently known of the origins and reception of the Bible in literature, art, music and film, in Jewish and Christian tradition, Western and non-Western traditions alike. The entry on the Psalms is several years away. Secondly, OUP published in 2011 *The Oxford Handbook of the Reception History of the Bible* with one chapter on the reception history of the Psalms by Katharine Dell (pp. 37-51). Thirdly, John Sawyer, one of the Blackwell editors in this Series, has produced his *Concise Dictionary of the Bible and its Reception* (Westminster John Knox, 2009). It has a brief but seminal entry on the psalms and their afterlife (pp. 214-215) and also includes several allusions to the psalms in other entries, as seen in the index (pp. 287-288).

Despite these new developments, this paperback edition of Volume One of *Psalms through the Centuries* is still unique. There is nothing quite like this one-authored paperback work on the reception history of psalmody, unified by one method and one purpose. Furthermore, Volume Two, a commentary on the Jewish and Christian reception of all the psalms, will also be distinctive. Each psalm will be presented as an 'anthology with a purpose', with its own distinctive reception history and its peculiar issues of interpretation. So the paperback edition of this, the first volume, is not only a means of making it easier for colleagues to purchase their own individual copies: it also announces that Volume Two, which will be a very different Psalms Commentary in its reception history focus on all the psalms, is to follow.

Works Cited

Numbers of psalms and verses from psalms always accord with the *NRSV* unless otherwise stated.

The size of the bibliography has meant that books and articles not explicitly used in the text have been placed on the Wiley website (www.wiley.com/go/gillingham) and are indicated in the footnotes by the use of italic script. All the website addresses found throughout this work are listed on the Bible Commentaries website at www.bbibcomm.net/.

Asterisks indicate terms explained in the glossary.

Introduction: Towards a Reception-History Commentary on the Psalms

Given the central place of the palms in both Jewish and Christian reception history, it is surprising that only two other works of this nature have previously been published. R.E. Prothero's *The Psalms in Human Life* (1903) is an intriguing study of the use of the psalms in the lives of individuals from early Christianity to 1900, whilst W.L. Holladay's *The Psalms through Three Thousand Years* (1993) is a more systematic treatment of the Jewish and Christian use of the psalms from their inception 'in David's day' up to the end of the twentieth century, focusing on Psalm 23. This book is closer to Holladay's in that it looks at the reception of psalmody through commentary, homily, translation, liturgy, literature, music and art. Its purpose, however, is different, for it is the first of two volumes, setting the scene for a forthcoming reception-history commentary on individual psalms.

A work of this sort has the inevitable problem of particularity. I write as an English-speaking Anglican woman, and it is impossible not to prefer some types of reception above others, however open-minded and even-handed I seek to be. Selecting what material to use has been difficult. Although nearly four thousand works have been consulted, the breadth of the project has meant that the discussion, footnotes and bibliography represent a small proportion of more detailed research. Furthermore, I have found a 'word-centred' survey of psalmody somewhat restrictive: other ways of 'hearing and seeing the psalms', not least through liturgy, prayer, music and art, have had to be described rather than experienced. And not only is this project necessarily selective, it is also diffuse. The maps at the beginning of each chapter illustrate the geographical expansion as psalmody spreads out from the Levant eastwards and westwards, eventually reaching the New World and beyond. (The book has an intentional bias towards psalmody in the English-speaking world, and from the fifteenth century onwards, in Britain in particular.)

The chapters are divided into six periods which each suggest different changes of emphasis in the reception of psalmody in both Jewish and Christian traditions. Each chapter looks at five types of reception history. The first is reception through *exposition*, and mainly comprises commentaries and introductions which expound the texts and ancient contexts of the psalms and their relationship with other parts of Scripture. The second is reception through *instruction*, and this includes sermons, tractates and devotional works, whereby the moral and spiritual meaning of psalmody is uppermost. The third is reception through *liturgy*; this is about the adaptation of the psalms both within public worship and in private prayer. The fourth is reception through *translation* – for example, from Hebrew into Greek, Latin, Aramaic and Syriac in the earliest periods, and (for our purposes) into Middle English, Elizabethan English and contemporary English. The fifth type is reception through *aesthetic representation*, which includes not only literary and poetic imitations, but also music, architecture and art.

The six chapters illustrate how these modes of reception function in different ways. The first, from the time of the Davidic monarchy in about 1000 BCE up to the fifth century of the Christian era, begins in an exclusively Jewish context, where expositions, didactic works and translations each suggest a bias towards interpreting the psalms as prophecies anticipating future redemption. This prophetic bias continues within the earliest Christian reception, both within the New Testament and within the writings of the early church fathers, particularly in the debates about the churches' relationship with Judaism and with the Graeco-Roman world; it is seen especially in commentaries, works of instruction and translations, and so follows a similar pattern to the ways in which the psalms were understood in Judaism. The difference is that the psalms are now read as prophecies which have been fulfilled, so that the 'psalms of David' are now seen as 'psalms of (and to) Christ'; by the end of this period, the different interpretations of psalmody within the two faiths are clearly apparent.

The second chapter covers the fifth to eleventh centuries, and illustrates first the innovations in the liturgical use of the psalms, both in Judaism and Christianity, both in public and private. Liturgical renewal brings about a proliferation of commentaries and devotional works, again with each faith tradition claiming the psalms as their own. This period ends with a striking innovation in Christian interpretation, namely the illuminations of psalm manuscripts, which enables theological difference to be expressed not only verbally but also in artistic representation.

In the third period, which encompasses the eleventh to fifteenth centuries, liturgy, instruction and exposition are the most prevalent modes of reception, and here we find evidence of acrimonious debates between Jews and Christians as to their variant different readings of particular psalms. Artistic representation continues, with some illumination now evident in Jewish prayer books. This period ends with another development in Christian tradition, namely the appearance of the psalms in literary works as well as in some experimental translations in Middle English.

In the fourth period, comprising the fifteenth to seventeenth centuries, two trends are particularly evident in Christian reception: that of further translation (which in turn influences liturgical renewal, poetic imitations and devotional works), and that of representations of psalmody through music as well as through art. Jewish reception, by contrast, reflects less concern for either translation or musical reception: there are some notable exceptions, but here there is more continuity with the previous centuries, especially in expositions and devotional works.

In the fifth period – the eighteenth and nineteenth centuries – innovations in Christian reception include expository works of a more rational and critical nature, which contrast starkly with other more spiritual studies and aesthetic works. Jewish reception comprises more liturgical and devotional works, although there is now increasing evidence of aesthetic representations.

The sixth period, covering the twentieth century up to the present day, illustrates just how much all five modes of reception co-exist in each faith tradition. A plethora of translations and liturgical innovations are most evident in Christian reception, most of which serve an ecumenical purpose. Furthermore, the wide variety of exegetical, didactic and aesthetic responses contributes to draw more closely together – in effect for the first time – Jewish and Christian interpretations. Alongside this more positive state of affairs, with the psalms offering new ways of reconciling differences both within each faith tradition and between them, there is a downside, because the vast amount of innovation and experimentation (particularly with the language of the psalms) begins to result in a loss of discourse with the rich heritage of the past.

This, then, is a skeleton outline of what readers will find in this book, whose purpose is to explore further the ways in which the five modes of reception wax and wane through the six different periods of reception history. It is a 'macro' look at the Psalter as a whole, with individual psalms used as illustrations, whilst the forthcoming commentary will be a 'micro' study of the reception history of individual psalms. One contribution this first volume makes to the second is that it allows us to determine which psalms have the richest reception history, and so which deserve the most attention by way of commentary (the index of psalms referred to here should be helpful in this respect). We should also be able to ascertain which stages in Jewish and Christian history use certain psalms, and which psalms illustrate specific issues of interpretation throughout their reception history.

Psalm 8 is a significant example in this respect. As will be seen in the following pages, it is frequently referred to by both Jews and Christians, and the most critical different stages in its reception history include the very earliest period, the Middle Ages, the Reformation period and the twentieth century: hence a commentary must focus on these periods. Psalm 8 also reflects one overriding issue throughout the history of interpretation – namely, the very different way it has been interpreted by Jews and Christians, and this is seen in four of the five modes of reception. The earliest controversies hinge upon different views about its *translation* (particularly of a verse in the middle of the psalm which speaks of 'the son of man') from the Hebrew into Greek, then into Latin, and eventually into English, particularly during the Middle Ages and the Reformation and then into contemporary times.

The contentions about translation have in turn generated a large number of *commentaries* and *devotional* works, which epitomize the division of opinion between Jews and Christians on various points of meaning, with Jewish interpreters favouring the psalm as a hymn about creation and Christian interpreters preferring to see it as a song of redemption – or a prophecy about the person and work of Jesus Christ now having been fulfilled. Jewish and Christian *artistic* portrayals of Psalm 8 illustrate further these differences. So in terms of translation, exegesis, devotional works and representation in art, Psalm 8 is rich in reception. The only type of representation not as prominent in this psalm is in fact the liturgical one; and because the psalm does not play a major part in many Jewish or Christian festivals apart from Ascension Day, its reception in liturgical terms means that its reception in musical terms is not notable either. A reception-history commentary will offer more specific illustrations of this particular psalm, but it should be possible to see how this first volume on the Psalter as a whole forms the backcloth against which individual psalms can be seen in clearer outline.[1]

In fact, reception study of psalmody, whether in a 'macro' or 'micro' form, can act as a prism to enable us to see larger issues at work in both Judaism and Christianity and their interaction with the cultures around them. This is not surprising; the Psalter has of course been a vital resource for defining both the Jewish and Christian faiths, both in public debate and in private reflection, a theme which will recur constantly throughout this book.

---

[1] For a fuller reception history of Psalm 8 see S. Gillingham (2007) (forthcoming).

FIGURE 0.1 Psalm 1 from the Utrecht *Psalter*: a ninth-century Christian illustration teaching the literal meaning of the first psalm, from a workshop in Rheims.
Source: Utrecht Psalter, psalm 1, f. iv, University Library Utrecht (Photography Frans L.T. Verdonk and Erik C.B.M. de Groot).

FIGURE 0.2 Psalm 150 in Chichester Cathedral by Marc Chagall: a twentieth-century celebration of Psalm 150 by a Jewish artist for Christian worship, also crafted at a workshop in Rheims.
Source: The Dean and Chapter of Chichester Cathedral. © ADAGP, Paris and DACS, London 2007.

The Eleventh Century BCE to the Fifth Century CE: Translation, Exposition, Instruction, Liturgy and the Prophetic Bias

Jewish Reception

From Composition to Compilation to Translation

The first millennium of reception history is the least complex, given that during this period the psalms were used exclusively in Jewish settings and within the defined geographical area of Syro-Palestine, Egypt and Babylon. However, our account begins where most commentaries end: the debates about the dates, authors and provenances of individual psalms are of minimal concern, because our emphasis is on the reception of individual psalms once the Psalter had become a recognized collection. So what follows is a brief summary of the stages leading to the compilation of the Psalter as a whole.

It seems fairly certain that many psalms were composed in the *pre-exilic period – psalms for the king to use in the Temple (for example, Psalms 2, 72, 89, 110 and 132), psalms which ratified the conviction that God would protect the city of Zion from invasion (such as Psalms 46, 48), and psalms which would be used in times of national distress (for example, Psalms 74, 77, 79, 80, 82). Other psalms with archaic language and Canaanite motifs are probably also early: these include Psalms 29 and 68. Some psalms may even be traced back to David himself (c.1000 BCE), although the title 'A Psalm of (or in Hebrew, 'to') David' is not a good guide to authorship as the psalm headings would have been added in the second Temple period. But all the psalms referred to above would have been preserved and reinterpreted during the period of exile in Babylon in the sixth century BCE. The so-called 'royal psalms' and 'Zion hymns' would have been used with an eye to the future, to encourage the community whose present experience would have made them question the confident faith expressed within them, and other psalms of distress (for example, Psalm 137) would have been added. Other additions would include

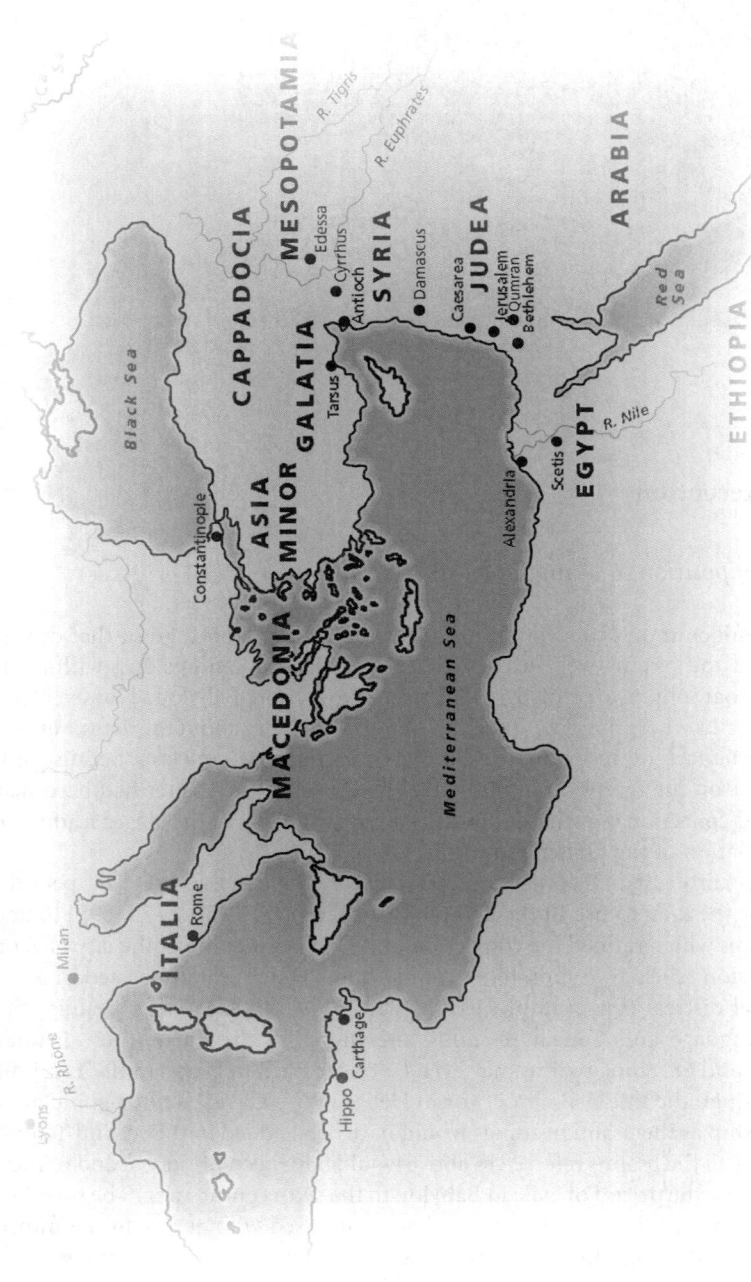

MAP 1.1 Jerusalem: the centre of psalmody for early Jewish and Christian communities.

the psalms celebrating God's kingship (for example, Psalms 47, 93, 95–9) which would have given the disenchanted exiles a new vision. However, given that these psalms have been scattered throughout the Psalter, a chronological arrangement was not the primary concern of the compilers.

After the exile, many psalms of a more personalized nature would have been added; the best examples are found within *'The Psalms of Ascents' (Psalms 120–34), which show how individual piety was incorporated into Temple worship. New hymns of praise, individual complaints and didactic psalms would also have been incorporated. Gradually psalms were organized into groups and then into collections, each given a heading to connect one with another, and later still, these collections would have been incorporated into the five different books which make up the Psalter as a whole.

The first book (Psalms 1–41) comprises mainly personal laments, and here the heading 'Psalm of David' dominates; this is a more homogenous work, comprising smaller groups of psalms (for example, Psalms 15–24). Books Two and Three (Psalms 42–72 and 73–89) form a second group, determined up to Psalm 83 by the prominent use of Elohim as a name for God, compared with the name Yahweh which is prevalent in Book One. Several smaller collections are evident here, and the title 'Psalm of David' is used only in Psalms 51–65 and 68–70. Books Four and Five (Psalms 90–106 and 107–50) form a third and final division, comprising one large collection (Psalms 120–34) and several smaller ones; here the psalms are mainly those of praise, and far fewer have superscriptions.

The adding of titles to individual psalms and the placing of psalms into collections and then into books thus mark the first stages of reception history. For example, the superscriptions give the psalm a different historical focus to that which the composer intended (the historical headings to psalms such as 3, 7, 18, 30, 34 and 51 now set these psalms in the life of King David as told in the books of 1–2 Samuel). Furthermore, by placing particular psalms next to those which have a different style and theology, as well as a different date, each psalm is read not only in its own light, but in the light of its neighbour. The best illustration is the way Psalm 1, a late psalm concerning the importance of meditating on the law, and Psalm 2, an early psalm suggesting an accession ceremony of the king, have been brought together to illustrate complementary themes, each key facets of Judaism – the 'Torah' (Psalm 1) and the 'Messiah' (Psalm 2). Given that by this time the Psalter would have been divided into five books, the juxtaposition of Psalms 1 and 2 suggest that here we have a second Torah, with David, not Moses, as the significant Messianic figure.

Although the precise details of this process are most unclear, up to this point of compilation – by the early Greek period, in about the third century BCE – the focal point is Jerusalem and the Temple, and the compiling and editing are being undertaken by scribes and priests living in Judah.[1]

---

[1] Most introductions to psalmody offer a fuller discussion of these issues; see for example L. Sabourin (1974); J. Day (1990); S.E. Gillingham (1994); C. Hassell Bullock (2002).

The process starts to become more untidy when we start to examine the reception of the psalms through translation. The best-known Greek translation of the Psalter (known as the Septuagint, or the *LXX) was intended for Hellenistic Jews, probably in Alexandria (although some would argue the actual provenance could be Palestine). This occurred fairly soon after the formation of the Hebrew Psalter in Jerusalem, probably around the second century BCE. The earliest extant manuscript of this Greek translation dates from some four hundred years later: it is an uncial codex of the entire Old Testament, called *Codex Vaticanus* ('B'); only the beginning (up to Genesis 46:8) is missing, and the Psalms are therefore intact.

Over the past thirty or so years, a good deal has been written about the relationship between the Greek and Hebrew Psalters, and the extent to which it was intended to be an accurate translation or (given that many of the Hebrew terms, not least in the superscriptions, do not seem to have been known in second-century Alexandria) more of an interpretation. Given that the translator was living at a time when Jewish hopes for a cataclysmic redemption were high, this could have influenced his work, giving it a more future-orientated, eschatological bias, a feature which might be seen in the way he interpreted the titles to the psalms. For example, some of the musical terms in the titles have not been understood, so that, for instance, the term 'for the choirmaster' in fifty-five psalms reads in the Greek 'for perpetuity' or 'for fulfilment' – a term which might imply a more future-orientated reading. Or again, the musical term 'Gittith' ('a stringed instrument') in Psalms 8, 81 and 84 is read by the Greek as 'a wine-press' – a term which might denote their use as harvest-psalms, but also could be a metaphor about harvesting on the day of final judgement. Furthermore, the persona of David is more apparent in the Greek Psalter, so that even more psalms are given Davidic headings, and an extra psalm celebrating David's victory over Goliath is added at the end: this might indicate a future hope in a David-like Messianic figure, although it could also be a recognition of David as a pious hero of the past. It could be that the translator was concerned to provide as accurate a rendering as he could, and an eschatological reading has been read into the Greek text some time later, especially by Jewish-Christian commentators.

Whichever view one takes, the Greek translation is very different in some places. Not only do the psalm titles reflect twenty or so omissions and seventeen expansions, but, more substantially, the Hebrew word for God is not given the unique term it has in the Hebrew (Yahweh), but is translated according to Jewish spoken practice usually as, simply, 'Lord'. And the system of dividing one psalm from another is different: the LXX unites Psalms 9–10, which share the same alphabetic structure in Hebrew, and similarly connects Psalms 114–15, and splits 116 and 147, thus causing a different system of numbering the psalms in the Hebrew and the Greek. Furthermore, difficult verses in Hebrew are sometimes rendered more comprehensible in the Greek (e.g. Psalm 40:6 reads in the Hebrew 'ears thou hast dug for me' whereas the Greek reads 'thou hast given me an open ear'). Even if some of these changes are a result of later developments in the Greek text (and there was clearly more than one Greek version, as we know from other Greek manuscripts dating from about this time), even the most cautious of scholars agree that this represents a new stage in the history of interpretation, inevitably bringing more Greek ideas and hopes for a better future into an earlier Hebrew version.[2]

Exposition: The Prophetic Bias

The discovery of other early Hebrew versions of the psalms at *Qumran offers further insights into the Septuagint translation. Amongst the Dead Sea Scrolls (DSS), over twenty-seven manuscripts of psalms, some of them commentaries rather than translations, many of them fragmentary, almost all in a Hebrew script, were found in eleven caves near the ruins of Qumran; two others were found at Masada and a further two at Nahal Heber and Nahal Seelim. It is now possible to compare variant readings in these scrolls with the Septuagint and the traditionally accepted Hebrew Massoretic Text, or *MT. The most important discoveries are from Caves 4 and 11, where copies of 126 of the 150 Hebrew psalms have been found, dating from the first and second centuries BCE (Cave 4) and the first century CE (Cave 11). There appear to be at least two different arrangements of the psalms. It is likely that at least two different 'Psalters', as well as multiple collections of parts of the Psalter, were used in the community. Like the LXX, the standard number is not 150 psalms; there are even three psalms in Syriac (Psalms 151, 154 and 155).

It seems that the first three books of the Psalter (Psalms 1–89) had a more stable history than the latter two. Scrolls which have several psalms from Books 1–3 (for example, 4QPs^a, which starts at Psalm 5 and ends at Psalm 69, although several psalms are missing) usually maintain the same order as the Hebrew Psalter and have no additional psalms amongst them. By contrast, 11QPs^a, the largest psalms scroll, which contains many of the psalms from Books 4–5 (starting with Psalm 101), does not maintain the order in the MT, and includes fifteen hitherto unknown psalms interspersed within it. For example, Psalm 101:1–8 is followed by Psalm 102:1–2 [+3–18], 18–29, then 103:1; this is followed by parts of Psalm 109, then similarly 118, then 104, and then 147; only the collection headed 'Songs of Ascent' keeps to the order of the Hebrew text. The additional psalms, found in the latter part of the scroll, indicate that psalms composed later (for example, a 'Plea for Deliverance' and an 'Apostrophe to Zion', both of which are found in

---

[2] A vast amount of literature has recently been written on this issue. For a more eschatological reading, see M. Rösel (2001) and J. Schaper (1995). For a more cautious approach, see A. Pietersma (2000b, 2001a, 2001b, 2005); also F. Austermann (2000); C.E. Cox (2001); M. Flashar (1912) ; A. van der Kooij (2000); S. Olofsson (1997); A. Soffer (1957); and J.M. Wevers (2001); E. Zenger (2001). For English translations of the Psalms from the LXX, see J.M. Dines (1994) and A. Pietersma (2000a); see also the German study of the Septuagint Psalms at www.unikoblenz.de/~sept/index2.html.

other scrolls) were just as authoritative as the earlier traditional ones. 11QPs[a] has fifty-six compositions in all; one is of David's last words (following parts of 2 Samuel 23:1–7), another concerns the inspiration of his compositions, and another two correspond to Psalm 151 in the LXX, thus reflecting the same Davidic emphasis as in the Greek Psalter. Some would argue that the remaining fifty-two psalms were a liturgical collection for fifty-two weeks of the year, although much of this depends on whether one sees the Qumran community using a lunar rather than solar calendar (and the latter is more likely). Whatever view one takes, this particular collection has a clear theology: its focus is the present and future salvation of God's elect who are inheritors of the promises made to David of old, with an emphasis on the psalms as prophecies awaiting fulfilment as much as on present application.

Another feature is the composition of new psalms based on old models. Some suggest personal, private use – for example, four psalms are to be recited against demons. Others indicate more public use: the *Hodayot*, or thanksgiving psalms, adapt the language of suffering and deliverance found in the biblical psalms. An interesting feature is the way that some of the language is also found in the Gospel accounts of the suffering of Jesus. Psalm 22:14–15, which speaks of sufferings in terms of an aching fever, is taken up in *Hodayot* 7:4; Psalm 22 is used repeatedly in the passion narratives of Jesus. Psalm 41:9, which speaks of betrayal by close friends, is used in *Hodayot* 5:23–4; John 12:18 also uses this verse in relation to Jesus. Psalm 69:21, which speaks of the thirst of the psalmist being relieved by being given vinegar to drink, is repeated in *Hodayot* 4:11; it is also in Mark 15:36. In addition to the *Hodayot*, other psalm-like copies have a more mystical orientation: the so-called 'Angelic Liturgy' or 'Songs for the Sabbath Sacrifice', imitating the praises of the angels in heaven, is an example of this.

As well as copying the psalms, other sectarian works at Qumran cite the traditional psalms explicitly or implicitly, interpreting them in the light of the events of their own time. The term used for this practice is *pesher*, a type of exegesis which is either a running commentary on a biblical text or a commentary on a group of texts (usually termed *'catena' or 'florilegium') arranged around a central idea. For example, in 4QFlorilegium, Psalms 1:1–2:1 are taken together along with parts of 2 Samuel 7:10–14, Is. 8:11, Ezekiel 44:10 and Daniel 12:10 to speak of the restoration of the Temple and the coming figure of the branch of David, the interpreter of the law. This undoubtedly has a prophetic emphasis. The same prophetic reading is evident in 11QMelchizedek: here Leviticus 25:9,13, Deuteronomy 15:2, Isaiah 52:7; 61:1–3 and Daniel 9:25 are used along with Psalms 7:7–9 and 82:1–2 to describe the redemption to be brought about by heavenly Melchizedek. Similarly 4QCatena combines psalmic and prophetic texts to speak of what is to happen to the community 'at the end of days'.

Fifteen other texts use the more continuous type of pesher, interpreting only one text at a time. Three of these are on the psalms. 1QpPs. is a pesher on parts of Psalm 68; 4QpPs[b], on Psalm 129:7–8; and 4QpPs[a], on parts of Psalms 37, 45 and 60. Here the emphasis is on the imminent fulfilment of the psalms in the life of the community: for example, Psalm 37:11 ('... the meek shall inherit the land') is interpreted literally concerning the physical vindication of the community's leader, the Teacher of Righteousness, over his enemy who attempted to kill him, the Wicked Priest.

In summary, the psalms scrolls at Qumran give examples of at least four aspects of reception history of the Psalter: copying of Hebrew texts; distinctive liturgical collections for both public and private prayer; new psalm-like imitations used to instruct the community in matters of faith; and, most significantly, brief commentaries on psalms, interpreting them especially with what might be termed a prophetic spirit, in that they saw the psalms as prophecies soon to be fulfilled, probably within their own generation.[3]

These four aspects are not unique to Qumran. For example, in terms of copying and translation, some individual psalms were already being translated in a paraphrase from the Hebrew into Aramaic, the vernacular language of the Jews in Palestine and Babylon. Although the entire written collection, known as the Targums, did not emerge until between the fourth and sixth centuries CE, Aramaic psalms were known earlier, illustrated by Jesus' cry of dereliction using Psalm 22:1, given in Aramaic in Mt. 27:46, and a citation of Psalm 68:19 in Ephesians 4:18 which is closer to the Targ Pss in Aramaic than to the MT. There is also evidence of psalms in Syriac later in this period: Ps. 151, in two sections, is different from the Greek version, and two additional psalms at Qumran (Psalms 154 and 155: one a didactic psalm, the other a prayer with a confession of sin similar to Psalm 51) are also in Syriac.[4]

Instruction through Imitations of Psalms

A feature noted at Qumran was the prophetic use of psalmody. Several other examples of this mode of interpretation are found in intertestamental Jewish writings written in Greek. One is the first book of *Maccabees*: 1 Macc. 7:16–17 states 'the flesh of thy saints and their blood they poured out around Jerusalem, and

---

[3] Studies of this subject are extensive, and the following references pertain only to the issues discussed above: cf. P.W. Flint (1992, 1994, 1997 and 1998); G.J. Brooke (*1979–81*, 1985, *1987*, *1994*); J.H. Eaton (2003), pp. 45–6; E. Glickler-Chazon (*1993a, 1993b, 1994*); M.P. Horgen (*1979*); J.A. Hughes (*2006*); T.H. Lim (*2002*); M. Mansoor (1961); F.G. Martinez (1996a, 1996b); S. Holm-Nielsen (1960a); J.P.M. van der Ploeg (*1967, 1971*, 1973, 1992); J.A. Sanders (1962, 1963, 1964, 1965, 1966b, 1967, *1974*); E.M. Schuller (1994–95, 1996); P.W. Skehan (1963, 1964, 1965a); E. Ulrich and E.M. Schuller (1994); B.Z. Wacholder (1988); G.H. Wilson (1983, 1985a, 1985b, 1997).

[4] On the psalms in Aramaic, see M. Bernstein (2005); E.M. Cook (2002); M.M. Stec (2005); M.Wilcox (1985); on the Syriac psalms, see R.J.V. Hiebert (2001, 2005); M. Noth (1930); H.F. van Rooy (1999, 2005); P.W. Skehan (1976); A.S. van der Woude (1974). Translations and commentaries of the psalms in Syriac does not take place until at least the mid-second century CE, and so will be dealt with more fully in the following chapter.

there was none to bury them', a phrase which is derived from the Greek translation of Psalm 78:2–3 (in Hebrew and English Psalm 79:2–3). The psalm refers to the suffering of the people at the time of the exile, in the sixth century, some four hundred years earlier. This description of the murder of the martyrs in Jerusalem in the second century BCE is a deliberate attempt to link the two events and to encourage the 'saints' (termed the Hasideans in 1 Macc. 7:13) to imitate the piety of the 'saints' (in the Hebrew, the Hasidim, as seen in Psalm 79:2). Another Greek text, also from about the first century BCE, is the *Psalms of Solomon*, and this also uses the psalms in a similarly didactic way: Psalms Solomon 17 recalls psalms about the protection of the Davidic king in Psalms 2, 89 and 132 and applies them to the impending punishment on the Roman nation after the capture of Jerusalem by Pompey in 64 BCE.[5]

A slightly later Jewish Greek text, probably from Alexandria, and probably dating from the latter part of the first century CE, also borrowed liberally from psalmody, but not so much in a prophetic spirit as in a homiletic one, in that its purpose was to show the superiority of Jewish wisdom above that of the Greeks. This is the *Wisdom of Solomon*: Wisdom 1:1, 6:1–2, 21 take up the language of Psalm 2:10–12, in its address to pagan nations to take note of the God of the Jews. For example, 'Love righteousness, you rulers of the earth, think of the Lord with goodness...' (Wisdom 1:1) has been influenced by 'Be warned, O rulers of the earth, serve the Lord with fear...' (Psalm 2:10–11). There are many more allusions to and citations of the psalms in Greek throughout *Wisdom of Solomon*: the most striking is Wisdom 15:15, concerning pagan idols which have 'eyes... nostrils... ears... fingers... feet' which they cannot see, smell, hear, feel or walk with – almost identical, except for the order, to Psalm 115:4–7 which speaks of idols with mouths, eyes, ears, nostrils, hands and feet in a similarly derogatory way. It is interesting to see how the LXX Psalms have been used by the writer of *Wisdom* in defence of the divine origins and hence ascendancy of Jewish wisdom, thus illustrating how psalmody was used didactically as well as prophetically.

In terms of other psalm-like compositions in addition to those found at Qumran, the evidence is abundant. Not only are there some fifteen outside the Psalms but within the Hebrew Bible (for example, the Song of Moses in Exodus 15, the Song of Deborah in Judges 5, the prayer of Hannah in 1 Samuel 1, and the prayer of Jonah in Jonah 2, all of which became included in the collection of 'canticles' or psalm-like hymns in later Christian liturgy), but there are many examples, in Greek, within the intertestamental literature. Some are imitations of personal prayers: taking examples from the Apocrypha, these include the prayers of Mordecai and Esther in the Greek additions to Esther; the prayer of Azariah and the Hymn of the Three Young Men in the Greek additions to Daniel; the prayer of Manasseh; and prayers in the book of Tobit (3:2–6, 11–15; 8:5–8). Others are more

---

[5] See A. van der Kooij (2001); U.A. Rappaport (1998).

eschatological and hymnic in form, breathed with a prophetic spirit concerning the salvation of Israel and the dawning of a new age, rather like the 'Apostrophe to Zion' at Qumran. Tobit 13 is a good example, as also is Baruch 4:5–5:9 (4:36–5:9 correspond with Psalms Solomon 11) and Ecclesiasticus (Ben Sira) 36:1–17. Others are more mystical prayers, like the 'Songs of the Sabbath Sacrifice' at Qumran: a good example is a later Slavonic translation from the Greek which in itself may go back to the Hebrew, called the 'Apocalypse of Abraham'. The best example is of the song which an angel teaches Abraham on his journey to heaven (17:8–18). Many of these imitations of psalmody mark the beginning of another form of reception – that of liturgical innovation.[6]

One other early Jewish interpreter of the Greek psalms is *Philo of Alexandria* (20B CE–40 CE). This reading of psalmody is very different from that at Qumran, for example. In his allegorical commentary on the Pentateuch, '*Philo Judaicus*', with an interest in God's supreme revelation through the Torah, cites some twenty psalms when highlighting moral or theological points in the books of Genesis and Exodus. Each psalm is introduced as if divinely inspired and written by David, and its instructional value is clear; nevertheless, according to Philo, David is basically a disciple of Moses, and David's role is to highlight the law. For example, in *De confusione linguarum 39*, on Genesis 11, the Tower of Babel story, Philo quotes from Ps. 31:19: 'As one of the disciples of Moses … prayed in his hymns and said, "Let their cunning lips be devoid of speech…"'. The psalms are thus witnesses to underscore Philo's exegetical points on the Torah. Hence when '*Philo Alexandrinus*', the philosopher with a concern for reasoned faith, takes a more allegorical approach, looking at deeper meanings hidden within the biblical texts, he does this with the Torah, but not with the psalms. This is for the same reason; the relation of the soul before God is paramount far more in the Torah than in the psalms. So Philo's concern *only* with the moral quality of the psalms contrasts well with other Jewish writers of his time, for example at Qumran, and in Maccabees; their value as prophecies, about to be fulfilled in the life of his community, is hardly evident.[7]

Christian Reception

Given that the first Christians were Jews, it is not surprising that when the New Testament writers and early church fathers use the psalms, their expositions echo

---

[6] See also G.J. Brooke (2004); P. Fiedler (1988); S. Gillingham (2002); S. Holm-Nielsen (1960b); G.W.E. Nickelsburg and M.E. Stone *(1983)*; O.H. Steck (1984); C. Thoma (1983); for online resources, see www.earlyjewishwritings.com/.

[7] See P. Jeffrey (2004); D. Runia (2001a).

the polemical and prophetic readings found in the Qumran scrolls and their instructional works reflect those in *Wisdom of Solomon* and Philo, similarly creating imitations of psalms. Most importantly they share a Greek translation – if not the LXX itself, something quite like it.

The Psalms as Prophecies in the New Testament

Over one-third of the 360 Old Testament quotations in the New Testament come from the psalms. Like both Philo and the sectarians at Qumran, the New Testament writers assume that David is the author of the entire Psalter. But there is one crucial difference: no longer is David the most important figure, writing psalms for instruction (as Philo emphasized) or as inspired prophecies (as Qumran upheld); instead, his authority has been superseded by Jesus Christ, of the Davidic line. The psalms may all be understood as 'by' David, but they are 'about' Jesus Christ, and so illustrate how the Old Testament is now fulfilled in his life and death.

The difference between the earlier Jewish and this Jewish-Christian emphasis is illustrated by comparing some of the psalms used at Qumran with the New Testament. Jesus Christ's vindication and resurrection (his being raised up, exalted, received by God, his sitting at the right hand of God) echo the language of royal psalms also used at Qumran. For example, all three Synoptic Gospels both cite and allude to Ps. 2:7 ('I will tell of the decree of the Lord: He said to me, "You are my son; today I have begotten you"'). At Qumran this psalm refers to an idealized future figure (e.g. in 4QFlor and 11QPs^c) whereas in the New Testament it applies specifically to Jesus. Ps. 118, referring to a figure coming in the name of the Lord on a great festal day, is used in all four Gospels (Mk. 11:9–10; Mt. 21:9 and 23:39; Lk. 13:35, 19:38; and Jn. 12:13) and also at Qumran. Parts of it are found in 11QPs^a and 4QPs^b ; in the latter, Ps. 118:1, 15 and 16 are followed by two apocryphal psalms called 'Plea for Deliverance' and 'Apostrophe to Zion', and in another scroll, 4QpPs^b, Ps. 118:26, 27 and 20 are read alongside parts of Ps. 127 and 129; together this illustrates how at Qumran the great festal day announcing the beginning of God's return to his people is still in the future. By contrast, in the Gospels, this day has come, and Jesus' entry into Jerusalem, when this psalm is used, marks it. 'Hosanna! [Save now!] Blessed is the one who comes in the name of the Lord!'

By contrast, some of the most popular lament psalms in the New Testament, chosen because they echo Jesus' suffering (his being betrayed, abandoned, troubled in spirit and delivered up), are rarely used at Qumran. For example, Psalms 22 and 69 are prominent in the Passion Narratives of all four Gospels; although the Qumran scrolls use other lament psalms, these two are hardly used (Ps. 22:15–17 occurs in 4QPs^f ; Ps.22: 4–9, 15–21 is found in the collection from Nahal Seelim; and parts of Ps. 69 are in 4QPs^a). And even here, the language of suffering is applied to the community of faith and not to any specific figure. By contrast, because parts of Psalms 22 and 69 fit, remarkably specifically, the sufferings of Jesus they are frequently used by the New Testament writers as ways of showing that his suffering was foreordained long ago.

Psalm 110, a royal psalm which is used in all four Gospels and in Hebrews, is also not found at Qumran, neither as a copy nor as part of a *pesher* commentary. This is extraordinary, given that verse 4 of this psalm ('You are a priest forever according to the order of Melchizedek') could have been an important commentary on Melchizedek returning to redeem Israel in 11QMelch. It is possible that given the debates in the Qumran community about the authority of the priesthood in the Jerusalem Temple, this psalm might have been too contentious. But for the New Testament writers it was an ideal way of illustrating the divine nature and priestly calling of Jesus Christ.[8]

Mark's Gospel

The allusion to Ps. 2:7 ('You are my son; today I have begotten you') in the accounts of both the baptism and transfiguration has already been noted. The acknowledgment by God 'This is my beloved Son, in whom I am well pleased' (Mk. 1:11 and 9:7; also Mt. 3:17 and 17:5, and Lk. 3:22 and 9:35) demonstrates that Jesus is the anointed Son of God, of Davidic lineage. The use at the baptism in Mk. 1:11, so early in the Gospel, suggests that Mark is using this idea of sonship and kingship to challenge imperial Rome. The use of Ps. 2:7 at the transfiguration in Mk. 9:7, where the verse is addressed to the disciples in the context of the prediction of Jesus' sufferings (Mk. 8:31), makes the same point as Jesus nears the end of his ministry. The final section of the Gospel (chapters 11–16) makes use of two other psalms which suggest the same theme. As Jesus enters Jerusalem, Ps. 118:25–6 ('Save us, we beseech thee O Lord ... Blessed is the one who comes in the name of the Lord') is put in the mouths of the crowds to show that Jesus is the promised king arriving on a festal day (Mk. 11:9–10). Mark follows this with the account of the cleansing of the Temple (Mk. 11:15–19) which is framed by the accounts of the cursing of the fig tree (11:12–14, 20–24), where the leaders, unlike the crowds, fail to acclaim Jesus. At the end of this sequence, in Mk. 12:10–11, Ps. 118 is used again: this

---

[8] Four psalms discussed here will recur in our assessment of the New Testament's use of the psalms. On the use of **Psalm 110**, see D.R. Alexander (2001); J. Dupont (1974); D.M. Hay (1973); M. Hengel (1993, E Tr 1995); E.E. Johnson (1992); O. Linton (1981); W.R.G. Loader (1978). On the use of **Psalm 118**, see M. Berder (1996); J.A. Sanders (1993); *J. Schröten (1995)*; J.R. Wagner (1997). On the use of **Psalm 2**, see N. Füglister (1988); J.W. Watts (1990); W. Weren (1989); J.T. Willis (1990). On the use of **Psalm 22**, see H.D. Lange (1972); J.L. Mays (1985); V.K. Robins (1992). For more general works which have informed the following discussion, see S.E. Balentine (1984*); G.T. Brooke (1998)*; A.Y. Collins (2003); R.J. Dillon (1987); C.A. Evans and J.A. Sanders (eds.) (1990); C.A. Evans (2005); *J.A. Fitzmyer (1960–1)*; D.A. Koch (1986); U.P. McCaffrey (1981); *D.J. Moo (1983)*; M.J. Mulder (ed.) (1988); S. Moyise and M. Menken (eds.) (2004); *H. Ringgren (1985)*; and A. Rose (1962).

time vv. 22–3 ('the stone that the builders rejected has become the chief cornerstone ...') is used to foretell that although Jesus is soon to be rejected as God's Son and the people's king, he will later be vindicated. This is followed in Mk: 12:36 by Ps. 110:1 ('The Lord says to my Lord, "Sit at my right hand until I make your enemies your footstool"') where Jesus appears to accept the title 'son of David' whilst at the same time claiming his authority over the Davidic king. (The same point is made in Mk. 14:62, when this verse is alluded to again.)

The accounts of the trial and crucifixion are punctuated with psalms about a righteous sufferer. Ps. 41:9 is used in Mk. 14:18 ('one of you will betray me') as if it is a prophetic text now being fulfilled. In the same way, Ps. 42:5,11 and 43:5 are alluded to in the prayer in Gethsemane, in Mk. 14:34 ('I am deeply grieved, even to death'); and on the cross, Ps. 69:21 ('for my thirst they gave me vinegar to drink') is evoked in Mk. 15:23 as Jesus is offered wine to drink. But it is Psalm 22 which dominates this sequence: see Ps. 22:18/Mk. 15:24, on the dividing of garments; Ps. 22:7/Mk. 15:29, on the derision of Jesus; Ps. 22:8/Mk. 15:30–31, on the taunting; Ps. 22:6/Mk. 15:32, on taunting Jesus to come down from the cross; and finally, Ps. 22:1/Mk. 15:34, on the cry of dereliction, uttered in Aramaic: 'My God, my God, why have you forsaken me?' So Mark's use of the psalms is profoundly theological: three psalms illustrate Jesus' conflict with the authorities and his future exaltation (Psalms 2, 110 and 118), and four others demonstrate that his exaltation can only be achieved through the path of suffering (Psalms 41; 42–3; 69; 22).[9]

Matthew's Gospel

Matthew has more allusions to psalms than Mark, in part because he also uses them didactically, to highlight Jesus' teaching. One example is the formulaic phrase 'Blessed is the man' (for example in Ps. 1:1, although the phrase occurs nearly thirty times in the Psalter), which is used in the Beatitudes in Mt. 5:2–12: this link back to the teaching of David shows Jesus as the teacher whose authority supersedes that not only of Moses but also of David. Another didactic use of a psalm is in Mt. 16:27 ('for he will repay everyone for what has been done') which has echoes of Ps. 62:13. A further example is in a psalm which Matthew shares with Luke. Psalm 91 is a didactic psalm, and vv. 11–12 are used in the account of the temptations (Mt. 4:6; also in Lk. 4:10–11). Earlier in the psalm we read of 'terror ... pestilence ... destruction' (vv. 3,5,6), which in the Aramaic version becomes the 'terror of demons ... the arrow of the angel of death'; Qumran includes Psalm 91 in a collection of four exorcism psalms (11QapocrPs) so its contents make it an appropriate psalm to be 'perverted' by the devil: 'If you are the Son of God, throw yourself

---

[9] On the use of the Psalms particularly in Mark, see A.Y. Collins (1997); J. Marcus (1992); and R. Watts (2004).

down [from the temple]; for it is written, 'He will command his angels concerning you ... on his hands they will bear you up ...' (vv. 11–12). The didactic lesson here is that just as Jesus resists false routes to power, by implication, his disciples must do the same. Two other psalms are also used didactically by both Matthew and Luke: Mt. 7:23 ('Go away from me, you evildoers') is also in Lk. 13:27 and is a reference to a Greek version of Ps. 6:10, and Mt. 13:32, on the birds of the air nesting in the trees, is also in Lk. 13:27 and taken from Ps. 104:12.

Elsewhere Matthew uses psalms, alongside other Old Testament quotations, to show how Jesus' life and words are in fulfilment of scripture (Mt. 1:22–23; 2:15, 17–18, 23; 4:14–16; 8:17; 12:17–21; 13:25; 21:4–5; 27:9–10). Mt. 13:35 is from a psalm: Ps. 78:2 ('I will utter my mouth in a parable ...') is used to explain how Jesus' teaching in parables is in fulfilment of prophecy. (Matthew may have had Is. 29:13–14 in mind, but Ps. 78:2 also fits the citation.) It is clear that Matthew thought of David the psalmist as a prophet: elsewhere, without an explicit fulfilment quotation, he marks out stages in Jesus' life to show implicitly how the words of the psalms are being fulfilled. In Mt. 3:17 and 17:5, Ps. 2:7 is used in the account of Jesus' baptism and transfiguration, like Mk. 1:11 and 9:7; Ps. 110:1, used in Mk. 12:36, is found in Mt. 22:44; Ps. 118:26 is used in Mt. 21:9, as in Mk. 11:9–10, and it occurs again in Mt. 23:39, after Jesus' lament over Jerusalem. (The fact that Psalm 118 is an important Passover psalm makes its use here, as Passover draws near, all the more apt.) Psalm 8:2 is cited in Mt. 21:16, with prophetic implications: in the psalm the young infants are singing praises to God, and here they are in the crowds praising Christ upon his entry into Jerusalem. Ps. 118:22–23, on the rejected stone becoming the head of the corner, which occurs in Mk. 12:10–11, is found in Mt. 21:42. The psalms of lament (Psalms 41, 42–3, 69, 22) used in Mark also occur in Matthew; as in Mark, Ps. 22 dominates (Mt. 27:35/Ps. 22:18; Mt. 27:43/ Ps. 22:8 [here expanding Mark] and Mt. 27:47/Ps. 22:1).

Matthew differs from Mark in that he uses the psalms more explicitly to show that Jesus is the new David as well as the new Moses – teaching, as did David, through psalmody, and bringing about a fulfilment of the words of the psalms in his own life and death. Like Mark, Matthew has no difficulty turning particular psalms Christwards, to show that Jesus is the son of David by adoption (Pss. 110; 118) and the Son of God by nature (Ps. 2) whose suffering is necessary as it leads to his future exaltation (Pss. 69 and 22).[10]

LUKE'S GOSPEL

Luke is unique amongst the Gospel writers in creating psalm-like compositions, following the practices at Qumran and in the Apocrypha. Placed in the mouths of Mary (Lk. 1:46–55), Zechariah (Lk. 1:68–79) and Simeon (Lk. 2:28–32), these 'new

---

[10] On the use of the psalms in Matthew, see M.J.J. Menken (2004) and S. Van Tilborg (1988).

psalms' speak of the dawning of a new age. Hence like Matthew, the prophetic spirit of psalmody is assumed, although, given Luke's particular liturgical appreciation of psalmody, his way of demonstrating this is different. (The liturgical emphasis is also evident in the way Luke, alone of the Gospels, uses the title 'Book of Psalms' [Lk. 20:42; also in Acts 1:20] and the term 'psalms' [Lk. 24:44; see Acts 13:33,35].)

Nevertheless, the prophetic element is made explicit: Luke follows Mark and Matthew in using Ps. 2:7 at the baptism and transfiguration (Lk. 3:22 and 9:35, with the addition 'My Son, my Chosen …'). Like Mark and Matthew, Luke also uses Pss. 110 and 118, albeit with a different twist. As in Matthew, Ps. 118:26 is twice used in Lk. 13:35 and 19:38, before the entry into Jerusalem: however, in 19:39 Luke adds 'Blessed is the *King* who comes in the Lord's name', to make his emphasis clear. And in Luke's schema, Psalm 118 comes at both the beginning and end of a journey narrative (chapters 13–19) from Galilee to Jerusalem, a journey which ends in Jesus' death. This psalm is important to Luke: Ps. 118:22 (the 'rejected stone') is alluded to in Lk. 20:17 at the end of the parable about the wicked tenants (it is also used in Acts 4:11, where it combines with Ps. 146): in Luke it shows that Jesus' rejection in Jerusalem, as the new Davidic king, is part of God's plan. Ps. 110:1 ('The Lord says to my Lord …') is used in Lk. 20:42–3: like Ps. 118, it is another important psalm in Luke, used also in Peter's first speech in Acts 2: 24–35. In the Gospel it shows that Jesus is both the son of David and yet David's 'Lord', and it is used in Acts to show how the disciples have to testify to the same truth.

Luke also takes up the psalms of the 'righteous sufferer' used by Mark and Matthew. Ps. 42:5 is found in Lk. 22:42, Ps. 22:17–18 in Lk. 23:34, and Ps. 69:21 in Lk. 23:36. In chapters 22 and 23, Luke also takes up another lament psalm, 88:4–13, in the allusions to Jesus being forsaken by all his friends. This psalm is most pertinent for Luke: Jesus may be forsaken by his friends, but he is not forsaken by God. Following from this, Luke does not include the cry from Ps. 22:1 ('My God, My God, why hast thou forsaken me?') on the cross, for this is too radical in its God-forsakenness: he chooses instead Ps. 31:5 ('… into thy hands I commit my spirit …') in Lk. 23:46. This has links with the ways in which the psalms are used in Acts: Ps. 16:11 is used in both Acts 2:25–8 and 13:35, as a clear statement that God will *not* abandon his Son in Hell. Hence the appropriateness of a committal into God's hands, rather than a cry of dereliction, from the cross.[11]

JOHN'S GOSPEL

John is perhaps the most unusual of the Gospels in his use of the psalms. He has little interest in royal psalms such Pss. 2 and 110. The only three psalms John uses

---

[11] On the use of the Psalms in Luke, see *R. Brown (1993)*; P. Doble (2004); *C.A. Evans and J.A. Sanders (1993a)*; D.R. Jones (1968); *C.A. Kimball (1994)*; N. Lohfink (1994); and J.R. Wagner (1997).

in a way similar to the Synoptics are Ps. 118, 22 and 41. Ps. 118 is used just once, to mark the entry into Jerusalem (Ps. 118:26, 'Blessed is he who comes in the name of the Lord', in Jn. 12:13). Psalm 22 is also used just once: Ps. 22:18 occurs in Jn. 19:24, and is prefaced by explicit 'fulfilment quotation' ('this was to fulfil what the scripture says, "They divided my clothes among themselves, and for my clothing they cast lots"'). Ps. 41:9 is found in Jn. 13:18, and again John brings in a 'fulfilment quotation' ('But it is to fulfill the scripture, "The one who ate my bread has lifted his heel against me"') which incidentally reveals in the Greek that John is not quoting from the Septuagint but from another version.

Like Luke, John has his own particular selection of psalms. Instead of using Psalm 110 in the discourse with the Jews about his divine origins, Jn. 10:34 takes up Ps. 82:6, a difficult psalm speaking of God's judgement on the deities of other nations; here it makes the point that those who reject Jesus as God will themselves be judged, like foreign deities, as strangers to God. (Small wonder that the interpretation of this psalm results in an attempted arrest, presumably for blasphemy, in Jn. 10:39.) Not surprisingly, given John's theology about the oneness of the Father and the Son (see Jn. 8:29 and 16:32, for example), John, like Luke, omits the cry of God-forsakenness in Ps. 22:1. Instead, the cry (not echoing any known psalm) is 'It is finished'. Another psalm used by John is 78, rich in references to the exodus from Egypt, which highlights the old exodus/new exodus motifs in Jn. 6:31 (Ps. 78:24–5) and Jn. 7:38 (Ps. 78:16,20): Jesus is seen as the living water and the bread from heaven, giving not only physical food (through the feeding of the five thousand) but also spiritual food and drink, in contrast to Moses' sole material provision of manna and water in the wilderness. Hence in the use of these two psalms Jesus is shown again to be greater than David (through Ps. 82) and greater than Moses (Ps. 78).

John's use of Ps. 69, a psalm of a 'righteous sufferer', is also different from the Synoptics': it occurs three times, and serves as another witness to the way in which Jesus' life and death is a fulfilment of prophecy. The psalm is first found early in the Gospel, at the time of the cleansing of the temple in Jn. 2:17: 'Zeal for thy house has consumed me' is from Ps. 69.9. The reference here may be intentionally profound: Ps. 69:8 refers to the psalmist being forsaken by his mother's sons, and in Jn. 2:12, Jesus has just been with his brothers and mother, before this act of cleansing took him away from them. Psalm 69 further illustrates well John's theme of human forsakenness (though not God forsakenness), as in Jn. 15:25, verse 4 is used ('they hated me without cause') to show how the disciples can expect to be hated as Christ too will be hated. The final allusion is of Ps. 69:21 in Jn. 19:28 ('I thirst').

In all these different ways, the prophetic use of the psalms is uppermost: six of the examples above are accompanied by explicit 'fulfilment quotations' (Pss. 69:9 in Jn. 2:17; 82:6 in Jn. 10:34; 118:26 in Jn. 12:13; 41:9 in Jn. 13:18; 69:4 in Jn. 15:25; and 22:18 in Jn. 19:24) – even more than in Matthew. John assumes the psalms are prophecies and points them Christwards, to illustrate Jesus' eternal sonship from the Jews' own scriptures; like Matthew, he uses the psalms to show Jesus is both greater than David and greater than Moses. It is significant that the affirmation of Thomas in Jn. 20:28 ('my Lord and my God!') picks up the addresses in the psalms always used of God, which here are applied to Jesus instead.[12]

THE ACTS OF THE APOSTLES

Here the psalms partly echo the theology and selection in Luke's Gospel. Often they are used explicitly as 'proof texts'. For example, Pss. 69:25 and 109:18 are used to justify the choice of Matthias in Acts 1:20; and in Peter's brief speech in Acts 4:8–12, the familiar Ps. 118:22 (the 'rejected stone' text) is used again. In three other key speeches, an interesting *midrashic use of psalmody is evident, rather like the way the Qumran texts interwove several psalms together to bring about an 'inner meaning' of the whole. In Peter's first speech in Acts 2:25–36, four psalms serve this end: in just two verses (vv. 34–5) Pss. 16:8–11; 89:4–5; 132:11, and Ps. 110:1 together show how Jesus is even greater than David, for he, unlike David, has risen from the dead. Peter's prayer upon release from prison in Acts 4:24–31 begins with a brief imitation of a thanksgiving hymn (rather like Luke 1–2), but this develops into a speech using both Pss. 146:6 and 2:1–2, to illustrate that 'now' is the time of the dawning of the kingdom of God. In the third speech (this time by Paul) in Acts 13:17–41, Pss. 89:21, 2:7 and 16:10 are used together to argue that Jesus is the Messiah. The use of the speech form to create a commentary on several interconnected psalms is quite different from the method used in the Gospels, although the underlying purpose, to show how the psalms are prophetic texts now being fulfilled, is very like that of the Gospels.[13]

PAULINE EPISTLES

In *Romans*, allusions to the psalms are more common than citations of them. The predominant use is didactic and rhetorical, defending Paul's authority as well as his theological polemic. For example, in a lengthy passage which demonstrates the sinfulness of both Jew and Greek (1:8–3:20), Rom. 2:6 alludes to Ps. 62:13; Rom. 3:4 to Ps. 51:4; and Rom. 3:10–18 is a 'catena' of Pss. 14:1–2 (53:1–2); 5:9; 140:3; 10:7 and 36:1, with a prophetic text (Is. 59:7–8) included as well. In the next passage (Romans 3:21–5:21), which argues for the justification of all sinners who have faith in Christ, Rom. 4:7–8 takes up Ps. 32:1–2 ('Blessed are those whose iniquities are forgiven …'). Occasionally, like the Gospel writers, familiar psalms are

---

[12] On the use of the Psalms in John, see *J. Ashton (1991)*; J. Beutler (1979); M Daly-Denton (2000 and 2004); *B.G. Schuchard (1992)*.
[13] On the use of the psalms in Acts, see *C.K. Barrett (1994)*; W.H. Bellinger (1990); *R.I. Denova (1997)*; P. Doble (2004); J. Dupont (1962).

used to show how Christ has fulfilled the prophecies of the old covenant: Rom 8:34 uses Ps. 110:1 to demonstrate that Jesus is greater than David, and Rom. 15:3 uses Ps. 69:9 to show Jesus as the righteous sufferer.

Another related use of psalmody is to remonstrate with the Jews. Although Paul uses more examples from the Law and the Prophets, Rom 11:9 takes up a psalm, namely 69:23–4 ('Let their eyes be darkened so they cannot see …') to show that the Jews' resistance to the Gospel is in part providential. Rom. 10:18 uses a psalm to defend the mission to the Gentiles: Ps. 19:4 ('Their voice has gone out to all the earth'), originally referring to the glory of God over the created order, now refers to how the Gentiles have understood the Gospel in ways the Jews cannot comprehend. Rom 15:9, adapting the Greek, uses Ps. 18:49 ('I will extol thee amongst the nations') again to defend the mission to the Gentiles; Ps. 117:1 ('Praise the Lord, O nations') is used similarly in Rom. 15:11. This is just a selection of the mosaic of psalms which defend the various themes in Paul's arguments in Romans: they are basically used as proof-texts, for instruction and for doctrine, so that a psalm's original meaning is less important than its contemporary appeal, with a key reason for their inclusion being their support for the mission to the Gentiles.

Other than in Romans, Paul's use of psalmody is not as extensive as texts from the Law and the Prophets. *Galatians* has just two allusions: in Gal. 2:16, Ps. 143:2 is used as part of an argument about God's justice ('Enter not into judgement with thy servant: for no man living is righteous before thee') and Gal. 3:16 alludes to Ps. 89:4–5, in its reference to an eternal covenant, but these are far from clear. Similarly in *1 and 2 Corinthians* the references are allusive. 1 Cor. 3:20, in the debate about the nature of wisdom, may be an allusion to Ps. 94:11; 1 Cor. 15:27, on the relationship between the church and Christ, may echo Ps. 8:7 ('all things are put in subjection under him'); 2 Cor. 4:13, on Paul's need to speak out in adverse situations, may allude to Ps. 116:10; and 2 Cor. 9:9, on giving to the poor, suggests Ps. 112:9. The use of the psalms to support Christian doctrine and practical morality has correspondences with the way psalmody is used in Romans.[14]

OTHER EPISTLES

Hebrews reflects a distinctive use of psalmody. Sometimes the writer uses a *pesher* commentary on just one psalmic text: Heb. 2:5–8 makes lengthy use of Ps. 8 ('… you have made them a little lower than God, and crowned them with glory and honor …' [v. 5]) to illustrate the humiliation and exaltation of Jesus; similarly Heb. 3:7–4:1 uses Ps. 95:7–11 several times (3:12–19/Ps. 95:5; 4:1–5/Ps. 95:3; 4:6–10/Ps. 95:2; 4;11–13/Ps. 95:11) in the plea for the people to repent ('*today* if you will hear his voice, harden not your heart'), applying the psalm to the present

---

[14] On psalmody in Pauline literature, see *J.P.G. Dunn (1998)*; *C.A. Evans and J.A. Sanders (eds.) (1993a)*; A.M. Harman (1969); R.A. Harrisville (1985); R.B. Hays (1993); S.C. Keesmat (2004); F. Mussner (1986); C.D. Stanley (1992); D.M. Swancutt (2004); H.H.D. Williams (2004).

moment. Another didactic use of psalmody is in Heb. 10:5–10 which takes up Ps. 40:7–9 in the teaching about a spiritual sacrifice being acceptable to God. Other examples are on a theme, taking up a string of familiar psalms (for example, Psalms 2 and 110) as well as other non-psalmic texts, like the use of *catena* at Qumran (for example, 4QFlor) to develop an argument. Heb. 1:5–13 draws from Ps. 2:7; 2 Sam. 7:14; Deut. 32:43; Pss. 97:7; 104:4; 45:6–7; 102:25–7 and 110:1 in an argument about Christ's superiority over the angels. Heb. 4:14–5:14 is an argument about Christ's eternal priesthood, drawing from Pss. 2:7 and 110:1–4. (Psalm 110:4 is used again to conclude the same point in Heb. 6:20.) Sometimes psalms are introduced by a formulaic quotation; at other times they are just alluded to. Sometimes they are used to address Christ as God; at other times they are used to describe his divine nature. The use of the psalms in Hebrews is complex, not least because the writer, rather like Philo, is as well versed in Platonic philosophy as in Jewish midrashic exegesis, so that what emerges is a good example of Jewish and Hellenistic exegesis of psalmody, seen through a Christian lens.[15]

1 Peter is notable for its use of the familiar 'rejected stone-text' (Ps. 118:22–3) found in 1 Pet. 2:4 and 7. (1 Pet. 2:4–10 uses a typical *catena* of texts, from the prophets and the law as well as from this psalm, under the theme of Christ as the 'corner stone' and the church as 'living stones'.) But it is Ps. 34, used only here within the New Testament (with the possible exception of Ps. 34:20 in Jn. 19:36), which makes 1 Peter most interesting: 1 Pet. 2:1 ('Rid yourselves, therefore, of all malice …') may well be alluding to Ps. 34:13; 1 Pet. 2:3 ('taste and see that the Lord is good') more clearly uses Ps. 34:8. And in the heart of the letter, 1 Pet. 3:10–12, Ps. 34:12–16 creates a long homily on loving one another. Both the psalms are connected with the key theme of this letter: Ps. 118 provides the model for the rejected/exalted Christ, and Ps. 34 offers a model of archetypal suffering which the church must expect if it is to follow Christ.[16] Hence in this letter we see especially the didactic use of psalmody is more apparent than prophetic use.

Ephesians is interesting in its use of Psalms 8 and 110 in Eph. 1:20–3. These two psalms are also used together in Hebrews and 1 Corinthians, as seen above, but Ephesians illustrates best why these two psalms occur together: their combined meaning is that the one who sits at the right hand of God (Ps. 110:1) is the one who has put all things in subjection under his feet (Ps. 8:6). Both psalms are thus now about the exaltation and dominion of Christ. Psalm 8 was originally a hymn to God the Creator, and Psalm 110, a psalm addressed to the king: it is interesting how much their meaning has changed. Ephesians is also noteworthy for its unusual use of Ps. 68:18 in Eph. 4:8–10, and provides a good example of the difficulty of knowing which Greek version the writer used. In the Hebrew, the text clearly reads 'you have *received* gifts among men', and the LXX translates this accordingly. But

---

[15] On the use of the psalms in Hebrews, see D.R. Anderson (2001); H.W. Attridge (1989, pp. 21–58, 113–121; 2004); P. Enns (1997); *L.D. Hurst (1990)*; S.E. Kistenmaker (1961); D.F. Leschert (1995).

[16] On the use of psalms in 1 Peter, see S. Woan (2004).

Eph. 4:8 reads 'when he ascended on high ... he *gave* gifts to men'. It may be that the author is refuting a way in which the psalm had been used in Jewish liturgy: a rabbinic text, Meg31a, refers to the use of this psalm at the Feast of Weeks (i.e. the festival of Pentecost) whose focus was on the *receiving* of the law from Moses on the mountain. The Christian writer here is stating that, whereas Christ *descended* from the mountain, he also *ascended* (to heaven) thus showing himself superior to Moses, and so was able to give the 'new law' (the Spirit of Pentecost) to his church. Here we see Jewish/Christian polemic packed tightly into the different translations of this one verse. These three psalms in Ephesians may not seem much: but they together offer another illustration of the use of psalmody in the early church.[17]

THE BOOK OF REVELATION

The psalms are important here because of their teaching about God's judgement on the nations and the salvation of the faithful. Occasionally psalm-like compositions, both hymns and laments, are used to make this point (for example, Rev. 4:8,11; 5:9–10; 7:15–17; 11:17–18 (see Ps. 95:1); 15:3–4 (see Ps. 86:8–10); 16:5–6; 18:4–8, 10, 14, 16–17, 19–20): these illustrate the influence of both psalmic forms and psalmic language, if not specific psalms. But it is the use of Psalm 2 – which typifies both positively and negatively the themes of judgement and salvation referred to above – which is most significant. In Rev. 2:26–27, the motif of the 'iron rod' (see Ps. 2:8–9) is used to highlight the authority of the church over the nations. The same use is evident in Rev. 19:15, which depicts the rider of the white horse (symbolizing the church) having power over the nations. A more negative use of Ps. 2:8–9 is found in Rev. 12:5, which refers to the male child born of a woman (where the enemy power is Rome). Ps. 2:1–2, by contrast, is alluded to in Rev. 11:15,18, which depicts God's sovereignty over the nations. Interestingly, Ps. 2:7, used so frequently as a prophetic text concerning the nature of Christ, does not appear at all in Revelation; nor is any other psalm like it specifically cited. The use of the psalmody here is much more subtle, without any specific proof texting.[18]

In conclusion, it is clear that the New Testament writers use the psalms both didactically and polemically. The didactic use has many similarities with the ways in which non-Christian Jews used psalmody; by contrast, their polemical use, reading psalms as prophecies now being fulfilled within the life of the Christian community and thus illustrating the superiority of the new covenant of Christ over the old covenant of David, is more divisive. It marks a break with the Jewish practices of reading psalmody throughout the first millennium BCE, and develops into a sophisticated approach throughout the period of the early church fathers.

---

[17] On the use of the psalms in Ephesians, see T. Moritz (1996; 2004); *J. Muddiman (2004)*.
[18] On the use of the psalms in Revelation, see *D.E. Aune (1997)*; J. Paulien (2001); S. Moyise (*1985*; 2004).

The Psalms as Prophecies in the Church Fathers

As the Jewish-Christian communities and then Gentile-Christian communities were established beyond Jerusalem and Palestine, and later beyond Caesarea and Antioch, and further into Asia Minor, Greece and Rome, the Graeco-Roman setting influenced another change in the way the psalms were read by Christian commentators. The emphasis was still polemical, but not so much to confront Jewish ways of reading the psalms as to respond to criticisms of Christian theology from Greek (often *neo-Platonic) philosophy. In addition, the second- and third-generation Christians had to confront an increase in divergent Christian beliefs and the rise of heresies (in part due to different Hellenistic contexts), especially about the nature of Christ's relationship with God. Again, the psalms were used as part of the discourse in refuting heresy, but this time with a different audience and a different purpose from the New Testament writers.

This period culminates, somewhat artificially, with the *Council of Chalcedon in 451. Throughout this time over twenty Greek or Latin writers produced commentaries or homilies on the psalms which are still extant today. Up until the time of Origen (184–254) the medium, like that of the New Testament, was more by way of letters, homilies, tractates; from Origen onwards, the genre of 'exegetical commentaries' begins to develop and expand. Throughout all this period, the psalms familiar to the New Testament writers are still very much in use – Psalms 2, 8, 110 and 118 as psalms testifying to Jesus as the 'new David' and Psalms 22 and 69 as witnessing to Jesus as the 'righteous sufferer'. In addition, other psalms which received little attention in the New Testament gain prominence, of which the most notable are Psalms 1, 34 and 45. The dominant interpretation of psalmody is still Christocentric, although, as will be seen, the approach gradually departs from the more Jewish-centred prophecy/fulfilment bias of the New Testament writers.[19]

THE APOLOGISTS

A Jewish audience is still presumed by some of the early Christian writers, known as *Apologists. Of these, *The First Epistle of Clement,* possibly written by Clement,

---

[19] Concerning the popular use of Psalms 1 and 45 in this period, relevant works include, on **Psalm 1,** D.A. Koch (1994); J. Maier (1987); and C. Waddell (1995); on **Psalm 34,** L.O. Eriksson (1991); and on **Psalm 45,** R.C. Hill (1993). More general works on the use of the psalms by the early church fathers include J. Allenbach (1975–7); D.L. Balas and D.J. Bingham (1998); P.F. Bradshaw (1995); B.E. Daley (2002 and 2004); B. Fischer (1991); E. Fergusson (ed.) 1990, 1998²; R.P.C. Hanson (1970); W. Horbury (1988); J. Irigoin (1994); O. Linton (1969); R. Loewe (1957); R.N. Longenecker (1975); J.M. Neale and R.F. Littledale (4 vols.: 1874–9); C. Reemts (2000); M.-J. Rondeau (1982–5); M. Saebø (ed.) (1996); F. Young, L. Ayres and A. Louth (eds.) (2004); The two most helpful websites for consulting texts in English translation are www.earlychristianwritings.com and www.ccel.org/fathers, and these will be referred to with respect to particular commentators.

Bishop of Rome, c.96 CE, uses the paraenetic approach of Philo, but here the psalms highlight the moral teachings of Jesus rather than the laws of the Pentateuch, thereby illustrating the superiority of Christ over David rather than – as did Philo – of Moses over David. The best example is in 1 Clement 36, concerning the use of Psalm 34 (a psalm used in 1 Peter); v. 1 says 'Come, children, listen to me!' which Clement interprets as Christ addressing us. 1 Clement 36 intersperses some thirty-two psalms with verses from Heb. 1:5–14: this illustrates well that, by the end of the first century, the psalms still had an authoritative use for Jewish Christians, alongside the New Testament.[20]

Justin Martyr (c.100–65), born in Palestine but mainly living in Rome, had contacts with non-Christian Jews and thus read the psalms, as did the New Testament writers, for their prophetic worth. His *Dialogue with Trypho* (c.160) uses Psalm 22 in this way. Not only was it unusual to offer a Christian exegesis of one entire psalm, but the emphasis throughout on this being a prediction of the passion of Christ is striking. Justin also uses this psalm in his other works: referring to Ps. 22: 16–18 ('My hands and feet have shriveled ... they stare and gloat over me ... they divide my clothes among themselves') Justin contends that 'David, the king and prophet, who says these words, has not suffered any of these things. But Jesus Christ had his hands stretched out' (I *Apol.* 35.6). The speaker of Psalm 22 is therefore Christ, not David, whose words were later to be fulfilled. What is new here is that Justin's reading is as much influenced by Greek neo-Platonism as it is by Jewish *midrash. Jesus Christ is now viewed as the timeless Word of God, and references to this Word pervade the psalms, sometimes speaking of Jesus' life, sometimes of his death and resurrection. Three examples must suffice. In Ps. 110:1 ('The Lord says to my Lord ...') and Ps. 45:6 ('Your throne, O God, endures for ever') are not in fact addresses to the king, but rather, because they could be speaking about two natures in the Godhead, they point towards 'the divine Christ'. Similarly, because Ps. 24:7–8 ('Lift up your heads, O gates ... that the King of glory may come in ... who is the King of Glory?') cannot refer to Solomon, as the community would know who he was, it must refer to Christ; and because it cannot refer to the Temple gates (which have been destroyed), the allusion must be to the gates of heaven; thus the meaning of the entire psalm is that it points to Christ's ascent into heaven (I *Apol.* 51; also *Dial.* 36 and 85).[21]

Irenaeus, c.130–200, Bishop of Lyons, uses Pss. 110 and 45 in a similar way to Justin. In two relevant works, *The Proof of Apostolic Preaching* and *Against Heresies*, the entire Old Testament – not only the Psalms – is subsumed under the category of the prophetic. However, the psalms are especially useful for a prophetic focus in stating the supersession of Christianity over Judaism. Unlikely psalms – also used by Justin – such as Ps. 21:5 ('splendour and honour thou dost bestow on him') and

---

[20] See S. Jellicoe (1972), and www.earlychristianwritings.com/text/1clement-lightfoot.html.
[21] See O. *Skarsaune (1987)*; also www.ccel.org/ccel/schaff/anf01.viii.iv.i.html (on *Dialogue with Trypho*).

Ps. 3:5 ('I lie down and sleep; I wake again, for the Lord sustains me') are used as witnesses to Christ's death and resurrection. But Irenaeus goes beyond Justin in his choice of other psalms. Not only Psalm 22, but also Psalm 69 (also used in the Gospels) testifies to Jesus' death and resurrection. And not only Psalm 24, but also Psalm 68 (vv. 17 ff.: 'Thou didst ascend the high mount') witnesses to Christ's ascension; not only Psalm 45, but also Psalm 132 (not least vv. 1–2 and 11 where David 'swears to the Lord') show Christ's authority over David and his rightful claim to be the Messiah because of his divine and human nature.[22]

Of the writings of *Tertullian of Carthage*, c.160–220, three relevant Latin works offer different examples of his use of the psalms to argue against opponents of the Christian faith. In *Answer to the Jews,* Tertullian (a convert at the age of thirty-seven) argued, like Irenaeus, against the Jewish interpretation of the Old Testament in general, using the psalms as illustrations of their misappropriation by the Jews. Tertullian uses Ps. 19:4 ('their voice has gone out into all the world') rather like Paul's use of this psalm in Romans, to show how salvation for the Gentiles has been prophesied in the psalms; whilst Pss. 132:17 ('I have prepared a lamp for my anointed one') and 72:15 ('May gold of Sheba be given to him') testify to Jesus as the Messiah prepared by David, fulfilled in part by the visit of the Magi at his birth (*Against the Jews,* Chs. IX and X). *Against Marcion* argues, conversely, against *Marcionism and its preference for New Testament scriptures over the Old, and here Tertullian uses the psalms as a bridge between the two covenants. He does this not only by taking psalms which have a positive evaluation of the Law (Psalms 1 and 119 in particular) but also specific verses, such as Ps. 82:1 ('God has taken his place in the divine council, in the midst of the gods he holds judgement'), which speaks, he argues, of other beings being judged as non-gods (*Against Marcion,* Bk. II Ch. XIX and Bk. I, Ch. VII; see also John 10:34). In *Against Praxeas* Tertullian contends with Christian *Gnosticism in general and with Praxeas in particular, in their denial of the divine nature of Christ as well as the Trinity. It begins with a quotation from Ps. 91:11 ('he will command his angels concerning you, to guard you in all your ways'), also used in Jesus' Temptations, to show how Praxeas is sowing similar seeds of doubt in the church at Rome as the devil tried to do to Christ (ch. I). Tertullian then uses the psalms to show how the divine nature of Christ is clearly evident in the psalms – typically, he uses Ps. 45:7 and 110:1 (chs. IV, XI and XIII). This is why Christians can use the psalms as an address to Jesus Christ as God: Tertullian uses Pss. 96, 23 and 34 in this respect.[23]

Although the authentic writings of *Hippolytus of Rome,* c.170–235, are difficult to establish, a few commentaries on individual psalms in Greek, and fragmentary

---

[22] See www.ccel.org/ccel/schaff/anf01.ix.i.html (*Against Heresies*).
[23] See *T.P. O'Malley (1967);* also www.ccel.org/ccel/schaff/anf03.iv.ix.i.html (*Answer to the Jews*); www.ccel.org/ccel/schaff/anf03.v.iv.ii.i.html (*Against Marcion);* www.ccel.org/ccel/schaff/anf03.v.ix.i.html (*Against Praxeas*).

verses on other psalms, are likely to have come from his hand. Like Tertullian, Hippolytus's works often address both the Marcionites, with their negative view of the Old Testament, and the *Montanists, with their enthusiasm for contemporary prophecy in the church. To show that the Old Testament has an inherent value, and that prophecy has an ancient foundation, Hippoloytus selects various psalms to show their worth as prophecies, pointing to the life and death of Christ. He speaks of the Psalms providing us with a 'new doctrine' after the law of Moses, in that it was David, more than Moses, who was deemed worthy of bearing the name of the Saviour. His commentary on Psalm 110 refutes Christian Gnosticism by way of a 'florilegium' which intersperses psalms with other biblical texts to create an overall Christological bias. And his commentary on Psalms 23 and 24 shows how Ps. 23 is about the death of Christ, and Ps. 24, about his resurrection and ascension. Taking Psalms 1 and 2 together, Psalm 1 is (surprisingly) about the birth of Christ; Psalm 2, about his passion.[24]

Both Tertullian and Hippolytus also give us insights as to how the psalms were viewed by their Gnostic opponents, who invented their own copies (the expression 'psalmoi idiotikoi' applied to all sorts of private compositions, but certainly included those of the Gnostics) in order to disseminate their own doctrines in hymnic forms. We know that a *Mandean Gnostic called Valentinus (c.100–175 CE) composed his own psalms; that by the third century the *Manicheans also composed their own copies – the more mystical *Psalms of the Festival of Bema* (Mercy Seat) and the *Psalms to Jesus* trace their origins back to this time; and, somewhat later, a sixth-century Gnostic work, *Codex Brucianus* from Upper Egypt, has examples of Gnostic hymns which echo the psalms ('... Hear me as I sing praises to thee, O Mystery who existest before every incomprehensible one ...'). It is clear that this type of imitation, defying the way the psalms were used as an increasingly important resource for the defence of orthodox Christian doctrine, was a popular way of offering an alternative belief – not of the hidden Christ redeeming mankind by his life and death, but rather, of human effort to reach the light of God. Both Tertullian and Hippolytus refer to such works, the latter explicitly. In *Philosophumena* V 10, which is a refutation of yet another Gnostic sect called the Naassenes who also denied the divinity of Christ, Hippolytus speaks of the ways in which they devised their own 'bible texts *and psalms*'. Hence the appeal by the Apologists to authentic biblical psalms is also in part to show up the counterfeit versions. It is small wonder that the Synod of Laodicaea in Phrygia, some time between 341 and 381 CE, stated that it was not permitted that privately composed psalms be read out in church, but only those in the canonical books.

---

[24] See www.ccel.org/fathers2/ANF-05/anf05-17.htm#P2768_891774 (a general work on the psalms) and www.ccel.org/fathers2/ANF-05/anf05-17.htm#P2773_892838 (commentaries on Psalms 2, 23–24 and 110).

Alexandrian Commentators

The early Apologists were constantly searching for hidden meanings which highlighted in varying ways the presence of Christ in the psalms. This is not such a large step from the ways in which the so-called *Alexandrian commentators of the eastern churches evince an allegorical reading of Scripture. Relevant writers include *Clement* (150–215), *Origen* (184–254) and *Athanasius,* Bishop of Alexandria (296–373). The real difference is one of emphasis – not so much 'proof-texting' from the psalms as using them as illustrations for a now more established body of Christian doctrine. Yet again, Philo of Alexandria's allegorical exegesis was an influence, and these writers applied to the psalms (and so to Christ) what Philo applied to the Pentateuch (and so to Moses). Greek philosophy was also of paramount importance: although there was still a small Jewish community in Alexandria, the most influential opponents of the Christian faith were Gnostics.

Clement spent most of his time in Alexandria, although he had to flee to Caesarea in his later years to avoid persecution. Like Justin Martyr, Clement uses the idea of Jesus as the eternal word (the '*Logos*'), and thus assumes that in the ancient psalms (more ancient even than Platonic philosophy) Jesus is eternally present. Ps. 78:1–2 ('... I will utter my mouth in a parable; I will utter dark sayings from of old' – a verse also used in Matthew's Gospel) is a key text in *Stromata* 5.32, which is a collection of miscellaneous sayings, for Clement sees that the reference is to the Logos opening up his mind to unlock the enigmatic truths of Scripture. There is, however, an important difference from Justin: when using familiar psalms such as 2, 45 and 110, Clement sees them as 'witnesses' to Christ, by David, rather than spoken by Christ himself, the inner meaning of which Christ the Logos can make clear. Clement understands that the eternal meaning (relating to Christ) is found in the temporal words of a psalm (spoken through the mouth of David). The psalms illustrate Christian doctrine and Christian living, rather than the reverse: thus Clement provides an important bridge between the essentially prophetic use of psalmody and the more allegorical use which succeeded him.[25]

Origen of Alexandria wrote some nine homilies on the psalms and commentaries on probably three of them (although Jerome reports the number to be some 120 homilies on sixty-three psalms and forty-five commentaries on forty psalms). From what limited extant material there is, it is clear that Origen's real gift is his ability to combine a textual, philological approach to the psalms (he was conversant in Hebrew, as his work on the *Hexapla* reveals) with a philosophical, Logos-based doctrine which was a development of Clement's allegorical approach. Origen was concerned on the one hand with the way that Judaism had failed to see the ultimate reality of Christ within the psalms; and on the other, with the way the Greeks still failed to see within the whole Old Testament the revelation of a God greater than their way of thinking. So in addressing Jews, Origen can compare the different readings in the Greek and Hebrew texts of Ps. 2:11–12 ('serve the Lord

---

[25] For Clement's writings in Stromata, see www.ccel.org/ccel/schaff/anf02.vi.iv.i.v.html.

with fear, with trembling kiss his feet') where he writes in detail as to what the expression 'kiss his feet' means, and he can speak about the Greek misquotation of Ps. 91:11–12 in Lk. 4:10–11 as 'the devil's exegetical blunder' (for how could Christ need the help of angels if he were the Son of God?); and in addressing Greeks, he can take Ps. 16:10 ('for you do not give me up to Sheol …') and Ps. 68:18 ('You ascended the high mount …') as witnesses to the resurrection and ascension of Christ respectively (*Homil. in Lucam* 10 and 27). Another significant aspect of Origen's studies of the psalms is his writing on the changes of speaker (an approach whose roots are already in Justin's and Tertullian's works), and he argued that the 'I' could be the human Christ identifying with humanity as well as the divine Christ vindicating his church. This way of reading became known as 'prosopological exegesis', influencing Augustine's interpretation of psalmody some 150 years later.[26]

Athanasius' exegetical use of the psalms is best seen in his *Letter to Marcellinus*, whose subject matter is how to interpret the Psalms. (This text was, by a strange sequence of events, included as a preface to the Psalter in the *Alexandrian Codex, and this popularized the work more than might have been expected.) In the letter, Athanasius outlines two categories of psalms – those which echo the movements of the soul (for example, Pss. 3; 11; 12; 51; 54; 56; 57; 142) and those which announce the coming of Christ (Pss. 87; 45; 2; 22; 88; 69; 138; 24; 47; 110; 72) (*Letter to Marcellinus 27*). Athanasius contends that the psalms are different from any other Old Testament book in this respect; firstly, they alone can take us through the voice of David to Christ himself, and secondly, they alone can help us recognize in them our own voice: they are like a garden, containing in one place everything necessary for our salvation, the human and the divine (*Letter to Marcellinus 2, 10, 11, 12*). Hence both the moral and prophetic qualities of the Psalter are emphasized together; if there is a search for inner meaning, this is for personal, spiritual instruction. Athanasius concludes that no extraneous alterations are to be made for the Psalms: they are to be chanted and sung in all their simplicity (*Letter to Marcellinus 31*). Furthermore, the personal piety of the psalmists, addressing our human needs, anticipates the Incarnation: this approach, demonstrating how the Incarnation was foreshadowed in the Old Testament, served Athanasius well in his stance against *Arianism. In brief, Athanasius saw the '*skopus*' (or goal) of all Scripture to be the person and work of Christ, to whom the Psalms, more than any other book in Scripture, bear witness. This has similarities with Origen's approach, but with a more spiritual and personal slant because it is seen through one particular letter.[27]

---

[26] For Origen's general works, see www.ccel.org/fathers2/ANF-04/anf04-40.htm#P6085_1027786. For his works on the psalms, see *Excerpta in Psalmum I, VI, XV, XVIII* MPG 12:1076–84, 1092–96; also *Libri in Psalmos (Praefetio et Fragmenta in diuersos Psalmos in catenis)* MPG 12: 1053–76, 1409-1686 ; MPG 17: 105–49.

[27] For the text of the letter, see www.athanasius.com/psalms/aletterm.htm. In addition to the general works referred to earlier, more particular studies on the use of the Psalms by Alexandrian Commentators include J.M. Auwers (1994) and J. Carleton Paget (1996) on the Greek fathers; *R.P.C. Hanson (1959)*, E. Muhlenberg (1987), and M. Wiles (1970), all on Origen; and G.C. Stead and H.-J. Sieben (both on Athanasius).

The Cappodocian Fathers

Of the *Cappodocian fathers, only *Basil of Caesarea* (330–79) and *Gregory of Nyssa* (335–95) wrote specifically on the psalms. Basil wrote some fifteen homilies on the psalms which have much in common with Athanasius': the Law, the Histories and Proverbs offer a special sort of teaching, but the use and profit of all three was to be found in the Psalter (*Prefix to Psalm 1*). Basil has a particular, practical slant. His homily on Ps. 15, for example, is about right behaviour, particularly regarding usury, but this is directed to the Christian, not the Jew; the Christian's ultimate goal is not the earthly city (Ps. 15:1) but heavenly Jerusalem. At times Basil leans towards allegory: he reads Ps. 29:3, 'The voice of the Lord is upon the waters', as a reference to the baptism of Christ, and because Ps. 45:6 ('Your throne, O God, endures forever …') is an address to Christ, the reference to myrrh in Ps. 45:8 refers to his birth and his burial. Nevertheless, overall the moral and spiritual appeal of the psalms is to the fore, with less evidence within the homilies, at least, of contending with the Christian heresies which so absorbed earlier Alexandrian writers on the Psalms.

If Basil is closer to Athanasius in his use of the psalms, *Gregory*, his brother, is closer to Origen. His work on the titles of the psalms (*In Inscriptiones Psalmorum*) is unique up to this point in time in the way it deals with the Psalter as a whole, rather than individual psalms. Gregory takes the five books of the Psalter and sees within the separate titles to each psalm a progressive account in five stages (what Gregory, following Greek philosophical terminology, calls '*akolouthia*' or sequence of changes) of the ascent of man's soul towards God (towards what is termed '*taxis*', or the given order of things). This progressive view of psalmody is not concerned with their chronological development in the history of Israel, but rather it is interested in a spiritual and mystical progression. For example, Psalm 1 concerns the quest for blessedness, with its sapiental teaching about the avoidance of evil; Psalm 2, so rich in Christian allusions since the time of the New Testament, is not developed in this way at all; according to Gregory, it is the consequence of Psalm 1 – what the one who seeks to be blessed can expect, namely victory over evil as promised by God. Psalm 3 continues this idea, in personal terms, and so on. Although Gregory never denies a specific Christian exegesis (indeed, his idea of '*theoria*' or meditation clearly points Christwards), his focus on the individual soul is very different from the prophetic proof-texting of some of the New Testament writers and early Apologists. His is a more mystical, neo-Platonist view in his sense that psalmody is about the origin and goal of the human soul: several scholars have noted shared concerns between Gregory and the later Proclus Diadochus (c.410–85), who was the last of the great Platonic teachers and was schooled in Alexandria before he taught in Athens. The Christian influences upon Gregory were undoubtedly Origen, Basil and to some extent Athanasius, in their mutual search for the *skopos* of psalmody (although for the other three this was expressed in relation to the person and work of Christ rather than the ascent of the soul to God). There may be rational difficulties in Gregory's expositions of some titles of the psalms;

but that he offers a unique contribution to the reception of the Psalter as a whole cannot be denied.[28]

ANTIOCHENE COMMENTATORS

Although they too were writing mainly in Greek for the eastern church, the *Antiochene commentators represent a very different approach to psalmody. Of these, the church historian *Eusebius* (260–340), Bishop of Caesarea in Palestine, offers an intermediate position, being less attracted to 'speculative' readings and more engaged with the textual and historical tradition. Origen had a great influence on Eusebius, the two having spent time together during the *Diocletian persecution when Origen had fled to Caesarea, and Eusebius was attracted as much to Origen's philological approach as to his allegorical method. Being concerned to bring some order into the ways in which the psalms had been used in their references to Christ, Eusebius used Origen's prosopological approach in order to identify, more analytically, the different speakers in the psalms. For example, in Ps. 2:7 ('You are my son; today I have begotten you'), David could not be 'begotten of God'; so this must refer to God addressing Christ. And in Ps. 16:10 ('For you do not give me up to Sheol') and in Ps. 30:3 ('O Lord, you brought up my soul from Sheol') David could not have returned from Sheol, so again, this must refer to Christ (*Demonstratio evangelica* II 16,1–8; III 2,71). By contrast, where the psalmist confesses his sin (Psalm 51) or his integrity (Psalm 26) the 'I' cannot be Christ: David is the speaker. Eusebius' *Commentary on the Psalms* (of which only Psalms 51:1–95:3 are extant) is a combination of a prophecy/fulfilment reading with a more literal and historical analysis. Eusebius's summary of the entire Psalter, by way of his reference to the titles of the psalms and their contents, became particularly well known owing to its inclusion in an introduction to the Psalms in the Alexandrian Codex, along with Athanasius' *Letter to Marcellinus*.

Three other writers of the Antiochene school use a more thoroughgoing historical approach with respect to psalmody. The first, *Diodore of Tarsus* (died c.390) tutored the other two, *Theodore of Mopsuestia* (350–429) and *John Chrysostom* (347–407) at Antioch. *Diodore's* legacy (one which some scholars admittedly have doubted) is a critical commentary on some fifty-one psalms; these he saw as a poetic gloss on the history of Israel from the time of David to the time of Hezekiah, and so served as a kind of commentary on Isaiah, Jeremiah and Samuel–Kings. According to Diodore, the psalms are about Hezekiah, not about Christ; David is still seen as the author of the psalms, speaking prophetically – but about Hezekiah,

---

[28] On the use of the Psalms by Basil, see www.ccel.org/ccel/schaff/npnf208.vi.ii.iii.html and *Homiliae super psalmos* MPG 29: 209–494. For translated texts of Gregory's commentary, see R.E. Heine (1995); for secondary literature, see W. Bloemendaal (1960); *M. Canevet (1983)*; A. Meredith (1996); H.P. Nasuti (2005); J. Reynard (1997); M.-J. Rondeau (1974).

not about Christ. For example, Diodore (in *Commentarii in Psalmos I–L*) reads Ps. 29 against the backcloth of the Assyrian attack in Hezekiah's day, quoting 2 Kings 19:35–6 as its background (the reference to the waters in v. 3, the cedars in v. 5, the oaks in v. 9a and the Temple in v. 9b are all read in this light). Similarly Diodore protests that Ps. 22 cannot be about Christ, who needed no confession of sin, but (taking this further than Eusebius) can only refer to Hezekiah's guilt, as in 2 Kgs. 19. In fact, very few psalms apply to Christ: the only convincing examples are Pss. 2, 8, 45 and 110.

Theodore of Mopsuestia, Bishop in Cilicia, also reads the psalms historically, but sees the fulfilment of David's 'prophecies' not in the time of Hezekiah and the Assyrians, but at the time of the exile in Babylon, and later still, in the days of Zerubbabel and the Persian restoration. Theodore's commentary on the psalms was his first work, and his comments on some eighty-one psalms are still extant. Refuting the neo-Platonic and allegorizing tendencies of the Alexandrian school, and following Diodore, his teacher, the historical context is thus all-important, although (with no knowledge of Hebrew, unlike his tutor) Theodore still sees that the meaning (*'dianoia'*) of the psalms is as important as the bare text (*'lexis'*). The psalms are all inspired by the spirit of David; David is a prophet; but prophecy's fulfilment is within the confines of the Old Testament. Following Diodore, a Christological interpretation is found in only four psalms: Pss. 2, 8, 45 and 110.

Theodore differs from Diodore in his more extensive use of 'typology'. He argues that the historical 'types' are contained within the Old Testament (from David through to Hezekiah and to Zerubbabel) and only rarely can one move, typologically, into New Testament times. His dictum could have been 'clarify Homer with Homer' – i.e. the psalms must be interpreted within the bounds of the Old Testament itself. For example, of Psalm 22, he argues that those who, in the light of the opening verse ('My God, my God, why hast thou forsaken me?'), apply it to Christ are 'guilty of no little rashness'. Hence the relevance of the psalms is in the light they shed on Old Testament religion; Theodore's rationale is to establish Christianity's roots firmly in Jewish soil, not in Greek religion. Accused of being too much of a Jewish sympathizer in this approach, Theodore responded by rejecting the Jewish titles of the psalms and replacing them with more fitting comments summarizing the contents of the psalm, following the tradition already initiated by Eusebius of Caesarea. Perhaps in the light of Gregory of Nyssa's commentary, Theodore vigorously refutes the value of the psalm titles (which at this stage were also discussed in a Syriac version as well as the Greek) in illuminating this quest. (Somewhat incongruously, Theodore's cautious, more literal reworking of these titles was used in the ninth-century Paris Psalter (containing some fifty psalms in prose) and so also became known in the western churches: it was even copied into early Irish Psalters as well, as will be illustrated in a later chapter.)

John Chrysostom, Bishop of Constantinople, also a student of Diodore, modified this approach. As well as offering information about Israel's history, the psalms had a unique didactic and spiritual value. In his homilies on over fifty-eight psalms, the historical context of the psalms is still a primary concern; precision of comment is all-important, and Chrysostom uses typology much less than Theodore. Most of Chrysostom's works on the psalms (4–13, 44–50, 109–18, 120–50) were delivered as homilies on particular occasions for the church in Constantinople, and their homiletic and practical bias is very clear. Chrysostom's concern with finding precepts for Christian morality in the psalms was in part a reaction to the more mystical and allegorizing approaches of the Alexandrians, and he avoided, as much as possible, the Christianizing of psalmody: in fact Ps. 110 was the only psalm where he offered some Christian application through typology, advocating that Christ must be the Lord spoken of by David in verse 1 (*Expositiones in Psalmos 110*). Having a strong incarnational theology, whereby he believed that God in Christ accommodated himself to our human weakness, his pastoral, homiletic stance, with its emphasis on the importance of good works, resulted in his being accused of *semi-Pelagianism.

Theodoret of Cyrrhus (393–460), Bishop in Syria, was in part responsible for the abolition of Tatian's *Diatessaron* in the Syriac church (c.423). This resulted in the increasing use of the *Peshitta* (Syriac) translation of the four Gospels and the Psalter. The Psalter had been translated into Syriac from the Hebrew, probably in Edessa, by the second century CE – whether by Jews or Christians is unclear, because it shows influence of the Jewish *Targums* and rabbinic sources as well as of Christian commentators in the eastern churches. The *Peshitta* became the standard Syriac text for the Psalms from the fifth century onwards and this promoted Theodoret's commentary on all 150 psalms. This has survived, but it is the prologue, explaining his method, which is the most interesting. Trying to avoid both an overly historicizing approach and too much of a moralistic bias, both of which claimed too much Jewish history and Jewish morality for the Christian cause, Theodoret (arguing against Theodore here) contended that the psalms must be interpreted not as a case against the Jews, but rather as prayers and prophecies for the household of faith. He sets out clear divisions between the literal and the typological approaches, although the literal/historical is still most important: Psalms 29, 30 and 33 pertain to Hezekiah, for example. Typology is only allowed when the speaker could not possibly be a human Davidic king (i.e. again, in Pss. 2, 8, 45, 110 – and, surprisingly, Ps. 22 and 72). Much of Theodoret's ministry was clouded by the divisions between orthodox Christianity and *Nestorianism, and his interpretations of the human and divine Jesus in the psalms led to his being accused of semi-Nestorianism.[29]

---

[29] Studies on use of the psalms by the Antiochenes include a general work by J.J. O'Keefe (2000), with specific works by Eusebius such as *Commentarius in Psalmos* found in MPG 30:81–104; MPG 23:441–1221. See also secondary literature such as Theodore's reading of psalmody by *R.A. Greer (1961)*; R.C. Hill (2004); M. Wiles (1970b) and *D.Z. Zaharopoulos (1989)*. Studies on Chrysostom and psalmody include R.C. Hill (1997; 1998a, 1998b). Works on Theodoret include B. Croke (1984) and J.N. Guinot (1994). Studies on the Syriac Psalms and the Peshitta include W.E. Barnes (1904); W. Bloemendaal (1960); *S. Hidal (1996)*; R.J.V. Hiebert (2005); J. Lund (1988; 1995); *L. van Rompay (1996)*; H.F. van Rooy (2005); A. Vogel (1951); and M.P. Weitzman (1982; *1999*).

Other Commentators of the Eastern Church

Three other significant contributors to the reception of psalmody, whose works in different ways influenced commentators in both the East and West, deserve mention here. The first represents that growing trend in new compositions imitating psalmody; the second is significant for his mystical yet practical work on how to pray the psalms; and the third is important for a commentary of the psalms which quotes and draws from the accumulative wisdom of the past.

Ephraim the Syrian (306–73) became a member of the church at Edessa, which, since the second century, had been heir not only to the Aramaic culture, but was also as close to the Graeco-Roman world in the West as it was to the Persian culture in the East. Hence the eclectic nature of Ephraim's hymns and prayers, which were popularized before the *Peshitta* translation of the psalms was established and before the Synod of Laodicaea which banned privately composed psalms for church use. Ephraim's compositions were designed to be sung by alternating choirs of nuns, as a means of countering the *Arian heresy of Bardesanes (a Syrian Gnostic poet) through Christian verse. Many of these compositions imitated psalmody in their use of strophes and refrains, of experimentation in rhythm and accent, rhyme and assonance, and acrostic forms. Ephraim's liturgical and doctrinal adaptation of psalmody was an important inspiration for western writers of hymns such as Ambrose of Milan, as will be seen shortly. One example, echoing the style of first two verses of Psalm 1, and illustrating how one could find the two natures of Christ in the psalms, reads:

> Blessed is the one who has not tasted
> > the bitter poison of the wisdom of the Greeks.
> Blessed is the one who has not let slip
> > the simplicity of the apostles ...
> Nature and Scripture
> > together carry
> The symbols of his humanity
> and of his divinity.

The second commentator is perhaps the best known of the Desert Fathers for his writings on psalmody and prayer. *Evagrius Ponticus* (345–99) spent time with the Cappodocians such as Basil in Caesarea and Gregory in Constantinople, and from there, via Jerusalem, with Alexandrians such as Origen, until he eventually joined a monastic community in northern Egypt. There he completed his *Scholia* on the Psalms. Evagrius assumed the Psalms summarized the whole of Scripture, and saw Christ the Creator and Jesus the one created present throughout them. Tradition has it that he prayed the psalms 100 times daily, each time followed by a period of silent prayer; *Scholia* is an exposition of the relationship between these two aspects of prayer, and Evagrius offers a dialectical relationship between an active engagement with the language of psalmody, with its rich imagery and vivid, diverse life-settings, and a more passive and receptive period of silent, apophatic prayer. Despite his being condemned of semi-Pelagianism by Justinian some 150 years later, Evagrius' work on the healing properties of psalmody was a huge influence on Christians, both monastic and lay, in both East and West, who used his writings as instruction on psalmody as a way of fighting temptation.

Hesychius of Jerusalem (dates uncertain: died c.433? 451), wrote in the midst of the Nestorian and Arian controversies, and continued an Alexandrian approach to psalmody. Although much of his life and works are shrouded in obscurity, *Fragmenta in Psalmos* is attributed to him. This is essentially a mystical commentary, showing the mystery of Christian dogma hidden in the psalms. Hesychus' greatest contribution was in the way he used other Christian commentators to interpret and give authority to his own works. This type of expansion to a commentary became known as the *'Gloss', and Hesychius was among the first to use it in a Greek work on the Psalms. It is most likely that he is the 'Hesychius' referred to frequently by writers using a more extensive (Latin) Gloss in the Middle Ages.[30]

Thus by the fourth century, the Christian use of the psalms, at least in the eastern churches, was becoming quite diverse. Most writers still agreed that the psalms were 'prophetic', but they understood 'prophetic inspiration' in different ways, and by the end of this period, a prophetic interpretation of the psalms was simply another way of offering a 'Christocentric' reading of them. It is nevertheless possible to identify three specific emphases. The most cautious one, exemplified by the Antiochenes, who were wary of the excesses of allegorical readings, was to see prophetic inspiration contained within the limits of the Old Testament alone; in this case, a more historical bias and practical application was given, with little emphasis on Christianizing the psalms. A second approach, begun by some of the New Testament writers, was to see prophetic inspiration within both the Old and the New Testaments, and to allow typology as the bridge between the two, whereby 'types' from the life of Christ (his birth, baptism, temptations, transfiguration, passion, death, resurrection, ascension) were prefigured in verses in the psalms. A third emphasis, seen especially in the Alexandrian approach, is to argue that the Old Testament is a temporal shadow of the eternal reality encapsulated in the New Testament. Here, a more allegorical approach dominates, and very little historical empathy is required: the Christocentric reading is primary, and this thus allows for a 'prophetic approach' in the broadest, neo-Platonic sense.

Commentators of the Western Church

Most of the Alexandrian, Cappodocian and Antiochene commentators belonged to that part of the Roman Empire which by 330 under Constantine represented

---

[30] On Ephraim, see S. Brock (*1983²*; 1998); S. Griffith at syrcom.cua.edu/Hugoye/vol1No2/HV1N2 Griffith.html; also K.E. McVey (1989). On Evagrius, see L. Dysinger (2005); J. McKinnon (1994); M.-J. Rondeau (1960); C. Stewart (2001). On Hesychius, see *M. Aubineau (1978–80)*.

Greek-speaking eastern Christianity, with Constantinople as the centre, and patriarchies in Antioch, Jerusalem and Alexandria, as well as in Rome. When we move across to Rome and to the Latin fathers of the western church, less diverse interpretations are evident. In part this is because of a prevailing pastoral and instructional emphasis throughout the western churches, still dominated at this time with the controversies related to the Arian heresy, a response to which resulted in emphasizing the spiritual meaning of psalmody in the life of the church. The best way of illustrating this is to take in turn the four great commentators of the western church (Hilary, Jerome, Ambrose and Augustine – the latter three later known as amongst the fathers of the western church, along with Gregory the Great, to be discussed later).

Hilary of Poitiers (315–67) wrote several homilies on the psalms. His paramount concern was the need for careful exegesis. Thus different psalms are expounded in different ways. Here Hilary develops Origen's prosopological method concerning the different speakers of the psalms. For example, in his introduction to Psalm 1, he speaks of the need to attend to the 'voice of the prophet'; this is quite different from the 'voice of the Father' in Ps. 89:19 ('I have exalted one chosen from the people, I have found my servant David') or the 'voice of the Son' in Ps. 18:43 ('... people whom I had not known served me ...'). In his *Homilies on the Psalms*, it is clear from a reading of Psalms 1, 53 and 130 that Hilary uses the psalms not to create doctrine, but rather, to illustrate it. In *Tractatus super Psalmum*, his actual commentary on the Psalms, of which Pss. 1–2, 9, 15–16, 53–71, 93 and 120–50 remain, his exegesis of Ps. 137 ('By the waters of Babylon, we sat down and wept when we remembered Zion') is a good illustration of the way he sought to combine both literal and allegorical readings (again, following Origen). First, Hilary gives attention to the questions about the meanings of the Babylonian irrigation system, the nature of the musical instruments and the types of willow trees; but then he moves on to reflect upon the spiritual longing for a secure resting place with God, a longing which is then applied to the Christian community in Hilary's day (perhaps a response to the uncertainties evoked during the reforms of Justinian, in which period Hilary is probably writing).

Jerome (342–420) represents a more cosmopolitan background, having been influenced by centres of Christianity in the East as well as the West. Born and brought up near Rome, his time in Antioch and Caesarea influenced his views of the literal and historical approaches to psalmody, whilst a period in Constantinople brought him under the influence of Gregory of Nyssa and the Cappodocians. From there he travelled to Egypt, where he was taught by an Alexandrian exegete, Didymus the Blind. It was his time in Bethlehem that saw the culmination of his works on the psalms, amongst which were three revisions and one translation of the Psalter and two commentaries on selected psalms which each reflect the eclectic nature of his theological method. For example, concerning translation, Jerome identified with Origen in understanding the inspiration of the psalms to be in the meaning they convey, not in the single words: 'sense for sense not word for word'. In Rome, between 382 and 385, he had revised the old Latin version of the Psalter (the '*Vetus Itola*', a second-century text from North Africa, which became known as the '*Psalterium Vetus*'), and then made a second revision by using the Greek versions, creating the '*Psalterium Romanum*'. In Caesarea, between 386 and 387, Jerome had made use of Origen's *Hexapla, and from this had revised the (Latin) liturgical text of the Roman church, which became known as the '*Psalterium Gallicanum*'. In 391–3, almost certainly in Bethlehem, he provided a new translation in Latin by use of the Hebrew (the '*Psalterium Hebraicum*' or '*Psalterium iuxta Hebraeos*'): this was for popular use, although the '*Psalterium Gallicanum*' became the best known because of its liturgical value, and, despite the plethora of other Greek and Latin versions at this time, this was the version which was included in Jerome's *Vulgate*. Jerome's translation was a remarkable feat at a time when there were no vowels in the text, no guides to pronunciation, no grammars, dictionaries or concordances to help with the Hebrew.

The fragments of Jerome's *Commentarioli* comprise annotations of psalms, which illustrate, like his translations, a concern for philology as much as interpretation. His *Tractatus* – a composite work on the psalms – reflects a more spiritual approach. The several different comments on the same psalm show his diverse emphases and methods: for example, in the *Commentarioli* on Psalm 1, Jerome asks why the psalm has no title, and, writing in Latin, compares it with the Hebrew and Greek. In *Tractatus*, his comments on Psalm 1 compare the psalm to a door of a great building, where the Holy Spirit gives the key through which the 'righteous man' can enter and so learn to be like Christ through acquiring the gift of wisdom (the 'tree' in v. 3 symbolizes wisdom). Hence Jerome not only avoids the Alexendrian reading, which identifies the ideal figure as Jesus Christ, but he also refutes the Jewish (and indeed Antiochene) belief that the ideal figure within this psalm might be King Josiah: rather, for Jerome, the saint is anyone and everyone who has been saved by Christ.

Ambrose of Milan (339–97, at one time tutor of Augustine) combined a more pragmatic reading of psalmody (like Hilary of Poitiers) with a neo-Platonist and more allegorical approach (like Origen), both of which enabled him to Christianize the psalms as much as possible. As Bishop of Milan (which by 352 was the capital of western Europe), his *Expositio Psalmi* sets a different trend in its attempt to give the psalms a 'sacramental discourse' within the teaching of the Roman church. For example, his *Expositio Psalmi* cxviii (Ps. 119 in our English versions), dating from about 388 CE, is a work of twenty-two addresses to his congregation, each one consisting of one psalm division. It is read both in a practical human-centred and theological Christ-centred way, with a concern throughout for its place in the life and teaching of the church.

Ambrose's ecclesial concerns resulted in his most distinctive contribution to the reception of the psalms: that of their role within liturgy. Although the eastern churches, represented by Diodore of Tarsus and Theodoret of Cyrrhus, had encouraged antiphonal singing, a tradition which seems to have been passed via Jerusalem to Antioch (Acts 11:19–30), and although Ephraim the Syrian established the tradition of singing hymns based upon psalms, its real development in the West is credited (at least, by Augustine) to Bishop Ambrose. He initiated a tradition which became known as 'Ambrosian Chant', and the psalms played a central part within it. Both congregation and choir were used, creating a *schola cantorum*, where music –often elaborate and ornate – was learnt and preserved. The music in Milan, composed in the context of the ongoing battle against Arianism, often had an eastern influence, adopting anti-Arian hymns from the East (like those of Ephraim) in order to protect the community at Rome from Arian heresy. (This is a curious reverse situation of the ways in which earlier the Gnostic heretics at the time of Justin, Irenaeus and Tertullian had composed their own copies of psalms – '*psalmoi idiotikoi*' – to detract from the Christian use of authentic psalms.) Several hymns today trace their origins back to Ambrose: of these, '*Aeterne rerum conditur*' ('*Eternal Creator of the World*': HAM No. 17) has clear overtones of Psalm 12; whereas '*Deus Creator Omnium*' ('*Lord, Creator of All Things*'), '*Iam surgit hora tertia*' ('*Now as the Third Hour begins*') and '*Veni Redemptor Gentium*' ('*Come Redeemer of the Nations*') are full of psalmic allusions from hymns of creation (for example, Psalms 8, 19, 33, 101 and 139) and the enthronement psalms (93–9). But authentic psalms were also used: in the Eucharist, they were sung antiphonally, in what has since been termed the Ambrosian Rite, between each of the readings from the Old Testament (usually the Prophets), Epistles and Gospels; often a further psalm was read, and other psalms were usually sung before and after the Lord's Prayer.

Augustine of Hippo (354–430) was born near Carthage, and after becoming a Christian, served the North African churches for most of his life. During his time in Milan (from about 387 onwards) he was baptized by Ambrose and his mentor's allegorical and Christianizing approach to the psalms undoubtedly influenced his own interpretation. Augustine's interest in psalmody was inspired by the comfort he had gained from the psalms shortly after his conversion from *Manicheanism in 390: it was precisely their suspicion of the Old Testament, and so of the psalms, which drove Augustine towards psalmody: 'My God, how I cried to you when I read the Psalms of David, songs of faith, utterances of devotion which allow no pride of spirit to enter in! ... How they kindled my love for you!' (*Confessions 9.4.8.*) His great work *The City of God* opens with a quotation from Ps. 87: 3 ('Glorious things are spoken of you, O city of God'). Not only the *Confessions*, but also letters and sermons, resound with explicit and implicit references to the psalms, which, in terms of his commentaries and works overall, were second only to the Gospel of John: on his account, Augustine made his own revision of the Psalter, probably using the Gallican Psalter.

Augustine's *Enarrationes in Psalmos* is the only collection of expositions on the *entire* Psalter from any of the fathers of the western church (this includes no fewer than thirty-two sermons on Ps. 119, all around 422, which coincided with his refutation of Pelagianism). Most of these expositions are from sermons preached at Hippo (Pss. 1–32, from some time between 392 and 396; Pss. 111–18, from c.400; and Pss. 120–34, c.406–7) although some are from his time at Carthage.

Hence the liturgy in which the sermons were preached gives them a distinctive church-based application. Many were influenced by Augustine's refutation not only of Pelagianism but also of *Donatism, and here, Augustine was able to use the psalms to illustrate a more universal ecclesial base for the Christian Gospel. He does not defend the old arguments of looking for *either* literal readings *or* inner meanings of the psalms; instead, he holds together a moral and Christological reading of the psalms and sees that the bridge between these two interpretations is the Christian church.

Taking the now developed prosopological reading, with its interest in the different speakers and different addressees in the psalms, Augustine proposes there are only two participants: Christ speaking as himself, as it were, as the 'Head', and Christ speaking on our behalf, as the 'Body', thus holding together the human voice (the voice of Christ through the Church) and the divine voice (the voice of Christ as the risen and ascended Lord). Hence Psalm 22, for example, with its cries for help, can be seen as '*Christ the Body*' speaking through the church (although in another sermon he notes that this could be Christ himself, 'whole Christ, man and God'). By contrast, Ps. 2:8 ('Ask of me and I will make the nations your heritage' is '*Christ the Head*' speaking, gathering together all the Gentiles into the one universal church. This is both a mystical and a homiletic approach to psalmody; it could be argued that its minimal attention to details literal and historical, and its thoroughgoing Christocentric approach, take it more in the direction of Alexandria than Antioch. Indeed, Augustine's unusual use of numbers in *Enarrationes in Psalmos* also takes him in an allegorical direction. For example, 'The Sheminith' in the title to Psalm 6 is interpreted as 'the octave', whereby the number eight signifies the day of Judgement, whilst his preoccupation with the numbers 3 (standing for the soul), 4 (the body), 7 (the human being), 10 (the Creator) and its multiples and additions (12, 40, 50, and even 153, as in Ps. 50) in other psalms further illustrate this bias. But overall, it was his method of using the psalms as the voice of Christ and the church working together which took the reading of psalmody into an altogether new direction.[31]

---

[31] On Hilary and psalmody, see *A.G.S. Anyanwu (1983)*; for selected texts from Hilary's *Homilies on the Psalms,* see www.ccel.org/ccel/schaff/npnf209.ii.vi.ii.i.html. Jerome's commentaries on psalmody are mostly in fragmentary form: see www.ccel.org/ccel/schaff/npnf206.iv.IV.html; for *Commentarioli in psalmos* see G. Morin (ed.) *CCSL 72 (1959) and CCSL 78 (1968)*; and for *Homilies on the Psalms* see M.L. Ewald FC 48, 57 (1964, 1967); also C.M. Cooper (1950); J.C. Howell (1987); *R. Kieffer (1996)*; D.P. McCarthy (1992); A.S. Pease (1907); *H.F.D. Sparks (1970)*. On Ambrose's works as they relate to psalmody, see www.ccel.org/ccel/schaff/npnf210.iii.vi.html; also *H.J. auf der Maur (1977)*; M. Petschenig CSEL 62 (1919) on Psalm 119; T.K. Carroll (2000) and H. Leeb (1967). For Augustine's expositions of psalmody, see www.ccel.org/ccel/schaff/npnf108.ii.i.html and www.newadvent.org/fathers/1801.htm; also V.J. Bourke (2001); P. Bright (1997); D.E. Dekkers and I. Fraipoint (eds.) (CCSL 38, 39, 40, 1956, 1990); E.T.S Hegbin and F. Corrigan (eds.) (ACW 29 1960); S. Poque (1986); *J.W. Wiles (1995)*; *D.F. Wright (1996)*.

Liturgical Adaptations of the Psalms

Christian Liturgy

Thus far the interpretation of the psalms since New Testament times has been assessed only from the contributions of significant Christian thinkers, noting in particular the trends of using the psalms didactically, polemically, and (in the cases of Origen, Jerome, and Augustine) as revisions or translations. Another important aspect of psalmody in this period – referred to briefly in the discussion of Ambrose – is the increasing emphasis on the psalms in Christian liturgy, and the practice of psalm- singing by ordinary believers, whether in Greek, Syriac or Latin.

It is all but impossible to trace any clear development of the standardized use of psalms in Christian liturgy throughout this period. That there were set hours of prayer in the morning and evening in some Christian communities is clear from the time of Clement of Rome (*1 Clem 40:1–4*) at the end of the first century, and Tertullian of Carthage, over a century later (*On Prayer* Ch 25). By the beginning of the third century, Hippolytus of Rome's *Homily on the Psalms* makes a plea for the churches to use the Psalter as a whole (the emphasis is very much on Psalms 1–2 as a Prologue to the Psalter) rather than individual psalms from here and there. By the middle of the third century, Eusebius of Caesarea (*Commentary on Psalm 64*) refers to the regular use of Psalm 141 for evening prayer and Psalm 63 for morning use. John Chrysostom (*Commentary on Psalm 140*) also speaks of Psalm 141 being chanted daily, as also Psalm 63 in morning prayer. He speaks of all types of worship having 'David first, last and midst', whether in church, at home, in the forum, in monasteries, or in the desert, a theme echoed by Jerome (*Epistle 46*) who speaks of the psalms being used in the fields as well as in the church, showing just how much the psalms were both memorized from liturgy and used in everyday life. The Greek *Apostolic Constitutions* (regulations for church order in Syria in about 380 CE) also prescribe the use of Psalm 63 for the morning and Psalm 141 for the evening. In the western churches, the Latin *Ordo Monasterii* (c.395 CE) describes regular psalms in the morning service (Psalms 63 and 90), whilst the travelling monk, John Cassian, notes in his *Institutes* that in the western monastic tradition, Psalms 63 and 119 were always used at the sunrise service, and Psalms 148–50 (known as 'lauds', from the Latin, 'hymns of praise') along with Psalm 51 were used at the first morning service. The use of Psalm 119 for morning prayer is further illustrated by Ambrose of Milan (*Expositio Ps. 119*), as also Psalm 141 at evening prayer (*Hexameron V 12:36*).

Clearly these practices were not uniform, but they give interesting information about the early use of psalms in liturgy. In terms of daily worship, the 'controversial' psalms, such as 2, 8, 45, 72, 110, 118 and 132, are hardly evident. Instead, the more personal psalms, whose 'themes' correspond with the everyday rhythm of prayer, are more prominent. Ps. 141:2 ('Let my prayer be counted as incense before you, and the lifting up of my hands as an evening sacrifice') thus suits evening worship; whilst Ps. 63:5 ('I meditate on you in the watches of the night') fits with early morning prayers, as do the complementary moods of praise (Psalms 148–50) and confession (Psalm 51) at the beginning the day. Each of these psalms was of course given a Christian 'overlay' in the additions of antiphons, doxologies and the '*Gloria Patri*', so that the overall effect, albeit less polemical than in the writings of the fathers, was still the 'Christianizing' of psalmody.

By the fourth century, monastic communities were fully established in the desert regions of Egypt, Cappodocia and Syria. The *monastic office* grew out of these communities, with different emphases in different places. In Scetis, near Cairo (according to John Cassion, who stayed there 380–99 CE, recorded in his *Institutes Books II and III*) there were two main offices, morning and evening, when, at each office, twelve psalms were read by a soloist, whilst the monks sat and prayed; after each psalm, they stood, prostrated themselves, and stood again, all in silent prayer. With the increasing number of psalms on Saturdays and Sundays, the whole Psalter would have been read in a week; some Syrian communities are known to have recited the whole Psalter even in a day, and, as we have seen, ascetic monks such as Evagrius Ponticus apparently achieved this 100 times a day. Of all the citations from and allusions to Scripture in Egyptian works such as *The Sayings of the Desert Fathers* from Egypt, the Psalms occur almost three times as many as any other Old Testament book (Isaiah and Genesis being the next most frequently used), only to be succeeded within Scripture as a whole by references from the Gospel of Matthew. And within the Syrian tradition, a work such as Theodoret of Cyrrhus's *A History of the Monks in Syria* reveals a similar phenomenon: the constant use of psalmody – often reciting some fifteen or twenty at a time – and the rumination upon them throughout the day armed the monks in their struggle against evil and in the formation of a holy life dependent only on God in a way no other biblical text could do. 'Prayer succeeded prayer, prayer succeeded psalmody, and both again were succeeded by reading the divine oracles … (and so) he put to sleep desire, anger, pride, and all the other wild beasts of the soul' (*Cyrrhus*, on the monks Marcianus, Publius and Zeno: pp. 38, 59 and 90).

Other monasteries were established near cities, where the practice was quite different: for example, near Bethlehem, where Cassion also stayed (382–3), there were offices at cockcrow (nocturn), sunrise (matins), then at the third, sixth and ninth hours, and in the evening, making six 'hours', with selected psalms, and a continuous reading of other psalms, at each. Basil of Caesarea refers to the seven hours of prayer in the monasteries of Cappodocia – one less in the morning, but three in the evening (Vespers, Compline, and the Midnight Vigil), where again selected psalms were read along with the continuous reading of other psalms; together these formed the main part of the office. 'Seven hours of prayer' was becoming the norm, with traditions differing in terms of one or two morning or one or two evening offices: hence the significance of Ps. 119:164 ('Seven times a day I praise you …'). The practice in monastic communities was to memorize the psalms by heart; postulants – many of whom would be illiterate – were required to learn as many as they were able, before being admitted. The assumption here was that the psalms embraced all Scripture, and therefore to learn them by heart (along with parts of the New Testament) was to embrace the essence of the Gospel.

After the so-called 'Peace of Constantine' in 312, with the gradual building of new churches and the burgeoning of public worship, the daily *cathedral office* became more important in churches both eastern and western. This office was clearly influenced by the monastic tradition, but it modified the seven or so hours of prayer to two – morning and evening prayer, thus encapsulating the rising sun and lighting of the evening lamps as symbols of Christ, the light of the world. The cathedral office was different in its emphasis on ritual, ceremony (with lights, incense, processions) and chant (with responsories, antiphons and hymns, usually performed by 'cantatorii') and it had a variety of ministers (bishops, presbyters, deacons, readers, psalmists). The selective use of a few appropriate psalms was more central than the continuous reading of a series of psalms in the monasteries, although it is clear that psalms were read continuously in some traditions: the Ambrosian rite, itself a combination of the monastic and cathedral offices, completed the Psalter overall once every two weeks, and the Roman and Gregorian rites, usually once every week. Throughout the western churches, by the third and fourth centuries, the tradition of hymn-singing – testified to as early as Tertullian, but better documented by the time of Ambrose – allowed the congregation further access to the psalms by way of imitated forms. Furthermore, the psalms were read in the cathedral eucharists through the liturgy of the word, after which the congregation often heard a homily on the psalms, as seen by Augustine's sermons, which were preached on the lectionary psalm.

As for the cathedral office in eastern churches, an intriguing fourth-century account of the liturgical use of the psalms in Jerusalem (in the early 380s) is given by a travelling Spanish nun named Egeria, who, in her description of an entire liturgical year, refers, for example, to the many liturgies of Holy Week, when psalms were both read and sung to depict dramatically the sufferings of Christ, after which the Gospels were read to explain how the psalms had been fulfilled in the life of Christ. Another example from the fourth century is from the church in Ethiopia, which divided the Psalter into fifteen parts, reading thirty psalms each day from Monday to Saturday, and the entire Psalter and New Testament canticles on Sunday. There was an emphasis on the reading and singing of psalms *per se*, rather than imitations of psalmody: Canon LIX of the Synod of Laodicea in 363 actually pronounced that 'No psalms composed by private individuals ... may be read in the church'. It is no overstatement to conclude that, in both East and West, monastic and cathedral traditions together bear witness to the ways in which the Psalter pervaded worship in ways more diverse than any other biblical book.[32]

---

[32] Works which have informed this survey, both generally and specifically, include D. Burton-Christie *(1993)*; G.P. Braulik (2004); P.F. Bradshaw and L.A. Hoffman (1991a); R.T. Beckwith (1995); H. Buchinger (1995); *D.J. Chitty (1995)*; *J. Daniélou (1956)*; C. Jones, G. Wainwright and E. Yarnold (1978); J.A. Lamb (1962); *J. Mateos (1967)*; R.E. Murphy (1992, 1994); K.S. Pedersen (1998); A. Stewart-Sykes (2001); W.F. Storey (1977); R. Taft (1986, 2004); Theodoret of Cyrrhus (ETr R.M. Price 1985); R.J. Tournay (1988); B. Ward (1975); and G. Wolfenden (1990).

Jewish Liturgy

Thus far it might appear that the only vibrant use of psalmody was in the Christian tradition. This is obviously not so: indeed, the tradition of morning and evening prayer has its origins in Judaism, both in the practice of the two daily sacrifices (probably before the Temple was destroyed), but certainly in later synagogue Sabbath practice. Not surprisingly, Jewish communities, having survived the fall of the Temple in 70 CE and their final expulsion from Jerusalem in the mid-130s, and then having been dispersed through the same regions as Christian communities, were seeking to re-establish their own identity. They, like the Christians, had suffered dreadfully during periods of persecution – for example, those of Trajan (111–13) and Marcus Aurelius (161–80), particularly in Gaul, Rome and North Africa, but especially those of Decius (249–51) and Valerian (253–60), when they were ordered to sacrifice to the Roman gods or be killed, and Diocletian (284–305), when their books and buildings were destroyed, and leaders of the community were deprived of their rights. Indeed, the Jews fared worse than the Christians. After the conversion of Constantine (312), the position of Christians in society gradually strengthened (with one notable exception in this period being Julian the Apostate's restoration of Hellenistic pagan practices between 361 and 363), whereas Jews, like pagans, were constantly disenfranchised and under attack. In these times, Jewish practices of prayer based upon their psalms were almost as important as the teachings from the Torah and Prophets; and, given that the Christians were appropriating these sacred prayers above all other texts as *their* sacred literature, the practice of keeping psalmody alive in the Jewish tradition was vitally important.

So although there were no particular Jewish commentators of the psalms throughout this period (Jewish exegesis being more of a developing process, in that it was beginning to amass abundant rabbinic literary traditions, but without the series of independent writings which exemplified the Christian tradition), the Psalter nevertheless had a prominent place in the liturgical traditions of Jewish communities. The psalms were used not only in Hebrew but also in Greek. They were also accessible by the end of the period under discussion in Aramaic, through the Targums, whose date of compilation is probably somewhere between the fourth and sixth centuries CE; this vernacular translation and explanatory commentary on the Hebrew text provided a unique resource for Jewish exegesis, for it was a vernacular edition of the Psalter which was not used by Christian writers in the same way that the Septuagint was.[33]

One of the best ways of understanding the use of psalmody in Jewish liturgical practices is by reference to the Mishnah. As a Hebrew commentary on the Torah,

---

[33] Because the date of the Targums on the Psalms is more likely to be sixth century at the earliest, a fuller discussion of the contribution of this translation to our understanding of psalmody has been left until the following chapter, and a list of the relevant literature is offered there.

possibly dating as early as the third century BCE, its six parts contain over forty references to psalms, mainly of prescriptions for reciting psalms in daily life and – somewhat arbitrarily – in times of drought (e.g. Psalms 120, 121, 130 and 102). Services are prescribed three times daily (adding afternoon prayer to that of morning and evening); appropriate psalms (what in Christian tradition became termed 'proper psalms') are prescribed for the entire day. Interestingly, these prescriptions are the same as the additional headings in the LXX: Psalm 23 (Hebrew 24) was for the first day of the week, Psalm 47 (Hebrew 48) for the second day, Psalm 93 (Hebrew 94) for the fourth, Psalm 92 (Hebrew 93) for the sixth, and Psalm 91 (Hebrew 92) for the Sabbath. Although the Septuagint has no headings to other psalms for the third and fifth days, the Mishnah also records Psalm 82 for Tuesday and Psalm 81 for Thursday. Although eastern and western traditions varied, Psalms 19, 33, 90, 91, 92, 93, 135, 136 and 145–50 were jointly used in Sabbath liturgy. Ps. 119:12a ('Blessed be thou, O Lord') is a repeated refrain in the eighteen Daily Benedictions. The daily liturgy of the *Amidah* (a prayer offered whilst standing) illustrates the way that other psalms were also used in morning prayer (Psalm 30, parts of Psalms 145–50 and Psalm 100 are the most frequently quoted) and in evening prayer (for example, Psalm 134). And for the annual festivals, the Hallel (Psalms 112–18) is designated for the Feast of the New Moon (along with Psalms 98 and 104, owing to their creation themes), Passover, Pentecost, Tabernacles (Psalm 12 is to read on the eighth day of this Feast) and the Feast of the Dedication of the Temple (along with Psalm 30). In addition, Psalm 7 is to be used at the Feast of Purim, Psalm 47 for the New Year Festival, and Psalms 103 and 150 on the Day of Atonement. Individual psalm verses are to be recited during Sabbath services: for example, whilst putting on the prayer shawl, Ps. 36:7–10 is read ('How precious is your steadfast love, O God! All people take refuge under the shadow of your wings. They feast on the abundance of your house, and you give them drink from the river of your delights ...'); and when the Torah scroll is taken from the ark and presented to the people, Ps. 34:3 ('O magnify the Lord with me, and let us exalt his name together') is recited.[34]

Several observations arise from this list of psalms. Firstly, rather like the Christian use of psalmody in liturgy, the controversial psalms, both within Jewish tradition itself and within the discourses between Jews and Christians (e.g. Psalms 2, 8, 22, 26, 45, 51, 68, 69, 72, 82, 89, 110, 118, 132), receive little attention: clearly liturgical occasions address different needs from polemical concerns. Psalms 2, 72

---

[34] A particularly useful resource on Jewish use of psalmody in this period has been W.L. Holladay (1993), pp. 134–60. More general works on psalmody, prayer and liturgy a this time include P.F. Bradshaw and L.A. Hoffman (eds.) 1991(a) and G. Wolfenden (1990), both referred to previously; also D. Barthelemy (1996); A. Bastiaensen (1989); M. Bernstein (2005); W.G. Braude (2 vols., 1959); H. Danby (1933); H.H. Donin (1980); I. Elbogen (1993); P. Fiedler (1988); A. Green (ed.) (1986); C. Kessler (1991); J.C. Kugel (1987); R. Loewe (1957); M. Maher (1994); J. Maier (1983); E.M. Menn (2004); J.J. Petuchowski (1972); R. Posner (et al. eds.) (1975); S.C. Reif (1983, 1993); G.F. Willems (1990).

and 110, all avowedly Messianic psalms in Christian tradition, hardly receive mention. Secondly, there is very little obvious overlap between Jewish and Christian psalmody in liturgy: although there is no common consensus in Christendom concerning the use of specific psalms for daily use, and although the Christian use of psalms revolves around the seven or more daily offices rather than constant weekly psalms, Psalms 24, 48, 82, 94, 81, 93 and 92 just do not appear frequently in Christian liturgy; the only real correspondence is the use of Psalms 148–50 in the morning prayer of the cathedral office. Thirdly, most of the psalms in Jewish liturgy are taken from the hymns (almost all of them are represented), in addition to psalms of confidence and thanksgiving and the wisdom psalms; very few individual and communal laments are represented – no more than one-sixth, overall. Jewish psalmody in daily, weekly and festival liturgy thus seems to be more about praise and rejoicing than about lament. Fourthly, taking the proportion of psalms used on a weekly basis, those listed above (psalms for one day of the week, or for one day of the year) are far less in number in Jewish tradition than in Christian liturgy. In the latter, the Psalter was read through if not once a week, then once a fortnight or once a month, but this was not a practice in Jewish communities.

A final word needs to be said about Jewish exegetical and didactic studies on the psalms, for from the first to fifth centuries CE they do not appear to have been as pervasive as in Christian communities. It is clear that many, indeed most, of the Christian commentators referred to previously were very much aware of a Jewish audience as well as the Gentile one – hostility to Jewish readings has been evident in the writings of Apologists (for example, Irenaeus and Tertullian), Alexandrians (particularly Origen) and Cappodocians (for example, Basil). The evidence of a large Jewish community at Antioch provoked hostility in the writings of Chrysostom, whilst the works of other Antiochenes such as Theodore and Theodoret often reveal a greater concern for dialogue. And in Jerome's works, the collaborative approach is more evident in his translation work, although a confrontational style is apparent in his expository work. So Jewish-Christian discourse about psalmody was a continuous issue throughout this period. The problem is that most of what we have is from the letters, tractates and commentaries of Christians, so our knowledge of the dialogue, in this period at least, is somewhat one-sided. As far as Jewish rabbinical works were concerned, from the second century onwards the compilation of *Midrashim was proliferating, but, as with the Targums and the Palestinian and Babylonian *Talmuds, the focus in each of these interpretative traditions was undoubtedly on the Law – and to a lesser extent, the Prophets. Although it is clear from the above works that a good deal of study and reflection on psalmody went on, it was not until the thirteenth century that the *Midrash Tehillim*, an important homiletic and liturgical commentary containing Jewish traditions concerning the psalms, was eventually produced: although its origins may be traced back to the third century, it took some thousand years of tradition before its authority was fully recognized. And although by the tenth century onwards Jewish tractates and commentaries (often highly vitriolic, as will be illustrated in a later chapter) begin to abound, in this earlier period, the evidence for it, as far as the psalms are concerned, is remarkably scanty.[35]

Concluding Observations

This chapter has shown how the reception psalmody, once focused in the earlier centuries BCE within Syro-Palestine, Egypt and Babylon, becomes increasingly diversified. By the beginning of the fifth century CE, not only had both Jewish and Christian communities spread through all the Mediterranean seaboard as far as Spain to the West and Byzantium to the East, but they had also settled further inland, into Gaul and Ireland, Italy and Greece; centres such as Rome and Constantinople, Alexandria and Antioch, Jerusalem and Carthage, Lyons and Caesarea, Edessa and Milan were all significant, testifying to the prominent and abundant use of the psalmody in both faith traditions. This diffuseness, as well as the growing differences between the two faith traditions, will become increasingly evident in the following chapters.

---

[35] Pertinent works on Jewish-Christian controversies during this period include *H. Bietenhard (1974)*; R. Devreesse (1939); *M.J. Edwards (ed.) (1999)*; *P.W. Haskins (1979)*; *C.H. Kraeling (1932)*; *S. Krauss (1894)*; *N.R.M. de Lange (1976a and 1976b)*, M. McNamara (2000), pp. 239–301; *W.A. Meeks and R.L. Wilken (1978)*; M. Simon (1986); and S.G. Wilson (1995);

The Fifth to Eleventh Centuries: Liturgy, Exposition, Artistic Representation

The reception of psalmody between the fifth and eleventh centuries is more difficult to hold together. In Christian traditions, the evidence for the *liturgical* use of psalmody is still vast, both in the eastern and western churches, and in both the cathedral and monastic offices. Similarly, *expositions* of the psalms, both practical and academic, although less innovative (attending to present controversies by deferring to the writings of the early fathers, thereby contributing to a kind of canonical commentary on psalmody which became known as the *Gloss), are found in abundance. These will be discussed along with *translations* and *didactic* works, again with respect to both the eastern and western churches. A separate discussion needs to be assigned to the most significant innovation in this period in Christian tradition – that which we have termed *aesthetic*, in the production of *illuminated manuscripts of Psalters, which even at this early stage is apparent in the churches in western and eastern Christendom.

By contrast, Jewish reception history during this period follows a different pattern. Several innovations are apparent in the *liturgical* use of psalmody. The other noteworthy development is the Jewish *exposition* of the psalms: at the latter end of the period commentators with philological and polemical concerns begin to come to the fore. This is helped by a significant *translation* which also includes *didactic* concerns: hence these latter three modes of reception will be discussed together. The most notable contrast with the Christian reception of the psalms is the paucity of *aesthetic* representation.

Christian Reception

Liturgy

These were troublesome centuries for the churches in the West. First came the gradual disintegration of the Roman empire after the fall of Rome to the Goths in 410, followed

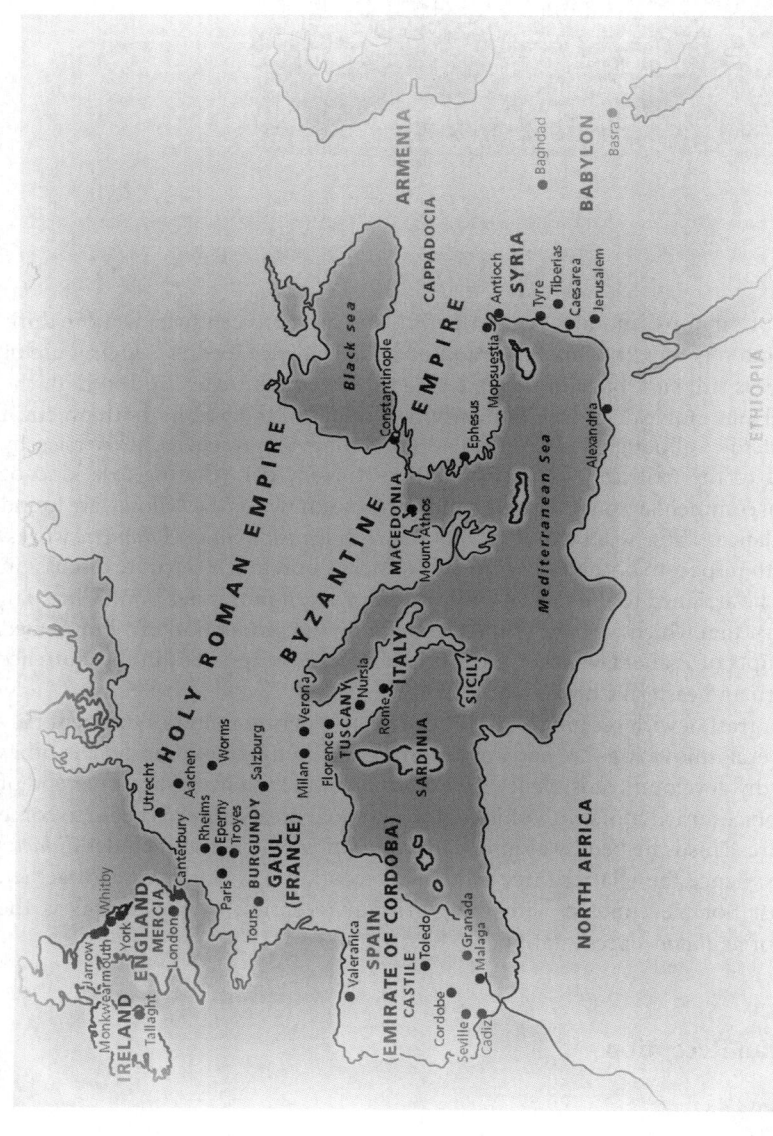

MAP 2.1 Rome: a centre of psalmody in the early Middle Ages.

by further Germanic invasions in the West and Persian victories in the East; then came the Visigoth conquests in Spain and South West France, followed by the capitulation of these countries (along with North Africa) to Islam in the seventh century. Nevertheless, the churches in France, England, Scotland, Ireland, Spain and Lombardy survived (just as the churches in Byzantium, between the sixth and seventh centuries, conquering then losing territories in North Africa, Spain, Italy, Sardinia and Sicily, also survived, even holding on to lands in southern Italy, Greece and Turkey). Although their continued existence is to be explained by factors beyond our scope – political, economic, social and religious – nevertheless, at the more unseen level, survival was undoubtedly helped by continuous prayer and worship within both the cathedral and monastic offices. And in this respect, a good deal is owed to the central place of psalmody within these offices, in both the West and East.

EASTERN CHURCHES

We have already noted the extensive influence of psalmody within different forms of eastern monasticism by the fifth century. In the *Armenian* churches, for example, whose origins go back to the figure of Gregory the Illuminator from Cappodocia, the church sang only psalms until the invention of the alphabet in the fifth century; this was probably accompanied by ancient folk melodies. As the rituals of the church developed, new sacred songs ('sharakans') were composed, many based upon the psalms, in distinctive Armenian chant – partly Persian-Arabic, partly Byzantine, and unique in its use of the tetrachord whereby the top and bottom notes remained fixed but the middle notes changed. Within the *Divine Liturgy, psalmody remained an integral part of church worship – a practice still apparent in Armenian churches worldwide today. For example, during the vesting of the priests before the service, in imitation of the elevated role of the king and high priest within the psalms, Psalm 132 is sung ('... Rise up O Lord, and go to your resting place ... let your priests be clothed with righteousness ...'); the procession from the vestry is accompanied by Psalm 26 ('... I wash my hands in innocence, and go around your altar, O Lord ...'); at the confession, the elders chant Psalm 100 ('... Know that the Lord is God ... It is he that made us, and we are his ...') followed by Psalm 43 ('... Send out your light and truth; let them lead me; let them bring me to your holy hill ...'). Still within the Liturgy, the prayers to the Holy Spirit, using forms attributed to St Gregory of Narek, are replete with allusions to the psalms. Following this, readings from Scripture are punctuated by verses from psalms; and after the bread and wine are brought to the altar, Ps. 24:7–10 is chanted ('Lift up your heads, O gates ... that the King of Glory may come in ...') and, during the distribution of the elements, Psalm 34 is sung ('... O taste and see that the Lord is good ...'). The Divine Liturgy ends with Psalm 28 ('O save your people and bless your heritage ...'), Psalm 113 ('Blessed be the name of the Lord from this time on and for evermore ...') and, again, Psalm 34 ('I will bless the Lord at all times ...').

If the Armenian churches testify to the ongoing practice of psalmody influenced by the monastic tradition from Cappodicia and Caeserea (the first Armenian bishop Leonius was Metropolitan of Caesarea), the Ethiopic church, dating from the third century and thus equally ancient, testifies also to an association with Syria (its first bishop, Frumentius, came from Tyre) but to a greater influence from Alexandria (where Athanasius was Bishop) and to the Egyptian (Coptic) monastic tradition. There are interesting similarities between these two churches. Ethiopic liturgy also has an ancient and lengthy oral tradition, centred around singing the psalms; it too gives psalmody a central place in the Divine Liturgy, and it too adopts prayers attributed to an early saint: Yared of Aksum dates from the sixth century, whilst the Armenian Gregory of Narek dates from the ninth century. Both liturgies are rich in citations and allusions to the psalms. The distinctive feature of the Ethiopic church is that it has traditionally been influenced by Jewish practices and Jewish symbolism, which explains why within the liturgy the psalms play a major part; furthermore, it has its own distinctive form of chanting psalmody, also partly Arabic, partly Byzantine in derivation, which, known as Fellasha chant, still survives today. And not only in the Divine Liturgy but also in the adaptation of the seven canonical hours of prayer taken from monastic practices, the psalms play a focal part: Psalms 148–50 are typically used at Lauds, Psalm 63 at Matins and Psalm 93 at Vespers, for example. Like the Armenian churches, the influence of this rite developed uninterruptedly until the Isalmic invasions of the seventh century.

Elsewhere in the eastern churches, the 'Byzantine Rite', developed first from the Liturgy of Basil of Caesarea for the churches in Antioch and later adapted by John Chrysostom for the churches in Constantinople, comprises mainly the Liturgy of the Divine Office and calendars of feasts and liturgical rubrics; this became the common practice throughout the Byzantine Empire and its influence is found in many Orthodox churches today. Here again we may note the extensive use of psalmody, both week by week and in the use of special psalms at festival times. The Psalter is organized into some twenty groups, each called a *kathisma* (using the Hebrew numbering of psalms, these contain Psalms 1–8; 9–17; 18–24; 25–32; 33–7; 38–46; 47–55; 56–64; 65–70; 71–7; 78–85; 86–91; 92–101; 102–5; 107–9; 110–18; 119:1–76; 120–34; 135–43; 144–50). Each *kathisma* is divided into three parts, each called a *stasis*, or *antiphon*. This organization then becomes the basis of determining which psalm reading should be used for each week. Usually the first two *kathismata* would be read at Matins and the last two would be read at Vespers, thus working through the entire Psalter within a week. (Throughout Lent, this was doubled, to make the reading twice weekly.) No *kathisma* was to be offered on Sunday Vespers, the key service being the Saturday Night Vigil: this began the cycle of services for the Sunday (Vespers, Matins, Divine Liturgy), and here yet more psalms were used, such as those for lighting lamps and for introducing Bible readings.

The psalms would usually be said in a recitative monotone; if they were sung at all, this would be unaccompanied, in unison, adapting a type of plainsong which is more enharmonic than the more diatonic chanting in the western churches. In addition, hymns imitating the psalms and giving them a Christian meaning were sung, as well as one or two of the *Canticles of the church. Overall, this model provided both variety and flexibility: different *kathismata* could be read at different times of the year, and on different days within the same part of the year. In all this, the regular recitation of the entire Psalter, whether once a day, once a week or once a month, was common practice: this is best illustrated by John Chrysostom, whose influence upon the Byzantine Rite and whose commentaries on the psalms we have already noted:

> If the faithful are keeping vigil in the church,
> David is first, middle, and last.
> If at dawn anyone wishes to sing hymns,
> David is first, middle, and last.
> In the holy monasteries, among the ranks of the heavenly warriors,
> David is first, middle, and last.
> In the convents of virgins, who are imitators of Mary,
> David is first, middle, and last.
> In the deserts where men hold converse with God,
> David is first, middle, and last.[1]

Western Churches

Within western Christendom, by the end of the fifth century, different collections of psalmody for specific liturgical uses began to take shape, in some ways mirroring the liturgical organization of the psalms in the eastern churches. The *Psalterium Feriale*, for example, was a work divided into eight sections to fit the daily offices; in some collections psalms were arranged in a liturgical order, according to the times of their recital throughout the week, along with other additions such as canticles, invitatories, versicles, antiphons and doxologies. The 'biblical Psalter' – in its various translations, mainly in Hebrew, Greek, Syriac and Latin – was still the obvious source for commentators, whilst 'liturgical Psalters' were an additional resource for monasteries and cathedrals.

A critical figure for the promotion of psalmody in the West is *Benedict of Nursia* (480–550), whose life and works are told through the *Dialogues* of Pope Gregory

---

[1] For information on the psalms in the eastern churches, see *W. Aymero and M. Joachim (eds.) (1970)*; M. Bailey (2000), also at jacwell.org/spring_summer2000/psalmic_music_in_orthodox_liturg.htm; J.A. Lamb (1962); *N.E. Maragos (1988)*; *R.P.E. Mercenier and F. Paris (1937, 1953)*; R. Taft (1986); *D.H. Touliatos-Banker (1984)*; *C. Vrionides (1980)*; K. Weitzmann (1980); H. Wybrew (1990); significant websites include www.orthodoxwiki.org/Psalter and www.orthodoxinfo.com/praxis/typicon_psalms. aspx. The Chrysostom quotation is taken from M Bailey ibid., where it is attributed to Pseudo-Chrysostom, *De poenitertia*, PG LXIV, 12–13, paraphrased in English by David Drillock (1997): Liturgical Song in the Worship of the Church, *St. Vladimir's Theological Quarterly* 41:2–3, 186.

the Great (540–604). The son of a Roman nobleman, Benedict was schooled in Rome, but left the city aged about twenty, during the period of Justinian's rule in Constantinople, to embrace an ascetic life of poverty and solitude. After some time as a hermit in a cave near Subiaco, for a brief period Benedict became abbot of a monastery nearby. Gregory writes that he then went on to found twelve monastic communities in the same region, each with twelve monks and a superior, whilst he served as abbot in the monastery he had founded at Monte Cassino.

The founding of new monastic communities necessitated the establishment of an appropriate Rule of life and prayer. The *Benedictine Rule* (in part dependent upon the 'Masters' Rule' associated with Basil of Caesarea) had an appeal because of its simplicity and its flexibility, and could be adapted in different ways in different monasteries. Its threefold emphasis on prayer, study and manual work gives central place to the daily offices, usually seven times a day, and within these hours of prayer (the '*opus Dei*') the psalms are used most of all. Much of the Rule deals with more practical domestic, disciplinary and moral issues, using the Gospels, Epistles and Psalms for guidance; yet even here, the psalms are the most frequently quoted texts. Even the Prologue to the Rule is full of references to the psalms, particularly those which were best known in liturgy: for example, Psalm 95, a prominent psalm in the first daily office ('Today, if you will hear his voice, harden not your hearts' [vv. 7–8]), Ps. 34, often used in eucharistic liturgy ('O taste and see that the Lord is good; happy are those who take refuge in him … Come, O children, listen to me; I will teach you the fear of the Lord …' [vv. 8, 11]) and Psalm 15 ('O Lord, who may abide in your tent? … Those who walk blamelessly, and do what is right …' [vv. 1–4]).

The part of the Rule which demonstrates the central place of psalmody is chapters 8–20, on praying the Divine Office. The first hour of prayer starts with '*Vigils*', at about 2.30 a.m.: the first prayer on Monday is from Psalm 51 ('O Lord, open my lips, and my mouth will declare your praise …' [v. 15]). Complete psalms to be used at this time include Psalm 3 ('I will lie down and sleep; I wake again, for the Lord sustains me' [v. 5]) and Psalm 95 ('O come, let us sing unto the Lord …' [v. 1]); these are read with appropriate *glorias* and antiphons, as in the other offices, along with a rotation of further twelve psalms, beginning at Psalm 21 onwards. '*Lauds*' (usually at about 6.00 a.m., or daybreak, and sometimes combined with the later office of *Prime*) starts with the whole of Psalm 51 (as a penitential prayer) and Psalm 67 ('May God be gracious to us and bless us and make his face to shine upon us …' [v. 1]) and always ends with the same psalms of praise, Psalms 148–50. On Sundays, selections from Psalm 118 are also used ('This is the day that the Lord has made …' [v. 24]) as well as Psalm 63 ('when I think of you on my bed, and meditate on you in the watches of the night …' [v. 6]). On weekdays, other psalms include 5 and 36 (Mondays); 43 and 57 (Tuesdays); 64 and 65 (Wednesdays); 88 and 90 (Thursdays); 76 and 92 (Fridays); and 143 (Saturdays). Sometimes this office begins with a call to prayer from Ps. 70:21 ('Be pleased, O God, to deliver me. O Lord, make haste to help me!'), followed by the recitation of three other psalms from between Psalms 1 and 20, and sections from Ps. 119 on Sundays. *Terce, Sext* and *None* (usually at 9.00 a.m., 12.00 p.m. and 3.00 p.m.) also have three psalms (from Psalms 120–28) and parts of Psalm 119 on Sundays, as with *Prime*; whilst *Vespers* (about 4.30 p.m.) includes the recital of four psalms (from 110–47) interspersed throughout the week, and *Compline* uses three set psalms – Psalm 4 ('I lie down and sleep; I wake again, for the Lord sustains me' [v. 5]), Psalm 91 ('You will not fear the terror of the night … or the pestilence that stalks in darkness …' [vv. 5 and 6]) and Psalm 134 ('Come, bless the Lord, all you servants of the Lord, who stand by night in the house of the Lord …' [v. 1]). It can be seen from this list that some psalms which had already become well established in liturgy, such as Psalm 51 as a psalm of penitence and Psalms 148–59 as *Lauds*, or praises, were still both used at the beginning of the day.

Like previous Rules associated with Basil in the East and Ambrose in the West, the Rule of Benedict promoted the recital of the whole Psalter once a week and so influenced the way in which some psalms became more prominent than others through liturgical use. Psalms 3, 4, 15, 34, 51, 63, 67, 70, 91, 95, 118, 134, 143 and 148–50 are repeatedly used, chosen on account of just one or two appropriate verses. In method this is very much like the 'proof-texting' of psalms in the New Testament, although, as was noted at the end of the previous chapter, in content this liturgical range of psalms is very different from those used in the New Testament and the early church fathers (i.e. Psalms 2, 8, 22, 26, 45, 51, 68, 69, 72, 82, 89, 110, 118 and 132).

The Rule, and adaptations of it, spread to other monastic communities throughout the western churches, particularly initially in Italy, northern France, England, Scotland and Ireland, resulting in the psalms having a central place in liturgy up to eight times a day (the cathedral offices, adopting only morning and evening prayer, normally used them twice a day, basically combining the four morning offices and the four evening offices into one). Between the seventh and eleventh centuries, the vast proportion of monastic communities throughout much of northern Europe, free from Islamic rule, were Benedictine, and adopted the Rule to a greater or lesser extent. This applied even to newly established orders; many of these also appropriated a Benedictine spirit, from the more flamboyant Cluniacs in Italy in the tenth century to the more rigorous Cistercians in France in the eleventh century. In whichever tradition, no other biblical book was as widely used as the Psalms. Even outside monastic communities, by the tenth century – in the eastern churches as well as in the west – the Psalter was so well known through its offices that it became a 'reading primer' for monks and nuns, and indeed for anyone who could afford to pay for lessons in literacy.[2]

In England, it is more than likely that it was the Benedictine Rule, along with the Old Latin Psalter, which was introduced to England through Pope Gregory by Augustine of Canterbury (c.595). A manuscript of the Rule in the Bodleian Library

---

[2] On the Benedictine Rule, see P. *Barry (1995)*; J.D. *Chittister (1992)*; P. *O'Donovan (1980)*; N. *Vest (1991)*; and E. de Waal (1984).

(Hatton 48 [4118]), probably written at Canterbury in about 700, suggests that Augustine was a Benedictine; if so, he would have brought this Rule with him. Even in Ireland, where Patrick's missionary work, commissioned through Bishop Germain of Auxerre and by Pope Celestine I, was too early (c.432) for implementing the Benedictine Rule, the imposition of some Rule is clear because the psalms also play such a vital role in monastic communities in Ireland. For example, the Columban Office, or *The Monk's Rule*, associated with the Irish missionary Columbanus (c.543–615) and now preserved at Bobbio monastery in Italy, prescribes that some seventy-five psalms are to be sung at Matins during the winter liturgy. And the Irish *Rule of Ailbe*, dating from the seventh century, has a lengthy section on personal devotion to Psalm 119, which required a hundred genuflexions at the recitation of the first 'Blessed' of this psalm. Or again, *The Rule of the Monastery of Tallaght*, dating from the mid-ninth century, amusingly records the payment of 'one milch cow' to the successful tutors of postulants who were able to recite the Psalter in its entirety, dividing David's psalms into three groups of fifty.

We possess over thirty documents, most of them written in Ireland, which provide insights into how the psalms were used there. Some are actual Psalters; several are in Jerome's *Hebraicum* text, others in the *Gallicanum*, and a few divide the Psalms into 'three fifties', each ending with the Lord's Prayer. The most recent discovery (in July 2006) of parts of a slim, large-format Psalter with wraparound vellum (possibly dating about 800 CE), unearthed by a digger in a south Midlands bog, suggests again, by the indication of illuminations for Psalms 1, 51 and 101, this Irish practice of dividing the Psalter up into 'three fifties'. Other documents are introductions; some are attributed to Jerome, one to St Columba, and one to Bede, and show the use of the Psalter in the *Divine Office and in private devotion. Others are *glossed commentaries, and these offer insights into the very different theological emphases emerging as psalms were copied and commented upon by different communities. On the one hand, a mystical and allegorical reading of the psalms is seen in the *Cathach of St. Columba*, a Gallican Psalter of Psalms 30:10–105:13. Dating from about 630, this Psalter uses psalm titles to indicate different speakers – the 'voices' are mainly of Christ, the Apostles and the Church – rather like the prosopological approaches used by the western fathers. On the other hand, a Hiberno-Latin commentary (now in the Vatican), dating from about 700 and with Irish glosses, has, somewhat surprisingly, psalm headings taken from the commentary of Theodore of Mopsuestia, and so attests a literal, historical tradition, reading all the psalms back into the life of David, with little Christian appropriation. Another is a ninth-century Latin translation of Theodore of Mopsuestia's commentary, preserved in two manuscripts now in Milan and Turin, whose glosses in old Irish highlight the typically historically orientated psalm headings. How Theodore's Syriac Psalms Commentary, translated into Greek and then into Latin, came to be copied in Ireland by the mid-seventh century is a mystery; but it shows us just how far psalms commentaries could travel through the cross-fertilization of the monastic Rule, not only via Benedict in the West and but also via Theodore in the East, and how different rules provided both continuity in the use of the psalms and diversity in their theological emphases.[3]

One innovatory liturgical use of the psalms during this period is in the Office of the Dead. The use of psalmody in funeral services goes back as early as John Chrysostom, when texts from the Psalter as well as from the books of Jeremiah and Job were used. Psalms 22, 23 and 116 were classified as the 'funeral psalms'. (The *Apostolic Constitutions*, also containing prayers for the burial of the dead, similarly affirms the use Psalm 116, with its emphasis on God's deliverance of the soul from death and the affirmation that the death of God's saints is precious in his eyes [vv. 7–8, 13–15]: Psalm 116 similarly is a key psalm in the Armenian rites of burial, and also the Coptic order – along with Psalms 51, 139 and 119.) Despite the obvious connection between psalmody and funeral rites, the Office of the Dead did not become prominent until the seventh or eighth century. Two features within the Office are shared by many of the churches in the West and several in the East. The first is a compilation of late night and early morning hours of prayer – Vespers, in late evening, Vigils, in the early night watches, and Lauds/Prime at dawn, leading to a climax in the celebration of the Eucharist. The second is the way in which this early 'dawn office' uses two particular groups of psalms – the Songs of Ascents (i.e. Psalms 120–34) and the increasingly popular penitential psalms (i.e. Psalms 6, 32, 38, 51, 102, 130 and 143), as well as other psalms, used in the burial liturgies of various church traditions, which allude to the state of the dead (e.g. Psalms 16, 23, 31, 83, 88, 116, 139). The creation of such an Office was to satisfy private devotion to the dead; and although it had no official standing in the Catholic church until the fifteenth century, it nevertheless reveals how, both in the rituals for death as well as for life, psalmody played another significant part in the liturgy of the Christian community.[4]

Exposition, Homily, Translation

EASTERN CHURCHES

Other than just two works, both from the churches in Syria, and both dating before Syria succumbed to Islamic rule (635) – one a commentary and the other a translation – the churches in the East were less prolific in producing expositions and homilies than those in the West. After the *Council of Ephesus in 431, Syriac Christianity favoured more the Alexandrian modes of interpretation, so that the commentary of Theodore of Mopsuestia was no longer as much revered as was,

---

[3] On the Psalms and the developing offices, especially in Ireland, see M. McNamara (1999 and 2000) and R.L. Ramsey (1912); also M.-J. Rondeau (1982–5); H.F. van Rooy (2005); and P. Salmon (1962).
[4] On the psalms in funeral liturgy and in the Office of the Dead, see C. Jones, G. Wainwright and E. Yarnold (1978); J.A. Lamb (1962); *G. Rowell (1977)*; and R. Taft (2004).

for example, that of Athanasius (a fact which makes the use of Theodore's commentary in the Irish church such an anomaly). The two Syriac works illustrate in different ways this change of emphasis.

The first psalms commentary to appear in Syriac (in about 542), written by the *'Monophysite' Daniel of Salah, was a concerted attempt to combine an Alexandrian reading with an Antiochene one. Daniel's commentary on Psalm 1, for example, illustrates the allegorical approach by reading the psalm as about the economy of the Word of God, whilst it illustrates the more literal approach by reading it as a reflection by David on the foolishness of Saul. Similarly, Daniel's commentary on Psalm 2 is read allegorically for its insights on Christ the Messiah, and in a literal sense by seeing it as having been written by David after he was anointed king.

In about 616 a translation of the psalms was made from the Greek into Syriac. This was based upon the fifth column of Origen's *Hexapla, so that the translation was known as the 'Syrohexaplaric Psalter'. It signified an important move away from the Aramaic *Peshitta with its Jewish emphasis and brought into focus a more Greek-based reading with its attendant Alexandrian emphasis.[5]

Western Churches

As has been seen, one influence in the West was the liturgical and prayerful contemplation of the psalms (often known as *lectio divina), which owes much to Benedict. Alongside this, a very different way of reading psalmody also begins to emerge, having its roots in commentators of the late fourth and early fifth centuries such as Eusebius, Ambrose and Augustine, but being a more systematic development of it. This marks the beginning of the use of the psalms for learning, or prayerful academic study.

Two great Christian commentators, both from Rome, each influenced by Augustine, and each using an Alexandrian reading of psalmody within a Latin setting, are *Cassiodorus* (485–580), who served as a Roman senator and then became a monk, and *Gregory the Great* (540–604), the son of a Roman senator, who, whilst in monastic orders, was elected Pope. These two writers influenced the developing tradition of a biblical *Gloss (a tradition which did not really mature until the eleventh century) by adding observations from the commentaries of the early fathers alongside their copies of the psalms. Psalm manuscripts started to produce the Latin text in a narrow central column, with the quotations from the fathers taking up the margins on either side (AU was used for Augustine, JER for Jerome, for example; later Cass was used to indicate Cassiodorus, and GR, Gregory).

---

[5] On Daniel of Salah, see D.G.K. Taylor (1998–99); on the Syrohexaplaric Psalter, see R.J.V. Hiebert (1989). See also J.-M. Auwers (1994); W. Bloemendaal (1960); R.J.V. Hiebert (2005); R.C. Hill (2004); H.F. van Rooy (2005); M. Saebø (ed.) (1996); and M. Wiles (1970b).

Cassiodorus played a major part in revising much of Jerome's *Psalterium Hebraicum*. But it was his commentary on the psalms, *Expositio Psalmorum*, which was his most important legacy for psalmody. It is a commentary written in the typical rhetorical style of the classical literary tradition, whereby one verse is offered which then interacts with other commentators (for example, Chrysostom, Hilary, Jerome, Ambrose and Augustine). It seeks to demonstrate the hidden presence of Christ throughout the psalms, using Augustine's commentary and homilies on the psalms (particularly evident in Cassiodorus' exegesis of Christ the Head and Christ the Body speaking through the psalms). It seems that the commentary was begun some time in the 540s, probably the first work since his conversion, written after leaving the service of high office in Ostrogothic Italy for Byzantine Constantinople, at the height of Justinian's rule. The allegorical reading of psalmody alongside the clear focus on Chalcedon orthodoxy concerning Christ, 'in' and 'of' two natures, shows the dialogue with the anti-*Nestorian concerns of this time.

Cassiodorus's distinctive contribution is his identification of twelve Christological categories of psalms according to their titles. The twelve categories are listed at the end of the lengthy Preface to the Commentary: firstly, their place in the liturgy of the Christian Church (here Cassiodorus was most interested in the 'Asaph' headings, which he believed originally designated synagogue use, and so now related to church use); secondly, their insights into the nature of God the Father (e.g. Psalms 2, 45, 110); thirdly, their reference to the enemies of Christ; fourthly, prayers to Christ to defeat the evil ways of man; fifthly, psalms of Christ's passion (e.g. Psalms 22, 35, 55, 69 and 109); sixth, the penitential psalms (Psalms 6, 32, 38, 51, 102, 130, 143 – here Cassiodorus builds upon Augustine's classification of these psalms and was among the first to categorize them as a separate collection); seventh, the prayers of Christ in his human nature; eighth, allegories of the life of Christ; ninth, the 'alleluia' psalms; tenth, the gradual psalms; eleventh, the prayers of the Trinity; and twelfth, the psalms of the exaltation of Christ (e.g. Psalms 8 and 68). Although some of these topics have much in common with the way the psalms are used in the New Testament and the church fathers, these twelve themes were never previously compiled together to create a theology of the Psalter as a whole. (It is true that a similar method was used by Eusebius and Theodore, and in a different way by Gregory of Nyssa, but the specific categorization around the two natures of Christ is quite different, making this altogether a more systematic and analytical work.)

An intriguing feature – again showing the influence of Augustine – is Cassiodorus's interest in the *numbers* of the psalms. Psalm 12 (in the Hebrew and English, Psalm 11), for example, ends with a long comment about the twelve tribes, twelve thrones and twelve apostles; Psalm 30 offers comments about the age of Joseph when Jesus was born, and the age of Jesus at his baptism; Psalm 150, bringing together the Psalter in its entirety, summarizes that here we have 'seventy psalms for the Old Testament, eighty for the New'. This is both an allegorical and an analytical commentary, and, given that the final revision took place when Cassiodorus was living in his monastic community in Squillace, southern Italy, it also reveals his practical and pastoral concerns. For example, his preface speaks of how the singing of psalms makes pleasant the silence of the night, beguiles the first hour of the day, consecrates the third hour, makes joyful the sixth hour through the breaking of bread, ends fasting at the ninth hour, and brings the last hours of day to a close, taking away darkness from the mind. As a whole, his commentary provides an extraordinary range of insights, bringing together the wisdom of the church fathers and establishing an authoritative tradition of earlier commentators in a way which anticipated the medieval commentators some four hundred years later; yet it is always pragmatic and spiritual in its ultimate concerns. It is not surprising that this work, along with that of Augustine, was one of the great influences in shaping later medieval interpretation of the psalms.[6]

Gregory the Great, the fourth 'father' of the western church, after Jerome, Ambrose and Augustine, is equally significant in his promotion of psalmody. By his early thirties Gregory had established his own Benedictine Monastery of St Andrew in Rome, having renounced his prefecture of Rome in the chaotic years which followed the final collapse of the Roman Empire under Justinian. Although his monastic calling was temporarily interrupted by being required to serve as papal nuncio at the Emperor's court at Constantinople, the Rule of Benedict was fundamental to him, whether in public political life or in private prayer as a monk. His hagiographic life of Benedict (part of *Dialogues*, written in 594, four years after being elected Pope) shows just how profoundly the Rule affected his understanding of prayer and worship as well as his pastoral care of the churches. Given the close relationship between the Rule and psalmody, his love of the psalms is apparent in two distinct ways.

The first is more scholarly and pastoral, and is evident in his commentaries and homilies on the psalms. Although the attribution of a commentary on the seven penitential psalms to him may not be authentic, his sermons on psalms such as 67:5 ('Let the peoples praise you, O God; let all the peoples praise you …') have survived, and more importantly, so has his work *Liber Regulae Pastoralis*, which concerns the pastoral care of Christians during his time as Abbot of St Andrews, from 573 onwards. The style of this work imitates the Benedictine Rule: it is a pastiche of verses mainly from the psalms. Here, unlike Benedict, Gregory applied a threefold exegesis – historical, allegorical and moral – in reading and applying the psalms. Firstly, they were read historically within the life of David; secondly, they were read in an allegorical way, finding their deeper meaning in and through Christ (here Gregory made use of several earlier commentators, especially Augustine and Cassiodorus); and thirdly, they were adapted for their moral lessons for the church in his day. This work was widely used by later commentators as far apart as Bede in the eighth century and Aquinas in the thirteenth.

---

[6] For an English Translation of Cassiodorus on the Psalms, see P.G. Walsh (1991, 1992, 1993). See also J.J. O'Donnell (1979, 1995, also at ccat.sas.upenn.edu/jod/texts/cassbook/toc.html; J.P. Halporn (*1981*, 1987); H.P. Nasuti (1999, 2005); M.-J. Rondeau (1982–5); A. Schokel (1989); P.G. Walsh (1998).

Gregory's most influential contribution to psalmody is liturgical (although because of its innovative use of music, it could also be classified as aesthetic), showing how vital the psalms were in keeping alive the spirit and identity of the church during turbulent times. For Gregory, it was by *hearing* psalmody as well as by *seeing* it which facilitated memorizing the psalms for daily prayer. Beginning within his monastic communities in Sicily, almost certainly founded upon the Benedictine Rule, and from 590 onwards in the cathedral offices in Rome, Gregory encouraged the tradition of plainsong, and in doing so, he transformed the use of the psalms in the daily office. As Pope, Gregory used his influence to extend this tradition throughout the ailing churches of Italy, France and England in particular: his commissioning of Augustine to Canterbury in 596–7 is one example of it.

'Gregorian Chant' became even more vast in its corpus of religious music than 'Ambrosian Chant', with its similar promotion of *schola. The difference is mainly in the way the psalm verses were sung – usually with three inflections at the beginning, middle and end of a line, rather than an intonation at the beginning and inflection at the end of a line, as in the Ambrosian tradition. Both types of chant are monophonic, and each is deceptively simple to learn yet striking to hear. Each psalm verse is divided into two, usually marked off by a colon. Each psalm tone consists of a reciting tone followed by an ending formula, fitted into each of these halves, the second having a more final-sounding ending formula. Since all the verses of the psalm itself have different number of syllables in Latin, the performers simply added repetitions of the reciting tone as needed, to fit the text. Of the some three thousand compositions dating from this time onwards (admittedly, some may instead be traced back to the later Pope Gregory II [715–31]), almost one-third were influenced by verses from the psalms. Some were used as 'introit psalms' at the beginning of the Mass; others, as 'gradual psalms' before the reading of the Gospel; and yet others, with antiphons and responses, at the appropriate hours in the Divine Office. So just as Benedict promoted the prayerful recitation of psalmody for all the community through monastic offices, Gregory encouraged their recitation through music, by professional singers, within the cathedral schools. Like the Ambrosian tradition, this is as much to do with the aesthetic reception of psalmody as it is the liturgical: the spiritual, prayerful *remembering* of a psalm is the most important, in either case.[7]

Moving from Rome to England, two native English commentators, albeit written mainly in Latin, are also important for their works on the psalms. *Venerable Bede* (c.673–735), a Benedictine monk and scholar at St Paul's monastery, Jarrow,

---

[7] See *S.C.L. Kessler (2000)*; E. Nowacki (1995). There are several different websites on Gregorian Plainchant, some more visual, some with recordings, some more informative. Four of these are: comp.uark.edu/~rlee/otherchant.html#resources; www.schuyesmans.be/gregoriaans/; www.beaufort. demon.co.uk/chant.htm; and www.grovemusic.com/shared/views/article.html?from=az&section= music.11726.

Northumberland, was schooled in the weekly recitation and memorization of the Psalter by his Abbot, Ceolfrith, from about the age of seven. He wrote much of his work in the period under the shadow cast by the Synod of Whitby (664), which attempted to reconcile missionary Roman Christianity with indigenous Celtic Christian spirituality, and on this account much of Bede's writing had an affinity with the pastoral spirit of Pope Gregory. Although, like Eusebius, Bede is mostly known as a church historian (his *Ecclesiastical History of the English People* is his best-known work), his contribution to psalmody is still significant.

The first is more scholarly. It is fairly certain that he knew, by heart, both the *Psalterium Hebraicum* and the *Psalterium Gallicanum* of Jerome. It is clear that he knew the *Psalterium Hebraicum* because this was the version used in the *Codex Amiatinus*, an extraordinary manuscript of the Psalter (to be discussed shortly) which was written during his lifetime at either the monastery of Jarrow or Monkwearmouth nearby. Bede used the Gallican Psalter in a work entitled *De Metris et Tropis*, which explored the poetry of the psalms by reading the Latin as lines of classical metres, in order to show that the poetry of David was as inspired as any pagan poet. A further scholarly use of the psalms is seen in Bede's sermons and tractates: these addressed the divisions in the church in England after the Synod of Whitby, and Bede here used the same approach as Gregory, applying three types of readings to the psalms (the literal, allegorical and moral) and adding to these (following in many ways the schema of John Cassian, whose works he probably knew) a fourth (typological). Like Gregory, Bede knew and used Cassiodorus' commentary (its existence at Jarrow at this time is fairly clear) as well as those of Augustine and Jerome; a piece on the psalm headings (*Tituli Psalmorum*) attributed to him is rich in allusions to these works. All of this is of course through the Latin medium: it is unclear as to whether Bede knew and used a translation of the Psalms in Old English attributed to a contemporary, Adhelm of Sherborne (640–709), but it is quite likely and certainly would make sense of Bede's pastoral and academic concerns.

Bede's second contribution is more devotional and, like Gregory, it is the result of his similar devotion to Benedictine spirituality. This is his *Abbreviated Psalter*, which consists of condensed renderings of psalms from Jerome's *Psalterium Hebraicum*. A precedent can be seen in, for example, the *Psalterium Feriale*, and it seems that Bede's purpose was to take from the Psalter a spiritual core, using verses which would have been most familiar from the offices. Hence most psalms retain only one or two verses (e.g., Pss. 2:10,12; 3:3,7; 4:1; 5:2,3,8; 6:1–4; 7:1–2; 8:1; 9:2; 11:7; 12:1; 13:2–6, and so on) and these would be those most used in liturgy, sometimes dependent upon a Christian reading of the psalm, sometimes upon its more general moral and spiritual qualities. A few psalms have up to ten verses (Psalm 119 has twenty-seven). Bede's concern was that less learned monks, and laypersons too, would be able to recite and memorize a more manageable portion of the Psalter, with the result that those wanting to learn more could move from the one or two verses to memorize the psalm as a whole. The only psalm Bede seems to omit, or at least translate differently, is Psalm 137, with its shocking curse at the end ('Blessed is he who takes your children and dashes them against the stones' [v. 9]). Instead Bede apparently reads this verse (it is the only verse given from the psalm) as 'Blessed is the man who fears the Lord'. This selective devotional version became a popular vehicle of prayer for the next four hundred years: its reduction of the Psalter to a minimal core contrasts with the expansion of it by means of a Gloss – a method which Bede used elsewhere in his more scholarly works.[8]

Alcuin of York (734–804), a pupil of Egbert who was a contemporary of Bede, continued the twofold tradition of scholarly and devotional works on the psalms. His earlier years were spent at the cathedral school in York, where he became both monk and deacon, and where he expanded the library with manuscripts collected on his travels to Rome and the Continent. (One of these almost certainly included Cassiodorus' Commentary on the Psalms.) His period in France began during the *Carolingian Renaissance, when, in 781, he was invited by Charlemagne (768–814) to take up residence in the 'Palace School', initially at Aachen. This was a period of comparative stability on the Continent, culminating with the crowning of Charlemagne as Holy Roman Emperor (800) by Pope Leo III in an attempt to re-create a focus of Christian authority in the west over and against Constantinople; Alcuin was, it seems, both protégé and tutor to Charlemagne, eventually becoming Abbot of Tours. In this atmosphere of learning and teaching, Alcuin wrote on scientific and literary issues as well as theological works. His most scholarly work on the psalms has not survived; this was his revision of Jerome's *Psalterium Hebraicum*, made between 797 and 801, which, like Cassiodorus before him, was an attempt to produce one coherent version at a time when there were many diverse readings of the text, with different versions even in the same churches and monasteries. Another way in which Alcuin followed the tradition of Cassiodorus was his short commentaries on the penitential psalms, as well as on Psalm 119 and the Psalms of Ascents; these are still extant, and, like Cassiodorus, the comments are organized according to 'quaestio' (questioning the meanings of particular phrases in the psalms) and 'glossaria' (giving answers by referring to a collection of earlier commentators). In this way Alcuin also contributed to the growing tradition of the Gloss and which led on to *Scholastic reading of the psalms.

Alcuin sent a copy of his commentaries to Bishop Arno of Salzburg, together with Bede's *Abbreviated Psalter*, which he clearly frequently used and loved. His own devotional work on the psalms, *De Psalmorum Usu Liber*, is in many ways inspired by Bede. However, Alcuin avoids those psalms which are part of the set lectionary in the offices of the church and instead uses less familiar but more personal ones. Taking as his premise, 'The Lord inhabits the Psalms', and reading the psalms as prophecies which anticipate the works and words of Christ, Alcuin

---

[8] G.H. Brown (1999); G.M. Browne (2002); R.N. Bailey (1983); *W.T. Foley and A.G. Holder (1999)*; J. Fraipoint (1955); *H. Mayr-Harting (1972, 1991³)*; B. Ward (*1990, 2002² a*; 1991, 2002² b).

sets out nine ways in which particular psalms could be used in private Christian devotion. At each point Alcuin quotes these psalms by their Latin titles, even when those of some psalms are identical, reflecting just how much he assumed his readers would know their psalms by heart, in spite of the fact they were not the psalms most repeatedly prayed through liturgy. The first use is for those who need to express confession and repentance, and for this Alcuin selects the penitential psalms first classified by Augustine and Cassiodorus: these are, with their headings, Psalms 6 and 38 both starting with 'Domine, ne in furore …' ('O Lord, do not rebuke me in your anger …'); Psalms 102 and 143, both beginning 'Domine exaudi' ('Hear my prayer, O Lord …'); and Psalms 32, 51, 130, each with different Latin superscriptions. The second use includes psalms which encourage spiritual joy and gladness: here Psalms 17, 25, 54, 67, 70, 71 and 86 are commented on. The third use is for times of thanksgiving: here Alcuin suggests the Alleluia Psalms (105–7; 111–18; 135; 136; 146–50). In times of temptation, Psalms 22, 64 and 69, the first and the last associated with the passion of Christ in the Gospels, are to be used; in times of weariness, Psalms 42, 84 and 63. In times of feeling abandoned by God, Psalms 13, 44, 57, 55 and 31 are suggested, and in times of prosperity, Psalms 34, 103 and 30. Psalm 119 is to be used for profound contemplation on the ways of God and his commands. To these eight uses, Alcuin adds a ninth more general one, namely meditation on the first and second coming of Christ expressed within the entire Psalter. (Here the word-play on 'meditation' in the Latin makes a further point: *intima mens* is about 'the depths of the mind' and *intenta mens*, about 'the well-focused mind'.) Like Bede, Alcuin's prayerful reading of the psalms was an important influence for some centuries to come.[9]

Artistic Representation

Illuminated Psalters in the Western Churches

One of the most striking features of the *Carolingian Renaissance, in part due to the continuous liturgical use of the psalms in monastic communities throughout this period, is the beginning of the practice of copying and then *illustrating* older Psalters. These books were produced both for public worship and private use, and were financed by wealthy patrons. Somewhat incongruously, the practice of illustration in western churches – especially in France and England, and also in Germany – began at the same time as *iconoclasticism spread in the eastern

---

[9] For an English version of Alcuin's reading of the psalms, see *D. Dales (2004)*. The Latin version is in J.P. Migne (1844–64, pp. 100–1). For a more personal account of the psalms in personal prayers and instruction, see M.A. Mayeski (1999) on Dhuoda of Septimania. See also B. Ward (1991, 2002[2] b) and M. Treschow, web.ubc.ca/okanagan/critical/faculty/treschow/psalms.html.

churches. Even in the West, manuscript illumination suffered a temporary setback in the so-called 'dark ages' of the late eighth and ninth centuries, when the Saracens invaded from the south of Europe, the Magyars from the east, and the Norwegians and Danes from the north and west; nevertheless, its influence can be seen throughout this entire period, and reached its high point later, between 1140–80 and 1220–70. Several illustrated manuscripts from Carolingian times deserve mention.

The simplest examples are of historicized initials, usually in one colour, marking out the first letter of an individual psalm. One of the earliest, with calligraphical details of Uncial letters, is the *Codex Amiatinus*, a huge seventh/eighth-century manuscript of some seventy-five pounds, comprising the entire Latin Vulgate and probably produced at one of the two Benedictine monasteries of Monkwearmouth and Jarrow, founded in the seventh century by Benedict Biscop and his disciple Ceolfrid. The *Psalter* in this Codex is actually the *Psalterium Hebraicum*, thus illustrating the popularity of this work there (as seen in the fact that this was the version used by Bede in his *Abbreviated Psalter*). Despite its northern provenance, the style of writing and illustrations reflect the influence of Italian scribes, thus illustrating the close communication between monasteries in England and Italy at this time. (The affinities of Amiatinus with Codex Grandior, produced in an Italian monastery founded by Cassiodorus, are interesting: the illustration in Amiatinus of Ezra the scribe mending and reading the Scriptures probably depicts not Ezra, but Cassiodorus, and so again illustrates the influence of this Italian commentator on monasteries as far north in England as Northumbria.) Amiatinus found its way to Burgundy, and by Carolingian times in the ninth century it was kept in Monte Amiata in southern Tuscany, from where, in 1786, after the suppression of the monastery, it was taken to Florence. As the first illustrated version of the psalms in England, the illustrations are minimal: they consist of historicized initials and the miniatures pertain to books outside the Psalter.[10]

One other early eighth-century example is important, because it is of an illustrated Psalter (albeit fragmentary) rather than an entire Hebrew Bible. The *Vespasian Psalter* was written in Mercia some time around 760, about the time of the threat from the Danes, and taken later to St Augustine's Canterbury. It has two historicized initials of Psalm 26 (of Jonathan and David shaking hands) and Psalm 52 (of David fighting a lion). Psalm 1 also suggests a historicized initial for the first letter of the first word, 'Blessed', depicting Samuel anointing David. The Psalter has one full miniature by way of a frontispiece (a motif found also in non-Christian texts of this period): it is of David playing the lyre. Now in the British Library, it is important for several other reasons. First, it contains a marginal *Gloss*, using the traditions of past psalmic commentators such as Jerome, Augustine, Gregory and

---

[10] See *R.L.S. Bruce-Mitford (1978)*; for images, see ccat.sas.upenn.edu/jod/texts/cassbook/amiatinus.pic.html (with an image of Ezra/Cassiodorus); see also J.F. Fenlon at www.newadvent.org/cathen/04081a.htm.

Cassiodorus; secondly, it is divided into eight liturgical divisions (Psalms 1, 27, 39, 51, 69, 81, 98, 110), akin to the *Psalterium Feriale*; thirdly, it sets out the psalms in clear verse units, whereby the beginning of a new verse starts a new line with a larger initial; and fourthly, it is an early interlinear Old English/Latin translation of the psalms (for example, Ps. 100:1 ['Rejoice in the Lord, all the earth'], in the Latin, reads 'Jubilate Deo, omnis terra', whilst the Old English is 'Wynsumiað gode, all earðe'). The interlinear translation, with its *Gloss*, some of which has been edited in the eleventh century, has helped scholars to understand more about the origins of medieval English.[11]

Throughout the last two centuries of the first millennium, two distinct styles of manuscript illustration are evident. The first is more opulent, gilded and colourful, and bears the marks of both Carolingian and Byzantine influence. The second is more agitated, sketchy, and uses an outline form. The latter is best represented by a most stunning manuscript, namely the *Utrecht Psalter*, made between about 820 and 835 at the Benedictine monastery of Hautvillers, near Eperny. One hundred and sixty-six dynamic dark brown ink and pen drawings accompany each psalm and a further sixteen *Canticles (including seven from the Old Testament and four from the New, as well as Psalm 151 and the Gloria and Apostles' Creed). The project was commissioned by Ebbo, Archbishop of Rheims and librarian to the Emperor Louis the Pious, who would have used artists from the School of Rheims. The text is of Jerome's Gallican Psalter, written mainly in rustic capitals: there are no word divisions, but several musical annotations. The more usual uncial style is used for the first word of the first line, which seems to have been added at a second stage. Headings to psalms have been added in red at a third stage; the draughtsmen would have worked on the available space left, and illustrated each psalm, verse by verse, usually with a literal and historical focus, setting it in the life of the author (often specifically identified as David). Several stock symbols recur: the 'enemies' are armed soldiers, the just are always unarmed, torn between angels and demons in their pursuit of the life of faith; the majesty of God is a hand from the sky and 'mercy' and 'truth' are always female figures with palm branches.

The most interesting feature, in the light of the Christianizing tendencies of the New Testament writers and the earlier commentators, is that only occasionally do the drawings display any obvious Christological emphasis: one exception is Ps. 16:10 ('You show me the path of life. In your presence there is fullness of joy; in your right hand are pleasures for evermore') which depicts the resurrection, with three

---

[11] For a clear website on this and the following illuminated Psalters from the eighth to fifteenth centuries, see www.geocities.com/indunna/manu; also www.groveart.com and www.newyorkcarver.com/museum.htm which have many relevant entries. For more general background, see *J.M. Backhouse (1979)*; *M.P. Brown (1994)*; *A. Grabar (1968)*; C.F.R. de Hamel (1986); *G. Schiller (1972)*; and J.J. Tikkanen (1975). For the Vespasian Psalter, the British Library reference is BL Cotton MS Vesp A I. For general works, see *J.J.G. Alexander (1978)*; G.H. Brown (1999); S. Kuhn (1965); J.J. Tikkanen (1975); D.H. Wright (1967); and for images of the Psalter, see www.fathom.com/course/10701049/session5.html.

women approaching Christ's tomb, and Christ drawing Adam and Eve out of Hell. There are a few others, including Ps. 22:16–18 ('For dogs are all around me; a company of evildoers encircles me ... They stare and gloat over me; they divide my clothes among themselves, and for my clothing they cast lots') which depicts two men digging by an empty cross; Ps. 74:12 ('Yet God my King is from of old, working salvation in the earth'), illustrated by two midwives bathing the Christ Child, with Mary on a mattress, and Joseph behind; and Ps. 116: 3,8,13 ('... the snares of death encompassed me; the pangs of Sheol laid hold on me ... For you have delivered my soul from death ... I will lift up the cup of salvation and call upon the name of the Lord') which portrays the crucifixion, with Mary, John and the psalmist holding the 'cup of salvation' which, somewhat crudely, catches the blood of Christ. But these are exceptions. Usually the illustrations belong to the more literal, historical type of exegesis, with strikingly vivid and detailed attention paid to the interpretation of the poetry within the life of the psalmist. An interesting example is of Psalm 44:23, which depicts a group of angels waking the Lord from his bed, representing the prayer 'Rouse thyself! Why sleepest thou, Lord? Awake! ...'[12]

Five other western Psalters from this period deserve mention. The *Stuttgart Psalter*, dating from c.830, probably from St Germain-des-Pres near Paris, has less verse-by-verse details than Utrecht, but its multi-coloured miniatures for each psalm have more Christianizing typological tendencies. For example, unlike the Utrecht Psalter, the 'tree' in Ps. 1:3 ('... they are like trees planted by streams of water, which yield their fruit in due season ...') is depicted as the cross of Christ. But the main interpretation is overall literal, with an emphasis which is both contemporary and didactic: Psalm 15, for example, is illustrated by a man bringing his money to Christ instead of lending it out at interest (as in Ps. 15:5: '... who do not lend money at interest, and do not take a bribe against the innocent ...') which fits with the teaching of the Carolingian rulers who, modelling their kingship on the pattern of sacral kingship of David, saw their function as protecting the poor, and so forbade usury on biblical authority. The *Verona Psalter*, dating between the seventh and eighth centuries, also has examples of separate illustrations, but in the margins, creating, as it were, an additional *Gloss* to the text. The *Troyes Psalter* (a version of the Gallican Psalter, commissioned in France for Henry I, some time before 850) depicts one miniature of Psalm 51 in golden rustic capitals, and other coloured historicized initials in blues, reds, greens and violets, and represents a striking contrast to the illumination in the Utrecht Psalter. The *Douce Psalter* (commissioned in the mid-ninth century, now in the Bodleian Library, Oxford) is of purple parchment, probably to suggest its 'imperial' appeal, with miniatures of Psalms 51 and 101 (suggesting therefore a tripartite division of the Psalter, with Psalm 1 missing) in silver and gold.

---

[12] See K. van der Horst, W. Noel and W.C.M. Wustefeld (eds.) (1996); for the extraordinarily vivid images from this Psalter, with commentary, see psalter.library.uu.nl, bibliomane.tripod.com/utrecht_psalter.htm and www.bodley.ox.ac.uk/oxlip/.

Perhaps the most interesting is the *Paris Psalter*, also from the ninth century, and now one of at least two *Paris Psalters* in the Bibliothèque nationale in Paris (here, MS 8824). It contains twelve full-page illustrations marking out typical Benedictine liturgical divisions; it is set out in two columns of Latin and English with nine ink drawings, in the style of the Utrecht Psalter, which are set between the Latin version on the first sixteen pages. But its significance is not in illustration alone. It is the first actual translation of the Psalter into Old English (others being interlinear glosses). The translation of the first fifty psalms, set out in prose, has been attributed to *King Alfred the Great* (849–99) because of the correspondences with his translation of another more pastoral work. Each of the prose psalms is headed with that twofold historical explanation of the psalm we have seen used in the Columban traditions in Irish Psalters, which looks back to Theodore of Mopsuestia. This is a Psalter which is rich in reception history.[13]

The most outstanding example of all is not from France or Italy or England, but from Spain. It is of the entire Bible: the Visigothic-Mozarabic Bible, now at St Isidore's in Leon, is dated by its miniaturist, Florencio, as 19 June 960 CE, and made in the Mozarabic Monastery of Valerañica, Castile. The colour and the details are in the illuminated initials, and the calligraphy is by Sancho. The text is Latin, probably pre-Jerome, and the commentary is Arabic; a type of *Gloss* is in the margins, and overall the work illustrates the influence of Visigothic, Catholic, Islamic and Carolingian features. The hundred or more miniatures reveal much about society in tenth-century Spain – its churches, palaces, costumes, armour, bullfighting on horseback and ordinary household goods – and all are still preserved in striking colour with vivid characterization, for example of eyes and hands; in all this, the Psalter is no exception. It is undoubtedly the most rare and exotic example of an illustrated Psalter within this period.[14]

ILLUMINATED PSALTERS IN THE EASTERN CHURCHES

The history of illuminated Psalters in the eastern churches is quite different, on account of the iconoclastic controversies; many examples depict the hostility felt towards those Islamic and Jewish fundamentalists whose doctrines and laws banned the depiction of the divine in images. The laws of iconoclasm, initiated by the Byzantine Emperor Leo III (680–741) in 726, lasting until 787, and revived between 815 and 843, created a good deal of unrest throughout Byzantium. (When various popes, for example Gregory II and Gregory III, opposed such measures, this divided further the churches of the East and West, and explains the different

---

[13] In addition to the more general references [note 11] images of the Stuttgart Psalter are at www.library.nd.edu/medieval_library/facsimiles/litfacs/stuttgart.html; for the Paris Psalter see M.J. Toswell (1995–1996) and the website www.aug.edu/augusta/psalms/.

[14] For images of this Bible, see www.fhvl.es/BIBLIA/bible_ingles.htm.

traditions of manuscript illumination at this time.) Not surprisingly, no illustrated Psalter in Greek before the ninth century has been found. The first example is from the ninth and tenth centuries, when the Coptic church began to produce ornamental pages with a strong Arabic design – known, for this reason, as carpet pages. Their function was to separate the various biblical books, and this tradition spread to Jewish illuminated manuscripts, especially in Islamic lands, and to Psalters in the eastern churches, by the eleventh and twelfth centuries.

The most notable example from this period is undoubtedly the ninth-century *Khludov Psalter*, from Constantinople. It has eighty miniatures, all with Christological themes, but unlike the *Utrecht Psalter*, these are taken from just one line of a given psalm, and the Christocentric illuminations are presented alongside quotations from earlier commentators on the psalms. This is a good example of 'reception history' in process, in the illustrating, copying and commenting of the psalms by way of received traditions: the *Khludov Psalter* has clearly been influenced by the *Utrecht Psalter*, or at the very least, by the traditions which evolved from it. A comparison of Psalm 1 in both manuscripts shows how similar the compositions and symbolism are, except for the way the *Khludov Psalter* presents its illustrations as marginal vignettes, suggesting this is a complementary part of the '*Gloss*', and the way this Psalter portrays the 'enemies' of the psalmist no longer as armed soldiers, but as three Jews. This is a clear comment on the iconoclastic stance of the Jews (although, interestingly, there is no pictorial comment on the Islamic pressure exerted on the emperors). This is again illustrated in Ps. 69:21 ('They gave me poison for food, and for my thirst they gave me vinegar to drink ...') with its drawing of Christ suffering on the cross, again tormented by Jews, giving the psalm a particular anti-Jewish rhetoric. Similarly by Ps. 25:1–6 ('To you, O Lord, I life up my soul. O my God, in you I trust; do not let me be put to shame; do not let my enemies exult over me ...') the iconoclasts are depicted as wiping out an icon of Christ himself.[15]

Although over eighty such illuminated Byzantine Psalters are still extant, mostly dating between the ninth and eleventh centuries, three deserve particular mention, because of their allegorical and Christological representations. The first, also from the ninth century, and now kept on Mount Athos, is the *Pantokrator Psalter*, with some ninety-seven images of Christ, the Virgin Mary and the saints in the margins. The second, the eleventh-century *Barberini Psalter*, now in the Vatican Museum, contains illustrations of Christ enthroned, with David and musicians in worship below, as well as of David playing the harp for the animals, and David slaying a lion and bear. The third was completed in 1066 by one Theodore of Caesarea for the monastery of Studious near Constantinople. Called the *Theodore Psalter*, it is now in the British Library. Its illustrations have many affinities with the ninth-century Khludov Psalter, and it is clearly a later development of it. Its marginal illustrations no longer refer to the historical times of the psalmist, but

---

[15] See K.A. Corrigen (1992); For an image and discussion of Psalm 25, see homepage.mac.com/paulstephenson/madison/byzantium/notes/illumination.html.

are more Christological (for example, Psalm 8 is now illustrated with a series of events from the life of Christ). Nevertheless, there are more contemporary and polemical representations, like those in the Khludov Psalter: Ps. 25:1–6 still depicts the iconographic persecutions. It is possible that this was a reminder to the patron, Abbot Michael, of the monastery of Studious, to hold fast to the traditions established by St Theodore: this is a many-layered text, intended both for private prayer and public liturgical use.[16]

It is clear that by the eleventh century the psalms were beginning to be appreciated more aesthetically. Other representations include ivory plaques of psalms, such as those on the Psalter of Charles the Bald [son of Judith, the second wife of Louis the Pious], which have illuminations similar to the Utrecht Psalter's scenes of Psalms 55 and 49. These have a blend of historical illustration, with a moral and contemporary application, alongside an allegorical and typological interpretation, with a specific Christian emphasis.

Jewish Reception

Liturgy

The Jewish reception of psalmody throughout this period had its own distinctive history, but it can still be assessed in the categories used for Christian reception. As far as the *liturgical* reception of psalmody is concerned during the *Talmudic period in Judaism, the prescriptions of the *Mishnah, discussed in the previous chapter, were the usual practice: these included Proper Psalms for days of the week, selected verses for recitation in public liturgy, and particular psalms for use in particular festivals.

By the *Gaonic period, a different development in the liturgical use of psalmody emerged amongst the Jews in Byzantine Syria and Palestine, one which was adapted in Spain by Arab-speaking Jews. These were the free poetic compositions, in Aramaic or Hebrew, which often used the form and language of the psalms, written for Sabbath worship and particular festivals, particularly the Passover, the New Year Festival and the Day of Atonement. (We have noted how this was also a practice in Christian tradition, both orthodox – such as Ambrose in the west and Ephraim of Syria in the east – and Gnostic, such as Valentinus). These poetic imitations of psalmody and other biblical texts, called *piyyutim*, were particularly important during the periods of Jewish persecution (for example, during the time of Justinian in Byzantium) when the reading from sacred books was forbidden and so creative expressions, preserved by memory, became a substitute for the text. The two main

---

[16] In addition to general references in notes 11 and 15, see also J.C. Anderson (1983, 1988, 1998); G.P. Schiemenz (1996); for an extended website on the Theodore Psalter, see www.ischool.utexas.edu/~slavman/hypertexts/Theodorepsalter.htm.

forms of expression were imitations of psalms of lament (for communal use, reflecting on the loss of homeland and of the Temple) and of psalms of penitence (for personal use, reflecting the Christian use of similar psalms and the need for individual forgiveness). As freer paraphrases of the text, in more lenient times they were interspersed with readings and recitations from the psalms, in this way allowing for a more musical expression in a liturgy: the *piyyut* was partly recited, partly sung.

For example, Yannai, a sixth-century composer of *piyyutim* from Palestine, specialized in *Kedushta, to be sung on the Sabbath, and the *Amidah, comprising nine sections, obeying rules of metre, length, stanza and rhyme, often using an acrostic form which spelt out his name through the beginning letters of the first word in each line. By the tenth century, this time in a *Sephardic Spain, Solomon ibn Gabirol (1021–51), born in Malaga, composed '*Adon Olam*' ('Eternal Lord'), a poem on the unity and providence of the God of Israel, in part a defence of Jewish faith, usually sung with actual psalms in morning worship, but also at night prayers – and still used today. Similarly Judah ha-Levi (1080–1140), of Toledo, produced a poem called '*Yom Layabasheh*', which, like Psalms 78, 105, 106, 135 and 136, celebrated the escape from Egypt and was sung on the seventh day of Passover.

By the tenth century this tradition was also prevalent amongst *Ashkenazi communities in Italy and northern Europe, and had developed into a complicated system of cantillation with metre, line-forms and end-rhymes. For example, in the eleventh century, Rabbi Meir ben Yitzhak, of Worms, wrote a forty-five double-verse *piyyut* – in Aramaic – for the Sabbath, about God the Creator of the World and Redeemer of His People, Israel. Every one of the ninety rhyming lines ended in 'ta', and the last twenty-three verses spelt out in acrostic form his name and his good deeds. The *piyyut* had its own melody, sung in alternate lines by the cantor and congregation. The correspondences with Gregorian plainsong as a vehicle for psalmody are clear, and are further demonstrated in just one of the hundreds of *piyyutim* found in a *Genizah in a synagogue in Cairo where we read how the poet, Amar, had the music for his poem provided by a converted Italian priest, Obadiah, who had settled in Egypt in about 1121.

Hence, not only was this tradition a supplement to psalmody (rather like the creation of hymn-singing in the western churches from Ambrose onwards), but, in turn, it also aided and inspired the actual *singing* of psalmody. And in Jewish worship, this alleviated a problematic issue. Polyphonic singing, women's voices and instrumental singing had been forbidden in the Babylonian Talmud (*Berakhot* 24a and *Sotah* 48a, for example) as a sign of mourning for the loss of the Jerusalem Temple. The introduction of singing in synagogue worship was in large measure due to the success of the *piyyutim* – albeit usually in monophonic form, led by a precentor and often accompanied by the (male) congregation. It is even likely that hitherto unknown *sigla in some versions of the Hebrew Bible could indicate different tones and pitches for the precentor to use during synagogue worship. The fact that the *sigla* used in these psalms (placed above or below syllables, subdividing verses) are very different from those used in parallel texts in other biblical narratives (for example, in Psalm 18 compared with the same prayer in 2 Samuel 22, and Ps. 105:1–5 compared with the same text in 1 Chron. 16:8–22) gives further support to the theory that by the twelfth century the psalms were at least chanted and sung in liturgy – not only in churches, East and West, but in synagogue worship, East and West, as well.

One other promotion of the Jewish liturgical use of psalmody was the establishing of a recognized prayer book. Because the psalms were not as extensively used in Jewish daily and weekly worship as they were in the Christian monastic and cathedral offices, it is not surprising that there is no evidence of anything like the *Ferial Psalter* in Judaism. But a fixed daily and weekly prayer book (the *'Siddur'*) gradually emerged: a sixth-century example is one compiled by Yoseh ben Yoseh, and a ninth-century work ('*Seder Tefillot Kol Ha-Shanah*' or 'Book of Prayers for the Entire Year'), by Amram Gaon of Sura, Babylon, was sent to the Jews in Spain, where, with the increasing interest in the Hebrew versions, it gradually became an authoritative guide in worship.

Although the psalms used in the *Siddur* were by no means as pervasive as those found in Christian *Missals and *Breviaries, they nevertheless played an important part. Psalm 145, with its theme of God's faithfulness from one generation to another, was used near the end of the morning service, as well as near the beginning of the afternoon service; Psalms 146–50 were similarly recited near the end of the morning service. In addition, verses from select psalms were used as part of the *pesukei de zimra*, used in the morning service (for example, Ps. 5:7 '… I will bow down toward your holy temple in awe of you …'; Ps. 26:8 'O Lord, I love the house in which you dwell, and the place where your glory resides …'; Ps. 69:13 'But as for me, my prayer is to you, O Lord …'; and a familiar verse in Christian liturgy, Ps. 95:6 'O come, let us worship and bow down, let us kneel before the Lord, our Maker!'). In addition, Psalm 100 usually preceded the *pesukei de zimra* on weekdays, and Psalms 19, 34, 90, 91, 135,136, 33, 92 and 93 were used for Sabbaths and festivals. At the end of the *Shema'* (Deuteronomy 6:4–5) which follows the *pesukei de zimra*, parts of Ps. 119:153–4 were read; and the *Shemonah esreh* which follows the *Shema'*, with the *Kedushah Blessing and the Priestly Blessing, also ended with psalm verses (for example, Ps. 19:14: 'Let the words of my mouth and the meditation of my heart be acceptable to you, O Lord, my rock and my redeeemer'; also Ps. 34:13 'Keep your tongue from evil, and your lips from speaking deceit'). After the Torah reading of the appropriate day, other psalms verses were used (for example, Ps. 84:4 'Happy are those who live in your house, ever singing your praise'; and Ps. 144:15 '… Happy are the people whose God is the Lord …'). And in the *Mahzor, Psalms 112–18 were frequently used.

Obviously there were local variations, and furthermore distinctive differences are to be found in Sephardi and Ashkenazi communities, but the general format – and one which continues to the present day – was the same: three services a day, with the afternoon service usually acting as a preface to the evening service with psalm verses used at the beginnings and ending of these services, and, in addition to the set psalm for the day, Psalm 145 and Psalms 146–50 were usually repeated daily. (Some scholars have argued that from this time, probably from Babylon, a 'triennal' method of reading psalmody arose, whereby each of the 150 psalms was read on the 150 (or so) Sabbaths over three years, copying the known practice of reading the Pentateuch in this way, but there is not yet enough evidence to substantiate this claim.)

Several associations between Jews and Christians, in the ways they used the psalms in liturgy, have already been noted. The examples from Jewish liturgy listed above show some interesting correspondences. Psalm 95 is used for morning prayer; Psalms 148–50 (in Jewish liturgy, Psalms 146–50) are also recited daily. Psalms 34 and 91 also reflect a significant overlap with their use in Christian liturgy. By contrast, Psalm 51, the psalm of penitence, features more in Christian liturgy; and Psalm 118, the festal psalm heralding the entrance of one 'who comes in the name of the Lord', is also used more in Christian worship. Although it features at Passover at the end of the Hallel, Jewish liturgy tends to prefer more the following psalm, with its exultation of Torah, as well as Psalm 19B. Jewish liturgy also prefers psalms with verses which speak of the beauty of the Temple (Pss. 5; 7; 26:8; 69:13; 84:4; 144:15) and of God's dealings with his people in the past (Psalms 112–18; Psalms 135–46) whilst the Christian choice of psalms is more spiritualized and personalized (for example, as well as Psalm 51, Psalms 3, 4, 63, 67, 134, 143 – using our previous list for Christian liturgical psalms). Furthermore, it is clear that during this period at least, Jewish writings on the Law, and to a lesser extant on the Prophets, were still more prominent, seen especially within various editions of *Targums and the Talmud, and their use of psalmody by the end of the eleventh century was not as pervasive as it had become in Christian liturgy. So, in terms of Jewish/Christian relations in their liturgical use of psalmody, there are notable affinities but some clear differences as well.[17]

Translation, Exposition, Homily

The most significant Jewish translation of the psalms, dating from about the sixth century, was the *Aramaic Targums on the Psalms* (TgPss), which clearly were produced in several different editions. Some twenty manuscripts containing some or all of TgPss are extant, the earliest being the late thirteenth century, each representing much earlier textual traditions. It is probable that older Aramaic versions of particular psalms, especially for use in liturgy, existed for centuries before the production of the Psalter as a whole, and this diffuse history would account in part

---

[17] General resources on poetic imitations of psalmody for liturgy and the use of the psalms in Jewish prayer books include P.F. Bradshaw and L.A. Hoffman (eds.) (1991a); H. Danby (1933); H.H. Donin (1980); I. Elbogen (1993); A. Green (ed.) 1986; *L.A. Hoffman and J.R. Walton (eds.) (1992)*; W.L. Holladay (1993); C. Kessler (1991); J. Maier (1983); M. Maher (1994); *J. Neusner (1983)*; R. Posner, U. Kaploun and S. Sohen (eds.) (1975); S.C. Reif (1983, 1993) and G.F. Willems (1990). On musical notation and the Massoretic Text, *see* S. Haïk-Vantoura (E Tr 1991).

for the textual diversity. For example, Psalm 108 refers to 'the wicked city of Rome' and to 'Constantinople, which is Edom' (v. 11) which would date it no later than the latter part of the fifth century. The Aramaic version, bringing the sacred Hebrew text into a common vernacular, compares in many ways with the production of the Septuagint for the Jews in Alexandria some eight hundred years earlier. But its difference is that it is not only a translation (usually quite a literal one, although frequently offering alternative readings) but that it also has many explanatory expansions of the translation, and these serve as a running commentary. By looking at these expansions, and comparing the changes and additions in the translation with the Hebrew versions, it is possible to see the particular concerns of the translators and compilers – for example, their interest in prayer, the Torah, prophecy, angels and demons, reward and punishment, exile, the nation's history, miracles, Temple and priesthood, the 'assembly of Israel' and the Messiah. Overall it reflects a reverent view of God, although here it is inconsistent in its translation of anthropomorphisms, sometimes using more general terms such as 'glory' and 'power' for God's 'face' or 'right hand', yet elsewhere freely adding extra details about God's hands, lips and ears; such differences again suggest that this is the work of a number of translators from different periods. But this production undoubtedly gave renewed attention to psalmody in the Aramaic-speaking communities in Syria, Babylon and Palestine – all, by the seventh century, under Islamic rule.[18]

Until Jewish exegetical works really began to develop, from the eleventh century onwards, scholarly work in psalmody took place by assembling the traditions of the past (akin to the ways in which Christian scholars used the traditions of earlier commentators to create Glosses on the Psalms) more than addressing the concerns of the present. The some twenty-six volumes of the Babylonian Talmud, dating from the sixth century onwards, containing passages both from the *Mishnah and from additional collections known as the *Gemara, frequently cited the psalms in legal, liturgical and homiletic discussions, using verses from different psalms to illustrate or answer or raise questions which had been raised in other texts, with the Torah presumed as the base text. For example, speaking of the provision of manna, reference is made to Ps. 78:23–4 ('... he opened the doors of heaven; he rained down on them manna to eat') which is then a reminder of Genesis 7:11, where the windows of heaven are opened at the time of Noah's Flood; returning to Psalm 78, this leads to a discussion of Ps. 23:5, where God is said to prepare a table in the presence of the psalmist's enemies (Babylonian Talmud: *Yoma 76a*). This relates to the liturgical use of psalmody in Christian tradition by its correspondences with the prescriptions in the various Rules in the monastic offices, whereby the literal, didactic, contemporary appeal is of primary concern. And whereas in the Christian tradition this is related back to the Gospels and Epistles,

---

[18] On the Targums, see especially D.M. Stec (2005); also M.J. Bernstein (1997, 2005); *D. Boyarin (1994)*; E.M. Cook (2002), also accessible more fully at www.tulane.edu/~ntcs/pss/tg_ps_index.htm; Y. Komlosh (1964); *E. Levine (1996)*; M. Maher (1994); L. Diez Marino (1982); J. Shunary (1966); also M. Wilcox (1985).

in the Jewish tradition the psalms go back to the ever-present authority of the Torah.[19]

A prominent concern in Jewish biblical exegesis was Hebrew philology and grammar (although this took some time before it was evidenced in exegeses of particular psalms). This interest in the Hebrew language thrived in Islamic Spain, between the eighth and tenth centuries, when collaboration between Jews and Arabs was unusually good (for example in Cordoba and Granada, first under the Emirate [756–927] and later under the Caliphate [929–1031]), and where cultured Jews spoke and wrote as much in Arabic as in Hebrew. Jews who had settled in Cadiz, Cordoba and Toledo as early as the fifth century were joined between the eighth and tenth centuries by Jews from Baghdad (at the time of the Ummayad Caliphate and then the Emirate of Cordoba), and, with growing settlements in Malaga, Granada and Seville, they formed the largest Jewish communities outside Babylon. Jews with a traditional affinity with Hebrew and Aramaic also needed to speak in Arabic, and in so doing traced the roots back to early Hebrew. By the end of the period under discussion the interest progressed from a more mathematical and linguistic study of the Hebrew language to a more philosophical enquiry: that it happened first in Spain, rather than in Italy or northern Africa (where traditional analytical Talmudic studies were still strong) or in the Frankish kingdoms (where mainly homiletic and juridical studies prevailed) is not surprising. *Hisdai ibn Shaprut* (940–66) is just one example of a leading patron of Hebrew studies in Cordoba.

This excursus is simply to illustrate how and why the scholarly interest in psalmody at this time was so minimal, especially when compared with Christian uses at this time. In fact we have to look to the eastern end of the Mediterranean for an example of the first significant Jewish commentator on the psalms. *Saadiah Gaon* (882–942) was born in Egypt and worked mainly in Palestine and Babylon, and was one of the first Jewish writers to translate the entire Hebrew Bible into Arabic, the language of Jews living under Islamic rule in Egypt and Syro-Palestine. Saadiah also wrote two introductions – the earliest much shorter than the other – on the psalms. He reads the psalms, as did Philo, as a 'second Pentateuch' – all by David 'the prophet', uttering 'divine speech' through human discourse. He uses contemporary arguments about the (eighteen) rhetorical modes of speech and musical melodic modes to reinforce his argument. He is at pains to show that the psalms we recite are not our own innovation (as the *piyyutim* had done) but rather, they have been handed down to us in a continuous tradition which goes back to David; nothing new must be added to them, for they contain 'divine speech' which began and ended with David, the inspired prophet. This means that, for our own day, their worth is for edification alone, akin to the Torah.

Much of Saadiah's work on the psalms was a polemical response to a Jewish sect called the *Karaites whose communities were mainly in Palestine and Egypt, and centred on Jerusalem. Rejecting the legal requirements of the Torah, Talmud and

---

[19] The example from the Talmud is taken from W.L. Holladay (1993), pp. 147–8. See also *D. Weiss-Halivni (1986)*.

Mishnah as well as all the oral legal traditions of Judaism, the Karaites had turned instead to the psalms as their authority and guide. They read them as prophetic prayers, relevant for all ages, especially their own; as prophecies with a contemporary ring they created hope in a new Messianic future, and according to the Karaites' reading of the psalms, that future concerned one place (Jerusalem) and one community who would worship there (the Karaites). Hence Saadiah's commentary was in response to them: by affirming the psalms were prophecies given to David, and by focusing on their historical setting and their didactic worth, he excludes the possibility of any contemporary prophetic appropriation.

Two Karaite writers wrote their own (Arabic) commentaries on the Psalms, in part a response to Gaon, demonstrating that an overly historical approach robbed the psalms of their present-day relevance, thus contradicting the prescriptions in rabbinical teaching such as the Mishnah about their importance as contemporary prayers. *Salmon ben Yeruham*, from Palestine/Egypt, born c.910, and *Yefet ben 'Ali Halevi*, from Basra, born c.930, were both known as 'mourners for Zion' and wrote in reply to Gaon's extreme historical emphasis on the psalms. They sought to demonstrate their value as prayers – to be used not only by an ancient exiled Jewish community in Babylon in the sixth century BCE but a present exiled community in the tenth century CE. On this account, the psalms were also to be read as present-day prophecies, interpreted through prayer. Their impact as poems went far further than Davidic authorship alone; there were many other psalmists, each interpreting the tradition of David, and these set a precedent for further interpretations shaping the community of their day. For example, taking Psalm 137 ('By the waters of Babylon, we sat down and wept'), Saadiah understood this as a psalm by David, and he re-read the psalm as if David was speaking, adding at the beginning of the psalm, to avoid anachronism, 'the people in exile will say ...'. By contrast, Yefet understood the psalm to be a composition whose actual context was the Babylonian exile, thus allowing a bridge between the past and present experience of exile in the tenth and eleventh centuries.

The Karaites' approach to psalmody is rather like the ways that the community at Qumran read the psalms in defending their claim to be God's elect people, and the reaction of Saadiah is rather like that of the Jews of the first and second centuries who reacted to the ways in which the Christians seized upon the prophetic element in psalmody and, turning the psalms Christwards, applied that element to their own day. But Saadiah was not addressing Christians, and nor were Yefet and Salmon affirming any Christian prophetic hermeneutic. The debate here is a brief example of the way that the Jewish prophetic interpretation of psalmody becomes important in one place for a short period of time, offering an important insight into polemical commentary solely from the Jewish tradition.[20]

---

[20] Saadiah's commentary is only available by Kafih in Hebrew, and Salmon's and Yefet's, only in manuscript form. Material for this assessment has therefore been dependent upon U. Simon (1991), especially the first two chapters, as well as M. Sokolow (1984); and H. Malter (1969) and L. Marwick (ed.) (1956).

Artistic Representation

Jewish adaptation of psalmody in musical or illustrated form is far lass apparent in this period. Given the teaching in the Law against graven images, and given the Jewish associations with the iconoclastic movement in the eastern churches, it is hard to find even a handful of examples of Jewish manuscript illumination or musical composition of any biblical text. The earliest examples are from the end of the ninth century, and, not surprisingly, are attributed to the Karaites from Tiberias, Palestine; but even here the illuminated manuscript is not from the psalms, but from the Prophets. Other examples can be found in Islamic Spain, where Jews wrote out psalms in Arabic as well as in Hebrew characters, using Islamic calligraphical ornamentation. This eventually led to geometric, fauna and floral designs illustrating manuscripts of psalms; so this is tradition which reaches maturation in the later centuries.[21]

Concluding Observations

We are now in a position to see the extent to which our five modes of reception are now found throughout both Jewish and Christian traditions. One of the most difficult to categorize, but undoubtedly the most pervasive, is the *liturgical* use of the psalms. In both Jewish and Christian forms of worship, both in public hymnody and in private prayer, it is almost certainly the continuous use of the psalms, or at the least, imitations of psalmody, which helped to preserve both faiths in their darkest periods. As early as Clement of Rome and Eusebius of Caesarea, and in the works of John Cassion and in the monastic and cathedral offices, as well as in the Mishnah, Targums and Talmud, the evidence is compelling. Although different traditions espoused different psalms, a good deal of continuity has been seen to exist between the two traditions, and in each the daily, weekly and monthly use of psalmody is paramount.

Almost as pervasive is the *didactic* mode of reception, relating the moral and spiritual elements of psalmody to members of a particular community. This approach has been seen in the Qumran scrolls and in Philo; it was also evident in Matthew, Acts and the Epistles, as well as in earlier church fathers such as John Chrysostom and Hilary of Poitiers. In this chapter it has been seen in the Mishnah and Targums as well as in the monastic Rules and the writings of Bede and Alcuin.

Exegetical works, also prevalent, take two forms. On the one hand, we find commentaries and homilies which are analytical, textual, philological and historical in emphasis, but which are directed towards a particular community rather than to

---

[21] See *J. Gutmann (1971); J. Leveen (1944);* and G. Sed-Rajna (1992).

heretics and opponents of the faith; they have a less polemical edge, and many could be classified as more moral and devotional works. They include the homilies of Augustine and the expositions of Cassiodorus, Bede and Alcuin, who each contributed to the formation of the Christian *Gloss*; and they also include the rabbinical discussions of the psalms in the Targums and Talmud and the inherited body of tradition which arises out of these works. On the other hand, other exegetical works, still analytical and textual in nature, can be highly polemical: these include the *pesher* commentaries and the *florigelia* at Qumran, the prophetic use of the psalms by the New Testament writers, and the commentaries from as early as Justin to as late as the Antiochene and Latin Fathers, as well as Jewish commentators such as Saadiah Gaon and the Kairites.

As for *translations* of psalmody, we have seen how there are particular periods when new translations are particularly abundant: in Judaism, this is marked by the Septuagint in the second century BCE and the Aramaic Targums in the sixth century CE. In Christendom, the third and fourth centuries are the most prolific, influenced by the works of Origen and Jerome. By contrast, there are other periods when such activity is minimal, for example in the tenth and eleventh centuries, when there was only some minor revision of received texts such as the Targums and Jerome, usually for liturgical purposes. At the very end of this period, a few Psalters in Old English begin to appear in Christian tradition: examples given earlier include the *Vespasian Psalter* and the *Paris Psalter*.

At this stage in history, the *aesthetic* representation of psalmody is mainly evident in Christian tradition. The earliest is through music, exemplified by the Ambrosian and Gregorian chants and the plainsong of the fifth and sixth centuries. Artistic depictions are apparent nearer the end of the first millennium, in illuminated and illustrated psalms manuscripts and prayer books in both western and eastern Christendom. Aesthetic representation develops more cautiously in Jewish tradition, both in music and in art, but its beginnings are found in the work of the *piyyutim* and in Arabic-influenced calligraphy.

Each of these five distinct (yet overlapping) types of reception bears witness to the differences between Jews and Christians in their interpretation and use of the psalms. The remaining four chapters, which will examine the reception of psalmody over the next thousand years, in both traditions, will continue to use these five ways of reading the psalms, with the differences between the two faiths constantly in mind.

The Eleventh to Fifteenth Centuries: Learning and Discerning

The diversity of material before us necessitates a focus which is increasingly on the reception of psalmody in the West. Of the five modes of reception, it will become clear that, in both Jewish and Christian traditions, *expositions of psalmody* are the most prolific; in part this is because of a new genre of disputatious works now undertaken by Jews as well as Christians, and in part it is due to a renewed interest in grammatical and linguistic questions within psalmody. The *aesthetic reception of psalmody* is also profuse, particularly in the ongoing production of illustrated manuscripts, mainly by Christians, but with some remarkable Jewish examples as well, not only in illuminated manuscripts and prayer books, but in church and synagogue architecture as well. The *didactic reception of psalmody* is also rich, with distinctive examples in each faith tradition. Perhaps surprisingly, the Christian use of the psalms in the *liturgy*, in both cathedral and monastic offices, is not as vibrant as in previous centuries; there are exceptions, not least in musical compositions, but the lack of innovation is partly due to the many social and political upheavals in both the East and West. The same applies to Jewish use of psalmody in liturgy, for similar reasons. As for *translations* of psalms, the most significant development is in the Christian tradition; focusing here specifically on the English medium, there are a few striking examples in Old and Middle English.

Because it is therefore possible to trace similar lines of development in both the Christian and Jewish reception of the psalms throughout this period, we shall assess their distinctive contributions alongside one another, under each of the five modes of reception.

Jewish and Christian Controversies through Exegetical Works

Preliminary Considerations

Between the eleventh and fifteenth centuries the most notable developments in psalmody were in the West. As the Byzantine church was spreading westwards and

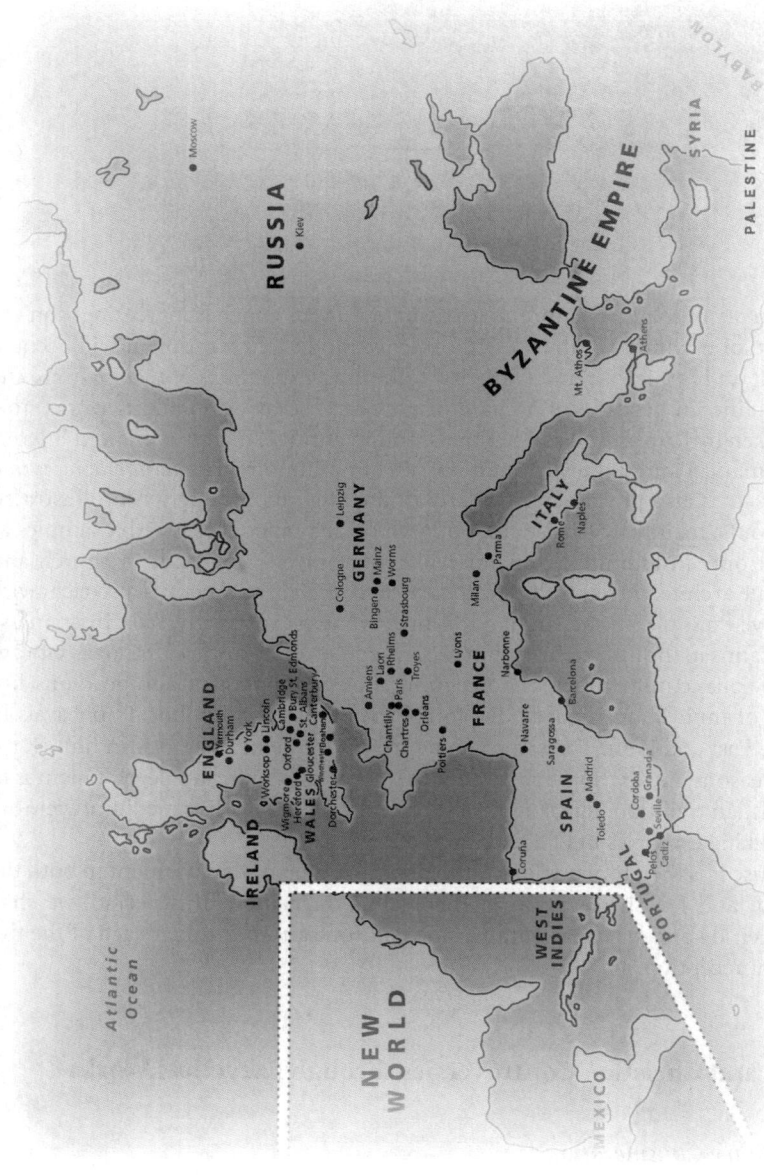

MAP 3.1 France: a centre of psalmody in the later Middle Ages.

southwards from Constantinople, into what is now southern Italy, Turkey and Greece, Catholic churches were expanding westwards and northwards into what is now Germany, northern Italy, France, Luxemburg, England, Ireland, Spain and Portugal. The 'Great Schism' between the churches of the East and the West, symbolically dated at 1054, the pillage of Constantinople during the fourth crusade (1202–4) and the eventual fall of the Byzantine Empire in 1453 created great instability in the eastern churches in Palestine, Syria and beyond; as far as psalmody is concerned, contemplative reflective works are more in evidence than the more critical and exegetical works which characterize the West. By contrast, the western churches, particularly after the Christian re-conquest of most of Spain between the twelfth and thirteenth centuries, were more actively engaged within a new atmosphere of learning.

Furthermore, Jewish migration to new Christian territories in the West meant that Jewish scholars, now also exposed to a greater freedom of intellectual enquiry, explored new ways of defending their faith, and one of these was in various types of disputatious writings – in many cases, as we shall see, using the psalms. In part, such works were in response to increasing persecution of Jews from the mid-twelfth century onwards, first in northern France and Rhineland, and later in England and throughout the Continent, so that, not surprisingly, Jewish writings became more strident against the Christian faith. Their provocation was on many levels. One example, important here because it relates to psalmody, is of the way in which Jewish faith was presented in Christian architecture and art in the burgeoning cathedrals in the twelfth and thirteenth centuries. An example in stained glass, influenced by the same genre in illuminated Psalters, is the increasing popularity, from the eleventh century onwards, of the *Jesse Tree: in northern France, the windows at Laon, Chartres, Amiens, Le Mans, St Denis and Sainte-Chapelle illustrate vividly a conviction that David was as much the guardian of the Christian faith as of the faith of the Jews. Another instance, this time in sculpture, is of two female figures (often one on each side of the crucified Christ), the one blindfold, dejected and turning aside, representing the 'false mother' of the Jewish synagogue, and the other exultant, responsive and receptive, depicting the 'true mother' of the Christian church. Examples of this new genre include the façades of the Notre Dame cathedrals in Paris and Strasbourg, as well as on the north porch of Chartres, and the south and west porches of Rheims; given that these were all places with growing Jewish communities, they served again to expose publicly what was seen as the inferior nature of the Jewish faith. At this point in time, the Jewish response did not use corresponding art forms; their rejoinder was necessarily through the written medium, and commentators who used the psalms in their disputatious works – from Paris, Troyes and Narbonne, and Barcelona, Cordoba and Seville, as we shall shortly see – railed against this Christian interpretation of the Jewish Scriptures. Their works (many using the psalms, and mostly in Hebrew) were designed for Jewish audiences, but, similar to the ways in which the early Christian fathers used only the written medium against Jewish interpretations of the psalms some eight hundred years earlier, the intention was that Christians would also 'take note'.

In France, which by the thirteenth century had once more become the intellectual and cultural centre of Europe, the influence of university schools in Paris, Laon, Chartres and Rheims, for example, and, in Norman England, in centres such as Canterbury and Oxford, intensified these more verbal disputes about the correct exposition of Scripture. Again, Christian scholars frequently used the psalms in these debates: these were the texts above all which Jews considered had been plundered most for Christian purposes, so in turn, Christians defended their use of them with a new vigour. By the fifteenth century, anti-Christian comments on the psalms by Jewish exegetes caused Christian commentators, into whose possession these works had passed, to respond by erasing 'offensive' Jewish comments, and the full range of the debate has now become legible under ultra-violet light.[1]

There were nevertheless a few eirenical exchanges of learning, both in France and in Spain. In Spain, for example, Jews were beginning to attain prominent positions, serving Christian rulers as bailiffs, tax farmers, doctors and creditors; and Jewish grammarians and philologists, with their particular skills in Semitic languages, were frequently consulted by Christian scholars who were beginning to recognize the need to re-examine the biblical texts more linguistically, not least in relation to their ancient origins. The school of translators in Toledo – also a place of dispute between the two faiths – is one example. And in France, Anglo-Norman Psalters appeared with Hebrew texts annotated with Latin. Just as Christian scholars needed to learn and read in Hebrew to give depth to their knowledge of their own tradition of interpretation in Greek and Latin, Jewish commentators wanted to know more about the Greek and Latin interpretation through a less familiar tradition; so at the linguistic level, if not the theological one, consultation was mutual, and counterbalanced the more polemical works.

But disputations were more the order of the day, and in each tradition an appropriate choice of exegetical methods was vital to show the reasonableness of one position and the lack of rational argument in the other. Both Jews and Christians started with two similar modes of interpretation – the interest in the plain literal meaning of the text and the interest in a hidden meaning – but by the end of this period, it is clear that these two emphases developed in different ways. Jewish commentators tended to favour the plain unembellished literal reading, which they termed 'sensus Judaicus' – a David-centred, Israel-centred *peshat. Because this avoided any Christian overlay, it became highly effective in anti-Christian polemic. Nevertheless, even in Jewish tradition, a hidden meaning could not be ignored; this had always been part of their tradition (the *pesher interpretation, for example, is found as early as Qumran) long before the Christians read their texts in this way. And, given the eschatological expectations in the eleventh and twelfth

---

[1] This example is from a manuscript in the Cambridge University Library (MS Add 1574), quoted in Rosenthal (1960) p. 117.

centuries, when Christians read the psalms as pointing towards a new *Messiah* who was Christ, as well as towards a new *Law* which was embodied in the person and work of Christ, Jewish commentators needed to find in these biblical texts references to the Messiah who was still to come and to the eternal validity of the Jewish Torah. This search for a hidden meaning was known as *derash*, and with it Jewish commentators added two other elements: *remez'*, which was a more explicitly allegorical reading, and *sod* (meaning 'secret' or 'mystery'), which was a more mystical interpretation. From the eleventh century onwards, in southern France and Spain where the *Kabbalah movement was particularly influential, such mystical readings were particularly popular amongst Jewish commentators. Originating in Spain (later popularized in Safed, Galilee), the mystical *Book of *Zohar*, based upon meditations upon the 'Splendour' of God as found in the Law, also affected more mystical readings of the psalms as they pointed to the coming Messiah and the eternal Law. Usually, however, most Jewish commentators held all these four readings together, rather than isolating just one. An acronym derived from this fourfold approach (*Pesher/Remez/Daresh/Sod*) was 'PaRDeS' and, as will be seen below, in spite of the disputatious setting in which these methods were used, they had much in common with the fourfold way Christians were reading the same texts.

Christian scholars also placed a new emphasis on the *literal* meaning; this was not so much because of specific historical interests as their new grammatical and philological concerns (including not only Hebrew but also Aramaic and Arabic). But the hidden meaning was paramount, as this enabled insights for a Christ-centred reading. So alongside with the literal reading, the *allegorical* reading (whereby every single Old Testament reference could be turned 'Christwards') was combined with a *typological* or *typical* reading which was based upon the contrast of (inferior) Old Testament events and theology with Christian events and theology, and the psalms were particularly useful for this purpose. In addition to the literal and combined allegorical/typological readings, Christians applied two others. One was the more contemplative *analogical* approach, praying the words of Scripture, close to the Jewish *sod*, but in this case more influenced by Christian monasticism. The other reading, known as *tropological*, was more morally inclined, with the purpose of showing how Old Testament practices had been superseded by the Christian teaching on morality, and, by inference, that the Jewish Law was now fulfilled in Christian teaching. Between the eleventh and fourteenth centuries these different Jewish and Christian fourfold modes of reading were most popular, and developed into most sophisticated forms.[2]

---

[2] This discussion has been informed by *A.S. Abulafia (1995)*; D. Berger (1979); G.H. Brown (1995, 1999); R. Chazan (2004); J. Cohen (1999); G. Dahan (2000); N. van Deusen (ed.) (1999); A. Finkelstein (1993); M.T. Gibson (1993); A. Grabois (1975); M. Idel (2000); U. Köpf (2000); D.J. Lasker (1994, 1999); R. Loewe (1957); H. De Lubec (1998); E Mâle (1913); E.I.J. Rosenthal (1964, 1969); N.M. Sarna (1971); M. Signer (1998); B. Smalley (1983); R.W. Southern (1953); G. Stemberger (2000); F.E. Talmage (1987); and K. Walsh and D. Wood (eds.) (1985).

Jewish Commentators

Taking the more historical, literal and philological commentaries by Jewish scholars first, the two earliest exegetes actually disputed more with the *Karaites than with Christians (although there is some awareness of shared differences with Christians as well). Both writers were Spanish-born, and both were influenced by Saadiah Gaon. *Moses ibn Giqatilah* (*Chiquitilla*) (died c.1080) was from Cordoba, but forced to live in Saragossa and then in southern France, and *Abraham ibn Ezra* (1089–1164) was from Navarre. Moses ibn Giqatilah was not only the first Jewish scholar to translate scientific works from Arabic into Hebrew, but, as a grammarian, he put this skill to good use by composing his own *piyyutim* (the best known is on the servant figure in Isaiah) and in compiling a commentary on the psalms, some of which has been lost, although parts of it have been found amongst the scrolls in the Cairo *Genizah. For Moses ibn Giqatilah, like Gaon, the psalms are poetic prayers, not prophecies; they are addresses *to* God, not words *from* God. As prayers and poems, they have distinctive literary styles and suggest a variety of dates, as early as the time of David and as late as the exile. Moses ibn Giqatilah was one of the first Jewish commentators to question Davidic authorship of all the psalms, proposing that some fourteen psalms were composed during the exile: all were without Davidic titles, such as those of the sons of Korah (Psalms 42, 46, 47, 84), of Asaph (Psalms 76, 78, 79, 81), of Ethan (Psalm 89) and anonymous psalms (Psalms 102, 106 119 and 137). He also accepted that even those with Davidic headings need not all have been written by David: some could have been written after his time (for example, psalms which refer to Zion as a place of sacrifice, as in Ps. 51:18–19, or Ps.110:2, because the Temple was not built until Solomon's time). His commentary was, nevertheless, essentially historical in orientation, in large part because of the philological interests. It was even more radical in its protest against the prophetic appropriation of psalmody than was the more overtly moral interpretation of Gaon some hundred years earlier.

Abraham ibn Ezra was influenced by Moses ibn Giqatilah's work. Forced out of Muslim Spain at the time when Muslim rule was acceding to the Christians, he wrote mainly in south-western France, and his work is more polemical in style. He too was fluent in Arabic as well as Hebrew, and his commentary on the psalms was also philological, with an emphasis on the straightforward *peshat. One of his ways of undermining the Karaites' reading was, like Moses ibn Giqatilah, to affirm the psalms' value as religious poems. But Abraham's concerns were broader than disputing with the Kairites. In one of his two introductions to Psalms 1 and 2 (*The First Recension to Psalms 1–2*, lines 30–2) he speaks of the poetry of the Ishmaelites (i.e. the Arabs) being about love and passion; that of the Edomites (i.e. the Christians of the western churches) about war and vengeance; that of the Greeks, about wisdom and discretion; and that of the Indians, about all sorts of parables. Only the ancient poetry of the Hebrews can reveal that God is the one and only God. Abraham ibn Ezra's defence of the ancient origins of monotheism in Jewish poetry sought to make several points: as a defence of poetry, it attacked the Karaite view of psalmody as prophecy; as a defence of monotheism, it attacked the

Christian interpretation of psalmody through their belief in the Trinity; and as a defence of the antiquity of psalmody, it attacked Islamic claims that Arabic poetry (and indeed, the Arabic language) was superior. By referring to the *religious quality* of the psalms – not least, the way the monotheistic beliefs constantly expressed within them clearly predated any of those which were so important in Islamic literature, Abraham claimed that both literary and theological superiority belonged to the Jews. It is not surprising that he composed a *piyyut* on God's calling of his people out from amongst the nations, and that parts of his commentary expound the belief in the election of the Jewish people over and against the nations.

A further way in which Abraham saw the superior quality of the Hebrew Psalms was, ironically, in their value as prophecies, but not, as the Karaites supposed, because they were texts about to be fulfilled in the present generation, but because they were ancient religious poems whose aesthetic quality pointed to their inspiration by God. Occasionally, owing to the worsening situation for Jews both in Spain and southern France, a contemporary element relevant for his own people, longing for redemption, was emphasized, but this was rare, and the more historical reading of the psalms as ancient religious poems – composed long before the emergence of either Christianity or Islam – was more prominent.

Throughout his expositions of the psalms, Abraham ibn Ezra makes constant use of the literal and grammatical authority of earlier rabbinical sources. This was of course a popular rabbinic technique since before the Christian era, as becomes evident later in the *Mishnah and *Talmud, but to use such annotations and quotations within a commentary, here on the psalms, marks the development of an important twelfth-century correspondence between Jewish and Christian commentators – the practice known as 'glossing' – what some would regard as the vandalizing of a received text in terms of its interpretive comments, but what others would see as a creative means of breathing new life and meaning into texts with as traditional a reading as the psalms.

Another Jewish commentator, also from Spain, wrote more polemically against both Islamic and Christian scholars. Although more of an introduction to the use of psalms than a commentary on the psalms, two studies by *Moses ibn Ezra* (1055–1138) from Andalusia (although he was expelled from Granada in 1090) focused, like Abraham ibn Ezra, on the poetic language of the psalms. Moses ibn Ezra used an unusual combination of Arabic poetics (a discipline popular with Islamic scholars at this time) harnessed to Hebrew philology (in which he was expert) and Greek philosophy (another discipline popular with Arabic scholars). His presumed audience is Jewish, but his criticisms are of both Christian and Muslim scholars. Moses ibn Ezra demonstrated that a study of Hebrew poetry – and hence of the poetry of the psalms – was essentially a rational and literary process, worthy of study in its own right.[3]

---

[3] On these three Spanish writers, see D. Frank (1995); V.B. Mann, T.F. Glick and J.D. Dodds (eds.) (1992); N.M. Sarna (1971); U. Simon (1991, 2000 [on Abraham ibn Ezra]) and M. Cohen (2000a [on Moses ibn Ezra]).

Rabbi Shlomo Yitzhaki (1040–1105), better known as *Rashi*, lived in northern France and his polemical works were directed primarily at Christian schools of exegesis there. Born in Troyes, and spending some fifteen years of rabbinic studies in Mainz and Worms, Rashi returned to Troyes where he probably established his own **yeshivah*. It was not until after the first Crusade in 1096 that Rashi began to defend more disputatiously the Jewish cause, understanding the psalms as prophecies relating to his own age, pointing to the Messiah and to the imminent redemption of Israel. Many of his comments are anti-Christian: Christians are the hated 'Edomites', stealing the heritage of the Jews; the 'Kittim' represent Christian Rome – i.e. in Rashi's time, the church of western Christendom. Using terminology from earlier Jewish writers, Rashi terms Christians as '*minim*' (heretics), as contrasted with the '*ma'amin*', the Jews who have the right belief.

As well as citing the psalms in other works, much of his psalms commentary was written during this later period. It is a lengthy work, full of grammatical and syntactical comment as well as expounding the *Mishnah, Aramaic Targums, Babylonian *Talmud and other Rabbinic sources (thereby continuing the tradition from Abraham ibn Ezra of a type of Jewish ˙Gloss) to bring out both the **peshat* and **derash* in the texts. By using the text alongside these ancient authorities, Rashi demonstrated that, for instance, Psalm 45 was about Israel, not the Church, and that Psalms 2, 22 and 89 spoke only about David and the Jews (and in the case of Psalm 22, about their sufferings), not about Jesus. A couple of more specific examples must suffice. In Ps. 2:7 ('You are my son ...') Rashi noted that although the word 'bar' in Aramaic could only mean 'son', in Hebrew it had various meanings as well as 'son', including 'pure in heart' and, in the plural, 'children (of Israel)'; hence the phrase in Psalm 2:7, ('You are my son; today I have begotten you ...') need not signify any one individual figure (and certainly not Christ) but the 'pure' or 'children' of God – i.e. the people of Israel, or Jewish community in his time. Similarly, in commenting on Psalm 22, Rashi proposed that verse 1 ('My God, My God, why have you forsaken me?') was a prayer of David with reference to the future exiles, and verse 28 ('For dominion belongs to the Lord, and he rules over nations'), used by Christians to explain the mission to the Gentiles, really concerned the time of Israel's imminent redemption, the days of their Messiah. So again, this had nothing to do with Christ. Rashi's purpose was to show that, insofar as there was any prophetic element in psalmody, it was awaiting imminent fulfilment (rather than, as the Karaites had written, already fulfilled) and this was to be in the life of the Jewish community of his own day. The commentary was later seen as one the earliest substantial refutations of the Christian interpretation – and, in Rashi's view, mistranslation – of psalmody.[4]

---

[4] A recent work on Rashi and psalmody is the translation of his commentary, with critical notes on the Hebrew and the sources, by M.I. Gruber (2004). See also *S.W. Baron (1941)*; *J. Bloch (1958)*; *B.J. Gelles (1981)*; D.L. Goodwin (2006), pp. 169–201; A. Grossman (1996, *2000*); H. Hailperin (1963); J.M. Rosenthal (1967); *E. Shereshevsky (1970)*; and *D.E. Timmer (1989)*.

Other Jewish psalmic commentators include *Joseph Karan* (1050–1125), also from northern France, who wrote a similar anti-Christian commentary with a literal and grammatical bias, and Rashi's grandson, *Rabbi Samuel Ben Meir*, known as *Rashbam* (?1080–?1160), from near Troyes. Rashbam's commentary on the Psalms, as his other commentaries, makes full use of texts and versions, not only of the Massoretic Text, but also of the Vulgate, comparing these with French, German and Spanish manuscripts. His purpose was to create a critical and analytical study of the text, getting as close as possible to the earliest versions and translations. Hence *peshat was primary: like his predecessors, Rashbam's commentary is grammatical, literal and historical in emphasis, refuting the 'hidden meanings' induced by a Christocentric reading. But, according to Rashbam, *derash should not be left to Christian exegetes alone: it was also important for Jewish commentators. By referring frequently to the Targums and Mishnah, Rashbam argued that the only *genuine* midrashic interpretation of psalmody was the Jewish one continued through a longer and more continuous history of interpretive tradition than that of Christian commentators. Given the growing popularity of Christians 'glossing' a commentary, it was vital for Jewish commentators such as Rashbam to use the equivalent of a Christian Gloss to refute Christian typology and allegory as more recent and more spurious.

Slightly later, *Joseph Bekhor Shor* (1130–1200), from Orleans in southern France, wrote a commentary which continued many of the concerns of Rashbam. He affirmed the historical origins and literary worth of all Hebrew poetry, especially the Psalms: hence again *peshat was primary. But, like Rashbam, Shor was concerned to use *derash more effectively than the Christians, and drawing from the rich resources of Jewish midrashic tradition, he sought to show that because Christian exegesis broke with Jewish tradition it was basically derivative and imitative.[5]

Anti-Christian polemic reached its height in the commentaries of the Kimchi family. The father, *Joseph Kimchi* (1105–70), and his two sons *Moses Kimchi* (d. 1190) and *David Kimchi* (1160–1235), were originally from Andalusia; they were forced to settle in Narbonne (ironically the seat of an Archbishop, with a thriving Christian community), but later spent time in northern France, where they were profoundly critical of the Christian schools of exegesis and the Christian justifications of the Crusades. In *Sefer ha-Berit*, or *The Book of the Covenant*, Joseph Kimchi wrote a series of imaginary interchanges of claims and counter-claims between a Jew and a Christian, citing several biblical texts. For example, near the end of his work, Psalm 72 is cited by the Christian to show it is a hymn of praise to Jesus Christ; the Jewish protagonist retorts by showing that the psalm could never have been intended to refer to Jesus, as kings and nations never bowed down to serve him (as indicated in Ps. 72:8–11) – indeed Muslims and Jews explicitly deny

---

[5] On Rashbam, see *A. Grossman (2000)*; *E.I.J. Rosenthal (1969)*; and M. Signer (2002). More general but relevant works include N. van Deusen and M.L. Colish (1999); *B. Smalley (1969)*; and *D.E. Timmer (1989)*.

his Lordship, so Christian exegesis does not stand up to the evidence. Similarly the Christian cites Psalm 110:1 ('The Lord says to my Lord, "Sit at my right hand ..."') to show that David must be speaking of another Lord, Christ, as well as of God; this gives the Jewish respondent great opportunity to show how Jerome has mistranslated the Hebrew ('my lord') to denote a divine figure, whilst the Hebrew, quite simply, means a human figure (the king), to whom God is speaking. The literal reading is thus sufficient. In this way the Christian argument, constantly defeated by the Jewish response, is shown to be fallacious.

Rabbi David Kimchi, known as *Radak*, did not produce such an explicitly polemic work, but instead included similar disputations in his commentaries. His commentary on different psalms (some forty-eight are still extant) is full of linguistic and philosophical observations (the latter gained as a student of Maimonides of Cordoba). David Kimchi uses a similar literary device as his father, quoting repeatedly a phrase which implied he knew had been coined by the Christians through having had some dialogue with them: for example, 'the Christians interpret this psalm as referring to Jesus (*or* 'that man'), but you must answer them ...'. Like Rashbam and Shor, David Kimchi drew heavily from the Talmud and from Jewish commentators, and aimed to show in philosophical terms that an appropriate use of Jewish *derash could still allow for the plain meaning, the *peshat*.

David Kimchi's focus was on the two Christian doctrines which at this time gave most offence to the Jews: that Christ was the Messiah – and so was greater than David, and that Christ was the fulfilment of the Law – and so was greater than Moses. Concerning the argument about the Law, he took psalms which spoke especially of the importance of the law (Psalms 1, 19 and 119) and argued that the law could only be understood literally; there could be no such thing as an allegorical command. The Torah, as transmitted from Moses to David, had always been understood literally, and always should be: it had eternal validity, could not be supplanted by another, and this is what the Torah psalms advocated. Concerning the argument about the Messiah, Kimchi's exegesis of Psalms 2, 45 and 110 is most pertinent in this respect: on both philological and philosophical terms, he argues that the references in Ps. 2:7 to 'you are my son, today have I adopted you', in Ps. 45:6 to 'Your throne, O God, endures forever and ever' and in Ps. 110:1 to 'The Lord says to my Lord ...' can only refer to David, not Christ. (In this way, his view of Psalm 2 and 45 is different from that of Rashi, who saw the one addressed to be Israel, not David.) In these psalms, Kimchi saw that Christian interpretations compromise the absolute uniqueness of the one God. God is an indivisible unity, and cannot address himself:

> If anybody were to say: *I have today born you* and the born one is of the same kind as the begetter, then answer them: 'in divinity it is not possible [to assume] father and son, for the Deity cannot be divided ... again, you say of God that the father said to the son *ask of me and I will give you nations as your inheritance*. If the son is God why should he ask his father? Has he no power over nations and the ends of the earth like him? ... (*Commentary on Psalm 2:7–8*, quoted in Rosenthal [1960], p. 128)

David Kimchi saw that the psalms were profoundly relevant for the Jewish people, in their present situation of an experience of perpetual exile. Refuting the Christian readings also of Psalms 16, 19, 22, 72 and 89, he conversely interpreted them as prophecies alluding to the Messiah, written at different times in Israel's history (i.e. not only by David) – but, like Rashi, as *prophecies as yet unfulfilled*. This is a spirited defence of Judaism by way of using of the psalms; its real audience is of course the Jews rather than the Christians, and it uses the psalms to provide a clear rejection of Jesus as the promised Messiah, and Jesus as the fulfilment of the Torah. The commentary also addressed the heightened eschatological expectations of the day by showing how the psalms speak of one who is to come. Overall it shows how skilled Kimchi was at holding together the literal and spiritual, the traditional and the contemporary.[6]

Christian Commentators

Christian commentators of the psalms were mostly affected by the growth of university schools, particularly those at Notre Dame, Chartres, St Victor and Laon. Although these schools were still part of an ecclesial tradition, predominantly Benedictine, with several scholars becoming bishops and archbishops, they performed a very different function from the monastic and cathedral schools. Their exegetical methods were very different from the *lectio divina* of the monasteries and the musical and liturgical emphases of the cathedral schools, and their theological concerns became increasingly detached from the *sacra pagina*. The emphasis was as much on law, medicine and the arts as on theology *per se*: the method of reading had more to do with asking questions of the text than giving answers from the text, and this was not as easily appropriated by those more familiar with the contemplative and liturgical use of psalmody.

Hence in relation to studies of the psalms, when answers were given (usually taken from an anthology of earlier interpreters, going back to Origen, Jerome, Augustine, Cassiodorus, Bede and Alcuin), they were open to further interpretation, and so further questions were asked. This was a type of exegesis which required a good deal of intellectual dexterity, and glosses – many of them in Anglo-Saxon, and later, Anglo-Norman – which had previously been simple explanations of Latin words not properly understood were written more at length either in the margins or above the lines of the word. In time these became so vast they had to be compiled into independent works on the whole Vulgate. Their popularity waxed (the high point being the thirteenth century) then (by the end of the fifteenth century)

---

[6] As well as more general works noted above, see the following works on David Kimchi: J. Baker and E.W. Nicholson (1973); J.B. Bosniak (1954); *M. Cohen (2000b)*; S.I. *Esterton (1935)*; R.G. Finch and G.H. Box (1919); E.I.J. *Rosenthal (1969)*; and F.E. Talmage (1975). The reference to Joseph Kimchi is from R. *Chazan (2004)* pp. 134–5 and p. 245.

waned – emulating, as we shall shortly see, the popularity of illuminated manuscripts, both being skills more appropriate to the pre-printing era. One of the earliest independent glosses, the *Glossa Ordinaria*, on the entire Vulgate, is often traced back to a ninth-century Benedictine German monk, Walafrid Strabo, working in the Carolingian court, and was expanded in this later period. Another, the *Glossa Interlinearis*, also on the whole Vulgate, with a more explicit Christological bias, is attributed to Anselm of Laon (d. 1117), who, having trained at the abbey of Bec under St Anselm of Canterbury, founded the school at Laon, where he was born.[7]

Anselm also helped to establish the *Victorine School* within the Abbey of St Victor in Paris in about 1109 along with William of Champeaux (1070–1121), one of his pupils, and the *Glossa Interlinearis* (on most of the Bible) became an important text in all the schools of northern France. The Abbey, together with those of Ste Genevieve and Notre Dame, formed the core of the university of Paris, and aimed to combine piety with learning. *Hugh St. Victor* (c.1096–1141), possibly from Ypres, Flanders, arrived at the Abbey in 1115, and stayed there all his life, becoming its Prior in 1133. Although perhaps best known as a Christian mystic (his work was based upon the 'three eyes of the rational soul' – thought, meditation, contemplation), his theological works frequently use the psalms. He sought to make acceptable the new scientific method in the university schools, and often did so by reference to Scripture: for example, his *Didascalicon*, a massive guide to the place of the arts in medieval study, draws frequently from Genesis in its discussion of the doctrine of creation and the potential and constraints of human knowledge, whilst his *Chronicon*, a compilation of genealogical and chronological tables, made use of the psalms as a technique for the art of memory, whereby the first verse of a psalm would lead to the rest by way of verses stored in the memory, so that remembering psalm texts became a paradigm for memorizing other data. Hugh also wrote a few notes – mainly for lectures – on selected psalms. *Notulae et Expositiones super Psalmos* uses a threefold approach to psalmody – historical, allegorical and moral, of which the first was most important – and demonstrates how the psalms are an important way of testing whether Scripture could be used as a resource for reasonable theology without undermining its spiritual worth. Hugh knew Hebrew, and because he frequently consulted with Jews about the Hebrew text of the Psalms he established more fruitful and collaborative relationships within a potentially disputatious climate.

Christian scholars throughout northern Europe stayed in the Abbey of St Victor, and one, probably originally from Wales, was *Andrew St. Victor* (c.1110 – 1175).

---

[7] The *Glossa Ordinaria*, which includes the Psalter, is to be found in Migne, P.L., CXIII and CXIV under the works of Strabo. The *Glossa Interlinearis* is in Migne, P.L., CLXII, 1187–1669, under the works of Anselm of Laon. On the rise of university schools and the use of glosses, see also G.H. Brown (1999); G. Dahan (2000); G.R. Evans (2000); K. Froehlich (2000); M.T. Gibson (1993); C. de Hamel (1984); U. Köpf (2000); M.P. Kuczynski (1995); H. Meyer (1986); and B. Smalley (1969, 1983).

He arrived in about 1130, and studied under Hugh St Victor, leaving for England in 1147; by about 1163 he became Prior of a Victorine Abbey in Wigmore, back in Wales. Hugh's influence upon Andrew is clear: as far as the psalms were concerned, Andrew was interested in integrating a *lectio divina* approach with scholastic exegesis, and like Hugh he acquired a first-hand knowledge of the Hebrew text. The grammatical and philological, and from this, the literal and historical, were his primary concern. Like his mentor, Andrew regularly consulted Jews, especially those in the *yeshivah founded by Rashi in northern France, about textual variants. Andrew was keen to avoid the Jewish charge that Christians had mistranslated the text, and so was at pains to start with the Hebrew original and the Greek translations, to search out as many textual variants as possible, and to amend the Latin when necessary. Sometimes he changed the Latin because of its archaisms, replacing the text with vernacular when necessary. No full-length commentary on the psalms remains; his significance is more the way his approach influenced his pupils who did write commentaries which have survived.

One such pupil was *Herbert of Bosham* (c.1120–94), from Sussex, who from about 1162 served in the household of (Archbishop) Thomas à Beckett, where amongst other roles he was his adviser on Scripture. After Thomas's death, Herbert came increasingly under the influence of the Victorine School, and especially of Andrew St Victor, both in Paris and at Wigmore. Herbert produced two important works on the psalms. The first is a 'Gloss' on the Psalter, now at Trinity College Cambridge, which is a compilation of both Christian and Jewish commentators; its typically Jewish emphasis is on David (and other composers of the 'faithful synagogue') being the authors of the psalms, rather than on Christ being the author, using David as a mouthpiece. Herbert's second work is a commentary on the psalms, probably begun some ten years before his death; it has been given recent attention because of a manuscript found in St Paul's Cathedral Library (MS2) in 1930. The influence of Andrew St Victor is clear – like Andrew, Herbert used Jerome's '*Psalterium Hebraicum*' based on the Hebrew, rather than the '*Psalterium Gallicanum*', which was Jerome's revision of the Latin liturgical text; like Andrew, Herbert's concern was grammatical and philological; and like Andrew, this concern led him to consult with Jewish writings (for example, he used Rashi's commentary, which in turn influenced his literal and historical reading of the psalms and his understanding of the future salvation of the Jews) and with Jewish scholars, both from Spain and in northern France. Although we know little of the biographical details of Herbert's life, his two works on the psalms offer an significant example of the way in which Christian exegetes of the psalms drew as much from the Jewish sources as the Christian tradition.

At about the same time, *Richard St Victor* (d. 1175) wrote a very different kind of commentary, applying the principles outlined in the Hugh's *Didascalicon* to the relationship between the teaching of Scripture and the arts within university education. Following Hugh rather than Andrew and Herbert, Richard understood that although grammatical and literal readings were necessary, they were a means to another end – that end being intelligent contemplation of God, and of Christ, the one hidden in the psalms, who gives us that vision of God. One of Richard's better-known commentaries was on the ecstatic visions of Ezekiel: his commentary on the psalms, *Mytice annotationes in Psalmos*, is another example of the same concerns.[8]

The tradition of glossed Bibles, and especially glossed Psalters, continued with *Gilbert of Poitiers* ('Gilbert de la Poiree' c.1080–1154), who spent time at Laon under Anselm, later teaching at Chartres and Paris before settling in Poitiers where he had been born and where he later became Bishop. He was essentially a philosopher, but his psalms commentary (written whilst at Laon, in about 1117) shows how much he enjoyed expanding and categorizing the received Gloss with various symbols and explanations of those symbols. His commentary is a model of what exegesis of biblical texts began to look like during this period, providing a type of map which charted its way through the vast terrain of interpretative methods. Believing the Psalter to be an anthology of diverse literary and theological types which had grown together rather haphazardly, Gilbert understood, like Cassiodorus before him, that the task of a commentator was to impose both theme and structure. Firstly, he stressed the importance of a proper *accessus to the glosses of the classical authors which outlined the subject matter before moving on to the method of procedure, the purpose of the work, and so on. This should lead on to a *divisio*, a selection of clear boundaries for the text, then an *expositio*, or exposition of the (Christian) meaning by reference to a traditional *Gloss*. Like Cassiodorus, Gilbert also enjoyed the resonance of the number twelve, and the twelve categories of Cassiodorus' Commentary formed the basis of his own *Gloss*. Finally, Gilbert showed how to use *dubia* and *questiones*, the exegetical questions which allowed some progression on to new issues of interpretation. The text of the psalms was presented in two columns, with each word to be glossed indicated by a larger initial.

Like many *scholastic commentators, Gilbert combined the literal with the spiritual, although in his case the overall emphasis is more Christocentric. Psalms 2, 8 and 19, for example, are each expounded as referring to the two natures of Christ; and Psalms 22 and 35 are each seen to contain hidden references to the passion and resurrection. Psalm 1, with its imagery of the 'tree' in verse 3 ('they are like trees planted by streams of water'), is read literally as a reference (in the singular) to the tree of life in the Garden of Eden, bearing the fruit of sin, but understood *spiritually* to mean the cross of Christ in the midst of the church on earth, bearing the fruit of redemption. Here Gilbert is building upon a received tradition, pointing to the authority of the exegetes of the past. His work marked an important stage along the road to a more formally accepted *Gloss*, and over fifty copies, dating between the twelfth and thirteenth centuries, are known to have been made in northern France and England.

---

[8] Hugh's works, including those on the psalms, are in Migne PL CLXXV-CLXXVII. Richard's *Mytice annotationes in Psalmos* is in Migne, P.L., CXCVI, 263–402, translated in E.R. Fairweather (ed.) (1956). For further discussions of the Victorines, see R. Berndt (2000); N. van Deusen (1999); G.R. Evans (2000); M.P. Kuczynski (1995); and B. Smalley (1983). On Herbert of Bosham, see E. de Visscher at www.uni-trier.de/uni/fb3/geschichte/cluse/eu/en_stip_devisscher.html and D.L. Goodwin (2006).

Another significant scholar at Laon was *Peter Lombard* (1100–60), who had spent time with the Victorines in Paris. His psalms commentary, his first work, represents another critical stage in the Gloss of the psalms. Lombard used three main sources. The first was a controversial commentary from the early twelfth century known as 'pseudo-Bede', which developed the idea of the Psalter as a single book (rather than five books brought together, as, for example, Jerome had argued) but, like an anthology, the works of several different poets. This commentary (which stops at Psalm 94) dealt with the historical, moral and mystical meanings of each individual psalm, drawing from the writings of the fathers and earlier commentators. The second source was Anselm's *Glossa Interlinearis*; and the third, the psalms commentary of Gilbert of Poitiers.

Lombard's *In Psalmos Davidicos Commentarii (Glossae Psalterii)* may have been a mix of different Glosses but it also had its own distinctive emphasis. In the first instance it advocates a historical reading, using David as the exemplar of faith (Lombard himself believed David to be the author of all the psalms), thus creating also a tropological bias; but it combined this with more typological and analogical concerns, whereby David was seen as the prophet of Christ and the church. Lombard divided the Psalter into six stages, each symbolizing the six ages of man, awaiting a seventh stage, the Coming of Christ. With its specific theology and rich reception history, Lombard's commentary on the entire Bible became the most important glossed commentary of all, known as *The Laon Gloss*; the version of the psalms was frequently cited, copied, studied (and further glossed) throughout the twelfth century.

Other less fixed 'running glosses' nevertheless continued in schools in northern France, Germany and England, showing the fluidity of the tradition at a time when the ethos was openness to new ideas – even when reading the psalms, with their more conservative setting in liturgy and prayer. For example, *Peter the Chanter* (d. 1197) of the school of Notre Dame, who never wrote a commentary on the psalms, nevertheless used different 'running glosses' from psalm commentaries in his other biblical works. And *Stephen Langton* (d. 1228), also at Notre Dame, later to become Archbishop of Canterbury, wrote his own 'running gloss' on the psalms which paid particular attention to Jewish traditions, differing from the school at Laon, and following more the early Victorine writers. And *Robert Grosseteste* (1168–1253), a Franciscan from Hereford who moved between Paris and Oxford, eventually becoming Bishop of Lincoln, wrote a commentary on the psalms, of which Psalms 79–100 are the best known; this used a Gloss which had so many references to Greek commentators (Basil, Gregory of Nyssa, Euseubius, Atahanasius, for example) that it seems he had a Greek *catena on the psalms as a source.[9]

---

[9] On the school at Laon, see *R. Berndt (2000)*; *G.R. Evans (2000)*; M.P. Kuczynski (1995); and B. Smalley (1983). On Gilbert, see T. Gross-Diaz (1996, 1999). For a translation of some of Lombard's commentary, see *A.J. Minnis and A.B. Scott (eds.) (1988a)*; visual examples of Lombard's Gloss are at scholar.library.csi.cuny.edu/~talarico/gloss004.htm and scholar.library.csi.cuny.edu/~talarico/gloss005.htm. On Robert Grosseteste, see M.R. James (1922) and www.grosseteste.com/bio.htm.

The Schools of Notre Dame, Chartres and St Victor were all Benedictine in foundation; Laon was Benedictine and Cistercian. A good example from a slightly different tradition is *Thomas Aquinas* (1225–74), a Dominican who moved between Naples, Paris and Cologne. His commentary on Psalms 1–54 was delivered as pastoral lectures to his Dominican *studium*, probably in Naples, near the end of his life (the commentary breaks off abruptly at Ps. 55:11).

In order to understand Aquinas's mode of exegesis, it is necessary to see how this is developed in his earlier works. *Summa Theologica* – a huge systematic summary of Christian theology – frequently refers to selected verses from psalms as a means of rooting theological enquiry in references to Scripture as well as tradition. From the *Summa*, and taking Psalm 8 as an example, v. 1 ('You have set your glory above the heavens') is used within the discourse about whether angels have bodies, and, in another place, whether Christ ascended above the heavens; v. 5 ('... you have made them [mortals] a little lower than God ...') is used within a discourse about whether the world will be renewed; v. 6 ff ('You have given them dominion over the works of your hands') is part of an objection as to whether God always loves more the better things, and elsewhere, whether man's happiness consists in wealth, and in another, whether it is lawful to be solicitous about temporal matters; and in another discourse, referring to vv. 7–8 (where the psalm speaks of 'sheep and oxen' being put under mortals' dominion) he asks whether there is any reasonable cause for ceremonial observances. In each of these examples, after the specific question is asked, a section beginning with the word *videtur* ('it seems that') offers arguments for what will later turn out to be an inadequate answer to that query. A brief section follows, beginning with the words *sed contra* ('but on the contrary'), which in turn introduces a different answer. A section labelled *responsio* ('response') finally presents arguments for what Aquinas considers the correct view. The question then closes with a refutation of the arguments presented in the *videtur* section.

If the *Summa* used psalms by way of *eisegesis, to inform part of a larger argument about doctrinal and practical issues engaging the Dominican community of the thirteenth century, Aquinas's psalms commentary (*Postilla super Psalmos*) adopts an *exegetical* method, developing the same rhetorical technique, but using it to a different end – to inform the life of prayer. A typical Aristotelian prologue is evident in most psalms, with its discussion of the four *causes* of the psalms: here Aquinas sees that their *matter* is Christ; their *form* is prayer (not prophecy); their *origin* is in the divinely inspired meaning of the words; and their *goal* is the Gospel. The psalms do not just illuminate the Gospels; they *are* the Gospel, and the evangelists interpret their meaning, rather than the reverse.

Psalm 8 again provides an interesting model. Here, Aquinas first offers his translation (of the Vulgate). The commentary follows, beginning with the *accessus*, which is a summary of the entire psalm:

> Above is the Psalm in which David prayed on account of his persecution; he sets the Psalm down for the purpose of giving thanks: and, first of all, he begins the Psalm with thanks for the benefits conferred upon the entire human race.

Aquinas then discusses in great detail the title of the psalm ('To the leader, according to The Gittith. A Psalm of David') which could be translated from the Latin as 'unto the end; for the winepresses; a psalm of David', and he concludes that this was offered by David at the new year vintage festival. By this stage it might seem that Aquinas is far from seeing the *matter* as Christ and the *goal* as the Gospel: but he quickly progresses to an idea of Israel as a vineyard as described in Isaiah 5:1–7; and from this, to the Church as the vineyard of God.

> He says therefore for the presses, that is, the circle of the church: and he calls the church a press, because, just as in a press the wine is separated from the lees, so in the church the good are separated from the evil by the work of the ministers: and if not in place, at least by their state of mind ... Likewise, the presses are the martyrdoms, in which the separation of the souls from the bodies is made, for when their bodies, which are tread upon in affliction and persecution for the name of Christ, at the same time remain in the earth, their souls arise to rest in the heavens.

One might think that these are innovative insights into the psalm: but although he never refers to it explicitly, Aquinas is using a glossed commentary on this psalm by Augustine and developed by Cassiodorus, compiled in the *Laon Gloss*, where exactly the same points about the vineyard and the church and the martyrs are made.

Thus far the commentary has only dealt with the psalm's title. The body of the psalm is then summarized in its two parts, and the exegesis which follows takes a similar pattern to the discussion of the psalm's title – a summary of the argument, raising questions, giving answers, raising further questions, illustrating the summary by reference to other biblical texts, then moving from the literal application to David, to Israel, to the church, with an emphasis on Christology particularly in the latter part. A gloss is often assumed, but it is rarely referred to explicitly within this psalm: instead it is incorporated into the argument as a way of taking the discussion forward.

Aquinas's use of the psalms in both the *Summa* and the commentary reveal the extent to which he believed the psalms belonged as much to the New Testament as to the Old, because he perceived in the Psalter a complete theology of the person and work of Christ. The commentary also reveals just how much he was influenced by Augustine's mode of exegesis; like Augustine, Aquinas understood the psalms to be prayers (first of David, then of Christ) rather than prophecies, to be used by the whole church throughout all time. The notable difference from Augustine is the expanded questioning approach: Aquinas raises questions in the commentary in the same way he does in the *Summa*. Nevertheless, the answers offered are emphatically Augustine's, even if they are received through the prism of Lombard's *Gloss*. And as Aquinas raises further questions to the answers given, giving further answers, it is as if yet another separate commentary arises; he was not unusual in this respect, and the extended comments became known as the *postillae*. In the case of Aquinas, these were sufficiently important for the incomplete commentary to be termed nevertheless *Postilla super Psalmos*.[10]

Three other psalms commentaries, all from the thirteenth century, deserve mention because of the diverse traditions they represent. The first is the work of a Franciscan from Paris. *Nicholas of Lyra* (1270–?1349) had good knowledge of Hebrew, and published a monumental commentary on most of the Bible with a consistently literal emphasis, which was in part a reaction to the more mystical and allegorical readings, and to the decline in philological and grammatical studies since the time of Andrew St Victor and the Victorine school. Like Aquinas, its extended comments (*postillae*) gave the commentary the title *Postillae Perpetuae in universam S. Scripturam*. Significantly, Nicholas used as his resources Jewish authorities (especially Rashi) as well as Christian commentators (especially Jerome) in addition to the *Glossa Ordinaire* of Anselm and the *Postillae* of Aquinas. This was the first biblical commentary eventually to be printed, and, along with Song of Songs, *Postilla super Psalterium et Cantica Canticorum* stands as a separate glossed commentary in its own right. Its significance is in the way it uses both Jewish and Christian authorities, even as late as the fourteenth century.

Nicholas of Lyra's commentary contrasts strikingly with another Parisian work, by *Philip the Chancellor* (1160–1236). As Chancellor of Notre Dame, Paris, Philip became responsible for much of the teaching at the burgeoning university school. He was a philosopher as well as a poet; his work *Summa de bono*, on the notion of goodness, anticipates his approach to psalmody just as Aquinas's *Summa* anticipated his commentary. Philip's *Distinctiones super psalterium* drew not so much on Jewish sources (as had Nicholas of Lyra) as from more rhetorical enquiry, more along the lines of Aquinas. It influenced another philosophical and tropological commentary written mainly in Paris but completed in Oxford by *Edmund of Abingdon* (1175–1240), later Archbishop of Canterbury, entitled *Moralitates super psalterium*. Like Nicholas and Philip, Edmund made abundant use of the *Glossa Ordinaire* and the *Postillae* of Aquinas; these together illustrate the growing significance of the use of received commentary traditions on the Psalter which often became as important as the text itself.[11]

With regard to both Jewish and Christian expositions of the psalms, one observation is paramount: that, at the very least, some dialogue between the two traditions is now more in evidence, sometimes of a disputatious nature, particularly in Jewish commentaries, at other times of a more collaborative enterprise, actually more evident in some Christian works. This mutual exchange of ideas invariably influenced other types of reception, of which the production of illustrated Psalters is one.

---

[10] See M. Rzeczkowski (1995); T.F. Ryan (2000); B. Smalley (1983); *T.G. Weinandy, D.A. Keating and J. Yocum (eds.) (2005)*. The text for Aquinas's use of Psalms in *Summa Theologica* is from www.globalserve.net/~bumblebee/ecclesia/summa/psalms.html and the quotations from Psalm 8 are from *Aquinas Translation Project coordinated by S. Loughlin Psalms Commentary*, at www4.desales.edu/~philtheo/loughlin/ATP/.

[11] On Nicholas, see T. Gross-Diaz (2000); *D. Klepper (2000)*; and A.J. Minnis and A.B. Scott (eds.) 1988b; on the other commentators, see also K. Froehlich (2000) and B. Smalley (1969, 1983).

Christian and Jewish Artists

In the twelfth and thirteenth centuries, at the same time as Jewish commentaries and Christian scholastic exegesis of psalmody were developing as distinctive literary genres, Christian communities in monasteries, cathedrals and abbeys, and Jewish communities in synagogues and *yeshivot* produced an increasing number of illustrated (and often glossed) Psalters and prayer books: these were not only for public use, but also for private devotion.

Christian Illumination

ILLUMINATED MANUSCRIPTS IN THE WEST

If glosses show a written concern with more than the text itself, it is not surprising that this extends to artistic illustrations of texts as well: Augustine's *Enarrationes in Psalmos*, as well as the glossed psalms of Gilbert of Poitiers, Peter Lombard and Herbert of Bosham, provide good examples of this, with scribes and artists augmenting the gloss sometimes by way of a more literal interpretation, and at others with a more specifically Christian emphasis.

An early example of a more historical and literal interpretation (following the tradition of the Utrecht Psalter, discussed in the previous chapter) is the *Harley Psalter*, made between 1010 and 1030 at Christ Church, Canterbury. It was probably originally inspired by Dunstan's reforms, and its colour representations are set in Carolingian *miniscules, using, overall, the Gallican text. The influence of the Utrecht Psalter, which was brought to the Cathedral Priory of Christ Church, Canterbury by about 1000, is clearly seen; even the very first illustrations for Psalms 1 and 2 make this clear, although in the Harley Psalter the drawings are placed before the text. Psalm 104 is an arresting example of the literal interpretation influenced by the Utrecht tradition: here the skies are stretched out like a tent (v. 2), with angels (and God himself?) depicted as 'riding on the winds' (v. 3); the sea is depicted with its ships and Leviathan 'sporting' in it (vv. 25–6), whilst young lions, in the bottom right, are seen seeking their prey and given their food from God (v. 21), and in the middle of the illustration, next to the cattle (v. 14), is a feast of those whose hearts are gladdened by wine and strengthened by bread (v. 15) Although incomplete, this work is an excellent example of a Frankish tradition in an English art form.[12]

---

[12] For more general works used throughout this survey, see the websites and resources listed in note 11 of the previous chapter. Also G.H. Brown (1999); W. Cahn (2004); *A. Fingernagel and C. Gastberger (2003)*; *R. Marks and N. Morgan (eds.) (1981)*; *N. Morgan (1992)*; *T.H. Ohlgren (ed.) (1972)*; *F. Wormald (1969)*. For the *Harley Psalter* (British Libary, Harley 603) see K. Van Der Horst, N.W. Noel and W.C.M. Wustefeld (1996), pp. 234–35; also N.W. Noel (1995).

A more ambitious example is the *Eadwine Psalter*, also made by the monks of Christ Church, Canterbury, between 1150 and 1160; it too shows the influence of the Utrecht Psalter, but from over a century later. This is a triplex text, in that it is set out in three columns, using the old Roman, with Anglo-Saxon interlinear glosses, the Gallican, with Latin interlinear and marginal glosses, and Hebrew translations of Jerome, with Anglo-Norman glosses. Not only does this then bear witness to the three cultural languages in twelfth-century England, but it also shows the gradual development of Anglo-Norman from Anglo-Saxon. This is the work of at least a dozen scribes and artists; each psalm has a prologue, commentary and concluding prayer. As well as line drawings for each psalm, most of which show again the influence of the Utrecht Psalter (or at least a tradition related to it), each major initial is fully illuminated whilst minor initials are set in silver and gold. The preface has a huge cycle of 'pictorial narratives', as well as a portrait of Eadwine, 'Prince of Scribes', along with a depiction of a comet, and plans of waterworks in the precinct of the cathedral priory (installed c.1160). In many ways this is a Psalter which reflects contemporary social concerns, as well as having obvious theological importance.

Another copy, known as the *Great Canterbury Psalter*, or the *Anglo-Catalan Psalter*, was made at about the same time as the Eadwine Psalter, but this was taken unfinished to Catalonia, where by the fourteenth century it was completed by Catalan artists, probably in Barcelona. Again, it has three parallel texts – Latin, Hebrew, and here, Catalan; its greatest difference from its predecessors is its lavish use of colour, its vivid characterization and its burnished gold backgrounds. A copy of it, recently undertaken by the Moleiro publishing house in Spain, is now in University College Chapel, Canterbury.[13]

The *Windmill Psalter* of 1270–90, the *Tickhill Psalter* of about 1310 and the *Luttrell Psalter* of about 1345 also follow the same tradition of literal, 'plain-sense' illustrations, although these three are very different from the Utrecht Psalter. The Windmill Psalter, yet again produced at Christ Church, Canterbury, is so called because in one of the many creation scenes it has the first known illustration of a windmill. The Tickhill Psalter is unfinished, but is set in a Gothic script with some 482 elaborate Gothic illustrations in the lower margins, many of which depict incidents in the lives of Saul, David and Solomon; in addition there are eight full-page illuminations, the first of which is a *Jesse Tree (a feature also found in the Windmill Psalter), the other seven being full-page initials depicting scenes from the life of David, thereby dividing the Psalter into eight liturgical parts, distributing

---

[13] For the Eadwine Psalter (Trinity College Cambridge MS R.17.1), see G.H. Brown (1999); K. Van Der Horst, N.W. Noel and W.C.M. Wustefeld (1996), pp. 236–9; M. Gibson, T.A. Heslop and R.W. Pfaff, (eds.) (1992); see also NASC Bible Translation Project on the Eadwine Psalter at www.geocities.com/Athens/Academy/4506/eadwine.html; For the Great Canterbury Psalter, now at the Bibliothèque Nationale, Paris (MS Lat 8846), see the website www.canterbury.ac.uk/News/newsRelease.asp?newsPk=515.

the Matins psalms for seven days of the week, with the eighth psalm being the Vespers psalm: the initials at Psalms 26, 38, 52, 68, 80, 97 and 109 make this clear. A second division is evident in another group of four large initials; the first initial is placed before the Preface which is taken from Peter Lombard's commentary on the psalms, and the others separate the Psalter into three groups of fifty, following the tradition in Irish Psalters. This Psalter was produced by John de Tickhill, who was Prior of Worksop in the early 1300s. The Luttrell Psalter, whose patron was Sir Geoffrey Luttrell of Irnham in Lincolnshire, is also divided into three parts, each separated by larger illuminated initials at the start of Psalms 1, 50 and 100. Its marginal illustrations – over two hundred out of some three hundred leaves – are exceptional. Biblical scenes mingle with depictions of saints and vignettes from daily life (it too depicts a windmill), thus creating an excellent resource for social comment of the day, being full of illustrations of Luttrell's family, of ordinary people at work, of people going to war, and of animals and plants.[14]

As well as more literal interpretations, many Christian Psalters, especially from France, have a more *typological and Christocentric emphasis. Several have full-page miniatures which illustrate scenes from the entire Old Testament history from Adam and Eve up to David, moving on to New Testament scenes from the annunciation and birth of Christ through to the miracles of his ministry, his death, resurrection and ascension, and finally, the last judgement. The thousand-year history between David and Christ is omitted completely; in order to bridge this gap, the *Jesse Tree was frequently depicted. In France, the best examples of more Christianized illustrations include the *Ingeborg Psalter*, now kept at Chantilly; this was made some time between 1193 and 1213 for Ingeborg of Denmark, the young rejected wife of Philip Augustus of France, who was obliged to withdraw for some ten years in convents in northern France. The first part of the Psalter contains a liturgical calendar (with signs of the zodiac as well as Christian symbols), followed by a Jesse Tree and twenty-seven full-page illustrations, from Genesis, Exodus and the Gospels. The Psalter begins with a full-page illuminated 'B' for Psalm 1, with Samuel anointing David; other large illustrated initials occur at Psalms 27, 39, 50, 51, 79, 81, 98, 102, 110 and 145, in each case, like Psalm 1, placing the psalm in the life-setting of king David. Throughout the Psalter David is clearly the exemplar of piety; Christian interpretation is found mainly in the illustrations at the beginning and the creeds, canticles and prayers at the end.

Another example from France is the *Psalter of Blanche of Castille*, mother of Louis IX, dated about 1235, with twenty-two miniatures, two on each page – first

---

[14] For the Windmill Psalter (Pierpont Morgan Library, M 102), see A. Bennett (1980); for the Tickhill Psalter (New York Public Library, Spencer Collection MS 26), see D.D. Egbert (1932); J. Fox (2000/2001); *J.J.G. Alexander, J.H. Marrow and L. Freeman Sandler (2006)*; see also www.nypl.org/research/chss/splenor/book26/book26.html. For the Luttrell Psalter (British Library MS 42130), see J. Backhouse (1989).

of an astronomer and then a scribe, then seven pictures from creation up to Jesse, and the rest from the New Testament finishing with the Last Judgement, again with the Jesse Tree separating them. (By contrast, the *Imola Psalter*, dated about 1200, sets the Jesse Tree within an enlarged 'Beatus' ('Blessed') initial which marks the first word of Psalm 1.) Finally, in the *St Louis Psalter*, belonging to King Louis IX (c.1254–70), and probably produced after his return from the Crusade in 1254, the text is preceded by some seventy-eight miniatures taken from the narratives between Genesis and Kings, with the subject choices reflecting political concerns of the thirteenth century: the figures of David at prayer set within the initials of the psalms to be read at Matins and Vespers suggest as much the piety of the King of France as of the King of Israel.

Christocentric examples from England include the *Tiberius Psalter*, made at Winchester in about 1050, again with an eightfold liturgical division. Its ink on parchment illustrations suffered fire damage in the eighteenth century, but one can still clearly see in the prefatory pictures a cycle of five scenes from the life of David, and eleven from the life of Christ. The scene 'The Harrowing of Hell' is particularly striking because it illustrates David as a prophet, heralding in Christ. The *Winchester Psalter* was possibly made at the Priory of St Swithun (or Hyde Abbey), between 1121 and 1161; the Jesse Tree here moves from Jesse, to a king who is probably David, to the Virgin Mary, then Christ, with the Holy Spirit at the very top. Two prophets holding scrolls stand on each side, again showing the prophetic reading of the psalms. The *Munich Psalter*, from around 1200, probably from Gloucester Abbey, has eighty full-page illustrations which use the typological motifs mainly from the Gospels. The *Westminster Psalter*, also around 1200, from Westminster Abbey, has several illustrations of the Virgin as well as a striking red and blue image of Christ in Glory.

An elaborate illumination depiction of the Jesse Tree is in the *Amesbury Psalter*, dating from about 1250, probably made for a nun at the Benedictine convent there; here the Jesse Tree is part of the historiated letter 'B' which begins Psalm 1 ('Beatus vir': 'Blessed is the man'), having a close relationship with a similar illumination in the Tickhall Psalter, some sixty years later. The *Gorleston Psalter*, commissioned in the mid-fourteenth century as one of three Psalters by a local wealthy patron from the village of the same name near Yarmouth, has its Jesse Tree just before Psalm 1. Another Psalter, probably by the same hand, is the *Macclesfield Psalter*, designed for a patron in East Anglia in the 1320s; this was only discovered in the early twenty-first century at Shirburn Castle, Oxfordshire, in the art collection of Lord Macclesfield, and in February 2005 was purchased and returned to East Anglia in the keeping of Fitzwilliam College, Cambridge. Its colourful, riotous illustrations display not only devotional imagery but also humorous, sometimes bizarre and often lewd depictions of people and animals. Rather like the Luttrell Psalter, it offers another excellent example of the confluence of religious and secular life in fourteenth-century England. It too has a Jesse Tree before Psalm 1, and one of the most arresting Christian illustrations is that of the Father and Son sitting on elaborate thrones as a preface to Psalm 110 ('The Lord said to my Lord, sit at my right hand').[15]

The *St Albans Psalter* offers another example of the relationship between Christ and David through a Jesse Tree. It was made around 1136–39, and like some of those in France, it is dedicated to a woman, in this case the anchoress Christina of Markyate (the dedication being found within the initial to Psalm 106). The book begins with a liturgical calendar, followed by forty full-page miniatures of the life of Christ, and a *quire of miscellaneous material; the letter B (from '*Beatus Vir*', or 'Blessed is the man …' from Ps. 1:1) indicates the start of the Psalter as a whole, and this is followed by the caption to Psalm 1 which reads 'The blessed David as psalmist uttered forth the Annunciation of the Holy Spirit'. Each psalm has historiated initials which usually illustrate in summary form the contents of the psalm: there are many similarities here with the Utrecht illustrations, although in the St Alban's Psalter everything is compressed into the framework of just one initial, followed by a short caption, in red ink, explaining the illustration.

But there are far more Christianized illustrations compared with Utrecht. For example, at the beginning of Psalm 42 ('As a deer longs for flowing streams, so my soul longs for you, O God …'), a hart (itself an allegory of the soul panting for the waters of baptism) is devouring a serpent (representing sin, which the soul devours). The Christological emphasis is further brought out by depicting Jesus as the main character in many of the initials, assuming he is therefore speaking through David, or at least is being spoken about by David. Tropological concerns are also apparent: for example, the iconography in the initial to Psalm 80, whose themes are remorse and penitence, shows two doves, representing sacrifices for sins of omission and commission; and before Psalm 112, which contrasts the fate of the righteous and wicked, the initial shows a monk giving clothing to the poor, as prescribed in the Rule of Benedict (Ps.112:9: 'They have distributed freely, they have given to the poor'). A better understanding of these illustrations would have required a good deal of knowledge of earlier glosses such as Augustine (for Psalm 42), Jerome (Psalm 80) and Benedict (Psalm 112).

The Psalter was commissioned by Geoffrey Gorham, Abbot of St Albans (1119–46) and several initials illustrate the relationship between the anchoress Christina and Geoffrey, as also does the accompanying 'Chanson of Alexis', an early example of Old French literature and language, which (along with a letter of Pope Gregory in French, three other pictures of Christ at Emmaus and a discourse on good and evil)

---

[15] Several of the above examples – for example of the Jesse Tree, David and Goliath and the Harrowing of Hell are to be found on the CD *Images of Salvation: The Story of the Bible through Medieval Art* (2004) also at the website www.york.ac.uk/inst/cms/candc. For the Tiberius Psalter (British Library MS Cotton Tiberius C VI) see G.H. Brown (1999); K.M. Openshaw (1992). For the Winchester Psalter (British Library MS Cotton Nero IV), see F. Wormald (1973); for the Amesbury Psalter (All Souls Library Oxford SM 0559), see *F. Wormald (1969)*; for the Gorleston Psalter (British Library MS Additional 49 622), see S.L. Cockerell (1907); for the Macclesfield Psalter, see S. Panayotova (2005) and www.fitzmuseum.cam.ac.uk/gallery/macclesfield/.

FIGURE 3.1 *St Albans Psalter*, Psalm 72 – close-up of the 'D' illustration showing the Christian focus.
Source: Dombibliothek Hildesheim, Hs St. God. 1 (Property of the Basilika of St. Godehard, Hildesheim) – see www.abdn.ac.uk/stalbanspsalter/english/copyright.shtml.

follows the miniatures and precedes the psalms. From this, another notable feature in this particular Psalter is the prominent place given to women. For example, the Christian miniatures illustrate women as active participants rather than passive supporters for the male characters: the miniature of Eve shows her giving and receiving the fruit, and in the Visitation two female attendants are present; in the Presentation, Joseph is absent; and the two Marys are both present at the Descent from the cross. Furthermore, in at least twenty of the illustrated initials, women are unusually visible: for example, the initial before the Psalm 72, a royal psalm, illustrates v. 10 ('… May the kings of Sheba and Seba bring gifts …') by depicting the adoration of the Magi, who are present before Mary and Christ alone. In the initial to Psalm 149, the call in v. 1 ('… Sing to the Lord a new song, his praise in the assembly of the faithful') is carried out by a group of women in a church. The initial to Psalm 106 features Christina praying for the monks of St Albans. This Psalter, now kept in St Godehard Church, Hildesheim, Germany, is another extraordinary example of both the social and theological concerns of the period.[16]

Illuminated Manuscripts in the East

Although our focus is now increasingly on reception history in the West, one example from the eastern churches deserves mention because its 300 miniatures and large illuminated initials reflect the influence of Byzantine illuminations discussed in the previous chapter and indicate that in some ways at least the reception of the psalms was still in process. The example is the *Kiev Psalter* of 1397, the only complete preserved Slavonic manuscript before the fifteenth century. The scribe, possibly Archdeacon Spyridon from Moscow, was working for his patron Bishop Mikhail of Smolensk, who was with Spyridon in Kiev between 1396 and 1397. The artist combined both Russian and Byzantine styles, being influenced by earlier iconographical works of art from Constantinople, as evidenced by the theological and polemical affinities with both the Khludov and Theodore Psalters. For example, the Khludov Psalter shows a bird resting on a column to illustrate Ps. 104:17 ('in them the birds build their nests; the stork has her home in the fir trees'); the Theodore Psalter has the same image for Ps. 102:7 ('I am like a lonely bird on a housetop'); the Kiev Psalter has three images between Psalms 102 and 104 – a stork in a tree (for Psalm 102), an eagle (Psalm 103), and several birds in a tree (Psalm 104). Another example is Psalm 22, where all three illustrations are found in both the Khludov and Kiev Psalters: the first depicts soldiers with heads of dogs, (following vv. 16 and 20 'for dogs are all around me …; … deliver my life from the power of the dog!'); the second is of Christ being nailed to a cross (v. 16: 'they pierced my hands and feet'); the third, of three men with a pile of clothing (v. 18: 'they divide my garments among them, and for my raiment they cast lots'). The soldiers are dressed not in Roman style, but that of eleventh-century Byzantium. A striking image is found in Psalm 78, illustrating vv. 69–70 ('He built his sanctuary like the high heavens … he chose David his servant …') and shows David at the foot of a mountain, pointing towards the summit where there is a shining icon of Mary and the infant Jesus: the image again has correspondences with both the Khuldov and Theodore Psalters. This one example shows that, before the fall

---

[16] The St. Albans Psalter is best viewed through the impressive online project of the University of Aberdeen, at www.abdn.ac.uk/stalbanspsalter. See also K. Haney (2002); and O. Pächt, C.R. Dodwell and F. Wormald (1960).

of Byzantium in 1453, illuminated Psalters continued to be as rich in Christian typology in the eastern churches as in the west.[17]

EXAMPLES IN STAINED GLASS

Although few examples have survived, stained glass windows, used increasingly in cathedrals and abbeys from the eleventh century onwards, reflect similar artistic forms to illustrations found in Psalters. One of the best examples is a window from the Gothic part of Canterbury Cathedral, dating from the latter part of the twelfth century, which depicts the siege of Canterbury by the Danes, and the picture is all but a replica of Psalm 60 in the *Harley Psalter*, which itself has been influenced by the same psalm in the *Utrecht Psalter*: given the presence of both Psalters at Canterbury, this is hardly surprising. Also at Canterbury, the medallion windows, dating from about 1200, have scenes from the Old and New Testaments which echo the typologies depicted in these two Psalters. Another example is at Sainte-Chapelle in Paris, built as a reliquary by Louis IX between 1242 and 1248, where, not surprisingly, the Genesis lancet window has a close relationship with the miniatures found in the thirteenth-century Psalter of St Louis: the most striking example is of Abraham's visitation by the three angels. Similarly at Laon Cathedral, the thirteenth-century windows reflect the influence of the twelfth-century Ingeborg Psalter, which was discussed earlier; both windows and Psalter date from the time of Philip Augustus (1180–1223), and the eastern lancet windows have several scenes which, stylistically, have clearly been influenced by the Psalter – those of the Flight to Egypt (here, developed in two medallions) and of Jesus' entry into Jerusalem, the Last Supper and Gethsemane are the most notable. And in Chartres cathedral, the most detailed references to two psalms is in the Symbolic Window of the Redemption, which has an extraordinary depiction of David with a pelican and its young, just beneath the medallion of Jesus being taken from the cross; the link between the two windows is the cry from Psalm 22 from the cross ('My God, my God, why hast thou forsaken me?'), ascribed to David. David holds a scroll on which is written, in Latin, 'I am like a pelican' (Ps. 102:6), recalling the belief that just as this bird killed its young and resurrected them on the third day with its blood, so too Jesus would be raised again on the third day.[18]

The *Jesse Tree, so popular in illustrated Psalters because of the David and Christ typology, is also found in early examples of stained glass. At the beginning of this chapter, in the context of Jewish-Christian disputations, we noted several examples of this feature in cathedrals of northern France. It also occurs in English architecture: the earliest instance is a fragment in a panel in the north aisle of the

---

[17] For the Kiev Psalter (Saltykov-Shchedrin Public Library, Leningrad MSF6 Kiev 1397) see T. Toranova, at www.currentmiddleages.org/artsci/docs/The_Kiev_Psalter.pdf; also G.P. Schiemenz (1996).
[18] For the Ingeborg Psalter, see F. Deuchler (1967); M.-M. Pinot de Villechenon and P. Chapu (1986–1987); see also www.photo.rmn.fr for illustrations. For the Saint Louis Psalter, see Y. Christe (2004).

nave in York Minster, dating from about 1170. Many abbeys and ordinary churches between the thirteenth and sixteenth centuries used the Jesse Tree. An unusual fourteenth-century example is in the north wall of the chancel at Dorchester Abbey, near Oxford, because it uses both stained glass and sculptures: the sleeping figure of Jesse is carved on the window ledge, and figurine ancestors of Christ, from David through to the (badly preserved) figure of Mary, rise in sculptured tendrils out of Jesse's side, whilst some sixteen stained glass inserts add other Old and New Testament figures to complete the typology. Another well-preserved example is in the east window of Margaretting Church, Essex, from about 1460, probably by John Prudde of Westminster; the reclining Jesse is at the base, and a vine grows from his side which forms into oval shapes, each with figures of kings; at each side is a prophetic figure, holding a scroll. The vine grows upwards till it ends with the Virgin Mary, then above her the figure of Christ, surrounded by the terminals of the vine. In each of these cases, Christ is seen as the culmination of the line of David, an interpretation which both influenced and was influenced by the reading of the Psalms of David as Psalms of Christ, as illustrated by the number of Psalters which used the Jesse trees as a key illustration, as we noted earlier.[19]

EXAMPLES IN PRAYER BOOKS

By the fourteenth century, hand-copied *Prymers became popular and their name, 'first prayers', suggests they were often used not just for personal devotion but also for teaching the laity to read. Over a third of the Psalter was used in these books – not only the selected psalms set by the Rule of Benedict for each hour throughout the day (especially Psalms 95, 8, 19, 24; 93, 100, 63, 67, 148, 149 150; 117, 118; 120, 121, 122; 123, 124, 125; 126, 127, 128; 13, 43, 129, 131; 119), but also seven psalms for Advent (i.e. the penitential psalms, Psalms 6, 32, 38, 51, 102, 130 and 143), psalms of the passion for Lent (usually Psalms 22 and 31:1–5), and psalms for Easter (i.e. the Psalms of Ascent, Psalms 120–34). With the emergence of the *Gütenberg Press by the fifteenth century, such books proliferated throughout Europe.

Whilst it became easier to print the written word, the printing of the illustrated word took longer to realize, and so the tradition of hand-painted prayer books (often with the illustrations added to printed versions) continued for some time. The larger copies for use in public worship, usually termed *Breviaries, and the smaller copies for private devotion, known as *Books of Hours, were often richly illustrated. Books of Hours were particularly popular amongst the laity between the fifteenth and sixteenth centuries, especially in France. The tradition of illustrated prayer books and illustrated portions of the Bible to aid the personal devotions of

---

[19] For a detailed illustration of Canterbury windows and Harley/Utrecht Psalters, see K. Van Der Horst, N.W. Noel and W.C.M. Wustefeld (1996), p. 143. Resources which have informed this discussion more generally include M.H. Caviness (1992); T. Dowley (ed.) (1990); J. Drury (1999); A. Grabar (1968); B.S. Levy (1992); A. Lockhart (ed.) (1994); R. Marks (1993); H. Read (ed.) (1960).

the laity also extended into the Netherlands and Rhineland, and into England, Italy and Spain.

The central text of the Books of Hours, like the Prymer, was the Little Office of the Blessed Virgin (or the 'Hours of the Virgin'), modelled on the Divine Office and the Canonical Hours of Prayer, but in this case it was illustrated. By applying images alongside the set psalms for the eight Hours of the Virgin, the illuminations gave these particular psalms (the list being much the same as that for the Prymer, above) as much a focus on Mary as on Christ alone. Typical illustrations would include the Annunciation (for Matins), the Visitation (Lauds), the Nativity (Prime), the Annunciation to the Shepherds (Terce), the Adoration of the Magi (Sext), the Presentation in the Temple (None), the Flight into Egypt (Vespers) and the Coronation of the Virgin (Compline). In addition to the Office of the Blessed Virgin, the Abbreviated Hours of the Cross and the Hours of the Holy Ghost as well as the Office of the Dead were often also included, each with illustrations and set psalms. For example, the penitential psalms (used before Advent and also in the Office of the Dead) were often illustrated with a miniature of Christ in Judgement, or occasional images of David playing the lyre, or of David and Goliath, or David kneeling in prayer; other images (evoking the idea of David the ideal penitent) would be of David watching Bathsheba, or David sending Uriah into battle. The *Belles Heures* or *Très Riches Heures* of Jean de Berry offer striking examples of this type of 'Selected Psalter' in its abbreviated liturgical form, along with the fourteen canticles of the church, richly illustrated in both a contemplative and instructional way. Other smaller Books of Hours, less lavishly illustrated, were 'Girdle Books', attached to girdles or belts of the pious layperson: one version is John Croke's *Psalms in English Verse* (c.1540).[20]

Jewish Illumination

Manuscripts

Our first example is of an entire Bible, which has 513 folios and no fewer than 334 miniatures, many of which are in the Psalms. *The Alba Bible* dates from 1422, and compares with the Mozarabic Bible, discussed in the previous chapter, which was the work of Christians living under Islamic rule in Spain in the tenth century, whereas the Alba Bible is the work of a Jew, living under Christian rule in the fifteenth century. Its origins are in Castile. It is a fine example of the ways in which Jewish culture had profoundly influenced Spanish life, especially in terms of the transitions between Arabic and Hebrew and Latin and the vernacular. A prominent churchman, Don Luis de Guzman, requested a Jewish rabbi, Moses Arragel de

---

[20] John Croke's Girdle Book on the Psalms is in the British Library, Stowe Ms 956. For aesthetic and liturgical resources which have informed the rest of this section, see G.H. Brown (1999); C. Jones, G. Wainwright and E. Yarnold (eds.) (1978); J.A. Lamb (1962); *R.L.P. Milburn (1969)*; E. Soltesz (1967); R. Taft (1986); and R. Webber (2000).

Guadalajara, to translate the Hebrew Bible into Castilian, as well as creating a commentary (or gloss), and, along with Christian artists, to advise on numerous illustrations. Rabbi Moses, although reluctant, was pressurized into the task by church authorities; as far as the psalms were concerned, neither translation nor commentary actually gave many concessions to Christian doctrine, for they included extracts from Rashi, the Talmud, the Midrashim and the Zohar, and Arragel further advised the Christian draughtsmen to create illustrations specifically depicting Jewish scriptural interpretations and religious objects. Nothing is known of Arragel after he completed the work by 1430; the text in fact caused much disputation in Toledo, and any hopes of Judeo-Christian reconciliation were anyway abandoned by 1492. Apparently the Bible was taken to a Franciscan monastery in Toledo, and by the seventeenth century it appeared in the library of Liria Palace, Madrid, where it is today.

The Alba Bible contains one distinct example of an illustrated Psalter which has Jewish influence. By the thirteenth century, Jews all over Europe – especially in Spain, Portugal, France, Germany and Italy – began to develop more and more the art of *decorated manuscripts*. With a few notable exceptions (for example, the *Karaites in ninth-century Tiberias), the precision and beauty of the Hebrew text had previously been expressed mainly through calligraphy; now it was increasingly extended to ornamentation. A common practice was to work floral motifs in gold from within words out to the margins, usually adding one other single colour and dark outlines. Earlier Christian ornamentation was undoubtedly an influence here. Carpet pages appeared between different biblical books, and symmetrical palmettes and geometrical designs were increasingly common: these suggest more Islamic influence. But actual 'narrative art' and figurative illustration, so much a part of Christian biblical illustration since the ninth century, was still rare. This type of Jewish art took time to develop: but gradually it was recognized that the sacred text deserved the same creative ornamentation and symbolic representation that had been lavished on the Jerusalem Temple, with its architecture, its gold, its silver, its jewels and precious stones. In fact, one of the earliest examples of explicit figurative art by Jews, found in the fourteenth-century Farhi Bible from Provence, is of Temple symbolism (the three courts were seen to correspond with the Law, Prophets and Writings in the canon) and of the holy vessels of the Temple.

Two contrasting examples of Jewish figurative art within the psalms must suffice. *The Parma Psalter* (c.1280) is from northern Italy, and *The Kennicott Bible* (c.1476) from north-western Spain. *The Parma Psalter* is the oldest Hebrew illustrated manuscript to have survived intact; its further value is in its inclusion of selected extracts from Abraham ibn Ezra's commentary on the psalms. The first word of each psalm is illuminated (there being no capital letters in the Hebrew script, historicized initials are less common) and pictures abound in the margins, many of musical instruments, often bringing out the instructional and literal meaning of the text. The artistic divisions are not according to eight or three, as was more common in Christian Psalters; instead, the geometric and linear decorations are found at the beginning of each of the five books of the Psalter, the first psalm of each of the five books having a much larger decorated word. The decorations are

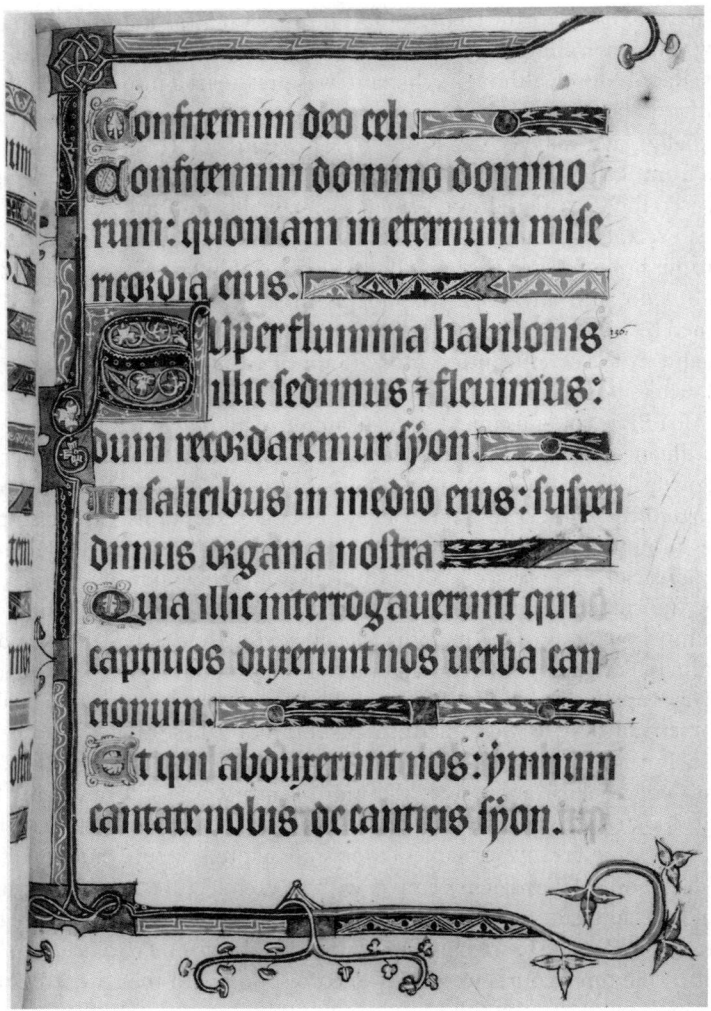

FIGURE 3.2   *Luttrell Psalter*: a Christian illustration of Psalm 137.
Source: British Library. For more detailed and fanciful illustrations, see the 'turning pages' of this Psalter at http: www.bl.uk/onlinegallery/ttp/ttpbooks.html

amongst the earliest examples of figures in Hebrew manuscripts – many have animal heads, but some are depicted as judges, rabbis and kings: their purpose is to summarize the didactic import of the rest of the psalm. Symbolism and allegory are rarely used: David, as the model of piety in all aspects of his life, is a key theme throughout. Considering the place of Jews in Italian society at this time (the *Fourth Lateran Council in 1215 marked an increase in Jewish persecution, the wearing of identity badges, forcing conversions and the burning of Jewish books),

FIGURE 3.3 *Parma Psalter*: a Jewish illustration of Psalm 137.
Source: Biblioteca Palatina, Parma, Italy – or facsimile available from Finns-books.com.

the production of such a lavish manuscript symbolizes an act of defiance by an (unknown) wealthy patron against Christian authorities. A good illustration of this is from Psalm 137: two figures, weeping, drawing water, with willow-like leaves framing the text, upon which are hanging lyres (or lutes?), show the ways in which the Jews in thirteenth-century Italy were able to identify by word and image with their exiled forebears in Babylon.

The Kennicott Bible, acquired by Benjamin Kennicott in 1771 and transferred to the Bodleian Library by 1872, is also set at a time of Jewish and Christian conflicts, but some two centuries later, in fifteenth-century Spain. Its Spanish setting could not be more different from that of the Alba Bible. The text, together with David

Kimchi's grammatical treatise to the Psalter, was copied by a scribe, Moses ibn Zabara, in 1476, commissioned for Isaac, the son of Don Solomon di Braga of Coruña. The artist is Joseph ibn Hayyim; the zoomorphic and anthropomorphic letters, the representations of flora, fauna, geometric designs, animals, birds, dragons, drolleries, and the vividly drawn pictures (for example, of King David on his throne) make it clear that this is an illustrated text to educate young Isaac. The fact that the symbols were taken from secular playing cards and Islamic carpet pages gives further weight to this; the project has some shared features with the didactic intentions of the artist of the Parma Psalter. But although elaborate decoration and figurative art abound, the illustrations rarely suggest an explicit illumination of the text itself: unlike the Parma Psalter, they are more constrained to ornamentation.

Hence, although the artist Joseph ibn Hayyim provided several full-page strikingly detailed illuminations (some fifteen pages at the beginning and twelve at the end, amidst Kimchi's treatise), he kept these distanced from the text. What ornamentation there is occurs to a higher degree in the Torah and the psalms. The Psalter, in its canonical place between Job and Proverbs, two books without any decoration, stands out in that it is prefaced by a vivid carpet page, and concluded with a quarter page of vivid pink and blue geometric decoration. Almost every page of the psalms has marginal decorations – of dragons, monkeys, fishes, flowers, drolleries; and every psalm has its own decoration (often zoomorphic and anthropomorphic, and hence usually unrelated to the sense of the text which follows) through the first word. Linear geometric patterns, in blues, reds and gold, divide up each book of the Psalter. Only Psalm 119, the psalm praising the importance of the Torah, set out in two columns of four-line stanzas, is alone in its lack of decorative art. In spite of the restraints inherent in the tradition, the heightened coloured decoration in this particular part of the Hebrew Bible shows just how distinctive the Psalter was for the Jewish scribe and artist – a characteristic undoubtedly influenced by his Christian contemporaries.[21]

SYNAGOGUE ARCHITECTURE

Through the decoration of stained glass windows, cathedral architecture embodied psalmody: the psalms were also used, albeit less figuratively, in synagogue architecture. Two examples must suffice, both from Spain. At Cordoba, a synagogue which was enlarged and reconstructed in the early thirteenth century, during a period of

[21] General resources on Jewish art and Hebrew illuminated manuscripts include K.P. Bland (2000); J. Gutmann (1971 and 1978); J. Leveen (1944); T. Metzger (1969; 1970–1); B. Narkiss (1982); and G. Sed-Rajna (1990, 1992). For the Alba Bible, see C.O. Nordström (1967). For the Parma Psalter (now in Biblioteca Palatina, Parma, MS Parm 1870 [De Rossi 510]), see M. Beit-Arié (1996) and T. Metzger (1977); illustrations from this manuscript may be found, for example, on www.facsimile-editions.com/en/pp/. For the Kennicott Bible (MS Kennicott I, Bodleian Library, with a bound introduction to the facsimile) see S. Edmunds (1983); also Bodleian Picture Book 11 (1957).

Christian tolerance after the re-conquest by Ferdinand III, still reveals the interesting combination of *Mudéjar stuccowork and psalm quotations all over the walls of the prayer hall. The square Hebrew characters were originally in beige on a blue background. For example, Pss. 138:2 and 27:4 are written together from the right side upwards to the left side of the arch surrounding the east-facing sanctuary: 'I bow down toward your holy temple and give thanks to **your name** for your steadfast love and faithfulness ... **One thing I asked** of the Lord, that will I seek after: **to live** in the house of the Lord all the days of my life, to behold the beauty of the Lord, and to inquire in his temple.' (Words in bold are those which still clearly remain in Hebrew.) Around the north wall are quotations from Pss. 95:6, 132:7 and 99:5 (all on the similar theme of worshipping God in his holy place) and then from Pss. 100:1–2, 86:9 and 95:1 (on the theme of God being worshipped by all peoples) with Pss. 29:2, 96:9, 66:4 and 22:27,28 underneath them (a selection of psalms which combines both themes above). On the south wall, ending with a rosette, Ps. 84:1–3 dominates ('How lovely is your dwelling place, O Lord of hosts ...'), and, in a similar vein, Pss. 13:5–6 and 26:8 are found after it. Above what were once windows two poignant verses are found: Ps. 122:6–9 ('Pray for the peace of Jerusalem ...') and Ps. 102:12–13 ('... You will rise up and have compassion on Zion ...'). Few of these psalms are those prescribed by the Mishnah for daily or festival use; they have been especially selected here to serve a more particular theological purpose, which is to illustrate how the synagogue symbolizes the Temple at Jerusalem. These quotations contrast with the illustrations of psalmody in churches, and reveal just how differently Jews and Christians saw the relationship between the physical and the spiritual in their use of sacred space; in the Jewish tradition, the more literal interpretation is found, and in Christian tradition, the approach is often more figurative and allusive.

The architecture of the synagogue El Tránsito in Toledo, built between 1336 and 1357 on the orders of Samuel Halevi Abulafia, diplomat and treasurer in the court of Peter I of Castile, tells a similar story. This synagogue was clearly even more luxurious than the one at Cordoba: the hipped roof is one of the best examples of Hispanic-Muslim carpentry, with the blues, greens, reds, oranges, whites and blacks and several Arabic inscriptions still visible. The walls, with pointed arches in their upper parts, reveal *Mudéjar influence in the stuccowork, with fruits, flowers and geometric designs. The Hebrew inscriptions are set amongst these, mainly on the east and west walls: they are in part historical, praising Samuel Halevi and King Peter, and partly biblical. As well as the psalms, passages from Chronicles, Kings and Exodus are also represented. On the east wall, Psalms 84 and 100 are found in complete form, with their corresponding themes of the joy of living in God's 'temple' and the Lord as Shepherd of his people. In addition, Pss. 17:1, 28:2, 68:35, 61:2, 86:6, 102:2, 18:3, 88:2, 5:7, 69:13, 52:8, 88:13, 73:17, 148:13, 99:1, and the whole of Psalm 111, and some of Psalms 133 and 121, all intertwined with floral and geometric designs, run along both the east and the west walls. The women's gallery has also references to the psalms, creating a high decorative frieze: Pss. 65:5–13, 30:1, 45:6–9, 138:1, 122:3–5 and parts of Psalms 67, 130 and 132 are most clearly evident, with the twin themes of God's provision from the natural

FIGURE 3.4   Jewish psalms and Arabic art in El Tránsito synagogue, Toledo, showing Arabic calligraphy and art alongside Jewish writing.
Source: Museo Sefardi, Toledo.

world and the joy of worshipping in his holy temple. Overall, this choice of psalms – again, with hardly any correspondences with those most frequently prescribed in the Mishnah – reveals two dominant themes: firstly, the synagogue as a place of prayer ('Hear a just cause, O Lord' [Ps. 17:1]; 'Hear the voice of my supplication' [Ps. 28:2]; 'From the end of the earth I call to you' [Ps. 62:1] 'Give ear O Lord to my prayer' [Ps. 86:6]; 'Incline your ear to me' [Ps. 102:2]; 'Let my prayer come before you …' [Ps. 88:2]) and, secondly, the synagogue as the holy place where God is ever-present for his people (Pss. 18:3; 52:8; 73:17; 133:1; 121:1). This again shows how the synagogue is a microcosm of the Temple – not as a place of sacrifice, but of prayer and praise, with the particular choice of psalms both serving and creating such a theology.[22]

PRAYER BOOKS

Between the thirteenth and fourteenth centuries, the decorations in Jewish prayer books suggest further correspondences with the decorative art in Christian Breviaries and Books of Hours. Two examples of public liturgical books must suffice, both from *Ashkenazi Jews in Germany, and similarly, two from more personal prayer books, in this case from *Sephardi Jews in Spain.

[22]   On the Cordoba and Toledo synagogue decorations, see J.P. del Rosal (1988).

From the thirteenth century, especially in Germany, the tradition developed of decorating the *Mahzor, with its stories, prayers, hymns, psalms and *piyyutim, for the festivals of the Jewish year. The psalms were fairly prominent in these texts, in that they were used in all three festivals of Passover, Weeks and Booths (for example, Psalms 112–18 creating the *Hallel which was a central part of Passover), and, as we have already seen, many Jewish prayers and *piyyutim allude to phrases from the psalms. In addition to ornamentation and word-painting in the margins and at the base of the manuscripts, the first illustrations of narrative art are evident, too: given that these public prayer books focus on the epics and stories found in Genesis and Exodus, this is obviously in the more literal and historical tradition. For example, the Worms Mahzor, finished in Rhineland in 1272, has full-page illustrations, of which one, the prayer at the beginning of the Day of Atonement ('He who opens the gates of mercy for us …'), provides another instance of Temple imagery: it is of a gateway to heaven, and above the archway is a heavenly city, whilst below the city, in the arch, are prayers, some of which are allusions to the psalms. Another, later, example is the Leipzig Mahzor, from Southern Germany, dating about 1320. Its most notable illustrations are of Abraham in Genesis and Moses in Exodus; here the figures are human but the faces are heads of birds, echoing in their human art form the decoration of the psalms in the late-thirteenth-century Parma Psalter of Italy. But because the faces in this prayer book are more deliberately deformed, they imitate more precisely another work aptly called the Birdshead Haggadah, demonstrating that there was still a reluctance to flout the ban on graven images.

With the gradual destruction of Jewish communities in Spain from 1391 onwards, and their final expulsion in 1492, centres of manuscript production gradually disappeared (although the workshops in Lisbon were able to preserve undamaged some twenty illustrated manuscripts). Before this, in thirteenth- and fourteenth-century Spain, the production of richly illustrated copies of Haggadot was quite prolific, mainly in areas which were under Christian rule – in Catalonia, Castile, Aragon and parts of Andalusia. The *Haggadah is really part of the Mahzor, in that this was the book which provided prayers and readings for the Passover. Its production as a separate familial prayer book, in part influenced by the prescriptions for the *Seder in the Mishnah, originated from ninth-century Babylon. Not surprisingly, the Haggadah comprises stories from Genesis and Exodus, interspersed with hymns, poems, prayers and psalms; of the latter, some are for the restoration of Jerusalem (e.g. Psalm 79, a lament on the destruction of the Temple) but the central place is given to the *Hallel, when Psalms 112–18 were sung or read before the Passover meal itself began.

Since the Passover is essentially a festive family ceremony, looking forward with hope on the basis of what God had done in the past, and given the instructional value of the Haggadah for children, the text was an ideal model for illustration. Decorations were made either in the margin and around the biblical text, or by images (miniatures) on separate pages. Two contrasting examples are the Golden Haggadah, from Barcelona, c.1320, and the Prato Haggadah, also from Spain, c.1300 (nothing is known further of the latter's provenance; it eventually ended up in Rome, and in the middle of the twentieth century was taken to New York). The *Golden Haggadah* contains several separate High Gothic miniatures of stylized figures in blues, reds and greens against a rich golden background, mainly illustrating stories from both Genesis and Exodus, whilst the *Prato Haggadah* has several Italian-Ashkenazic additions, also Gothic in style, with gold and silver leaf and sumptuous blues and reds, and is more an ornamentation than illustration of the text. A fascinating example is the folio which illustrates the opening 'Hallelujah' to Psalms 113–14, which were sung before the formal meal began ('Hallelujah! … When Israel went out of Egypt, the house of Jacob from a people of strange

FIGURE 3.5   Illustrations of Psalms 113 and 114 in the Prato Haggadah, folio 33r.
Source: Courtesy of The Library of The Jewish Theological Seminary (www.jtsa.edu/library/conservation/prato/gallery.shtml).

language, Judah became God's sanctuary, Israel his dominion' [Pss. 113:1 and 114:1]). The decoration has tendrils supporting birds and animals emerging from the two letters 'l' in Hebrew of the word 'Hallelujah'.

Just as there were clear differences in the use of the psalms in church and synagogue architecture, so too with the decoration of liturgical and prayer books there are clear differences between Christian and Jewish traditions. First, a far smaller number of psalms are included in Jewish works, because here the central text is the Torah — especially the narratives of Genesis and Exodus; this compares with the large number of psalms (often used as if they were part of the Christian Gospel) depicted in the daily offices in the Books of Hours. Secondly, in the Mahzor and Haggadah the psalms are used in a literal and historical way, to highlight the escape from Egypt; this is very different from the more predominant typological and Christological illustrations of psalms in liturgical and devotional works.[23]

Christian and Jewish Didactic Works

Christian Writers

The predominant pastoral use of psalmody within western Christian tradition throughout this period has its roots in Augustine's homiletic commentaries, in Cassiodorus' *Expositio Psalmorum*, and in Gregory the Great's and Bede's homilies on the psalms: the focus is on the twin themes of the 'moral life of David' and the 'moral life of Christ', and is expressed in various running glosses. But a notable development in the period under discussion, in terms of the edifying use of psalmody, is the use of the *lament psalms* in two different ways — for the private confession of guilt and for more public protests of innocence.

Confessions of guilt pertain mainly to the so-called *penitential psalms*. The seven psalms used for confessing sins (i.e. Psalms 6, 32, 38, 51, 102, 130, 143) were identified as early as Augustine and used by Cassiodorus and later by Alcuin, with the main theological emphasis being God's anger against human sin and the need to claim forgiveness. Their use by the ninth century in the Office of the Dead and before the Advent offices gave them a prominent place in private devotion, and their recognition increased when they were included together in Prymers and Books of Hours, depicting the various acts of penitence in David's life. Translations and

---

[23] For the *Worms Mahzor* (Jewish National and University Library, Jerusalem, MS 4°781/1), see M. Beit-Arié (ed.) (1985); B. Narkiss (1985). For the *Leipzig Mahzor* (Leipzig Universitätsbibliothek MS 1102 / I-II), as it relates to the illustration of birds' heads, see I. Fishof (ed.) (1994), pp. 58–9. The *Golden Haggadah* (British Library Add. 27210), is now available online under www.bl.uk/onlinegallery/ttp/ttpbooks.html; see also B. Narkiss (1996); *Sed-Rajna (1992)*; and Y.H. Yerushalmi (1974). The *Prato Haggadah* (Library of the Jewish Theological Seminary of New York, Mic. 9478) is at www.jtsa.edu/library/conservation/prato/.

commentaries on these seven psalms are in evidence from the eleventh century onwards: a typical example, now in the Cambridge University Library, is *The Seven Psalms*, a Middle English translation of a French commentary, by Dame Eleanor Hull, who was attached to a house of Benedictine nuns dependent upon the Abbey of St. Albans. The French commentary must have been composed after 1189, the year of the Fall of Jerusalem, because it refers to it; the translation, which has also some decoration of initial letters, was made during the 1420s after Eleanor Hull was widowed. The moral emphasis in this commentary is paramount.

It is unclear why these particular seven psalms were first chosen: four at least (Psalms 6, 38, 102, 143) have little explicit repentance and penitence, whilst other psalms would fare much better (for example, Psalm 25 'For your name's sake, O Lord, pardon my guilt, for it is great' in v. 11). But the consistency of the selection is due in part to the influence of the authority of Augustine and Cassiodorus and Alcuin, through the glosses. By the fourteenth century another theological emphasis is ascribed to them, focusing less on averting God's anger and more on confessing particular individual sins, in imitation of David (though not, of course, of Christ). By linking single words of these psalms with the words which encapsulated the seven deadly sins, a tradition arose whereby Psalm 6 was the psalm to be used against Anger; Psalm 32, against Pride; Psalm 38, against Gluttony; Psalm 51, against Luxury; Psalm 102, against Greed; Psalm 130, against Envy; and Psalm 143, against Sloth. Gradually this act of prayer was attached to other acts of piety – the need to 'buy off' individual sins through the sacrament of penance and indulgences. (This emphasis on using the penitential psalms to focus on particular sins could not be more different from that of Luther nearly two centuries later: his first publication in 1517, *The Seven Penitential Psalms*, was about the sin of all human nature, which God in Christ had 'bought off' – without the need for paying indulgences for particular sins.)

If penitential psalms were read as prayers imitating the life experiences of David which led to individual reparation, other psalms which protested the innocence of the suppliant were read as prophecies uttered by David demanding religious reform in the fifteenth-century Catholic church. The best examples are found in the *Lollards' glosses within the various copies of the Psalter of Richard Rolle, a work which had a wide circulation between about 1410 and 1450. The Lollards, as disciples of Wycliffe, were equally as persecuted as he had been for their anti-ecclesiastical stance (exemplified by their identification of Archbishop Arundel as the Antichrist for his enforcement of the Constitutions of 1408 against owning vernacular scriptures and preaching without a licence). Sometimes traditionally ascribed penitential psalms were used for this purpose: their moral tone was now used as means of praying for vindication, asking God to pour down judgement against the leaders of the church establishment. Psalm 51, for example, traditionally seen to have been a response by David to the prophet Nathan's indictment of his adulterous affair with Bathsheba narrated in 1 Samuel 12, was taken up by the Lollards as if they were the prophetic speakers communicating their indictment to those in ecclesial power: like David, the church leaders should acknowledge their iniquity and sin (Ps. 51:3 'For I know my transgressions, and my sin is ever before me') and if they did not, God would judge them.

But the Lollards also created glosses on other psalms, such as 35 ('Contend O Lord with those who contend against me; fight against those who fight against me!' [v. 1]), linking it with a cross-reference to 1 Peter 3: 13 ('Now who will harm you if you are eager to do what is good?'). And Psalm 22 was seen as a description of their own distress ('For dogs are all around me; a company of evildoers encircles me ...' [v. 16]), again implying that God would vindicate them in the sight of their enemies. And Psalm 109, with its sequence of horrific curses on the psalmist's enemies, was again applied to the church leaders, whilst the end of the psalm ('For he stands at the right hand of the needy, to save them from those who would condemn them to death' – v. 31) was seen as a prophecy applying now to the Lollard cause: God was on their side as they were both suffering and needy. This might be called using the psalms for 'moral prophesying'. The clearest examples of this use of psalms are in a Lollard Treatise, *Lanterne of Lizt*, written shortly after 1408, which quotes repeatedly from the psalms (first in Latin, then in the vernacular), to show that the present persecutions were first prophesied by David himself. For example, Ps. 10:1 [Ps. 9:21 in the Latin]) 'Why Lord, do you stand far off? Why do you hide yourself in times of trouble?' is seen as David prophesying in prescience of the Lollards' experience of the evils of the early fifteenth century.

The difficulty is that by using the figure of David as a model for moral authority, the psalms can work for opposite causes. Just as the Lollards used particular psalms to appeal to their cause, those who opposed them used other psalms to condemn it. For example, John Lydgate (?1370–1449), a Benedictine monk from Bury St Edmunds, who, during his education which was probably at Gloucester College, Oxford, came under the royal patronage of the Lancastrian Prince of Wales, later Henry V, wrote a poem for the king just after the Lollard revolt of 1413, entitled *Defence of the Holy Church*. In it Henry V is identified with David – providing he takes actions to suppress once and for all Lollard heresy throughout his realm. Lydgate rewrites Psalm 137 ('By the rivers of Babylon – there we sat down and there we wept, when we remembered Zion ...', as in v. 1) to show that the church had created its own Babylonian captivity, imprisoned by its inability to drive out heresy, and it must, under the new David, break free; even the dreadful language of cursing at the end of the psalm is used by Lydgate to provide a rationale for a just punishment of the heretic Lollards – just as they had used Psalm 109, with its similar curses, to attack the establishment. So Henry, like king David, must trust the Lord who alone is his light and salvation (Ps. 27:1). Like the Lollards, Lydgate believed that the psalms were moral prophecies in the process of being fulfilled in his day; but his perception of the fulfilment of these 'psalmic prophecies' is entirely different from theirs.[24]

---

[24] On the twofold use of psalmody discussed here, see M.P. Kuczynski (1995) pp. 51–77 and H.P. Nasuti (1999). Regarding Lollard glosses, of the eleven glossed manuscripts which have been found, the most significant include British Library MS Royal 18 C.26; MS Lambeth Palace 34; Bodleian Library, Oxford MS Bodley 554, Harvard University MS Richardson 36 and University College Library, Oxford MS 74. On the Lollard/Lydgate controversies, see *A. Hudson (1998); W.J. Courtenay (1985); H. Hargreaves (1969)*; and especially M.P. Kuczynski (1995, pp. 151–88), (1997), (1998).

By the thirteenth century, a rather more unusual way of using the psalms as instruction became increasingly popular amongst the laity. Its origins can be traced back to ninth-century Ireland, where the recital of the 150 psalms (in three groups of fifty) during one day was commonplace for Irish monks. Lay people who wished to join in, but could neither read nor memorize the psalms, participated by reciting the Lord's Prayer, in the first instance after every psalm. A way of keeping count of the psalms was by filling a leather pouch with 150 pebbles, or by tying a thin rope with 150 knots; a simplification of this was to use fifty pebbles or fifty knots and repeat these three times. (By the tenth century it seems that, in some Celtic churches, the 'Hail Mary' sometimes replaced the Lord's Prayer.) By the thirteenth century, popularized by St Dominic of Castile (1170–1221), founder of the Dominican Order, the practice had spread through the Continent and into England. Following from this, adapting a tradition as old as Cassiodorus, whereby the entire Psalter was understood as veiled prophecies concerning the life, death and resurrection of Jesus, the Psalter was divided into three 'rosariums', and the knotted rope (in fifties) became a means of meditating upon three aspects of the life, death and resurrection of Christ as hidden in the psalms. Between each psalm, or after every ten psalms, either the Lord's Prayer or Hail Mary (or praise of Jesus, or angelic salutations) was recited.

By the fifteenth century, this practice, using what by now had been termed a rosary, had developed into praying the entire Psalter by way of the Joyful, Sorrowful and Glorious Mysteries of Mary, as the one through whom the fulfilment of the prophecies in the psalms had come about. The Hail Mary was therefore the dominant prayer offered between groups of psalms, which were recited over the course of a week rather than one day. (There are obvious correspondences here with the use of psalms in the Eight Hours of the Virgin, in the Books of Hours, discussed earlier.) The 'Joyful Mysteries' took up two or three different weekdays, and reflected upon the Annunciation (Psalms 1–10,) Visitation (Psalms 11–20), Birth of Jesus (Psalms 21–30), Presentation in the Temple (Psalms 31–40), and the Finding in the Temple (Psalms 41–50). The 'Sorrowful Mysteries' were usually on two other weekdays, and prayed through the Agony in the Garden (Psalms 51–60), the Scourging at the Pillar (Psalms 61–70), the Crowning of Thorns (Psalms 71–80), the Carrying of the Cross (Psalms 81–90), and the Crucifixion (Psalms 91–100). The 'Glorious Mysteries' were usually on Wednesdays and Sundays, and dwelt upon the Resurrection (Psalms 101–10), the Ascension (Psalms 111–20), the Descent of the Holy Spirit (Psalms 121–30), the Assumption of Mary (Psalms 131–40), and the Coronation of Mary (Psalms 141–50). Particular psalm verses were singled out of each psalm as most appropriate for meditation (for example, Pss. 1:1–2; 2:8; 3:4; 4:7; 5:3; 6:3; 7:8; 8:3; 9:10; 10:12). The knotted rope became a string, first with wooden blocks and then with beads on it; and by the late fifteenth century woodcut picture prints were printed, usually not with 150 pictures but usually with some ten, each to signify both a Hail Mary and an Our Father bead. One striking example is by Alberto da Castello, from Venice, dating c.1521.[25]

---

[25] See P. Huyck (1994) and the website on rosary psalms at www.presentationministries.com.

Jewish Writers

The didactic use of the psalms became equally important in Jewish tradition at this time. Saadya Gaon's earlier concern to present the psalms as a second Pentateuch, whereby divine speech is given a distinctly moral emphasis, may have been a reaction to the Karaite controversy, but it anticipated a work which was finalized by the thirteenth century and which focused almost entirely on the moral appeal of psalmody. This is the *Midrash Tehillim*, the most important Jewish commentary, as far as the didactic use of the Psalms is concerned. The sources for this collection go back to the third century, when reference is made to a *Haggadah-de-Tehillim*, a midrashic work on the psalms, with which Rabbi Hiyya was so absorbed that he failed to greet Rabbi Simeon, son of the great Rabbi Judah I (Gen. Rabbah 33:3). This suggests the beginning of a midrashic commentary. The rabbinical sources quoted in *Midrash Tehillim* are almost all Palestinian, and no rabbi after the Talmudic period is quoted by name, thus indicating that the formative place of both the oral and written traditions was Palestine and the formative dates were between the second and sixth centuries CE. It is likely that a first recension of the commentary was made in *Gaonic times, by the second half of the ninth century. This was possibly only for Psalms 1–118, for various other copies of just this collection have been found, the most important being the *Constantinople Midrash* of 1512; if so, Psalms 119–50 were added some time later (with the exception of Psalm 119, the commentary on the rest of these psalms is less expansive than in the earlier collection, which suggests some difference between these two parts). Up until the thirteenth century various accretions were made, until copies emerged in more or less the form we have it today (although Psalms 123 and 131 were missing). The unity of the collection is affirmed through the titles – first by the ten authors mentioned (Adam, Melchizedek, Abraham, Moses, David, Solomon, Asaph, and three sons of Korah) and secondly through the ten types of song referred to within the superscriptions overall (glory, melody, psalm, song, praise, prayer, blessing, thanksgiving, Hallelujah, and exultation).

It is extraordinary that, given the amount of midrashic, Mishnaic and Talmudic material on the Torah which had already been accepted as authoritative by the end of the Talmudic period, *Midrash Tehillim* took some thousand years in the making before it emerged as a similar (though not equal) authority. This points again to the way in which the psalms in Jewish tradition were overshadowed by the Torah, and to a lesser extent by the Prophets, a factor which has been frequently noted as it contrasts strikingly with the centrality of the psalms *alongside* the Gospels from at least the third century onwards in Christian tradition.

What makes *Midrash Tehillim* so obviously a didactic commentary is the development of a series of homilies, often on almost each word of the psalm (as is the case with Psalms 1 and 4), sometimes on just the first and final verses (for example, Psalms 124, 144, 150) but usually taking the text verse by verse. First the word or verse is quoted, usually alongside another verse (not necessarily from the psalms) which is seen to shed light on it. Sometimes this is by using a catchword principle ('Shepherd'; 'Vine'; 'rejoice'; 'sin'); sometimes it is by making a subtle word connection (for example, from Ps. 53:1 'The fool has said in his heart, there is no God' the connection is made to 1 Samuel 25:38,25, concerning David, Abigail and Nabal – for the word 'fool' and the proper name 'Nabal' are the same in Hebrew); and sometimes it is by using the second verse as a moral summary of the first (the title to Psalm 52, for example, which sets the psalm in the conflicts between David and Saul, is explained by a verse from Ecclesiastes 5:5, on appropriate speech). Then follow various interpretations of the citation, which give it the feel of a gloss, albeit a distinctly Jewish one: 'Rabbi A taught ... Rabbi B said in the name of Rabbi C ... Rabbi D interpreted ... Rabbi E and Rabbi F said in the name of Rabbi G ...'.

This is not simply a literal, historical commentary, although there is clearly an interest in the early (usually Davidic) context of most psalms: it is homiletic, tracing its teachings back to the authority of the Law, and given that the rabbis upheld that each word had 'seventy meanings' (seventy being symbolic of an infinite number) its interest is in finding multiple meanings of the text and relating these back to the Law. So titles of psalms and numerical values of the Hebrew letters are explored for their inner meanings. Ps. 9:3, which reads 'I will rejoice in you', promotes a discussion on the two Hebrew letters which comprise 'in you', arguing that because they signify the number twenty-two, which is the number of letters in the Hebrew alphabet, this must mean a reference to the written Torah which causes the psalmist to rejoice. Or again, Ps. 19:2 ('Day to day pours forth speech, and night to night declares knowledge') promotes a discussion on the theme of 'day' and 'night' and is a reminder of Moses receiving the tables of the Law in the wilderness for 'forty days and nights' (Exod. 34:28); this leads on to an observation that one must therefore study the Written Law by day, and the Oral Law by night. Noting that Moses is called 'My Beloved' (*dwdy* in Hebrew), and the sum of the numerical value of the letters of *dwdy* is twenty-four, this is seen to refer to the twenty-four books of Written Law. That the whole psalm is therefore really about the law, and not so much about creation, is apparently ratified by its second half which praises the value of the law above everything else. Similar numerical observations, bringing out the deeper meaning of the text, and relating it back to the time of Moses and the importance of the law (rather like the way Philo used the psalms) are found in Pss. 25.5 and 27.4. Other examples include interchanging the letters of Hebrew words to effect a deeper meaning (Pss. 87.6 and 90.13), using acrostic forms (Pss. 3.3 and 5.5), and reassessing defective readings (Pss. 9.1 and 80.3).

The search for hidden meanings through the Law has obvious similarities with the Christian search for hidden meanings through the Gospel. So it is not surprising that this approach is found in Christian commentaries from the same period – those of Andrew of St Victor, Herbert of Bosham and Nicholas of Lyra, for example, who aligned themselves to a Jewish reading. One of the most interesting comparisons is with Thomas Aquinas's commentary on the psalms. Take again Psalm 8: through the title ('To the leader: according to the Gittith. A Psalm of David') Aquinas made rapid connections between the 'Gittith', or winepress, Israel as the vineyard in need of pruning, and the church as the new vineyard of God producing new wine in the martyrs of faith. By contrast, *Midrash Tehillim* 8.1, commenting also on the 'winepress', sees it as a symbol of judgement on the Gentiles, quoting Joel 4:13, referring to the fall of Babylon, using Jer. 51:33. Then follows a sequence of texts for four metaphors for redemption – grape-gathering, harvest, a pregnant woman, and spices – all of which lead to confirm the ultimate triumph of God's people. The meaning gleaned by Jews and Christians from the text could not be more different.

In terms of some overall moral tone, a key theme (in this case, like that in the Christian collections of penitential psalms) is '*imitatio David*'. Assumed as the author of all the psalms, David is the ideal model for prayer. Even in Ps. 30.3, commenting on the title of the psalm, which terms it as a song for the dedication of the Temple (thus referring to a time after David), *Midrash Tehillim* observes, by taking a verse from Ps. 61.4 ('Let me abide in your tent forever'), that, according to Rabbi Judah, this means David prayed that 'For ever may my Psalms be sung in houses of prayer and houses of study'. David is also the model for prayer in daily life (Ps. 61.3). He is the ideal intercessor for others (Pss. 25.5,14; 31.2,3,6) even praying for the future of his people (Ps. 17.9). He is the figure of humility (Pss. 17.13; 116.8) and the model of obedience (Ps. 27.2). Furthermore, the literal meaning in Hebrew of the Davidic headings ('to David, a psalm') is an indication of the gift of inspiration falling directly upon him through the spirit of prophecy (Pss. 24.3; 57.4). This is what makes him a prophet alongside Moses (Ps. 1.2). His song foreshadows the days of the Messiah when it will be sung again (Ps. 18.5). He is even ascribed a Messianic character (Ps. 70.1).

Midrash Tehillim offers an important illustration of collective rabbinical homilies on the psalms, and reveals the method of connecting the text with its past interpreters, as did a 'running gloss' for Christian interpreters. But there is one difference: because the authorities quoted in *Midrash Tehillim* cease by the sixth century, this is very much about the importance of the tradition from the past, rather than, as in the Christian use of the gloss, its ongoing appropriation in the present (taking, as just one example, the way in which Lombard's glossed commentary built upon Gilbert's commentary). Further, the purpose of *Midrash Tehillim* is of course entirely different from Christian works, best illustrated by its references to David. In *Midrash Tehillim* David's moral authority is like that in Gaon's commentary, and before that, in the works of Philo, where he is seen as the one who points back to the greater authority of the Law and Moses; this compares with the figure of David in later Christian works on the psalms where David points forward to the person of Christ. To put this slightly differently, in *Midrash Tehillim* the psalms are imbued with authority because of the way they highlight the Mosaic Law through the witness of David, whilst in Christian commentaries, the importance of the psalms is because they open up new possibilities of meaning through the way they can be turned 'Christwards'.[26]

---

[26] See W.G. Braude (1959); A.C. Feuer (ed.) (1985); *L. Jacobs (1973)*; E.M. Menn (2001, 2004); and L. Rabbinowitz (1935–6).

Christian and Jewish Liturgy

Christian Adaptations

THE EAST

The fortunes of eastern Christendom were quite different from the churches in the West, and some explanation is required in order to appreciate the different changes in liturgical psalmody which were taking place in the western churches. In the eastern churches the expansive and perpetual repetition of the psalms, which had been such an integral part of both cathedral and monastic prayer, became severely threatened until, by the time of the Fall of Constantinople in 1493, the sung offices (for example at Vespers and Great Vespers on Saturday evening) were rarely used. Between the eleventh and fifteenth centuries, not only Byzantium but also Syria and Palestine became part of this decline – one which was brought about as much by the actions of churches in the West as by Islam from the East. The Crusades indirectly brought about the fall of Edessa to the Turks in 1144, and similarly the reoccupation of Jerusalem under Saladin the Turk in 1187. One of the consequences in Palestine was the disruption and eventual cessation of the Sabaïtic rites (so named from the monastery of Mount Sabos, near Jerusalem), with their elaborate Eucharistic psalmody and the weekly recitation of the whole Psalter in the Divine Office. Similarly in Constantinople, starting with the Latin occupation between 1204 and 1261 and ending with the Ottoman occupation of 1453, the monastic offices of Mount Studious (the place of origin of the eleventh-century Theodore Psalter, with its Studite rites of liturgy) also gradually came to an end. With other churches in ruins, the liturgical practices of the cathedral church of Hagia Sophia were also terminated: as had happened in Aleppo, in 1124, the church was transformed into a mosque. Byzantine rites still continued in monasteries such as Athos and Meteora in Greece and St Catherine's Monastery on Mount Sinai, but the fall of Byzantium had a lasting impact on the fortunes of both cathedral and monastic liturgies in the East, and with it, what had previously been the central role of psalmody in worship and prayer.

THE WEST

In the late fourteenth and fifteenth centuries in western Christendom, despite the retreat of Islam, and despite the greater freedom of intellectual enquiry, and even despite the proliferation of piety and devotion through new Psalters and Breviaries, the cathedral and monastic offices (and so too the role of psalmody) was also by no means in continual good shape, although the factors which brought this about were less dramatic than in the churches in the East.

The decline can be traced back to the twelfth and thirteenth centuries, when the dominant cathedral ministry, dependent upon the focus of the one bishop, was critically transformed by the proliferation of outlying churches and chapels, each with their own clergy. But there were just not enough clergy to maintain the regular, daily offices of prayer in each locality; in many areas the offices either withered or became privatized, so that local priests, still using their Breviaries, had to say the psalms and the offices on their own. In addition, the cathedral offices were perceived by many as remote, overly excessive in devotion, and just too long, with their choirs, cantors and intricate plainchant. Psalmody seemed to be subsumed under, rather than enhanced by, the accompanying music: the cantatorii sang increasingly complex melodies prepared for the psalmic texts, and many of the doxologies, antiphons, gloria, versicles and responses composed for the Mass, which had in the first instance been closely linked to verses from the psalms, gave less and less prominence to these texts. Meanwhile, the monastic offices, with their simpler and more contemplative reading of the psalms, survived independently. The singing was in a simpler form, a rhythmic prose which was a medium for reflection, but here too the offices were less compelling for the laity: here too they were reckoned to be remote from the ordinary people. In part, the growth of more personal Prymers and Books of Hours, each maintaining the prayer of the psalms as a private rather than public devotion, is a consequence of this. Movements advocating a more fervent lay piety began to develop from the thirteenth century onwards: examples include the Waldenses of Lyons, later in Lombardy and Germany, and the Humiliati of Milan, both of which advocated a simple faith and simple lifestyle. Hence the outward forms of the cathedral and monastic offices continued, but by the end of this period, throughout the Continent and in England, a movement which encouraged a more personal use of psalmody, away from public liturgy, was beginning to develop.[27]

There were of course exceptions, both in cathedral and monastic offices, and one of these, from the early twelfth century, is an anthology of musical compositions which used the psalms in entirely new ways. Although no prolific musical tradition is really evident until the early sixteenth century, manuscripts dating from the ninth century demonstrate just how much the psalms were used in Eucharistic liturgy, despite the degeneration in later centuries. One of the key musical innovations was an experimentation with melodic modes; these pertained to a theological rationale in making a musical transition, in liturgy, between the Old and New Testaments – a rationale similarly expressed in Christian commentaries and illuminated manuscripts, but here, in music.

An exceptional anthology, from twelfth-century Germany, is that of *Hildegard of Bingen*, abbess and visionary mystic (1098–1179). As was often the custom for a

---

[27] For further discussions of liturgy during this period, see (on the eastern churches) C. Jones, G. Wainwright and E. Yarnold (1978); A. Lingas (2004); *O. Strunk (1977)*; and R.F. Taft (1991); and (on the western churches) see P.F. Bradshaw and L.A. Hoffman (eds.) (1991a); *S.J.P. van Dijk (1969)*; J. Dyer (1989, 1999); M.E. Fassler (ed.) (2001); M.E. Fassler and R.A. Baltzer (eds.) (2000); *J. Harper (1991)*; W.L. Holladay (1993); *U. Köpf (2000)*; J.W. McKinnon (1999); W.F. Storey (1977); and R. Taft (1986, 2004).

tenth child, Hildegard was offered as a 'tithe' to the church at birth, and by the age of eight was living in the Benedictine monastery of Disibodenburg. She learnt how to read from the Latin Psalter, and was immersed in liturgy and prayer some four hours a day through the Benedictine offices. The theology and imagery of psalmody, imbibed through the liturgy, played an important part in Hildegard's formation. She wrote her first known theological work, *Sci vias Domini* (*Know the Ways of the Lord*), aged thirty, a commentary on one of the most familiar psalms in the Benedictine offices – Psalm 150. But her music came later. She did not begin to compose until nearly forty, but the outpouring of the visions she saw and the voices she heard inspired her to sing plainchant in new ways.

Hildegard's originality is the way she increases the ascent and descent melody by some four or five notes whilst extending over two and half octaves (and all this using just one syllable of a word), giving her rendering a haunting and lingering resonance. In her *Book of Divine Works*, probably written between 1163–73, we read:

> Underneath all the texts, all the sacred psalms and canticles, these watery varieties of sounds and silences, terrifying, mysterious, whirling and sometimes gestating and gentle must somehow be felt in the pulse, ebb, and flow of the music that sings in me. My new song must float like a feather on the breath of God.

Her plainsong was collected into a work of over seventy melodies, composed in Latin, for use both at the Mass and also in the Daily Offices; called *Symphonia armonie celestium revelationum* (*Symphony of the Harmony of Celestial Revelation*), it included forty-three antiphons (short passages usually sung before, after or between each verse of a psalm; here twenty-eight are actual psalm antiphons, to be sung between the verses of a set psalm), sixteen responsories (passages chosen to follow Scripture readings, whether 'great responsaries' at Matins or 'short responsaries' for the other offices), seven sequences (chants sung at the Mass between the Alleluia and the Gospel), five hymns, a Kyrie and an Alleluia. These are dedicated variously to the Father and the Son, to the Holy Spirit, to the Virgin, to St Ursula, to the angels and saints of the church, to virgins, widows and innocents. The imagery of the dawning of a new age, of light after darkness, of renewed creation and of new birth is everywhere apparent, and some of the most frequently used Benedictine psalms have clearly influenced many of the motifs in this collection – for example, those sung at Lauds (Psalms 67; 93; 100; 148–50) which resonate with similar imagery. Certainly allusions to the psalms are frequent. For example, 'Rejoice, daughter of Zion in the exalted dawn', from a song to Ursula, is reminiscent of Ps. 9:14 ('in the gates of daughter Zion, I rejoice …') and Ps. 149:2 ('Let the children of Zion rejoice in their King'). Or again, a song to the Holy Spirit, 'Let all the world praise you', has resonances with psalms such as 66:3 ('Let all the peoples praise you, O God'), or 150:6 ('Let everything that breathes praise the Lord!').

Because her compositions were originally intended only for her own Benedictine community, and because of their visionary emphasis and their feminine concerns, they are quite different from the plainchant traditions associated with Ambrose and Gregory, although they are clearly a development of them. There is a sense in which Hildegard is the first to offer a 'musical gloss' on the psalms, in that what she composes is more than an exact rendering of the psalms themselves.[28]

Jewish Adaptations

Jewish liturgy, and with it the ongoing use of psalmody, underwent critical changes throughout this period, and these have a certain equivalence with the churches in the East, not least because many of these were initiated by the churches in the West. The expulsion of Jews from French royal domains in 1182, the First Lateran Council regulating Jewish affairs in 1215, the public burning of the Talmud and Jewish books in Paris and disputations in Barcelona in the mid-thirteenth century, the expulsion of Jews from England and Wales in 1290, further persecution and violence at the end of the thirteenth and fourteenth centuries throughout France, Germany and Spain, the anti-*converso* riots in Toledo in 1449, and finally the expulsion of Jews from Spain in 1492 – all these events not only disrupted but forcibly prevented continuity of worship for Jews all over Europe. Yet, as has been seen through our examples of commentaries, illuminated prayer books, and not least the *Midrash Tehillim*, the tradition of psalmody was maintained in other ways. And, as in earlier times of persecution, through the tradition of *piyyutim*, some liturgical creativity continued. Some of the best-known hymns, composed as *Zemirot* (songs) for the Sabbath liturgy, have allusions to the psalms. For example, *Adon Olam* ('Lord of the World') was composed in the eleventh century in Valencia by Solomon ibn Gabirol, with the last words alluding to Ps. 118:6 ('With the Lord on my side I do not fear. What can mortals do to me?').[29]

Translation in Christian Tradition

Because throughout this period Jews usually sang or read the psalms in Hebrew, they rarely needed to translate them into the language of the countries in which they had settled (a practice which, apart from the earlier Aramaic versions, did not change significantly until the late nineteenth century). Thus only in Christian

---

[28] For musical use of psalmody generally, and the use of melodic modes as musical expressions of the theological transference from Jewish to Christian interpretations, see N. van Deusen and M.L. Colish (1999). On Hildegard and psalmody, see *M. Fox (ed.) (1987)* and M. Fassler (2004); for a translation and commentary on *Symphony* (Dewndermonde, St Pieters-and-Paulusabdij, Codex 9) see B. Newman (1988); for a musical interpretation, see Deutsche Harmonia Mundi, 'Symphoniae: Spiritual Songs', Hyperion CD A66039. See also www.staff.uni-mainz.de/horst/hildegard/ for further resources.

[29] On Jewish liturgy, resources which informed this discussion include *R. Chazan (2004)*; A. Green (1986); L.A. Hoffman (2004); C. Kessler (1991); J.C. Kugel (1987); and S.C. Reif (1993).

tradition is there any early evidence of psalmody in the vernacular. And even here it is limited: England, greatly influenced by Norman culture, had become more Latinate than had been the case in earlier Anglo-Saxon times, and Latin was the language used in the courts, in science, in literature, in politics – and in the church. So what follows is a survey of Christian exceptions.

From the ninth century onwards there were at least fifteen Psalters with marginal and interlinear glosses in Old English: these include the *Vespasian Psalter*, the *Paris Psalter* and the *Eadwine Psalter*, each of which has been discussed previously. Another example is the fourteenth-century *West Midlands Psalter*, which has a glossed Vulgate and Middle English prose translation of all the psalms (these are followed by eleven canticles and the Athanasian Creed, and the whole collection is probably wrongly attributed to William of Shoreham, vicar of Chart Sutton in Kent, because one manuscript was bound up with a copy of his poems). Taking Ps. 1:1 as an example, the Latin reads '*Beatus vir, qui non abiit in consilio impiorum, et in via peccatorum non stetit*'; the Middle English reads 'Blesced be þe man þat ȝede nouȝt in þe counseil of wicked, ne stode nouȝt in þe waie of sinȝeres'.

The West Midlands Psalter has no commentary. By contrast, the *Psalter of Richard Rolle*, also from the mid-fourteenth century, contains a Latin text followed by a verse-by-verse translation and commentary in Middle English. (This work was taken up as part of the *Lollard cause in the fifteenth century, as we saw earlier.) For Rolle, the Psalter was, perhaps paradoxically, a moral yet mystical bridge between the physical world of words and heavenly realities. The commentary is mainly a translation of Lombard, and as Rolle states in his introduction, its purpose was not simply to present a vernacular version of the Psalter but to allow those who knew no Latin to come to some knowledge of it. It is written in a rather stolid and literal dialect, yet it soon spread to the south of England and was much copied (and altered) by Wycliffe's Lollard followers, as was discussed earlier. Ps. 1:1 reads: 'Blisful man þe whilk oway ȝed noght in þe counsaile of wicked, and in þe way of sinful stode noght'.

The tumultuous times of the fourteenth century, which resulted not only in the lack of vitality in the cathedral and monastic offices but also in the decline of earlier creativity expressed in scholastic exegesis and manuscript illumination, also played a part in the lack of recognition of these vernacular editions of the psalms. The natural disasters (the 'little ice age', followed by the famine of 1315–17 and the Black Death of 1346–61, decimated one-third of Europe's population) as well as the political, social and ecclesial unrest (for example, the beginning of the Hundred Years War in 1337, the Peasants' Revolt in England in 1381, and the schism within the Catholic Church [1378–1417] between church authorities at Rome and Avignon) resulted in less of a focus on innovation and more of an emphasis on received tradition. Hence the language of psalmody, as with the rest of Scripture, was either the Latin text which Augustine had used, or Jerome's Latin, in one of its three versions – the *Romanum*, used in the south of England and introduced by Augustine of Canterbury; the *Gallicanum*, used in the Norman churches and brought into the north of England by Irish missionaries; and the *Hebraicum*, which was used by scholars, but not in liturgy. (The irony was that Jerome's intentions, in the fourth and fifth centuries, had been to translate the Psalter into a language which could be used and understood by many – hence 'the Vulgate', for common use.) Nevertheless, until the end of the fifteenth century, Latin Bibles and Latin Psalters were to remain the norm – not only in England, but throughout Europe.

One challenge to the status quo at this time was *John Wycliffe* (1330–84), whose objective was to wrest control of Scripture out of the hands of both the authorities in the church and the scholars in the university schools, and make it more accessible to the laity. Wycliffe's opposition to the abuse of power both in church and university, whether the philosophical scepticism of scholastic theology, or the veneration of saints and the doctrine of transubstantiation of ecclesial theology, and not least his criticism of the papacy itself, brought about his condemnation by Pope Gregory XI in 1377 and by the Council of Oxford University in 1381.

Hence the two vernacular editions of the Bible which are associated with his name (although almost certainly not his work) were treated with deep suspicion by church and university authorities alike. A stilted 'Early Version' of the Old Testament was made between 1382 and 1384; about thirty copies have survived, some with illustration and illumination. This translation has been associated with a Lollard follower of Wycliffe, Nicholas de Herford. Ps. 1:1 here reads 'Blisful the man, that went not awei in the counseil of vnpitouse, and in the wei off sinful stod not'. The so-called 'Late Version' of 1388, attributed to another Lollard leader, John Purvey, has a more idiomatic slant, and Ps. 1:1 reads: 'Blessid is the man, that gede not in the council of wicked men; and stood not in the weie of synneris'. Only those copies which omitted the Prologue with its denunciations of ecclesiastical authorities were allowed official use; but the ban on all copies by Archbishop Arundel in 1408 (itself directed not so much against a new translation as against the way it had been interpreted by the Lollards) brought an end to the production of other Wycliffite versions. Nevertheless (as has been noted already), in their private sectarian gatherings, Wycliffe's followers, the Lollards, continued to use their own vernacular editions of the entire Bible, annotating the Psalms with their own revision of Rolle's Psalter.[30]

Throughout the difficult years of the fourteenth century, another influence on reception of psalmody in the vernacular was the emergent literary culture, whereby works composed in Middle English offered an alternative to the culture of Latin and Norman French (although the latter was beginning to die out in England by this time). The two best-known examples, both contemporaries of Wycliffe and both using the psalms in their works, are William Langland (?1332–87), credited

---

[30] For the West Midlands Psalter (British Library Additional 17376) see K.D. Buelbring (ed.) (1891); for the Psalter of Richard Rolle, see J.A. Alford (1995); R. Allen (trans.) (1988); D. Everett (1922 and 1923); G. Hodgson (trans.) (1928); and M.P. Kuczynski (1997). On Wycliffe and the Lollards, see *W.J. Courtenay (1985)*; *H. Hargreaves (1969)*; G. Jackson (ed.) (1999); M.P. Kuczynski (1995); *G. Shepherd (1969)*; *K. Walsh and D. Wood (eds.) (1985)*.

with the composition of *Piers Plowman* in about 1377, and Geoffrey Chaucer (1342–1400), whose *Canterbury Tales* are dated between 1387 and 1400.

Langland's persona, Will the Dreamer, gives us an indication of Langland's own profession, which may well have been a 'Psalter clerk', or a reader of the psalms (in Latin) in the offices:

> The lomes þat ich laboure with and lyflode deserue
> Ys pater-noster and my prymer, placebo and dirige,
> And my suter som tyme, and my seuene psalms.
> This ich segge for hure soules of suche as me helpen … (VI. 45–8)

The references to his Prymer, Psalter and 'seven psalms' at the very least explain Langland's high regard for the psalms throughout his work, an esteem held by poet and the created character alike (although Will the Dreamer only 'remembers' the psalms and does not read them, being a humble ploughman). The psalms are quoted some 107 times in the B version of the three versions of the poem; they occur over ten times in Passus V, especially in relation to the confession of the seven deadly sins, and some ten times in Passus XVIII (the account of the passion and the allegory of the Four Daughters of God). The majority of the other quotations unite around the themes of repentance and the infinite mercy of God, and of the need for human mercy to imitate the mercy received from God. Psalm 51 ('Miserere mei deus') plays a significant part in Passus V, and Psalm 85, with its thanksgiving for sins forgiven ('You forgave the iniquity of your people; you pardoned all their sins' – v. 2), is an important part of Passus XVIII, with its discourse on the relationship between Justice and Truth. Psalm 51 is again important here: v. 4 ('Against you, you alone, have I sinned, and done what is evil in your sight, so that you are justified in your sentence and blameless in your judgement') is spoken by Christ himself in the poem to illustrate his ability to absolve sins, having borne the sins of all.

Specific quotations are given in Latin. But there is also a remarkable occurrence of psalms in the vernacular. In III, 234–45, Conscience also argues from the psalms: first Ps. 15:1 ('Domine, quis habitabit in tabernaculo tuo?') is quoted in Latin, then it is translated into the vernacular ('Lord, who shal wonye in thi wones with thyne holy seintes, Or resten in þyne holy hilles: þis askeþ Dauid'), and then the answer to Ps. 15:1, found in Ps.15:2, is given in the Latin ('Qui ingreditur sin macula …'). The 'translation' and commentary (using, it seems, some of Augustine's Gloss on this psalm) illustrate the ways in which Conscience, as a model of pious devotion, could draw from a wide store of psalmic sayings. A similar use of psalmody is found in Anima's speech in Passus XV, where the text is Ps. 1:1–2, quoted in Latin, again followed by an interpretation in vernacular speech. And in Passus VII, Piers himself uses the same format: Ps. 23:4 ('Even though I walk through the darkest valley, I fear no evil …') is quoted in Latin, without translation, at the point when Piers is challenged by a priest that he has received no real pardon; this makes the point that the text itself has its own direct authority. But Piers ends his rebuff to the priest with a vernacular paraphrase from Ps. 42:3 ('Fuerunt michi lacrime mee panes die ac nocte ...') which is then followed by the Latin of this verse, which illustrates both the direct authority of the text and Piers' appropriation of it. This movement between the Latin text and the Middle English translation not only highlights Piers' insight and devotion over that of the priest, but it also illustrates the possibility of learning pious devotion not only from the Vulgate Psalter but also from the psalms in the 'vulgar' dialect of the day.

Simple piety is to pray the psalms in a spirit of integrity; the vehicle of the language, be it Latin or the vernacular, is less important than the spirit in which it is prayed, as seen in the quotation from Passus VI, referring to the psalm of 'Beati omnes' – Psalm 128, quoting in Latin part of verse 2:

> The Sauter seith in the psalme of Beati omnes,
> The freke that fedeth hymself with his feithful labour,
> He is blessed by the book in body and in soule:
> **Labores manuum tuarum** &c.

Although Chaucer did not use the psalms as frequently as Langland, he nevertheless applies a similar contrast of Latin and vernacular versions. In 'The Summoner's Tale' (lines 269–73), when the Summoner seeks to expose a certain friar as a beggar and hypocrite who abuses the simple hospitality of Thomas and his wife, the Latin quotation again adds to the satire:

> Whan they for soules seye the psalm of davit;
> Lo, 'bur!' they seye, 'cor meum eructavit!'

Like Langland, Chaucer is quick to defend a simple and commonsensical piety which comes from a humble and practical reading of the psalms, along with the wisdom of Proverbs and the Greek poets, as in *The Manciple's Tale* (lines 344–46):

> Reed salomon, so wys and honurable;
> Reed david in his psalmes, reed senekke.
> My sone, spek nat, but with thyn heed thou bekke.

On one occasion, in the very first lines of 'The Prioress's Tale', Chaucer, like Langland, also provides a vernacular translation of a psalm:

> O Lord our Lord! thy name how marvellous
> Is in this large world y-spread! (quoth she)
> For not only thy laude precious praise
> Performed is by men of high degree,
> But by the mouth of children thy bounte
> Performed is, for on the breast sucking
> Sometimes showe they thy herying.

The quotation is from Ps. 8:1–2 ('O Lord, our Sovereign, how majestic is your name in all the earth! You have set your glory above the heavens. Out of the mouths of babes and infants you have founded a bulwark because of your foes …'). So although *Canterbury Tales* does not use the psalms as much as *Piers Plowman*, a similar interest in the form and content of psalmody as a medium for personal devotion is nevertheless evident, and each produces psalmody in both Latin and Middle English in order to achieve this end.[31]

One other new venture which raises critical questions about the language, translation, culture and ideology of the psalms within the Christian tradition, which is at the cusp of the period under discussion and the period to be discussed in the following chapter, is the so-called voyages of discovery, from the late 1440s onwards. Beginning with explorations in Africa (from Portugal), the Americas (from Spain), and in Asia and north America (from France and England), and with motives which focused more on the competition for trade than on religious zeal, these nevertheless provoked a good deal of Christian rhetoric about a new world order, and friars and priests usually played an important part in baptism and catechesis in new communities overseas. Nevertheless, the overall effect of the spread of Christendom into new lands raised questions about whether a Latin Psalter, for example, could really serve the liturgical needs of young Christian communities in Africa and Asia. These issues became more pressing in the sixteenth century, in the Jesuit missions initiated by Ignatius Loyola (1491–1556) in Europe and Palestine, and Frances Xavier (1506–82) in India. Although there are several later examples of Amerindian choristers attached to Jesuit communities singing the Offices or the Little Hours of the Virgin in Latin, and composing polyphonic psalm settings from the Latin for the Mass, and of Mesoamerican monastic communities covering their cells with Latin inscriptions of the psalms (for example, in the sixteenth-century Augustinian monastery of Malinalco, Mexico), there are many other telling examples from the fifteenth century onwards of prayer and hymnbooks overseas being produced in the vernacular. Another example from Mexico is a hymnbook of canticles for Sundays and major feast days which was composed in the Náhuatl language by Fray Bernardino de Sahagún, called *Psalmodia Christiana*; it was published in Mexico City in 1583, and was to be sung whilst dancing.

The voyages of discovery also elicited an intense expectation of living on the brink of a utopian age, which was itself part of the final stages of world history. Imagery of a new Jerusalem and a newly found paradise appeared frequently in English literature from this time onwards (*Utopia* by Sir Thomas More (1516), *The Faerie Queene* by Edmund Spenser (1580), Shakespeare's *Tempest* (c.1611)

---

[31] For an online version of Langland, which enables a search of verses from psalms, see worldebooklibrary.com/eBooks/WorldeBookLibrary.com/piersplowman.htm. For Chaucer online, with a similar search capacity, see www.kankedort.net/. See also *L. Besserman (1988)*; and M.P. Kuczynski (1995, 1999).

and *Paradise Lost and Regained* by John Milton (1677) being obvious examples) and, as will be seen in the next chapter, much utopian imagery borrows from the language and ideology from the psalms. A late-fifteenth-century example is the 1497 *Isabella *Breviary*, owned by Isabella of Castile, patron of Columbus's 1492 voyage to the New World, which is full of illustrations to psalms, reflecting the sense of anticipation of building a new Temple as a sign of a glorious new age: behind this imagery is the anticipation of the discovery of new lands and the belief that the expulsion of the Moors from the Iberian peninsular was to be a foretaste of the re-conquest of Jerusalem. The (anachronistic) illustrations of David before the Temple for Psalm 146 ('Praise the Lord, O my soul!') and before the Songs of Ascents to Jerusalem at the beginning of Psalm 120 are particularly relevant in this respect (noting here that Ferdinand of Aragón held the title 'King of Jerusalem').

Christopher Columbus himself was both the recipient and inspiration of such expectations: his *El Libro de las Profecias* (*The Book of Prophecies*), co-written with his son and chaplain in 1502, is a compilation of the various biblical texts which refer to the hidden islands (of Seba, Ophir, Tarshish and the like) to demonstrate that Columbus was the new Solomon just as Ferdinand was the new David. Psalms such as 72:10 ('May the kings of Tarshish and of the isles render him tribute, may the kings of Sheba and Seba bring gifts …'), 97:1 ('The Lord is king! Let the earth rejoice; let the many coastlands be glad!') and 19:4 ('… yet their voice goes out through all the earth, and their words to the end of the world') were seen as prophecies in the process of fulfilment through the discovery of the West Indies (which of course at the time were believed to be islands to the east of Europe, the islands which would herald the end of history by receiving the Gospel). Hence Christopher ('Christ-bearer') Columbus saw himself incarnating a divine mission: the words of Ps. 2:7–8 ('You are my son; today I have begotten you. Ask of me, and I will make the nations your heritage, and the ends of the earth your possession') were applied several times both to the Spanish monarch and to himself. A *Polyglot Psalter dating from 1516, written in Latin, Hebrew, Greek, Arabic and Aramaic, was commissioned by Cardinal Francisco Ximénez de Cisneros in Spain in order that upon Christ's return, Christians could converse with him in their native languages: and here, a lengthy eulogy of several folios concerning Columbus and his achievements is added exactly after Ps. 19:4 ('… their voice goes out through all the earth, and their words to the end of the world …').

The ways in which the psalms inspired political ideologies will be brought out further in the following chapter; but it is significant that, at the end of this period under discussion, the Psalter, particularly when conveyed through the vernacular, still was able to infuse political aspirations with apocalyptic hopes.[32]

---

[32] On de Sahagún's *Psalmodia Christiana*, see A. Anderson (1993); L. Burkhart, 1995. On the *Isabella Breviary* (British Library Additional MS 18851) see J. Backhouse (1993) and J. Lara (2004). On Christopher Columbus, see H. Avalos (1996); J. Fleming (1991); J. Lara (2004); *A. Prosperi (1992)*; and *P.M. Watts (1985)*.

Concluding Observations

The reception of psalmody throughout this period has thus both negative aspects – for example, in the disputatious works between Jews and Christians, and in some decline of the vibrancy of the psalms in both the cathedral and monastic offices – but there are also many positive features. One example is the beginning of some collaboration between Jews and Christians concerning the grammar and language of the psalms. Another is the richness of manuscript illustration, developed in distinctive ways by both Jews and Christians, thus opening up new possibilities of reading the psalms which went beyond textual and verbal responses alone. In Christian tradition, the experimentation with plainchant, as evidenced in the works of Hildegard of Bingen, illustrates that this more imaginative and creative response to the psalms can be expressed through music as well. Another example, evident this time in both faiths, is the rise of lay piety, expressed in primers and prayer books and in *haggadot* and *sedarim*, as well as in new works such as *Midrash Tehillim* and in new acts of Christian piety focused, for example, on the penitential psalms; as a result, we see a new lay appreciation of the moral and pastoral relevance of the psalms. A final positive feature, and one which is more western and Christian, is the beginning of the process of translating psalmody from a Latin to a vernacular medium, whether through literary works such as *Piers Plowman*, or through glosses to Psalters written in the vernacular, or even through deliberate translations, such as those associated with Richard Rolle and with John Wycliffe and the Lollards. In all this, compared with the first millennium, we see both continuity and change in these different kinds of reception, and the enormous transformation which took place in the next three centuries is more explicable on account of it.

The Fifteenth to Seventeenth Centuries: Democratization and Dissemination

In Christian tradition, on the Continent and then in England, the most striking development in the sixteenth and seventeenth centuries is the proliferation of *translations* of the psalms. Linked to this is an abundance of new *liturgical* material, a feature which contrasts again with the lack of real progress in the preceding four centuries. New translations and new liturgies fostered a few significant *commentaries* on the psalms and a few *didactic works*; the latter are interesting because they illustrate new ways of reading the psalms politically, a feature quite different from the more traditional types of sermons and devotional works. The first half of this chapter will therefore assess these four modes of reception alongside one another, under the broad category of '*reception as translation*'.

The *aesthetic representation* of psalmody will be dealt with separately in the final part of this chapter. Although the illumination of Psalters is not as profuse as in earlier centuries (though access to printing produced some interesting developments in both Christian and Jewish tradition), two other artistic forms gain prominence – namely *literary imitation* and *musical composition*. New poetic imitations of psalmody were of course influenced by the increase in vernacular versions; and although many musical arrangements were still set in Latin, experimentation with the psalms in the vernacular created new musical possibilities as well. Furthermore, given that most compositions were for worship, in Protestant, Reformed, Anglican and Catholic churches (and, as we shall see, occasionally for a Jewish audience as well), another shared concern is with translation and liturgy. Hence although the second part of this chapter will focus on '*reception as aesthetic representation*', the issues here are very much related to the discussion in the first part of the chapter.

Reception as Translation: Christian Responses

Commentary, Liturgy, Homily and Translation on the Continent

In this period the number of commentators on the psalms, so prolific in the Middle Ages, begins to decrease. In part this is because there were fewer opportunities for

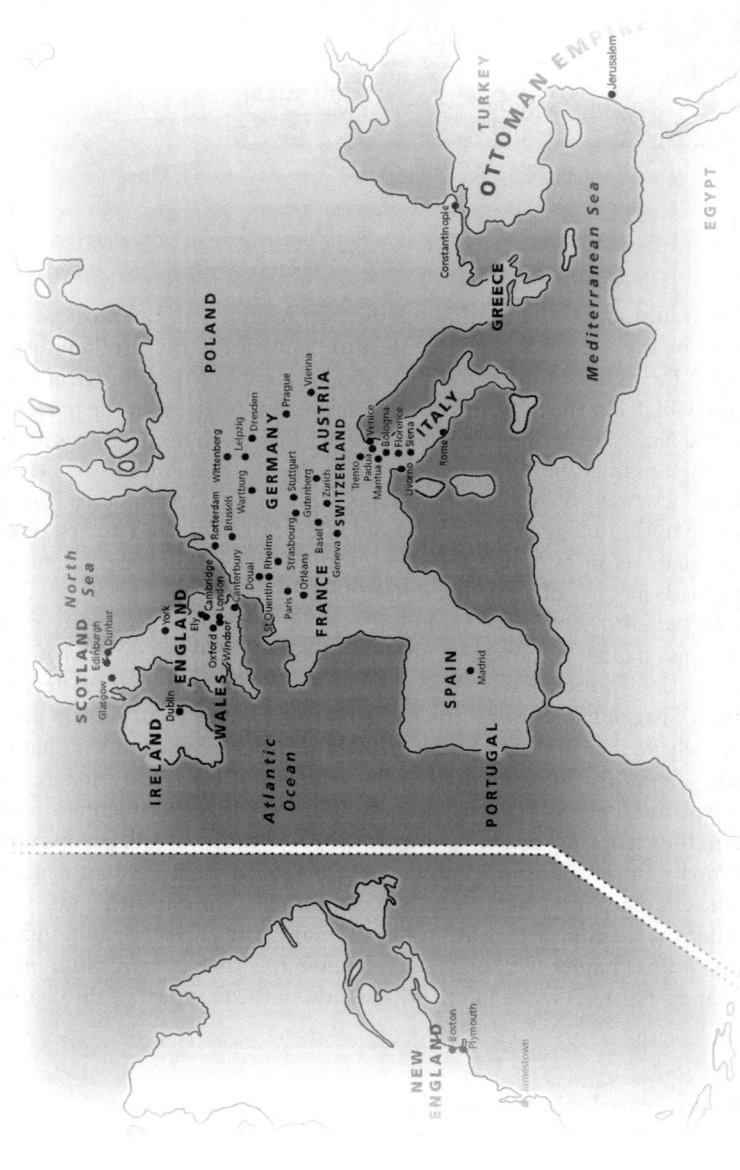

MAP 4.1 From England, Scotland and western Europe to the New World: centres of psalmody during Reformation and Commonwealth times.

Jewish–Christian disputation and dialogue: after the Jews' expulsion from Spain and Portugal, Jewish centres in the West were reduced to the 'ghettos' in, for example, Rome and Venice, and to the *Judengassen in parts of Germany, and, by the middle of the sixteenth century, in the Calvinist Dutch Republic and Poland, where religious toleration was more established. Hence centres of learning like those in Spain and France, which created opportunities for the discourse which influenced many Jewish and Christian commentaries, were no longer an influence. Furthermore, more pressing political and ecclesiastical concerns focused attention on the psalms in practical and immediate ways, so that scholastic studies and commentary writing became a less pressing matter. Although we could list a number of less known commentators on the psalms, both Jewish and Christian, there are very few early exegetes who merit particular attention: the emphasis is much more on translation than on commentary *per se*. Indeed, other than individuals such as Erasmus, whose works influenced later reformers, only two – Martin Luther and John Calvin – produced significant commentaries on the psalms in the early Reformation period.[1]

Desiderius Erasmus Roterdamus (1469–1536) never actually translated the psalms into any vernacular; indeed, his choice of text as the Greek-based Latin translation of Jerome illustrates that his concern was as much to get back to the earlier Greek Old Testament as to offer any vernacular version. Nor did he even complete his intended commentary on the whole Psalter ('Who indeed has not written on the Psalms?' he once wrote). His cosmopolitan background suggests some comparisons with Jerome's, over a thousand years earlier: born near Rotterdam, Erasmus travelled to Paris, Oxford, Cambridge, Italy and Germany, so was well acquainted with the theological debates of the early sixteenth century, and his works were as much an influence in England as on the Continent. His reading of the psalms was important because it combined both philological and grammatical concerns with an emphasis on more hidden analogical and tropological readings: Erasmus was keen to apply the psalms to issues facing the church at a critical time. His *Enarratio in Primum Psalmum*, a commentary on Psalm 1, was published in 1516, six months before his entire New Testament translation of the Vulgate appeared; '*Iuxta tropologiam potissimum*' was its subtitle, showing that Erasmus's primary concern was not only with the language of the psalm but also with its moral (tropological) lessons and its Christian message (that temptation can be overcome with due meditation upon Christ – a theme which anticipated Luther's reading of the same psalm). His exposition (*enarratio*) of Psalm 1 was followed in 1522 by a commentary (*commentarius*) on Psalm 2, in 1524 by a paraphrase (*paraphrases*) on Psalm 3, and in 1525 by a sermon (*concio*) on Psalm 4, after which he then abandoned any order and wrote until his death in 1536 on a

---

[1] Resources which have informed this chapter and which are not used in later footnotes include C. Bradshaw (1996); E. Duffy (1992); G.R. Evans (1985); C. Hill (1993); R.G. Hobbs (1990); J. Lara (2004); D. MacCulloch (1992, 1995 [ed.], 1996, 2003); A. Milton (1995); R.A. Muller and J.L. Thompson (1996 [ed]); H.O. Oberman (1992); J.S. Preus (1969); I. Rashkow (1990a, 1990b); and K. Shuger (1994).

selection of psalms, including Psalms 23, 34, 39 ('expositions'), Psalms 15, 29, 84 ('treatises' or titled commentaries) and Psalm 86 (a sermon).

In spite of his concern with ancient and classical culture, Erasmus (unlike Jerome) did not know Hebrew; his preference was for Greek and Latin, and indeed, many of his commentaries have anti-Semitic tendencies. Nowhere is this more evident than in his commentary on Psalm 2, running to over seventy pages. For example, of Ps. 2:6 ('I have set my king on Zion, my holy hill') Erasmus' initial historical interpretation is that the psalm is about David's defeat of the Jebusites and his rebuilding of Zion. However, he then contends that this interpretation is 'the letter that kills'; Christians prefer 'to drink the new wine of our king': David's kingdom was destroyed, Zion became no more than a point on a map, but Christ's reign in a heavenly realm will last forever. Nevertheless, Erasmus' usual approach was at least to consider the Hebrew (through other commentators, Jerome not least) as well as the Greek, before he used the Latin: in fact, it was his attempt to translate the Hebrew 'Zion' as 'watchtower' which enabled him to interpret the text in Christian terms, whereby Zion became the watchtower from which the Christian Gospel was preached. As with Psalm 1, it is the *Christian* application which governs his exegesis more than the philological and grammatical concerns.

Nevertheless, other commentaries show a variety of interests. Psalm 29, for example, with its references to the sevenfold voice of God echoing over the waters, is discussed in the context of the proposals for war against the Turks, a theme he returned to again with a lengthy appeal to this psalm in his *De Bello Turcico*; Erasmus interprets the 'waters' as the Christian peoples, tossed about by their passions and false doctrines, over whom God sits in judgement (here Erasmus is implying the Turkish victory was God's judgement on the church) but protecting those who hear his voice. His sermon on Psalm 4 centres on the redemptive words from the cross, yet also refers to scholarly disagreements between the Hebrew, Greek and Latin in verse 4 ('when you are disturbed [or "angry"] do not sin'), concluding that 'God had allowed the differences of the copyists'. So although Erasmus's own interests were more about concealed Christian meanings and contemporary Christian application, it was in fact his interest in the pre-Jerome Greek texts which raised questions about whether one should use the Vulgate alone and which actual language – Latin, Greek or Hebrew – should form the basis for a translation, if indeed one was to make a translation at all.[2]

William Tyndale (1494?–1536) knew Hebrew as well as Greek and Latin, although, unlike Erasmus, he was more interested in translation than commentary. Tyndale, like Wycliffe, believed that the authority of Scripture was above the authority of the church, and his opposition to the church's dependence on the Vulgate as the ultimate source of authority placed him at odds with the ecclesiastical establishment. One of the most important differences between Wycliffe and

---

[2] For published and translated works on the psalms, see D. Erasmus (1997); for a translation of *De Bello Turcico*, see E. Rummel (1990 [ed.]); see also *J.W. Aldridge (1966)*; *L. Bouyer (1969)*; M.J. Heath (1991); and G.W.H. Lampe (1969).

Tyndale was that, by the latter part of the fifteenth century, the latter could disseminate his work to a greater degree through the printing presses – at least on the Continent, where he had more political freedom: because of opposition to his theological motives by figures such as Thomas More and Archbishop Warham, Tyndale was never able to publish his translations in England. By the 1520s he had fled to Germany, and although he produced there the first printed translation of the New Testament in English, his attempt to import this into England was thwarted, for the copies were burnt by officials of the Bishop of London upon their arrival at the London Docks. Until his death in 1535, Tyndale was in constant hiding throughout Europe, and although he translated over half of the Old Testament during this time, he never managed to produce a final version of the psalms. His lack of success was undoubtedly due to the extraordinary circumstances of the last part of his life, just before the Church in England separated from the Catholic Church.

By a savage irony, in 1535, at Vilvorde near Brussels, Tyndale was burnt at the stake for heresy, the very same year that *Miles Coverdale* (1488–1568) was publishing, probably in Zurich, an English copy of the complete Bible, which, without Tyndale's dissensions in prefaces and notes, was acceptable both to the king and ecclesiastical establishment. Like Tyndale, Coverdale was more interested in translation than commentary. For his translation, he consulted other German and Latin versions, and of the five versions it seems he used, it is likely that one of the others was Tyndale's: Coverdale had in fact met Tyndale in 1529, when they worked together on the Pentateuch and the New Testament. But Coverdale was very different from Tyndale: for example, the Greek and Hebrew – with which Tyndale, in spite of the censure of his works, was more cognizant – were less important to him. In his Bible translation overall, Coverdale's work is of a man under pressure, often verbose, and frequently inconsistent in his choice of words (for example, 'penance' and 'repentance', and 'priests' and 'elders', were often used for the same two Latin words), but his task was to produce a complete version as soon as possible. By contrast, Tyndale's translation, had it survived in its entirety, would have represented the work of a lifetime, with attention given to the original languages, and to precision and exactitude of expression. Coverdale's Bible contained a preface addressed to Henry VIII, comparing him to Moses, David and Josiah, rebuking his earlier conduct whilst commending his repentance of faith: it was sent to England, and, perhaps surprisingly, was given royal approval (ironically, implicitly sanctioning the influence of Tyndale within parts of this version, not least in the psalms). The consultations with bishops and scholars revealed that Coverdale's Bible had 'errors, but not heresies'.

Coverdale's two acknowledged resources for his translation of the psalms were the Vulgate (for example, he kept the Latin forms of Hebrew names) as well as Luther's 1524 German translation. For example, Ps. 68:31 ('... Let bronze be brought from Egypt; let Ethiopia hasten to stretch out its hands to God ...') reads, in Coverdale, 'Then shall the princes come out of Egypt: the Morians' land shall soon stretch out her hands unto God', where the odd expression 'Morians' land' is a direct translation of Luther's 'Mohrenlande'. This was a translation with limitations, but of all of the books in the Bible, despite our earlier observations, the Psalter is his most effective work. Coverdale developed here a form which is best typified as *prose rhythm*, influenced in part from the Latinate plainchant traditions of psalmody going back to Ambrose and Gregory. Each psalm verse is set in two half-lines to reflect – intuitively, albeit not always with linguistic accuracy – the characteristic parallelism of the Hebrew poetry. The poetry is more in the balance of sense than rhythm or metre, which meant that in liturgical recital, the balance could be achieved by creating a pause between one half-line and another, and any irregularity in the rhythm could be compensated by chanting, singing and musical accompaniment. One example, from the beginning of Psalm 150, must suffice:

1. O praise God in his holiness: praise him in the firmament of his power.
2. Praise him in his noble acts: praise him according to his excellent goodness.
3. Praise him in the sound of the trumpet: praise him upon the lute and harp.

The period before and after Anne Boleyn's execution brought Coverdale's publication under suspicion, because of her support of both Tyndale and Coverdale. So by 1537, another translation, Matthew's Bible, had appeared, the work of John Rogers, whose pen name was Thomas Matthew, but his version was essentially a combination of Coverdale's Old Testament and Tyndale's New Testament, with over 2,000 controversial marginal notes. As far as the Psalms were concerned, the revision was only of some grammatical infelicities, for few of the changes noted (for example, Pss. 17:13, 32:10, 42:11, 94:15) have any controversial theological points within them. By 1539 the 'Great Bible' appeared, which on the king's order was to be used in every church in the realm. It was so called because it was larger than both Coverdale's and Matthew's; although without the controversial marginal notes, it included a good deal of their work.

In a new era of independence from Rome, an English Bible was an important symbol of, firstly, the authority of Scripture over that of Rome, and, secondly, the King's sole right, as Supreme Head of the Church, over any such publication. The consequence of the subsequent reforms for the reception of psalmody in English was momentous. Within just four years, between 1536 and 1540, over 250 centres of monastic spirituality were destroyed, with only seven monastic cathedrals and Westminster Abbey surviving (and through all this Henry 'glossed' his own Psalter with notes which justified his actions against what he saw as excessive devotion to ritual). Hence as the continual (Latin) use of the psalms in the monastic office disintegrated, the vernacular use of psalmody became an enforced practice in the church offices – first Coverdale's Bible, then Matthew's Bible, then the Great Bible. By 1543, in an attempt to create some liturgical unity, Henry's Act for the Advancement of True Religion banned all public and private expositions of Scripture in English ('being of the craft, false and untrue translation of Tyndale') except the Great Bible. Only those men of a high enough social standing were permitted to read privately, with the interesting exception being the recitation of

Psalms, Prymers, Ave Marias and the Creeds, which were deemed to be more personal, beyond political dispute.

However, despite the other versions which were popularized after 1535, it was the Psalter from Coverdale's Bible which, after Henry's death, was incorporated by the Act of Uniformity in 1549 into Cranmer's *Book of Common Prayer*. As well as its artistic merit, another reason for its success was, again, its appearance within an extraordinary period of history. Latin psalms were less widespread in the monastic offices, whilst, ironically, vernacular psalms also were dwindling in the cathedrals and parishes, because Cranmer had replaced the various offices with just morning and evening prayer, with almost no hymnody (to avoid singing in Latin). So the 1549 publication of the *Book of Common Prayer*, which was essentially a revision of the Latin material from the Roman *Breviary and the *Sarum Rite*, was in part an attempt to redress this imbalance, and hence to increase the role of the psalms in liturgy: for example, Psalm 95 (the '*Venite*') was now always to be used at morning prayer, following the monastic office, and a 'psalm for the day' was always prescribed at Communion. In addition, the rubrics instructed that the recitation of the entire Psalter should be completed over the course of a month, including Matins and Evensong as well as Communion. By including Coverdale's version in this prayer book, it became, by default, the official liturgical resource for psalmody, ratified further by its being made compulsory by an Act of Parliament in 1552. And its potential for a variety of representations, by way of public singing and private recitation, added to its popularity because of its flexibility. (Its ongoing familiarity into the seventeenth century led to its inclusion in the revised 1662 *Book of Common Prayer*, thus guaranteeing its use to the present day.)[3]

If Erasmus is noteworthy for his commentaries on selected psalms, and Coverdale, using Tyndale, more noteworthy for translations of psalmody, then *Martin Luther* (1483–1546) combines commentary with translation. His attachment to the psalms began in 1505, as an Augustinian friar and later priest, when he followed the daily practice of the canonical hours of prayer. But Luther had a high regard for the intellectual demands of the Psalter as well. His first theology lectures for the University of Wittenberg in 1513 were on Psalms 1–126; these made full use of various *glosses, referring extensively to Augustine, Strabo, Lyra and Lombard, using an edition called the *Quincuplex Psalter* printed in France in 1509, which included the Latin, French, Gallican, Hebrew and Greek versions. Luther's own copies contain further explanatory glosses written around and between the lines for the edification of his students, as well as a separate manuscript containing *scholia*, on further theological issues raised by the psalms. Indeed, tradition has it that he arranged for his students to have printed Psalters with very wide margins so they could create their own glosses, which could complement the received traditions

---

[3] On Tyndale generally, and Coverdale in particular, see *R.H. Bainton (1970)*; *D.C. Steinmetz (1990)*; *R.H. Worth Jr (2000)*.

found in the medieval commentaries. His better-known lectures on Romans and Galatians were not given until some two years later: hence it could be argued that the psalms were as formative as any biblical book in his theological thinking about the triumph of the grace of God over human sinfulness.

For example, in his Christological interpretation of Psalm 51, showing how the Christian is made righteous in Christ, Luther read this psalm as a prophecy made in the person of the church, serving as a model for all would-be penitents to use independently of the payment indulgences: if they prayed the psalm with faith in God, they would receive directly God's mercy through Christ. This analysis is typical of Luther's more psychological approach: the psalms pertain to the life experiences of the saints of God, then and now, dealing with all that is necessary in praying to God. The publication of Psalm 51 was as part of Luther's commentary on the seven penitential psalms (referred to in the previous chapter). Throughout the collection as a whole, Luther takes an Augustinian line of interpretation, hearing not only the voice of David (especially in Psalms 32 and 51) but also the voice of the people (as in Psalms 102, 130 and 143) which together foreshadow the voice of Christ (who is the one who 'remembers us' as he shares our suffering, although not our sin, as in Psalms 6 and 38). This approach allows Luther to detach Christ from the weakness of human sin (in that it is David and the people speaking) whilst also allowing Christ to deal with the effects of that sin. This work was published in 1519, two years after Luther had posted the ninety-five theses against the door of Wittenberg Castle Church, and consequentially faced the opposition of church authorities at Rome. The political as well as theological symbolism in publishing the penitential psalms at this point in time could not have been clearer: it defied the authority of Pope Leo X and his *Cum Postquam*, also made in 1519, against indulgences, and witnessed instead to a personal faith in Christ alone to deal with sin.

As for Luther's other commentaries on the psalms, some are from his lectures, some from his sermons. They date from as early as 1513 until his death in 1546. Their significance is the way they illustrate the tensions in his theological approach to the Old Testament in general and the Psalms in particular. Taking for granted the traditional four ways of interpreting the Psalms (literal, allegorical, moral, mystical), Luther struggled with the right balance of interpretation. On the one hand, he repudiated allegorical interpretations of psalmody, seeing them as too much associated with Roman Catholic exegesis; but on the other hand, his pursuit of practical and devotional Christian meaning led him to look for that which was 'hidden' within the psalms, resulting in his compromising an adherence to the literal sense alone. During his earlier period at Wittenberg, this compromise was worked out by making Christ, not David, the one who gave 'literal sense' to the psalms, and several of the commentaries from this time are as anti-Semitic as were those of Erasmus before him. Psalm 1, for example, is literally about the way Jesus did not give in to the perverse and adulterous pursuits of the Judaism of his day: here Luther reads 'the wicked … the sinners … the scoffers' in v. 1 as the Jews, who, spiritually and literally, have been 'like the chaff which the wind blows away' (v. 4). Luther circumvents the problem in Hebrew of the law being a 'delight' for meditation (v. 2) by following the Vulgate translation which implies that the law comes from faith in God which Christ give us the 'free will' (*voluntas*) to obey. Psalm 2 concerns the fury of both Jews and Gentiles against Christ in his passion; and Psalm 3 is a complaint of Christ against the Jews. All these readings, centred on Christ rather than David, Luther sees as the *literal* interpretation of a given psalm. Of his earlier commentaries, Psalm 51 is one of the very few psalms where Luther assumes the literal sense starts with David (and his adultery with Bathsheba), although even here, as was observed earlier, David is still speaking as the prophetic voice of the church.

However, in the later commentaries Luther increasingly adopted a more Davidic-centred emphasis as the focus of his literal interpretation. This involved writing increasingly about the *tropological value of a psalm. But this in turn raised another theological issue. In advocating an interpretation of psalmody whereby the 'voice of Christ' no longer determined the ultimate worth, Luther implied that the moral life of the Old Testament psalmists *per se* was a model for faith; and hence his argument for the unique act of the grace of God in Christ was compromised. Luther circumvented this problem by stating that the psalmists' faith was 'temporal' – i.e. still working within the confines of obedience to the law, awaiting the promise of a greater ('eternal') reality. The psalmists' faith therefore created a bridge between the 'literal' world of the Old Testament and the 'spiritual' world of the New. One of the most significant places where Luther works this out is in his many commentaries on Psalm 119, the last of which was published in about 1539, where he sees the teaching on the law as anticipating the coming of Christ, rather than being (an allegory) about him.

Overall, a reading of Luther's commentaries on the psalms, which stretch over some thirty years, allows one to see the various theological shifts of thought between Luther's emphasis first on the literal and then on the spiritual meaning, between Old Testament (Jewish) faith (in works) and New Testament (Christian) faith (in God's grace). The psalms, because they were the object of real affection and an inspiration towards the reform of the church, were also a challenge to the overall consistency of Protestant theology.

Luther's interest in commentaries on the psalms was closely related to his commitment to create a German translation of them. He had achieved this by 1524, shortly after his return to Wittenberg from exile in Wartburg. His translation was by no means the first in German: there were already some fourteen printed versions of the entire Bible in the Middle High German dialect and some three in Low German. However, his was the most provocative, not so much in the publication itself as in the theological motivation which inspired it. This was the same motivation which had prevented Tyndale achieving the same success in England, for both concurred that a vernacular version meant that the Vulgate Psalter was no longer the ultimate authority in church teaching and practice. Furthermore, Luther's translation was not dependent upon on the Vulgate alone: indeed, he is said to have hated Jerome's 'monkish bias'. Despite the anti-Jewish bias in some of his commentaries, he frequently consulted appropriate glosses which used the Hebrew, such as Nicholas of Lyra and those known to Jewish rabbis; for the Greek, he conferred with his contemporary, Melanchthon, as well as consulting Erasmus's commentaries. He further sought out older Latin versions, and he used some of the editions in Middle High German and Low German. His concern was to create a scholarly version of the psalms as well as one with which the laity could be familiar. But his overall purpose was to produce 'whole psalms, not just parts of them', avoiding the fragmentation of psalmody which was increasingly the practice in chants and choral works in Latin. This very much affected Luther's motivation in reforming the liturgy, an issue which was closely related to his understanding of the purpose and relevance of entire psalms.

Luther's timing of his translation of the Psalms, a year after the publication of a hymnbook in 1523 which contained some six metrical paraphrases of the psalms, was again not coincidental. Erasmus had said of the church music of his day that it was so constructed that the congregation could not hear one distinct word, and Luther clearly wished to reform the liturgy, but, given his relationship with the church after the *Diet of Worms at Nürnberg, he had to progress cautiously. His initial concern was to preserve the Latinized liturgy so that instead of the choir performing the entire Office or Mass, the singing of metrical psalmody by the whole congregation could be encouraged. Gradually Luther began to remove many of the chants and choral songs, especially when he felt that the performance was what he termed 'a work', made in order to achieve God's grace: to him it seemed that congregational participation was far more appropriate because it elicited a response to God's mercy rather than promoted a quest to earn it. By 1526 he had already published the mass and order of service in German, and was increasingly encouraging the singing of hymns and psalms by the entire congregation. Probably the best known of his metrical psalms, written some time between 1527 and 1529, is *Ein Feste Burg ist unser Gott*, from Psalm 46. Even in the English translation (the one below is by F.H. Hedge [1853], with some minor revisions), the rhyme, rhythm and verse structure are clear; and as well as the implicit references to the political and ecclesial struggles in the first verse, we may note the 'Christianizing' of the psalm in the second:

Ein feste Burg ist unser Gott,	A mighty fortress is our God,
ein gute Wehr und Waffen.	A sword and shield victorious;
Er hilft uns frei aus aller Not,	He breaks the cruel oppressor's rod
die uns jetzt hat betroffen.	And wins salvation glorious.
Der altböse Feind	The old satanic foe
mit Ernst er's jetzt meint;	Has sworn to work us woe!
groß Macht und viel List	With craft and dreadful might
sein grausam Rüstung ist,	He arms himself to fight
auf Erd ist nicht seinsgleichen.	On earth he has no equal.

Mit unsrer Macht ist nichts getan,	No strength of ours can match his might!
wir sind gar bald verloren;	We would be lost, rejected.
es streit' für uns der rechte Mann,	But now a champion comes to fight,
den Gott hat selbst erkoren.	Whom God himself perfected.
Fragst du, wer der ist?	You ask who this may be?
Er heißt Jesus Christ,	The Lord of hosts is he!
der Herr Zebaoth,	Christ Jesus, mighty Lord,
und ist kein andrer Gott,	God's only Son, adored.
das Feld muß er behalten.	He holds the field victorious.

Singing 'the whole psalm' was the key issue here, eliciting understanding of the words of the entire prayer through community participation. This was why Luther encouraged not only the singing but also the preaching of entire psalms, rather than single verses, as happened in the Latin liturgy. (Other reformers took a more stringent line: *Ulrich Zwingli* (1484–1531) of Zurich, another reformer whose theological views often clashed with both Luther and Calvin, was a grammarian competent in Hebrew, Greek, Latin and German, yet he prevented his congregation from singing any of the psalms, lest they imbibed any Roman heresies in doing so. Psalms were restricted to preaching and recitation only.[4])

A somewhat different approach to the translation and use of the psalms in liturgy is found in Luther's younger contemporary, *John Calvin* (1509–64). Whereas Luther was a Saxon peasant whose father was a miner, Calvin was from the French middle class and his father was an attorney. Calvin was never ordained into the Catholic church; he was mainly educated in Paris, specializing in arts, philosophy and law. Unlike Luther (whom he never met), Calvin did not publish any vernacular translations of the Bible: his cousin, Peter Olivetan, a former Franciscan, was the first Protestant to publish a French translation in 1535. It seems that, unlike Luther, Calvin's 'conversion' from Catholicism to Protestantism was gradual, occurring some time between his training as a lawyer in Orléans in 1528, when he started to read the New Testament in Greek, and his commencement of theological study under the influence of his Greek tutor, Melchior Woldmar, in 1531. The decisive moment was his contribution to an All Saints Day address by the rector of the University of Paris, Nicholas Cop, which clearly aligned both of them to Reformation doctrine, forcing them to flee from Paris in 1533. Calvin sought protection in Basel, where his intellectual and teaching skills resulted in his being a focal point for the reformation cause in Switzerland. By 1536 he had begun to study Hebrew, had written the first draft of the *Institutes of Christian Religion*, and had moved on to Geneva, where he remained, with the exception of a brief 'exile'

---

[4] For works on Luther and psalmody, see C. Black (1985); *H. Bornkamm (1983)*; *P.N. Brooks (1983 [ed.])*; *R.G. Davies (1946)*; *J. Goldingay (1982)*; *D. MacCulloch (2003)*; *H.C. Oswald (1974)*; *J.S. Preus (1967, 1969)*; O.C. Rupprecht (1983); D.C. Steinmetz (*1979*, 1980); also U.F.W. Bauer at www.arts.ualberta.ca/JHS/Articles/article8.htm; for Luther's teaching on Psalm 46, see *P.N. Brooks (1997)*, pp. 3–14; and, for Luther's works, with a search capacity for referencing his citations of psalms, see www.ccel.org/l/luther.

in Strasbourg from 1538 to 1541, for the rest of his life, becoming a prominent leader of the Protestant movement in France and Switzerland from that base. Hence unlike Luther, who began his studies with the Psalms, Calvin's writings on psalmody really only commenced in Geneva, and intensified during his time in Strasbourg. But from 1538 onwards, no other biblical book took as much of his time and energy.

It is interesting to see how Calvin, a generation apart from Luther, approached psalmody in a more orderly, rational and pragmatic way. His love of the psalms was not the consequence of, and a reaction to, that Augustinian discipline which had inspired Luther, but was the result of a straightforward desire to nurture lay piety by '*sola scriptura*', which cause the words of the psalms served admirably. In Strasbourg Calvin encountered striking ways of appropriating the psalms for this purpose, for there Martin Bucer (very much under the influence of Lutheran Protestantism) had since 1524 been introducing metrical hymns and psalms, set to music, into the liturgy of his German-speaking congregation. Believing profoundly in congregational participation, Calvin could see how metrical psalmody promoted the laity's use of the psalms. By 1539 he had published his first collection of twenty-two metrical psalms, helped by Clément Marot, a French court poet: some six are attributed to Calvin himself. These versions, like Bucer's and Luther's, were paraphrases of the psalms into a metrical, rhyming version (in his case in French), and they were accompanied by both new and traditional easily memorable 'religious' tunes (some of German origin). Against the same background of debates about the abuse of indulgences as Luther, it is interesting to see how, like Luther's concern with the penitential psalms, those which comprised Calvin's first collection were almost entirely about penitence and forgiveness (Psalms 32, 51, 103 and 130 by Marot, and Psalms 25 and 36 by Calvin), in addition to others asking God's protection from enemies (Psalms 3, 46, 912, 114, 137 and 143), which also have similarities with Luther's translations of psalms such as Psalm 46.

Upon his rehabilitation in Geneva in 1541, Calvin sought to promote the use of psalmody further still, but with several constraints: whereas Bucer, like Luther, encouraged all kinds of texts and polyphonic melodies, both sacred and secular, Calvin determined to give exclusive priority to the psalms alone, to allow no other types of hymns, no organs, and no other musical instruments; singing had to be done in unison. The practice of 'lining out' comes from this time: the first line of a psalm was sung by the choirmaster, to be repeated by the congregation until it became familiar. This was in stark contrast to Catholic liturgical practices, where the psalms, sung by cantors and choirs in Latin plainchant, afforded the congregation little chance to participate. By 1543, Marot, who had also moved to Geneva to avoid persecution in France, had versified into French a further thirty-nine psalms, which were set to music by Louis Bourgeois. In spite of the initial strictures about singing in unison with no musical accompaniment, polyphonic singing was gradually introduced under the influence of Bourgeois, although Calvin always taught that unison was the purest form for worship in church. The psalms were composed to increasingly irregular metres (over one hundred in all) each of which attempted to correspond to the various moods of the psalms. For example, Psalm 51, as a confession for sin, was set in a dark lament-like metre, whilst Psalm 19, a hymn concerning God's provision in creation and in the law, was set in a brighter celebratory rhythm. These contrasted with the more conventional and sedate Latinate renditions, and gave them additional novelty. Their simplicity and directness meant that they could be easily memorized so that they could be sung not only in the churches, but also in homes and at work, and by women and children as well as by priests and leading members of the laity. (In spite of his strictures against secular music, Calvin did not disapprove of the 'sacred' being taken into the 'secular': it was the reverse of which he disapproved.)

Below is an example of the metrical versification of Psalm 46, the same psalm illustrated for Luther previously, in a later English imitation of the French form. Luther's version has nine lines, and both in the German and the English the metre is variable (8.7.8.7.6.6.6.6.7, which, it could be argued, added to the dramatic quality of the psalm). The metrical version below, following the line forms and metre of its French counterpart, is simpler; it has eight lines, and the clear metrical beat (9.9.8.8.9.9.8.8) changes only every two lines, with a refrain as the last two lines of each verse. It could be argued that Luther's version is more interesting and colourful, whilst the one associated with Calvin is more distinct and memorable.[5]

> God is our refuge and salvation,
> our present help in tribulation.
> We will not fear though earth may shake,
> for God will keep us mid the quake
> Mountains may fall into the ocean,
> but we will not fear such commotion.
> With us the Lord of Hosts shall dwell
> the mighty God of Israel.

Further expansions to the French edition of the 'Genevan Psalter' were made in 1551 and 1562, using texts by Théodore de Bèze, John Calvin's successor at Geneva, with the music of Claude Goudimel as an accompaniment. By 1562, all 150 psalms, set to at least 125 different tunes, had been published. Inspired by the traditions of Ambrose and Augustine, Calvin's Psalter was sung by the Genevan congregation within twenty-five weeks, allowing therefore for six or seven psalms a week. Twenty-seven thousand copies of the Geneva Psalter were printed in the first two years. Hence the practice spread beyond the church in Geneva: Protestant congregations, not only in England, but also across France, Italy, the Netherlands and Scotland sang to the same tunes and metrical forms but in their own language. Hence this restored what had progressively been lost in the public performance of psalmody since the initiatives of Ambrose and then Gregory some thousand years earlier – the recitation and enjoyment of the psalms through singing them in their

---

[5] The English version of Psalm 46 is by D.T. Koyzis, and this and musical version of many of the Psalms in the *Geneva Psalter* is to be found at genevanpsalter.redeemer.ca/psalm_texts.htm. See also www.smithcreekmusic.com/Hymnology/Metrical.Psalmody/French.metrical.psalmody.html.

vernacular, by the laity as well as by the clergy, by women and children as well as by men, outside church services as well as within them.

Given the reformers' passionate defence of the dictum of *sola scriptura*, and Calvin's insistence that only the psalms, and no non-scriptural hymns, should be used in worship, it is ironic that metrical psalmody familiarized the laity not so much with the texts of the psalms themselves as with paraphrases of them. In Geneva, this issue of seeming to 'dilute' the text of the psalms was in part countered by Calvin's voluminous production of sermons, lectures and commentaries, bringing the actual texts of the psalms before his congregation.

Twenty-eight of Calvin's sermons were published in French, usually using the Latin text rather than a vernacular version. It is significant that, like Luther, Calvin focused especially on Psalm 119: twenty-two sermons, all dating from 1554, are on this psalm, seeking to show the importance of God's mercy working through the law, but as a response to (rather than a prerequisite of) the Gospel. As far as lectures on the psalms are concerned, Calvin focused on this form nearer the end of his ministry, between 1552 and 1556, rather than at the very beginning of it, as did Luther; here one sees the sharp mind of the lawyer, and the linguistic skills of one versed in Hebrew, Greek and Latin.

It should be clear by now that Calvin was more of an inspiration for metrical psalmody rather than a great composer of it. His most significant personal contribution to psalmody is in his commentaries and exegetical works. These amount to some 2,400 in all; the five-volume commentary, first published in Latin in 1558, and in French in 1557, was almost twice the length of the 1559 edition of *The Institutes*. The Preface extols the Psalms above all other books in its teaching on 'the single liberality of God toward his Church, and of all his works'. The commentary in part emerged from Calvin's weekly discussion group on the Psalms, *Congrégations*, between 1555 and 1559. His systematic, orderly approach is evident in both structure and analysis. First, each introduction discusses the author, place, provenance, date and contents of the particular psalm. Then, after translating the text directly from the Hebrew (Calvin used the Hebraist Louis Budé and also consulted with Jewish scholars), he presents detailed grammatical and philological notes. After this follows the comment, which is in part doctrinal and theological, in part moral and practical, the latter tending to move from the moral life of David to the implications of the psalms in the life of Christ and the life of the church – 'to behold David, as in a mirror', Calvin states in his Preface.

The overall approach is thus pragmatic and historically orientated, with a reading of David as an example of faith. Calvin usually applied the model of the human David rather than that of David the prophet. For example, Psalm 23 is about what God achieved for David, and not (initially) David speaking prophetically about what Christ, as the Good Shepherd, did for us. This is clearly very different from Luther's more prophetic and Christocentric approach. In Calvin's work the Christianizing aspect is often absent and the practical concerns are to the fore. For example, Psalm 20, probably composed for the king before setting out to battle, is read both in terms of its ancient royal setting and as a prayer for all Christians to use when fighting for the kingdom of God. What attracted Calvin to identify so much with the life of David in the psalms were the parallels between David's life and his own, in the movement from obscurity to prominent leadership, and in his sufferings and afflictions which resulted from such elevation. (The fact that what might have been identifiable for Calvin in the life of David was not necessarily the same for the average members of his congregation does not seem to be duly noted in the commentary.) His pragmatic bias is expressed in the Preface: the psalms stir us up to 'perform' piety: they are 'the anatomy of the soul'.

This 'David-centred' approach allowed Calvin to read more freely those verses which were difficult to relate to Christ. These are mostly the same texts which in the earlier centuries Jews disputed with Christians, and it is here that Calvin's interpretation is less anti-Semitic than is Luther's, in that Calvin comments on the psalms firstly through an Old Testament lens, and only later through a New Testament one. Ps. 22:20 ('Deliver my soul from the sword, my life from the power of the dog!') is a good example; here Calvin points out that this could not primarily refer to Christ, for God did in fact give him up to death, whereas its application to David is appropriate on several occasions where he was spared death. Only secondarily does it refer to Christ, whom God ultimately redeemed from death through the resurrection. Hence its relevance for the believer is more through the life of David (for there may be many moments when we are spared death) than through the life of Christ (for none of us using the psalm can experience literally in this life victory over death through resurrection).

On other occasions Calvin starts with a Davidic-centred reading and then interprets David's experience as foreshadowing that of Christ: Ps. 18:35–8 is a good example, where David's sufferings are seen to anticipate or prefigure those of Christ; Psalms 2, 20 and 72 are read in a similar way, rather than in a more immediately Messianic mode. (Perhaps it was a more republican stance which impelled Calvin to read royal psalms such as 2, 18, 20 and 72 as less about a present and future king and more practically about David's life experiences.) This David-centred approach nevertheless gave Calvin the same problems with which Luther had to contend, concerning the nature of the faith of psalmists: if David's faith and experiences are so central, what difference does the Gospel really add to them? At this point Calvin has to introduce a more Christological and 'Messianic' argument, not unlike Luther's: David's (sacral) kingdom was a type, foreshadowing Christ's (messianic) kingdom, representing a physical promise of what Christ would bring about in spiritual terms, and the psalms are the vehicle for this hope.[6]

---

[6] For works on Calvin and psalmody, see *B.G. Armstrong (1998)*; A. Cabaniss (1985); M. Carbonnier-Burkard (1997); *R.G. Davies (1946)*; J.A. de Jong (1994); C. Eire (2004); *H.J. Forstman (1962)*; *P.T. Fuhrmann (1952)*; *C. Garside (1979)*; R.A. Hasler (1965); *H.-J. Kraus (1977)*; S. Jones (2004); J.L. Mays (1988; 1990); B. Pitkin (1993); *D.L. Puckett (1995)*; W.S. Reid (1971); S.H. Russell (1968); J.T. VanderWilt (1995); J.D. Witvliet (1997). For Calvin's own works on psalmody, see E Tr J. Anderson (1948–49) and J. Dillenberger (1975 [ed.]) and www.ccel.org/ccel/calvin/calcom08.html; www.ccel.org/ccel/calvin/calcom09.html; www.ccel.org/ccel/calvin/calcom10.html; www.ccel.org/ccel/calvin/calcom11.html; www.ccel.org/ccel/calvin/calcom12.html.

Calvin's huge commentary on the psalms, translated into English by Arthur Golding in 1571, was amongst the last major works of its kind for some two centuries, eclipsing to a large extent other psalm commentaries which had been published before it (for example, Reuchlin's German commentary on the seven penitential psalms in 1512; Bucer's commentary on selected psalms in 1526; and the commentaries of the Catholics Cajetan [1530] and Pellican [1532] and Münster [1534–35]). Later examples after Calvin, also less well known, include Protestant works such as Selnecker (1581), Hugo Grotius (1645) and, from England, Henry Hammond (1659) – the latter two combining literal and grammatical readings with the help of Jewish scholarship – as well as Gesner (1609) and Amryaldus (1662). Catholic commentaries include those of Agellius (1606), Corderius (1643) and Hulsius (1650) as well as a pioneering work known as the *Biblia Maxima*, completed in France by *John de la Haye* in 1660, of which Volume VI is on the psalms, which is a digest of earlier Catholic literal and grammatical exegesis, from the scholastic period onwards, summarizing contributions and creating a further Gloss by referring to earlier adaptations of the texts and versions.

Liturgy, Homily and Translation in England and Scotland

Translation brings with it a new kind of democratization, in that anyone who can read (or hear) and then memorize a psalm may now creatively use it. But it also introduces diffusion, in that whereas Greek or Latin versions, despite their local variations, gave a sense of continuity throughout the churches East and West, vernacular versions required a more specific appropriation to their own linguistic culture. One has only to compare the reception of local translations of psalmody in more Catholic Portugal and Spain with that in the more Protestant churches in the Netherlands and Germany, or metrical psalmody in Switzerland and in France with the various versions in England and Scotland, to see how impossible it is to talk any longer in terms of a common practice of psalmody in liturgy.

Liturgy

Returning to England, it is clear that here, as on the Continent, several different versions of psalmody were beginning to develop. The fortunes of the *Vulgate* waxed and waned, both in public and in private, returning briefly to its earlier status during Mary's reign. The fortunes of *Coverdale's Psalter*, included in the *Book of Common Prayer (BCP)* in 1549, nevertheless also waxed and waned until the beginning of the reign of Elizabeth in 1559, when it became an important resource for public recitation. In 1549 Robert Crowley's *Psalms* popularized four-part harmonies to selected psalms; by contrast, in 1550 John Marbeck's *Booke of Common Praier* reinstated simple Gregorian plainsong-like tunes for psalmody. At the other end of the spectrum, by the 1540s metrical psalmody – brought initially to England by Dutch Protestants fleeing persecution – was also beginning its appeal within the English churches. Whether in plainsong, harmony, singing in metrical form, or reading and recitation, the psalms played a significant part within a climate of liturgical change.

Reference has already been made to two *prose versions* of the psalms which were published in the 1530s: Matthew's Bible, and the Great Bible. Other significant editions of the entire Bible were to follow, the first of which was the *Geneva Bible*. Geneva in the mid-sixteenth century was undoubtedly the centre for Bible translation. Inspired by the success elsewhere of Luther's 1534 edition and Zwingli's 1527–29 German editions, either entire Bibles or at least New Testaments were published in Italian (1555), French (22 editions by the end of the 1550s), Spanish (1556–57), Greek (1551) and Latin (1556, 1567). Miles Coverdale, driven into exile by anti-Protestant policies after Mary Tudor became Queen of England in 1553, along with other Protestants such as John Foxe (a reformer of the Scottish church) and William Whittingham (who became Calvin's brother-in-law), settled in Geneva, where, protected by the civic authorities, he and they were able to produce another even more Protestant English Bible which needed the permission of neither England nor Rome. The *Geneva Bible* contained a prose version of Psalms, using, like other Old Testament books, both the Hebrew (aided by Christopher Goodman) and Greek (mainly Whittingham's work), hence being the first public English version of the psalms to be translated entirely from the Greek and Hebrew. This was the first English edition to maintain verse divisions, and to use italics for words which were not originally in the Hebrew. The New Testament was produced in 1557, in many respects a revised and corrected edition of Tyndale's 1534 version, whilst the Old Testament with Preface was published in 1560. After the death of Mary in 1558 and the accession of Elizabeth in 1559, the Geneva Bible was printed and disseminated in England (with a suitable laudatory dedication to Elizabeth, drawing parallels between the queen and king David). It maintained many anti-Catholic marginal annotations, not dissimilar from glosses, and by 1560 some ten editions had appeared.

By 1568 the *Bishops' Bible* was produced, a compromise edition of the Great Bible and the Geneva Bible, but this never really gained acceptance, and certainly not privately. After the death in 1575 of its editor, Archbishop Parker, the Geneva Bible flourished all the more, and for some eighty years dominated the field. This was the Bible of Shakespeare, of Oliver Cromwell and the Puritans: even the King James version of 1611 (which used it as a resource for translation) could not immediately overtake its popularity and over 100 editions had been made by the end of Elizabeth's forty-five-year reign. More than anything, it was its anti-Catholic stance which gave it immediate popularity (through the Calvinist Reformer, John Knox).

The Geneva Bible was popular amongst the reformers because of its Calvinistic origins. But in spite of its high esteem, by the beginning of the seventeenth century new moves were made to supersede it: the impetus for creating the *King James Bible* in 1611 (the 'Authorized Version', or AV, but from now on to be termed the *KJB*) was as much political as theological. James I stated at the 1604 conference at Hampton that, of all the Bibles translated into English before his time, he considered the Geneva Bible to be the worst – a prejudice influenced more by the Republican commentary in the notes of the Geneva Bible than by its accuracy or its anti-Catholic tendencies. The result was that in 1604, scholars of Oxford and Cambridge, with good knowledge of both Hebrew and Greek, as well as other church dignitaries with good knowledge of the Latin and literary English of their day, were presented to the Privy Council and divided into six companies (two to sit at Oxford, two at Cambridge, two at Westminster) with some eight translators in each, to divide the Bible into six portions and produce a translation 'fit for the king ... which was neither republican in sympathy, nor puritan-biased, nor catholic'. One of the Cambridge Committees was responsible for the section from 1 Chronicles to Ecclesiastes (i.e. including Psalms). Two of the Cambridge scholars who were part of this company died early, before its completion; for whatever reasons, this section is considered to be the least fluent and distinguished of the six, with the possible exception of Job and Psalms. But three years were spent on the translation, using, in addition to the Hebrew, Greek and Latin sources (which at that time were more modest than the translators would have liked), Tyndale's version (which was an enormous influence) and, perhaps surprisingly, the Geneva Bible.

Another publication contemporary with the *KJB* was the *Douai Rheims* version of 1609, a translation by English Catholics who had had to flee to Douai (and after some time, to Rheims) from where, over some fifty years, they produced their own English version, as part of the Counter Reformation. This translation was almost entirely dependent upon the Vulgate. As far as Psalms is concerned, it retains a prose form and its style has several Latinized expressions. For example, Ps. 4:9–10 reads: 'In peace in the self same I will sleep, and I will rest: For thou, O Lord, singularly hast settled me in hope'. The translation was never really successful: only one extra edition was made before the end of the seventeenth century.

As for the *KJB*, a further three years were spent on the revision and marginal references. Accuracy, 'middle level English' and theological parity for all parties were the agreed criteria throughout. The following examples contrast part of Psalm 1 taken from the *Geneva Bible*, the *KJB* and the *Douai Rheims* version: they illustrate how the style of the *KJB* is crisper, and the parallelism of the Hebrew is better preserved; the *KJB* also took more care in the translations of Hebrew terms, which in this instance were more clearly theological than political ('ungodly' for 'wicked'; 'congregation' for 'council' or 'assembly').[7]

Geneva Bible
1. Blessed is the man that doeth not walk in the counsel of the wicked, nor stand in the way of sinners, nor sit in ye seat of the scornful: ...
3. For he shall be like a tree planted by the rivers of waters, that will bring forth her fruit in due season: whose leaf shall not fade: so whatsoever he shall do, shall prosper.

---

[7] On prose translations of the psalms, see *R.H. Bainton (1970)*; G.W.H. Lampe (1969); and on the Geneva Bible, see www.genevabible.org/Geneva.html.

King James Bible
1. Blessed is the man that walketh not in the counsel of the ungodly, nor standeth in the way of sinners, nor sitteth in the seat of the scornful. ...
3. And he shall be like a tree planted by the rivers of water, that bringeth forth his fruit in his season; his leaf also shall not wither; and whatsoever he doeth shall prosper.

Douai Rheims
1. Blessed is the man who hath not walked in the counsel of the ungodly, nor stood in the way of sinners, not sat in the chair of pestilence; ...
3. And he shall be like a tree which is planted near the running waters, which shall bring forth its fruit, in due season. And his leaf shall not fall off: and all whatsoever he shall do shall prosper.

Very different renderings of psalmody were provided by *English metrical versions*, which took from their French and German counterparts not only the principles of paraphrase, metre and rhyme, but also some of the tunes which regulated the form and made for easy memorization. Even Coverdale experimented with this genre, composing thirteen metrical psalms in English as early as 1535 in a version entitled *Goostly Psalmes and Spirituall Songs*, which was rejected by Henry VIII (and indeed copies of it were symbolically burnt at Paul's Cross in 1546) in favour of his prose-rhythm version. The most popular metre was the ballad form (rhyming lines of fourteen syllables, printed in couplets of eight and six) because there was quite a range of tunes which could fit them. Amongst the better known of these are Bourgeois' Old 100th, originally set to Psalm 100, but in the English metrical form more commonly used with the doxology 'Praise God from whom all blessings flow'; also familiar are the Old 113th, for 'I'll praise my maker while I've breath'; and the Old 134th, for 'Stand up and bless the Lord'. Metrical psalmody became increasingly popular amongst the dissenters and nonconformists in England; although it was adopted in some parish churches, it was less used because the emphasis on outward form (in terms of metre and rhyme) over content (in terms of an accurate rendering of the original) allowed for too much poetic licence in the theological and social comment.

Of the metrical versions in English in circulation after the death of Henry, the most well known is a version by Thomas Sternhold and John Hopkins, called *The Whole Book of Psalms*, published in 1549 as a courtly edition which was designed for private prayer. It was dedicated to Edward VI, referring to the fact that the king enjoyed this new form of psalmody: it actually contained only forty-four psalms, Sternhold having contributed some thirty-seven, dying before the collection could be completed. It was suppressed during the reign of Mary Tudor, but was widely used in Geneva, where it was revised and republished four times. The first Geneva edition was in 1556, to which Whittingham contributed a further nine psalms. Each psalm was now set to music, with a mix of French, German and English tunes, and the collection became used in public singing. The third version in 1561 contained a further twenty-five psalms by the Scottish churchman William Kethe, which were later included in *The Scottish Psalter* of 1650.

By 1562 John Daye had published an entire metrical Psalter in England, including in it some of the newly composed psalms from Geneva and from Dutch Protestant churches, as well as compositions from *The Whole Book of Psalms*. This was the first complete English version of metrical psalmody set to music, and it became known first as *The Anglo-Geneva Psalter*, but eventually simply as *Sternhold and Hopkins*. The Preface to the 1567 version stated that it was 'newly set forth and allowed to be song in all churches, of all the people together, before and after morning and evening prayer: as also before and after the sermon, and moreover in private houses, for their godly solace and comfort, laying aparte all ungodly songes and ballardes, which tend onely to the nourishyng of vice, and corrupting of youth'.

By 1600 this Psalter had gone through seventy-eight editions, and was given royal approval to be used in all churches, chapels and congregations in the land. Despite the many alternative metrical versions, it became known as the 'old version', and was the most popular until the 'new version' of Tate and Brady in 1696. Nevertheless, although some versions were published bound into prayer books, they were not universally acceptable; as well as prose versions such as the Geneva Bible, the older Latin plainsong and Coverdale's Psalter were obvious alternatives. Below is a comparison of four versions of Psalm 23, firstly from Coverdale, then the *Geneva Bible*, and then from Sternhold and Whittingham.

Coverdale (the heading, still in Latin, is *Dominus regit me*)
1. The Lord is my shepherd: therefore can I lack nothing.
2. He shall feed me in a green pasture: and lead me forth beside the waters of comfort.
3. He shall convert my soul: and bring me forth in the paths of righteousness, for his Name's sake.

The Geneva Bible
1. A Psalm of David. The Lord is my shepherd, I shall not want. 2. He maketh me to rest in green pasture, and leadeth me by the still waters. 3. He restoreth my soul, and leadeth me in the paths of righteousness for his Name's sake.

Sternhold's version
1 My Shepherd is the living Lord,
nothing therefore I need:
In pastures fair, near pleasant streams,
he setteth me to feed.
2 He shall convert and glad my soul,
and bring my mind in frame
To walk in paths of righteousness
for his most holy Name.

Whittingham's version
1 The Lord is only my support,
and he that doth me feed;
How can I then lack any thing,
whereof I stand in need?
2 In pastures green he feedeth me,
where I do safely lie,
And after leads me to the streams
which run most pleasantly.
3 And when I find myself near lost,
then doth he me home take,
conducting me in his right paths,
e'en for his own Name's sake.

Coverdale's version certainly has more rhythm, and preserves more faithfully the 'parallelism' in the Hebrew text, but it has neither metre nor rhyme. The Geneva Bible attempts neither rhythm, metre nor rhyme, being a more literal and precise translation. Sternhold's and Whittingham's versions have a more popular appeal; although less faithful to the Hebrew, they establish the metrical patterns which became so dominant in later English psalmody: the 'iambic heptameter', or the 8.6.8.6. common metre [CM], is used in both versions here (although they also frequently used the 6.6.8.6. short metre and the 8.8.8.8. long metre), allowing for easy memorization and repetition.

Of other rival metrical psalters, four from England are best known. An early one is *Archbishop Matthew Parker's* translation, published by John Daye in 1567, called *The Whole Psalter translated into English Metre*. Originally intended for private rather than pubic use, its significance was its harmonization of well-known melodies used for the metrical psalms, eight of which, in four parts, were the work of the court musician Thomas Tallis (whose works will be discussed later). The tunes used the eight *modes developed by musical theorists in the Middle Ages, each representing eight different musical types – meek, sad, angry, fawning, delighting, lamenting, robust, gentle – for which the scale and pace of music provided appropriate accompaniment.

Another, very different, Psalter is by *George Wither* (1588–1667), a Parliamentarian who, despite fighting in Cromwell's army in the Civil War, nevertheless dedicated his 1619 *Preparation to the Psalter* to Prince Charles, son of James I, and his 1632 *Psalmes of David* to Princess Elizabeth. He published his *Canonical Hymns and Spiritual Songs* in 1623 and obtained a royal patent compelling printers to produce it for the next fifty-one years as part of every copy of the *Psalm Book in Metre*. Wither's sources were certainly not the original languages, but rather a composite of the various several English versions of the day. He considered the Sternhold and Hopkins version too barren and superficial, and yet was similarly concerned to preserve the brevity and simplicity of the Psalter so that it could be more easily memorized and used. A comparison of Ps. 27:1 shows the differences between the versions. Sternhold and Hopkins is longer, and perhaps more crude, but there are many similarities in the style in spite of the different rhythm (Withers is 8.8.8.8; Sternhold and Hopkins is 8.6.8.6).

Wither's version
God is my light, my health, mine aid,
My life's defence: whom should I fear?
When wicked foes my death assayed,
They tripped and fell, and ruined were.

Sternhold and Hopkins' version
The Lord is both my health and light,
shall man make me dismayed?
Since God doth give me strength and might,
why should I be afraid?
While that my foes with all their strength
began with me to brawl,
Thinking to eat me up, at length
themselves have caught the fall.

Another metrical version was published by George Sandys, son of the Archbishop of York; Sandys was an inveterate traveller, an ardent Royalist, and belonged for some time to a great artistic entourage at Great Tew. His *Paraphrase upon the Psalmes of David* was published during this period, in 1636. Unlike Wither, Sandys' version was intentionally more aesthetic and elegant, experimenting with a variety of metres; and it was intended as much for private prayer as for public liturgy. (It was the version used by Charles I whilst awaiting execution.) Sandys published his Psalter with new tunes to show off the variable metre. The composer was Henry Lawes of the Chapel Royal, making this a version for a more refined liturgical taste. Psalm 1, with an implicit pun on the name of its composer, reads:

> That man is truly blest, who never strayes
> By false advice, nor walks in Sinners wayes;
> Nor sits infected with their scornful pride,
> Who God contemne, and Pietie deride.
> But wholly fixeth his sincere delight
> On heavenly Lawes; those studies day and night.

Psalmes of David From the New translation of the Bible Turned into Meter (1651) was a version by Henry King, Bishop of Chichester, and was a reaction to the overly elegant style of Sandys. His version was intended as yet another improvement on Sternhold and Hopkins. The 8.6.8.6 metre reflects this, as does the inclusion of popular tunes from that version. The only real innovation was the frequent attempt at an *aabb* rhyming scheme, which, given the metrical constraints, made the flow of sense somewhat unnatural. Compare King's version of Psalm 1 with that of Sandys given earlier:

> The man is blest whose feet not tread
> By wicked counsailes led:
> Nor stands in that perverted way,
> In which the Sinners stray;
> Nor joynes himselfe unto the chaire
> Where Scorners seated are;
> But in God's Law both dayes and nights
> To meditate delights.

Although none of these publications supplanted Sternhold and Hopkins, by the end of the seventeenth century that version had clearly become outdated by comparison with so many other versions which were seen to be more aesthetically pleasing. John Wilmot (1647–80), Earl of Rochester, wrote:

> Sternhold and Hopkins had great qualms
> When they translated David's psalms
> To make the heart full glad;

> But had it been poor David's fate
> To hear thee sing, and them translate
> By God! 'twould have made him mad.

Sternhold and Hopkins was replaced in 1696 by what became known as the 'new version', the compilation of the Poet Laureate Nahum Tate and Nicholas Brady, chaplain to William and Mary, and later, to Queen Anne. This version experimented with metres: some ten psalms are in an unusual 8.8.8 metre, and forty others use longer and more complex metres than those of the 'old version'. Furthermore, like *The Scottish Psalter* (see below), it claimed to be closer in translation and poetic form to the Hebrew. The new version later became known as a 'Whig' Psalter, because of its occasional slights on the monarchy; nevertheless, its overall appeal to popular piety and its memorable use of metrical forms resulted in Tate and Brady still being part of hymnody today. The best example is probably Psalm 34: 'Through all the changing scenes of life, in trouble and in joy / The praises of my God shall still my heart and tongue employ'. To gain a comparison with versions offered earlier, below is part of Psalm 23:

> 1. The Lord himself, the mighty Lord,
> Vouchsafes to be my guide;
> The shepherd, by whose constant care
> My wants are all supplied.
>
> 2. In tender grass he makes me feed
> and gently there respose;
> Then leads me to cool shades, and where
> Refreshing water flows.

Turning briefly to Scotland, metrical psalmody in Congregationalist and Presbyterian churches there was as popular as in Geneva. John Knox returned thence to Edinburgh in 1559, where Genevan metrical psalms were revised and published in 1564 as the *Book of Common Order*: it contained not only all the psalms in metrical form, but also metrical translations of canticles such as the *Nunc Dimittis* and *Magnificat*, as well as a rendering of the Apostles' Creed. By 1644, some seventy editions had been published; in the earliest editions provisions made for singing included over forty popular Genevan tunes, far more than in the English versions, but, until 1635, following Calvinistic practice, only singing in unison was allowed. Eventually, by 1650, the General Assembly of the Church of Scotland approved a revised version, called *The Scottish Psalter*. This was essentially the work of one Francis Rous, whose work had been thoroughly examined by a committee over a six-year period for its accuracy of translation from the Hebrew, and rendering of metre and rhyme. This scrutiny stood the test of time: with the exception of some modernization of spelling, *The Scottish Psalter* is still sung today, and its version of Psalm 23 is amongst the best known amongst all types of English-speaking Christians:

> 1 The Lord's my shepherd, I'll not want.
> 2 He makes me down to lie

> In pastures green: he leadeth me
> the quiet waters by.[8]

In seventeenth-century England, it was Coverdale's psalms which were the most commonly used in Anglican liturgy. The *Book of Common Prayer* underwent a controversial revision by Archbishop Laud in 1637 for the Scottish Episcopal Church under the authority of Charles I, but the most significant revision came in 1662 after the restoration of the monarchy. The Communion Service still followed the order of the old Missal, and although more unscriptural parts were cut out, a Gradual Psalm was still appointed for daily use. The reduction of eight offices to just morning and evening prayer meant it became more difficult to work through the entire Psalter once every week or fortnight; so one solution was now to take a complete psalm for each daily service and allot a number of psalms to particular weeks. (The only exception was Psalm 119, to be divided into four or five portions.) In the first week, Psalms 1–37 were to be used; in week 2, Psalms 38–74; in week 3, Psalms 75–106; in week 4, Psalms 107–38; and for the remaining days of week 5, Psalms 139–50. *Proper psalms included the following: for Christmas Day, Psalms 19, 45, 85, 89, 110, 132; for Ash Wednesday, Psalms 6, 32, 38, 102, 130, 143; for Good Friday, Psalms 22, 40, 54, 69, 88; for Easter Day, Psalms 2, 57, 111, 113, 114, 118; for Ascension Day, Psalms 8, 15, 21, 24, 47, 108; for Whitsunday, Psalms 48, 68, 104, 145. (This list of *proper psalms explains the prominence of some psalms in musical compositions, in that the composers were supposed to set their music to psalms appropriate for particular festive occasions, especially Christmas and Easter.) Usually the psalms were simply recited by the congregation as a whole, or chanted by a choir, using different forms of plainsong, or sung by the congregation in a form of 'Anglican plainchant', working on a basic system of ten notes, with four notes sustained in the first part of the line, and six notes in the latter part. Furthermore, versicles and responses and collects, citing or alluding to the language of psalmody, were used throughout the service, the best example being the uses of Pss. 51:15 ('O Lord, open my lips, and my mouth will declare your praise') and 70:1 ('Be pleased, O God, to deliver me. O Lord, make haste to help me!') at the beginning of both morning and evening prayer. In all this variation Coverdale's version, with its great flexibility, was mainly adapted. Metrical psalms were also used, with the advantage that congregations could participate more easily, and their place would be before and after the sermon.

There are some parallels in the *Catholic revisions* to liturgy in the sixteenth century. Against the background of the decay in the parish and cathedral offices described in the previous chapter, the Catholic church set about some reform of

---

[8] On the *Geneva Psalter*, see W.S. Pratt (1933); on Tate and Brady's version, see www.cgmusic.com/workshop/newver_frame.htm; on Scottish psalmody, see P. Millar (1949) and www.smithcreekmusic.com/Hymnology/Metrical.Psalmody/Scottish.psalmody.html; on Wither, Sandys and King, see H. Hamlin (2004), pp. 51–84; for Wither's psalms, see L. Wieder (1995) on Psalms 11, 27, 48 and 142; on Wither's Psalter, see J. Doelman (1993). For the John Wilmot quotation, see *D.M. Vieth (2002 [ed.]), pp. 22–3.*

its daily offices, but using the Gallican Psalter or Vulgate Psalms instead of, for example, Coverdale, or metrical psalms, or the Psalms in the Great Bible. Revisions of the Breviary began as early as 1523–4 under Pope Clement VII, only to be distracted by the sack of Rome by Charles V in 1527. But by 1535, a revision undertaken by the Spanish cardinal Quiñones was published, and its popularity was evidenced in that eleven further printings occurred within a year. The various councils of Trent (1545–7, 1551–2, and especially 1562–3) attempted to keep the process of Catholic reform alive, and by 1568, under Pope Pius V, a revised version of the Breviary was finally approved, and this then lasted some three hundred years (until further reforms and the *Divinu Afflatu* Bull of Pius X in 1911).

The 1568 *Roman Breviary* was not as radical as Cranmer's 1549 version had been: although it pruned the offices dramatically, it still maintained the traditional Hours of Prayer, taking three psalms sequentially through each of the eight Hours, day by day, as before, so that the Psalter was to be read during the course of a week, rather than a month, as in the Anglican liturgy. This was possible only because the *Roman Breviary* was intended more for recitation by the clergy than for lay use: it was essentially a means of preserving the Benedictine and other monastic traditions. The 1568 edition prescribed several different psalms from the 1535 revision by Quiñones, and of course there were differences in local use, but the continuity in the prescription is clearly evident.

This change in Catholic liturgy also established for some further three hundred years the use of Latin as the unifying medium of worship in general and psalmody in particular. But as far as psalmody is concerned, there is a continuity of form (though not of language) between Catholic and Anglican usage, in that psalms were used in both traditions for the Introit (either an entire psalm, or a psalm using one of its verses as an antiphon and the rest of the psalm recited, or sung by a choir, around it), and the Gradual Psalm, used with the Alleluia and *Tract between the lessons, was also an established tradition. For the Offertory and Communion, versicles from psalms were used in both traditions, often antiphonally.

The key difference was that in Catholic liturgy congregational recitation and chanting of psalms in the vernacular, and the singing of metrical psalmody, was seen not only as bad practice, but also deficient in the refusal to take seriously the authority of the Vulgate. After the first Council of Trent in 1545, the use of some vernacular in the Mass was in fact permitted, but it was restricted to the Gospel and the sermon; the psalms were still to be offered in Latin, usually with choir, orchestra and trained soloists, and the most a Catholic congregation could use of vernacular psalms would be in short extracts, for example at the *introit and the offertory. English Catholics in the early seventeenth century could of course read the Psalms in the Douai-Rheims version (1609: this was revised by Calloner in 1750) – but this was for private reading, and rarely for public liturgy.[9]

---

[9] On the psalms and liturgy in the sixteenth and seventeenth centuries, see D. Baker and J. Welsby (1993); R. Box (1996); P.F. Bradshaw and L.A. Hoffman (1991a [eds.]); F. Cabrol (1934); *S.J.P. van Dijk (1969)*; W.L. Holladay (1993), pp.191–237; C. Jones, G. Wainwright and E. Yarnold (1978); J.A. Lamb (1962); M.H. Shepherd (1976); R. Taft (1986, 2004); and N. Wallwork (1977).

Homily

We now turn to the didactic use of the psalms, much of which is connected with liturgy. The genre of homilies on the psalms (for which Calvin is so famed) becomes increasingly vast and diffuse, so we shall focus on just one innovatory aspect of it – one whose antecedents go back to Lydgate and the Lollards – namely the political reading of the psalms. This is first seen through the use of marginal and interlinear glosses; in some ways the notes made by Henry VIII in his own version of the Psalter, justifying through psalm verses the *dissolution of the monasteries, belong to this genre, as also do those of James I, which reveal his distaste for the Geneva Bible. A different example is found in the paraphrases on the psalms by Henry Howard, Earl of Surrey, a Christian in the tradition of both Wycliffe and Tyndale, beheaded for political treason in 1547, whose glosses on the psalms of the innocent sufferer reflect the same indignant outrage against the monarch as did the Lollards against their king some two hundred years earlier.

But the most pervasive political appropriation is through the medium of metrical psalmody: being paraphrases, ideological concerns can be read into the text to a greater degree. For example, in the Scottish Civil War of 1559–67, metrical psalmody was used as battle hymnody by the Parliamentary armies. Psalm 46 was popular, especially in its form in the Scottish Metrical Psalter, produced by John Knox shortly after the founding of the Church of Scotland in 1560. Selections of the psalm, taken here from the Sternhold and Hopkins (and later Whittingham) version, illustrate the contemporary concerns, similar to the way that Martin Luther and John Calvin used the psalm previously:

1 The Lord is our defense and aid,
the strength whereby we stand;
When we with woe are much dismayed
he is our help at hand ...

9 By him all wars are hushed and gone,
though countries did conspire;
Their bows and spears he brake each one,
their chariots burnt with fire.

10 Be still therefore, and know that I
am God, and therefore will
Among the heathen people be
highly exalted still.

11 The Lord of hosts doth us defend,
he is our strength and tow'r;
On Jacob's God we do depend,
and on his mighty pow'r.

Similarly, on the Continent, in the *Wars of Religion from 1562 onwards, the Huguenot armies in France sang the psalms in polyphonic form, as a means of establishing unity and identity in the face of Catholic opposition. This was part of the Calvinist attempt to take over the governments in anti-Reformation countries – an attempt which almost succeeded in France, and did succeed in Holland and Scotland. (The psalms were never used as battle hymns in this way in England, possibly because Reformers never had to face Catholic armies in this way.) A whole new range of hitherto less used psalms – not only Psalm 46 but also Psalms 24, 68, 91, 118 and 124 – came into favour during these times. These were the psalms whose references to God's victory over his people's enemies, and God's fighting with his people's armies, were interpreted in a literal contemporary sense. Ps. 68:1 is a good example: 'Let God rise up, let his enemies be scattered'. This was sung in its French metrical form by the persecuted Huguenots, who called it their 'Song of Battles', believing that when they sang it, the enemy knew their military fervour. The Scottish Psalter of 1650, a close relative of the Geneva version, captures the mood of this psalm:

> 1 Let God arise, and scatterèd
> let all his en'mies be;
> And let all those that do him hate
> before his presence flee.
> 2 As smoke is driv'n, so drive thou them;
> as fire melts wax away,
> Before God's face let wicked men
> so perish and decay.

Other examples abound. Ps. 118:1 ('O give thanks to the Lord, for he is good; his steadfast love endures for ever!') was sung by the forces of Henry of Navarre before the Battle of Coutras in 1587; Ps. 124:1 ('If it had not been the Lord who was on our side, let Israel now say') was sung in Marot's version by the people of Orléans when the Prince de Condé arrived at the beginning of the Civil War in Orléans in April 1562, with the refrain changed to '… Let Orléans now say'; Ps. 37:12 ('The wicked plot against the righteous, and gnash their teeth at him') was sung by the armies of William of Orange in 1568 against the forces of Philip of Spain. Other examples include portions of Pss. 2:8–9 and 149:7–9 (concerning the breaking of nations with a rod of iron, and the binding of kings in fetters and chains) and Ps. 58:1 ('Do you decree what is right, you mighty lords?') which were used as a critique of the monarchy. Each was sung in unison, in metrical rhyming form: they are but a few of the many examples of what became widespread popular practice amongst Calvinist forces throughout the sixteenth century.

The same custom was in evidence in the Civil War in England a century or so later. Although Cromwell privately used the Geneva Bible, between 1641 and 1649 he nevertheless ensured that all his forces possessed copies of the Sternhold and Hopkins version of the psalms, and popularized them in the manner of the Huguenots. Thus, for example, at the Battle of Marston Moor in 1644, when an allied army of Parliamentary and Scottish troops led by Sir Thomas Fairfax and Lord Manchester forced the Royalists to surrender, Cromwell applied Ps. 83:11–18 to the victory of the Parliamentary forces. Parts of this, from *Sternhold and Hopkins*, are offered below:

> 11 Make them now and their lords appear
> like Zeb and Oreb then;
> As Zebu and Zalmana were,
> the kings of Midian:
>
> 12 Who said, let us throughout the land,
> in all the coasts abroad,
> Possess and take into our hand
> the fair houses of God.

13 Turn them, O God, with storms so fast,
as wheels that have no stay;
Or like the chaff which men do cast
with wind to fly away …

16 Lord, bring them all, I thee desire,
to such rebuke and shame,
That it may cause them to enquire,
and learn to seek thy Name:

17 And let them daily more and more
to shame and slander fall,
And in rebuke and obloquy
confound and sink them all;

18 That they may know and understand
thou art the God most high
And that thou dost with mighty hand
the world rule constantly.

The practice continued into the Commonwealth period: in 1650, when the Presbyterian Scots invited the exiled Charles II to be their new king and the Scottish army was routed at the Battle of Dunbar, Ps. 117 was sung as a victory song as Cromwell entered Edinburgh:

1 O All ye nations of the world,
praise ye the Lord always;
And all ye people every where
set forth his noble praise:

2 For great his kindness is to us,
his truth doth not decay;
Wherefore praise ye the Lord our God,
praise ye the Lord always.

An interesting example of a royalist reading of the psalms in England is *Edward Hyde*, exiled to Jersey in the late 1640s, who began there his *Contemplations and Reflections upon the Psalms of David, Applying those Devotions to the Troubles of the Times*. Hyde, in reaction to the Cromwellian use of psalmody, argued that if one was to read the psalms politically this should be done from a historical perspective, assuming they applied primarily to David's own times, and that the most appropriate contemporary use of them was as personal and private devotion.

The following discussion, on the use of psalms in America, begins in the seventeenth century but continues well into the mid-eighteenth century, when metrical psalmody had developed into hymns which were little more than very loose paraphrases of a number of psalms. Thus what follows belongs partly to this chapter and partly to the next, but for the sake of continuity we shall deal with the whole topic here.

The *Jamestown settlers of 1607 used Sternhold and Hopkins metrical psalms, in part a result of their Puritan aversion to Coverdale's Psalter. The *Pilgrim Fathers who landed in Plymouth, Massachusetts in 1620 also used metrical psalmody, preferring, however, the 1612 *Book of Psalms* by Henry Ainsworth, a grammarian with good knowledge of Hebrew, whose works (including a commentary on the Psalms in 1626) included consultations with rabbis. His metrical psalms, like the Scottish Psalter, used tunes original to the French version of the Geneva Psalter, published earlier for the congregations in Amsterdam; as well as Genevan tunes, there were also some thirty-nine tunes of English origin, and Dutch melodies as well. The first Psalter to be written and printed in America itself was compiled in 1640 by the group of Puritans who had settled around Boston in the Massachusetts Bay Colony; called *The Whole Book of Psalmes Faithfully Translated into English Metre*, it became known as the *Bay Psalm Book*. It owed much to the work of John Cotton, but its Genevan roots did not allow for anything other than singing in unison, using the tunes from Thomas Ravencroft's Psalter of 1621. Two further versions, which placed theological correctness above aesthetic considerations, followed in 1647 and 1651: these became known as the *New England Psalm Book*.

The real influence behind this was actually an English hymn-writer, *Isaac Watts* (1674–1748). His first hymn based on the psalms was the result of a challenge by his father (a Dissenter, who had spent time in Southampton Gaol for his non-conformist beliefs) that he would be unable to improve upon the metrical psalmody of Tate and Brady or the prose psalmody of Coverdale. The result was 'A Short Essay Toward the Improvement of Psalmody' published in 1707, where Watts made it clear that he followed more the contemporizing hymnic tradition of Luther than the less flexible metrical tradition of Calvin. By 1719 *Psalms of David Imitated in the Language of the New Testament* had been published. Its intention was 'to make David speak the common sense and language of a Christian' – to imitate, but not to copy, ancient writings. Watts still wrote in metre (and most of his 138 hymns based on the psalms were produced in the familiar forms of common metre [8.6.8.6], short metre [6.6.8.6] and long metre [8.8.8.8]).

Many of Watts' 'psalmic hymns' are more explicitly Christian. The best known include a setting based upon Psalm 72 ('Give the king your justice, O God, and your righteousness to a king's son … May he live while the sun endures, and as long as the moon, throughout all generations') for which the first verse of Watts' hymns runs:

> Jesus shall reign where'er the sun
> Doth his successive journeys run.
> His kingdom stretch from shore to shore
> Till moons shall wax and wane no more.

Watts' paraphrase of Psalm 98 ('Make a joyful noise to the Lord, all the earth, break forth into joyous song and sing praises …' [v. 4]), helped by a well-known melody associated with George Handel in England (although more likely to be the work of Lowell Mason in America), is now a well-known Christmas Carol:

> Joy to the World; the Lord is come!
> Let earth receive her King;
> Let every heart prepare Him room,
> and heaven and nature sing, and heaven and nature sing …'

Other hymns have political connotations; some are explicit, and even those more implicit, such as Psalm 90 ('Lord, you have been our dwelling place in all generations …'), which Watts transposed as the well-known hymn, 'Our God our help in ages past', has been used at several royal occasions up to the present day, including the funeral of King Edward VII, the unveiling of the Queen Victoria Memorial before Buckingham Palace and at the Investiture of Edward, Prince of Wales:

> Our God, our help in ages past,
> Our hope for years to come,

> Our shelter from the stormy blast,
> And our eternal home.
>
> Under the shadow of Thy throne
> Still may we dwell secure;
> Sufficient is Thine arm alone,
> And our defence is sure.

Twenty-eight hymns contain explicit political language, thirteen with specific references to eighteenth-century Britain. These include Psalm 60 ('O God, you have rejected us, broken our defences; you have been angry; now restore us!'), which is headed 'On a Day of Humiliation from Disappointments in War' and runs as follows:

> 1 Lord, hast thou cast the nation off?
> Must we for ever mourn?
> Wilt thou indulge immortal wrath?
> Shall mercy ne'er return? ...
>
> 3 Great Britain shakes beneath thy stroke
> And dreads thy threat'ning hand;
> O heal the island thou hast broke,
> Confirm the wav'ring land ...
>
> 5 Go with our armies to the fight,
> Like a confed'rate God;
> In vain confed'rate powers unite
> Against thy lifted rod.
>
> 6 Our troops shall gain a wide renown
> By thine assisting hand;
> 'Tis God that treads the mighty down,
> And makes the feeble stand.

Psalm 67 ('May God be gracious to us and bless us, and make his face to shine upon us') is a thanksgiving hymn, which Watts gives even more nationalistic overtones:

> 1 Shine, mighty God, on Britain shine
> With beams of heavenly grace
> Reveal thy power through all our coasts
> And show thy smiling face.
>
> 4 Sing to the Lord, ye distant lands
> Sing loud with solemn voice
> While British tongues exalt his praise
> And British hearts rejoice.

Psalm 47 ('Clap your hands, all you peoples; shout to God with loud songs of joy ...') has a strong sense of election in its combined themes of the elevation of the king, the ascension of Christ, and Britain's inheritance of the promises to Israel:

> In Israel stood his ancient throne
> He loved that chosen race
> But now he calls the world his own
> And heathens taste his grace
>
> The British Islands are the Lord's
> There Abraham's God is known
> While powers and princes, shields and swords
> Submit before his throne.

Similarly Psalm 100 ('Make a joyful noise to the Lord, all the earth ...') has Britain at the centre of its praise:

> Sing to the Lord with joyful voice
> Let every land his name adore

> The British Isles shall send the noise
> Across the ocean to the shore.

Ps. 19:4 ('yet their voice goes out through all the earth ...') is more specific still: 'Ye British lands rejoice where he reveals his word'. Psalm 135 begins 'O Britain, Know thy Living God'; Psalm 115, 'A Psalm for the Fifth of November' runs 'O Britain, trust the Lord ... and Britain blest the Lord that built the skies'. Psalm 75 is subtitled 'Power and Government belong to God alone. Applied to the Glorious Revolution by King William, or the Happy Succession of George I to the Throne'.

Watts sent samples of his hymns to the Puritan colony in Massachusetts; he owned a copy of *The Bay Psalm Book*, and added to it his own imitation of Psalm 107 – 'A Psalm for New England'. Selections from this run as follows:

> 3 Where nothing dwelt but beasts of prey,   4 They sow the fields, and trees they plant,
> Or men as fierce and wild as they,   Whose yearly fruit supplies their want;
> He bids th' oppressed and poor repair,   Their race grows up from fruitful stocks,
> And builds them towns and cities there.   Their wealth increases with their flocks.
>
> 5 Thus they are blessed; but if they sin,
> He lets the heathen nations in;
> A savage crew invades their lands,
> Their princes die by barb'rous hands.

Watts' *Psalms of David Imitated* became popular in New England; preachers such as George Whitefield and Jonathan Edwards in the *First Great Awakening in the 1740s used them. John Wesley used at least fourteen of Watts' hymns in his own collection when he was in America, founding Methodist congregations. The British references become generalized: of Psalm 19, he writes 'Ye happy lands rejoice'; and of Psalm 47, he changes Watts' 'The British lands are the Lord's' to 'Remotest nations are the Lord's'. Somewhat ironically, before and during the American War of Independence (1775–88), the previously British-orientated psalms composed by Watts became increasingly Americanized.

One of the best known American composers is *William Billings* (1746–1800), son of a Boston shopkeeper and a self-taught tutor in singing the psalms, whose *New England Psalm-Singer* of 1770 (the first Hymn Book of the Psalms by an American composer, with all-American tunes) had enormous influence during the American Revolution. Billings saw psalmody as an art to be imitated: he composed nearly 350 pieces, with a four-part unaccompanied chorus (no instrumental music and no solo songs) to be used in schools and churches. His *The Singing Master's Assistant* (Boston, 1778) went through four editions, and his *The Psalm-Singer's Amusement* (Boston, 1781), a more flamboyant version of fugues, with their overlapping texts and more complicated hymn tunes, was also popular. Although without formal training, Billings sought to imitate Renaissance choral music of his day, without following all the rules of cadence and modulation; he took a line at a time, changing metre in order to express best the sense of the words. The principal melody was provided by the tenor voice, the bass was added as a counterpoint, then the treble, and the counter tenor was used to fill in missing parts of the harmony. His most notable hymn was 'Chester', the unofficial hymn of the American Revolution, which is still in popular use today; although written in psalm-like style ('... We'll fear them not; – we trust in God, – New England's God for ever reigns'), it was not taken directly from any one psalm. But a clear example of political appropriation is of Psalm 137, written during the British occupation of Boston, entitled 'Lamentation over Boston', which, like the psalm it is based upon, starts reflectively but ends with angry resolve:

> By the Rivers of Watertown we sat down and wept, when we remember'd thee, O Boston ...
> For they that held them in bondage requir'd of them to take up arms against their brethren. Forbid it, Lord.
> God forbid! Forbid it Lord, God forbid! that those who have sucked Bostonian Breasts should thirst for American Blood! ...
> If I forget thee, if I forget thee, yea if I do not remember thee, let my numbers cease to flow, then be my Muse unkind; then let my tongue forget to move and ever be confin'd ...

John Mycall's edition of the psalms in 1787 had a similar appeal, with similar revisions: Psalm 75 now gains a new subtitle, 'Applied to the Glorious Revolution in America, July 4th, 1776'. References to 'the king' (for example in Psalm 21) are substituted by 'our rulers'; and Ps. 135:19 ('O house of Israel, bless the Lord!') Mycall reproduces as 'New England, know thy living God'. Later American editions of the psalms as hymns by Joel Barlow in 1795 and Timothy Dwight in 1800 made changes with a more Christianized influence (Psalm 137, 'I love thy Kingdom, Lord' is a well-known example from Dwight) which, theologically, had as much a popular appeal in New England as the political copies had done. It is incongruous that, by the end of the eighteenth century, with the exception of the deep south, a reform movement had suppressed the appeal of Billings in favour of more European tastes.[10]

---

[10] On the Earl of Surrey and the Psalms, see W.A. Sessions (1996). For more general resources, see H. Hamlin (2004); and R. Zim (1981). On the psalms as battle-hymns, see W.S. Reid (1971). On Watts and his influence on American psalmody, see J.H. Dorenkamp (1972); J.M. Hull (2002); R.A. Stackhouse (1997); L.R. Stallings (1978). For Watts' own versions of the psalms, see I. Watts (1719; reprint 1816) and for online versions of Watts' psalmody, see www.ccel.org/ccel/watts/psalmshymns.i.html and www.cyberhymnal.org/bio/w/a/t/watts_i.htm.

Reception as Aesthetic Representation: Jewish and Christian Responses

Jewish Reception through Art and Music

Thus far this survey has not only excluded much of what was being published in other languages in parts of Catholic Europe, but has also omitted a discussion of changes in attitudes to psalmody in *Jewish tradition*. In part this is because it was not until some two centuries later, through *Reform Judaism in Germany and eastern Europe, that the translation of the Hebrew Bible into vernacular languages became an issue in Judaism; some isolated exceptions include a Ladino translation of the Psalter from Constantinople in 1540, and a Yiddish version from Venice in 1545. More typically, during the period under discussion here, Hebrew was seen as the God-given means of preserving Jewish identity, performing the same function as Latin had done in the Christian churches in the earlier period.

An increasing phenomenon in the mid-sixteenth and seventeenth centuries is that Protestants attempted to refute the Latin text by reference to the Hebrew 'original', whilst Catholics, predictably opposed to such a position, became increasingly hostile to Hebrew writings. On the Continent, using the authority of the Council of Trent, Catholics attacked earlier Jewish exegetes such as Rashi and put restrictions on the printing of their commentaries, unless such anti-Christian propaganda was erased. But this is not to say that Protestants always collaborated with Jews: Luther's attitude to the Jews in his later life has already been noted, marked by his frustration at their resistance to repentance. At about the same time as the Council of Trent, his pamphlets equating the Jews with the Devil were in circulation, with the insistence that their books, homes and synagogues were burnt, that their rabbis were banned, and that they were to be expelled from the protection afforded by Christian towns.

Despite all this, anti-Christian tracts by Jewish commentators using the psalms, as seen in the previous chapter, are a rare phenomenon. Any innovation in the reception of psalmody in Judaism is in fact more *aesthetic* than through a disputatious commentary. In part this was helped by the rise of Jewish printing presses, firstly in Italy, especially in Venice, but later in Mantua, Padua, Bologna, Florence and Ferrara, and also in Germany and Holland. The earliest aesthetic works are restrained artistic ornamentation of the Hebrew text (although nothing quite like the *Parma Psalter*, discussed earlier, has survived from Italian presses in this period). The most popular medium in doing this was in new editions of Passover prayer books, known as *Haggadoth*, where the 'gateway image' became a fashionable motif to be used on title pages. The image was popularized by Daniel Bomberg (1483–1553), the Venetian Christian printer of Hebrew books, and the verse, in Hebrew, was from Ps. 118:20 ('This is the gate of the Lord; the righteous shall enter through it'), heavily decorated with baroque forms and architectural elements symbolizing the Temple. (Earlier evidence of this motif was seen in our discussion in the previous chapter of the thirteenth-century *Worms *Mahzor.*) The tradition was continued in the 1540s in the Augsburg printing presses of Jacob ben Asher, and in the 1550s by Ruffinelli of Mantua (where the temple symbolism included the twisted columns of St Peter's, Rome, which at the time were believed to have been part of Solomon's Temple).

Temple illustrations allude to verses from the psalms, but they do not use whole psalms. More complete representations are found in Haggadoth, such as the one printed by Solomon ha-Kohen in Prague in 1526, which has some sixty woodcuts, in a clear bold type, with ornately decorated letters beginning new sections, some of which highlight the psalms used in the *Hallel. Another is an edition printed by Jacob ben Asher in Mantua in 1550, clearly reflecting the influence of the Prague prayer book in terms of type and text, but with more Italian-influenced figurative illustrations, far bolder than the previous centuries. A third is *Amsterdam Haggadah*, first printed by a Jewish proselyte, Abraham ben Jacob, in 1695, this time using copper-engraved illustrations, but showing the clear influence of Christian figurative art, taken from illustrations by a Christian Swiss artist, Matthäus Merian in his *Icones biblicae* [Basel, 1625–6]. This last Hagaddah is most celebrated for its first known Hebrew map, showing the land of Israel as a separate entity.

These examples demonstrate the continuity of the tradition of Jewish illustrations discussed in the previous chapter. But one other most surprising aesthetic innovation can be seen at this time – the Jewish rendering of the psalms in music. The unusual nature of this development can only be appreciated in the light of Jewish tradition: as a symbol of mourning for the lost musical practices of the destroyed Temple, the law (for example, in the Babylonian Talmud, as in *Sotah* 48a) banned the use of musical instruments in the synagogue (admittedly there were local exceptions concerning Sabbaths and holy days), and prohibited the voice of a woman to be heard in synagogue worship (Babylonian Talmud, *Berakhot* 24a). Since the end of the second Temple period, cantillation was thus performed by the *hazzan, who regulated the rhythm and the elaboration in the melodies by intuitive local customs, and where a response was returned, it was by male voices and in unison. (The tradition of the *piyyutim belongs to the same genre.) The different form of **te'amim* in the poetic books of Psalms, Proverbs and Job is believed to go back to this type of recitation of psalmody, although it is unclear whether the accents serve a rhythmic or melodic purpose. Certainly there were no uniformly accepted chants which accompanied psalmody, as in Gregorian plainchant. Indeed, synagogue cantillation resisted the Christian view that most psalm verses could be sung by the balancing of the two halves which were parallel in terms of sense: Jewish tradition upheld that a large number of verses were tripartite, and thus required more elaborate recitation notes added to the additional syllables at the end of the verse (often a tone higher or lower than the first part of the verse). Obviously there was a good deal of variation: cantillation took different forms in Sephardic liturgy (with its past Arabic influence and the teachings of Maimonides who distinguished between secular and sacred use) compared with

Ashkenazi worship (with its practice of silent recitation, influenced by two very different Germanic and Ottoman cultures). But the overall impact of the ban on music and psalmody had implications everywhere on composition, choral arrangements and professional performance, and it was not really until the Emancipation of the Jews in Europe in the second half of the eighteenth century (which will be discussed in the following chapter) that the laws became relaxed and musical creativity began to develop.

Nevertheless, given the explosion of musical arrangements of psalmody in Christian churches – a feature to which we shall turn shortly – it would have been surprising if this had not influenced Jewish culture as well. One of the communities bearing witness to this was the old Sephardic community in Venice, which moved to Livorno in the eighteenth century, and whose synagogue, at the time of Emancipation, became a focus for experimentation in choral music, even using the organ: many manuscripts dating from this time reveal practices which could be traced back to seventeenth-century Venice, Ferrara and Mantua in particular, and to one Jewish composer in particular.

Salamone Rossi (c.1570–1628) rose to prominence as a court musician for Duke Vicenzo I in Mantua from 1587. A singer and violinist, and a colleague of Monteverdi during his time in Mantua between 1592 and 1612, Rossi became a prominent composer, pioneering what became known as the 'trio sonata'. He composed several books of madrigals and instrumental works, probably being the first Jewish musician to print Hebrew music. But Rossi did not only publish music for public performance: his collection of Hebrew motets for selected psalms shows how he intended his works to be used for sacred as well as for secular purposes. In 1623 he had published *Ha-Shirim Asher li-Shelomo* – a collection of thirty-three psalms, hymns and liturgical poems to be used on festive synagogue occasions, as well as for the 'study hall, the house of bride and groom, and private homes'. His rationale for this was the writings of his friend Rabbi Leon Modena (1571–1648) who re-examined Jewish laws to demonstrate that choral works in synagogues should not merit disapproval. Hence Rossi skilfully grafted his works onto a received tradition: he used the acceptable idea of *melismatic chanting of psalms, and but avoided using any recognizable musical settings; instead he used his own compositions, very much influenced by the tradition of plainchant in the church of Mantua, and added polyphonic elaborations, to be sung in three to eight voice parts, including sopranos and altos as well. Rossi thus in part deferred to the prohibition against music: his entire collection was sung by an unaccompanied chorus, with the understanding that if the performance took place outside a synagogue, instruments could be used.

Of his psalmic compositions, some six are most notable, mainly for the way that Rossi elucidated the meaning of the words from the music. For example, Psalm 137 ('By the waters of Babylon, we sat down and wept') is for four voices, beginning with a chromatic progression depicting the word 'wept', and a flowing passage in unison for the word 'river'; the hanging up of harps is achieved first by lowering the key by a semitone, with an unexpected F sharp in the soprano part at the end of the phrase, whilst the call for revenge at the end of the psalm ('Destroy it! Destroy it!') takes on repeated harsh chords. Psalm 80 ('Give ear, O Shepherd of Israel, you who lead Joseph like a flock') Rossi entitled *Elohim Hashivenu*, because of its thrice-repeated refrain 'Restore us, O God' in verses 3, 7 and 19. The motet is divided into three parts, each progressively intensifying the plea for restoration by using contrasting bass and soprano parts, ending in the final verse (with its highest hopes) with the highest note throughout, top E. Psalm 128 has a three-voice setting, with a good deal of contrapuntal play between the treble and bass parts; the same word-painting is evident, with the word *shir* (song) as a melisma, the rejoicing over family life in quicker triple metre, and a long polyphonic development on the word 'Shalom' at the end. Psalm 121 is another psalm notable for its contrasts; here Rossi brings this out by a five-voice setting with similar combinations of voices making both colour and texture. Other psalms in the collection include Psalm 84, whose contents provide a similar use of contrasts between polyphony and homophony, Psalm 92 (whose heading links it with Sabbath observance) and Psalm 146, a psalm which Rossi used to create the contrasts between 'Hallelu' and 'Yah'.

Rossi was exceptional for his time, and not surprisingly a good deal of his work was criticized for its overtly Christian influence. His work disappeared after his death, to be rediscovered and revived a century later in the synagogue at Livorno. This marks a fitting end to our assessment of the Jewish reception of psalmody in this period: our survey of reception through art and music must therefore return to the Christian tradition, beginning first with illuminations of the psalms.[11]

Christian Reception through Art, Literary Imitation and Music

Artistic Representation

In terms of pictorial representations, the illumination of Books of Hours, Breviaries and manuscripts continued, especially in Catholic churches, until the middle of the sixteenth century. But several factors contributed to the demise of these art forms, both in Catholic and Protestant traditions. First, as was noted earlier, the Council of Trent, culminating in the pronouncement of Pius V in 1568, in an attempt to unify its church, reduced the diverse texts to one standard *Breviary, which was followed by the publication of the *Missal in 1570. A similar phenomenon is evident in Protestant England, where the *Book of Common Prayer* from

---

[11] For more general resources on Jewish music in the Renaissance and Reformation periods, see www.grovemusic.com/. On Rossi, see *I. Adler (1967)* and J. Jacobson (1988). Of the many websites on Rossi, those which have access to samples of his music include www.myjewishlearning.com/culture/Music/TOSynagogueMusic/Rossi.htm and www.zamir.org/composers/rossi/rossi-mon.html and www.hom.com/topics/choir/rossi.htm.

1549 onwards had the same effect in preventing too much diversification of texts for both public and private prayer. Furthermore, easier access to printing presses meant that private hand-illuminated manuscripts and Books of Hours became much more expensive and more difficult to produce: although the printed copies initially imitated the Gothic style of manuscripts (errors included), the lavish decoration and illumination became less of a trend. Copies did not disappear entirely, of course: the *Heures de Notre Dame, à l'usage de Rome, Latin et François* of Anne Blanchard, with its expansive borders and illustrated rubrics, was published in both Latin and French in 1519. But personal, private prayer books underwent some demise as the printing of such texts took over, each with limited illuminations.

This did not mean that the art of illustration died out completely. A few different forms of experimentation, dependent now upon the printing presses, are still in evidence. For example, as woodcut engraving and then copper engraving gained popular appeal, this was applied to texts of the psalms. This form of art took some time to develop. The first major printed Bible, the Gutenberg Bible (1455), had movable metal type and a geometrically proportioned layout; its main form of decoration was in illuminated initials at the beginning of different books and chapters, including those in the Psalms. By contrast, the Psalter published in Mainz in 1457 by Fust and Schoeffer was remarkable for its use of colour printing, albeit again only in its initials. However, most Psalters were now produced as hymnbooks to accompany printed prayer books, and decoration was kept to the minimum of border illustration and decoration of initial letters. The emphasis was far more on the word read, and preached, heard and sung: the visual impact of psalmody in both public and private devotion was minimal at this time, particularly when compared with the rich and diverse tradition which had preceded it.

The main influence of psalmody in art and sculpture is to be found in the idealized figure of David. Sometimes this is linked with the psalms of penitence (where David is depicted with Bathsheba), sometimes it is influenced by frontispieces of Psalters (David playing the lyre), sometimes it is simply of the heroic figure alone, reflecting both the Renaissance concerns with figures of antiquity and Humanistic interests in the portrayal of the human form. One might argue that there was an Italian obsession with the figure of David (probably more a Classical Greek or Roman representation than a Semitic one), in works as various as Donatello's David, first of David alone, in marble (1409) and then of David and Goliath, in bronze (1430, followed by Verrocchio's representation, in bronze, between 1473 and 1475, and later, by Michelangelo's David (1504) and, much later, by Bernini's David (1623–34). The depiction of David and Bathsheba is represented by artists as various as Lucas Cranach I (1526), Virgil Solis's pen and ink sketch (1540–50), Francesco de Rossi Salviali in Rome (1552–4), Jon Massys of France (1562), and the haunting depiction of David and Uriah by Rembrandt (1665). It could be argued that these are examples taken from narratives about David; but an interest in David undoubtedly derives from psalmody, as seen more explicitly in 'David playing the harp' by Rembrandt (1656), and later, by Jan de Bray (1670). David and Goliath, although not an explicit theme of the psalms (other than in the apocryphal Psalm 151), was read into the life of David in psalms which spoke of personal attack and physical violation: Caravaggio's three paintings of David and Goliath (1600; 1606–7; 1609–10) suffice as just one illustration of the development of a theme. An explicit reference to the Psalter is found in a painting by the Counter Reformation artist, Domenico Manetti (1609–63), whose work 'Jesus discussing the Psalms with Catherine of Siena' is found in Palezzo Pubblico, Siena.[12]

LITERARY IMITATION

There is a sense in which 'word-pictures' begin to replace the art of illumination, in that the more pragmatic and theological concerns of translation transformed into a sophisticated experimentation with the 'words' themselves, at a time when the rules of grammar, spelling, vocabulary and style were still very much in their infancy. Here again the psalms received more attention than any other biblical book, in part due their poetic form, in part due to their liturgical history. Few of these poets knew Hebrew; many of them were closely associated with those who had composed metrical psalms for liturgy or for social and political comment, and like them, they assumed that Hebrew originals must have been composed in a quantitative classical metre, if they were inspired to an even greater degree than the Greek and Latin models.

An early example is *Thomas Wyatt* (1503–42), a courtier poet for Henry VIII, whose travels for the king brought Italian styles to his writing: Wyatt used Dante's interlocking rhyming schema from his *Divine Comedy* (noting that Dante himself used Psalm 114 ['When Israel went out from Egypt ...'] at the beginning of *Purgatorio*, when it is sung by souls arriving on the shores of Mount Purgatory). Wyatt also adapted into English *Petrarchan Italian sonnets with their characteristic rhyming couplets. His first poems to be published in 1549, seven years after his death, were not his vast secular collection of sonnets, odes and satires but his *Certain Psalms ... Drawn into English Metre*. Wyatt also compiled an unusual version of the seven penitential psalms in *terza rima*, using a prose paraphrase composed in 1534 by the Italian Aretino: this collection included Italian-influenced prosody as a commentary between each psalm, to depict David's penitence for his adultery with Bathsheba, with clear allusions to the poet's own personal situation.

---

[12] For general resources on the Christian illumination of psalmody in this period, see H. Hermann (1956); A. Lockhart (1994 [ed.]) and H. Read (1960 [ed.]). Of the many websites on the images of David (and of the David of the Psalms) in art, the most useful are www.groveart.com/; www2.evansville.edu/ecoleweb/imagesD.html#prophdavid;www.artcyclopedia.com/scripts/tsearch.pl?t=David&type=2; and www.wga.hu/index1.html.

Wyatt's work influenced *Philip Sidney* (1554–86) who also applied an innovative use of metre to the first 43 psalms when he rendered them into English verse. Psalms 7 and 30, for example, use the same unusual *terza rima* that Wyatt used. Many of Sidney's poems used hexameters, particularly where the subject matter required an imitation of royal style, as with Psalms 2 and 18: 'He nobly saves his King, and kindness keeps in store / For David his Anoynt, and his seed ever more'. Another form Sidney adapted was the Latin *Sapphic model: Psalm 6, imitating a lover's complaint, is in stanzas with three lines of iambic pentameter of ten beats, and a concluding line as a dimeter of five beats:

> Lord, let not me, a worme, by Thee be shent,
>   While Thou art in the heat of Thy displeasure:
>   Nor let Thy rage, of my due punishment
>   Become my measure.

A comparison of the 8:7:8:7 metre of the creation hymn, Psalm 19, with the 8:6:4:8:6:4 metre in the psalm of confidence, Psalm 23, shows how effectively the different metres are utilized within a rhyming schema:

> The heavenly frame sets forth the fame
> Of him that only thunders;
> The firmament, so strangely bent,
> Shows his handworking wonders.
> Day unto day doth it display,
> Their course doth it acknowledge,
> And night to night succeeding right
> In darkness teach clear knowledge ...

The Lord, the Lord my shepherd is,	He me revives: leads me the way,
And so can never I	Which righteousness doth take,
Taste misery.	For his name's sake.
He rests me in green pasture his:	Yea though I should through valleys stray,
By waters still, and sweet	Of death's dark shade, I will
He guides my feet.	No whit fear ill.

After his death in 1586, Philip Sidney's sister, *Mary Sidney, Countess of Pembroke* (1561–1621), revised his collection and added Psalms 44–150. Her background equipped her well for this task. Having been invited to the court of Elizabeth I in 1575, she subsequently married Henry Herbert, Earl of Pembroke, and her home at Wilton House became the setting for various well-known poets, musicians, artists and dramatists; Spenser, Jonson, Marlowe and probably Shakespeare were frequent guests. As for her own literary work, of which *The Sydney Psalter* is but a part, the variety of metres and the aesthetic quality of the poetry outclassed even those of her brother. Hexameters were chosen when the metre highlighted subject matter which was either royal or heroic, as in Psalms 76 and 141. The *sapphic mode was used for Psalm 125, and the *elegiac mode for Psalm 114, with longer lines of alternating 12:8 metre:

> At what tyme Jacobs race did leave of Aegypt take
> And Aegypts barbrous folk forsake ...

A *Spenserian sonnet was used for Psalm 100, and a *Petrarchan sonnet for Psalm 150. Psalm 117 was set out as an acrostic, the first letters of each lining spelling out PRAISTHELORD. The originality of the varied use of line lengths (4:6:8) along with unusual rhyming is most evident in Psalm 92:

> O lovly thing,
> to sing and praises frame,
> to thee, ô lord, and thy high name
> with early spring
> thy bounty to display,
> thy truth when night hath vanquisht day
> yes so to sing
> that ten string'd instrument
> with lute, and harp, and voice consent.

The Sidney Psalter was inspired by a dislike for what was seen as the 'unadorned literalism', both of Coverdale's version and the Geneva Bible, as well as a distaste for the lack of artistic and aesthetic concerns in the metrical versions. Originality, freshness and imagination were vital. For example, in order to bring out the dialogical nature of a psalm, Sydney used conversational syntax, with questions, exclamations and interruptions, but in a restrained way: 'Ah! Cast me not from thee: take not againe / Thy breathing grace! Againe thy comfort send me' (Ps. 51:33–4) and 'What speake I? O lett me heare / What he speakes for speake he will' (Ps. 85:21–2).

Such an approach to psalmody would have been unthinkable some fifty years previously, not only in literary but also social terms: although not the first woman to publish psalmody in this way, Mary Sidney was perhaps the most skilled. Anne Vaughan Lock (c.1533–c.1607) preceded Mary Sidney; her appendage of 'Meditations of a Penitent Sinner' to her translation of some of Calvin's sermons in 1560, with its rich allusions to the sin of both male and female in Psalm 51, is another example of a female composer. Another is Isabella Whitney (c.1540–c.1580), who in her work *A Sweet Nosegay, or Pleasant Posy Containing a Hundred and Ten Philosophical Flowers* (1573) includes a lament on human frailty in a letter to one 'C.B.' which has several allusions to the contrition expressed in Psalm 51. Mary Sidney was undoubtedly the most innovative female poet at this time, not least where psalmody was concerned; but although exceptional, she was not alone.[13]

Four other (male) poets in this period deserve brief mention for their aesthetic and personal imitations of the psalms. The first is George Gascoigne (1539–c.1577) His use of the penitential psalm 130, in his anthology *Posies* (1575), was a reflection on his own misspent years, by playing upon the love of David and Bathsheba, which he deemed to have been the subject of this psalm; his choice of archaic diction and excessive alliteration make it an extraordinary poem:

> From depth of doole wherein my soule doth dwell,
> From heavy heart which harbours in my brest,
> From troubled sprite which sildome taketh rest,
> From hope of heaven, from dreade of darksome hell.
> O gracious God, to thee I crye and yell ...

The second poet is *Francis Bacon* (1561–1626), whose *Translation of Certain Psalms into English Verse* (1625) is a rendering of seven psalms (1, 12, 90, 104, 126, 137, 149) into different quantitative metres, dedicated to 'my very good friend', George Herbert. The first verse of Psalm 90 shows just how different this version is from that of Isaac Watt's version, written later but referred to earlier:

> O Lord, thou art our home, to whom we fly,
>   And so hast always been from age to age:
> Before the hills did intercept the eye,
>   Or that the frame was up of earthly stage,
> One God thou wert, and art, and still shall be;
> The line of time, it doth not measure thee.

A third example is Henry Vaughan (1622–95), best known for his poetic depictions of God as Creator in his use of Psalms 65, 104 and 121 in *Silex Scintillans* (1650 and 1655). Two stanzas from the middle of Psalm 104 (vv. 10–15) show just how much Vaughan transposed his love of the countryside of Brecknockshire and Herefordshire into the psalms which spoke of knowing God through nature:

> Thou from thy upper springs above, from those
>   Chambers of rain, where heaven's large bottle lie,

---

[13] On psalmody and the Sidneys, see B.W. Fisken (1985); R. Greene (1990); H. Hamlin (2004), pp. 102–7; M.P Hannay, N.J. Kinnamon and M.G. Brennan (1998 [eds.]); R.E. Pritchard (1992 [ed.]); J.C.A. Rathmell (1963 [ed.]); T.L. Steinberg (1995); K.M. Swain (1999); R. Todd (1987); L. Wieder (1995 [ed.]) on Philip Sidney's versions of Psalms 10, 13, 18, 22, 24, 26, 31, 37, 40, 41 and Mary Sidney Herbert's versions of Psalms 44, 45, 50, 52, 56, 59, 62, 66, 69, 71, 75, 76, 84, 92. 93, 96, 98, 99, 108, 111, 117, 119, 122, 129, 134, 138, 139, 144, 147; see also R. Zim (1981). On women and psalmody in this period, see *D. Clarke (2000 [ed.])*; M. P. Hannay (1991, 2001); and S. Trill (1996a and 1996b).

> Dost water the parched hills, whose breaches close
>   Healed by the showers from high.
>
> Grass for the cattle, and herbs for man's use
>   Thou makest to grow: these (blessed by thee) the earth
> Brings forth, with wine, oil, bread: all which infuse
>   To man's heart strength and mirth.

A fourth example – and perhaps the most original – is by Samuel Woodford (1636–1700), whose *Paraphrase upon the Psalms of David* (1667) was influenced by the creative use of quantitative metres in the Sidney Psalter. This was a translation of the entire Psalter into *Pindaric odes – using a three-part symmetrical structure for every single psalm, whatever its length, whereby the third part retained a different metre from the first (strophe) and second (antistrophe). The second part of Psalm 84, in 10.10.10.10.10.10 metre, runs as follows:

> So lovely is Thy Temple, and so fair,
> So like Thy self, that with desire I faint;
> My heart and flesh cry out to see Thee there,
> And could bear any thing but this restraint:
> My Soul do's on its old Remembrance feed
> And new desires by my long absence breed.[14]

As well as imitations of psalmody into poetic forms, the influence of psalmody pervaded other forms of literature of the period. It is clear that just as Luther's Bible and its successors anticipated the golden age of German literature, when Protestant writers, poets and dramatists as various as Lessing, Herder, Goethe and Schiller each adapted in their works commonly known biblical quotations, so too the English Bibles of the sixteenth and seventeenth centuries permeated the language and style of much English literature. Therefore this means that when a phrase becomes an idiom in common parlance, its origin may not in fact be the well-known author or poet who publicly used it, but rather, a vernacular biblical quotation behind it, for which the author is simply the medium.

An obvious example is *William Shakespeare* (1564–1616). His collected works offer allusions to over sixty different psalms. His source was almost certainly the Geneva Bible; given that the *KJB* was published in 1611, some five years before his death, and that it took some time before it overtook the popularity of the Geneva Bible, it is more likely that his allusions to psalmody are from the latter translation. But others have had a different view. An article in the *Times* some forty years ago

---

[14] For further observations on the four extracts from Gascoigne, Bacon, Vaughan and Woodford, see H. Hamlin (2004), pp. 111–18 (on Gascoigne), pp. 136–9 (on Vaughan), p. 77–8 and 107–10 (on Woodford); and L. Wieder (1995 [ed.]), on Bacon's version of Psalms 12, 90 and 126, and Vaughan's version of Psalm 65, 104 and 121.

popularized the idea that Shakespeare had a particular hand in the translation of some of the Psalms for the *KJB*. The key evidence was from Psalm 46: Shakespeare would have been 46 in 1610, the year before the publication, and when one reads in 46 words from the beginning of Ps. 46:1 (starting with 'God'), and then 46 words from the end of Ps. 46:11 (after the rubric 'Selah'), one gets a combination of words 'shake+speare'. Was this some secret coding by Shakespeare himself, or maybe a birthday attribution by the translators? Another view presumes that Shakespeare had a hand in Psalm 23, as his birthday fell on 23 April. However, it is more likely that the fifty-four translators possibly did not recognize the literary worth of Shakespeare for what it was (noting that Sir Thomas Bodley wrote to the Keeper of the Books, Thomas James, as late as 1598, telling him not to fill the library with those 'Baggage Books' – i.e. the folios of Shakespeare), but rather used their own committee of clerics, academics and theologians.

But that Shakespeare freely used psalmody is beyond dispute. To take just three examples from the Tragedies: first, the phrase which compares life to a 'span of a hand' in *Othello* ii.3.72 has resonances with a phrase from Ps. 39:5 which describes a life as 'a few handbreadths'; secondly, in *Hamlet* iii.3.45–6, the question about guilt, whether there is 'rain enough in the sweet heavens to wash it white as snow' is undoubtedly a citation of Ps. 51:7 – 'Wash me, and I shall be whiter than snow'; and thirdly, the reference to 'the way of dusty death' in *Macbeth* v. 5.23–27 is an echo of Ps. 22:15, 'the dust of death'. To take two illustrations from the Comedies: the unusual expression 'apple of the eye' in *Midsummer Night's Dream* iii.2.104 has its counterpart in Ps. 17:8 'Guard me as the apple of the eye'; and the expression 'fire seven times tried' in the *Merchant of Venice* ii.9.63–64 has allusions to Ps. 12:6, concerning God's promises which are like refined silver, 'purified seven times'. Or to take the Histories, the reference in *King Richard III* v. 3.110 which speaks of the 'bruising irons of wrath', with its allusions to the power of the king, under God, over the nations, leads back to Ps. 2:8, with its reference to the nations being chastised by the king, under God, with a rod of iron; whilst in *King Richard II* i.3.160–163, the complaint about the inability to speak one's native language in exile, so that the tongue is like an 'unstringed viol or harp', surely has allusions to Ps. 137:2, where the exiles, complaining they are unable to sing their native songs in a strange land, speak of hanging up their harps on willows. Shakespeare may not have imitated the psalms in the same manner as some of the poets referred to previously, but that he was able to experiment with the new forms and styles provided by various English versions, there is no doubt.[15]

One could cite countless examples of the practice of adapting different vernacular versions of psalmody in sixteenth- and seventeenth-century literary circles in England. Brief mention should be made of the Puritan, *John Bunyan* (1628–88), whose *Pilgrim's Progress* occasionally uses verses from psalms (Christian's

---

[15] On Shakespeare and psalmody, see *W. Burgess (1968)*; *R. Noble (1935)*; N. Shaheen (1999); and D.C. Steinmetz (1990 [ed.]).

sinking in the mire, for example, is accompanied by a verse from Ps. 69:1–2 and Hopeful's attempts to save him quote from Ps. 73:4–5), thus providing another example of the ways in which by this time the use of the psalms were part of common discourse.

A more substantial discussion is required of three other major poets of this period whose use of psalmody in each case is both versatile and distinctive. *John Donne* (1571/2–1631), a convert from Catholicism by 1610, was a moderate conformist, being ordained in 1615 to a royal chaplaincy under James I, and from that time serving first James and then Charles I, from 1621 at St Paul's. Although Donne used phrases from the psalms freely, in a manner akin to Shakespeare, he does not seem to have composed any imitations of specific psalms: his approach to psalmody was undoubtedly more pastoral, personal and devotional, increasingly so after his marriage to seventeen-year-old Mary in 1601 and her death in 1617. *George Herbert* (1593–1633) spent a good deal longer than Donne in academic life, becoming Reader in Rhetoric at Cambridge in 1618 and Public Orator from 1620 to 1628. His marriage in 1630 and the final three years of his life as a parish priest in Bemerton, near Salisbury, offers further comparisons with Donne (in fact, the two knew each other well, for Herbert's mother had provided a home for the then impoverished John and the young Mary after John's father had rejected him). Using the psalms as freely as Donne, he was also the composer of at least one imitation of a psalm. By contrast, *John Milton* (1608–74) experimented with actual compositions of psalms whilst still a student at Cambridge aged fifteen; his knowledge of Hebrew as well as Greek and Latin gave his appreciation of the psalms a different emphasis. And unlike Herbert, he was more associated with the political turmoil of his day, first composing eulogies to bishops and to William and Mary, yet by 1641 criticizing bishops and kings for apostasy and supporting the cause of Cromwell in the Civil War. He undoubtedly shared with Donne and Herbert a personal devotion to the psalms as prayer, but (rather like Isaac Watts, discussed earlier), he also saw the psalms as vehicles through which his dissenting political views could implicitly be made known. Taken together, these three great figures reveal the breadth and variety of the influence of psalmody by the middle of the seventeenth century – 'Protestants' who shared the same concern for the importance of the words of psalmody, yet each crafting the words in different ways and to different ends. Their different contributions merit a more detailed discussion.

Donne's appreciation of the genius of *The Sidney Psalter* is seen in his commendation of it in his poem 'Upon Translation of Psalms by Sir Philip Sidney and the Countess of Pembroke, his Sister'.

> … Fix we our praises therefore on this one
> That, as thy blessed Spirit fell upon
> These Psalms' first author in a cloven tongue
> – For 'twas a double power by which he sung
> the highest matter in the noblest form –
> So thou hast cleft that Spirit, to perform

> That work again, and shed it here, upon
> Two, by their bloods, and by Thy Spirit one;
> A brother and a sister, made by Thee
> The organ, where Thou are the harmony.

As Dean of St Paul's, Donne frequently chose as texts for preaching to the courts of King James and then King Charles verses from the psalms: two of the best known are Ps. 11:3 ('If the foundations are destroyed, what can the righteous do?') preached on 3 April 1625, and another known as 'Death's Duel', delivered before the King at Whitehall at the beginning of Lent, 1630, being the last public sermon before his death, on Ps. 68:20 ('… to God, the Lord, belongs escape from death').

Although none of Donne's psalms imitated the psalms in the lyrical manner of the Sidneys, many of his Holy Sonnets were inspired by the piety of the psalmists. It seems his two sources were the *KJB* and Coverdale. A striking example is found at the end of his poem, 'A Litanie', where the phrase from the penitential Ps. 51:15 ('O Lord, open my lips, and my mouth will declare your praise') is recalled in 'That we may locke our eares, Lord open mine … That we may open our eares, Lord lock thine … Heare us, weake echoes, O thou eare, and cry'. But for Donne, to preach and teach from the psalms was the most important service of all. As he recalled in a sermon, the Psalms are the 'Manna of the Church'.[16]

The psalms pervade Herbert's collection of some seventy religious poems, published posthumously in 1633 as *The Temple*: for example, Ps. 29:9 (8) is on the title page, and Herbert's version, which is that of neither the *KJB* nor the Geneva Bible, but probably Coverdale, reads 'In his Temple doth every man speak his honour' (the *KJB* and the Geneva Bible have 'glory'). Given his Salisbury connection, another source for Herbert's psalmody was almost certainly Thomas Ravencroft's *The Whole Booke of Psalmes* (1621), set to harmony. A few examples of Herbert's approach to the psalms must suffice. In Antiphon I, the opening lines of the chorus,

> Let all the world in ev'ry corner sing
> My God and King!

echoes many of the psalms, such as Ps. 150:6 ('Let every thing that breathes praise the Lord'), the Matins Psalm, 95:1 ('O come, let us sing to the Lord') and Ps. 100: 1 ('Make a joyful noise to the Lord, all the earth!'). The words of the response in line 9

> The church with psalms must shout,
> No doore can keep them out:

---

[16] On Donne and psalmody, see R. Dubinski (1986); J.M. Mueller (1971 [ed]); D.B. Quinn (1958; 1962); and H. Hamlin (2004), pp. 131–3 (on his praise to the Sidneys).

> But above all, the heart
> Must bear the longest part

underlines the importance of psalmody in this respect. Similarly, the frequent references to singing, whether of God's name, his praise or his victories (for example, in 'Praise II', 10; 'The Dedication', 4; 'Love I', 13; 'Easter-Wings', 9) again echo the psalmists' calls to praise (as in Pss. 59:16–17, 61:8, 144:9). Images, such as man as a fruitful tree (from 'Man', lines 7–8) have echoes from Pss. 1:3, 52:8 and 92:12. The phrases 'Who hath dealt his mercies so' and 'He our foes in pieces brake' (lines 4 and 13 of Antiphon II) have allusions to Psalm 136, with its refrain 'for his steadfast love (or, mercies) endure forever' and its reference to the striking down of kings and enemies in vv. 17 ff.

A poem where the connection with psalmody is most subtly developed is 'Easter', where the calls to praise God have clear associations with the Proper Psalm for Easter, Psalm 57:

> Rise heart; thy Lord is risen. Sing his praise
> Without delays,
> Who takes thee by the hand, that thou likewise
> With him mayst rise :
> That, as his death calcined thee to dust,
> His life may make thee gold, and much more just.
>
> Awake, my lute, and struggle for thy part
> With all thy art.
> The crosse taught all wood to resound his name
> Who bore the same.
> His stretched sinews taught all strings, what key
> Is best to celebrate this most high day.

Ps. 57:7–10 reads:

> My heart is steadfast, O God,
> My heart is steadfast.
> I will sing and make melody.
> Awake my soul!
> Awake, O harp and lyre!
> I will awake the dawn …

Similarly we may note the connection between the *Proper Psalm for Whitsuntide, Psalm 104, and the poem 'Providence':

> When th'earth was dry, thou mad'st a sea of wet:
> When that lay gather'd, thou didst broach the mountains (lines 113–14)
>
> You cover it with the deep as with a garment;
> the waters stood up above the mountains'. (Ps. 104:6)

Another example concerning the times and seasons (lines 57–8) echoes 104: 19–20; the 'cupboard serves the world; the meat is set' (lines 49–50) echoes 104:14, 27; and 'the windes grew gard'ners, and the clouds good fountains' (lines 115–16) echoes 104:3.

The above illustrations have been taken from Herbert's psalms which imitate hymnic forms: those which mimic the laments and thanksgivings have similarly evocative associations: for example, 'Thou art still my God' has echoes of the many lament psalms which use this expression (Pss. 4:1, 5:2, 7:1, 13:3, for example), and 'But Thou shalt answer, Lord, for me' is found in Pss. 38:15 and 86:7. It may therefore seem strange that Herbert actually translated only one psalm into quantitative verse – Psalm 23. One might argue that had he not died at forty, there would have been others (some would argue there are at least five more). But of all the versions of this psalm, Herbert's is as compelling as any.

> The God of love my shepherd is,
> And he that doth me feed:
> While he is mine, and I am his,
> What can I want or need?
>
> He leads me to the tender grasse,
> Where I both feed and rest;
> Then to the streams that gently passe:
> In both I have the best ...
>
> Yea, in deaths shadie black abode
> Well may I walk, not fear:
> For thou art with me; and thy rod
> To guide, thy staff to bear.[17]

Finally, *John Milton* (1608–74) wrote poems within the literary tradition of Sidney and Sandys (he considered Sternhold and Hopkins to be too 'bumbling and literal'), but his knowledge of Hebrew required him to stay more faithful to the original, collaborating with Jewish scholars and acquiring some knowledge of midrashic commentaries, and even of Rashi, if only through sixteenth-century Latin translations, as seen in his allusions and echoes in *Paradise Lost*. The use of Hebrew was a point which Milton was always keen to make, even placing such ideals on the lips of Jesus, when facing the temptations, in *Paradise Regained* [4.331–49].) Hence when Milton translated the psalms, he did so directly from the Hebrew, italicizing words where it was difficult to find an English equivalent. And, like Donne and Herbert, his works are full of psalmic allusions. A few examples from *Paradise Lost* must suffice. In Book VII, 205–9 the lines

---

[17] On Herbert and Psalmody, see *C. Bloch (1985)*; *C. Freer (1972)*; N. Kinnamon (1981); *D. Norton (1993)*; and L. Wieder (1995 [ed.]), for Herbert's version of Psalms 23.

> Attendant on thir Lord: Heav'n op'nd wide
> Her ever during Gates, Harmonious sound
> On golden Hinges moving, to let forth
> The King of Glorie in his powerful Word

echo Ps. 24:7–10 ('Lift up your heads, O gates! And be lifted up, O ancient doors! that the King of glory may come in …'), whilst the reference to God uplifting the poor and humbling the proud in XII, 564–570

> His providence, and on him sole depend,
> Merciful over all his works, with good
> Still overcoming evil, and by small
> Accomplishing great things, by things deemd weak
> Subverting worldy strong, and worldly wise
> By simply meek; that suffering for Truths sake
> Is fortitude to highest victorie …

has similar echoes of Ps. 145:14–20, where God 'upholds all who are falling, and raises up all who are bowed down'. And in *Paradise Regained*, Milton speaks of Sion's songs 'to all true tastes excelling' (IV, 334–49).

As well as alluding to psalms, Milton also composed several imitations of them. Psalms 114 and 136 were composed when he was only fifteen. Psalm 136, with its English updated, is now a well-known hymn sung to the French tune 'Midi', as skilled as any metrical psalm:

> Let us with a glad-some mind
>   Praise the Lord, for He is kind;
> For His mercies shall endure,
>   Ever faithful, ever sure.
>
> Let us sound His name abroad,
>   For of gods He is the God;
> For His mercies shall endure,
>   Ever faithful, ever sure …

It is probably Milton's imitations of Psalms 80–8 in 1648, just before he became blind, which are the most interesting. Some have argued that Milton chose them as possible samples to be used in the new Scottish Psalter, to replace the Sternhold and Hopkins version, a decision which had been made by the Westminster Assembly in that same year. This might have been the case, for Milton chose the common 8.6.8.6 metre so popular in Scottish psalmody, and clearly intended this to be as accurate a translation as possible, using the Greek and Latin and Hebrew, with the consequence that his concern to explain original meanings created an expansion in the English translation. It is strange, however, why he should have chosen this particular collection of psalms, which does not even comprise a discrete unit within the Psalter as a whole. The year 1648 was also the time when the Independents were rallying for a second Civil War. It is quite likely that, given his political sympathies at the time, Milton was making a political commentary from this group of psalms. The first two have explicit references to Israel's escape from Egypt (for example, Ps. 80:8–9 'You brought a vine out of Egypt'; also 81:5 'he made a decree in Joseph, when he went over the land of Egypt') when they fled from the Pharaoh's enslavement under their hero, Moses. (It is interesting that the other two psalms, 114 and 136, also concern the Exodus theme, and that Milton rewrote his version of Psalm 114 in his mid-twenties.) It is not too difficult to see the parallels between Israel and the Reformers, between Pharaoh and the kings and bishops – and between Cromwell and Moses. As was noted earlier with regard to Cromwell's particular use of the Psalms as Battle Hymns, such an approach would not be unusual. And given that Milton's friend and colleague, Andrew Marvell, also working for Cromwell, composed poetry in the same vein ('Bermudas' and 'Upon Appleton House' being just two examples), it would actually be more surprising if Milton had not taken this approach. Indeed, some of his sonnets, written between 1640 and 1650, do this, and his prose writings, referring to the bishops as 'Egyptian taskmasters', hold the same view: *Animadversions* (1641) is the best example of it. Furthermore, underlying all this ideology was the theological belief in the power and sovereignty of God – or, to put this in the Christian thinking of Milton's day, the 'fifth monarchy', the rule of Christ at the end of time. His metrical version of Psalm 80 could certainly give weight to this view; sections of his adaptation are given below.

> Thou Shepherd that dost Israel keep
> Give ear in time of need,
> Who leadest like a flock of sheep
> Thy loved Josephs seed,
>
> Upon the man of thy right hand
> Let thy good hand be laid,
> Upon the Son of Man, whom thou
> Strong for thyself hast made.
>
> Turn us again, thy grace divine
> To us O God vouchsafe;
> Cause thou thy face on us to shine
> And then we shall be safe ...
>
> Return us, and thy grace divine
> Lord God of Hosts voutsafe,
> Cause thou thy face on us to shine,
> And then we shall be safe.

In 1653, as his blindness worsened, Milton composed copies of Psalms 1–8. This was an entirely different enterprise, more of an experiment in versification than translation, as it had been for Psalms 80–8. Much of this was in imitation of the still popular Sidney Psalter, using variable forms of metre and versification and rhyme: each psalm was different, whether in heroic couplets (Psalm 1) or Italian tercets (Psalm 2) or different six-line stanzas (Psalms 3, 4, 7) or four-line stanzas (Psalms 5, 6) or six-line (Psalm 7) or eight-line (Psalm 8). The collection is clearly more an artistic representation of the psalms for their own sake, rather than aspiring for any ideological ends. Psalm 8 is a good example of this:

> When I behold thy Heavens, thy Fingers art,
> The Moon and Starrs which thou so bright hast set,
> In the pure firmament, then saith my heart,
> O what is man that thou remembrest yet,
> And think'st upon him; or of man begot
> That him thou visit'st and of him art found;
> Scarce to be less then Gods, thou mad'st his lot,
> With honour and with state thou hast him crown'd.

Psalms 80–8 were intended more for public use; Psalms 1–8, probably for private reading. It may well have his blindness which prevented Milton accomplishing more on the psalms. But that they were both an ideological challenge and a personal comfort in all his suffering is beyond doubt.[18]

Musical Representation

If poetic imitation is about the art of 'seeing' as well as 'hearing' a psalm, musical compositions, which proliferate from the fifteenth century onwards in the same way that illustrated manuscripts became increasingly popular in the previous five centuries, is more focused on the 'hearing' of a psalm. From what has been discussed previously, it might seem that the main musical medium for psalmody was congregational singing – particularly through metrical psalms. Although this is undoubtedly the case in the non-conformist churches, this period shows enormous musical advances within both the Catholic and Protestant traditions.[19] Taking *Catholic composers* first, beginning with Josquin des Prez (who was influential by the beginning of the sixteenth century) and ending with Vivaldi (who, born in 1678, falls into the period leading up to the middle of the eighteenth century), we shall see that psalmody plays a remarkable part in so many Catholic and Protestant works.

Although it may seem strange to start this assessment with a French composer, *Josquin des Prez* (?1450–1521) wrote innovatory motet settings for many psalms which influenced many later composers both on the Continent and in England. Little is known of his early years; he probably came from Condé or St Quentin,

---

[18] On Milton and psalmody, see E.C. Baldwin (1919); M. Boddy (1966); J.C. Fleck (1928); J.K. Hale (1987, 1994, 1995); H. Hamlin (2004), pp. 74–6, 139–44 ; W.B. Hunter (1961); M.A. Radzinowicz (1989); and L. Wieder (1995 [ed.]) for Milton's version of Psalms 2, 7, 80, 85, 87 and 136.

[19] A key resource for the following discussion has been www.grovemusic.com/ (with subscriber login); also 'Psalm Settings at the Proms' from the *BBC Proms Programme, 14 July – 9 September 2000*; see for example S. Johnson (2000), pp. 15–19.

and moved freely between patrons in France (including François I) and to the papal chapel in Rome (1489). Motets had, in the Middle Ages, become more secularized; but using this form for many psalms, with the characteristic tenor rhythm offset by overlapping two or three upper voices in faster style, Josquin popularized both the contents of the psalms and the art form at the same time. His earliest psalm motets include 'Memor esto verbi tui' from Ps. 119:49–64 ('Remember your word to your servant, in which you have made me hope') which, it is said, was composed to remind an early patron of promises not yet fulfilled), and 'Qui habitat' from Psalm 91 ('You who live in the shelter of the Most High'). His later works, composed at the beginning of the fifteenth century, on the penitential psalms, such as 'De Profundis', on Psalm 130 ('Out of the depths') and 'Miserere mei Deus', on Psalm 51 ('Have mercy on me'), had a notable influence on later English and Italian composers such as Tallis and Byrd, and Palestrina, Giovanni and Allegri, all of whom used the motet genre with Latin psalms.[20]

Christopher Tye (c.1505–73) was an English composer who studied and sang at King's College Cambridge and then at Ely Cathedral. Introduced to the court of Edward in the 1550s by Richard Cox, previously Archdeacon of Ely and erstwhile tutor to the prince, Tye served in the royal chapel under both Edward and Mary. His Latin church music was thus mainly for official, courtly occasions, and includes settings to Psalm 149, 'Cantate Domino' ('Sing to the Lord'), to Ps. 119:9, 'In quo corrigit' ('How can young people keep their way pure?') and to Psalm 47, 'Omnes gentes, plaudite manibus' ('Clap your hands, all you peoples'). His English church music includes settings to Psalm 31 ('O Lord, deliver me'), Psalm 25 ('My trust, O Lord') and Psalm 130 ('From the depth I called to thee'). He returned to his old post at Ely in 1558, got ordained, and rarely performed in the court again.[21]

Thomas Tallis (c.1514–85), like Josquin and Tye, was a Catholic who also had to learn to survive as a court composer during political turmoil. His post as organist of Waltham Abbey was forfeited upon the dissolution of the abbey, yet in 1542 he was appointed to the Chapel Royal, where he remained as organist, singer and composer through the reigns of Henry, Edward, Mary and Elizabeth, mainly because of his ability to reinvent his music for changing liturgical and theological styles – canticles and hymns and psalms for Matins and Evensong, anthems and motets and settings for the Mass – so that he adapted almost every genre used during the sixteenth century. He was able to transform his earliest votive antiphons in Latin into more Christocentric motets which were pleasing to Cromwell and Cranmer. He was one of the first musicians able to write in the chordal, syllabic (one-note-one-syllable) style required for the new liturgy of the Church in England: 'Remember not, O Lord God', which is taken from Pss. 79:8–10 and 100:3, is typical of this genre. He could turn a text such as 'Gaude gloriosa' into epithets

---

[20] For a website on Josquin's music, see www.josquin.com/.
[21] For a website which plays some of Tye's music, see www.cyberhymnal.org/bio/t/y/tye_c.htm.

directed not only to the Virgin Mary but also to Queen Mary herself, and his seven-voice mass 'Puer natus est nobis' was composed at the time when it was believed Mary was expecting an heir. He maintained his Catholic stance by composing Latin chant-based choral 'psalm-motets', in the style of Josquin, for Elizabeth's private chapel: 'Laudate Dominum' (Psalm 150) and 'Domine quis habitat' (Psalm 15) are probably from this period. A major contribution to psalmody was his eight four-voice psalm tunes for Archbishop Parker's 1567 Psalter, discussed earlier. Using the traditional eight church *modes', Tallis was able to providing a wealth of contrasting emotions by adapting the pace and tone of the music to his particular choice of psalms: Psalm 1 has as its title '*The first is meek: devout to see*'; Psalm 68 has '*The second is sad: in majesty*'; Psalm 2 has '*The third doth rage: and roughly brayeth*'; Psalm 95 has '*The fourth doth fawn: and flattery playeth*'; Psalm 42 has '*The fifth delighteth, and laugheth the more*'; Psalm 5 has '*The sixth bewaileth: it weepeth full sore*'; Psalm 52 has '*The seventh treadeth stout: in forward race*'; and Psalm 67 has '*The eighth goeth mild: in modest pace*'. (A ninth, 'Come Holy Ghost', known now as Tallis's Ordinal, or Tallis's Canon, was added at the end of music section.) Tallis's great forty-part motet, 'Spem in alium nunquam habui' ('I have no faith in any other than God'), possibly taken from Ps. 56:4,11 ('in God I trust: I am not afraid: what can flesh do to me?'), with its pace, texture and harmonic rhythm, was sung in an English-text version as 'Sing and Glorify Heaven's High Majesty' at the investiture ceremonies of Henry and Charles as Prince of Wales in 1610 and 1616 respectively.[22]

William Byrd (c.1542–1623) studied mainly under Tallis. After serving as organist at Lincoln Cathedral from 1563, by 1570 he became a lay clerk in the Chapel Royal; by 1575, he was elected organist. He was one of the first English composers to write madrigals, whilst also being a prolific composer of church music. In 1575, along with Tallis, he was granted sole rights to print his music: this accounts in part for the popularity of their compositions. Byrd, too, lived in unsettling political times during the reigns of Elizabeth and James I, yet remained a faithful Catholic, in spite of having to leave London with his family in 1593 to live more safely in the parish of Stondon Massey, Essex. Works which are relevant to psalmody include his 1588 *Psalms, Sonnets and Songs of Sadness and Pietie*', which included English settings for Psalms 47, 54, 84 and 100, his 1607 *Gradualia*, a collection of Latin graduals for the Mass for the major feasts (the '*Propers') of the church year, including Marian votive masses, and his 1611 *Psalms, Songs and Sonnets, Some Solemn, Others Joyful, Framed to the Life of the Words, Fit for Voyces or Viols, etc*, which has English settings for Psalms 114, 55, 119 and 24; his famous three masses, for three, four and five voices respectively, also use verses from the psalms. His ability to produce music for psalmody, in rich and concise polyphonic modes, to suit both Anglican and Catholic liturgy, in English as well as Latin, for

---

[22] For a website with Tallis's music, see www.bbc.co.uk/music/profiles/tallis.shtml. On Tallis and psalmody, see L. Ellinwood (1971 [ed]); and T. Knighton (2005), pp. 12–16.

secular as well as sacred use, earned him the Latin epigram in *Gradualia* as 'Father of British Music'.[23]

Several other English composers served first in cathedral choirs and then in the Chapel Royal, like Tye, Tallis and Byrd, and although their range was obviously far more vast than psalmody alone, the settings they composed for (mainly) office psalms are still popular today. One example is *William (John) Blitheman* (1525–91), who served at St Paul's in the 1540s, Christ Church Oxford in the 1550s, and the Chapel Royal from 1558 to 1591, succeeding Tallis as organist there in 1585. His setting of an evening psalm, Psalm 4 'In pace' ('I will both lie down and sleep in peace') is amongst his best known. Similarly, *Thomas Morley* (1557–1602) served at Norwich Cathedral, at Oxford, at St Paul's and, by 1592, after the death of Blitheman, at the Chapel Royal. Noted for his popularizing of Italian music, particularly the madrigal and ballet forms, for an English audience, and admired by Queen Elizabeth, he was given Byrd's patent after his death, and was thus able to safeguard his own publishing rights. One of his best-known psalm compositions is the English version of Psalm 130: 'Out of the deep have I called unto thee, Lord hear my voice'.

A title sometimes used of Byrd was 'a British Palestrina'. *Giovanni Pierluigi da Palestrina* (c.1515–94) was perhaps the greatest composer of liturgical music of his time. From a modest background, by 1551 his talent took him from choirmaster at Palestrina to Rome as *maestro di cappella* at St Peter's, and, upon the publication of a volume of masses dedicated to Julius III (previously Bishop of Palestrina), he was given membership of the papal chapel in 1554, in spite of not being ordained. This was the period of implementing the reforms of the Council of Trent concerning the Tridentine Mass with its need for new compositions to bring the Latin to life, and in spite of opposition and jealousy from colleagues, by 1571 Palestrina had risen to prominence as composer to the royal chapel and director of music at St Philip's Oratory. By the end of his life Palestrina had composed some 140 madrigals, both sacred and secular, some 250 motets, 33 settings to the Magnificat, some 70 hymns and setting to psalms, 104 Masses, 68 offertories, as well as versions of Gregorian chant (for Pope Gregory XIII) and motets to Song of Songs and Lamentations. Of his many polychoral compositions to Latin text of the psalms, perhaps the most poignant, composed after the death of his wife in 1580, is 'Super flumina Babylonis', from Psalm 137.[24]

Giovanni Gabrieli (1558–1613) is known almost entirely for his church music whilst organist at St Mark's, Venice, where, under the patronage of the Venetian Doges, he used the spatial acoustics of the Basilica to create antiphonal compositions between singers and instrumentalists, of which his eight-part *Jubilate* (from the opening words in Latin to Psalm 66: 'Iubilate Deo omnis terra') sung antiphonally

---

[23] For a website with Byrd's music on the psalms, see www.geocities.com/Vienna/2820/byrd.html.
[24] For a website with Palestrina's music on the psalms, see www-atdp.berkeley.edu/9931/htsai/palestrina.html.

between a double choir and brass is amongst the best known. Also noteworthy is his 'Timor et tremor' ('Fear and Trembling'), which is a grand and personal response to the psalms, intended for use in Holy Week, but not published until after his death, which takes up lines from Pss. 55:5–6, 57:2 and 61:2 as well as the *Te Deum*, juxtaposing the fear of mortality with trust in God through a polychoral motet form. Gabrieli was tutor to Heinrich Schütz between 1575 and 1579, and influenced greatly the latter's polychoral work on the psalms, to be discussed shortly. His madrigals and motets, composed for from six to some twenty voices, as well as a vast number of instrumentalists, were for State occasions as well as those in the Venetian church; the best known are his settings for Mass composed after the end of the plague epidemic between 1575 and 1577. Other psalmodic works include settings to the Latin text of Psalms 22 (1587), 119, 128, 34, 8, 102, 55, 135, 51, 47 (all published in 1597) and Psalms 9, 54, 57 (published posthumously in 1615).

Claudio Monteverdi (1567–1643) served as a string player from 1591 onwards in the court of Duke Vincenzo Gonzaga in Mantua, where he worked with Salamone Rossi. In 1613, shortly after the dedication of his *Vespers* (1610) to Pope Paul V, he was appointed as *maestro di cappella* at St Marks, Venice, on the death of Giovanni. His compositions were as influential in theatrical performance as in church music, especially nearer the end of his life, when he composed several scores for Venetian opera and ballet, as well as a vast amount of chamber music and madrigals. As for liturgy, Monteverdi composed numerous settings to masses, many vesper psalms (he composed three different motets for Psalm 1, for example) and numerous canticles and hymns, as well as his well-known setting to the Marian antiphon *Salve regina*. The psalms which are used in the *Vespers* of 1610 are nevertheless his most important legacy to psalmody. After the introduction 'Deus in adiutorium meum intende' (O God, make speed to save me'), the five vesper psalms chosen by Monteverdi are each given a dramatically different setting: Psalm 110 is set to a six-voice choir with six instruments, Psalm 113 to an eight-voice choir, Psalm 122 to five voices, Psalm 127 to a ten-voice choir, and Psalm 147 to two choirs of three voices; each psalm is interspersed with a motet, and the concluding pieces are an antiphon to Mary, 'Ave maris stella', with 2 choirs and soloists, followed by the Magnificat. This spectacular use of plainchant, set to a concertato form, with varying numbers of soloists, choirs and orchestra of strings and brass, is a superb example of Baroque style in church music at this time.

The final sixteenth-century Catholic composer whose contribution to psalmody was considerable is *Gregario Allegri* (1582–1652). Born in Rome, he joined the papal choir of Pope Urban VIII as an alto in 1629, and was elected *maestro di cappella* in the Sistine Chapel in 1650. Part of his renown is the result of his revision of Palestrina's psalms and hymns; other psalmic compositions included motets and antiphons for Masses, and a couple of studies of Lamentations. However, his best known work, publicized on account of its constant revision due to its prominence in the Tenebrae offices of Holy week, is his *Miserere Mei Deus*, composed in about 1638. This is a setting of Psalm 51 ('Have mercy on me, O God'), traditionally sung as plainchant by two choirs, one placed at a distance from the main choir, using high-rising soprano voices which rise and swell in contrast to the full strength of the choirs, who also alternate with tenors and basses, ending in unison for the last half-verse. The custom was to improvise embellishments, and this was what Allegri provided, creating an orchestral and choral piece, provided by tenors and basses, lasting some fifteen minutes, using intense repetition, with a soaring treble voice leading towards a spectacular finale, to symbolize the relief of forgiveness attained through prayer. It is said that the fourteen-year-old Mozart, upon hearing it in the Sistine Chapel, was able to transcribe it all from memory, thus breaking its carefully guarded place in papal worship.

With the exception of Vivaldi, most of the following composers are, broadly speaking, *Protestant*. A common feature unifying both Catholic and Protestant musicians throughout this period is the interest in experimentation – a feature which contrasts, somewhat surprisingly, with the more restrained musical tradition of psalmody in the Reformed churches, with their greater commitment to the memorization of the psalmic texts by using a clear melody and predictable rhythm.

One good example of the blend of Catholic and Protestant influences is seen in the five hundred or so compositions of *Heinrich Schütz* (1585–1672), who used applied Italian (Catholic) techniques to German (Lutheran) sacred music. The Lutheran spirit is clearly evident in the ways in which the music brings to life the meaning of the words (which reveal a good deal of private devotion despite their public function), whilst the Catholic form is seen in the range of musical genres used – madrigals, motets, concertos, requiems and passions. Schütz, originally from Saxony, spent some five years in Venice from 1608 to 1613, where Gabrieli was his tutor; he left St Mark's just as Monteverdi was beginning his time there. Back in Dresden as organist and musical director, these years were constantly marked by the effects of the Thirty Years War (Schütz went without pay for two years in the 1620s), but this did not prevent compositions such as the setting to Psalm 98 'Singet dem Herrn ein neues Lied' ('Sing unto the Lord a new song') being used in the three-day festival to celebrate the centenary of the Reformation in October 1617: the psalm's words as well as its delivery, with its double choirs and elaborate melodic lines, clearly influenced by Italian style, leading to a grandiose conclusion, suited the occasion well. By 1619 Schütz had made his first collection of sacred music – on the Psalms. *Psalmen Davids sampt etlichen Moteten und Concerten* used the same, now familiar, genre of motet concertos of his Venetian tutor, Gabrieli. Schütz returned to the Psalms again and again – after the death of his wife in 1625, after only six years of marriage, he directed his grief into the *Becker Psalter* (1628), transforming popular paraphrases of psalmody by Cornelius Becker into the motet genre, sometimes in German, sometimes in Latin. It seems that Schütz always intended to create a second volume of his *Psalmen Davids*; even in 1671, aged 86, he composed thirteen double-choir motets for eight voices, of which the best known are on Psalms 100 and 119. Like Luther himself, Schütz was somewhat obsessed with Psalm 119: not only did he compose several arrangements of it throughout his life, but this became his 'funeral text', in that his 1674 setting of it resulted in Ps. 119:54 ('Your statutes have been my songs wherever I make my home') being performed at his funeral.[25]

Orlando Gibbons (1583–1625) and his son *Christopher Gibbons* (1615–76) are the most notable English (Protestant) composers of psalmody in the late sixteenth and seventeenth centuries. Both served in the Chapel Royal, Orlando for the last ten years of his life, and Christopher as a chorister to Charles I until 1638, and again, after the Restoration, to Charles II. Both composed a number of Psalm settings for the short services, mostly to the English texts, which adopted polyphonic singing (for between four and eight voices) to organ accompaniment. Orlando's 'O clap your hands' (Psalm 47, the psalm used for Evensong on Ascension Day, although it may well have been composed for his Oxford DMus ceremony) is perhaps his best-known work, composed for two four-part choirs; his rendering of verse 5 ('God has gone up with a shout, the Lord with the sound of the trumpet') shows a dramatic use of polyphony and especially of the tenor voices. Christopher's rendering of Psalm 13 ('How long wilt thou forget me') is simpler, by contrast, using the organ and two solo trebles.

Johann Pachelbel (1653–1706), organist in Vienna from 1674, and later in Erfurt and Stuttgart and Nuremberg, also composed psalm settings mainly in his native language, German (one exception being his setting to *Exsurgat Deus*, from Psalm 68). Although his chorales and Magnificat settings are the most renowned of his sacred music, nevertheless, following the tradition of Schütz, Pachelbel also adapted Catholic styles for German psalms, and used many motet and concerto settings for his texts, often using Vesper psalms. Psalm 46 ('God is our refuge and strength'), Psalm 96 ('Praise God in his Holiness') and Psalm 150 ('Praise God in his holiness') are good examples of his particular motet style, where the melody is held over several long notes, phrase by phrase, to draw out the meaning of the German version. His particular skill was the use of the solo voice, backed by several instruments, with a choral response: the setting to Ps. 118:24 ('This is the day which the Lord has made') as an aria for a ceremony at Erfurt at which the citizens professed allegiance to the emissaries of the Elector Karl Heinrich of Mainz (1679) is an example of this, where the soloist sings 'So is denn dies der Tag', and the choir, 'Vivat'.

It is impossible to do justice to the many varied settings of the psalms by members of the Bach family. Taking their most prolific composer, *Johann Sebastian Bach* (1685–1750), as just one example, his eleven hundred compositions include vocal, organ, keyboard, and solo instrumental music, as well as chamber works and concertos and orchestral suites and canons. His vocal works amount to well over five hundred compositions – some two hundred sacred cantatas (a further hundred or so have been lost) and another twenty secular cantatas, as well as some

---

[25] For a website on Schütz's *Psalms of David*, see www.naxos.com/catalogue/item.asp?item_code=8.553044.

two hundred chorales, some seventy spiritual songs, seven motets, at least twelve masses, five passions, three oratorios, three wedding chorales, and ten arias.[26]

Obviously many of these are pervaded with the language of the psalms; Bach was a pious Lutheran, and possessed some of Luther's commentaries on the Psalms. During his most creative period at Leipzig between 1723 and 1729, when he served the four churches and taught at the choir school, many of his compositions for civic occasions borrow freely from the imagery of the psalms which speak of God's protection of his city; the German version of Psalm 46:5 'God is in the midst of the city; it shall not be moved', one of Luther's earliest metrical psalms, is a clear example of this [BWV 303 and BWV 80b]). Most of his motets use language from the psalms: 'Lobet den Herrn, alle Heiden', from Psalm 117, is amongst the best known (although some speculate whether this is in fact Bach's own work), which is a good example of vocal polyphony, expanding this two-verse psalm into three contrasting sections, with a four-voice choir throughout each one, leading to a triumphant paeon of praise in festive style in its final 'Alleluja'. At least thirty of his two hundred sacred cantatas borrow from the psalms in this way, and some of the psalms he used in entirety. For example, Psalm 23 was used in three different sacred cantatas, each with a striking use of solo voice and instruments, in each case as this was the set psalm for the second Sunday after Easter: once in 1724 (*'Du Hirte Israel, hore'*: BWV 104), again in 1725 (*'Ich bin ein guter Hirt'*: BWV 85), when Bach adapted Becker's version of this psalm, and then in 1731 (*'Der Herr ist mein getreuer Hirt'*: BWV 112) when he used Meuslin's version.

Other psalms, or verses from psalms, according to their listings in Sundays and feast days throughout the liturgical year, were used similarly – not only in the cantata form, but for chorales as well. Amongst the chorales, the best known include Psalms 137 (BWV 267), 124 (BWV 258), 127 (BWV 438) and 67 (BWV 312). In each case the words follow the rules of metrical psalmody; an example from Psalm 67 has the *abab* rhyme, and 8.8.8.8 rhythm: 'Es woll uns Gott genädig sein / und seinen Segen geben; / sein Antlitz uns mit hellem Schein / erleucht zum ewgen Leben' ('May to us God his mercy show / and his salvation give us; / his face on us with radiant beams / pour light for life eternal'). But the above examples are but a few of a much richer range, including also Psalms 6 (BWV 338), 14 (BWV 308), 51 (BWV 305), 86 (BWV 372), 103 (BWV 390), 121 (BWV 427), 136 (BWV 286), 147 (BWV 374) 149 (BWV 411) and 150 (BWV 1126). Bach's distinctive contribution to Lutheran and Germanic psalmody was that although he is undoubtedly indebted to Vivaldi's orchestral work, for example transcribing several of his concertos to the keyboard, nevertheless, as far as his sacred works were concerned, he worked more independently of Italian, Catholic influence; he never once visited Italy, and for most of his life stayed close to Eisenach, the town of his birth, whether at Weimar, Köthen or Leipzig, where he stayed from 1723 till his death.

---

[26] Because of the sheer volume of works, the following discussion will also offer the BWV (*Bach-Werke-Verzeichnis*) as used, for example, on www.bachcentral.com/bwv.html. For a website with access to Bach's recordings on the Psalms, see www.jsbach.org/. See also U. Meyer (1997).

G.F. Handel (1685–1759) provides an extraordinary example of a musician committed increasingly to secular and state compositions, yet also of a composer whose occasional works on the psalms have been long-lasting. Handel is known as an English composer of German birth; and after his time serving the church at Halle (1703), it could be argued that he was no longer a composer of church music, although psalmic compositions occur everywhere in his broader concerns. Operas and librettos became increasingly dominant, as is evident from his time in Hamburg and later in Rome (1707). But even here, Handel is a good Lutheran: his *Dixit Dominus* (Psalm 110) and *Nisi Dominus* (Psalm 127) in 1707 and his other Vesper psalms, such as Psalms 113 and 127, illustrate his commitment to 'the text' of psalmody, although some would argue this was simply a prelude to his engagement with operatic scores, such as those he composed in Naples, Florence and Venice, until his arrival in England in 1711. It is possible to argue that the psalms increasingly became a means to another end: 'As Pants the Hart' (Psalm 42) was Handel's first English anthem (1711–12), and it was a means to his earning royal approval in the court of Queen Anne – a position which took him till 1727 to attain.

From a position of some financial security in the church of St Lawrence, Whitchurch, from 1717, Handel composed a few sacred renditions of the psalms, but mainly his interest was in performance – of opera, and oratorios, such as *The Messiah, Samson, Solomon, Saul* and *Israel in Egypt*. In the latter, Handel uses the national psalms with their hopes of restoration (Psalms 78, 105, 106). In *Saul*, Psalm 8 is used, most unusually, as David's victory song after his defeat of Goliath. And in *The Messiah*, which uses many extracts from the Prophets and Gospels, Part Two takes up verses from psalms, perhaps predictably from all those which had prophetic connotations when used in the Gospels: the tenor recitatives 'All they that see him laugh him to scorn' (from Ps. 22:7) and 'He Trusted in God' (Ps. 22:8) and 'Thy rebuke hath broken his heart' (from Ps. 69:21) use the psalms from the passion narratives; whilst the soprano air 'But thou didst not leave his soul in hell' is from Ps. 16:10, and the chorus response, 'Lift up your heads, O ye gates' is from Ps. 24:7–10; similarly the mezzo-soprano air 'Thou art gone up on high' is from Ps. 68:18, followed by the chorus 'The Lord gave the word', from verse 11 of the same psalm; and the later chorus 'Let us break their bonds asunder' is from Ps. 2:3. (This psalm is also used in 'Why do the nations so furiously rage together?' [Ps. 2:1–2]; 'He that dwelleth in heaven' [Ps. 2:4]; and 'Thou shalt break them' [Ps. 2:9].) By the 1730s Handel's main use of the psalms was in public ceremonies, such as his composition of 'This the Day' (Ps. 118:24) for the wedding, in 1734, of one of his favourite pupils, the Princess Royal. Hence in respect to psalmody, the concerns of J.S. Bach and G.F. Handel may be contrasted, in that the former suggests a more personal devotion to the psalms, whilst the latter appropriates them for more public occasions.[27]

The Purcell family of musicians and court composers was as diffuse in English culture in the seventeenth and eighteenth centuries as the Bach family was in

---

[27] For a website with access to Handel's compositions of psalms (through subscription) see www.classicalarchives.com/handel.html.

Germany. For this reason, the psalm settings by the greatest of them, *Henry Purcell* (1659–95) must suffice, in part because they make such a contrast to the more personal and devotional works of Bach. Henry Purcell was a court musician, beginning as a boy chorister in the Chapel Royal, which under Oliver Cromwell had almost dwindled away, but by 1660 began to emerge from the shadows again. By 1677 Purcell had become composer for the violins at court, and rose to the position of court composer for Charles II between 1680 and 1685, which meant that his vocation was to allow the psalms to serve more of a public purpose. This was the period when psalm settings for the regular services, anthems of psalms, verse anthems from psalms – for solo voices, choir, organ or strings – occupied Purcell's time. Settings for Psalms 8, 86, 72, 27, 65 and 102 may be dated from this period, as well as 'Rejoice in the Lord always' (from Psalms 97 and 105), known as the Bell Anthem because the symphony has a descending octave peal of bells in the bass, possibly from 1683–4. From this same time also is 'Jehova, quam multi hostes mei!', from Psalm 3 ('O Lord, how many are my foes!'), one of only two Latin motets composed by Purcell, this one in 1682 for the private Roman Catholic chapel of Charles II's queen, Catherine of Braganza; it undoubtedly was in tune with the political sensitivities of the time, exemplified by Purcell's use of the bass voice near the end ('I am not afraid of ten thousands of people') complemented by the chorus in triple metre, 'Deliverance belongs to the Lord'. Purcell's symphony with anthems with orchestra, performed for Charles II in 1685 as a setting to the royal psalm, 45: 'My heart is inditing' also comes from this time. The accession of James II and the revival of Catholicism were clearly difficult, although Purcell wrote 'I was glad when they said unto me' (Psalm 122) for the occasion; but secular music rather than sacred music was preferable until 1688, with the exile of James II. This situation was reversed after the coronation of William and Mary in 1689, as the court was now no longer the vibrant musical centre it had been under the Stuarts, and Purcell became more occupied with theatrical compositions than with liturgical psalmody. Nevertheless, he composed 'Praise the Lord, O Jerusalem' (Ps. 116:19) for the coronation at Westminster Abbey, and in 1695 his simple and striking 'Thou knowest, O Lord', from Psalm 139, was used at Mary's funeral in 1695, as well as at Purcell's own funeral, some six months later.

Antonio Vivaldi (1678–1741) takes our survey of the reception of psalmody back to Venice, where he was born. Unlike Purcell, Vivaldi preferred to avoid the world of politics rather than engage musically with it. Since Vivaldi is best known for his energy and vitality as a virtuoso violinist (he composed some five hundred concerti) with a love of opera (some twenty-two are ascribed to his name), it may be difficult to appreciate where he and psalmody coincide. But he produced some forty cantatas and some sixty sacred works, most of which were during his time as teacher (later, musical director) at the Conservatorio della Pieta, a State-run music school for orphaned girls, a period which divided roughly into two stages – from 1703/4 for some fifteen years, and later from 1735 for some four years.[28]

---

[28] For ease of reference, the catalogue number of Vivaldi's work on psalmody is given alongside its title. For Vivaldi's compositions of psalmody, see www.classicalarchives.com/vivaldi.html.

Two-thirds of his seventeen psalm settings come from these two periods; the rest were for patrons outside Venice. It was during the earlier period here that he pioneered the solo concerto form, which experimented with the contrasts between solo voice and orchestra, a genre evident in his large-scale choral and orchestral works, such as the *Gloria* – and also in some of his psalms. *Nisi Dominus* (RV 608), a work in nine movements starting with Psalm 127, is typical of this, from Vivaldi's earlier time at Pieta; so too is the long piece of some 420 bars (*Beatus Vir*: RV 597) using Psalm 112 (one of the five Vespers psalms, Psalms 110–14), which experiments with solo voice and viola, although this piece was later refashioned for *in due cori* – two ensembles of soloists, choir and orchestra, creating vast and alternating blocks of sound, with strikingly simple unison where the mood required it. Another Vespers psalm, Ps. 70:1 (*Domine ad adjuvandum* RV 593), which forms the opening words to the evening service, was conceived from the outset as a 'double choir' work, although ends with a haunting 'Gloria' by solo soprano. Yet another Vespers psalm, Psalm 110, is used in *Dixit Dominus* (RV594), which sustains a spectacular 'double choir' effect throughout, with contrapuntal texture often in eight parts. By contrast, *Laudate Dominum* (RV 606), from the two verses which comprise Psalm 117, experiments with unison violins and solo voice and choir, leading progressively to the climax of the psalm, *misericordia* – 'the mercy of the Lord which endures for ever'. Many of the features here may be compared with Bach's use of the same psalm.

A collection of five psalms (RV 604, RV 609, RV 795, RV 789, RV 803), now all believed to be the work of Vivaldi, date from about 1739: *In Exitu Israel* (RV 604) is a composition from Psalms 114–115, composed for Easter Sunday at Pieta, 1739; Psalms 112 and 127 are again evident, echoing his earlier work, this time using a single choir, in changing keys and different harmonic patterns, intended to contrast with the orchestra. Vivaldi's work on the psalms is illustrative of his work as a whole: even though he was ordained, (although he rarely said Mass, 'on account of his ill-health'), the psalms were more important mainly as the opportunity for musical experiments and dramatic performances, reflecting more his theatrical interest in orchestra and opera; the medium of the music is more important than the words themselves, a feature which becomes increasingly evident in the musical compositions of psalms in the period to be discussed in the following chapter.

Concluding Observations

What we have witnessed through this period of some three hundred years is, as our chapter title suggested, the 'democratization' of psalmody in Christendom, in that psalms could now be used in the vernacular by laity and clergy alike, and similarly the 'dissemination' of the psalms, in that psalms could now be used, publicly and privately, anywhere – not only in churches but in the home, at work, at war and at leisure. The creativity applied to the *illuminations* of psalms within the

Catholic tradition in previous centuries is now echoed as it is applied to the *words* of psalmody within the Reformed and Protestant traditions. Related to this renewed interest in the written words of the psalms, the extraordinary escalation of new translations affected the reception of the psalms in at least three other areas – in liturgy, instruction, and aesthetic representations (including not only art, but also music, poetry and drama).

The witness to psalmody in Jewish tradition is less dramatically marked: it could be argued that the 'democratization' and 'dissemination' of the psalms had been evolving in Judaism since the very first centuries, with the emphasis on the use of the psalms in daily life and in family worship, and so a reform of this nature was less pressing, and a very different sort of reform was to come in later centuries when the political and social circumstances were more congenial. Nevertheless, Jewish reception offers its most striking contributions in aesthetic ways, through music and art.

One less prominent example of the reception of psalmody during this period is the publication of theological and exegetical commentaries – a surprising factor, given the emphasis on the *words* of the psalms in translation and imitation. Significant exceptions are provided by the few scholars who propelled the Reformation cause forward (mainly Erasmus, Luther and Calvin, and others in the seventeenth century such as the commentary by Matthew Poole [1685] and Richard Simon [whose English version appeared in 1682]). But overall, this period, so full of literary and artistic creativity as far as the psalms were concerned, was one which at the same time offered less critical and practical exegesis of them. This situation changes again by the end of the eighteenth century, when, as we shall see, exegetical and devotional works become as popular as literary and artistic compositions, whilst liturgically influenced works and vernacular versions are far less in evidence.

The Eighteenth and Nineteenth Centuries: Secularization and Revitalization

The closer one comes to modern times, the more difficult it is to disentangle distinctively English developments from the complex global context in which the reception of psalmody now takes place. And because of the growing secularization of British culture, psalmody, like other parts of the Bible, is interwoven with other religious, political, social and intellectual developments, so that it is impossible to discuss certain aspects of reception without reference to some of the ideals of the *Enlightenment as they impact upon the psalms.

Nevertheless, it is still possible to chart the now familiar five modes of reception. One notable difference between this period and the previous chapter is that the main trends of reception there are minimal here, and vice versa. For example, there is now a vast increase in *commentaries and introductions*, many of which are more critical and detached from church tradition. There is also a plethora of *devotional and instructional* works, mainly for private use, which are partly a reaction to the more analytical exegetical works. Only the *aesthetic representations* of psalmody continue more or less as before, comprising mainly literary and musical compositions; there are fewer new artistic examples, and several of the musical compositions are now intended for a secular performance, again illustrating the detachment of psalmody from church tradition. *Liturgical* innovations are now minimal – a striking contrast with the sixteenth and seventeenth centuries, given the amount of liturgical reform involving psalmody at that time; other than musical compositions for liturgy, and further experimentations in hymnody, there is little innovation in the reception of psalmody in worship. Likewise, new *translations* of the psalms, particularly those for public worship, are far less in evidence – another feature which is quite different from the plethora of translations which we saw in the previous chapter.

These observations concern the Christian reception of psalmody. The Jewish reception continues to evolve in an independent and distinctive way (for example, *Haskalah* had its repercussions in Judaism a good deal later than in the Christian traditions), and so will be discussed separately. It will be seen in this case that the psalms play a major part in *liturgical renewal* and *didactic works*, both in conservative and reformed traditions; and in the latter, *exegetical works* as well as *musical*

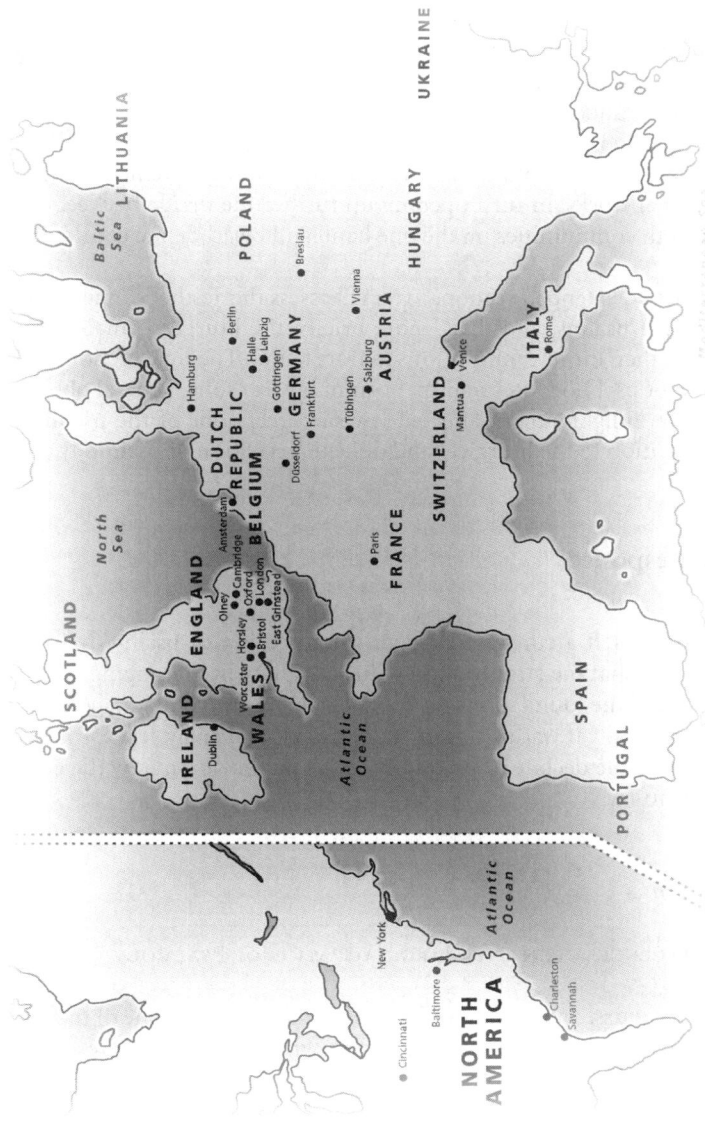

MAP 5.1 Great Britain, Europe and America: the spread of psalmody during the Enlightenment period.

compositions using the psalms begin to emerge. However, there is little evidence of *translations* of the psalms into the vernacular: this does not really feature until the start of the twentieth century.

We shall examine the first two most prolific modes of Christian reception – expositions of psalms and devotional studies – in two major sections. We shall first look at the ways in which, from the beginning of the eighteenth century onwards, increasing tendencies towards *secularization* influenced more analytical and critical works, written under the influence of the Enlightenment spirit. Contrasting with this, we shall then look at incidents of *revitalization* in Christian traditions throughout the same two centuries, noting the ways in which these movements encouraged more devotional works, in turn opening up further the divide between readings inspired by faith communities on the one hand and by academic communities on the other.

After these two extended sections, we shall assess the aesthetic, mainly musical, responses to the psalms, and then, more briefly, the liturgical (mainly hymnic) reception, and then the few innovations in translation. The final section will assess the reception of psalmody in Judaism, beginning with some general observations about how the Enlightenment affected Jewish perceptions of the psalms, giving particular attention to the liturgical and didactic reception of psalmody.

Christian Responses

The Reformation left a curious effect on the reception of psalmody in western Christendom, in that the stress on individual lay piety in the singing and praying of the psalms laid the foundations for more detached and individual critical study as well, and ironically it was this more independent and analytical spirit that contributed to a notable decline of psalmody in the public domain by the end of the nineteenth century.[1]

Exegetical Works

SECULAR INFLUENCES UPON THE MARGINALIZATION OF PSALMODY

It might not be at first apparent how the rise of *humanism, as one of the key characteristics of the *Enlightenment, could affect writings on the psalms. *Immanuel*

---

[1] General resources used in both sections on secularization and revitalization include J. *Drury (ed.) (1989)*; J.H. Eaton (1999, 2003); N. *Frei (1974)*; S.L. *Greenslade (1963)*; W.L. Holladay (1993); J.L. Houlden (1995); D.R. Jones (1963); E.G.H. Kraeling (1955); J. Rogerson (1984); J. Shaw (2001); K. Sloan (ed.) (2004).

Kant of Königsberg (1724–1804) was probably the first to use the term 'Aufklärung' or 'Enlightenment' for the process of change which had swept through Britain and France, Germany, the Dutch Republic and the American colonies from the middle of the seventeenth century onwards. His essay *'What is Enlightenment?'* (1785) illustrates the growing confidence that the natural world could give answers to problems which had previously assumed a supernatural explanation, and it was this belief in human progress channelled through a secular state and economic liberty which led to consensus that there was less need to plead for an interventionist God. Although Kant still professed a *Deist faith, his rejection of traditional beliefs and practices was otherwise typical of the response to 'absolutism' which had manifested itself not only in the monarchies and assumed powers of the state but also in the overbearing nature of ecclesiastical authority throughout eighteenth-century Europe.

This is not the place to offer a critique of the Enlightenment, except to say that it was profoundly inconsistent in allowing the questioning of everything except its own ideology, and in believing that everything was possible, except divine intervention. But the Enlightenment certainly transformed exegetical studies of the psalms. No longer was the interpreter constrained by a community of faith which had guarded the psalms in the history of tradition; gradually everything became open to question. And given the pervasiveness of the psalms in the previous centuries – in translation, in liturgy, in literary and musical culture – and their earlier use at critical moments in both church and state, this was a significant change in their status quo.

A century previously, scientists such as *Francis Bacon* (1561–1626), whose works had influenced the experimental *empiricism of scientists in the eighteenth century, could still publish poetic imitations of the psalms (as we saw in the previous chapter). His metrical versions of Psalms 12, 90 and 126 are amongst his best known, and the latter part of Psalm 90 epitomizes his facility, as a seventeenth-century scientist and poet, in holding the two worlds of scientific enquiry and psalmody in tension:

> Teach us, O Lord, to number well our days,
>   Thereby our hearts to wisdom to apply;
> For that which guides man best in all his ways,
>   Is meditation of mortality.
>   This bubble light, this vapor of our breath,
>   Teach us to consecrate to hour of death.[2]

By contrast, by the middle of the eighteenth century, scientific writings exuded such confidence that the world-view of the psalmists began to look as if it belonged to an older order of things. A fitting example of a scientist who lived during this

---

[2] See L. Wieder (ed.) (1999), pp. 137–8.

period of transition, who, like Bacon, still maintained an interest in theology as well as science, is *Isaac Newton* (1642–1727). As a mathematician and physicist, his investigation into the workings of gravity, light and colour also presupposed a personal belief in the ordering of the natural world and a creative force behind it; yet Newton was more critical of traditional faith and ecclesiastical orthodoxy than Bacon had been. Newton's views exemplify the way in which the authority of the Church was slowly being supplanted by a new authority – that of Nature, whose appeal came not from an invisible heavenly world above but from the tangible world all around. After Newton, we see an increasing confidence that answers to our existence could be provided by classifying and understanding the natural world without explicit reference to God: the Enlightenment Gallery in the British Museum, where one can view just how diverse and pervasive this classification of the natural world was, is a good illustration of this intellectual mood by the mid-eighteenth century. It is not surprising that even Newton's numerous theological works have nothing to say about the psalms: unlike Bacon, they were simply considered less relevant.

It was not only the questions raised by humanism and science that brought the world of the psalmists under threat. A different example, amongst the *philosophes on the Continent, is *Voltaire* (1694–1778) who, in 1756, was invited by Madame de Pompadour, mistress of Louis XV, to produce a paraphrase of the psalms. Voltaire (who had some interesting views on the psalms, for example once writing that '[David] breathes nothing but blood') reputedly turned the request down with the reply that he was 'not the right man for the Psalms'. By 1759 he had nevertheless translated Song of Songs and Ecclesiastes: love songs and reflections on wisdom were a more appropriate choice for an 'Enlightenment man' than pious and liturgically influenced works such as the psalms.

A more general factor which contributed to the marginalizing of psalmody was the so-called 'industrial revolution'. The slow progression from an essentially agricultural economy to a capitalist urban one, with England playing a leading part within Europe as a whole, had an enormous effect on traditional Christianity. By the mid-nineteenth century, Britain had a 50 per cent share in the European trade of manufactured goods, and at that point the success was seen as the practical consequence of what Enlightenment thinkers in the eighteenth century had been aspiring to in theory. Even the inevitable downside – cramped living and working conditions with low wages and long hours, fast-growing conurbations with waterborne diseases such as cholera and typhoid – did not dispel the confidence in material progress, and in the power of human achievement. This in turn raised further questions about the continuing relevance of the God of the psalmists who helped those who could not help themselves and whose resources came from an invisible and immaterial world beyond. The dramatic fall in church attendance by the middle of the nineteenth century, and with this the decline in the familiar knowledge and use of the psalms which had been such a part of the intellectual, artistic and liturgical culture since the Reformation, were telling examples of the transformation that was taking place.

A more particular way in which the psalms again appeared irrelevant – especially in France and America, although there were consequences too in England – was on account of their assumptions about the close relationship between religion, king and state. One of the paradoxes of the eighteenth and nineteenth centuries was the way in which the Enlightenment interest in liberal and tolerant values took place within intensely nationalistic and often intolerant cultures, interrupted frequently by civil and international wars, the latter intensified by the fact that the Reformation had resulted in a demarcation of boundaries between an essentially Catholic France, Spain, Portugal, Poland, Belgium, Italy, Austria and Hungary, and a Protestant Britain, Scandinavia and Switzerland, with Germany being Protestant in the north and Catholic in the south. The two notable Declarations of Human Rights, both following intense periods of war – in America in 1776 and in France in 1789 – were each founded upon a belief in human progress, renouncing any inherited shackles of religion, advocating the separation of church and state, and rejecting the ideal of kingship. The absolute authority of the monarchy, from Charlemagne to Louis XIV of France, and from the Saxons and Normans to the Tudors and Stuarts in England, had taken much of its theological rationale about the Divine Right of Kings from the Psalms of David. But now the old model of the state, founded on monarchic rule, was being replaced by the new model of Republican Rome (for even more than Classical Greece, Rome, in its eighteenth-century idealized form, suggested fairness, virtue and reasonable governance: the 'Grand Tour' which necessitated the completion of education in Italy to imbibe the culture of Rome, Venice, Florence and Naples was a typical example of this way of thinking). Against this new world order, the psalmists' views of a close relationship between the Hebrew monarch and the Temple cult, and hence between politics and religion, were seen by Enlightenment thinkers as insidious: the God of the psalmists was too readily associated with more traditional establishment values which encouraged superstitious and excessive devotion: it would not be going too far to say that Jupiter, for example, now had more of an appeal than had Yahweh of the Psalms.

Debates about the Authorship and Purpose of the Psalms

Given these different examples of the apparent irrelevance of psalmody in an Enlightened Age, it might seem incongruous to find evidence that this nevertheless produced some interesting and creative studies on the psalms. For example, at least from the early nineteenth century onwards, in England and Germany in particular, several psalms commentators began to read the psalms not so much from the standpoint of any royalist propaganda but from the highly relevant standpoint of their teaching about national identity. In part this was because of the questions raised about kingship and the psalms; in part, too, it was because David's influence in psalmody was being questioned in academic theological circles in a manner resembling that of the questions about Jesus' influence in the Gospels. One of the most thorough treatments of questions of national identity and psalmody was by

Rudolph Smend, in a German publication in 1888, which consistently interpreted the 'I' of the psalmists as the personification of the entire community. Smend argued that the enemies in the psalms were other nations rather than personal adversaries of the king. In part this was a reaction against a privatized pietistic reading of psalmody, and in part it was a means of avoiding the issue of Davidic authorship; but it was also an informed response to the contemporary nationalistic issues. Another well-known German work which proposed a similar corporate interpretation is *Julius Wellhausen*'s Polychrome Bible on the Psalms (1898). In England, in a commentary aptly titled *The Book of Psalms or the Praises of Israel* (1891; revised edition 1904), *Thomas Kelly Cheyne* offered a similar interpretation of most of the psalms. A further example is the commentary published in both America and Britain by *C.A. and E.G. Briggs* (1906–7), with its emphasis on the role of the entire community in psalmody, whether in the few psalms from before the exile, or those composed in exile, or in those – the majority – which were seen now to have been composed in the Persian and Greek periods.

Briggs' commentary – and to a certain extent those of Wellhausen and Cheyne – offer an interesting shift of emphasis compared with Smend's work, for in these other commentaries we read that the community within the psalms is as much a *religious* entity as it is a *nationalistic* one. This was influenced by a growing consensus, by the end of the nineteenth century, that most of the psalms were composed during *Maccabean times in the second century BCE. Here the nationalistic reading was given a different twist as psalms were seen as compositions by heroic and pious radicals who were part of the popular uprising known as the *Hasidim*; their fight was for a renewed national identity, combined with religious devotion, against the internal conflicts and the harshness of a pagan Greek state. This was still a corporate, community-centred reading of the psalms, and it allowed the commentators and the readers to 'fight', through the psalmists, the oppressive policies of both church and state. A typical German commentary was by *Justus Olshausen* (1853), who dated the majority of psalms to the second and first centuries BCE. (Psalm 137, 'By the waters of Babylon', was thus read as one of the earliest psalms, because of its presumed exilic reference.) This late dating allowed for a better explanation of the royal psalms (for example, Psalms 2, 45, 72, 89) for they were thus no longer Davidic compositions to be used to defend the rights of kings, but were seen to be written some eight hundred years later by members of the *Hasidim* in support of the Maccabean princes in their fight to wrest power from Hellenistic rule. Amongst the best-known English scholars of this persuasion are *William Robertson Smith* (1889 and 1890) and *Samuel R. Driver* (1897): neither wrote commentaries on the psalms, but each assumed the late dating of the psalms and the consequent communal concerns of the psalmists in their broader works on Israelite religion and the Old Testament.[3]

---

[3] For commentaries and other Old Testament works referred to here, see C.A. and E.G. Briggs (1906 and 1907); T.K. Cheyne (1891, *1904*); *S.R. Driver (1897 and 1915)*; H.W. Furness and J. Wellhausen (1898); J. Olshausen (1853); and R. Smend (1888) and *W.R. Smith (1889 and 1890)*.

QUESTIONS ABOUT THE HISTORICAL VALUE OF THE PSALMS

Up until the eighteenth century, most scholars who wrote about the psalms had appealed in different ways to the testimony of history for a reasonable faith. In the eighteenth century it became fashionable to bypass difficult questions of the contemporary relevance of psalmody and to analyse instead the texts of the psalms as examples of ancient poetry. This sort of historically orientated reading was helped by the legacy of the Reformers, with their emphasis on the plain and literal meaning of the Psalms as a reaction to the allegorical readings of medieval commentators. The Reformers had also been interested in the ancient text of the psalms for other reasons: they often turned to the Hebrew original and to the Greek and Latin versions, and they evaluated the psalms along the lines of grammar and philology, and their textual interest had been to create either new church translations or literary imitations of psalmody as part of the general intellectual discourse of the sixteenth and seventeenth centuries.

By the eighteenth century, however, exegetes were reading these texts analytically for their own sake, avoiding the more theological issues of authority or inspiration which had so preoccupied scholastic and Reformation commentators, and focusing on the text as an ancient artefact, creating grammatical and philological classifications more in the Enlightenment spirit. A well-known example is the German *Johann David Michaelis*'s glossed annotations in his commentary on Psalms and Proverbs published in 1745 which offered historical and linguistic notes on individual psalms for those without the original languages. Examples from England include an expanded revision of *Benjamin Kennicott*'s collated manuscripts and exegetical commentaries on various psalms ('intended to correct the grammatical errors of the text', as the frontispiece makes clear) produced by *The Revd. H. Dimmock* as early as 1791, which was reprinted several times into the nineteenth century. The verse-by-verse text-critical and philological studies of the psalms by *Stephen Street* (1790) also used Kennicott's work on the psalms, noting errors and repetitions and offering various alternative readings to the text, and this also went through numerous further publications. These sorts of 'text-critical' works allowed scholars to work within an Enlightenment spirit without having to answer Enlightenment questions about their contemporary relevance.[4]

However, by the 1830s, the more historically orientated approach to the psalms suffered a setback when the historical rug was pulled away – ironically by other theologians. The most significant example is of New Testament scholars such as *Ferdinand Christian Baur* and *David Friedrich Strauss*, both of the University of Tübingen, who argued that the New Testament books were too late to have historical value, and instead the Gospels were more significant for their moral teaching and more theologically interesting for the use of myths rather than for any

---

[4] For text-critical works referred to here, see F. Baethgen (1892); H. Dimmock (1791); H.W. Furness and J. Wellhausen (1898); H. Hupfeld (1888); S. Street (1790).

witness to historical 'truth'. This historically sceptical emphasis was soon applied to Old Testament studies, especially to Genesis and Psalms.

In some academic circles, this simply perpetuated the interest in the psalms as ancient texts, for it allowed commentators to avoid not only contemporary questions but questions about precise historical dating as well. *Hermann Hupfeld*'s four-volume commentary (1855–62), revised by W. Nowack in 1888, shows how uncertainties about the dates of the psalms could be complemented by confident assertions of a grammatical and philological kind, whilst *Friedrich Baethgen*'s 1892 commentary shows a similar focus, emending the text by use of older commentaries and early versions, and attending more to the metrical forms of the psalms. Other commentators, such as *Julius Wellhausen* noted earlier, produced works which were not entirely text-critical, but even his was a commentary whose critical edition of the Hebrew text was supplemented by endnotes which were predominantly textual and grammatical.

Historical questions about Jesus' relation to the Gospels had parallels with similar questions about David's relation to the psalms; the growing interest in myth and ritual meant that these, rather than history, were seen as the vehicles for communicating not only the ideas in the Gospels but also the prayers of the psalms. Several scholars, building upon what was becoming known of the literature and religion of other cultures in the ancient Near East (particularly in Mesopotamia) and in Egypt, emphasized increasingly the cultic life of the psalms, the adaptations of myths, the use of rituals, and the importance of the festivals for which some psalms might have been composed. It is interesting to see how gradually the text-critical interest in grammatical and philological classification transmuted into an interest in the classification of the *forms* of the psalms and how their different categories fitted more generally into what was known of ancient Near Eastern religious culture. This is a very different brand of commentary from anything which had taken place before; not only is it working more independently of church tradition – a feature also shared with many text-critical commentators – but it is far removed from the emphasis in previous centuries on the Davidic authorship of the psalms and hence on the relationship between David and Jesus.

The three main protagonists of what became known as **Gattungsgeschichte*, or 'form-criticism', were German, but their influence is seen in most English-language commentaries on the psalms from the nineteenth century onwards. In a work published in 1807, *W.M.L. de Wette* (1780–1849) was amongst the first to argue that there were four main types of psalms – individual laments, national laments, psalms reflecting on evil in the world, and *theodicy psalms; writing at a time when there was still some confidence in what could be known historically about psalmody, de Wette argued that one could date the psalms by discerning what was authentic and what was a copy within these types. His 1811 commentary on the psalms, whose second edition in 1823 made use of the Hebrew lexicon published by Gesenius, a Hebrew grammarian at Halle, expanded the original four into six types – hymns, national psalms about the history of the people of God (Psalms 78, 105, 1–6, 114), Zion and Temple hymns (Psalms 15, 24, 68, 81, 87, 132,

134, 135), royal psalms (Psalms 2, 20, 21, 45, 72), laments (further divided into six sub-groups, both individual and national) and reflective psalms including those expressing confidence in God. In this work, which overlapped with some of the more radical debates about the historical value of the psalms, de Wette sought to be less dogmatic about what can be known of the precise historical setting on account of the psalm-type, preferring to offer more aesthetic comments on the text and structure of the psalm as a whole. His work in turn influenced *Wilhelm Gesenius* (1786–1842), whose lectures on the psalms between 1826 and 1827 (also therefore at the very beginning of the historical controversies) bear a striking resemblance to the six psalm-types advocated by de Wette. The hymns are subdivided into four categories – praise of God in nature, as protector of the Hebrew nation, as protector of all people, and praise of God's very nature – but the Temple hymns and reflective psalms, laments, royal psalms and historical psalms all correspond in large measure to de Wette's classification.

These were of course not the first attempts to classify the psalms. We saw earlier how Cassiodorus created twelve categories of psalms – but these were in terms of their relationship to the life, death and resurrection of Jesus Christ. Gilbert of Poitiers also categorized miscellaneous types of psalms – but again, this was also part of a Christian world-view imposed onto the psalms. Nineteenth-century classification (bearing in mind the Enlightenment interest in this sort of task) was much more about the psalms in their general ancient setting; there is rarely any recourse to a Christian reading, as the task of these commentators was to provide a reasonable academic discourse.

The greatest champion of form-criticism was *Hermann Gunkel* (1862–1932), who began as a New Testament scholar and soon produced studies on Genesis and then on the psalms, and who was therefore very much aware of the problems posed by the Tübingen School. Gunkel's best-known works are his essay on selected psalms in 1904, and his 1926 commentary on the psalms, and his unfinished introduction (completed by his pupil Begrich and published a year after his death in 1932), but much of his groundwork was done in the late nineteenth century. Like de Wette and Gesenius, Gunkel circumvented discussions about the historical settings of the psalms by classifying the psalms by their different types and refusing to be drawn on their precise date and provenance. His affiliation with the *History of Religions School in late-nineteenth-century Germany persuaded him that the psalmists were influenced by the same mythical and ritual world as found in other ancient Near Eastern cultures – and it was these very elements which invested them with new life and meaning. Following the ways in which New Testament scholars were now looking at the Gospels primarily for their ethical value, Gunkel also emphasized their moral and pious teaching of the psalmists, following here *tropological readings of his predecessors.

Gunkel's greatest legacy is his refinement of the history of forms (or genres) of psalms within the history of religion, and he undoubtedly gave the academic study of psalmody a new focus at a critical juncture in its development. Although he affirmed that the two most basic psalm-types were prayer and praise, he nevertheless advocated five or six pure *Gattungen as a development of these: the hymn (under which he sometimes included communal thanksgivings, historical psalms ['holy legends']), Zion hymns and Enthronement hymns, the community lament, the individual lament, the individual thanksgiving, and the royal psalms. Other mixed types, which Gunkel saw as later post-exilic developments, included the wisdom psalms and prophetic psalms, individual and communal psalms of confidence, and responsorial entrance liturgies such as Psalms 15 and 24. Although Gunkel has often been criticized for inconsistency of method (for example, the royal psalms and the later mixed types are judged more on account of content than form), his several publications brought about a new confidence in the psalms' place in the developing Hebrew religion, and few academic works on the psalms today are devoid of reference to him.[5]

The interest in setting the psalms in relation to the myths and rituals of other cultures of the ancient Near East was further aided by a growing interest in archaeological discoveries. The origins can be traced back to acquisitions from Egypt after Napoleon's Egyptian campaigns between 1798 and 1801; British interest in Egypt and Mesopotamia continued as a result of the concern to preserve trade routes to India via the Red Sea and the Persian Gulf. British and French archaeologists discovered artefacts of the great ancient cultures within the Nile and Tigris/Euphrates valleys and these in turn raised questions about how such clay tablets, pots, seals and inscriptions related to the history and religion of Israel. The formation of different archaeological societies (for example, The Palestine Exploration Fund [1865] and the Society of Biblical Archaeology [1870]) provided an important forum for this quest and aroused much interest in the myths and rituals of the ancient Near East and the place of biblical literature within this broader context.

Hence by the mid-nineteenth century, commentators were paying increasing attention to the 'foreignness' of the psalms, and to the elements of polytheism as well as monotheism expressed within them. That this is again a far cry from earlier Davidic-centred, Christian-orientated readings goes without saying. The preference for later Maccabean dating meant that the interest began with comparisons with the Persian and Greek cultures; by the twentieth century, when commentators began to assume (again) a pre-exilic date for many psalms, the mythological and polytheistic motifs in the psalms began to be seen more in the context of Egyptian, Babylonian and Canaanite cultures. Psalms such as Pss. 82:1, which speaks of God dwelling amongst a council of deities, 89:6–7, which compares God to other heavenly beings, and 74:13–14, which speaks of God in combat with Leviathan, then began to be read in a new light. Similarly, it was not until the twentieth century that seminal works were written about the special religious status of the king at a particular annual festival which was like that in other ancient Near

---

[5] On form-critical studies of the psalms, *J. Rogerson (1984)*, pp. 44–9 (on de Wette) and pp. 56–7 (on Gesenius' unpublished lectures). See also W.M.L. de Wette (1811, 1823²) and H. Gunkel (1904, 1913).

Eastern cultures (here examining royal psalms such as 2, 45, 72, 89 and 110 in a new way). So it took some time for this understanding of ancient Near Eastern mythology to be applied explicitly to the psalms because of the nineteenth-century preoccupation with a later date. Nevertheless, scholars such as Briggs and Cheyne began to note how psalms such as Ps. 19:1–6, in praise of God's creation of the sun, might have been composed to refute hymns to the Babylonian sun-god, Shamash, and Psalm 104, also a creation hymn, might have been similarly influenced by Babylonian (although not yet any mention of Egyptian) ideas.[6]

So, by the end of the nineteenth century, psalmic scholars, as part of a larger body of biblical commentators and biblical theologians, pursued their critical and analytical interests either by avoiding nineteenth-century historical scepticism and historical relativism and attending to the nature of the text *per se* or by joining forces with sceptics and relativists and reading the psalms within the more general context of the ancient Near East. There were of course many who sought to hold together the concerns of secular culture and church allegiance, but this was always fraught with tension. A telling example of the growing tensions between the academy and the church is from America, where between 1891 and 1893 a heresy trial of *Charles Briggs* took place. His work on a Hebrew lexicon with Francis Brown and Samuel Driver (known and used still as '*BDB*') was already very much in progress, and his studies of the psalms was only just beginning. At his inaugural lecture as Professor in Biblical Theology at Union Theological Seminary, New York, Briggs called for a critical revision of the relationship between faith and scholarship, for the removing of 'dead orthodoxy' and 'effete ecclesiasticism' by which the church had prevented freedom of academic discourse. For this he had to face a two-year legal process and was eventually suspended from the Presbyterian ministry. By 1906–7 his two-volume critical commentary on the psalms (written with his daughter in the International Critical Commentary series) had appeared, as had the lexicon, with a Doctor of Letters from Oxford University in recognition of his contribution to scholarship. But it was at some cost.[7]

Devotional Works

A very different way of dealing with this divide has some associations with the stance taken by many of the early church fathers, who chose not so much to utilize Hellenistic philosophical methods as to castigate them, and to appeal to a different world order as an alternative authority. The following section will assess the

---

[6] See T.K. Cheyne (1891), pp. 201–2, on both psalms; and C.A. and E.G. Briggs, Vol. I (1906), pp. 166–8 (on Psalm 19), and Vol. II (1907) pp. 331–4 (on Psalm 104).

[7] *Essays and Reviews* (1860) contains Jowett's paper on Holy Scripture; see also *C. Gore (ed.) (1890)*. A striking account of Briggs' trial is to be found on the sea of faith website at www.sofn.org.uk/DOCTRINE/health%20or%20heresy%20appendix%20two.htm.

different ways in which eighteenth- and nineteenth-century writers sought to preserve the best of more traditional readings of the psalms.

REVIVALIST INFLUENCES

It is not surprising that within this increasingly secularized climate, a number of revivalist movements appeared throughout Europe, each giving rise to distinctive spiritual writings and songs, frequently using the psalms as a resource for spiritual direction. On the Continent, such movements include *Jansenism in France, Spain and Italy and the *Moravians in Protestant Germany. Here the emphasis on lay spirituality – exemplified by family prayers, Sunday observance, honest work, grace before meals – meant that the Psalms could provide the same ideal nourishment for personal faith as might be seen in the use of Books of Hours in the Middle Ages. In the First Great *Awakening between about 1730 and 1770 in America, for example, *Puritan revivalist movements focused intensely on psalmody: their uses of the psalms in the seventeenth and eighteenth centuries were discussed in the previous chapter in relation to new translations and the new psalmic hymns of Isaac Watts, and their influence contributed a good deal in the so-called Second *Awakening in the early nineteenth century.

There are several examples of didactic and devotional works on the psalms in England. As well as *Puritanism, other early revivalist movements included the *Quakers under George Fox as early as the middle of the seventeenth century, the Methodist movement of John and Charles Wesley, as well as non-conformist hymn-writers such as Philip Doddridge, and, within Anglicanism, hymn-writers such as William Cowper and John Newton. Nineteenth-century movements which used the psalms for preaching and teaching include a low church evangelical revivalist movement initially associated with F.B. Meyer and Charles Spurgeon, socialist writers such as John Ruskin, *high church reformers of the Church of England whose best-known adherents were John Henry Newman, John Neale, John Keble and Edward Pusey, and a handful of women hymn-writers, who include Charlotte Elliott, Cecil Frances Alexander and Catherine Winkworth. Although their expressions of faith and theological emphases were all very different, they each shared a common concern to read the psalms in a specifically faith-inspired way, and sought to keep alive old traditions in a time of great change. In part this was because they felt responsible for their own communities of faith, and in part it was to feed a spiritual hunger which they perceived lay beyond their own congregations at a time of comparative material abundance yet much political, social and intellectual uncertainty. Their writings, taken together, illustrate yet again the separation between the study of psalmody inspired by Enlightenment ideals, worked out more in the life of the universities, and the more traditional appropriation of the psalms, applied to the individual life of the believer and the corporate life of the church.

One of the more unusual examples of this, as it relates to psalmody, is the Quakers. From the time of its founder, *George Fox* (1624–91), hymn-singing was seen only as the result of an experience of the inner light of the Spirit of God working with the spirit of the individual; mouthing the words of another was forbidden, and hence the singing of hymns and reading of traditional prayers were prohibited too. The psalms thus created a particular problem: neither the metrical hymnody of Sternhold and Hopkins nor the more measured version of Coverdale was allowed. It was not until 1817 that a Quaker leader, David Willson, attempted to incorporate congregational singing into the meetings for worship: he did so by composing a hymn – sometimes based upon words from a psalm – but never repeating it, so that the words would be 'lined out' with the leader, then the choir, then the congregation singing them back – an activity which could take some thirty minutes to complete. It was not until the middle of the nineteenth century that the first Quaker hymnbook was produced. This meant that in the earlier period, if the psalms were to be used at all, they were to be used in private. A clear example of this is the Quaker *Elizabeth Fry* (1780–1845) to whom the psalms were read as part of her own education by her Quaker mother, and who in turn read from and preached from the psalms to the women in Newgate prison, eventually by 1817 setting up a school there – in which again the reading of the psalms played a part. Singing them in worship was still forbidden; but being taught them devotionally as prayers and praises was another matter, thus offering an interesting illustration of the privatized response to psalmody at this time.[8]

A difficult contributor to categorize is *William Law* (1686–1761). By becoming a non-Juror in 1714 (on the death of Queen Anne) he was prevented from taking up either university or parish posts, so his preaching ministry was through his books. *A Serious Call to a Devout and Holy Life* (1728), with its appeal for holy living through integrity of spirit and determined obedience, had a seminal influence on both the Wesley brothers. Chapter XV is on the chanting and singing of the psalms in private devotion. Dryly and directly Law defends such practice even for those with no musical skill and with little opportunity for private space. Singing is different from reading a psalm, for the former 'signifies a motion of the voice suitable to the motions of the heart', and 'devotion of the heart breaks out into outward acts of prayer', evoking within us a spirit of spontaneous thanksgiving and genuine devotion to God. Singing is the outward act which supports our inner attitude of mind, where both body and soul work together to join, in our imagination, with 'holy David with his hands on his harp, and his eyes fixed on heaven'. Law ends his written sermon with an exaltation on the singing of Psalms 34, 96, 103, 111, 146 and 147.[9]

---

[8] On the Quakers and psalmody, see T.H.S. Wallace (2003); also www.haverford.edu/library/quakermusic/
[9] See *W. Law (1951)*; also at www.ccel.org/ccel/law/serious_call.toc.html.

Enlightenment thinkers were accomplished at reasoned argument, but few of them were similarly accomplished at celebration and song, and what composers such as Isaac Watts had achieved for the singing of the psalms in public worship, preachers such as Law were able to achieve for singing psalmody as part of private devotion. *John Wesley* (1703–1791) was indebted to both: he published parts of Law's *A Serious Call* in 1744, and Watts' *Psalms of David Imitated* was one of his main resources when he was establishing new Methodist congregations in America at the time of the First Great *Awakening. He and his brother *Charles Wesley* (1707–1788) had been made particularly aware of the appeal of hymn-singing in 1735 when, on board the *Simmons* bound for Georgia, they faced violent storms at sea, and were much comforted by the singing of a company of German *Moravian evangelical colonists travelling with them. By 1737, under the influence of the Moravians, *The Collection of Psalms and Hymns* was published in America: nearly half of these hymns were by Watts. Many others were translations by John Wesley from German metrical psalms, through the influence of the Moravians. The hymn-book was printed in a different form in England in 1738; an expanded version, also published by John Wesley, which included hymns by several evangelical hymn writers of that time, appeared in 1780. In effect, these early editions were the first hymnbook of the Anglican Church. Over a hundred of the hymns are from the psalms, and include well-known hymns of praise, whose origins can be traced back as early as the sixteenth century:

> The spacious firmament on high,
> With all the blue ethereal sky,
> And spangled heavens, a shining frame,
> Their great Original proclaim.
> *(Joseph Addison [1712]: Psalm 19)*

> All people that on earth do dwell,
> Sing to the Lord with cheerful voice:
> Him serve with fear, his praise forth tell;
> Come ye before him and rejoice.
> *(William Kethe [1561]: Psalm 100)*

> O worship the King, All glorious above;
> O gratefully sing His power and his love:
> Our shield and defender, The Ancient of days,
> Pavilioned in splendour, And girded with praise.
> *(Robert Grant, following Kethe's version [1561]: Psalm 104)*

> Praise, O praise our God and king!
> Hymns of adoration sing;
> For his mercies still endure
> Ever faithful, ever sure ...
> *(Henry Baker, added in the 1861 edition, following John Milton's 'Let us with a Gladsome Mind' [1623] on Psalm 136)*

As well as hymns of praise, other more personal prayers include metrical versions of Psalms, for example, Psalms 34 and 42–3:

> Through all the changing scenes of life,
> In trouble and in joy,
> The praises of my God shall still
> My heart and tongue employ.
>
> *(Tate and Brady [1698]: Psalm 34)*

> As pants the hart for cooling streams,
> When heated in the chase,
> So longs my soul, O God, for thee,
> And thy refreshing grace.
>
> *(Tate and Brady [1696]: Psalms 42–3)*

Some hymns were more clearly Christianized. For example, Psalm 45, a wedding hymn for a Davidic king, becomes a psalm of praise to Christ, the bridegroom of the church ('My heart is full of Christ, and longs its glorious matter to declare …') and Psalm 97, a psalm celebrating the kingship of Israel's God, is transformed into a variant version of the Christian creed ('Rejoice, the Lord is King! Your Lord and King adore').

After only four months in Georgia, Charles Wesley had to return to England owing to ill health; despite being ordained and having already been dubbed by his contemporaries at Oxford a 'Methodist' because of the 'Holy Club' which was founded at Lincoln College, it was not until 21 May, 1738, back in Oxford, that he had what, in his view, was a conversion experience. The text which impelled him was Psalm 40:3, 'He hath put a new song in my mouth; many will see and fear and will trust in the Lord.' By the next day he had composed his first hymn, which was possibly 'And can it be that I should gain/An interest in my Saviour's blood?' This was the first of some 6,500 hymns he composed; most Methodist Hymnals today would contain well over a hundred of Wesley's hymns, and with the spirit of Watts as his influence, many metrical psalm-like hymns are included amongst them.

John Wesley had also returned to England by 1738. It was at St Paul's Cathedral in the afternoon of 24 May, 1738, that he heard the choir sing Psalm 130: 'Out of the deep have I called unto Thee, O Lord; Lord, hear my voice'. In the evening of the same day, whilst listening to the reading of Luther's preface to Romans at a Moravian assembly in Aldersgate Street, he experienced a similar intense conversion as had Charles some three days earlier. From 1739 onwards he too was producing scriptural passages in hymnic form, most of which, in his case, were translations of German hymns. John was less original than his brother in this respect, although together they became known as the 'Poets of Methodism', with a passion to reach the unconverted masses in England who were labouring under the strains of the industrial revolution, through simple preaching and the singing of hymns and psalms.

Another significant eighteenth-century hymn-writer was *Philip Doddridge* (1702–51). A non-conformist preacher from Northamptonshire, a friend of the Wesleys and a contributor to John Wesley's Hymnal, his regular practice was to follow his sermon with a metrical hymn which he had composed on the same theme. Sometimes these would be read rather than sung by the congregation; if they proved popular, the music would be added later. Many of these were imitations of psalms: for example, a sermon preached in Leicester in June 1739 pleading for repentance and faith was taken from Ps. 119:158 ('I beheld the transgressors, and was grieved, because they kept not thy law') and was followed by a hymn on the same verse, but with a very different Christian overlay:

> Arise, my tenderest thoughts, arise,
> To torrents melt my streaming eyes!
> And thou, my heart, with anguish feel
> Those evils which thou can'st not heal!
>
> See human nature sunk in shame!
> See scandals pour'd on Jesus' name!
> The Father wounded through the Son!
> The world abus'd, the soul undone!

The Anglican Church lost a good deal of creativity when, after the Wesleys' deaths (in 1788 and 1791), it eventually parted company with Methodism. But by the mid-eighteenth century Anglicanism was beginning to produce hymn-writers of its own, in figures such as *John Newton* (1725–1807) and *William Cowper* (1731–1800). Newton was sent to serve on his father's slave-ship aged eleven; some seven years later, by then its captain, he had a conversion experience whilst reading Thomas à Kempis' *Imitation of Christ*. Under the influence of George Whitefield and the Wesleys, this impelled him to set about improving the lot of his slaves, and then to attempt to eradicate the system which oppressed them. By 1764 Newton was ordained into the Anglican church, having already written countless hymns; the best known is probably *Amazing Grace*, written shortly after his conversion, inspired by David's prayer in 1 Chronicles 17:16–17 (a text which has correspondences with Psalm 89) and sung to an American folk melody from the slave plantations, 'Loving Lambs'. Specific psalms were also an influence: Newton's *Glorious Things of Thee are Spoken* is from Psalm 87:

> Glorious things of thee are spoken,
> Zion, city of our God!
> He, whose word cannot be broken,
> Formed thee for his own abode.
> On the Rock of ages founded,
> What can shake thy sure repose?

>   With salvation's walls surrounded,
>   Thou may'st smile at all thy foes ...

William Cowper had been a lawyer, but his bouts of depression resulted in his being committed to a religious asylum in his early forties, from where he was eventually sent to Olney, where Newton was the incumbent. It was through Newton's counsel and support that he was encouraged to write hymns. The best known of these are *O for a closer walk with God* and *God moves in a mysterious way*. By 1779 Newton and Cowper had together published a collection known as *Olney Hymns*, whose purpose was to help their congregation at Olney, in the church or at prayer meetings in The Great House, to memorize Christian teaching through poetry, believing that if they had set it in prose, the congregation would be more likely to forget it. Of about three hundred and fifty hymns, some seventy were by Cowper. Unlike the Wesleys' hymnals, these were originally intended for a local parish; but like the Wesleys', they also included various metrical paraphrases of the psalms. Partly from Cowper's influence, the general tenor of the hymnbook resembles more the psalms of lament than psalms of praise: Newton's *Glorious Things* (using Psalm 87) is one of the few with a celebratory theme, whilst *When Israel was from Egypt freed* is another, based upon Ps. 107:7. One-third of the hymnbook is from verses of Scripture, and although very few of the original compositions are Christian versions of entire psalms (one, from Psalm 91, *That man no guard nor weapons needs / whose heart the blood of Jesus knows*, and another, from Psalm 6, *In mercy not in wrath rebuke*, are exceptions), some thirty are taken from specific verses of psalms, and in almost every case, the Christian reading of the psalm is uppermost.[10]

One of the great *non-conformist preachers of the nineteenth century who lived and breathed the Psalms was *Charles Spurgeon* (1834–92). Many of his sermons at New Park Street Chapel in Southwark were taken from psalms; but his lasting contribution was his seven-volume *Treasury of David*, which was a scholarly but popular exposition of every psalm, published in weekly instalments over a twenty-year period in London Metropolitan Tabernacle's periodical, *The Sword and the Trowel*. The completed parts were published in seven volumes; within ten years, 120,000 sets had been sold. Each exposition started with the title of the psalm, then a division of the psalm verse by verse, followed by further explanatory

---

[10] On Charles Welsey and the psalms, see *J.R. Tyson (ed.) (1989)*; the website of Emory University offers access to his poetic version of the psalms at www.pitts.emory.edu/archives/text/mss159.html; see also www.smithcreekmusic.com/Hymnology/Wesleys/Charles.Wesley.html and www.ccel.org/w/wesley/hymn/title.html, which shows the two editions of Charles Wesley's hymnbook by theme and by title. On John Wesley, see A.C. Outler (1980); his explanatory notes on the psalms are to be found at www.christnotes.org/commentary.php?com=wes&b=19. On Philip Doddridge and psalmody, see www.evangelical-times.org/Articles/Mar02/mar02a10.htm. On John Newton, William Cowper and Olney Hymns, see www.ccel.org/ccel/newton/olneyhymns.toc.html.

notes and other 'quaint sayings', and ending with a section 'Hints to the Village Preacher', which was a simplified survey of the earlier exposition.

This was essentially a conservative and evangelical commentary, although because it was aimed both at the educated laity and also at preachers who sought to educate an illiterate audience, Spurgeon offered something for everyone. The Christological theme was uppermost, especially with the royal psalms. For example, of Psalm 45, traditionally a royal wedding psalm, he writes 'Some see Solomon and Pharaoh's daughter only – they are short-sighted; others see Solomon and Christ – they are cross-eyed; well-focused spiritual eyes see Jesus only ... as the heavenly bridegroom speaks to his earthly spouse, the church ...'. The exposition ends with the hymn 'When morning gilds the skies ...'. Of Psalm 110, Spurgeon writes that it is a 'coronation psalm, when Christ is bidden to take his throne'. Even non-royal psalms receive a Davidic and Christian emphasis. Of Psalm 8, Spurgeon surmises whether the 'Gittith' in the title might suggest that this is a song sung over Goliath of Gath; he notes how the psalm has been termed 'The Song of the Astronomer', and explains how this is because our eyes are lifted above this world to the heavens beyond. It shows us how God the Creator cares not only for 'Adam in his kingdom' but also for 'the second Adam who is Christ, ... who applied the psalm to himself (Matt. 21:16)'. As for Psalm 19, often seen to be a composition of two separate parts, Spurgeon affirms instead its unity as David the shepherd boy was its author – the one who knew of the two great books, Nature (the 'world-book' which shows God's glory [vv. 1–6]) and Scripture (the 'word-book' which reveals God's grace [vv. 7–11]) – in other words, the book of Creation in Genesis and the book of Moses' Law in Exodus. God wrote them both; and David the psalmist thus praises God for both, and ends by praying for his grace (vv. 12–14).

Spurgeon's exposition excels in clarity and simplicity; it falls into neither the literal nor allegorical category, being both practical and Christological. Its nearest companion work is that of Spurgeon's colleague *Frederick B. Meyer*, who wrote many devotional works on biblical characters, and whose *David – Shepherd, Psalmist, King*, published in 1910, is amongst the best known. These works are very much at the other end of the spectrum from the more academic text-critical and form-critical commentaries from this period noted earlier.[11]

Another nineteenth-century scholar who wrote about psalmody was *John Ruskin* (1819–1900). Neither low church nor high church, neither liberal nor catholic, he was something of all of these, and the broad spectrum of psalmody fostered his own breadth of moral and political thinking and his passion for beauty, truth and realism in art. For Ruskin, who had been taught the psalms by his mother from childhood, the psalms were a systematic collection 'of personal, economical and political prudence for all life'. His was more of a private piety than anything overtly public; instead of using metrical psalmody or Anglican chant, his personal devotions appear to have been from the Sydneys' translations of the psalms. His works engage

---

[11] See F.B. Meyer (1910) and C.H. Spurgeon (*1857*, 1860–67, 1887). The *Treasury of David* is found at eword.gospelcom.net/comments/spurgeon/psalm.htm.

with psalmody by way of allusion as well as quotation, and it is clear that the psalms of Creation and the Law ('both practical and unadorned') were the most valued. His reading of Psalms 19 and 119 could not be more different from Spurgeon's, however: here the law *per se* is his aid to personal piety, rather than the evangelical re-reading of the 'law of grace' through Christ. Many of Ruskin's personal letters and his autobiography, *Praeterita* (1886–9), reveal how he saw how such psalms compelled believers to be angry about iniquity and poverty and oppression, impelling them to work with God in the restoration of justice and dignity for all mankind throughout all creation.[12]

As well as inspiring non-conformist preachers and pastors of this period, the psalms provided a resource for High Church Anglicans as well. The most obvious examples are found amongst the *Tractarians; they understood the period of the early church fathers as definitive in matters of Christian doctrine and practice, and so neither the metrical psalmody of the Reformation, nor unadorned evangelical vignettes, nor liberal social ideals, nor critical Enlightenment commentaries were amongst their primary concerns.

John Henry Newman (1801–90), one of the 'founding fathers' of the movement before he left the Anglican church in 1845 to become a Roman Catholic (believing that to hold any *via media* between Protestants and Catholics through the Anglican church seemed an impossible ideal), wrote several papers on psalmody. His works on the psalms have two recurrent themes: the primacy of singing psalms and canticles in church liturgy, and the need for the contemporary renderings of the early Latin and Greek hymnody of the early church. (An interesting parallel may be drawn here with John Wesley, for whom the first three centuries of the church and the *BCP* were also normative; but whereas Wesley's response was to create contemporary metrical psalmody inspired by early church practice and present-day experience, Newman's was to create metrical translations of already existing hymns from the early church and order them as part of the Christian Year.) For Newman, the authority of these ancient hymns lay in the way they had been absorbed, over several generations, into the worship of the early churches, and had so remained in use; by contrast, the spontaneous outpourings of metrical psalmody (here Newman was almost certainly thinking of versions such as Sternhold and Hopkins, which he saw as trite and superficial in content and style) waxed and waned within a generation or two. Newman's reverence for the early church fathers meant that in his papers and sermons he applied the same typological (although not usually allegorical) ways of reading the psalms as they too had done. For example, a sermon preached in 1840 unashamedly takes a Christological reading of many of the psalms, seeing David as a type of Christ. Psalms 2, 22, 45, 69, 72 and 110 are all included: they 'breathe of Christ'. (The suffering Christ of Psalms 22 and 69 was particularly important to him.)

---

[12] Some of these observations have been informed by an unpublished paper by Andrew Tate, 'Ruskin and the Psalms', given at a conference hosted by the Centre of Reception History, Oxford, at All Souls College on 24 April 2004.

Newman's *Dream of Gerontius* (1865) also takes up some important psalms: Gerontius dies with the words of Ps. 31:5 on his lips ('Into thy hand I commit my spirit') and as his soul and its guardian ascend to heaven, the angelic choirs sing *Praise to the Holiest in the Height* – probably inspired by the opening lines of Psalms 147 and 150. As his soul temporarily descends to purgatory, the souls in the guardian prison sing a paraphrase of Psalm 90:

> 'Lord, thou hast been our dwelling place in all generations ... Before the mountains were brought forth, or ever thou hadst formed the earth and the world, even from everlasting to everlasting, thou art God ... For a thousand years in thy sight are but as yesterday when it is past, and as a watch in the night ...'

If Newman utilized the psalms essentially in his preaching and poetry and in published papers which discuss the place of psalmody and hymnody in the life of the ancient and contemporary church, *John Mason Neale* (1818–66), who shared Newman's interest in the patristic period, used his gifts in actually transposing ancient and medieval Greek and Latin hymns (some of which were themselves modelled on psalms) into English. After a university education at Cambridge, which gave him a good classical background, he was ordained priest in 1842. Chronic ill health prevented him undertaking parish work, so he had to accept the position of warden at Sackville College almshouse in East Grinstead, a position he held from 1846 until his death. Here he used his pastoral gifts to work amongst the poor; but this also provided him with the opportunity for composing, translating and expounding the works of the psalms by the early fathers. Like Newman, Neale believed that other new compositions in the vernacular from the Reformation onwards had put into disuse some of the greatest ancient hymnody of the Western church, and he considered his was an essential contribution to the more long-lasting liturgy of the Anglican church. His best-known hymns with correspondences from psalms include *Before the ending of the day*, a translation of a Latin fifth- or sixth-century hymn (*Te lucis ante terminum*) which takes up parts of the evening prayer, Psalm 4; *All glory laud and honour*, taken from Theodulph of Orleans (about 820) with its associations with Psalm 150; *Jerusalem the Golden*, a translation from Bernard of Cluny's hymn of about 1145, using parts of Psalms 48 and 87; *Christ is made the sure foundation*, from a seventh-century Latin hymn, from Ps. 118:19–24; and *In days of old on Sinai the Lord Almighty came*, from an eighth-century hymn by Cosmas of Jerusalem, using some of Psalm 68. Over an eighth of the hymns in *Hymns Ancient and Modern* are by Neale, many of which are allusions to psalmody and some of which are based on entire psalms.

In addition, Neale also produced a great work of patristic exegesis in his *Commentary on the Psalms from the Primitive and Mediaeval Writers* which was published, posthumously, in four volumes (1874) in association with R.F. Littledale, and has been a widely respected resource for all sorts of commentators and preachers of the psalms. Spurgeon, for example, referred to it many times, and it is still a seminal resource for understanding the reception of the psalms from the time of the early church fathers to the Middle Ages (and was used in the earlier chapters of this book).

Like Newman and Neale, *John Keble* (1792–1866) also contributed a good deal to our understanding and use of psalmody through hymnody and poetry. But unlike Neale, Keble composed more contemporary imitations of actual psalms. Neither Newman nor Neale was particularly concerned with producing metrical psalmody, but Keble was ideally suited for this challenge. Between 1831 and 1836 he was Professor of Poetry in Oxford, and as the conflicts surrounding the *Tracts of the Times* intensified, he left Oxford to be Vicar of Horsley, where he stayed until his death. Hence his feel for poetry was both academic and pastoral, as is evident from his *Psalter in English Verse* (1839). Originally it had been hoped that it could be licensed by the Bishop of Oxford for use in worship throughout the Oxford Diocese, but it became clear that it was beyond the bishop's jurisdiction to license anything like an *Oxford Psalter*; so Keble and Pusey (who had also become involved in this project) circumvented this problem, with permission, by printing on the title page 'By a Member of the University of Oxford, Adapted for the Most Part to Tunes in Common Use, By Permission to the Lord Bishop of Oxford'. Keble's preface to this book makes it clear that he had problems producing this version: Hebrew psalms were composed to be chanted, not sung, so Keble felt he had often had to constrict the Hebrew verse to a single line instead of half a stanza, trying to maintain some four stanzas overall for each psalm. This meant that he felt he had often missed the more profound resonances in the Hebrew on account of trying to give due attention to the balance of form with content. Keble's version of Psalm 51 illustrates how this is a version as much for private prayer as public liturgy, a factor which might also explain why the *Oxford Psalter* was not as widely used as other metrical psalm books:

(Part I)
By all thy pitying care
Forgive me, Lord, I pray;
With melting heart receive my prayer,
Blot all my guilt away…
(Part III)
The joy of Thy redeeming light
Restore me, Lord, again;
And with thy free and princely Sp'rit
My weary heart sustain…

(Part II)
Behold me shap'd with mortal stains,
My mother me conceiv's in sin:-
But lo! Pure Truth in heart and reins
And Wisdom deeply seal'd within…

A spirit bruis'd, that mourns apart,
Is God's own sacrifice;
A broken and a contrite heart
Thou wilt not, Lord, despise.

A more popular work was *The Christian Year* (1827, revised edition published in 1897 after Keble's death), partly because this was of more liturgical interest, containing hymns for the mornings and evening and Sundays and Holy Days from Advent to Trinity, with a second volume comprising hymns for the rest of the liturgical year, for some Saints' Days, and for other special occasions. Although each hymn is prefaced by a biblical text, none of these are from any psalm, although the psalms' influence is seen in various phrases within the verses. For example, the hymn set for the sixth Sunday after Trinity is entitled 'The Psalmist Repenting', and takes up parts of Psalm 51 (the version, with its four-line stanzas and *abab* rhyme, is perhaps more arresting than the one in Keble's Psalter). The portion below, also of Psalm 51, shows how in this version Keble tried to get to the meaning in terms of the sense as much as the sound:

> There drink: and when ye are at rest,
> With that free Spirit blest,
> Who to the contrite can dispense,
> The princely heart of innocence,
> If ever, floating from faint earthly lyre,
> Was wafted to your soul one high desire,
> By all the trembling hope ye feel,
> Think on the minstrel as ye kneel ...

If Newman was the preacher and teacher of the psalms, Neale the expert in interpreting and understanding patristic uses of psalmody, and Keble the great producer of metrical psalms, *Edward Pusey* (1800–82) was the skilled Hebraist and grammarian. Pusey had a well-known dislike for the rationalistic character of German theology, on account of what he saw as superficial moralizing and its lack of reference to the place of the Old Testament in salvation history. But as Regius Professor of Hebrew at Oxford, from 1828 onwards he also had ample opportunity to develop a particular interest in the psalms in their Hebrew original, and he used this gift in helping Keble with his *Psalter in English Verse* – so much so that Keble would not include anything in a metrical psalm which Pusey did not consider accurate, even though it might have ruined Keble's sense of rhyme and rhythm. These psalms, in Keble's own words, had to 'tread step by step with the sacred text', and Pusey provided this: such scholarly help had been absent in the making of, for example, the Sternhold and Hopkins and Tate and Brady Psalters.

Another genre used by Tractarians was that of devotional commentaries. Writing at the end of the century, *Fr. Richard Meux Benson* of the Cowley Fathers wrote on Psalm 119 in a work *The Way of Holiness*, and on the Psalter as a whole in *The War Songs of the Prince of Peace*. Some interesting comparisons could be made between the quest for holiness through meditation on the psalms advocated by Tractarians such as Benson and by non-conformist writers such as Charles Spurgeon who were writing at the same time – each interpreting the psalms in a consistently Christological way, but the former through a more mystical and sacramental piety and the latter through a more pragmatic and scripture-centred approach.[13]

---

[13] On J.H. Newman and the psalms, see L.F. Barmann (1964); T. Dearing (1966); and B. Fischer (1986). See also J.M. Neale and R.F. Littledale (1874–1879); and J. Keble (1827 and 1839). 'Project Canterbury' has several useful entries: for Keble and *The Christian Year*, see anglicanhistory.org/keble/index.html; for Neale, see anglicanhistory.org/neale/index.html; for Newman, see anglicanhistory.org/newman/index.html, which includes his preface to *Hymni Ecclesiae* with its discussion of the psalms in the church; for Pusey, see anglicanhistory.org/pusey/index.html and for Benson, see Benson (1991) and anglicanhistory.org/benson/index.html.

These five members of the Oxford Movement played interesting complementary roles in bringing new aspects of psalmody and hymnody into the church at this critical period. They represent an interesting contrast with another, more disparate selection of women composers who used some psalms as a resource for hymnody.

Charlotte Elliott (1789–1848) lived most of her life in Brighton, and was the composer of hymns such as 'Just as I am', possibly from the time of her conversion. Many of her one hundred and fifty hymns, written in a simple, repetitive devotional style, were composed to help the sick and suffering, and were included in an edition of *Psalms and Hymns* (revised edition 1935) by her brother, the Revd H.V. Elliott.

Cecil Frances Alexander (1823–95), an Irish poet from Dublin, composed hymns based more explicitly upon psalms: her 'All Things Bright and Beautiful' (1848), written for children, was from Psalm 104, and was later included in a hymnbook for children edited by John Keble. Her best-known hymn, 'There is a Green Hill Far Away', is typical of the simple devotion which is evident in her other hymns based upon psalms, for example, 'The Golden Gates are Lifted Up' (1858), from Psalm 24; all three hymns were included in the *Church of Ireland Hymnal* (1873).

Catherine Winkworth (1827–78) spent some of her earlier years in Germany, and when she finally settled in Bristol she published an English translation of well-known German hymns in *Lyra Germanica* (1853), which by 1857 was in its fifth edition, encouraging her to write a second volume which was equally popular. Many of the hymns were from the psalms: her translation of Luther, as 'From Deepest Woe I Cry to Thee', is from Psalm 130; whilst that of George Weissel, 'Lift up Your Heads, Ye Mighty Gates', is from Psalm 24; 'Open Now the Gates of Beauty', from Benjamin Schmolet, uses Ps. 100:4. Her two best-known hymns are both from psalms: 'Now Thank We All our God', from Martin Rinkart, suggests Ps. 126:2,3 (which itself may have influenced a similar text, Ecclesiasticus 50:22–4), and 'Praise to the Lord, the Almighty', from Philip Nicolai, is from Psalm 103.[14]

LITERARY WORKS AND POETIC IMITATIONS

Undoubtedly the most formative literary scholar in this entire period, whose works were published in the late eighteenth century but whose influence on later commentators has been seminal, was *Robert Lowth* (1710–87). Lowth took seriously not only the distinctive linguistic features of Hebrew psalmody, but also the nature

---

[14] On Elliott, see H.V. Elliott (ed.) (1835); also www.cyberhymnal.org/bio/e/l/elliott_c.htm which lists all her hymns; on Alexander, see *A.P. Graves (1930)*; also www.cyberhymnal.org/bio/a/l/e/alexander_cfh.htm; on Winkworth, see www.cyberhymnal.org/bio/w/i/n/winkworth_c.htm and www.ccel.org/w/winkworth/.

of its poetic forms, and his publications on psalmody, whilst not strictly devotional, fall more into the instructional and aesthetic category of reception than that of critical exegetical works. Preceding John Keble as Praelector of Poetry at Oxford, Lowth delivered some thirty-four lectures between 1741 and 1750 on the nature of Hebrew Poetry, which were published in Latin in 1753 and in English in 1787. Five were on the Psalms. Lowth demonstrated with great lucidity the distinctive features of Hebrew poetry – its economical style, its simplicity, brevity and uniformity of expression – and compared it with the more copious and flowing poetic measures of Greek or Latin. Its essence, according to Lowth, was encapsulated in the term 'poetic parallelism'. He broke up the continuous text of the psalms into short 'parallel' lines, and identified three types of parallelism: synonymous, where the same idea is repeated in a different way; antithetic, where two ideas are presented as contrasts; and synthetic, where two ideas together comprise one greater idea. Examples of synonymous parallelism, taken from the NRSV, would be Psalm 31:10:

> For my life is spent with sorrow, and my years with sighing;
> my strength fails because of my misery, and my bones waste away.

Antithetic parallelism is found in Ps. 34:10:

> The young lions suffer want and hunger,
> but those who seek the LORD lack no good thing.

In Lecture XIX, Lowth uses Ps. 19:8 ff. as an example of synthetic parallelism. A more modern version, the NRSV, runs as follows:

> The precepts of the Lord are right, rejoicing the heart;
> the commandment of the Lord is clear, enlightening the eyes;
> the fear of the Lord is pure, enduring forever;
> the ordinances of the Lord are true and righteous altogether.

Lowth was in many ways expanding the understanding of psalmody expressed in Coverdale's translation and Anglican plainchant – a genre well known to his Oxford audience. In addition, Lowth was applying that typical eighteenth-century interest in classification to psalmody. Although he was uncertain as to whether the actual psalmists worked more according to convention rules or from intuition, he showed his predominantly literate audience (but one which could not read Hebrew) how psalmody was as much an art form to be *heard* (as music and song in poetic form) as it was to be *read* (as a literary artefact). In some respects Lowth's work overlaps with the textual critics referred to earlier; but he infused a potentially dry discipline of philological exegesis with a more imaginative appreciation of these ancient poetic forms.[15]

---

[15] See B. Hepworth *(1978)*; and R. Lowth, (1753, 1787; reprint 1995).

INFLUENCES FROM THE ROMANTIC MOVEMENT

The interest in foreign cultures (which as we saw earlier is found in critical commentaries which looked at the psalms in the context of the ancient Near East) also had a notable influence on both didactic and aesthetic works on the psalms. The *Romantic Movement, and the sincerity and enthusiasm of the contributors (who usually looked as much to the Middle Ages as to Classical cultures for their sense of mystery and their quirky creativity) could not have contrasted more starkly with the more rationalist and detached works of many Enlightenment thinkers.

Although on the Continent the Romantic Movement really developed in the wake of the French Revolution, when it became clear that both traditional Christianity and analytical scepticism had broken down, it actually has its roots much earlier, in works engaging not only with Christianity, but also with the vitality of all religious experience. In Germany, the works of F. von Schiller (1759–1805) and Johan Wolfgang von Goethe (1749–1832), with their portrayal of charismatic heroes and their elevation of creative genius, belong to this; so, too, does the growing fascination with folklore – for example, the Grimm brothers' fairy tales, and J.G. von Herder's folk songs. This interest in folk culture, and in the ethnic origins of primitive peoples, fuelled a new appreciation of Hebrew poetry, of which the psalms, seen now as the products of the folk religion of the primitive world, were prominent examples: this was one of the issues which Robert Lowth developed in his seminal lectures on Hebrew poetry.

Romanticism, with its fascination with the bizarre, the remote, the mysterious, and even the weird and the occult, gave rise to a huge range of imaginative responses, many of which affected readings of the psalms. Travel to particularly exotic places became increasingly popular, encouraging travel diaries about hitherto unknown peoples in hitherto unknown parts of the natural world. Contributors sought to portray in literature, poetry, music and art the vitality of feelings of dependence between the divine and the human (or, at least, between nature and humanity) and of the importance of experience above reason, of imagination above scientific analysis, of liberty from political and reasonable correctness in art forms, relationships and social conventions. The essence of Romantic works is best seen in the almost universally shared response to nature – although quite different from the elevation of the natural order which was seen in relation to humanist and scientific works earlier. No longer was nature seen as part of a mechanistic universe, to be observed by natural laws – as argued by, for example, Kant – but a landscape, a place of natural beauty, both at home and abroad, to be enjoyed. From this, human life no longer comprised mechanisms which were to be analysed, but humanity was a gift to be embraced in all its pains and joys. The psalms, with their emphasis on the celebration of God in nature, and their focus on the vicissitudes of human experience with and without the presence of God, took on a new meaning in the literary enterprises of this period.

Rather surprisingly, a list of Romantic *literati* offers few examples of British poets using or adapting the psalms: one might expect, for example, works by William Blake

(1757–1827), William Wordsworth (1770–1850), Charles Lamb (1775–1834), P.B. Shelley (1792–1822) or John Keats (1795–1821). For most British Romantic writers, the focus was on more unorthodox literary ideas than those found in psalmody, and they composed different kinds of poetry from those which had previously been inspired by English translations of the psalms. Nevertheless, a handful of Christian Romantics used the psalms to contrast the heroic figure of David with Jesus Christ. One example is James Montgomery's *Songs of Zion, being Imitations of the Psalms* (1822); his hymn 'Hail to the Lord's Anointed' is perhaps the best known, borrowing from royal psalms 110 and 72 in particular:

> Hail to the Lord's Anointed,
> great David's greater Son!
> Hail, in the time appointed,
> his reign on earth begun!
> He comes to break oppression,
> to set the captive free,
> to take away transgression,
> and rule in equity.

Another example is Robert Burns' version of Psalm 1:

> The man, in life wherever placed,
> Hath happiness in store,
> Who walks not in the wicked's way,
> Nor learns their guilty lore!
>
> Nor from the seat of scornful pride
> Casts forth his eyes abroad,
> But with humility and awe
> Still walks before his God. ...

Yet another is Coleridge's adaptation of Psalm 46:

> God is our strength and our refuge: therefore will we not tremble
> Though the earth be removed and though the perpetual mountains
> Sink in the swell of the ocean! God is our strength and our refuge.
> There is a river the flowing whereof shall gladden the city,
> Hallelujah! The city of God! Jehovah shall help her ...[16]

One way in which the Romantic Movement influenced other didactic works on the psalms was by encouraging a more individualistic approach to religious poetry. Several writers offer detailed autobiographies of the psalmists: they sometimes

---

[16] On the Romantics and the Bible, see *M. Roston (1965)*. The quotations from Coleridge and Burns are from L. Wieder (ed.) (1999), pp. 69 and 7 respectively; see also J. Montgomery (1822).

presume the *persona* to be David, but more often they assume the supplicant to be a different figure, one who is imbued with a heroic and charismatic spirit, and who, rather like a prophet, champions the cause of high ethical values founded upon the belief in one God. *Alfred Rahlfs'* German account of the poor in the psalms (1892) is a good example of the ways in which the 'I' speaking in the psalms is a deprived Jew, afflicted by the political and social tensions evidenced in the post-exilic period, championing his rights. Hermann Gunkel's pupil, *Emile Balla*, expanded Gunkel's ideas in a publication in 1912 which read the 'I' form in the psalms as independent post-exilic composers who had been influenced by the piety of earlier prophets. *Bernhard Duhm* (1899) offered a similar interpretation, although he dated these psalms later still, in *Maccabean times. English-speaking commentaries were developing similar ideas at the same time. A study by *William Davison* (1893) argues that the psalmists were private individuals, mainly writing in the post-exilic period up to Maccabean times, and that their piety was infused with the earlier piety of the prophets. In his impressive commentary (1902), *Alexander F. Kirkpatrick* writes in his preface of the way the psalms 'come straight "from the heart to the heart" and the several depths of the spirit' (p. v). Affirming that the 'I' is an individual at prayer, Kirkpatrick was more open to a pre-exilic date – even from David himself – for many of the psalms. Another most important example, because it is one of the earliest reception history accounts of the psalms, is Roland Prothero's *The Psalms in Human Life* (1903), which examines not so much the psalms' composers as the psalms' readers, and looks at the ways in which the psalms have been used in everyday experience by the great and the good, in public and private, from second Temple days until the nineteenth century. This is a vital resource for our understanding of the significance of the psalms in the lives of countless individuals in Christian history, and has been widely consulted in this book.[17]

COMMENTARIES

Commentaries on the psalms were not only of the genre which, with their measure of detachment, imbibed the Enlightenment spirit: several writers used commentaries to demonstrate that a more traditional, Christ-centred way of reading psalmody was still important. Two examples must suffice.

Franz Delitzsch's 1867 revised edition is of his two-volume commentary on the Psalms (1859–60). In it Delitzsch writes disparagingly about de Wette, noting that although his style is precise and clear, and although he opened up a new epoch in psalm-exposition, his research on the psalms is too sceptical, because he did not sufficiently recognize their place in the history of redemption. Delitzsch is typical

---

[17] On the individual and the psalms, see E. Balla (1912); B. Duhm (1899); W.T. Davison (1893); A.F. Kirkpatrick (1902); R. Prothero (1903); and A. Rahlfs (1892).

of the divide in psalmic studies by the mid-nineteenth century: no longer is the tension between historical/literal and allegorical/typological approaches, each working from a faith-centred position, but between what were seen by those within a confessional tradition as 'faithful' and 'faithless' works. Delitzsch's own introduction to the commentary (for which, interestingly, he consulted at length with a Jewish scholar, Seligmann Baer) considers how the Psalms relate to the prophecy of the future Christ, how they spiritualize legal sacrifice, and how they relate to the New Testament teaching on the righteousness of faith, and life after death.

Hence it is not surprising that Delitzsch commends the more explicitly Christian four-volume work on the Psalms by Ernst Hengstenberg, de Wette's successor at Berlin University; the commentary was translated from its German original (1842–47) into English by 1876. Although Hengstenberg argued more than Delitzsch would have done for the traditional position of Davidic authorship, his appeal to the moral and pious value of the psalms set within a specifically Christian reading, and his defence of biblical inspiration and authority all suited Delitzsch's concerns ideally. 'The much abused commentary ... set the exposition of the Psalms in its right relation to the church once more, and was not confined to the historico-grammatical function of exposition.'[18]

Thus far we have observed highly rational, verbal responses to psalmody, whether working with or against the grain of the Enlightenment. What follows is a quite different genre.

Musical Reception

The greatest influence upon this reception of psalmody in the eighteenth century was the *Romantic Movement, enabling the psalms to evoke the imagination not only through poetry and literature but also through the musical medium as well. This influence within psalmody was long-lasting, continuing until the early part of the twentieth century – at least, if one applies generally accepted criteria such as intense emotional expression, experimentation with harmony and melody and rhapsodic forms.

It is intriguing that many composers of psalms espoused a traditional Christian faith in their earlier life but later denounced it. Beethoven, for example, was baptized a Catholic but was drawn to *Deism, and Schubert, similarly baptized a Catholic, later pronounced himself a sceptic; Brahms and Schumann renounced their Protestant faith in their early years, and both, like Beethoven, were later attracted to Deism. This means that their psalmic compositions have a rather different emphasis from those church composers of earlier centuries whose works were written from a more explicitly Christian perspective. In the works we have

---

[18] See F. Delitzsch (1859–60; E Tr 1986; the quotation is from 1986, p. 63). See also E. Hengstenberg (1842–1849; E Tr 1851).

discussed in earlier chapters, the interpretation of the traditional faith of the psalmists is more pious and Christian; in many of these later Romantic composers, it is more numinous and Deist. Here the different persuasion allowed more independent creativity, for, neither under the control of church patronage, nor often even personally committed to any church tradition, composers could afford to experiment more with individual expression of emotion – for example, modulation to distant keys, chromatic experiments, free use of dissonance, polyphony, changing orchestral colour, and repetition of movements one within another. Where this affects psalmody is that the texts became part of the process of experimentation rather than an end in themselves. Because many psalms in this period were composed not for sacred liturgy but as a secular performance, rather like the performance of opera (which was an increasingly popular medium of nineteenth-century Romantic music), they became drawn into large-scale choral works with religious themes, and were adapted to suit the concert hall or theatre rather than the church.[19]

An early composer who was interested in both sacred and secular settings for psalmody, and who was still largely dependent upon church patronage, was *Josef Haydn* (1732–1809) from Vienna. Like Vivaldi, Haydn was particularly interested in opera and the theatre, but he also composed several sacred works. His first and last compositions were Masses – his *Missa Brevis*, probably from 1749, was followed by eleven others, the last six being part of his duty in his last years in the court of the family of Nikolaus Esterházy – one mass for each summer on the princess's nameday, where the psalms featured, but more implicitly. Explicit psalmic compositions are evident in Haydn's *Lauda Sion* hymns, using part of the last five psalms of the Psalter, from the 1750s and 1760s, and his motet arrangement of Psalm 137, *Super flumina Babylonis*, in 1772. Ps. 113:9 is also the basis for his '*Non Nobis Domine*', in 1786. After his two stays in England between 1791 and 1792 and again between 1794 and 1795, when his symphonies were well received, the publication of Handel's oratorios inspired him, on his return to Vienna, to compose large-scale works such as *The Creation* and *The Seasons*. In spite of this, Haydn's most important musical contribution to psalmody was actually during his time in England: his six 'English Psalms' (26:5–8; 31:21–4; 41:12–16; 50:1–6; 61:6–8; 69:13–17), dated around 1794, offer an interesting example of how a Catholic, who was adept at concert hall performance, could arrange the psalms to music for the Protestant churches as well.[20]

Ludwig van Beethoven (1770–1827) is not a name that comes immediately to mind with respect to psalmody. Like Haydn, Beethoven worked under patronage, but by contrast he composed for, and performed mainly in, Viennese salons rather than in churches, and even his most 'sacred' compositions, which were Masses, were commissions

---

[19] The most important resource in what follows has been the Grove music web-pages, at www.grovemusic.com/index.html (each time under the appropriate composer). Other web-pages or secondary literature on individual composers will be referred to where relevant.

[20] A recording of Haydn's English Psalms is produced by Hyperion (67150) *Haydn and His English Friends* (Psalmody; The Parley of Instruments, director Peter Holman).

for performance outside regular liturgy. His *Mass in D* (*Missa Solemnis:* 1819–23) was intended to be performed at the ceremony where a patron, Rudolph, Archduke of Austria, was to be made Archbishop of Olmütz in Moravia, and although it was never completed in time, it comprises typically a five-part composition – the *Kyrie*, the *Gloria*, the *Credo*, the *Sanctus*, and the *Agnus Dei*; here, in Beethoven's translation of the Latin into German, several psalms are alluded to through the language of the vernacular liturgy. Similar examples are found in his *Ode to Joy*, based on an adaptation of Schiller's text, in the fourth movement of the *Ninth Symphony*, in the common language about the protection of the nation and the celebration of creation.

Felix Mendelssohn (1809–47) contributed to psalmody in a quite different way. Although from the 1820s to his death in 1847 he worked mainly in Düsseldorf, Leipzig and Berlin, he was profoundly influenced by Beethoven, and his music reflects the tension between the Classical and Romantic influences of that time. As well as composing orchestral and chamber music and a vast number of choral and vocal works for the concert hall, Mendelssohn also composed a number of oratorios and sacred works for the church. Although he was baptized (and from then on given the surname 'Bartholdy' whilst still young, when his family converted to Christianity), his Jewish origins counted against him for some time after his death, when anti-Semitic sentiments were rife (promoted, for example, by Wagner). Nevertheless, the popularity of his great religious oratorios ultimately survived: *St Paul* was first performed in 1836, and was possibly composed as a tribute to his father, also a Jewish-Christian convert to Christianity; his use of Psalm 51, as a penitential psalm to express Paul's repentance after his conversion, is a poignant work. His Jewish-Christian background meant that the large-scale settings of psalms were an intuitive choice, and furthermore they provided the opportunity to experiment with choral cantatas. Most of these were composed mainly for use outside church worship, and include Psalms 115 (1830), 42 (1837), 95 (1838), 114 (1839) and 98 (1843). Of the sacred works which Mendelssohn composed for an English audience, a striking example is an interpretation of Psalm 55 (1844) entitled *Hear my Prayer*, as well as the performance of *Elijah* for the Birmingham Festival in 1846, which, using the theme of a great Old Testament prophet in a way which echoed his oratorio on Paul, included several psalms, for example Psalms 6, 7, 10, 86, 88, 91, 93, 121, 128, 55, 16, 108, 25 and 104. Other notable psalmic compositions include Psalm 66 (1822), performed with a double female chorus, Psalm 5 (1839), Psalm 31 (1839) and Psalm 100 (1844), the latter of which was written after being invited by King Friedrich Wilhelm IV to be Kappelmeister of Leipzig cathedral. In addition, Mendelssohn experimented with various psalms melodies and harmonizations (one notable collection is of Psalms 2, 24, 31, 91, 93, 98 and 100) and another composition of three psalms was performed together in 1849 shortly after his death (Psalms 2, 43, 22).[21]

---

[21] A recording of Psalms 42 and 115 by Mendelssohn is produced by Harmonia Mundi (HM C901272) as *Mendelssohn: Psaumes/Ave Maria* (Paris Chapelle Royal Chorus, Ghent Collegium Vocale; conductor Philippe Herreweghe).

Robert Schumann (1810–56) was as interested in Romantic literature as in its music; this undoubtedly affected his compositional style, which in turn influenced later Romantic composers. His best-known psalms compositions come at the beginning and end of his musical career. Whilst still a schoolboy aged about eleven at Zwickau, one of his very earliest compositions was a setting to Psalm 150 in 1822 (although this was not performed until 1997). And in 1823, he set a text to music on Psalm 8, based upon a translation by the Benedictine Abbot of Melk, Maximilian Stadler, who had been a close friend of Mozart. A few years before his death in Düsseldorf, whilst fighting long periods of depression and insanity, he composed, for liturgical performance, a *Missa Sacra* (1852–3) and a *Requiem* (1852), in which liturgical allusions to the psalms played a part.

Like Schumann, *Johannes Brahms* (1833–97), at least in his formative years, was as inspired by Romantic literature, especially by German poets and national folklore, as he was by music. Some of his earlier piano sonatas, choral works and folksongs, composed mainly during his time at Hamburg, are examples of this. Some of his early choral works were for women's, men's and mixed choirs, experimenting in fugal variations and counterpoint and chorale-like melodies, inspired by Schumann's similar compositions: the most pertinent here is the second of his *Two Motets* (1856–60), which included a setting of verses from Psalm 51. Another work, *Begräbnisgesang* (1858), a funeral song, anticipating the second movement of his *Requiem*, is a further choral experiment which alludes to the preoccupation with mortality expressed in psalms such as 88 and 90.

But the best-known of Brahms' psalmic works are within his *German Requiem* (1865–8), which illustrate his growing mastery of choral and orchestral styles, and his ability to transform the rich polyphonic harmonies of the late Renaissance period to suit the Romantic interests of his day. His skill at ornamentation, expanding large themes from small ideas, pervades this work. However, as a Deist, Brahms could never intend this to be a liturgical performance, a point he made clear by avoiding all references to the Latin texts. The Requiem was also notably lacking in references to any central tenets of the Christian faith (there is no mention of Christ at all), for Brahms wished his work to have a more universal appeal, offering more a consolation for the living than a memorial for the dead. It may have been his mother's death, or it might have been the death of his dear friend, Robert Schumann, which impelled the work, although it is more likely that the work was shaped by several concerns, not least Brahms' own fascination with mortality and immortality. He brought together fifteen passages from Luther's Bible to create seven movements: three of these are from the psalms. In the first movement, a passage in German from Matthew 5:4 is complemented by Ps. 126:5–6 ('May those who sow in tears reap with shouts of joy'). In the third movement we hear Ps. 39:4–7 ('Let me know my end'); whilst the fourth movement, a meditation on the first part of Psalm 84 ('How lovely is your dwelling place, O Lord of hosts!'), takes up the rhythm of a Viennese waltz. This is perhaps the best example thus far of psalmody expanding beyond the traditional frontiers, now serving a more universal cause than bound up exclusively with Jewish and Christian concerns.[22]

The other great Romantic composer with psalmic interests, native to Vienna rather than performing and composing there, is *Franz Schubert* (1797–1828). As well as having a reputation for orchestral, piano and chamber music, Schubert's peculiar legacy was his German 'Lieder', with their rich melodies and subtle harmonies, many of which were composed as sacred music. As a child Schubert attended Mass regularly, although later, after he contracted syphilis, his faith, somewhat challenged, evolved into a form of Christian humanism. His composition of psalmody is mainly evident in his Masses. He wrote four of the six of these between 1814 and 1816, and the influence of Beethoven and Mozart is clearly apparent, even to the degree with which he used the Latin Mass text, albeit with greater flexibility. Schubert nevertheless composed for the Viennese church rather than the concert hall. The last of the six Masses, in E flat, which alludes to verses from the psalms, is the most interesting, in that its frequent changes in mood through an extraordinary wide range of melody and harmony seem to suggest this has much to do with Schubert's own inner spiritual life. He was also drawn to Jewish Messianism, and his setting of Psalm 92 in Hebrew, which was probably commissioned by the cantor of the Viennese synagogue, Salomon Sulzer, was an attempt to defuse anti-Semitism in Vienna. Two other psalm arrangements were of Psalm 23 (using the translation from the Hebrew by Moses Mendelssohn) in 1820, and of Psalm 8 (like Schumann, using Stadler's version) in 1823.[23]

The most significant English composer associated with the Romantic Movement who also arranged accompaniments for psalms is Edward Elgar (1857–1934). Drawing much of his inspiration from the Worcestershire countryside, from British culture and from his continental contemporaries, Elgar's symphonies, oratorios and his nationalistic works gave him huge popular appeal. By the time he had started the major choral work using Newman's *The Dream of Gerontius* (1900), he had already established himself with his *Enigma Variations* and *Sea Pictures*, both performed in 1899. In *The Dream* Elgar demonstrated something of his personal Catholic faith, and, despite the muted reception and Elgar's consequent distress at its first performance, it placed him as amongst the best of British performers of his day because of its universal import – the death of everyman. In *The Dream* Elgar set to music Newman's psalms – Ps. 31:5 ('into thy hands I commend my spirit'), Psalms 147 and 150 as the subtext for 'Praise to the Holiest', and especially Psalm 90, sung as Gerontius descends to purgatory. Later, Elgar composed other liturgical works from Psalms: in 1907 he arranged two single chants for the *Venite* (Psalm 95), and two double chants for more nationalistic Psalms 68

---

[22] On the German Requiem, see *D. Beller-McKenna (1995)* and M. Musgrave (1996). One of the many recordings is by Deutsche Grammophon (Universal 469 658-2), *Johannes Brahms: Ein deutsches Requiem* (Czech Philharmonic, Giuseppe Sinopoli).

[23] One recording of both Psalms 92 and 23 is by Lambourne Productions (ASIN B000003W01), *Schubert, Psalms and Part-Songs* (London Sinfonia, Conductor Jane Glover).

and 75. In 1912 he also wrote an accompaniment to Psalm 48 for a service at Westminster Abbey. But, in terms of psalmody, nothing perhaps excels his dramatic use of Psalm 90, with its balance of expression from orchestra and choir and soloists alike.[24]

Obviously, not all the musical settings of the psalms throughout the eighteenth and nineteenth centuries were performed within the tradition of Romanticism. Although not as drawn to church music as he was to other forms, *Wolfgang Amadeus Mozart* (1756–91) also wrote a few psalms settings for the Catholic liturgy. His relatively short life, until the last ten years, was spent mainly in Salzburg in the employment of the Prince Archbishop of Colloredo: however, of his some 626 compositions, only in the early, itinerant years between about 1770 and 1780 is there any real evidence of sacred music. His earlier years, which also involved much travelling all over Europe as his father searched (unsuccessfully) for better patronage for his gifted son than Salzburg could provide, were a time of experimentation, both at the keyboard and with strings, and here Mozart produced countless sonatas, minuets, arias, quartets, and some symphonies, but few sacred works. His later years, in Vienna (1781–91) reveal incredible industry, focusing increasingly on secular works such as his operas (which apparently he enjoyed composing most, and *The Magic Flute* and *The Marriage of Figaro* gave him the recognition he craved) as well as canons, concertos, oratorios and dance music and songs; other than his unfinished Requiem, in these last stages there is little sacred music in evidence. In part this was due to his gradual refutation of his earlier Christian faith: he became a freemason in 1784 and espoused Deism.

Hence the years 1770–80, whilst working for his patron in Salzburg, were the period when Mozart composed most of his fifteen Masses, as well as his church sonatas, and three compositions for Vespers. The Vespers provided him with the best opportunity to experiment with psalmody. *Dixit Dominus* was composed in 1774; *Vespers in C*, in 1779; and a further *Vespers in C*, in 1780. This last composition, made just before irreconcilable differences with both his father and the Prince-Archbishop caused him finally to leave Vienna, offers the best insight into Mozart's interpretation of psalmody. It is a work in five keys, with a range of styles applied completely differently to each of the five appointed Vesper psalms and the Magnificat. The first, 'Dixit Dominus', is a highly orchestrated accompaniment to Psalm 110; the second, 'Confitebor tibi Domine' (Psalm 111), works at a more relaxed pace, to allow the solo quartet to dominate; the third, 'Beatus vir', from Psalm 112, is faster, with a soloist soprano used to ornament the text ('exaltabitur' being an example of such elaboration). The fourth, 'Laudate pueri', from Psalm 113, this time in D minor, takes a fugal style, with dramatic leaps into the diminished seventh; the fifth, 'Laudate Dominum' on Psalm 117, is more ethereal, with a lilting accompaniment, using strings, a small organ and a bassoon to accompany a

---

[24] On Elgar's sacred music, see J. *Allison (1995)*; one recording of the *Dream of Gerontius* (which was part of the BBC Proms Programme 25 July 2005) is by the Hallé Orchestra (conductor J. Barbirolli) by Baker (EMI CM S5 73579-2).

soprano solo; whilst the sixth, the Magnificat itself, returns to the key of C major to bring the whole piece to a gratifying conclusion. In spite of Mozart's being bound to ecclesiastical patronage, this is as close to theatrical performance as it could be, and quite a distance removed from the Gregorian plainchant normally used for Vespers, giving Mozart in this respect some affinity with the sacred music of Haydn, Handel and Vivaldi in the enjoyment of the performance for its own sake.[25]

Although the actual composition of the work is really within the twentieth century, mention must also be made of *Edvard Grieg* (1843–1907), Norway's most famous composer, because, like many of the composers above, Grieg's *Four Psalms* (1906) took the psalms away from the church and into the cafés and restaurants. Grieg was a Unitarian, having a difficult relationship with the Church from his youth, despising what he saw as its abuse of power. And although he could not accept that Jesus Christ was the Son of God, he fully affirmed the importance of his teachings in contemporary life, and so this, one of the last of his works, represented a new grasp of faith in tension with unbelief. *Four Psalms* is a combination of Norwegian folk music with old religious texts imitating psalmic forms. The first two texts were by Hans Adolf Brorson ('God's Son hath set me free' and 'How far is thy face'), and Grieg brought to them a highly creative rhythm and harmony, with the soloist singing in the key of B major, and the choir responding in B minor. The third psalmic text, by Hans Thomissøn ('Jesus Christ our Lord is risen') is the most overtly liturgical, with an intermittent refrain of 'Kyrie Eleison'; the fourth, by Laurentius Laurentil ('In Heav'n Above'), has complex harmonies evoking a hymnic form about the mysteries of creation. As far as innovative and more secularized works on the psalms are concerned, marking the end of one century and the beginning of another, Grieg offers a striking example.[26]

By contrast, the British composers Sir Hubert Parry and Sir Charles Villiers Stanford wrote primarily for liturgical purposes, for which they received their stipends. (The same is the case with their later contemporaries, Ralph Vaughan Williams, Herbert Howells and William Walton, to be discussed in the following chapter.)

Hubert Parry (1848–1918) was given his first musical training at St George's Chapel. He did not enter a musical career immediately, but his lessons in piano technique with Edward Dannreuther, a Wagnerite, enabled Parry to meet the composer and to attend several of his concert performances in England. Wagner's

---

[25] Several editions of Mozart's complete works have appeared as part of the Mozart Jubilee Celebrations (2006), including the 1780 *Vespers in C* in *In Search of Mozart* (filmed and directed by Phil Grabsky); a highly rated recording is the Warner Classics Mozart Edition 2564623372, *Mozart: Complete Sacred Music* (13 CD set: Concentus Musicus Wien, conductor Nikolaus Harnoncourt) which includes all three Vespers compositions and the Masses. For a website which lists all the works and with full bibliography see www.mozartproject.org/index.html.

[26] *Four Psalms* (Op. 74) is found in a recording by Hyperion (CDH 55236), *At Twilight* (D. Wilson-Johnson [baritone] and P. Agnew [tenor], conductor Stephen Layton), which comprises polyphonic works by Percy Grainger and Edvard Grieg.

influence cannot be overestimated; his large-scale symphonic and oratorio experimentations in his early years bear witness to this. Yet, as his own musical career was emerging, Parry also composed smaller-scale chorales and motets, some written for church and cathedral liturgy, although others, nearer the end of his life, were composed for state occasions. His arrangements of psalms – some as chorales, others as motets, or anthems, or sacred symphonies – were prolific; amongst the best known are his *De Profundis* (Psalm 130), which was written in 1891 as a commission for Hereford Cathedral. His *I was glad* (Psalm 122) was also a public commission, composed for the coronation ceremony of Edward VII in Westminster Abbey in 1902 and revised in 1911 for the coronation of George V. *God is our Hope* (Psalm 46) was composed similarly for St Paul's, in 1913. Parry's chorale *Praise God from whom all blessings flow* (using the words of Thomas Ken's version from 1674) is a collection of psalm texts, the first from Ps. 17:15, and the last, as a doxology, from Psalm 149. As for motets based upon psalms, his most moving is probably *Let me know mine end*, based upon Psalm 39, composed in 1918 as one of his *Six Songs of Farewell*, showing just how much the First World War had affected him. He died the same year.[27]

Charles Stanford (1852–1924) was the son of a Protestant lawyer in Dublin. His musical talents flourished during his undergraduate days in Cambridge. By 1874, he had already composed various piano concertos and accompaniments to evening services. A period in Germany brought him under the influence of Brahms – an inspiration which becomes evident in his choral and orchestral works. Many of Stanford's arrangements of psalms were for particular occasions in the Anglican liturgical year, bringing new harmonious and recurrent themes to familiar texts. Some were for entire services ('Service in B flat' [1879] and 'Evening Service in A' [1880] are early examples), and others were of the canticles sung at morning and evening prayer; Psalm 96 ('O sing unto the Lord a new song') is one of the latter. Other compositions were of particular psalms designated for particular services. Of these, the most memorable include Psalm 46 ('God is our hope and strength', in 1877), an early version of Psalm 150 ('O praise God in His Holiness', also in 1877), an anthem on Psalm 23 (1886), a version of Psalm 24 ('The earth is the Lord's' in 1924) and of Psalm 57 ('Be merciful unto me', in 1928), and his three psalms for the evening service on the thirtieth day of the month (Psalms 147–50).[28]

Apart from the last two liturgical composers of psalmody, the other representations illustrate a major innovation in the reception of psalmody in this period,

---

[27] 'I was Glad' is found on *Rejoice! British Choral Music* (RRC 1040) recorded by the Choir of Clare College, Cambridge (conductor Timothy Brown); a notable recording of 'Six Songs of Farewell' is by Guild (GMCD 7132) by the Vasari Singers (conductor Jeremy Backhouse).

[28] On Stanford's and Parry's contribution to British sacred music, see J.A. *Fuller Maitland (1934)*; one recording which includes several of the psalms listed here is *The Charles Villiers Stanford Music Collection* (Decca British Music Collection 2894038429) with the London Philharmonic Choir (director Roger Norrington) and Oxford New College Choir (director Edward Higginbottom), which includes Psalms 96 and 150 and the Service in B Flat.

namely its progressive secularization, a factor clearly evident in academic writings but now in aesthetic works as well. Surprisingly, this tendency is not as evident in the artistic depiction of psalms until the twentieth century: in spite of the Romantic interest in hero figures and national folklore, portrayals of King David, whether through sculpture or through painting, with a few exceptions, ceased to be popular after Rembrandt's works on David in the mid-seventeenth century. Neither impressionist painters, in their reaction to Romanticism and with their interest in the play of light and shade in pastoral landscapes, nor the pre-Raphaelite school, with their interest in folklore and a bygone age in art, seem to have found much inspiration in the life of David, nor in the religion of Israel. John Ruskin is a notable exception here, and even he wrote about the psalms rather than used them to any degree in his artistic works.

Thus, unlike musical representations of psalmody which were used not only in the sacred but also increasingly in secular life, artistic representations in the eighteenth and nineteenth centuries were restricted mainly to church use, where the most obvious medium was stained glass. There were some exceptions: an amusing one is in the imposing dining hall at Keble College, Oxford, whose stained glass windows contain some fifty-five quotations from the psalms; all are the first words of a psalm, or sections of Psalm 119, and the word 'God' or 'Lord' is either included in each verse, or would be in the verse following the one used; the architect, *William Butterfield*, wished to remind those leaving the hall of spiritual as well as physical sustenance. For example, the first verse of Psalm 121 reads: 'I have lifted up mine eyes unto the hills. Whence will my help come?'

Reception through Liturgy

The introduction to this chapter noted how liturgical works involving the psalms are less distinctive in this period than in the preceding one. However, if we include here the various imitations of psalmody in hymnody, in the (by now) several denominations of the churches in England, and the numerous musical works for both Catholic and Protestant worship, the reception of psalmody in this respect has some vibrancy. The main contrast with the sixteenth and seventeenth centuries is that these examples are responses to what is already in place in liturgy, rather than, as in the earlier period, innovative aids to liturgical reform.[29]

However, the differences between the Catholic, Anglican and Reformed renderings of psalmody in liturgy are quite striking. Setting aside the monastic offices – which were beginning to reappear throughout the eighteenth and nineteenth centuries, returning in the main to the traditions established before the Reformation – the

---

[29] Resources which have informed this discussion on liturgy and psalmody include P.F. Bradshaw and L.A. Hoffman (eds.) (1991a); C. Jones, G. Wainwright and E. Yarnold (eds.) (1978); J.A. Lamb (1962); B. Payne (1709, 1731) and R. Taft (1986).

diverse uses of psalmody in church liturgy give food for thought, and explain in some ways why in the twentieth century there were so many initiatives in ecumenism and liturgical reform. For example, in the Catholic liturgy, a problem which was manifest at the beginning of the Reformation period, that busy Catholic priests found themselves unable to perform all seven daily offices and the prescriptions to read the entire Psalter – in Latin – within a week were becoming burdensome, was not yet resolved (and was not done until the reforms initiated by the Second Vatican Council in the twentieth century).

By contrast, the liturgical practice of psalmody was less onerous for Anglican priests, for since the Reformation the prescription was only daily Morning Prayer (with its reduction of three offices, Matins, Lauds and Prime, into one) and daily Evening Prayer (with two offices, Vespers and Compline, being combined into one). The language medium was of course the vernacular, and the psalms were read over an entire month rather than within a week. But the psalms were used for critical occasions, too: an interesting publication in the early part of the eighteenth century was *The Parish Clerk's Guide*, which was compiled by Benjamin Payne, clerk of St Anne's, Blackfriars, 'to help in the selection of psalms suitable to times and occasions' and went into several editions. Psalm 1 was for use at the assizes; Psalm 46, after an earthquake; Psalm 90, following traditional Protestant use, at funerals; Psalm 91, in times of plague or sickness; Psalm 124, on the Fifth of November; and Psalms 127 and 128, at weddings.

By the beginning of the nineteenth century, the psalms were read in Anglican services as much as they were sung. Attempts to create more singing of psalms and hymns – for example by reformers such as Thomas Cotterill, who in 1819 published a collection to be used in Sheffield Cathedral, and the Moravian James Montgomery's *The Christian Psalmist* (1825) – were met with resistance by the church establishment, who associated this more with the practices of the reformed churches. The emphasis placed on Sunday Eucharist by the end of the nineteenth century (in large measure due to the Oxford Movement) brought additional *Proper Psalms into the Sunday services in Anglican worship, and although this increased the numbers of psalms used, it made no difference to the daily recitation of them. It was really due to the Oxford Movement that by the late nineteenth century, psalm-like hymns by Keble, Newman and Neale, for example, were introduced into the Anglican liturgy: *Hymns Ancient and Modern* was published first in 1861, and after the second edition in 1875 it became a highly popular hymnal, containing versions of several psalms, with some (for example Psalms 67, 72, 84, 100 and 148) being used in two forms.

In the Reformed churches, the practice was still metrical psalmody, with the most popular version still being Tate and Brady. Sunday Communion services would use up to four metrical psalms – usually before the confession, before the blessing, before Communion, and before the final benediction. But because there was far less prescription about the exact number and which types of psalms were to be used, there was certainly no sense of having to read through the entire Psalter within a week or a month as in the Anglican and Catholic churches.

The strengths and weaknesses of all three traditions should be clear – the importance of reading regularly through the entire Psalter could be seen as a vital practice in an age of secularization, but an appropriate use of specific psalms has an equivalent appeal.

Translations of Psalmody

Compared with the previous two centuries, new translations of the psalms were by no means as fashionable in the eighteenth and nineteenth centuries. However, with the new ease in communication and publication, older translations were now more easily disseminated; and with this the importance of vernacular translations continued, not into English, but rather from English into other languages which were now being encountered on the mission field.

In the eighteenth century communication of new ideas was accelerated in part through the founding of public libraries and museums, public gardens, salons, coffee houses (there were some five hundred of these in London alone by the middle of the eighteenth century) and in part through a rapid increase in the facilities of publishing. Public places were used not only for exchange of commerce, but for entertainment, and the promotion of social, political, moral, philosophical and theological views. Newspapers, pamphlets and cartoons publicized current opinions with great speed, and the propagation of information expanded in the nineteenth century through, for example, the sponsorship of public lectures, a greater proliferation of journals and tracts. By the 1870s, modes of communication such as the telegraph and telephone made an enormous difference not just to the confident pursuit of knowledge, but to the quick reception of it.

The speed of communication had several consequences for the reception of the Psalms. First, it speeded up the already abundant publications of academic works of a more critical, Enlightenment-inspired nature, and facilitated translations of Continental literature which were brought before the literate public in England: for example, the German commentaries, hitherto unread by those without fluent knowledge of these languages, were now translated and made more widely accessible. By the end of the nineteenth century and at the beginning of the twentieth, new Commentary Series were being established – the International Critical Commentary, serving both American and British readership, the Expositors' Bible, the Century Bible and the Cambridge Bible – all with their own commentaries on the book of Psalms, and their scholarship was more readily available for a literate audience.

At the other end of the spectrum, the speed of communication also furthered the popularity of more devotional, moral and hymnic works. Spurgeon's weekly publication of his *Psalms of David* is but one example of it. *The Pictorial Sunday Book* (1845) and *Daily Bible Illustrations Vol. V, Job and the Poetical Books* (1877), both works of John Kitto (1804–54), are other examples. Each of these books, designed especially for family use, contained engravings illustrating scenes from the psalms.

Nevertheless, the ease of publication did not result in new translations of the psalms into English. It could be argued that there were so many intellectual and social changes for the Christian churches throughout these two centuries that to maintain the constancy of a familiar version of Scripture was more of a blessing than a hindrance. As was seen in liturgical uses of the psalms during this time, the different church traditions also had different attitudes to vernacular psalmody. For example, Catholic churches simply republished editions of the Vulgate-based Douay-Rheims translation dating from 1582 (for the New Testament) and 1609 (for the Old Testament). Given the social and religious constraints on practising Catholics until the late eighteenth century, this state of affairs is hardly surprising: Richard Challoner, who served secretly as a bishop in London, began in 1750 to make revisions to the Douay-Rheims Bible, deferring mainly to the Vulgate and not to the Greek and Hebrew; his fifth edition (1772) was the normative edition until 1911. Taking Ps. 23:1–2 (22:1–2 in Challoner's version) as a familiar example, the stilted nature of this translation (set in prose) is clear:

The Lord ruleth me: and I shall want nothing. He hath set me in a place of pasture. He hath brought me up, on the water of refreshment: He hath converted my soul ...

As for the Reformed and Anglican churches, the first alternative to the *KJV* was the *English Revised Version* (1881–5), whose only difference, apart from the decision in this edition to omit the Apocrypha, was simply formal changes to style. The same applies to the 1901 *American Standard Version*, which was also a direct, literal revision of the *KJV*. A comparison of Ps. 23:1–2 in the *ASV* should show some of the differences with the *Douay-Rheims* and the similarities with the better-known *KJV*:

Jehovah is my shepherd; I shall not want. He maketh me to lie down in green pastures; He leadeth me beside still waters. He restoreth my soul ...

By the end of the nineteenth century, the most vital and prolific translations of the psalms were, paradoxically, from vernacular English into other languages, through the auspices of various newly-founded missionary societies. Most of this was done by Protestant societies rather than Catholic ones; the latter usually sent priests who taught the catechisms and liturgy in the Latin medium, whereas Protestants tended to send out laypeople whose interest in Scripture in the vernacular impelled them to translate, print and publish into as many other languages as possible. More often than not their translation would be from the English version without the medium of Hebrew, Greek and Latin; natives were taught to read and write from the Bible, and the Gospels and Psalms were often the first (and sometimes only) texts they could read. A very early example, using the English version alone as a base, is John Eliot's *Indian Bible* (or *Up-Biblum God*) which was published as early as 1655 for the Algonquin American Indians in their 'Natick' dialect; given there was no alphabet, Eliot invented one using the roman script, and taught them

FIGURE 5.1   Illustration of Psalm 2 in the Pictorial Sunday book.
Source: John Kitto.

FIGURE 5.2   Illustration of Psalm 3 in the Pictorial Sunday book.
Source: John Kitto.

to read and write from firstly the Gospels and later the Old Testament, including the Psalms. Ps. 8:1 ('O Lord, our Sovereign, how majestic is your name in all the earth!'), for example, reads as follows: 'Woi Jehovah num Manittoom, uttoh nukkukque wunnegen koowefuonk wame muttaohket!'[30] By 1800 some sixty-six languages had some portion of Scripture in their own tongue, many of them sponsored by missionary societies, such as the Society for the Proclamation of the Gospel (1698) and the Society for the Propagation of the Gospel (1701), each of which was influenced

---

[30] Taken from *Eliot's Bible*, 1663, 1685²

FIGURE 5.3 Illustration of Psalm 8 in the Pictorial Sunday book.
Source: John Kitto.

FIGURE 5.4 Illustration of Psalm 12 in the Pictorial Sunday book.
Source: John Kitto.

by Eliot's pioneering work, and the English Baptist Society (1792), the London Missionary Society (1795), and the Church Missionary Society (1799).

In most cases, the working principle was that although scholarly advice about the original versions was preferred, it was better for the 'pagans' to have some version of Scripture rather than no version at all. A typical example is *William Carey* (1761–1834), who started as a totally untrained missionary in Calcutta in 1793, and by 1801 had began to translate, print and publish the Bible into Bengali, finishing the Old Testament in 1809, and beginning a translation into Hindustani in 1811 which was completed in 1818. By 1834 Carey was responsible for some twenty different Indian translations, most of them produced from his headquarters at Serampore, using mostly the English *KJV*. The vast number of translations made 'abroad' throughout the nineteenth century contrasts starkly with the dearth of English translations 'at home'. The alphabetical list in *The Historical Catalogue of Printed Editions of Holy Scriptures in the Library of the British and Foreign Bible Society*, published between 1903 and 1911, runs to three volumes: just working through the first few pages listing Psalters printed in languages beginning with 'A', there are entries as various as Accra (from West Africa) in 1861, Ainu (from Japan) in 1896, Albanian (first published in Constantine) in 1868, Amharic (from Abyssinia) in 1833, revised in 1860 and 1872, and a selection of psalms in Aneityum (in the New Hebrides) in 1863; this gives a flavour of the diversity of copies of the Psalms, sponsored with funds and personnel from the British and Foreign Bible Society.[31]

Jewish Responses

Reception as Translation and Liturgy

Although the effects of the Enlightenment were experienced some time later within Judaism, the reception of psalmody within Jewish tradition throughout the eighteenth and nineteenth centuries still had to engage with the same issues facing the Christian churches. The roots of the Jewish Enlightenment, with the consequences of 'secularizing' faith, may be traced in part to seventeenth-century Holland – to *Baruch Spinoza* (1632–77), who combined a study of medieval Jewish theology with natural sciences and natural philosophy, arguing – in many ways anticipating Newton – that theology and the sciences were interdependent disciplines. Excommunicated from his Jewish community in Amsterdam, Spinoza then wrote substantial works on ethics, natural law, and on God's oneness with nature. Although, like Newton, he had little creative interest in psalmody, he exemplifies a

---

[31] On Eliot, Carey and missionary Bibles, see *C. de Hamel (2001)*, pp. 270–97. and more generally, *E. Fenn (1963)*. The Psalms quoted from the BFBS Catalogue (1903–1911) are from Vol. II.

typical Enlightenment thinker, albeit one estranged from the Jewish establishment, whose influence was consequently mainly felt outside his community.[32]

By contrast, a century later, in Berlin, *Moses Mendelssohn* (1729–86: grandfather of the composer) provided a more acceptable philosophical defence of Judaism, and so is considered, by virtue of his reasonable but more orthodox approach, to be the true father of the Jewish Enlightenment, hailed as a 'Jewish Plato', or a 'Jewish Socrates'. Mendelssohn was in part influenced by his lifelong friendship with the Christian author and playwright Gotthold Lessing, whose liberal theology led Mendelssohn to argue that universal truths can reasonably be known by all peoples everywhere. For Mendelssohn the Jew, the implications were that belief about God, both universal and Jewish, was open to debate. Seeking to prevent the further isolationism of Judaism, Mendelssohn tried to find ways of bridging the gap between a natural theology which could encompass Gentile belief and a revealed theology which embraced Judaism through the Torah. His interest in the psalms lay mainly in his interest in *translating* them (along with the Torah) from the Hebrew into the German vernacular. The translation, with a short grammatical commentary, was first published in 1783; this was the version which was used for musical settings to the psalms by Schubert, for example.

Mendelssohn died before the period of Jewish *Emancipation really began, and hence his contribution to it was constrained by the circumstances of his time. But the effects of Emancipation were tremendous (albeit also complex), as one nation-state after another granted citizenship to the Jews (for example, Holland in 1796; France, in part through the mediation of Napoleon, in 1800; Italy between 1848 and 1870; Germany in 1871; Britain in 1890 – paradoxically some sixteen years after Disraeli was prime minister). Previous economic, social and religious restraints were gradually removed (although political leaders constantly objected to the Jews' new-found concessions and imposed further constrictions). Hence the *Haskalah* gradually spread throughout Europe through the processes of Emancipation. Hebrew literary magazines and tracts and journals began to appear in Germany, Austria, and later in Russia. By 1863, the Society for the Promotion of Culture among the Jews was founded. The dissemination of information, as we saw in Christian circles, led to a greater involvement in Enlightenment debate, which in turn affected new approaches to the psalms, as we shall shortly see.

At the very beginning of the nineteenth century, some Jews sought to transcend their Jewishness by undergoing conversion, and several new Jewish-Christian sects were established, amongst the first being the one founded by David Friedländer in Berlin in 1811. Similar groups began to develop in England by the middle of the

---

[32] Resources which have been used in the following analysis include D. Barthelemy (1996); *D. Cohn-Sherbok (1994)*; H.H. Donin (1980); I. Elbogen (1993); P. Johnson (1987); R. Liberles (1995); M. Maher (1994); and R. Posner, U. Kaploun and S. Sohen (eds.) (1975); D. Rechter (2002); *D.B. Ruderman (2000)*; A. Sutcliffe (2003).

nineteenth century, when a large number of Sephardic families also underwent conversion. An example from Germany is Felix Mendelssohn, the grandson of Moses Mendelssohn, referred to above; as a Christian composer Felix would use the text of his grandfather's translation for his arrangements of the psalms. Hence, although this resulted in mainly *Christian* aesthetic representations of psalmody – through music, vernacular poetry, and art – the Jewish origins of a vast amount of creativity, both sacred and secular, may be traced back to the nineteenth-century process of assimilation.

The greater the willingness to integrate, the greater the contribution Jewish scholars were able to make in constructive Enlightenment debates. Many emancipated Jews became freemasons, and several founded Masonic lodges where ideas could be heard and discussed. One typical example in England is David Levi (1742–1801), whose public debates with the radical *Unitarian scientist Joseph Priestley became well known; Levi was also a key opponent of Christian Hebraic scholars such as Benjamin Kennicott, whose emendations to the pointing of the psalms from the MT to make the readings more compatible with the Christian faith caused much Jewish opposition from other quarters, as well as of Robert Lowth, whose views of Hebrew poetry Levi found to be supersessionist and patronizing. Levi's rationale was that Jewish commentators had been looking at the Hebrew texts in this way from as early as the eleventh century in Spain (through the work of scholars discussed earlier, such as Moses ibn Giqatilah and Abraham ibn Ezra) and later, in France (Rashi, Rashbam and Radak being notable examples): he saw that it was the task of Jewish scholars who belonged to this long-established tradition to refute and refine Christian textual commentaries. Some of the scholars Levi took to task were those who had written on the psalms, such as Kennicott and Street in England, and Hupfeld and Baethgen in Germany.

One consequence of this process of assimilation and public discourse was liturgical reform. One of Levi's lasting contributions as far as psalmody was concerned was *The Translation of the Hebrew Prayers and Services into English* (1789–93), and, in 1794, a separate translation of the *Seder*. Some of this translation also offered a critical commentary of the *KJV*, particularly of those parts which were used in daily, weekly and annual worship. Because of their dominant place in daily and weekly liturgy, both the translation and commentary used a number of psalms; these included some of the daily psalms which were prescribed in the *Mishnah* (Psalms 24, 48, 82, 81, 94, 93 and 92, ending with the Sabbath psalm), and those used at morning prayer in the *Pesukei de zimra* (Psalms 100 and 145–50), as well as others used at evening prayer (including Psalms 84, 144, 115, 141, 145) and yet others prescribed for the *Amidah* (Psalms 30, 145, 150 and 100 for the morning, and Psalm 134 for the evening). As for the *Seder*, weekly psalms which Levi also had to attend to included the Sabbath psalms (Psalms 95–9 and 29, concluding with Psalms 92 and 93 on the Friday evening, Psalms 19, 34, 90, 91, 135, 136, 33, 92 and 93 for the following morning, and Psalm 145 for the Sabbath evening). Festival psalms included the Hallel Psalms (112–18) used on the three main festival occasions; Psalm 7, used at Purim; and Psalms 103 and 150, for the Day of Atonement.

It is interesting to see how this first vernacular version of some of the psalms, inspired entirely by liturgical concerns, corresponds – over two hundred years later – with what had taken place in Christian tradition. It took some further fifty years before the first publication of all the psalms – and indeed of the whole Hebrew Bible – in English appeared: this was by *Isaac Leeser* in 1852, and like Mendelssohn's German version, it was a work of individual initiative: authorized translations did not appear until the twentieth century.[33]

Reception as Homily and Exegesis

A very different Jewish response to Enlightenment questions within Judaism was the *Hasidic movement, founded by Baal Shem Tov in Lithuania in the eighteenth century, spreading later to Poland. This laid stress on an ecstatic and mystical approach to an omnipresent God, emphasizing the ascent of the soul through the upper realms of heavenly places, while relegating intellectual study (and with this, analytical study of the Torah) to a secondary position, after mystical prayer. These practices influenced very different *didactic* and devotional works on the psalms.

Perhaps the most relevant here is that of *Rabbi Nachman of Breslov* (1772–1810), grandson of Baal Shem Tov, who was the founder of a particular Hasidic group which began in Bratslev, Ukraine (his name was changed to 'Breslov' because the Hebrew translation ['Bris-lev'] meant 'covenant of the heart', and it was this heart-felt meditation on the spirit of the Torah which Nachman sought to inspire in his followers). This was a mystical, *kabbalistic movement which affirmed the sacredness of numbers ascribed to Hebrew letters: the number ten was highly significant, expressed for example in the Ten *Sefirot*, the Ten Commandments, and the Ten Lost Tribes. Hence Nachman chose ten Psalms – 16, 32, 41, 42, 59, 77, 90, 105, 137 and 150 – which he believed had a unique therapeutic quality, and when used together, chanted in Hebrew, he believed could atone for sins (in the first instance it seems he advocated their use especially to atone for night-time emissions, but this particular appropriation was later generalized). These psalms, known as *The Psalms of Tikkun ha-kelali* or *Psalms for General Healing*, were to be sung especially when making pilgrimage (at the time of the Jewish New Year) to Nachman's grave: by singing these psalms at his graveside, the supplicant would be cleansed from sin forever. In Nachman's words: 'I will intercede for anyone who recites these ten psalms, and gives to charity. No matter how serious his sins and transgressions, I will do everything in my power to save him and cleanse him … By his forelocks I will pull him out of Gehennom!' The quasi-magical, messianic-orientated use of these psalms – in some ways corresponding to the seven penitential psalms in Christian tradition – has continued within parts of the Hasidic movement up to the

---

[33] On Mendelssohn, see *A. Arkush (1994)* and *D. Sorkin (1996)*; on Levi, see *J.J. Petuchowski (1968)* and *D.B. Ruderman (2000)*.

present day, and Rabbi Nachman of Breslov is still seen as one of the greatest *Hasidic teachers and has thousands of followers, especially in Israel. His works have been expanded by discovering secret words from the numerical value of the first letter of the second line and last letter of the last line of each psalm, and musical notations have been similarly created from the letters so that their mystical quality is enhanced even more. Devotional books on these ten psalms abound: one of the most recent is edited by Rabbi Simcha Weintraub.[34]

At the opposite end of the spectrum, concerned with the more liturgical and exegetical use of psalmody, is Reform Judaism, whose earliest founders include Israel Jacobson of Westphalia, at the beginning of the nineteenth century, in the wake of the French Revolution. The Reform movement gained much ground in the mid-nineteenth century, first in Germany, later in England (the West London Synagogue was built in 1842) and in America, whither large numbers of sympathetic Jews emigrated. Whether on the Continent, in England or in the New World, the concern of Reformed Jews was to find a rationale for closer assimilation and toleration between Jews and Gentiles. The means necessary to achieve this end interestingly echoed those of the Protestant churches some three hundred years earlier. The services began to have sermons, choirs and organs, with congregational participation. Jewish hymns were composed, and were set to the melodies of German folk songs, Italian court songs and Protestant hymn tunes, and were sometimes accompanied by an organ and cantor. There was a new emphasis on the equality of men and women in synagogue prayer, and on the transformation of ancient traditions, in this case, the practice of circumcision and rigid Sabbath observance.

Reform Judaism resulted in at least two changes in the ways in which the psalms were read. The first was a consequence of their affirmation that their present homeland, wherever it was, should be seen as 'the new Zion'. Hence references to being 'in exile', to the hope for return to Israel and Zion, to special election, to a Messianic figure, were either amended or read in a different way: this resulted in the spiritualizing of psalmody in a way that was reminiscent of some Christian readings around the time of the Reformation. For example, the daily psalms, such as 24, 48, 81, 82, 92, 93 and 94, were now interpreted (often using the vernacular rather than Hebrew) in a non-literal, non-Zionist way, and psalm-like hymns which spoke instead of the more universal concerns of God as Creator (for example Psalms 8, 33, 104) were popularized as well. (This 'anti-Zionist' stance proved actually to be short-lived, due to the failure of full assimilation and to responses to the rise of Zionism by the beginning of the twentieth century – a Zionism which nearly chose Psalm 126 'When the Lord restored the fortunes of Zion, we were like those who dream' as its national anthem. By 1948, Reform Judaism had reversed these earlier 'new-Zionist' views entirely.)

---

[34] See S. Weintraub (1994); there are many websites on the Ten Psalms of Tikkun HaKlali, of which one of the most clear is www.geocities.com/rahelmusic/tikkunhaklali.html.

A second effect on the reading of psalmody in Reform Judaism was the result of the influence of secular learning, which was beginning to supplement even Talmudic and Mishnaic studies. By the 1830s, Jewish Reform rabbis, such as Abraham Geiger in Germany, began to write about Jewish history in the context of world history, whilst Solomon Formstecher wrote about the religion of nature and the religion of the spirit as these beliefs affected Jews and Gentiles alike. It is not surprising that in Judaism, Reform Jews were the first to produce more critical exegetical studies of the psalms, where critical issues such as the multiple authorship and later dating and historical anachronisms were given full exposure, thus marking a departure from the more traditional text-critical and didactic and devotional commentaries which had been the norm since Medieval times, although (unlike some Christian commentaries of this time) this was of course still within the context of a faith-based community. One of the first places where this type of commentary flourished was the Hebrew Union College, Cincinnati, founded by Rabbi Isaac Mayer Wise in 1875, although Reform Jews in New York, Baltimore, London, Hamburg, Frankfort and Breslau were also beginning to write similar works on biblical books. By the beginning of the twentieth century these authors had entered into an effective dialogue with Christian academics, as will be seen in the following chapter.

Aesthetic Responses

These changes had further consequences for more aesthetic responses to psalmody, especially through music. In the Ashkenazi synagogue at Vienna, where the Romantic influence of Beethoven and Schubert was potent, *Solomon Sulzer* (1804–90) initiated choral compositions which were sung to a classical *a capella* choir; Schubert wrote his setting for the Sabbath psalm, Psalm 92 (D942), from the German translation of Moses Mendelssohn for this choir. Sulzer also revised musical notations of old Jewish melodies to enable psalm- and hymn-singing to be accompanied by old folk tunes: at least two known publications are from the psalms (Psalms 111 and 134). Similarly, growing Reform congregations in Paris, London and Berlin developed a repertoire of hymns, many of them based upon psalms, with harmony and counterpoint, giving full expression to choirs, cantors and musical instruments.

Louis Lewandowski (1823–94) initiated similar innovations for the Jewish community in Berlin: there the congregation used choirs, cantors and organ. At least six of his arrangements, dating between the 1870s and 1880s, are from the psalms (24; 92; 93; 95; 103:15–17; and 150). And *Samuel Naumberg* (1817–80), known as the 'Jewish French composer', arranged at least two psalms to music (24 and 100). Sephardic communities in Italy were not dissimilar: the earlier influence of Salamone Rossi's choral settings of hymns and psalms in Venice, for example, continued, and in synagogues in Padua and Mantua, as well, psalms and hymns were sung by cantors and by members of the congregation, with strophic melodies and polyphonic harmonies. Almost all of the psalms were for singing in daily liturgy – Psalms 24, 92 and 93 for morning prayer, Psalm 134 for evening prayer, and Psalms 100 and 150 for the *Pesukei de zimra and *Amidah.

Yet again, this nineteenth-century reform is an echo of what had already taken place in the Christian reception of the psalms; the only difference was that, at this stage, the Jewish tradition offers little evidence of musical compositions of psalmody for secular performances in the theatre and concert hall (although this was to follow in the early twentieth century, as will be seen in the following chapter). Similarly, in the reception of the psalms through art, although the eighteenth and nineteenth centuries provide good evidence of the continuing tradition of calligraphy and decorative designs of prayer books now in the vernacular, both in Sephardic and Ashkenazi traditions, representative art in psalmody outside liturgy, for secular exhibitions and the like, did not really begin until the twentieth century, especially after 1948.[35]

Concluding Observations

Within both Jewish and Christian traditions over these two centuries, all our five modes of reception of psalmody are evident, albeit expressed in different ways in each tradition. Liturgical reforms adapting psalms are more prevalent in Jewish tradition, whilst critical exegetical commentaries and faith-centred devotional works using the psalms are more dominant in Christian tradition. Vernacular translations into English are not prevalent in either tradition: for Christians, this is partly due to the amount of reform in previous centuries, and for Jews, this is mainly because this is still a period of conservatism where public, authorized versions are concerned. Finally, both traditions share an increasing interest in aesthetic responses to the psalms, particularly in music, with the greatest innovation occurring in the Christian tradition, where the psalms are now 'performed' not only for church worship but also for the concert hall.

In all these five modes of reception, despite the nuances within each tradition, one common thread has interwoven throughout this chapter: that of the growing divide between the critical and confessional use of the psalms – or of the tension between the influence of the academy and a faith-centred community. This tension is more intensely experienced at this stage in Christian tradition, but it is beginning in Judaism as well; it is increasingly evident in the twentieth century, when different Christian churches responded by taking more ecumenical initiatives

---

[35] On the growing Jewish aesthetic responses to the psalms through art and music, see K. Bland (1999) and L.I. Levine (2002) [both on art] and P.V. Bohlman (2002) [on music]. An excellent website listing other Jewish compositions of psalmody and choral music in the nineteenth (but mainly twentieth) century is www.zamir.org/db/index.html.

to provide a more unified response in the face of a perceived enemy, and when Jews and Christians tried to deal with it by putting aside some traditional differences and working more collaboratively in their understanding of a common inheritance. Only time will tell if this is a permanent resolution, in the face of a long reception history; but it registers important progress, and it will be the focus of our discussion in our final chapter.

The Twentieth to Twenty-First Centuries: Pluralism and Ecumenism

Whereas by the Reformation period it had become clear that, because of the abundance of material, our focus had to be increasingly on the reception of psalmody in the West, and by the eighteenth century, our emphasis had to be on the English-language medium, in this chapter the remit has to be narrower still. The material requiring investigation is now so extensive that not only has the focus to be on the English language, but the location has to be more exclusively psalmody within Britain, with selected works, mainly from Europe and America, providing further insights where appropriate.

The last chapter argued that the effect of the *Enlightenment on the reception of the psalms was that many began to see them as irrelevant or inappropriate, and the only way they served Enlightenment interests was when critical scholars read them with little reference to the present community of faith. In this chapter, the legacy of Enlightenment thinking continues to be a theme, although it will be seen that by the latter part of the twentieth century a very different way of thinking, namely *Post-modernism, had provided unexpected opportunities for the reception of psalmody. Its liberal openness to pluralism and hence to new ways of thinking has in part encouraged Jews and Christians (whose approaches to the psalms have, despite a few exceptions, traditionally been far apart) to begin to take new initiatives towards mutual collaboration in the ways they use the psalms. This has made little impact on the relevance of psalmody within a secular culture – the gradual but dramatic drop in church and synagogue attendance bears some witness to this – but at least it illustrates the reversal of a two-thousand-year tradition of disputation about the psalms within the two faith traditions.

Some general observations should make this point clear at the outset. For example, in matters of critical scholarship, increasingly throughout the latter half of the twentieth century Jewish and Christian scholars have worked together on new aspects of studying the psalms which concern them all. This has included the investment of joint expertise in Septuagint, Targum and Qumran studies, which has resulted in (often annual) conferences and the joint publication of papers. Further symposia on the theology, history of interpretation and literary shape of

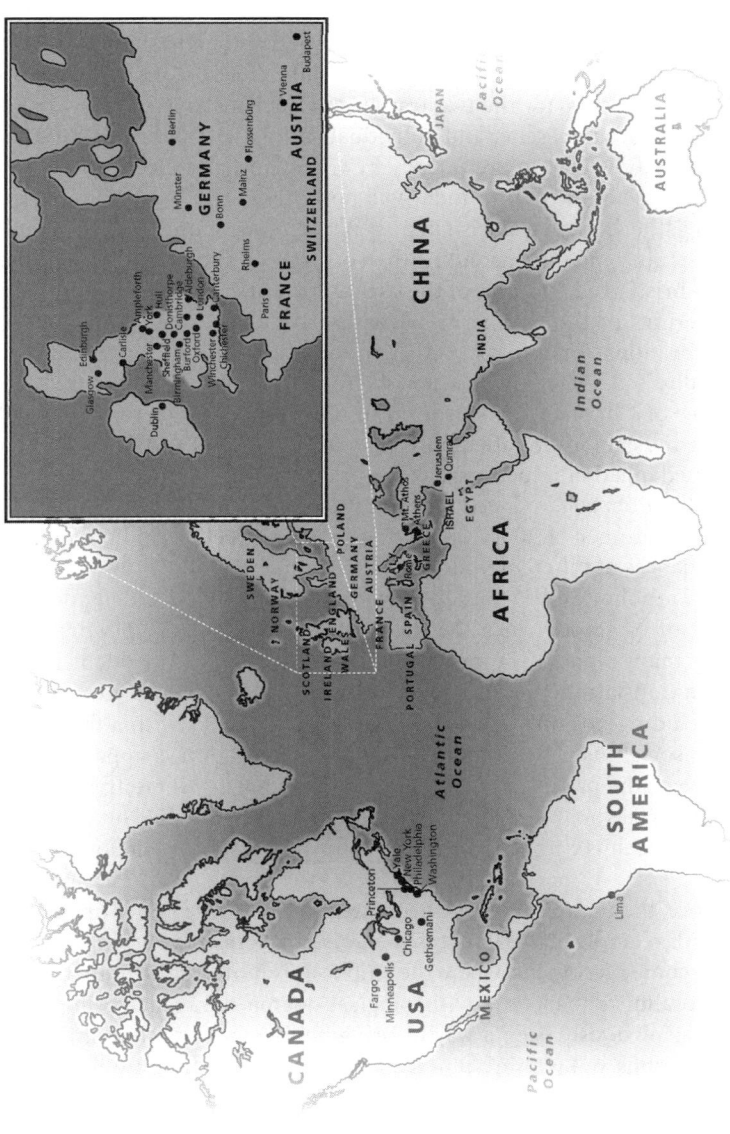

MAP 6.1 Great Britain and the English-speaking world: the spread of psalmody within the twentieth century.

the Psalter, resulting in other joint publications, have also been a feature of the past thirty years and more. Such collaboration has not been confined to academia. The *Council of Christians and Jews*, founded in 1942 against the backdrop of the Second World War and the Holocaust through the initiatives of Chief Rabbi Hertz and Archbishop Temple, has done much to promote respect and understanding between the two faiths; amongst its many projects has been the creation of a forum, in both synagogues and churches, for the two traditions to debate constructively the different ways each reads the Psalter and individual psalms. Jewish devotional studies of the psalms are now read appreciatively by Christians, and vice versa. Retreats encouraging the use of the psalms today will now often include a Jewish presence at a Christian gathering and a Christian presence at a Jewish one, with the emphasis more on listening and understanding than on arguing and defending a particular position. Christian adaptations of the psalms for worship often now use Jewish musical renderings of the psalms, and Jewish artists have often contributed to Christian celebrations (for example, Bernstein and Chagall at Chichester Cathedral, which we shall discuss later), whilst Jewish translators of the psalms frequently seek the advice of Christian scholars. And in music and art, where more secular performances and exhibitions are increasingly in vogue, Jews and Christians have also participated together in performing the psalms: a well-publicized example in England was the *Promenade Concerts* (the 'BBC Proms') in the Royal Albert Hall throughout the summer of 2000, which over an eight-week period offered some thirty performances of different psalms.

Similarly, Catholics and Protestants, who traditionally have defended their different uses of psalmody since the Reformation, particularly in worship, are now showing many signs of rapprochement. Collaboration is evident in work being done on translation, in ecumenical liturgies, and in edited academic works (the latter including not only commentaries but also works with a feminist, or ecological, or social justice emphasis). Similar collaboration is apparent in the devotional use of the psalms, as well as in music and art – where frequently we can see that the issues are more about what new light is being shed on our understanding of the psalms rather than about following a specific denominational correctness.

Furthermore, the psalms have also been used to encourage better understanding in interfaith relationships. Here it is the *universal* concerns within the psalms which have become a key focus, where the emphasis is more on the human experiences of the psalmists than on any theological dogma the reader brings to the psalm. This has obviously been a way of bringing together Jewish and Christian readers of the psalms, but within a pluralistic age it has more recently also brought together those from other faiths and those with no fixed religious commitment at all. Rather than reading the psalms through the life of David, or through Jesus Christ, those of all faiths read them as universal life-centred prayers to their deity, emphasizing what is typical and common to all humanity within them. In a century dominated in Britain by, for example, international warfare, economic uncertainty, threats of nuclear destruction, terrorism and ecological disasters, causing suffering at the individual, national and international level, the psalms (of all the books in Scripture) have been able to address issues which have a relevance for all humankind. Collectively they speak with a helpful poetic ambiguity about international and national affairs, about social injustice, about threats to society and the nation, whilst also addressing the full range of individual suffering. It is not that the psalms provide ready-made answers: but against the growing consciousness that a predominantly materialistic culture does not necessarily have all the solutions either, it is becoming evident that these ancient patterns of prayer and protest are still able to address most profoundly what it means to be fully human.[1]

So whether between Christians and Jews, Catholics and Protestants, or different faith communities, the psalms have served as a catalyst for a new understanding and creative partnerships. Our assessment of the use of psalmody in the now familiar five modes of reception will explore this further. Firstly, we shall examine the proliferation of new *translations* of the Psalter, noting how this relates to the large number of *liturgical* reforms since the end of the Second World War. We shall then look at the ways in which new *commentaries and critical introductions* also reflect a spirit of greater collaboration. This will lead to a discussion of *didactic works*, noting that whereas the previous two centuries witnessed a good deal of tension between more critical publications and works with more spiritual concerns, by the end of the twentieth century many writers sought to combine more creatively the two disciplines. Finally, we shall look at the various *aesthetic responses* to the psalms, particularly in music and art, and whilst recognizing that each tradition still has its own distinctive emphasis, we shall see how an innovative experimentation has given the psalms a more universal appeal and with it a newer appreciation of what each tradition can creatively offer. Because of the increasing

---

[1] Some of the following references to examples referred to here have actually been published at the beginning of the twenty-first century, but they still reflect an earlier history of mutual collaboration. For Jewish/Christian works on Septuagint studies, see for example A. Aejmelaeus and U. Quast (eds.) (2000); R.J.V. Hiebert, C.E. Cox and P.J. Gentry (eds.) (2001); and *S. Olofsson (1997)*. For shared works on Targumic studies, see for example *E.M. Cook (2002)*; and on Qumran, examples include U. Dahmen (ed.) (2003); D. Dimont (ed.) (1992); *D.W. Perry and S.P. Ricks (eds.) (1995)*; and *E. Ulrich and J.C. VanderKam (eds.) (1994)*. For joint works on the reception of the psalms, see H.W. Attridge and M.E. Fassler (eds.) (2004); P.W. Flint and P.D. Miller (eds.) (2005); F.L. Hossfeld and E. Zenger (1998); M.J. Mulder and P.B. Dirksen (eds.) (1988); and M. Saebø (ed.) (1996, 2000); Jewish works on using the prayerful use of psalmody widely used by Christians include *R. Alter (1990)*, *H. Levine (1995)* and *J. Magonet (1994)*. On the Council of Christians and Jews, see www.ccj.org.uk. Chagall's and Bernstein's works will be discussed at the end of the chapter. On the 'Psalms at the Proms', see *BBC Proms: 14 July – 9 September 2000 Programme* also at www.bbc.co.uk/proms. On interfaith readings, see for example *J.H. Eaton (1990)*; N. Fischer (2003); B. Griffiths and Roland R. Roper (eds.) (1996); and T. Merton (1956). In the more recent phenomenon of interfaith services, the psalms are frequently used as prayers and hymns about the human condition. And they are still used at state occasions – royal weddings, funerals, memorial services, and liturgies of prayer and thanksgiving at times of national crises – when those participating are often of different faiths and none.

cooperation between Jews and Christians in their understanding and use of psalmody, the two traditions will in this case be assessed alongside one another.[2]

Christian and Jewish Translations of Psalmody

The increase in the flow of information from the first decade of the twentieth century to the last has undoubtedly contributed to the newer collaboration between the different traditions. The move from telegraph to telephone to wireless to mobile and electronic mail, and from the big screen to private television to the World Wide Web, in just over a century, has resulted in immediate access to global events. Not only has this speed of communication facilitated more open debates about the use of psalmody, but it has also led to a greater experimentation with new forms: this is especially evident in the many different new translations which reflect the concern to provide contemporary versions for the ever-changing needs of society.

There has been a huge increase in translations for preaching and teaching, and a similar explosion of translations intended for private study and prayer. Many of these have been part of initiatives involving the Bible as a whole, although the large number of translations commissioned to accompany liturgical changes is more directed to just the Psalter. Compared with the paucity of new English translations in the eighteenth and nineteenth centuries, this has more resonance with the proliferation of new versions and literary imitations in the sixteenth and seventeenth centuries. Although the terms used today may be different ('formal equivalence', denoting a literal word-for-word version, 'dynamic equivalence', describing a more free meaning-orientated version, and 'an idiomatic approach' being more of a paraphrase), the approaches to translating the psalms some four centuries ago – about accuracy, singability, aesthetics and contemporary appeal – are still the same today. The only real difference is that whereas some four centuries ago allusions to psalms, whether from Coverdale or the *Geneva Bible* or the *KJV*, were frequent in secular poetry, drama and fiction – for example, in works as diverse as Shakespeare, Bunyan, Donne, Herbert and Milton – that is rarely the practice today. The sheer volume of translations makes a common literary and liturgical discourse virtually impossible.

The first types of translation to be assessed will be those which were made for preaching and teaching, and for study and prayer. Here all three approaches – the literal, the meaning-orientated and the idiomatic – are used in varying degrees. Translations intended for use in worship are different, because there the main

---

[2] General resources which have informed this preliminary discussion include R.E. Clements (1985); J.H. Eaton (*1999*, 2003); J.C. Endres (2002); *A. Hastings (2001)*; P.S. Hawkins (2004); W.L. Holladay (1993); and *J.L. Houlden (ed.) (1995)*.

concern is their 'singability', and a meaning-orientated approach conveying some poetic style is more dominant, and these will be assessed later.

Within the Catholic church, the most seminal translations of Psalms outside those commissioned especially for liturgy may be traced back to the initiatives of the Dominicans at the École Biblique in Jerusalem: this was in part the consequence of the work of the Pontifical Biblical Commission in the early 1940s and the resultant encyclical in 1943, *Divino afflante Spiritu*, which allowed Catholic scholars to pursue historical criticism and to work from the Greek and Hebrew as well as the Latin. Raymond Tournay was responsible for the French version of the Psalms in *La Bible de Jérusalem* (1948–54), and although the idea of a study Bible which assimilated much critical scholarship was opposed by many conservative Catholics, a parallel British version, *The Jerusalem Bible (JB)*, was completed by 1966. This was dependent upon the work of the French translators, and also used American Catholic scholars such as Mitchell Dahood with respect to the Canaanite influence pervading many psalms. This was the first widely acceptable and scholarly Catholic version of the Psalms (and indeed of the whole Bible) in English since the *Douay-Rheims* version in the seventeenth century and was the first English translation made by Catholics on the basis of the Greek and Hebrew texts rather than on the Vulgate. It did not seek to promote any specifically Catholic doctrine, but became known for being more ecumenical, literary and scholarly. As far as the Psalms were concerned, the most obvious changes were the use of 'you' not 'thou' when addressing God, and the use of 'Yahweh' instead of God (following its French counterpart); but the translators did not tackle the emergent issue of gender-inclusive language.

Following the revision of the French edition in 1973, an expanded and heavily revised version, *The New Jerusalem Bible (NJB)*, appeared in 1985 and is now the most widely used Catholic version outside the United States. Dom. Henry Wansbrough was the chief editor, working with a slightly larger team of Catholic scholars than for the first version. Wansbrough also had particular responsibility for the version of the Psalms. Efforts were made throughout to adopt more inclusive language; the following example from Ps. 34:6,8 illustrates how the concern to be more literal than literary and more accurate than aesthetic does not make an easy compromise where inclusive language is concerned. In the *KJV* the verses read

> 6 'This poor man cried, and the LORD heard him,
>   and saved him out of all his troubles ....
> 8 O taste and see that the LORD is good:
>   blessed is the man that trusteth in him.'

whereas the improved *NJB* version is

> 6 'A pauper calls out and Yahweh hears,
>   saves him from all his troubles ...

> 8 Taste and see that Yahweh is good.
> How blessed are those who take refuge in him.'

The first line in verse 6 has changed in the *NJB*, following more accurately the Hebrew which reads, more simply, 'The Lord heard'; but because the Hebrew has masculine pronouns in the second line of verse 6, the masculine orientation is retained, in order to preserve the singular subject from the first line; the result is that fully inclusive language has to be compromised. However, because in verse 8 the Hebrew imperatives in the first line and the Hebrew for 'blessed' in the second line are in the plural, more inclusive language can be used.

Since the early 1960s the issue of inclusive language has dogged all Bible translators. As far as psalmody is concerned, the key issues are the use of masculine pronouns and of masculine language for God. A critical problem, illustrated in Psalm 34 above, is when to leave in the word 'man'. For example, by leaving the word in Psalm 1:1, 'Blessed is the *man* ...' the psalm could have a very different theological interpretation, in drawing out a typology between humans and Christ, whereas by translating the verse 'Blessed are those ...', the more universal appropriation is clear. The same issue applies to this phrase as it occurs in Pss. 32:2; 40:4; 84:12; 94:12 and 112:1. In each case translators had to ask: are we speaking of Christ, or are we speaking of everyone, and hence is the psalm about us, or about Christ? A similar problem is how to translate the term 'son of man', for example in Pss. 8:4; 80:15, and 144:3. For those who wish to read it as a title, anticipating a Messianic or Christian reading, it should be left as it is; for others who prefer to read the term more inclusively, it is changed to a term such as 'child of Adam' or 'humans' or 'mortals'. Ps. 22:6 is a good example. In the *KJV* it reads 'But I am a worm, and no man; a reproach of men, and despised of the people' which in the *NJB* becomes 'But I am a worm, less than human, scorn of mankind, contempt of the people'. Sometimes the issue of masculinity can be avoided because of the different changes in person which occur so often in the psalms, whereby a first or second person singular or plural is more gender free (in English) than the third person. In other places, kinship terms such as 'brother' 'father' 'son' 'forefather' implicitly include women members, too; hence the translation in these cases should be 'kin' or 'ancestor' or 'family member', or the word can be erased altogether. So in Ps. 86:16, which in the *KJV* reads 'O turn unto me, and have mercy upon me; give thy strength unto thy servant, and save the son of thine handmaid', becomes in the *NJB* 'Turn to me and pity me. Give to your servant your strength, to the child of your servant your saving help'. The problem is more difficult when it comes to masculine language for God, because of the vast array of male images and metaphors for God in the psalms – the most obvious being those describing God as King and Father, although others such as Warrior, Shepherd and Judge also have, with a few exceptions, masculine connotations. The disagreements between those who value the accuracy and the traditional resonance of the language and those who wish to eliminate all male references for modernist or feminist reasons are particularly acute where the psalms are concerned, as these are hymns and prayers from God's people (male and female) to their God (who is neither male nor female). Every version shows how compromises have had to be made in order to meet the cultural needs of our day, when issues of exclusion by gender, race or religion are so paramount.

The most radical attempt to achieve this to date has probably been *The New Testament and Psalms: An Inclusive Version* (1995) edited by Victor Gold. 'God as Father' becomes God as Parent (Ps. 103:13), Guardian (Ps. 68:5) or Protector (Ps. 89:16). Occasionally, as in the Lord's Prayer, the term 'Father-Mother' is used. God is never described in the third person masculine in the psalms, but instead is directly addressed ('God') or given the second person form of address. 'Man' and 'Son of Man' become 'human beings' and 'mortals' (Ps. 8:4). Not only have all male references been eliminated, but also references to 'darkness' are amended to 'night' (as offensive to race and colour), references to God's 'right hand' are changed to God's 'mighty hand' or 'side', as offensive to left-handed people (see Pss. 16:8 'God is at my side' and 16:11 'In your mighty hand are pleasures forevermore'). Any pejorative or exclusivist references to people on account of gender, race, religion, colour or physical disability are amended by means of alternative renderings or paraphrase. The result is that although the criterion of 'being in vogue' might have been met, the criteria of aesthetic quality and accuracy (and, if to be used in worship, 'singability') are sometimes more difficult to attain.

Another example of contemporaneity is a change of format as well as of style. If the purpose of a version is for preaching or teaching or study, the poetic format, it could be argued, matters less; and given that some psalms were written in a prose style in continuous lines in some Qumran scrolls, and given that the *KJV* (unlike Coverdale) sets the psalms out in prose format, significant precedents could be claimed. The following prose version, considered for publication by OUP, has also a clear Christian overlay. Ps. 2:1–3, for example, produces a very different effect:

> What fools the nations are to rage against the Lord! How strange that men should try to outwit God! For leaders of the nations have been called to plot against the Lord and his Messiah, Christ the King. 'Come, let us break his chains,' they say, 'and free ourselves from all this slavery to God.'

Several other versions, mainly from Protestant churches, illustrate how these criteria have been applied in different ways. *The Living Bible* (*LB*: 1971), for example, is basically a paraphrase by an American, Kenneth Taylor; its publication by Tyndale House displays its evangelical leanings. The main criticisms relate to the fact that the entire translation is essentially by one man. In the psalms, where poetic ambiguity is of the essence, infelicitous turns of phrases and lapses of theological sensitivity might have been erased through greater consultation with experts in Hebrew, Greek and Latin. Some of this has been corrected in the *New Living Translation* (*NLT*: 1996), which is similarly a paraphrase version for easy reading. Ps. 8:4 reads: 'What are mortals that you should think of us, mere humans that you should care for us?' whilst Ps. 34:6 reads: 'I cried out to the LORD in my suffering, and he heard me. He set me free from all my fears'.

The Good News Bible (*GNB*: 1976) was originally intended for non-native English speakers encountered on the mission field. Its concern was to create 'thought for thought' rather than 'word for word'. Its simple everyday language makes it especially suitable for children and for those learning English, whilst the line drawings by Annie Vallotton bring the text to life. The psalms provided a particular challenge in conveying ancient poetic prayer-forms into colloquial speech: although there are inevitable infelicities, the line drawings compensate by illustrating the poetic ambiguities most strikingly. Ps. 8:4, with a line-drawing of someone with their hands outstretched to the heavens, reads 'What are human beings, that you think of them; mere mortals, that you care for them?'; Ps. 34:6 reads 'The helpless call to him, and he answers; he saves them from all their troubles'.

The *New International Version* (*NIV*: 1978; revised 1984) was undertaken by a hundred international scholars from twenty different Protestant denominations over a period of ten years. It is one of the most popular Protestant English versions, having sold over one hundred and fifty million copies worldwide. Many editions contain study guides and charts and maps. Although it does not lend itself easily for liturgical and musical use, it is a reliable study version for private and public reading. Ps. 8:4 reads, fairly traditionally, 'What is man that you are mindful of him, the son of man that you care for him?' and Ps. 34:6 is similarly conservative: 'This poor man called, and the LORD heard him; he saved him out of all his troubles'.

The *New King James Version* (*NKJV*: 1982) was a revision of the *KJV*, seeking to preserve the classic cadences from 1611 whilst updating some of the vocabulary and grammar. Its adherence to the *KJV* meant that it did not alter the text substantially, even though recent manuscripts suggested new readings: this is a translation of 'complete equivalence', staying as close to the Elizabethan syntax (rather than using the Hebrew or Greek original languages) as possible. This is a compromise version, for by placing modern words into a more archaic presentation, it is rendered in a language no one has ever really spoken. In Ps. 8:4 all that has changed is the address to God: 'What is man that *You* are mindful of him, And the son of man that *You* visit him?' and in Ps. 34:6, again retaining the masculine orientation, the only difference is in the first verb (the non-existent masculine pronoun following the second verb is retained as in the *KJV*): 'This poor man cried *out*, and the LORD heard *him*, And saved him out of all his troubles'.

The *New Revised Standard Version* (*NRSV*: 1990) was an update of the *Revised Standard Version* (*RSV*: 1952), which was itself a Protestant revision of the *KJV*. The *NRSV* aimed to achieve as accurate a translation as possible by reference to recently found manuscripts, whilst also modernizing the English, and exhibiting a more thorough use of gender-inclusive language. Designed for both academic and devotional use, it is published with and without the Apocrypha and Deuterocanonical books, and a further edition follows the Old Testament books in Vulgate order. Nearly three dozen Protestant denominations use it, as well as a small number of Orthodox churches. Ps. 8:4, for example, reads 'What are human beings that you are mindful of them, mortals that you care for them?', and Ps. 34:6 similarly has a more contemporary ring: 'This poor soul cried, and was heard by the LORD, and was saved from every trouble'.

Roman Catholics gave the *NRSV* a mixed reception on account of the inclusive language issue. Their text prescribed for lectionary use (the *NJB* being primarily for teaching and personal study) had been the *Common Bible* (*CB*: 1973), which was identical to the *RSV*, except it had the Apocrypha and Deuterocanonical books as well. The *English Standard Version* (*ESV*: 2001) is a revision which does not use gender-inclusive language as radically, and this is the version used more not only by Catholics, but by many evangelicals as well. Ps. 8:4 maintains a more traditional form: 'What is man that you are mindful of him, and the son of man that you care for him?' as also does Ps. 34:6: 'This poor man cried, and the LORD heard him and saved him out of all his troubles'.

The *Revised English Bible* (*REB*: 1989) is a revision of the *New English Bible* (*NEB*: 1970). It is essentially another study Bible for public and private reading, and its use has been widely supported by the Baptist churches, the Churches of England, Scotland, Ireland and Wales, the Quakers, the Methodist churches, the United Reformed Church, the Salvation Army and the Roman Catholic churches in England, Scotland, Ireland and Wales. Its use of inclusive language is more moderate, albeit more evident than in the *NEB*. But it does try to avoid masculine pronouns when the original word is clearly neuter. Many would argue that this is a good compromise ecumenical version; others would see its poetic style as rather flat and uninspiring. Its rendering of Pss. 8:4 and 34:6,8 is the same as the *NEB*.

The *Contemporary English Version* (*CEV*: 1995) was intended for those with little or no knowledge of the language of the Bible, and it takes care to make biblical terms and phrases as simple as possible to read. This is a visual rather than aural version: every effort has been made to make the text 'look good', so that parallelism and different lengths of line forms are not observed as rigidly as in more traditional versions. The *CEV* uses inclusive language consistently, adapting it as much as possible for humanity but not for God, where the 'you' form of address is usually used. Its paraphrase version has the same difficulties as the *LB* and the *GNB*, although the overall effect, because of the format, is more striking. Ps. 8:4 has none of the Christian overlay in the 'Son of Man' imagery. It reads:

> Then I ask, 'Why do you care
> about us humans?
> Why are you concerned
> for us weaklings?'

Ps. 34:6 is hardly close to the Hebrew, but it creates, rather loosely, the same sense:

> 'I was a nobody, but I prayed,
> and then the Lord saved me
> from all my troubles.'

Of the many other individual examples which could be highlighted, perhaps one stands out above the rest. This is *The Lincoln Psalter* (1997) by Gordon Jackson, who, in his Preface, writes about the ways in which the psalms 'then and now' speak within a living tradition. He admits to a 'poetic irritation' with half-hearted attempts to replicate the style and form of the psalms in twentieth-century cultural terms. His version is a homage to Coverdale, using both his technique of arresting idiomatic imagery and concerns to make the psalms contemporary. Jackson's representation of Ps. 1:1 'O how *well off* he will be whose nose has not been led by know-alls …' is a way of showing how in Hebrew thinking blessing was seen in terms of prosperity and how the Christian God is as concerned with the material as with the spiritual. Contemporary idioms (and not a little social critique) are evident in the rest of Psalm 1: 'In a just society they will have no place, on Judgement Day they will not have a leg to stand on'. This version might be compared with David Rosenberg's Hebrew interpretation of the psalms in *Blues of the Sky* (1976), to be discussed shortly.

A very different example is the 1,219 pages of *A Translator's Handbook on the Psalms* (1991), where Robert G. Bratcher and William D. Reyburn offer principles of translation for those from any church tradition, without knowledge of Hebrew or Greek – especially in mission contexts – who want to understand the theory and practice of translation. Each psalm has a commentary-type explanation, both etymological and theological, of the various turns of phrase which might be used from the Hebrew and which English synonyms might suit in each case. This is a vital book for those wishing to create their own version of the psalms.

Compared with the number of Catholic versions in the mid-sixties and mid-eighties, and the proliferation of Protestant versions, starting with the *RSV* in 1952 and continuing into the 1970s, 80s and 90s, the small number of English versions published by the Orthodox churches (one notable publication, in the nineties) and the Jewish communities in England (mainly two, in the 1970s and 80s) is minimal.

For example, the Orthodox church, which serves the hundred or so Orthodox congregations in the United Kingdom, affiliated with the Patriarchates of Antioch, or Constantinople, or Moscow, or the Russian Orthodox Church outside Russia, or the Coptic Orthodox Church, has one seminal translation in English as an aid to private prayer and study of the psalms: this is *The Orthodox Study Bible: New Testament and Psalms* (1993). Based on the *NKJV*, but using the Septuagint for its commentary, it illustrates the value placed on psalmody in that it is the first of the Old Testament books to be translated into an authorized English version. The short commentary given beneath each psalm points to its use throughout the liturgical year, and, where relevant, to its interpretation in the New Testament: Psalm 8, for example, is the communion hymn for 'Lazarus Saturday', the day before Psalm Sunday, also to be sung at Palm Sunday Matins. The reader is told to read Hebrews 2:5–9 for the 'best commentary' on the psalm. On Psalm 34, we are told that verse 8 ('O taste and see that the Lord is good') has given the psalm a central place at Holy Communion, as it is understood to describe the act of receiving the Body and Blood of Christ.

As for Jewish versions of the Hebrew Bible in English, we have seen in the previous chapter that the earliest translations started with Mendelssohn's German translation in the late eighteenth century, but that it was not until 1917 that the first major English version was published, known as *The Jewish Society Publication Bible*, whose main purpose was to take advantage of scholarship, both Jewish and Christian, and its two key sources were therefore the *Massoretic Text and the *KJV*. By the 1950s Jewish scholars of all traditions cooperated in producing *The New Jewish Version*, which appeared in full in 1985. This is considered the best translation today. Rabbis and Jewish leaders from both Reform and Conservative Judaism approve of it, especially because it combines the best of major Jewish medieval scholarship (rather than the Talmud and later rabbinic commentaries, as preferred by Orthodox Jews) with modern studies of the Hebrew Bible, whilst focusing on the Massoretic Text. One illustration is the way that proper names have been transliterated, rather than anglicized: for example, part of the superscription to Psalm 9 is left as ' *'almuth labben'* (the Hebrew meaning is unclear), and that to Psalm 45 is left 'on *shoshannim'* (again the Hebrew is unclear, but the English translation, presuming it to be a hymn tune, is usually 'upon the Lilies'). Other superscriptions are dealt with in a similar way, showing the importance of retaining the Hebrew when the meaning is unknown.

This was the text used in the Soncino Press in *The Psalms. Hebrew Text and English Translation* by Abraham Cohen, with the Hebrew and English versions set side by side, and a summary of the content, then the brief commentary (mainly of a historical-critical and theological nature, with some reference to the rabbinical traditions) set out below. It was also the text used in *The Jewish Study Bible* (2003). Forty contributors offer both Jewish and Christian readers insights into the various traditions of Jewish biblical exegesis, through essays, maps, charts, and study notes. Adele Berlin and Marc Brettler were responsible for the psalms: the introduction has both scholarly and spiritual emphases, and the running commentary beside the text offers different translations of Hebrew words with a theological interpretation of it from a Jewish perspective, with some restrained use of rabbinical comment, also referring to other parts of the Hebrew Bible illustrating theological and literary points. The introduction to Psalm 8 compares it with other creation hymns, and the commentary on Ps. 8: 6–9 uses Genesis 1:26–30 to show how the verse is about all humans and not about any coming figure. (Nevertheless, the translation of Ps. 8:5 [8:4 in the *NRSV*] reads: 'What is man that you have been mindful of him, mortal man that You have taken note of him …') The commentary to Psalm 34 stresses that this is about all who depend on God, but again the translation of 34:7 (34:5 in the *NRSV*), following the Hebrew more accurately, reads 'Here was a lowly man who called, and the Lord listened, and delivered him from all his troubles'.

Orthodox Jews use in the main *The Stone Edition of the Tanach* (also called the *Artscroll Tanach*) founded by Mesorah Publications in 1976. *Tehillim: The Book of Psalms* (published in two volumes as early as 1977, revised in 1985 and 1995) is a popular edition, although it has been criticized for trying to smooth out differences between the plain meaning and later commentators, rather than presenting a straight translation. Like the Soncino Psalms, it contains the Hebrew text on one side of the page and a new translation on the other, with a running commentary below. Both translation and commentary are by Rabbi Avrohom Chaim Feuer, using a multitude of Talmudic, Midrashic and Rabbinic sources to explain each psalm. The translation of Ps. 8:5 (8:4 in *NRSV*) is quite different from *The Jewish Study Bible*, reading 'What is the frail human that You should remember him? And what is the son of mortal man that You should be mindful of him?' whilst the commentary gives no hint of any need for a gender-inclusive interpretation. The commentary to Ps. 34:7 reads the verse as if it was David speaking, so the translation reads 'This poor man called and *HASHEM hears – and from all his troubles He saved him'.

This survey of different translations illustrates in some detail the problem which was aired at the beginning of this section: the proliferation of new translations now makes any common discourse for psalmody a real problem within faith communities, a problem which is exacerbated by the ignorance of Scripture in general and of the Psalms in particular within a predominantly secular culture. This is the first time in the history of reception that such fragmentation is evident: initially common discourse was possible through the medium of Hebrew, then Greek, then Latin, and since the Reformation through an authorized vernacular, such as the *Coverdale*, or *KJV*.[3]

Liturgy and Psalmody in Christian and Jewish Traditions

In the Christian churches, liturgical editions of the Psalter were impelled by two principal issues: ecumenism, in the main, and mission, in part. The earliest ecumenical initiatives began with joint meetings of missionary societies between 1888 and 1900; this resulted in the Edinburgh Conference of 1910, and

---

[3] Resources for the study of translations include R.J. Clifford (2004); D. Frost (1981); W.L. Holladay (1993); and *J.P. Lewis (1981)*. Websites on Christian translations of psalmody include www.bible-researcher.com/versbib10.html; www.cofe.anglican.org/worship/liturgy/commonworship/texts/lect/scriptver.html or www.cofe.anglican.org/worship/liturgy/commonworship/texts/psalter/psalter.html; www.catholic-ew.org.uk/liturgy; and www.orthodoxengland.btinternet.co.uk. Those on Jewish translations include www.breslov.com/bible and www.artscroll.com. Publication details concerning the different translations listed here are given in the bibliography.

continued to the Faith and Order Movement founded at Lausanne in 1927, culminating in the World Council of Churches which was formed in 1948 (the constitution was actually drafted in 1938 but not brought into practice until after the Second World War). Since the early part of the twentieth century, therefore, Protestant, Reformed and Orthodox churches in particular (Catholic representatives did not attend until 1968 in the wake of the second Vatican Council) have sought to understand what the terms 'faith' and 'order' mean within their own tradition and in the traditions of others. This led to liturgical innovations which in turn required new translations of the Bible for worship. The psalms have implicitly helped in the ecumenical process, because they are the prayer book of all denominations, who appropriate many of the same psalms for the similar liturgical occasions (such as morning and evening prayer, and communion).

In part a response to the ecumenical initiatives of the British Council of Churches, founded in 1947 (itself a response to the World Council of Churches initiatives of 1938), the Joint Liturgical Group was set up in England in 1963; its key members were representatives of all the Protestant and Free Churches and the liturgical reforms which resulted from this focused especially on the use of psalmody. By 1968 *The Daily Office* (edited by R.C.D. Jasper) was published as an ecumenical project. Given the lack of prescriptive readings of scripture in the Free Churches, *The Daily Office* included a new lectionary for using the psalms at Communion, Morning and Evening Prayer and the Daily Offices, working through the Psalter four times (rather than twelve times, as prescribed in *BCP*) during the course of a year. This new lectionary made some radical innovations as far as psalmody was concerned, building upon recommendations made in the 1928 Prayer Book. Several psalms were omitted, being considered unsuitable for public worship. These included the so-called cursing psalms. Psalms 58, 59, 60, 79, 83, 109 and 120 were totally omitted, and the 'cursing verses' from Psalms 2, 5, 6, 7, 11, 17, 18, 21, 28, 35, 44, 54, 55, 63, 68, 69, 75, 89, 101, 135, 136, 137, 139, 140, 141, 143 and 149 were also taken out. Other omissions were psalms which had doublets (for example, Psalms 14 and 108 were omitted, and their parallels, 53, 57:1–11 and 60:5–12, were left in, although oddly Psalms 70 and 40:13–17, which were also doublets, were both included); the long historical psalms (Psalms 78, 105, 106); psalms which were more regularly used in the Offices (Psalms 95, 100, 134); and the use of Psalm 119 over different Sundays. Traditional psalms such as 63 (for Morning Prayer) and 98, 67 and 141 (for Evening Prayer) ceased to be used predominantly in these services, and were used instead as lectionary readings. Furthermore, instead of a numerical sequence, the selection of psalms was more thematic – with attendant problems that the same psalm could occur in Evening Prayer of, say, week 2, and in Morning Prayer of week 3. In spite of the thematic arrangement, it was often difficult to match the subject matter of a psalm with the actual services. But this was all in the interests of ecumenism: the Free Churches had to compromise by having more prescription, and the Anglican churches, which since the sixteenth century had always used a psalms lectionary, by having more flexibility.[4]

Ecumenical and liturgical reforms not only affect lectionary readings of the Psalter; they also have an impact on what version of the psalms is to be read. Most of the earlier translations were designed for public and private reading and study rather than for singing and responsorial psalmody. So *The Revised Psalter*, commissioned under Archbishop Fisher in the late 1950s, was a translation designed to accompany *The Daily Office*. It was produced in 1963; literary consultants included both T.S. Eliot and C.S. Lewis, the translation being made by reference to other English versions, using the Hebrew only occasionally. Although it provided one of the first ecumenical versions, and was thus a viable alternative to Coverdale (which even today would still require an Act of Parliament were it to be revoked altogether), *The Revised Psalter* was deemed to be not radical enough, especially once the issue of inclusive language began to be more pressing.

The Daily Office and its recommended *Revised Psalter* was a compromise solution. The difference between the Free Churches and Anglicanism is that for the former, hymnody forms the backbone of worship, whereas in Anglicanism, liturgy forms the backbone in which both psalms and hymns play their part. Hence in the Free Churches, because fewer entire psalms were usually used, congregations knew the Psalter as a whole less and less, and were familiar only with smaller portions of selected psalms. Yet what they knew, they knew well, particularly in the metrical forms of hymnody. For example, in the German hymnbooks of the Lutheran churches, the French hymnbooks of the Continental Reformed churches, and the hymnbooks of the Scottish Presbyterian churches, almost a third of their contents are metrical psalms in the form of hymns; these are well-known favourites, but the result is that they rarely know the Psalter as a whole.

The Methodist churches come closest to Anglican practice: the United Methodist Church website is notably prescriptive in its use of psalmody for its new lectionary, and the 1999 *Worship Book* uses Psalm 95 (the *Venite*) always for Morning Prayer, following Anglican practice, and Psalm 100 (the *Jubilate*) for Evening Prayer (used

---

[4] Full details of the service books and revised Psalters and hymnbooks in what follows are given in the bibliography at the end. Resources which have informed the following discussion on Christian liturgy and psalmody include R. Box (1996); P.F. Bradshaw and L.A. Hoffman (eds.) (1991b); R.J. Clifford (2005); *D. Daniélou (1956)*; D. Drillock (1997); D.L. Frost (1981); A. Gelston (1975); H.H. Guthrie *(1981)*; C. Jones, G. Wainwright and E. Yarnold (eds.) (1978); J.A. Lamb (1962); G. Lathrop (2004); R. Leaver (ed.) (1984); A. Lingas (2004); A.G. Murray (1966); I. Nowell (1993); G. Ramshaw and G. Lathrop (eds.) (1993); *A. Schmemann (1986)*; M.H. Shepherd (1976); R. Taft (2004); *P. Toon (2003)*; and *K.B. Westerfield-Tucker (2001)*. On Jewish liturgy and psalmody, resources include H.H. Donin (1980); I. Elbogen (1993); C. Kessler (1991); M. Maher (1994); S.C. Reif (1983); and G.F. Willems (1990). Important websites for what follows include the Catholic www.adoremus.org; the Methodist www.gbod.org/worship; the Anglican www.oremus.org/liturgy/tcw/#psalter; the Orthodox jacwell.org/spring_summer2000/psalmic_music_in_orthodox_liturg.htm; and the Jewish www.jewfaq.org/liturgy.htm.

in Anglican practice in Morning Prayer), prescribing one other specific psalm daily in addition to these. Following ancient traditions from Chrysostom to the Middle Ages, its recommended use of psalms in pastoral services is strikingly similar to the Anglican usage: Psalms 23, 27, 42, 90, 116, 118, 121 and 139 are suggested for funerals, and 121 and 128 for weddings – a prescription which is almost identical to that prescribed for Catholic usage. But there are of course many differences in the two lectionaries, as well as in the way the psalms are sung or recited throughout the year. In short, although there are corresponding uses in all the church traditions, in spite of ecumenical concerns, each church tradition still appropriates the psalms in its worship in different ways.

A distinctive feature of Anglican liturgy has been working through the Psalter as a whole. But the prescriptions in the 1662 *BCP* created an increasing problem for any modernization. As early as 1913 the Archbishops of Canterbury and York set up a committee to revise errors and obscurities that, in the light of nineteenth-century scholarship, had become increasingly marked. The 1928 Prayer Book was the outcome of this. Its two most significant changes to the Psalms were, firstly, the beginning of the practice of bracketing verses which were unsuitable for worship (a practice which was more radically pursued in the 1968 *Daily Office*, as we saw above), and secondly, the provision of a lectionary whereby 'proper psalms' were used each Sunday throughout the year, as well as at major festivals, and so omitted from lectionary readings, to make it easier to get through the entire Psalter (which, unlike the *Daily Office*, still followed a numerical order) every three months.

The 1960s onwards represent a period of ongoing liturgical change in the Church of England. In part responding to the innovations of the Joint Liturgical Group, in part recognizing the need to update the 1928 Prayer Book, Series II Holy Communion was introduced between 1967 and 1968: the notable change here was the reinstatement of a psalm between the Old and New Testament readings (interestingly, a change introduced in Catholic reforms, also in the 1960s, after the Second Vatican Council). A revised edition in 1970 prescribed the use of the psalms for a thirteen-week cycle, and this was cut to a ten-week cycle by 1976.

By 1972, the Liturgical Commission recommended an entirely new version of the Psalter. Instead of using other English versions, such as the *Revised Psalter* of 1963, it was agreed that this should work from the original Hebrew; and instead of using one translator, a panel of experts was chosen, consisting of eight Hebrew scholars (surprisingly not one was Jewish, although many were known for their Jewish-Christian collaborations) and one literary expert, David Frost, from the University of Cambridge. Draft translations of one psalm were produced by one member, discussed by the panel until an agreed version was reached, and then given to David Frost for literary emendation, who in turn took it back to the Hebrew panel; once a final agreement had been reached, it was released to a group of musicians as a test for its singability. Twenty-five psalms were published in 1973, and introduced into the revised Series III Service of Communion, then into the revised Morning and Evening Prayer (1974), as a means of congregational experimentation. The whole liturgical Psalter was produced in 1977 where it was first included in the newly revised *Australian Prayer Book* (1978) before it was introduced into the *Alternative Service Book* of the Church of England (1980). The Church of England Synod still expressed some opposition to it: the *ASB* was published in two editions, one with and one without the Psalter. However, the edition with the *Liturgical Psalter* (as it became known: its earlier title had been *The Psalms: a New Translation for Liturgy*) was the more popular, and has become a yardstick for other liturgical revisions in the Anglican Communion, including, in the 1980s, those in Canada, Ireland, South Africa and New Zealand. The approach to the cursing psalms was more conservative: some eighty-eight verses were 'bracketed off', in the cursing psalms, following the recommendations as in the 1928 Prayer Book and the *Daily Office*, but these could of course still be used. Nevertheless, the days of all the Anglican Church using an unadulterated Psalter in Anglican worship were over.

The *ASB* was only meant to run for a decade, although in the end it went on to two. Hence in 2000 a further Prayer Book, *Common Worship*, was introduced, and the *Liturgical Psalter* was ousted for yet another liturgical translation. This was an anglicized version of the *Ecusa Psalter*, an American version made in 1979 and revised in 1992 and 1997, and used in the *Book of Common Prayer* of the Episcopal Church in the United States. Instead of a team of Hebraists working on the text, this English revision was predominantly the work of David Stancliffe, Bishop of Salisbury, in consultation with Hebraists such as John Eaton, John Rogerson, Anthony Gelston and John Barton. Begun in 1997, it was published as a draft text in 1998, revised in 1999, and finally included in *Common Worship* in 2000. Its virtues were that it attempted to imitate the cadences of Coverdale without having too many archaic intrusions, and it made a real attempt to produce all-inclusive language. The final version offered a wide variety of ways of using the psalms musically – not only through Anglican chant and a responsorial style inspired by the French composer Joseph Gelineau, but also offering other translations which allowed the psalms also to be sung following the pattern of the Free Churches, in choruses and metrical psalms. A selective comparison between parts of Psalm 8 should make these points clear:

Liturgical Psalter: Psalm 8
     5   What is man, that you should be mindful of him:
           or the son of man, that you should care for him?
     6   Yet you have made him little less than a god:
           and have crowned him with glory and honour …

Common Worship Psalter: Psalm 8
     5   What is man, that you should be mindful of him; *
           And the son of man, that you should seek him out?
     6   You have made him little lower than the angels *
           And crown him with glory and honour …

Interestingly, a second inclusive language alternative is given for these verses:

> 5 What are mortals, that you should be mindful of them; *
> mere human beings, that you should seek them out?
> 6 You have made them little lower than the angels *
> and crown them with glory and honour ...

Unusually, *Common Worship* offers yet another version of this psalm, this time with refrain:

> I see your handiwork in the heavens:
> the moon and the stars you set in place.
> **Your glory reaches beyond the stars.**
> What is humankind that you remember them,
> the human race that you care for them?
> **Your glory reaches beyond the stars.**

Throughout the twentieth century Roman Catholicism was also undertaking the most far-reaching liturgical reforms since the *Council of Trent (1545–63). The First *Vatican Council (1868–70), under Pope Pius IX, had been more preoccupied with matters of church unity than with liturgical innovation, and the first *Pontifical Bible Commission (from 1901 onwards) had been more concerned with Modernist controversies and issues raised by biblical criticism. In both cases, a liturgy which was based upon the Latin language was deemed to bind the entire church together, protecting it against heresy without and schism within. It was not until 1941, when Pope Pius XII commissioned the Pontifical Biblical Commission to produce a more elevated revision of the Vulgate Psalter, working from the Hebrew, that liturgical reform seemed more possible; the version produced in 1945 was for priests to use in the Daily Offices. The independent publication of the Psalter in English in 1947 by the converted Catholic *Ronald Knox* (1888–1957) was also part of this process, for Knox was a classics graduate with a trained eye for good English style. Psalm 46, a Zion Hymn, reads, for example: 'God is our refuge and stronghold; sovereign aid he has brought us in the hour of peril. Not for us to be afraid, though earth should tumble about us, and the hills be carried away into the depths of the sea ...'. Once it became evident that educated Catholics could read and pray the psalms in an elevated English style in private, to use them in the vernacular in liturgy also seemed possible, particularly in the context of liturgical changes taking place in other churches at this time.

Another seminal figure in this process was *Joseph Gelineau* (b. 1921): his adaptation of some of the Psalms from La Bible de Jérusalem into four-part settings, using Gregorian plainsong alongside suggestions of old folksongs, paradoxically brought an ancient Catholic tradition going back to Ambrose and Gregory into the twentieth century. By 1969 a setting of the whole Psalter had been published, and an English group, 'The Grail', translated them and so brought this kind of singing of the psalms into the English churches, with congregational participation in the repetition of key verses: this became increasingly used not only in Catholic but also in Protestant churches. The emphasis on the regular stress, of two, three or four beats in each line – even though the number of syllables can change dramatically – gives the impression of 'sung-speech', and echoes Hebrew poetry which, most would agree, is about regular rhythmic stress rather than counting syllables. Each verse in this sung-speech rhythm could be sung by choirs and cantors: the antiphons, taking up one verse of the psalms and usually sung to 2.4 time, are an important way of encouraging congregational participation, and are used at least three times in each psalm. Although more popular in American churches than in those in Britain, this type of psalm-singing nevertheless influenced many other forms of liturgy – including that in the *Common Worship Psalter*, for example.

After the Second *Vatican Council (1962–5) called by Pope John XXIII, modernization was now deemed possible on a more formal level, and this affected the use of psalmody in worship in at least two ways. A special commission to revise the liturgy, to go behind the decrees of the Council of Trent to the practices of the early church fathers, with the aim of involving the fuller participation of the whole congregation, resulted in the publication of *The Sacramentory* (the revision of readings for the Mass) in 1969 and *The Liturgy of the Hours* (the revision of the Daily Office) in 1970. In the Missal, Psalm antiphons in English were now used at the beginning, middle and ending of the Mass; and after the Old Testament reading, selected parts of a responsorial psalm (usually still in Latin) was sung by a cantor or read by a lector, with the congregation now participating with an antiphonal refrain usually taken from the beginning of the psalm. And in the Daily Offices, overworked priests were now given formal permission to pray four times a day, rather than eight: no longer had they to emulate the ideal practices of the monastic orders. Morning Prayer conflated Vigils and Lauds (Prime was suppressed) – with Psalm 95 ('Venite exultemus Domino' – 'O come, let us sing unto the Lord!') as the traditional invitatory psalm, as in the Anglican and Methodist traditions. Daytime Prayer conflated Terce, Sext and None; Evening Prayer was the former Vespers; and Night Prayer, Compline. The Psalms were now read four times a day, with no more than three psalms per office, over a four-week period: selected psalms are used for particular days, and the remaining psalms are used generally in numerical order.

A critical stage in the revision of the Psalter in Latin was the publication of the *Nova Vulgata* in 1979 – this time not the revision of Jerome, but an entirely new translation from the Hebrew. This is the version which was deemed most appropriate for the Mass: vernacular versions were more appropriate for the Daily Office. *The Grail Psalter* (published as *The Psalms: A New Inclusive-Language Version* or *The Psalms: The Grail Translation* in 1963) shows just how far vernacular revision was moving at this time. Taken from the *New Jerusalem Bible*, this was designed particularly for liturgical use in simple, contemporary English; it was revised in 1984 and 1993, and was the translation used by 'The Grail' when they adapted

Gelineau's plainsong into English. A further Catholic version, *The ICEL Psalter*, published by the International Commission on English in the Liturgy, was produced in 1995, along with a shorter breviary of psalms to be used at morning and evening prayer. The *ICEL* version in particular has been controversial, mainly because of its ideological stance in terms of gender-inclusiveness, and has met with some resistance from Catholic Bishops, not least in America. Taking again Psalm 1:1 as an example, the *ICEL* translation was considered inappropriate not only because of its looser form but also because its all-inclusiveness prevented a Christological interpretation by applying the psalms to everyone:

> If you would be happy:
> never walk with the wicked,
> never stand with sinners,
> never sit among cynics,
> but delight in the Lord's teaching
> and study it day and night.

The Catholic *NJB*, with its similar human-centred reading, interestingly provoked little criticism:

1 How blessed is anyone who rejects the advice of the wicked and does not take a stand in the path that sinners tread, nor a seat in company with cynics,
2 but who delights in the law of Yahweh and murmurs his law day and night.

Thus far this discussion of liturgy has focused on the directives given by various church traditions in the publications of Psalters and the prescriptions in how they should be read. But other liturgical changes were taking place throughout the twentieth century which encouraged the congregational singing of psalms in many different church traditions. Some of these sought to refine the singing of Anglican chant: *The New Cathedral Psalter* (1910) and *The Psalter Newly Pointed* (1925), which made use of 'sung-speech rhythm', and *The Oxford Psalter* (1929) are early examples of it. More recently, the publication by RSCM in 1981 of Anglican chants geared to the *ASB*, and in 2000 of several books, to accompany *CW*, each furthered congregational psalm-singing: the words and music edition of *The Common Worship Psalter pointed for Anglican Chant* is a good example, as well as *Music for Common Worship I*, which contains an anthology of Psalms and Canticles with four different ways of chanting them: a simple form of plainsong, Anglican chant, 'cantor' chants, and simple chant. (Examples of Psalms 8 and 34 from this version of psalmody were referred to earlier.) On a more ecumenical level, *New Hymns for All Seasons* appeared in 1970, with some fifteen metrical psalms by the Roman Catholic composer James Quinn. *Psalm Praise* appeared in 1973, with some seventy-six psalms, paraphrased by contemporary Christian composers such as Jonathan Barnes, Michael Baughen, Margaret Bowdler, Timothy Dudley-Smith, Christopher Idle, Hilary Newsom, Michael Perry, Michael Saward, Jim Seddon and David Wilson; they were set to melody, using metre as well as rhyme, and incorporated canticles and chants. *Ways of Singing the Psalms* (1984) is a collection of psalm texts set as canons. *A New Metrical Psalter*, published by the Episcopal Church in the USA, was published in 1986. *Psalms for Today* appeared in 1990: it contained 133 psalms, set to over two hundred psalm settings, many of which were already well-known hymn-tunes, others being set as chants or responsorial versions. It had an ecumenical group of composers, and in addition to some of the writers used for *Psalm Praise*, it also included writers such as Brian Foley, Fred Kaan, Keith Landis, David Mowbray, Paul Wigmore and Barbara Wolloett. The collection made its début at the Royal Albert Hall in the same year. And in 2001, the American *Selah Psalter*, containing forty-seven psalms for use with the Free Churches' lectionary, appeared: 'If I take the Wings of the Morning', from Psalm 139, by Rae Whitney, and 'With Humble Justice Clad and Crowned', from Psalm 72, by Brian Wren, are perhaps the best known, and indicate the Christian emphasis of this version.

A number of works of psalms are also sung to reggae, folk, blues, jazz, and *a cappella* music: one example must suffice. In July 2004, a five-day conference, 'Celebrating the Psalms', was organized by the Hymn Society in the United States and Canada at Collegeville, Minnesota, when psalms were sung to almost every imaginable form, ancient and modern, in order to show the breadth of experimentation which is now possible throughout both Jewish and Christian different traditions. Hence, in terms of psalmody set to music for liturgy, this last century has preserved the best of older psalmic forms – from the Ambrosian and Gregorian plainsong from the fourth and sixth centuries, Catholic and Anglican chants and responsorial psalmody and Protestant metrical psalms from the sixteenth and seventeenth centuries, hymnody from the nineteenth century – and added many innovations today. Pluralism and ecumenism are undoubtedly the hallmarks here.

One striking example of preservation and innovation of psalmody is the work of the Taizé Community in Burgundy, begun as a Protestant monastic community during the Second World War by *Roger Schutz* (1915–2005). This is now a centre of renewal for both Catholics and Protestants, bringing together young people for international meetings throughout much of the year. Contemplative prayer and social justice have been its key themes; and one of the best-known ways of communicating these has been through its chants. Most of these are in Latin (not because of Catholic insistence, but because of its extra-national status), and their simplicity and repetitive nature make them suitable for meditative singing. Examples of psalms used in this way (reflecting in some ways the influence of Gelineau, but using more repetition and harmony-less 'sung speech') include *Miserere Mei* ('Have mercy on me, for I am alone and poor': Ps. 25:16); *Misericordias Domini* ('The steadfast love of the Lord': Ps. 89:2); *Laudate Dominum* ('Praise the Lord, all you nations': Ps. 117:1); and *Miserere Nobis* ('Have mercy on us' – from Ps. 123:3).[5]

---

[5] For the Minnesota Conference, see www.thehymnsociety.org/conference2004r.html. For the Taizé community, see www.taize.fr/en.

Much has been made in earlier chapters about the use of psalmody in the monastic office, contrasting it with what has been termed the cathedral office. By the twentieth century, the office was carried out in various ways in diverse monastic communities, revealing a difference between the theoretical ideal and reasonable practice. Comparing two Benedictine communities as diverse as the Catholic monastic community at Ampleforth, Yorkshire, with the Anglican mixed community at Burford, near Oxford, a great deal of flexibility is apparent in the application of the psalm cursus prescribed by the Rule. Indeed, the *Thesaurus* published by the Abbotts' Congress in 1972 along with their *Directory for the Celebration of the Work of God* makes it clear that the Rule itself was not a mere reproduction of an existing Office, but was itself a reform, thus allowing the Abbott the freedom to adapt it further to suit local needs. 'Pluralism' in the celebration of the *Opus Dei* is thus deemed as appropriate as in church liturgy, providing it takes place within an established structure. The *Directory* expounds, for example, that Lauds and Vespers are the 'strong moments' in the Benedictine day; that besides the Eucharist, at least three Hours must be celebrated daily; that each Hour must consist of psalmody, hymn, reading, prayers; and that at least seventy-five psalms must be said each week, and the whole Psalter, within a period of four weeks. This is the structure: providing this takes place, any pattern of psalmody may be used (the *Directory* offers four very different patterns) and responses, versicles and antiphons can follow local practice. Burford Priory, for example, uses a two-week cycle and recites approximately seventy verses at Lauds (where Psalm 63 is also used, in its traditional place) and fifty at Vespers (where Psalm 141 is used similarly) with fewer verses used for the Little Hours, and groups the psalms, where possible, around liturgical themes (Sunday: Creation/ Resurrection; Tuesday: People of God; Friday: the Passion) rather than using a consecutive numerical order.[6]

The tensions between preserving ancient traditions and embracing changes are nowhere better illustrated than in the liturgical use of the psalms in the Orthodox churches. In many ways this is because issues concerning the psalms which have given so much conflict in other church traditions – such as the use of the vernacular in liturgy, the tensions between reciting the psalms in prose and singing them in a paraphrased form, and the different lectionary use of psalmody in the Eucharist and the Daily Offices – were in part resolved in Orthodoxy much earlier. By the time of the rise of the Byzantine Empire in the fifth century the psalms were sung and recited in the language of the people, psalm-like hymns were always used alongside the psalms themselves, and the practice of *kathismata* corresponds with lectionary use. Hence, as far as psalmody is concerned within Orthodox churches in England (where there are some hundred parishes belonging to one of the four main Orthodox traditions from Syria, Greece and Russia), these have faced quite

---

[6] On the Directory for the use of the psalms in the Monastic Offices, see A.M. Field (ed.) (2001); M.E. Johnson (ed.) (2005); M. Casey (1994); and R. Taft (1986).

different contemporary issues in the reception of psalmody not only in translation but also in worship. The main concern is the extent to which congregations participate in using them (the psalms are usually recited or sung by a reader or cantor, and if sung, the response is by a choir), and the extent to which they should have instrumental accompaniment (in Syrian Orthodoxy, for example, until the middle of the twentieth century the practice had always been unaccompanied singing). There are correspondences with other church traditions: an important issue is the gradual erosion of responsorial psalms within the Divine Office: lengthy psalms, rather than hymns and antiphons, are the casualties where pastoral concerns or matters of convenience in three-hour liturgies are primary. To counter this, American works such as Alexander Schmemann's publications on orthodox liturgical theology (1986) and the musical contributions of David Drillock (1984–5) and Mark Bailey (2000) have already done a good deal to reinstate the more central place of responsorial psalmody within liturgy, which 'perfectly echoes the responsorial nature of the Christian faith' (Bailey). Furthermore, in Greece, the practice of monasteries such as Simonpetra and Vatopaidi, both on Mount Athos, as well as liturgical innovations at university chapels such as those at Athens (where its choir is named 'The Maestors of the Psaltic Art') and Thessalonica have also gone some way to point a way forward in practice.

The changes in Jewish liturgy, as they affect psalmody, reflect the same concerns as the Orthodox churches for greater continuity with the past. Most of the innovations – in Reform Judaism, at least – had already taken place in the nineteenth century (and have thus been discussed already). But some changes are apparent. *Siddurim were published in new forms – with better layout, typography and binding – but the essential order of the daily, Sabbath and festival services, and of the use of the psalms within them, has stayed the same. For the Sabbath day, Psalm 92, with its superscription 'for the Sabbath', has always been an obvious choice, along with Psalm 29, whose drama of the voice of God corresponds with the Torah being returned to the Ark, as well as Psalms 95–9. For Hanukkah, Psalm 30, with its superscription 'a song at the dedication of the temple', has always been an equally clear choice, as also Psalm 47 (with verse 5 referring to the sounding of the *shofar); and the themes of Psalms 24, 27 and 130 have always made them appropriate for the New Year and Day of Atonement. For more personal use, Psalms 145–50 have consistently been used as morning psalms; Psalm 3 (see verse 5: 'I lie down and sleep; I wake again, for the Lord sustains me') has always been used along with the recitation of the *Shem'a before going to sleep; Psalm 16, following an ancient ninth-century burial liturgy called *Tzidduk Ha-dan, is to be used for funerals and mourning (see verse 10, 'For you do not give me up to Sheol, or let your faithful one see the Pit'); Psalm 23, for the sick or funerals; Psalm 39, for a house of mourning; and Psalm 139, for the sick. The daily psalms, 48, 82, 94, 81 for Monday through to Thursday, have remained constant. In brief (and here, very different from Christian liturgy) the psalms used for liturgical occasions in the twentieth century are the same as those known to have been used in the fourth and fifth centuries.

Of all the denominations, Orthodox Jews have been the most concerned with preserving the traditions of the past: their recent liturgical works, most of them in Hebrew, are best illustrated in *The Complete Artscroll Siddur* (1984; revised 1989 and 2003) which has an English commentary and English rubrics alongside the Hebrew text. For Conservative Jews and *Reconstructionist Jews, despite their various theological differences, in terms of the liturgical use of the psalms, the styles and formats of their *Siddurim* may vary, but their structure is the same, and with this, the use of psalmody – almost always in Hebrew rather than the vernacular – is the same.

Hence it is Reform Judaism that has undergone the greatest innovation, with its services in the vernacular and the introduction of new melodies for singing the psalms and prayers. Their *Union Prayer Book*, published in 1894, revised in 1924 and again in 1940, is almost all in English, and hence reads from left to right. In 1975 this was replaced by *Sha'arai Tefillah: Gates of Prayer* (the double title speaks for itself; many of the changes are revisions of the earlier more universalist, anti-Zionist stance, as a result of the Second World War). In 1996, the 1975 edition of the *Union Prayer Book* was replaced by *Gates of Prayer: A Gender Sensitive Prayer Book* which appropriated inclusive language as a response to the same challenges experienced by the Christian churches. The order of the services and the use of psalms are much the same as those listed earlier. The difference is of course their vernacular use, thus echoing very much the reforms of Catholic Liturgy in the twentieth century, with their changes from Latin, rather than Hebrew. Much of the experimentation of musical settings of psalmody is from the Reform tradition. Websites abound offering examples of Jewish chants to aid meditation and prayer: *Ashreynu* ('How lucky we are') is but one example which includes a selection from the psalms.

One striking example of an individual presentation of the psalms is that of David Rosenberg, a self-confessed 'poet scholar', whose *Blues of the Sky* (1976) is an intuitive/Hebraic response. This is evident in his translation of Psalm 1 (and which might be compared with Gordon Jackson's version, noted earlier): the version starts:

> Happy the one
> lightly stepping over
> paper hearts of men
> and out of the way
> of mind-locked reality
> the masks of sincerity
> he steps from his place at the glib café …

Verse 4 is particularly striking in its description of the wicked:

> bitter men turn dry
> blowing in the wind

> like yesterday's paper
> unable to stand
> in the gathering
> light ...

Psalm 23 is similarly evocative:

> The Lord is my shepherd
> and keeps me from wanting
> what I can't have
> lush green grass is set
> around me and crystal water
> to graze by ...

Several observations may be drawn from these fifty years of liturgical innovation which has brought the psalms into full prominence not only in Anglican, Reformed, Catholic and Orthodox traditions but in Jewish worship as well. The first observation is a salutary one: it is clear that, in spite of the plethora of examples indicating that the churches are attempting to change as society changes, at this point in time this has had little effect on 'mission'. Church attendance has dropped alarmingly over this century, so that by the time of the 2001 Census, even though some forty-two million people – over two-thirds of the population of the UK – considered themselves Christian, only just over an eighth of these regularly attended Christian worship. Hence liturgical reforms of psalmody have not only left a good deal of secular society untouched; they have also affected a very small proportion of those who profess a Christian faith.

However, if there has been less success in mission, there has at least been some in terms of 'ecumenism'. There is undoubtedly a growing awareness of the diverse practices, not only in the different Christian traditions, but also between Christians and Jews: this is because the Psalter, more than any other part of the Bible, represents a common tradition of prayer and praise to the same God, and in the context of a society which increasingly questions the existence of that God, a concern for unity against a common threat – secularism and the decline of religious belief – has, albeit gradually, been the outcome. In this sense, uniformity, as Cranmer envisaged it, is not only impossible to attain but is now undesirable; hence pluralism is perhaps no bad thing.

Exegetical Studies, Christian and Jewish

We noted in the last chapter just how different publications on the psalms were compared with most works dating before the Enlightenment – for example, the preoccupation with defending Davidic authorship or with reading the psalms as prayers of, by or to Christ is far less in evidence in these later works. Before the First World War, text-critical studies, so popular in the nineteenth century, continued (one of the greatest commentators here being C.A. Briggs) but the *historical-critical concerns also gradually diversified, and by the inter-war years historical approaches to psalmody took on several different forms. By the end of the Second World War, however, increasing historical scepticism resulted in a renewed interest in theological meaning – an academic concern which was more capable of being shared with others writing from a more confessional stance. By the 1980s the theological concerns transmuted into an emphasis on the psalms as literary artefacts, with a renewed interest, for example, in their poetic forms, their linguistic ploys, and the literary relationship between one psalm and another. By the turn of the century this concern was still dominant, but the literary interest was now more in the Psalter as a whole rather than smaller psalmic units.[7]

This gradual change of emphasis can be measured through the various reviews of psalmic studies which were published periodically throughout the century. Between ten- and twenty-year intervals, the Society of Old Testament Study sponsored a review of the most significant studies over that period. The first two, *The People and the Book* (1925) and *Record and Revelation* (1938), looked at the psalms only through essays on Israelite religion: here the interest is mainly on what they can inform us about Israel's myths and rituals, implied in the psalms, in a broader ancient Near Eastern setting. *The Old Testament and Modern Study* (1951) and *Tradition and Interpretation* (1979) each included specific articles on the Psalms, by A.R. Johnson and J. Eaton respectively, and each demonstrated an ongoing historical interest in the different ways we can understand the psalms in their ancient context, with Eaton picking up the more theological interests of various commentators. The two latest editions, *The World of Ancient Israel* (1989) and *Text in Context* (2000), have no specific chapters on psalmody, even though there are entries on law, prophecy, wisdom, historiography (and, in 1989, a separate one on apocalyptic) in each. It would seem that the sheer diversity of opinion – and, to some extent, the small number of English scholars writing creatively on the psalms since 1979 – prevented a specific article on the subject. It is only when looking at more recent specific surveys on the psalms by, for example, J. Kenneth Kuntz (1994), Erich Zenger (1994), Thorne Wittstruck (1994), J-M. Auwers (1997), J. Eaton (1999) and David Howard (1997), as well as a special edition of the journal *Interpretation* (1992) which was devoted to the psalms, that one becomes aware just how much the emphasis changed in the 1980s. Each reviewer concurs that the interest has shifted from questions about ancient setting to a concern with the theological meaning of the psalms and with the literary composition of the Psalter as a whole and in its smaller parts. The growing interest in different literary methods

---

[7] Because much of what has been recently published reflects what was taking shape in the latter part of the twentieth century, several of the following works will have a publication date in the early twenty-first century.

of reading their poetry shows just how much the emphasis has shifted from the text of the psalm to the reader of the psalm.[8]

So much for a brief synopsis of the changes in exegetical works on the psalms throughout the twentieth century: in order to understand how and why this took place, we need to look first at the different ways in which the historical-critical method evolved from the beginning of the twentieth century, when the historical questions which dominated exegetical studies at the end of the previous one continued. Three emphases from the nineteenth century continued into the twentieth. The first was a *communal/national interpretation*, by way of reading the 'I' of the psalmists either as the community speaking as a corporate personality, or as the king speaking on behalf the nation; in this case the preference was for a *pre-exilic dating. The second was a more *personal and individualized interpretation*, whereby the 'I' was either some heroic leader of the community or a figure, like the prophets, with an exceptionally personal and intimate relationship with God; here a *post-exilic dating, when it was presumed there was more emphasis on individual spirituality, was more usually presumed. The third historical emphasis, linked especially to the first, was to interpret psalmody *in the context of the ancient Near East*, either to demonstrate the historical worth of the psalms by way of archaeology, or to illustrate the similarity of Israel's religion to others by way of examining corresponding myths and rituals.

Although his main publications have been discussed in the previous chapter, because his roots were really in the nineteenth century, *Hermann Gunkel* (1862–1932) made contributions in all these three areas, and has continued to be a seminal influence through most of the twentieth century. Most commentaries even today would still make use of his classification of psalmody (an account of which was offered in the previous chapter) and his 1933 German commentary, completed by Joachim Begrich after his death, was translated into English by James Nogalski as recently as 1998. Gunkel's concern was to reconcile a historical-critical study of the settings of the psalms with a more spiritual understanding of the lives of the psalmists; certainly his view can serve a variety of different persuasions, in that it encompasses the individual, the royal/national, and the ancient Near Eastern influences upon psalmody. For example, Gunkel argued that many of the psalmists were pious individuals, influenced by the earlier piety of the prophets and using earlier forms of psalmody which had now been lost, and so were writing in the post-exilic times; but he also contended that, although most pre-exilic psalmody has been lost, it had been communal in orientation and had once been part of lively cultic drama, centred around the king, with practices akin to the myths and rituals in Mesopotamia.

---

[8] Details of the relevant literature will be acknowledged in footnotes only where there is insufficient information in the text. More comprehensive details of the books referred to in the text are given in the bibliography. So for the Society of Old Testament Studies' reviews on the psalms, here given in chronological order, see *A.S. Peake (ed.) (1925)*; *H. Wheeler Robinson (ed.) (1938)*; *A.R. Johnson (ed.) (1951)*; *G.W. Anderson (ed.) (1979)*; *R.E. Clements (ed.) (1989)*; and *A.D.H. Mayes (ed.) (2000)*.

Above all, Gunkel's most significant contribution was the classification of all the psalms into appropriate cultic settings, by way of their different forms. Starting with the most general types of all, 'prayer' and 'praise', and then subdividing each, this ultimately allowed for a great deal of freedom regarding dating. For example, the 'royal psalms' (2, 18, 20, 21, 45, 72, 89, 101, 110, 132, 144), which Gunkel so ascribed because of their specific references to the role of the king in worship, were actually pre-exilic, whilst psalms exuding a piety independent of the cult – the so-called 'spiritual songs', which comprised mainly individual laments, such as Psalms 40 (v. 7), 51 (vv. 18–19), and 69 (v. 31) – and the 'wisdom psalms' (1, 19, 37, 49, 73, 112, 119, 127, 128, 139) were post-exilic. Most psalms scholars working within the historical-critical remit, whether Catholic or Protestant, would all claim to have been influenced in some way by Gunkel. Some, for example, have built upon his view of individual piety, others have expanded his view of the psalmists' relationship with the prophets, and others have modified his views on earlier psalmody and the pre-exilic cult.[9]

Of the later exegetes, one stands out as having shaped the work of others. This is the Norwegian scholar, *Sigmund Mowinckel* (1884–1965), who was profoundly influenced by Gunkel when studying with him in Giessen in 1908. Mowinckel also studied with the Danish anthropologist, Vilhelm Grønbech, and these two influences impelled him to examine further the dramatic power of the cult and the effects of ancient Near Eastern myths and rituals on pre-exilic psalmody. Accepting Gunkel's form-critical analysis of the psalms, he nevertheless reversed some of his other views. First, Mowinckel held that the psalms were not late developments of now lost pre-exilic psalms, but they *are* pre-exilic – not only the royal psalms, as Gunkel proposed (Mowinckel's first publication in 1916 was on the royal psalms), but also many of the laments, hymns, thanksgivings, which would also have been used by the king, whom he saw as 'a veritable incarnation of the national god', following practices elsewhere in the ancient Near East. Therefore, claimed Mowinckel, almost all Gunkel's psalmic forms (some wisdom psalms were a possible exception) had been composed for the pre-exilic cult. Mowinckel argued that there was one great cultic drama, held for several days at autumn-time: this he termed

---

[9] Of the following influential commentators who have been influenced by Gunkel, only one seminal publication has usually been included with the date of the English edition, where appropriate, following it. The list has had to be selective, and omits scholars such as Mowinckel, Weiser, Kraus, Johnson and Eaton who are referred to in more detail in the following discussion, but it nevertheless illustrates the extent of Gunkel's influence in Continental, American and British scholarship. Those who have adapted Gunkel's views on individual piety include E. Balla (1912); M. Buttenweiser (1938); S.R. Driver (1915); R. Kittel (1905); and M Löhr (1922). Those who have expanded Gunkel's views on the prophetic influence in the psalms include P. Bonnard (1960) and *R. Tournay (1988/1991)*. Those who have modified Gunkel's views about psalmody in post-exilic times to argue for a pre-exilic setting include J. Begrich and H. Gunkel (1933); *A. Bentzen (1941)*; H. Birkeland (1955); *I Engnell (1943)*; *S.H. Hooke (1933, 1955)*; W.O.E. Oesterley (1939); *J.P. Peters (1922)*; E. Podechard (1949); *G. von Rad (1962, 1965)*; H. Ringgren (1963); and *G. Widengren (1937)*.

'the enthronement festival', because, like the corresponding spring (*akitu) festival in Babylon, it celebrated the kingship of God through enacting the great ancient Near Eastern myths of creation and re-creation via the ritual role of the king. From this, Mowinckel revised Gunkel's ideas in another way, arguing that the psalmists, not the prophets, were the innovative composers, and it was they who influenced the forms and styles of the great prophets such as Jeremiah and second Isaiah, not the reverse. The psalms thus become central to Israel's early life, influencing through liturgical enactment later prophets, later wisdom writings, and even parts of the Torah. Mowinckel undoubtedly continued what Gunkel had started, in bringing the psalms centre-stage in historical-critical studies of the Bible as a whole.

Mowinckel's approach is often termed 'cult-functional' rather than 'form-critical', because he used the forms of the psalms as a means of determining another end – their place in a so-called enthronement festival. His seminal publications include a six-volume work in German between 1921 and 1924, culminating in a two-volume work in 1951, later translated into English as *The Psalms in Israel's Worship* (1962). In this latter work, the index indicates that almost every psalm in the Psalter is seen as a composition for the enthronement festival: these include not only the *enthronement psalms which begin with 'The Lord reigns!' (i.e. Psalms 47, 93, 95–9) and not only Gunkel's royal psalms, which often refer to the king's rule in the light of God's heavenly rule (for example, Psalms 2, 18, 89, 110), but also psalms which suggest the enactment of ancient Near Eastern myths (for example, Psalms 74 and 79, which refer to God subduing a chaos monster of the deep at the start of creation, and Psalm 82, which speaks of God in a heavenly council with other deities). Mowinckel also included in this festival psalms which suggest prophetic liturgies (Psalms 50 and 81, for example), creation psalms (Psalms 8, 19, 29, 33 and 104, for example) and historical psalms (such as Psalms 78, 105, 106). In fact, Mowinckel included in passing most of the hymns and laments, which he supposed had been composed to enact out the heights and depths of this great festival at the turn of the year.

That there was an important autumnal festival in pre-exilic Israel is beyond doubt (Exodus 23:16 and 34:22 note it, and a later text, Leviticus 23:23 ff., points to it, for example) and it is also quite possible that some psalms, not least some creation psalms and those celebrating God's world rule, might have been composed for it. But to discuss one hundred and forty-one psalms in relation to the festival (only Psalms 4, 25, 70, 100, 111, 141, 143, 147 and 148 receive no mention in the index to his 1962 work) has echoes of the 'pan-Davidic' or exclusively Christ-centred emphasis from previous centuries and misjudges the diversity of the psalms, in terms of both date and provenance and cultic and life settings.

Nevertheless, Mowinckel's work, combined with Gunkel's, has had enormous influence upon exegetical studies throughout the twentieth century. Modifications of Mowinckel are expressed, for example, by two seminal German scholars, *Artur Weiser* and *Hans-Joachim Kraus*, which they popularized in their respective commentaries (1962; and 1988–9). Weiser argued that instead of the psalms being used at an autumn enthronement festival they were mainly composed for an autumnal covenant renewal festival, at which the stories of the escape from Egypt and the recital of the laws on Sinai were recited. Kraus proposed instead that the great occasion was a Royal Zion Festival, celebrating, by the adaptation of Canaanite myths used in the Jerusalem cult, God's choice and protection of Jerusalem. Given the uncertainties in the previous century about what could be known about the date and provenance of the psalms, and given Gunkel's more cautious approach in refusing to commit himself to precise settings for the psalms, these three scholars – Mowinckel, Weiser and Kraus – certainly attempted to reverse this trend of historical scepticism. Their imaginative reconstruction of psalmody has attracted many, but the differences between them show their work as just this – imaginative reconstruction in the face of a good deal of cynicism about historical criticism.

Three English commentators merit particular mention. The first two, who have already been noted because of their reviews on the state of psalm studies in the twentieth century, are *Aubrey Johnson* (1901–85) and *John Eaton* (1927–2007). Each has highlighted further the importance of pre-exilic Temple cultic drama for understanding psalmody. Each expands Mowinckel's views about the king's ritual enactment of myths in worship (and so highlights the Davidic impress in psalmody through this lens) and each develops Mowinckel's theory about the cultic prophets being composers and performers of the psalms. In *Sacral Kingship in Ancient Israel* (1955), Johnson focused on the way in which the festival represented God's defeat of darkness and death, which the king enacted and brought about in both ritual and military ways. Johnson developed these ideas in *The Cultic Prophet and Israel's Psalmody* (1979) and argued for the prominence of the prophets alongside the king in the cult, noting how the prophets contributed to the *eschatological emphasis in psalmody (for example, Psalms 47, 93, 95–9). Johnson's views remained, like Mowinckel's, essentially historical-critical; Eaton's works, by contrast, were more diverse. His earlier publications were undoubtedly historical-critical studies, such as *Kingship and the Psalms* (1976), *Vision in Worship: The Relation of Prophecy and Liturgy in the Old Testament* (1981) and his assessment of the music used for psalmody in *The Psalms come Alive: an Introduction to the Psalms through the Arts* (1984). However, Eaton also represented the growing interest in the theology and literature of psalmody, as seen in his later works such as *The Psalms of the Way and the Kingdom* (1995) and *The Psalms. A Historical and Spiritual Commentary with an Introduction and New Translation* (2003), the latter of which also takes seriously the resonance of the psalms down the ages as well as their contemporary use.

The third English scholar, Michael Goulder, defies categorization. His many books and articles include *The Psalms of the Sons of Korah* (1982), *The Prayers of David (Psalms 51–72)* (1990), *The Psalms of Asaph and the Pentateuch* (1996) and *The Psalms of the Return* (Book V, Psalms 107–50) (1998). Goulder's approach is either to align smaller portions of the Psalter with different liturgical occasions in ancient Israel or to arrange them alongside the narrative material, such as that of the history of the monarchy in the books of Samuel. One of his earliest papers, 'The Fourth Book of the Psalter' (1975), argues that Psalms 90–106 were compositions to be read each night and morning for the eight-day Feast of Tabernacles; whilst the work noted above on the second collection of the Psalms of David (1990) argues that Psalms 51–72 were compositions for king David, recording his sufferings during the last years of his life, with the narrative accounts in Samuel being the background to this tradition. Goulder's innovative work in many ways anticipated the more literary interests in the smaller collections in the Psalter to be discussed below.

Gunkel's form-critical studies have had a long-lasting significance, and two seminal scholars, one German and the other American, have developed this approach in distinctive ways. Claus Westermann (1909–2000) argued in *Praise and Lament in the Psalms* (1981), for example, that the psalmic forms need not imply every time a worship event, but rather that they pertain, more basically, to a 'life-event': in this way the experiences of the psalmists can be understood across the centuries through shared human experiences today. Instead of Gunkel's numerous form-critical categories, Westermann proposed only two: petition and prayer, both of which were as much 'life-centred' as 'cult-centred'. His commentary, *The Living Psalms* (1989), applies this more specifically to individual psalms. Gunkel's form-critical emphasis continues to be modified by the American, Walter Brueggemann. Taking up terms used by a French scholar, Paul Ricoeur, Brueggemann argued in *The Message of the Psalms* (1984) for three different types of psalms: those of disorientation (mainly laments, with the experience of loss or oppression), those of reorientation (mainly thanksgivings, with the experience of restoration and recovery), and those of orientation (the hymns, which focus on wholeness and well-being in the presence of God). According to Brueggemann, one of each of these life-experiences is dominant in each psalm. *The Psalms and the Life of Faith* (1995; edited by P.D. Miller) applies this more particularly to individual psalms. For Brueggemann, as for Westermann, the cultic connection is kept in the background: for example, his *David's Truth in Israel's Imagination and Memory* (1985) is a far cry from views about ancient sacral kingship, but stresses more the relevance of David then and now. By emphasizing the life-experiences of the psalmists, both scholars have made a positive contribution in bridging the gap between critical studies in the academy and didactic studies for the church, as we shall see when we look at didactic works on the psalms.

A number of scholars have also used the form-critical approach but combined it with different disciplines, such as anthropology or social-scientific criticism, and have sought to demonstrate that the psalms did not have to pertain to a public Temple cult, arguing instead that the term 'cult' is a heterogeneous term and it can also include the practice of popular religion at various local sanctuaries. Two influential scholars, *Reiner Albertz* and *Erhard Gerstenberger*, both once students working with Westermann, have each argued for the ways in which the psalms were used for rites of passage in popular religion. One of Albertz's most recent works which has been translated into English is 'Religion in pre-exilic Israel' and 'Religion in Israel during and after the exile' (2002) and this argues for the ways in which psalmody has been used in popular worship in pre-exilic and post-exilic Israel. Gerstenberger presents a fairly similar thesis, although he emphasizes more the role of post-exilic worship at local cultic centres, and he is more precise in the application of his proposals to specific psalms, as seen in the English translation of his *Psalms. Part 1, with an Introduction to Cultic Poetry* (1988) and *Psalms, Part 2, and Lamentations* (2001). These scholars, although the most recent and most influential today, were not the first to argue in this way. The other works are mainly in German, and include one as early as 1928, when *Hans Schmidt* proposed that the lament psalms were compositions for individuals to use when they were falsely accused and brought to trial. *Lienhard Delekat*, in a publication in 1967, and *Othmar Keel*, in 1969, similarly interpreted the individual laments as ritual texts to be used by those coming to take refuge in a local sanctuary. In 1970 *Walter Beyerlin* argued that psalms preoccupied with the fear of death were ritual texts composed for those who had had a near-experience of death. *Klaus Seybold*, in a publication in 1973, argued that psalms which indicate some form of sickness were composed as incantations for supplicants to use against illness and sorcery. And in 2001, in a larger work on the plurality of Israelite religion, the Jewish scholar Ziony Zevit argued similarly that the psalms were once ritual texts for polytheistic cults, like those composed in Babylon and Egypt.

Another legacy of Gunkel's was his interest in the psalms in the context of the ancient Near East. This was encouraged not only by the increasing number of artefacts, texts and inscriptions found in Mesopotamia, but by two particular discoveries much closer to Israel itself. The first were from Ras Shamra, an ancient trading port in Syria. Beginning in the late 1920s, a French-led team set about deciphering the cuneiform tablets at a huge site discovered there, written in *Ugaritic and Akkadian, and dating from between the fourteenth and twelfth centuries BCE. Amongst the letters, royal charters, and legal, administrative and financial texts were several epic poems, many of which, predating Israel's psalmody by at least four hundred years, described the myths of creation in terms that correspond with Pss. 74:13–14, and 89:10–11, which describe God dividing the seas and breaking the heads of sea-serpents. These epic poems also depict the gods dwelling or appearing on mountains in ways reminiscent of Psalms 48:1–3 and 68:7–10. Descriptions of the Most High God of the pantheon, who was called El, and whose throne had been established from primordial times, bore similarities to Pss. 44:1–4, 47:8–9 and 93:1–2. Psalms 29 and 93, describing God being heard through the elements of thunder and lightning, were also understood in new ways because of their close correspondences with Ugaritic texts. Overall these pointed clearly to a poetic tradition out of which Semitic poetry developed, including that found in the psalms. Even their styles were similar: the balance of ideas set in alternate lines, the word-pairing (for example light/darkness; sea/river; earth/deep; laughter/joy;

tent/dwelling; strength/might; justice/righteousness) and the use of repeated refrains are all evident in each tradition. One specific example must suffice:

> now, thine enemies O Ba'l
> now, thine enemies thou shalt smite
> now, thou shalt destroy thy foes …
> *(Ba'l and 'Anat Cycle: CTA 2: iv. 8–9)*

> for, lo, thy enemies, O Lord,
> for, lo, thy enemies shall perish
> all evildoers shall be scattered
> *(Psalm 92:9)*

These discoveries showed that Hebrew poetry, including psalmody, is by no means a unique phenomenon. Compared with exegetical works of earlier centuries, this could not be further removed from the view of David as the principal author of psalmody or of Christ as the one hidden in the psalms. But one other consequence should be noted, in the light of the ecumenical interests noted earlier: the end result of working in a site such as at Ras Shamra gave rise to greater collaboration between Catholic and Protestant scholars. One of the most influential commentaries which applies much of this material to individual psalms is by a Catholic exegete, *Mitchell Dahood*, whose three-volume *Anchor Bible Commentary* (1966, 1968, 1970), albeit often excessive in its enthusiasm for finding correspondences with Ugarit, has undoubtedly linked Canaanite and Israelite poetry together as part of a common cultural influence, and whose influence in the Psalms version of the *JB* has already been noted. Another Catholic exegete is *Joseph Coppens* (1946), whilst Protestant contributors include *William Albright* (1968) and, more recently, *John Day* (1985).

A second example of psalmody in its ancient Near Eastern setting, again by way of applying archaeological data to the psalms, is Qumran. Here this gives rise to collaborative works which include not only Catholic and Protestant scholars but also Christians and Jews. This site and these findings have already been discussed, as they impinge upon psalmody, in the first chapter. These twenty-seven or so manuscripts, found amongst the eleven caves at Qumran, have given rise to a number of works which compare the psalms in these scrolls with those in the Massoretic Text, as well as works which examine the ways in which older psalms have been imitated to form new compositions. One of the most interesting examples from a reception history point of view, noted in our first chapter, is of commentaries on groups of psalms which are given a particular prophetic bias. In the material which has been published since 1948, much of it the result of international conferences and particular projects, it is now common to find Jewish and Christian scholars working side by side. Of those who have contributed papers or books on the Psalms and Qumran, Catholic and Protestant scholars as diverse as P. Auffret, G. Brooke. J. Carmignac, U. Dahmen, P.W. Flint, F.L. Hossfeld, J.A. Sanders, P.W. Skehan, G.H. Wilson and E. Zenger are found in works alongside

Jewish scholars again as diverse as D. Blumenthal, E. Chazon, E. Eshel, M. Horen, A. Hurwitz, S. Talmon, E. Tov, V. Vermes and Y. Yadin. Such collaboration would have been impossible to envisage a century ago.[10]

A third example of the study of psalmody in its ancient Near Eastern setting is of iconography as it relates to psalmody. In *The Symbolism of the Biblical World* (1978), Othmar Keel examines concepts such as creation, destructive forces, the Temple, and the king and man before God, and offers over five hundred and fifty illustrations, most of them from the psalms, which show just how much their symbolic and mythical world-view is the same as that elsewhere in the ancient Near East. The difference between word-painting in psalmody and iconographical works in the ancient Near East is another striking example of how impossible it is now to look at the psalms without reference to their broader cultural setting.

Another popular approach has been to look at the theological message of the psalms, arising out of initiatives by theologians with more confessional interests writing theologies of the Old Testament/Hebrew Bible as a whole. Between the 1940s and 1990s, Christian scholars such as *Edmond Jacob* from France (1958), and, from Germany, *Walter Eichrodt* (1961 and 1967), *Gerhard von Rad* (1962 and 1965) and *Klaus Seybold* (1990), and from England, *Norman Snaith* (1944) and *Harold Henry Rowley* (1961), and from America, *G. Ernest Wright* (1960) and *Brevard Childs* (1992) all wrote different accounts of the theological 'centre' of the Old Testament, whether it was in monotheism, or salvation history, or covenant, or responses of faith, or creation and redemption. At the same time, a number of Theologies of the Psalter began to appear, particularly in Germany and America, of which seminal examples include those by *Hans-Joachim Kraus* (1986) and *Walter Brueggemann* (1988) and *J. Clinton McCann* (1993) and *David Mitchell* (1997). Kraus's *Theology of the Psalms* applied a more historical and *redactional approach to the psalms, especially to the use of the royal and Zion traditions within them, whilst Brueggemann's *Israel's Praise: Doxology against Idolatry and Ideology* applied a more theological and rhetorical approach to bring the psalms into the twentieth century. J. Clinton McCann's *A Theological Introduction to the Book of Psalms: The Psalms as Torah* looked through both a historical and literary lens at a twofold centre of psalmody – the reign of God and the importance of Torah. David Mitchell's *The Message of the Psalter: An Eschatological Program in the Book of Psalms* argued for one centre, namely its future hope, with the theme of David being played down on account of the failure of the monarchy. Many other works along one or both of these lines could be quoted – *John Eaton* (1995) who

---

[10] The list of scholars noted here has been taken from the bibliography in U. Dahmen (2003), pp. 319–40. Each of them has produced seminal works which impinge in different ways on psalmody at Qumran. The following publications are of just one relevant work on the psalms from each: for example, Christian scholars such as P. Auffret (1979–81); G.J. Brooke (1989–90); J. Carmignac (1961); U. Dahmen (2003); P.W. Flint (1997); F.L. Hossfeld and E. Zenger (2005); J.A. Sanders (1965); P.W. Skehan (1975); and G.H. Wilson (1985) are found in works alongside Jewish scholars such as *D. Blumenthal (1998); E. Eshel (1998); A. Hurvitz (1964–6); S. Talmon (1989); E. Tov (1996); and Y. Yadin (1966).*

argued through the voice of ten key psalms commentators for a didactic and eschatological centre, *Mattias Millard* (1994) who proposed that the key theme was the Torah, *Jerome Creach* (1996) whose view was that God as Refuge was the overriding theme, and *Patrick Miller* (2004) who proposed that obedience to the law was a central theme. Two features are noteworthy in all these works. First, little reference is made to the 'figure of David' as the theological centre, showing how twentieth-century psalm studies have entirely changed the Davidic focus which was so marked from the first to seventeenth centuries. Secondly, it is clear that modern scholars who emphasize a twofold theology, namely a hope for the future in its eschatology and direction for the present in its instruction (McCann and Eaton being seminal scholars in this respect), are, paradoxically, very close to the prophetic and didactic emphases found in the psalms in the five or so centuries before Christ and the five or so centuries of the Christian era.

Theological and literary interests are also evident in large-scale commentaries on the Psalms published since the Second World War. Setting aside the more obviously historical-critical works by Weiser (English version 1962), Dahood (1966, 1968, 1970) and Kraus (English versions 1988 and 1989), other examples include *Arthur Anderson*'s two-volume work in the New Century Bible Series (1972), based on the RSV, which takes seriously the Psalter as a liturgical manual, for ancient times and now; *Cyril Rodd*'s two-volume work for Epworth Bible commentaries (1963 and 1964), designed for teaching and preaching; *John Eaton*'s one-volume commentary in the Torch Series (1967) and his recent historical and spiritual commentary (2003); *Carroll Stuhlmueller*'s two-volume commentary (1983) with its historical, literary and theological concerns; *James Mays*' commentary in the Interpretation series (1994) which looks more at the language and literary shape of each psalm than at any historical-critical issues; and the three-volume *Word Bible Commentary* by Peter Craigie (*Psalms 1–50*: 1983), *Marvin Tate* (*Psalms 51–100*: 1990) and *Leslie Allen* (*Psalms 101–150*: 1983, revised edition 2002), which has both a scholarly and spiritual purpose. More recently, Richard Clifford's two-volume commentary (2002 and 2003) offers a specific literary, exegetical, theological and ethical look at each psalm, and Samuel Terrien's huge one-volume commentary (2003) examines each psalm through its ancient setting, literary genre, relationship to the New Testament, and the strophic structure unifying the theological message. The theological and literary concerns in these commentaries – the development of ideas about God, about his relationship with his people, about their guide to right living – paved the way not only for the greater collaboration between exegetical and devotional works but also showed affinities with the new wave of literary works on the Psalter as a whole.

Another approach has been to write Introductions to the Psalter. These are aimed, like psalms commentaries, either at students or at church ministers and often are expansions of what one would find at the beginning of a commentary, dealing with literary, historical and theological issues. Those familiar to English readers of the psalms, published over the past thirty years or so, include studies by *Peter Ackroyd* (1978), *Leopold Sabourin* (1974), *John Day* (1990), *Klaus Seybold*

(1990), *Susan Gillingham* (1994), *James Crenshaw* (2001), *C. Hassell Bullock* (2001), and, most recently, an edited work by *Philip Johnson* and *David Firth* (2005). As the century progresses and emphases change, the approach taken in the introduction is different, in that theological and literary concerns dominate over the historical ones, independent of whether it is aimed at a more academic or pastoral readership.

The new rise of writings with a literary emphasis alongside the theological one has been the consequence of other changes which were happening in biblical studies at large. New biblical approaches, still part of historical criticism, included *redactional studies and *canon-critical studies; each was interested in the final form of the text. Redaction-criticism was initially more concerned with single units of psalms (such as Psalm 19, with its two parts, or Psalm 108, joining together Pss. 57:1–11 and 60:5–12, or Psalm 144, with its clear relation to Psalm 18, and Psalm 135, with its clear relation to Psalm 115) or with smaller collections of psalms, determined by their headings (the Davidic collections, the *Asaph and Korah collections, the Songs of Ascents, for example). Canon-criticism was more concerned with the overall structure of the Psalter itself as used in the early versions, and with the ultimate purpose it served, particularly in relation to Psalm 1 (private prayer) and Psalm 150 (public praise). This emphasized the role of individual editors and collectors; although still interested in historical-critical studies, canon-criticism impelled scholars to look more at the end of the process, i.e. at the final form of the text. Other approaches developed alongside these, which were no longer really historical in emphasis at all. One was rhetorical studies, which looked at the text as a vehicle of persuasion for the contemporary reader – examining issues such as social justice, spirituality and gender. Another was *reader-response criticism, which looked at the performative value of the psalms as texts for use in public liturgy and private prayer, also moving the agenda away from a text-centred approach to a reader-centred one.

One of the most important writers responsible for much of what was later written on the *literary* arrangement of the Psalter as a whole and the function of the smaller collections of psalms within it has been *Gerald Wilson*. His work had been influenced by the canonical studies of his mentor, *Brevard Childs*, who also wrote on the canonical shape of the Psalter, in a seminal article on the function of the superscriptions of the psalms in *Journal of Semitic Studies* (1971). Wilson had also been influenced by the form-critical accounts of the final shape of the Psalter by both Westermann and Brueggemann. In *Praise and Lament in the Psalms* (1965, English edition 1981), Westermann had looked at the comparative placing of the laments in the first part of the Psalter and the hymns in the second part, and had noted a significant change between the end of Book Three (Psalm 89) and the beginning of Book Four (Psalm 90). Wilson's monograph, *The Editing of the Hebrew Psalter* (1985), used the editorial arrangements in Mesopotamian collections of hymns from as early as the third millennium BCE and in the Qumran psalms from the second century BCE manuscripts for comparison with the arrangements of the Psalter. His conclusion, that the first three books (Psalms 1–41, 42–72, 73–89) have many indications of special editorial arranging, with the royal psalms (2, 72, 89) playing a major part in this, whilst the latter two books (Psalms 90–106, 107–50) have very little, has many ramifications. It would seem that Psalms 1–89 give real prominence to the covenant between God and the Davidic king, and the cry of dereliction at the end of Psalm 89:49 ('Lord, where is your steadfast love of old, which by your faithfulness you swore to David?') shows the despair at the demise of the Davidic monarchy with which this first collection ended, whilst Psalms 90–150 compensate for these shattered hopes by focusing more on the eternal kingship of God himself, and on the importance of right living in the here and now (wisdom-influenced psalms, such as 90–1, 107 and 145, are found at the seams of these collections). This division of the Psalter, and the clarification of royal/wisdom features in its literary arrangement, have become the focus of much psalmic study since Wilson's work. Although many have sought to modify it – in that wisdom psalms are also found at the seams of the first three books (Psalms 1, 73) and royal psalms, in the latter two books (Psalms 110, 132, and 144, alongside 145), many today would accept the literary structure of the Psalter.

Since this work, three particular literary-orientated trends have been evident, and each represents a cultural setting of the different scholars involved. In *America*, exemplified by papers read at the Psalms Group of the Society of Biblical Literature in 1989 and 1990, published in part as *The Shape and Shaping of the Psalter* (1993), the interest has been essentially literary and theological, either with respect to the Psalter as a whole, or with respect to the smaller collections. The book speaks of a new approach to the Psalter; it echoes a good deal of what had been in the journal *Interpretation* a year earlier, and includes articles by James Mays, Walter Brueggemann, Gerald Wilson and David Howard who each place this new research in its reception-history context, followed by others who apply the theory to specific groups of psalms. Patrick Miller looks at how the first two psalms anticipate the literary structure of the whole; Wilson looks again at editorial linkages between the psalms (surprisingly, the discovery that many psalms had been deliberately set alongside others with the same linguistic motifs had only been really examined before by J.A. Alexander [1850], F. Delitzsch [1881] and C. Barth [1976]), and Howard examines this in detail with regard to Psalms 90–4, which form an introduction to Book Four of the Psalms. Several monographs have since followed. Howard's *The Structure of Psalms 93–100* (1997) is an expanded study of his earlier theory; Nancy de Claissé-Walford's *Reading from the Beginning* (1997) looks at psalms which introduce particular sections (Psalms 1–2, 3, 42, 73, 90, 107, 146–150); Carleen Madolfo examines the rhetorical voices of the lament psalms in *God in the Dock* (2002); and Robert Cole assesses the structure of Psalms 73–89 in *The Shape and Message of Book III* (2000).

Just one year later after McCann's edited work in America, a similar study, *Neue Wege der Psalmenforschung*, appeared in Germany (1994), which was also the result of a *Society of Biblical Literature Conference*, this time in Münster, in 1993. This includes several other papers on the smaller collections, such as Patrick Miller on Psalms 15–24, Klaus Seybold on the Asaph Psalms, Erich Zenger on the Koharite

Psalms, and Frank-Lothar Hossfeld on the *Enthronement Psalms. The difference in analysis and in emphasis between these works and those of Gunkel and Mowinckel at the beginning of the century could not be more pronounced, as each of these scholars looks at the psalms in relation to each other as literary and theological texts, rather than as isolated units operating in an ancient ritual drama. The essential difference between this and its American counterpart is the interest in *how* these smaller collections took shape as well as *why* this happened – in other words, an interest in *redactional* as well as *rhetorical* issues (and so reflecting historical-critical concerns alongside theological ones). Since then this line of enquiry has been followed by a number of larger works on smaller collections. Notable examples from Germany include Norbert Lohfink's work on the redaction of the prayers of the psalms (1992), and a large number of publications, mostly co-edited, by F.L. Hossfeld and E. Zenger. These include two out of three volumes of a German commentary in 1993 and 2000 and the first volume of a commentary in English in 2005, which lists all their previous works (mainly in German) on theological and redactional shaping of the smaller collections in the Psalter. In addition, a seminal article – by Zenger alone – on the new literary method in psalmic studies in 1994 offers a clear explanation of this change of emphasis in psalmic studies.

The third context in which this literary-critical debate has taken place is France. There is some evidence that French scholars were producing work of this sort some fifteen years earlier, including *Emile Beaucamp's* work on the Psalms of Ascents (1979), but these have not been part of the same collaborative enterprise as in America or Germany. Their works, nevertheless, are marked by a detailed assessment of the language and structures of individual psalms and their relationship with each other. The two best-known writers, *Pierre Auffret* (1982, 1995) and the French Canadian *Marc Girard* (1984 and 1994–6), assess the psalms by way of their repetitions and parallelisms, finding alternating or concentric patterns within them, and tend to focus more on the literary unity of individual psalms (offering many useful insights): they also reflect a scholarly discourse mainly between themselves.

No centre for collaborative studies in British publications has been evident since the 1990s, although works by *Norman Whybray* (1996), *John Eaton* (1995), *Alisdair Hunter* (1999) and *Susan Gillingham* (2005, 2006) might be named. Perhaps the more recent interest in the reception history of psalmody, represented in this book and also in an earlier work by the American *William Holladay* (1993), might indicate where psalmic studies might next develop in the English-speaking world. Certainly the reception-history focus is evident in two very recent books on the same theme. The edited work *Psalms in Community: Jewish and Christian Textual, Liturgical, and Artistic Traditions* by Harold Attridge and Margot Fassler (2004), which was the result of a symposium at Yale University on the reception of the psalms in formative Jewish and Christian traditions and contemporary practice, includes papers by both Jewish and Christian scholars on this very issue. And the edited work *The Book of Psalms: Composition and Reception* by Peter Flint and Patrick Miller (2005) draws Jewish and Christian contributors together in the project of looking at the shaping of single psalms, at the smaller collections of the Psalter, at the reception of psalmody in Judaism and Christianity, and at the Theology of the Psalter as a whole (Adele Berlin, Moshe Bernstein, Walter Brueggemann, Richard Clifford, Nancy de Claissé-Walford, Peter Flint, Erhard Gerstenberger, Michael Goulder, J. Clinton McCann, Patrick Miller, Gerald Wilson and Erich Zenger being amongst the chief contributors, all of whom have already been referred to previously).

Somewhere in between the historical-critical and the literary-critical approaches are the multitude of works on Hebrew poetry which focus in detail on the psalms, of which there have been a great many publications, particularly since the middle of the twentieth century. Some have looked mainly at the textual and philological issues, often applying some of the archaeological evidence from Ugarit and Qumran, for example; others assess mainly the structural and linguistic evidence. Of the reviews on this issue, the two by Kenneth Kuntz in *Current in Research: Biblical Studies* (1998, 1999) are particularly helpful. Of the more general works, the most important and measured for understanding better both the rhythm and the parallelism of the poetry of the psalms are works by both Jewish and Christian scholars, including *Stephen Geller* (1979), *James Kugel* (1981), *Wilfred Watson* (1984 and 1994), *Adele Berlin* (1985), *Alonso Schökel* (1988) and *Robert Alter* (1985, 1990). Others have applied theories of poetry to enable some understanding of the original music of psalmody, the most notable being *Suzanne Haïk-Vantoura* (1991) whose results can be found and heard on the website King David's Harp (www.rakkav.com) and also a more general study of music in ancient Israel by *Joahim Braun* (2002), who discusses the superscriptions of the psalms in this context. Others have more specific interests: of these, those who have worked further on Ugaritic patterns, such as the work on the structures of Canaanite and Hebrew poetry by *William van der Meer and Johannes C. de Moor* (1988) and on the counting of syllables by *Noel Freedman* (1980), deserve mention. Other similar works include an analysis of the structures of psalms with refrains by *Paul Raabe* (1990), an assessment of the strophic structures of individual psalms by *Jan Fokkelman* (2002) and an imaginative and iconic look at the poetic metaphors in selected psalms by *William Brown* (2002). Together, these demonstrate how much psalmic studies is now a discipline very much dependent on both historical/textual and literary/linguistic studies from outside its own remit.

To conclude this account of twentieth-century psalm exegesis, much of it, at least until the 1970s, was quite different from the earlier trends in reception history. For example, in spite of the interest in the pre-exilic monarchic cult, it was most unusual to write about the central figure of David himself, and more the norm to write about the vital role played by the kings in general and the nation as a whole, and religious leaders such as priests and prophets. In this sense 'David' was no longer a model of piety (and certainly not a 'type' before Christ) but a figurehead, a paradigmatic figure of kingship. Furthermore, scholars could write about the prominence of the prophets in the psalms, but it was rare that the psalms were seen as prophetic texts with the sort of contemporary application which was evidenced in the New Testament writers and early church fathers. Or again, when scholars described the eschatological hopes in the Psalter, they did so mainly within the context of an ancient Near Eastern festival, with little concern as to how to apply this sort of theology into any other culture. And given the amount of attention paid to the importance of the cult at a time when liturgical innovation was so rife, few scholars seem to have made connections between the anthropological models within the ancient world and the changes within their own culture. It was not until literary, reader-centred approaches to the Psalter really developed that more connections were made with what was happening in church and society; this in turn enriched historical studies and created a greater rapprochement with those who had a more devotional understanding of the Psalter, echoing more the integrated concerns of past commentators such as Gregory, Augustine and Cassiodorus.

This survey, because of its breadth, has had to focus more on the scholars and commentators than on the psalms themselves. In part this was also due to the fact that the interest has often been on the Psalter as a whole rather than on individual psalms – whether seen in historical-critical studies which examined psalms in the context of Israelite religion, or in literary-critical studies which discusses the shaping of the entire Psalter. (This is best illustrated by the fact that the first two reviews sponsored by the Society of Old Testament Studies, as well as the last two reviews, have no separate entry which examines individual psalms.) But this does not mean that, in twentieth-century exegetical studies, there are no significant psalms which repeatedly claim attention. In the earlier part of the century the key psalms were those which seemed to reflect the same myths and rituals as those in the ancient Near East: examples include the royal psalms such as 2, 45, 72, 89 and 110; the enthronement hymns, such as 47, 93, 95–9; and others, such as 8, 18, 46, 48, 74, 82 and 104, which each appear to contain vestiges of ancient Near Eastern myths. In the latter part of the century the key psalms have been those which are found at the 'seams' of the Psalter, at the beginning or end of smaller collections: these especially include Psalms 1 and 2; 72 and 73; 89 and 90; and 150; and psalms within two larger collections, Psalms 93–100 (celebrating the kingship of God) and Psalms 120–34 (the so-called *Psalms of Ascents). Hence Psalms 2, 72, 89 and Psalms 93, 95–9 are particularly important, in that they all serve the interests of very different exegetical methods.

It is important to note as well the positive elements which have emerged from this vast array of exegetical works. First, the ecumenical interests which have been evident in the previous two areas of the reception of the psalms – translations and liturgical innovations – can also be seen here. Not only have Catholic and Protestant commentators been working more closely together (especially since the Second Biblical Commission of 1942, and more particularly after the Second Vatican Council in 1965) – on projects such as Ugaritic poetry and Qumran, on textual and literary readings of the psalms, on commentaries and edited works – but Christian and Jewish exegetes have similarly been drawn into closer collaboration, for example on the language and poetic style of the psalms, and on the understanding of psalmody within its wider cultural setting. It was only at the beginning of the twentieth century that Friedrich Delitzsch (the son of the Jewish convert and Psalms exegete Franz Delitzsch) wrote a stark refutation of the Psalter with a distinctively anti-Semitic bias: its Jewish particularism, its reliance on the Torah as a means of salvation, its reliance on dubious historical events such as the Exodus, its materialism, its thoughts of hatred towards enemies, its melancholy view of life after death – like the rest of the Old Testament – made it 'a veritable hodge-podge of erroneous, incredible, undependable figures ... a veritable labyrinth of false portrayals, misleading reworkings, revisions and transposition ... in short, a book full of intentional and unintentional deceptions, in part self-deceptions, a very dangerous book, in the use of which the greatest care is necessary'.[11] Such observations would be unlikely to be expressed today. By contrast, when publications appear, such as Albert Pietersma's *The New Translation of the Septuagint: The Psalms* (2000), David Stec's *Targum of Psalms* (2005) and Ulrich Dahmen's edited work in German on the significance of *11QPs^a* at Qumran (2003), these are works which now affect Jews and Christians alike, and together they illustrate how, on the whole, exegetical works on psalmody are now being pursued in a more eirenical spirit than in previous centuries.

Devotional Works, Christian and Jewish

The more striking illustrations are in the Jewish tradition, which because of its particular history will be dealt with separately. More practical works in the Christian tradition will be assessed first.

One early example is by *Dietrich Bonhoeffer* (1906–45), for whom theology and opposition to national socialism in Germany were all of a piece. His leadership of the *Confessing Church (along with Martin Niemueller and Karl Barth) is well known, as also is his advocacy for the Jews, and his participation in 1938 in the Abwehr resistance in the wake of the pogroms: his role in helping Jews to escape to Switzerland contributed to his arrest in 1943 and his death in Flossenbürg concentration camp in 1945. What is less well known is Bonhoeffer's attachment to the psalms, which, as a priest, he prayed at least twice daily. He felt that it was in the psalms that human suffering and a God of love were most exposed: in an early sermon on Psalm 42 ('As a deer longs for flowing streams, so my soul longs for you, O God. My soul thirsts for God, for the living God. When shall I come and behold the face of God?') Bonhoeffer is quick to identify the sufferer, thirsting for God, with Christ on the cross: 'I thirst'. In his *The Psalms. Prayer Book of the Bible* (not actually published in English until 1970) Bonhoeffer speaks of the rhythm of

---

[11] The quotation is taken from Kraeling (1955) p. 158, and although it refers to the Old Testament as a whole, it follows a lengthy criticism of the psalms.

prayer in the psalms: first we read how David and other psalmists pray for themselves and the world around them; then we see how Christ, the suffering Christ, also prays for himself, his disciples and the world; and lastly we see how and why we too can pray. For Bonhoeffer, the God who is concealed in the world is revealed through the words of the psalmist. In a comment pencilled in the Bible he had at Flossenbürg, next to Ps. 74:8–11 ('They said to themselves, "We will utterly subdue them"; they burned all the meeting places of God in the land / ... How long, O God, is the foe to scoff? Is the enemy to revile thy name for ever?') Bonhoeffer simply wrote the date: 9.11.38 – the date of *Kristallnacht*, marking the start of the pogroms. Bonhoeffer also found imprinted in the psalms the suffering of God with the Jewish people: 'Only the one who cries out for the Jews may also sing the Gregorian chants'.

Suffering was one theme Bonhoeffer took from the psalms; paradoxically, life, in all its fullness, was another. His frequent meditations on Psalm 119, with its promise of blessing for obedience, may seem a total contrast with what he gleaned from the psalms of suffering. Yet for Bonhoeffer, the two tenets of faith were complementary, with God's grace mediating between them. On this account the psalms of creation were also a vital witness, and they are the first group of psalms Bonhoeffer commented on in his book on the psalms and prayer. Faith and life; religion and politics; church and society were held together in Bonhoeffer's theology, a tension which was relieved by his turning to the psalms and by his showing others, Jews and Christians alike, how they could turn to them too.[12]

There are very few other examples to match this practical and theological use of psalmody in the twentieth century: those who have suffered have not written much explicitly on the psalms, and those who have written on psalmody in this way have not had to undergo anything like Bonhoeffer's experience. The most striking works have actually been written in the past twenty-five years. In *Prayer, Praise and Politics: Reflections on the Psalms* (1973), *Edmund Hill* looks at the social and political implications arising from reading, for example, Psalms 1, 2, 32, 125, 145, 87 and 81. *John Hargreaves' A Guide to the Psalms* (2005) has an ecumenical, practical and worldwide perspective, intended for use amongst students internationally for whom English is a second language, and in the psalms chosen for a closer reading one can see the movement between a great variety of cultures, ancient and modern. *J. David Pleins* in *The Psalms. Songs of Tragedy, Hope and Justice* (1993) deals with issues of community and leadership by looking at the forms of the psalms. The Canadian Catholic priest *Marc Girard* has written *The Psalms: Mirror of the Poor* (1996), although the tendency here is to see the poor in spiritual rather than material terms. *Stephen Breck Reid* has produced two relevant works. *Listening in. A Multicultural Reading of the Psalms* (1997) begins with contemporary culture and moves back into the world of the psalmists, whilst his edited volume, *Psalms and Practice: Worship, Virtue and Authority* (2002), with its

---

[12] See D. Bonhoeffer (1954, 1970); also *E. Bethge (1970 (especially pp. 101 ff.)*; and P.D. Miller (1994).

'performative' readings of psalmody, includes a most pertinent article by *Gerald Wilson*, 'Songs for the City: Interpreting Biblical Psalms in an Urban Context'. A very different work is the entry on the psalms by *David Tuesday Adamo*, from Nigeria, in the *Global Bible Commentary* (2004), who, following the brief of the entire commentary, namely to bring different global life-settings to bear upon the Bible, brings a Third-World understanding of culture to bear upon the world of the psalmists. Adamo shows how particular psalms, when used in a tribal society, have a therapeutic importance – for stomach trouble, for barrenness, infant mortality, for safe delivery of babies, for safety in travel, and potent words of protection, for example. So some examples of practical and ethical worth are to be found: but they are few.

Other works have a more feminist slant. Given the rise of feminist biblical criticism from the early 1970s onwards, and given the issue of inclusive language and psalmody, one might have expected that a number of feminist writers would have engaged with the psalms. But here, too, there are few promoters. Three feminist Bible commentaries have appeared since the 1990s, each with entries on the psalms, but these have more to say about biblical studies in general than the Psalms in particular. *The Women's Bible Commentary*, edited by Carol A. Newsom and Sharon H. Ringe, was published in 1992 and revised in 1998; the article by *Kathleen A. Farmer* looks at psalms women sang outside the Psalter (Miriam, Deborah, Hannah, Judith, Mary), at the inclusive voice of women in the psalms (by focusing on psalms which use the first person singular and plural), and at a few psalms which best represent women's experience. In 2002, the 900-page *IVP Women's Bible Commentary* edited by Catherine C. Kroeger and Mary J. Evans was published, with some one hundred and thirty articles as well as papers from over a hundred contributors, mainly women, on reading the Bible 'through the biblical, sociological and psychological concerns of women'. *Philippe Carter* writes in a similar vein to Kathleen Farmer on women as psalmists, and *Gwynneth M.N. Raikes* offers a commentary on the Psalms with women's experiences in dialogue with the psalmists'. In 2003 *Elizabeth Cady Stanton*'s *Women's Bible* (1895) was republished with the additional title *A Classic Feminist Perspective*; in contrast to most other biblical books, the article on the psalms is extremely brief, with comments only on Psalms 45 and 51. These examples reveal that feminist studies of psalmody are very much in their infancy.

Perhaps the two most striking contributions are articles in *A Feminist Companion to the Bible: Wisdom and Psalms* (Second Series: 1998) edited by Athalya Brenner and Carole Fontaine, for they show the scope for women to grapple more with the individual psalms of lament: *Ulrike Bail* writes on violence against women in Psalm 55, and *Beth Tanner*, on the unspoken cries in Psalm 109. But other than this, there are few entire books devoted to the psalms. *Swallow's Nest: A Feminine Reading of the Psalms* (1992) is a notable exception, combining the practical (albeit individual) with the devotional: here *Marchiene Vroon Rienstra* offers a paraphrase of selected psalms using a four-week cycle with three different themes for each day – morning, noon and evening. This is an intentionally exclusivist version of psalmody – for women, not for men. Rienstra fits every single psalm into a life-experience of women – women ministers, widows, nuns, pregnant women, homemakers, women struggling for peace in the Middle East, Jewish women who have escaped concentration camps, women diplomats and women executives, homeless women, refugee women, women rabbis, women who have been sexually harassed: the list goes on, as each theme is complemented with other appropriate hymns and readings (many by women). Again using parts of Ps. 34:1–6, her rendering is as follows:

> I will bless and praise El Shaddai continually!
> I will glory in God …
> When a poor woman cries, God hears her.
> El Shaddai saves her through and in all her troubles.
> The angel of El Shaddai's presence surrounds all those who trust Her.
> She saves them from all her difficulties.
> O taste and see how good God is!
> Blessed are the women who take refuge in Her!

When it comes to works of a more spiritual and personal nature, there are perhaps too many, indicating that some quality control is necessary. Only the more stimulating examples deserve attention in what follows.

One classic work is by *Thomas Merton* (1915–68). In some ways, Merton, a converted Catholic who spent the last twenty-seven years of his life in Gethsemani, an ascetic Trappist order in Kentucky, echoes Bonhoeffer in his use of psalmody, for his life also was dedicated to political action (he became a prominent member of the peace movement by the 1960s). He was also committed to understanding other faiths: just as Bonhoeffer embraced Judaism, Merton did the same with Buddhism and East–West monastic dialogue. His little booklet *Praying the Psalms*, published in 1956 and again in 1957, reflects this inter-faith concern. Where Merton differs from Bonhoeffer is that his practical application of psalmody is to enable his readers to participate more fully in the liturgy of the church as much as in life in the world (although for Merton, like Bonhoeffer, the two were of course inseparable). Merton's reading of the psalms of suffering – including his understanding of Psalm 42 – have many echoes of Bonhoeffer's.

Reflections on the Psalms, by *C.S. Lewis* (1898–1963) was the first religious book he had written after an interval of some ten years, and was first published in 1958. With characteristic wisdom yet diffidence ('I write as one amateur to another') Lewis writes about the difficulties and enlightenments he had encountered over the years of using the psalms since his conversion in 1929; his writing is distinctive in that his literary and classical training makes him sensitive to the poetic ambiguities of the psalms, whilst his wrestling with a reasonable faith reveals a sensitivity to their theological inconsistencies. The book takes seriously the psalms in their ancient setting (the cursing psalms, the dark view of death in the psalms, and the psalms which speak of the self-righteousness of the sufferer pose particular problems), but Lewis also looks at them in their Christian setting (what he terms their 'second meanings') and in our daily experience. It is difficult to find a more psychologically shrewd and spiritually profound writing on psalmody in the twentieth century.

The earlier discussion of exegetical commentaries highlighted the point that many academic works now seek to bridge the gap between critical study of the psalms and praying them. In addition to that list of commentaries, which were more academic and critical than contemporary and devotional, other commentaries with the reverse emphasis might be added to that list. The most obvious is a pair of two-volume works for personal bible study: The Daily Study Bible Series, initiated by William Barclay, has *George Knight* as the contributor on the psalms (1982 and 1983), and the Bible Reading Fellowship uses *Donald Coggan* in a similar way (1998 and 1999). Three other commentaries deserve mention. In *The Vitality of Worship. A Commentary on the Book of Psalms* (1998), *Robert Davidson* looks at the Psalter with specific theological and liturgical concerns, both Jewish and Christian, ancient and modern. *Praying the Psalms. A Commentary* (2001) by *Stanley L. Jaki*, who has recited the entire Psalter once a week for the past sixty years, and so builds upon this experience, is to help readers recite the psalms as 'living prayers in a troubled world'. A very different book, *Berit Olam. Studies in Hebrew Narrative and Poetry. Psalms* (2001) by *Konrad Schaefer*, a Benedictine monk in Cuernavaca, Mexico, is an illuminating assessment of the rhetoric and poetic structures of the psalms with the intention of helping reader to enjoy each psalm both as a poem and a prayer.

Of the vast number of other devotional works in English, the following are amongst the most significant. In *Doors of Perception* (1978), *Peter Ackroyd*, writing as a biblical scholar then at King's College, London, helps the reader engage with both the language and thought-world of the psalms for a more profound religious appreciation of them. *Dermot Cox*, a Catholic scholar at the Gregorian University in Rome, in *The Psalms in the Life of God's People* (1984) shows how the psalms may be prayed as God's word to the whole faith community. *Mark Smith*, a Catholic American academic, explores the language and world-view of the psalmists in *Psalms. The Divine Journey* (1987), and relates these to our pilgrimage to God today. *Patrick Rodger*, successively Bishop of Manchester and Oxford, looks at the different worlds of the psalmists and readers today in *Songs in a Strange Land* (1989), and shows how the two can coincide in worship of the same God. *Jim Cotter*, an Anglican priest, has produced a fine three-volume collection of meditations on the psalms (*Through Desert Places* [1989] on Psalms 1–50; *By Stony Paths* [1991] on Psalms 51–100; and *Towards the City* [1993] on Psalms 101–150), connecting the faith of the psalmists with everyday life, not least in areas of sexuality and personal healing. *Martin Israel*, also an Anglican priest, uses *A Light on the Path: An Exploration of Integrity through the Psalms* (1990) to show how the Psalms are still 'a treasury of human spiritual experience', moving between the glory of God and the human condition. *Roland Murphy*, a Catholic Carmelite, offers a brief introduction and commentary on the riches of the psalms ('how to read, pray, study and enjoy the Psalms') in *The Gift of the Psalms* (1993). *Eugene Peterson*, a pastor and professor in spiritual theology in the United States, offers in *Psalms* (1994) a fresh and earthy translation of the psalms in contemporary idiom. *The Psalms: Ancient Poetry of the Spirit* (1997) is an anthology of one hundred psalms in various translations, with a foreword by R.S. Thomas, to illustrate the poetic qualities and range of human experience represented in them. *Jerome Creach*, an American scholar, presents in *Psalms* (1998) ten key psalms as bible study material for use in small groups, giving due attention to their background and contemporary worth. In *Spotlight on the Psalms* (2001) and in the following three booklets (2002) *Paul Inglesby*, an Orthodox priest from Somerset, offers fresh and contemporary reflections on all the psalms. *Ronald Dale*, a Methodist minister, provides a contemporary lively anthology to accompany each psalm in *Windows on the Psalms* (2001), setting them within the three-year lectionary of the Methodist church. *John Rogerson*, writing as both scholar and Anglican priest in *The Psalms in Daily Life* (2001), offers a fresh translation of forty-one psalms, dealing critically but positively with their ancient settings and their relevance today. *Brian Pickett*, also a parish priest, in *Songs for the Journey. The Psalms in Liturgy and Life* (2002), looks at how the psalms can lead the individual throughout the pilgrimage of life, using examples from both Jewish and Christian tradition. In *Journey through the Psalms* (2002), *Denise Dombkowski Hopkins*, an American academic, helps the reader approach God with the same emotional intensity as she believed the psalmists had, applying a multi-media approach to bring the psalms into a contemporary setting through artwork, song and poetry. *David Adam* applies his reading of *Poems of the Western Highlanders* to one hundred and forty psalms in *Music of the Heart. New Psalms in the Celtic Tradition* (2004), under headings such as singing, seeking, sorrowing, straying and saved. *Voicing God's Psalms* (2005) is the work of *Calvin Seerveld*, an American pastor, and comes with a CD; it is a fresh translation of thirty-seven psalms, highlighting both their 'rough and tender tenor', with creative ideas for their use in private and public worship. One has only to add to this the innumerable websites which similarly seek to move from the ancient to the contemporary settings of psalmody in the life of the individual and the life of the church (a useful site which is a link to many other sites is home.earthlink.net/~apex_ps/links.html) to ascertain that this aspect of psalmody, designed mainly to help personal prayer, is still a popular medium, and, as the list above revealed, is an ecumenical exercise shared by Catholic, Protestant and Orthodox writers alike.

We have left an account of Jewish reflections of the psalms until now, because two experiences in Jewish history have influenced devotional works on the psalms in a distinctive way: the rise of Zionism, and the controversial place of Jerusalem in psalmody, and profound innocent suffering not least during the Holocaust years. The rise of Zionism – a movement with complex beginnings, from the later part of the nineteenth century to the early part of the twentieth, was in part a response to the anti-Semitism which broke out at that time in France, Germany, Russia and Central Europe. Applying this directly to the Psalms, it is here that the very psalms which were originally deemed less acceptable in Reform Judaism increasingly became most significant, and verses such as 48:2; 51:18; 53:6; 87:2; 99:2; 102:16, 21; 122:2–7; 125:1; 128:5–6; 132:13–14; 135:21; 137:5–7; 146:10; and 147:2 were highly significant, with Psalms 122 and 137 in particular encapsulating Zionist hopes. For many Jews, however, much depends on how one reads verses such as these: when taken literally, their references to Zion exacerbate tensions both within Judaism and between Jews, Christians and Moslems, but when taken more spiritually, they become a means of building bridges between the three monotheistic traditions who each in different ways respect the worth of these psalms.

The twentieth century also brought with it an intensified period of suffering. From the violent persecution of the pogroms in Russia in the late nineteenth and early twentieth centuries and again in Poland and Germany in the 1930s, to life in the ghettoes before the Second World War and in the concentration camps during it, it is moving to read of the ways in which their ancient traditions inspired and encouraged Jewish believers during and after the *Shoah*. Psalm 44 has been understood by many Jews as the Holocaust Psalm; vv. 11–13, for example, read:

> Thou hast made us like sheep for slaughter, and hast scattered us among the nations. Thou hast sold thy people for a trifle, demanding no high price for them. Thou hast made us the taunt of our neighbors, the derision and scorn of those about us.

Stories emerge of those who prayed the psalms on the point of death, and of those who prayed them just to stay alive, and of psalms written on scraps of paper being passed from hand to hand. It was the lament psalms which meant the most: Ps. 22:1, for example, ('My God, my God, why have you forsaken me? Why are you so far from helping me, from the words of my groaning?') evokes the sufferings of the *Shoah*. It has always been the psalms which have been read or sung at Holocaust Memorial Services, by Jews and Christians alike. Pope John Paul II summed up this response to psalmody well in his address at the Yad Vashem Memorial site in 2000, when he started and ended with the lament psalm 31:13–15:

> I have passed out of mind like one who is dead;
> I have become like a broken vessel.
> For I hear the whispering of many – terror all around!
> as they scheme together against me,
> as they plot to take my life.
> But I trust in you, O LORD; I say, 'You are my God.'

Because the psalms of lament both reach deep down into the terrors of human suffering and reach high up in the hope for a new world order founded on God, this is perhaps why the many imitations of psalms, following the ancient tradition of *piyyutim, have been termed 'Holocaust Psalms', and there are many examples of these. One collection is by *Jacqueline Osherow; Dead Men's Praise* (1999) offers a stunning collection of poems which reflects the heights and depths of her Jewish heritage in *terza rima*. In the section 'Scattered Psalms', 'Psalm 37 at Auschwitz' is a dry, matter-of-fact meditation on Ps. 37:25, used as a Grace after meals: 'I was young; I've also grown old, and I've never seen a righteous man forsaken or his children begging bread' which ends

> I know it sounds crazy, but couldn't one of them –
> Not that it matters, they all died anyway –
> But still, so many people, and enough time
> For reciting what the dying are supposed to say
>
> (*Hear, O Israel*, et cetera) *and* a psalm.
> Or not even a whole psalm. Just one line.
> All those people waiting. Couldn't one of them
> Have mumbled to a brother, a father, a son
>
> (The women, of course, were on another line
> And this was not a psalm they would have known),
> *Just a little longer and there will be no wicked one;*
> *Just a little longer … he'll be gone.*

Another example is a translation published in *Contemporary Review* (2003) by Thomas Orszag-Land of a work by *Miklos Radnoti*, which echoes Psalm 74:

> *Wandering Jews: A new Hebrew psalm*
> Our altars all crumbled to dust
> our psalms were choked on ash
> our altars lost their lustre
> our altars, the future, died …
>
> And thus our bones were broken
> our consciousness tormented …
> and our altars crumbled to dust
> and our psalms, they lost their lustre
> and thus our infants fell silent
> and thus our menfolk grew lame
> as the women were lit like torches
> and our ancient prayers fell silent
> and all, but all met the flames …[13]

Most Jewish spiritual writings which use the psalms address post-Holocaust theology in one way or another. *Robert Alter*, who teaches Hebrew and comparative literature in California, has an article on psalmody in *The Literary Guide to the*

---

[13] The poem by Osherow (1999) is taken from pp. 60–4. Radnoti's poem is quoted in *Eva Lang (2003)*, pp. 2ff.

Bible (1989), and whilst being a literary assessment of the repetitions, allusions and structures, it also comments pertinently on themes of suffering in selected psalms. Another work with a literary focus, which also offers a number of insights into reception history, is *Sing unto God a New Song. A Contemporary Reading of the Psalms* (1995) where *Herbert Levine*, a Reconstructionist Jewish scholar, looks at the way the performance of psalmody has enabled the Jews to have a dialogue with their tradition of national tragedies, from the destruction of the First Temple up to the *Shoah* itself; the psalms are 'dialogic speech acts' which find meaning in a world which is full of both senseless violence and redemptive love. *Jonathan Magonet* applies a fresh and illuminating approach in *A Rabbi Reads the Psalms* (1994). He draws from his experience of teaching the Psalms at Leo Baeck College and first explains the literary features of psalmody ('Biblical Poetry for Beginners' and 'David Sings the Blues: on Concentric Psalms') which those not able to read Hebrew would miss, such as plays on words, word order, rhyme and rhythm and their poetic structure. He then takes a fascinating new look at thirteen familiar psalms (including Psalm 22, referred to above, using a dialogue between rabbinic comment and contemporary observation). Here Magonet brings the Jewish riches of psalmody to a universal audience.

These examples reveal a real rapprochement between Jewish and Christian traditions. Many of the Christian devotional works could be adopted by Jewish readers, and the converse is the case with the Jewish writings above. Obviously old controversies continue – for example, a book by J.R. Church, entitled *Hidden Prophecies in the Psalms* (1990), finds allusions to contemporary events in the psalms (Psalm 48 alludes to the birth of Israel in 1948, Psalms 39–45 correspond to 1939–45, the years of the Holocaust, and Psalm 17, to the liberation of Jerusalem in 1917, for example) in a way which is reminiscent of the literal application of prophecies which divided Christians and Jews in early Christian writings and in later Karaite works in the Middle Ages. And conversely, in commentaries such as the *Schofield Reference Bible* (first published in 1909, still published in revised forms today), the *dispensationalist and supersessionist readings of the psalms still prevail; but both these examples are exceptions within a much more constructive trend, which is one of a new kind of dialogue opening up between Jewish and Christian readers of the psalms.

Aesthetic Responses, Christian and Jewish

Aesthetic enjoyment of psalmody is now shared reciprocally by Jews and Christians alike and in each tradition we see their adaptation in secular life as well as in the synagogue and church. The two main areas again concern music and art.

Within both Christian and Jewish artistic representation, the works have been used mainly in faith communities: dominant art forms of the twentieth century, such as impressionism, expressionism, futurism, cubism, surrealism and art deco have rarely been given expression in depictions of the psalms; Chagall's interests in expressionism and cubism as expressed in his psalms illustrations are notable exceptions. Hence pictorial art has taken a different course from music, where adaptations of psalmody include an increasingly secular and universalistic appeal.[14]

One obvious example in art of the artistic representation of psalmody is through the medium of stained glass. Two very different Christian artists, each working in the latter quarter of the last century, deserve mention. The first is an American liturgical designer, *David Hetland*, who specializes in vast mosaics and stained glass, many depicting themes from the psalms. One striking example is in a chapel in a retirement centre for the elderly in Fargo, North Dakota; the series of fourteen-feet-wide stained glass windows, in typically vivid colours, placed high above the chapel walls, is entitled *From the Psalms*, and appropriately for their purpose, they are taken mainly from Psalms 27 and 108. The second example is by a Scottish designer, *Alec Galloway*, whose two modern glass windows in the church of St John the Evangelist, in Donisthorpe, tell the story in colour of how this erstwhile colliery town in the Midlands was gradually transformed into a heritage trail on account of its location on the edge of the National Forest. Galloway's contrasting windows depict the decline of the mining industry through the ochre, yellow and tawny hues of flames and fire, alongside the regeneration of the area through luxuriant verdant vegetation. Each window has an appropriate psalm verse below it. The one for decline is 'In his hands are the depths of the earth' (from the morning psalm, the Venite: Ps. 95:4) and the other for vitalization is 'All the trees of the forest shall sing for joy' (Ps. 96:12).[15]

Ironically, the most powerful expression of psalmic themes in stained glass in churches is by an artist who had to overcome not only the Jewish taboo of figuration in art but also the use of his works in churches. *Marc Chagall* (1887–1985) was over seventy when he received his first commission to work in stained glass – the Notre Dame baptistery glass at Assy, Savoy; Chagall wrote about the theological conflict he felt about this, not only from the point of Jewish creativity, but also because of the Christian context. Yet somehow he was able to embrace both worlds – his most famous windows in the early 1960s are of the twelve tribes of Israel in the synagogue at the Hadassah Medical Centre in Jerusalem and the World Peace Windows at the United Nations, New York. Of the many other (mainly Christian) examples – in the cathedrals at Metz and Rheims, in New York State and Tudeley, England, and in Zurich, Nice, Sarrebourg and at Mayence – two examples stand out, because they are of the psalms.

---

[14] The following discussion has used the resources on psalmody and art in the Grove art web-pages, at www.groveart.com/shared/views/home.html (each time under appropriate artists).
[15] For a visual representation of Hetland's use of the psalms in stained glass, see www.hetland.com/details/artist.htm. On Galloway's stained glass at Donisthorpe, see www.shielaglass.co.uk

As a Russian-born Jew with French citizenship, Chagall was moved by initiatives to create a monument of the reconciliation between France and Germany and Jews and Christians in the post-war years; the decision, aged ninety, to accept an invitation to create what was in fact his last monumental work in St Stephan's Church, Mainz (ironically the home of the Gutenberg printing press), was both unusual and apposite. St Stephan's had been almost completely destroyed in the Second World War, and the designs, which Chagall had in fact begun in etching forms as early as 1958, are from both the Old and New Testaments. He managed to complete nine of the twenty-eight portals: the vast expanse of various shades of blue in the glass in the central chancel windows sets the background for his typical 'free-floating imagery', comprising narratives from creation to crucifixion, but it is in the transept windows below, where the themes are more abstract, that the imagery from the psalms is used in subtle ways to witness to the healing nature of the project.

A work which was completed just before this, in 1978, is of single window in the north quire aisle at Chichester Cathedral. If Mainz was about reconciliation using blue as the dominant colour, this window was about celebration (the cathedral had had its nine-hundredth anniversary in 1975) with the primary colour as clarion red. It was commissioned by a well-known patron of the arts, Walter Hussey, who had retired as Dean the previous year, and was made by Charles Marq at his workshop in Rheims (the birthplace of the Utrecht Psalter). Chagall had found that working with the very general theme of worship of God was rather difficult, so Hussey suggested that Psalm 150 ('Let everything that hath breath, praise the Lord'), which would show all mankind caught up in worship, would be a choice which would give some focus to Chagall's creativity; this psalm clearly inspired the artist, now just ninety, and he completed the maquette in over a year. The finished work is extraordinary. It brings alive everything which represents Romanesque tradition, yet in contemporary form: the exuberance and vitality are created by fiery reds broken by greens and blues and yellows, and the small figures and animals, with their several musical instruments, each contribute to the window displaying a sense of fun and jubilation. At the top of the window is David, sitting rather uncomfortably on a donkey, playing his harp.

Chagall's monumental art forms were many – from mosaics and tapestries for the Knesset, to ceilings for opera houses in Paris and New York – but his interest in psalmody was also in the smaller detail. In this respect, again somewhat ironically given his Jewish background, he moved much further than many other artists using psalmody, in making the psalms available not only in faith traditions, but more universally as well. In 1930 he was commissioned by Vollard to create a series of etchings for an illustrated Bible; Vollard died before their completion, and Chagall's sufferings in the Second World War prevented further work; they were eventually published in 1955 with several additions. In these are several depictions of David – with Absalom, with Saul, with Bathsheba – which act as a narrative to the psalms with relevant superscriptions (for example, Psalm 3, on Absalom; Psalms 18, 52, 54, 57 and 59, on Saul; and Psalm 51, on Bathsheba). Between 1958 and 1959 Chagall produced another work, *Dessins pour la Bible*, with twenty-four colour lithographs and over ninety black and white representations on the retro pages. Two of these are from Psalm 1. In 1979, some three years after beginning the stained glass project at Mainz, and two years after Chichester, Chagall also made a series of thirty etchings from the psalms, entitled *Psaumes de David*. In their brown ink medium, and in their literal and moral interpretation, one is reminded of the illustrations in the Utrecht Psalter recast in the more contemporary form of Russian expressionism, for example. The most memorable include Psalm 114 (a Hallel psalm which recounts the escape from the sea), Psalm 25 (where the sun shines down on the righteous man) and Psalm 31 (where the psalmist is protected by a flying angel).[16]

Few other Jewish artists have produced works on the psalms as popular and as innovative as Chagall's. Nevertheless, 'psalm art', whereby prayers and praises are deemed to have as much potential for graphic illustration as the more specific themes of the narrative parts of the Hebrew Bible, is a medium which has fascinated Jewish poets and artists especially since the Second World War. Several contemporary websites testify to this, of which one example must suffice: the American *Irwin Davis* has created several mystical representations of psalms popular in Kabbalistic Judaism (for example, Psalm 91), and transformed these into twelve simple but evocative psalm drawings for each month of the year – Psalm 91 for January, Psalm 8 for July, Psalm 1 for October, and Psalm 150 for December, for example.[17]

Four Christian projects on psalmody and art deserve mention. Of these, the first had a very clear mission to represent psalmody within contemporary secular life. *Arthur Wragg* (1903–76), in *Psalms for Modern Life* (1934), uses raw and shockingly powerful black and white cartoon-like images from the psalms to illustrate the themes of social justice which could emanate from them. Wragg was anxious to show that the psalms of David could speak to our contemporary *physical* condition – at a time when poverty, unemployment, prison reform and the threat of war were frightening realities. Psalm 4, for example, has as its caption verse 2, 'O ye sons of men, how long will ye turn my glory into shame?' and portrays a naked pregnant girl sitting forsaken in an attic room. Psalm 142 has a young unemployed man crouched by a battered dustbin in the freezing cold, with the caption from verse 5 'I said, "Thou art my refuge and my portion in the land of the living"'. A few of the cartoons are specifically Christian: Psalm 22 illustrates man's inhumanity to man, with poverty, murder and suicide depicted between Christ's pierced hands. The cartoons were not intended so much to offend as to

---

[16] On Chagall's use of biblical imagery in art, see *J. Chatelain (1973)*; J-M. Foray and F. Rossini-Paquet (2000); B. Harshav (1994), pp. 51–87; and J.B. Rosensaft (1987). On the psalms windows at Mainz Cathedral, see www.mainz.de/WGAPublisher/online/html/default/mkuz-5v9lmb.en.html. On Psalm 150 at Chichester Cathedral, see P. Foster (ed.) (2002) and www.chichestercathedral.co.uk/. Some of the thirty etchings from the psalms can be seen at various online auctioneers: see for example www.centaurgalleries.com.

[17] On Davis' psalms paintings, see judaism.about.com/library/2_artlit/bl_artpsalms_a.htm. For a website with Jewish (mystical) interpretations of almost all the psalms, see jfroger.club.fr/berger/ang/berger.html.

FIGURE 6.1 Psalm 142 by Arthur Wragg. 'Thou art my refuge and my portion in the land of the living' (v.5).
Source: Reproduced from Arthur Wragg: *Twentieth-century Artist, Prophet and Jester* by courtesy of Sansom & Company Ltd (www.sansomandcompany.co.uk).

provoke: with a telling foreword from the cleric and popular broadcaster Dick Sheppard, the book was – unexpectedly – an immediate success, going into four editions in its first year, and receiving many notices in the popular press. In some ways it anticipated the brutal questioning of the psalmists by Jewish survivors of the *Shoah*; in other ways it corresponded with the more universal appropriation of psalmody by later feminist writers such as Marchiene Vroon Rienstra.[18]

---

[18] See A. Wragg (1934). On Wragg's use of psalmody in art, see J. Brook (2001).

The Twentieth to Twenty-First Centuries 295

Figure 6.2 Psalm 22 by Arthur Wragg. 'My God, my God, why hast thou forsaken me?' (v.11).
Source: Reproduced from Arthur Wragg: *Twentieth-century Artist, Prophet and Jester* by courtesy of Sansom & Company Ltd.

If Wragg's was a book designed to shake secular society through graphic interpretations, *Michael Jessing*'s (b. 1953) more recent representations of the psalms at the turn of the century are perhaps more designed to shake the church by showing to believers their universal appeal. His psalm-like series of paintings, with geometric and curvilinear compositions and highly symbolic style, some of them based on dreams and others on ancient Near Eastern mythology, some with hints of pre-Raphaelite art, have now been published as *The Book of Psalms* (2001). Psalm 1 is a striking depiction of the godly man bathed in light, with the unrighteous tumbling into the abyss; Psalm 8 depicts a young father, mother and child, with hints of angels and light, looking up to the heavens from where God's glory is revealed. One of the most graphic psalms is Psalm 23 – not so much a reflection of the peaceful pastures as of the escape from the horrors of the valley of the shadow of death. By contrast, the psalm of praise in Psalm 148 depicts a prophet-like figure weaving his way through a maze of upturned palms.[19]

Roger Wagner (b. 1957) is a Christian artist whose experiments in wood engravings to illustrate the psalms are a conscious echo of the Reformation tradition, exemplified best by Albrecht Dürer's illustrations for the *Lübeck Bible of 1494. Wagner's *Book of Praises* is being published in hand-bound copies in five volumes, on all the psalms in each of the five books of the Psalter. The first volume appeared in

[19] See M. Jessing (2001), also at www.m-jessing.supanet.com/.

FIGURE 6.3 Psalm 148 by Michael Jessing. 'Praise the Lord from the heavens; praise him in the heights!'(v.1).
Source: Michael Jessing (www.m–jessing.supanet.com).

1994, and was an expansion of an earlier work of engravings and poems, *In a Strange Land* (1988), which included images of the then desolate London docklands against the background of Psalm 137. *Book of Praises* includes a fresh and vivid translation of the psalms, using red ink for Hebrew and black for the English, with a woodcut placed between the two versions to illustrate a key theme in each psalm. Sometimes the languages interlace, sometimes they run separately down the page, sometimes they create a parallel spread, and the woodcut design varies from page to page. Wagner works on themes such as faith overcoming despair, peace and redemption overcoming the chaotic forces of nature, and judgement and suffering

FIGURE 6.4 Psalm 42 by Roger Wagner. 'As a deer longs for flowing streams, so my soul longs for you, O God' (v.1).
Source: Book of Praises by Roger Wagner, Volume 2. The Besalel Press © Roger Wagner (www.rogerwagner.co.uk).

held in the love of God. In imitation of Renaissance art he uses pastoral scenes (Suffolk landscapes and Oxfordshire countryside occur frequently) to act like vignettes for the reader to enter into an English scene through the Hebrew mindset in a contemporary and contemplative way. If this work continues into its projected five volumes, it will mark an extraordinary feat in contemporary psalmodic art – and, like Chagall's lithographs and etchings, in a form available for anyone.[20]

A final example of the visual representation of psalmody takes us back to illuminated manuscripts some five hundred years ago. A group of artisans – including the Queen's calligrapher and a number of highly skilled Benedictine monks – have been combining the latest in computer technology with medieval 'quill and vellum' methods with the aim of producing the first illuminated Bible since the sixteenth century. The project, *St John's Bible*, is not only on the psalms; it will measure two by three feet, and is scheduled to take eight years to complete, at a cost of eight million pounds. But of the some two hundred illuminations carried out to date, several thus far are on the psalms. Psalm 107 is a typical example, with its vibrant colours reflecting a celebration of creation.[21]

---

[20] See R. Wagner (1994). On Wagner's art and psalmody, see R. Martin (1995) also at www.imagejournal.org/back/010/martin_essay.asp
[21] On the St John's Bible, see www.saintjohnsbible.org/.

As for the reception of psalmody in music, their liturgically inspired use has already been highlighted in our earlier discussion of the new adaptations for worship – namely through plainchant, graduals, antiphons, introits, motets, anthems, metrical hymns, choruses and the like. So we deal here with musical compositions which, although in many cases intended for church or synagogue use, have in most cases also been adapted for public performance. Focusing first on Christian composers in the British tradition, the best-known examples of psalmodic music include *Ralph Vaughan Williams, Herbert Howells, William Walton, Michael Tippett, Benjamin Britten, John Harvey* and *John Rutter*, most of whose works encompass both the church and the concert hall.[22]

Ralph Vaughan Williams (1872–1958) was born in Gloucestershire and received his initial training at the Royal College of Music from Hubert Parry and Charles Stanford; they also influenced Vaughan Williams' enthusiasm for Brahms. Vaughan Williams' compositions include many different genres, especially studies in English folksong (for which he became known as the great champion of the British heritage), but encompassing also chamber and ballet music, operas, symphonies, and music for brass bands. Described by his second wife as 'a cheerful agnostic', he nevertheless enjoyed Anglican church music, and indeed one of his earliest compositions was *Super Flumina Babylonis* (Psalm 137), for the Royal College of Music in 1892. In 1906 he became editor of the *English Hymnal*, and choral and sacred works became a natural part of his other compositions. Of the choral works, two were arrangements of Psalm 100: *The Hundredth Psalm* (1929) is a choral cantata for mixed chorus and orchestra, and *The Old Hundredth Psalm Tune* is a four-part chorus, with organ, orchestra and congregational participation, arranged for the coronation of 1952 in Westminster Abbey. His sacred works on psalmody include *O Clap your Hands* (Psalm 47) in 1920; *Lord, thou hast been our refuge* (Psalm 90) in 1921; *O How Amiable* (Psalm 84) in 1934, composed especially for the Abinger Church Pageant; a solo for the piano, accompanied by chorus and orchestra, called 'The Old 104th Psalm Tune', whose choral text used Sternhold and Hopkins, entitled *Fantasia (Quasi Variazione)* in 1949; *O Taste and See* (Ps. 34:8) in 1952; and *Psalm 23* (1951) which was incorporated into Williams' contemplative morality opera, *The Pilgrim's Progress* (1906–52). Other later works include *Te Deum and Benedictus* (1954), set to familiar metrical psalm tunes, for unison or mixed voices with organ or piano accompaniment, and *A Choral Flourish* (1956), using Psalms 22 and 33, with a mixed chorus, organ and two trumpets.[23]

Herbert Howells (1892–1983) was also born in Gloucestershire, and similarly came under the influence of Parry, Wood and Stanford when at the Royal College of Music (where he himself later taught from 1920 almost until his death). Not

---

[22] A key resource for psalmody and music has again been the Grove music web-pages, at www.grovemusic.com/index.html (each time under the appropriate composer) and www.classical.net. Where relevant, the programme notes for *BBC Psalms Proms Programme, 14 July – 9 September 2000* have also been used.

[23] For a selection of Williams' works on the psalms, including 90, 47 and 100, see *A Portrait of Vaughan Williams* (conductors S. Darlington and W. Boughton), Nimbus 1999, ASIN B000001757.

surprisingly, amongst his mentors were those in the quintessentially English tradition – Elgar, Walton and Vaughan Williams – and their diatonic influence is heard in Howells' composition of songs, chamber and orchestral pieces, particularly in his earlier years. One of his first psalm-inspired works was *Three Psalm Preludes: Set One*, composed in 1915–16, whilst still a student at the Royal College of Music; the first setting, from Psalm 34, is noted for its sonorous ascent and descent as it follows the mood of the psalm. A second set of *Three Psalm Preludes* appeared in 1938–9. But other than these, the psalms did not play a marked part in Howells' public composition until the 1940s, although they were used in private works. One unpublished example, composed in 1917 at the time of Howells' severe ill-health and the death of a close friend in the war, is of Psalm 137 ('By the Waters of Babylon'). The shadow of this illness combined with the early death of his son in 1935 had a marked effect on the elegiac style of two other compositions which used two psalms: *Requiem* (written in 1936 but not released until 1980) has a profound sense of transience and loss, and its two mixed *a capella* choirs (at times with ten parts in each) use the well-known funeral psalms, 23 and 121, in a most evocative way. And in a similar requiem-like piece, *Hymnus Paradisi* (1938 but not performed until 1950), the same two psalms appear. Soon after this, Howells' love of Anglican cathedral music and architecture became invested in more public psalmody, as he continually experimented with choral texture, acoustic resonance and chromatic mood changes. *The Four Anthems* (1941) was the first example: all four psalms – 'O Pray for the Peace of Jerusalem' (Psalm 122), 'We have heard with our Ears' (Psalm 44), 'Like as the Hart' (Psalm 42) and 'Let God Arise' (Psalm 68) – echo the heights and depths and light and darkness of cathedral space, as they resonate again with the theme of transience and loss, yet of hope and faith. This is also the evident theme in a composition from 1944, *God has gone up* (Psalm 47). Howell's greatest public setting of psalmody was probably his *Behold O God our Defender* (Ps. 84:9–10), composed for the royal coronation in 1952 (another version, using Howells' text, was set by John Scott at the end of the service celebrating the Queen's Golden Jubilee in 2002). Other psalms composed in a similar vein include *Jubilate Deo* (Psalm 100), composed in 1967; *One Thing have I desired* (Ps. 84:10), from 1968; and *Exultate Deo* (Psalm 81), from 1977. Amongst the most moving, in this later phase, is Howells' representation of a psalm 'once-removed': *Let all the World in every Corner Sing* (1976) is taken from the words of George Herbert's hymn, which itself appears to be from a blend of Pss. 95:1, 100:1 and 150:6.[24]

William Walton (1902–83) is often regarded as the major English composer between Vaughan Williams and Benjamin Britten. Although his works, like theirs, include many genres (from his unaccompanied choral work, *Litany*, composed in 1916 whilst still at Christ Church Cathedral School, Oxford, through settings of songs and poems, and the *Viola Concerto* (1928–9), to his opera, *Troilus and Cressida*

---

[24] For Howells' *Psalm-Prelude in D Minor*, see 'Psalm Settings at the Proms' from the *BBC Proms Programme, Monday 17 July 2000*, pp. 20–2. For a selection of Howells' works on the psalms, including 42–3, 23, 121, see *Howells: Requiem* (conductor C. Robinson), Naxos 1999, ASIN B000026D1K.

between 1947 and 1954), very few examples are of psalms. One exception is *Jubilate Deo*, set to Coverdale's version of Psalm 100 for the English Bach Festival at Christ Church in 1972. But the most fascinating use of psalmody is to be found in *Belshazzar's Feast* (1930–1, revised in 1948 and again in 1959), intended to draw satirical parallels between the excesses and eventual judgement upon the Babylonian monarchy and Edwardian society. Here Psalm 137 is used dramatically to depict the Jewish people's anguish at their captivity, and, by contrast, Psalm 81, to depict their joyful celebration as the Babylonian kingdom falls. In this way Walton typified – more than Williams and Howells – the use of the psalms as performance rather than as an integrated part of liturgy.[25]

In his earlier lyrical and diatonic works, which included symphony, opera, string quartet, sonata, and concerto, *Michael Tippett* (1905–98) reflected the influence of Beethoven and Romantic composers of the nineteenth century. It may seem out of place to include Tippett at all, for his only choral work on a psalm (*Psalm in C* with the pun on Psalm 100) was not published. But his increasing experimentation with new styles – including Black American genres such as jazz, blues and rap – allows one to view him as a highly original imitator of the genre of the lament psalm. An appropriate example is *The Five Spirituals*, composed by 1941 as his angry response to *Kristallnacht*, combining a modern *a capella* chorus with the more improvisatory Negro Blues to depict outrage at the exploitation of human dignity. These spirituals were eventually included in the oratorio *A Child of our Time* (1944). They might be seen to imitate the way Bach used chorales (with words from psalms) in his Passions, and certainly T.S. Eliot's libretto gives them every appearance of psalm-like laments. Yet again the performative aspect of psalmody, moving out from the cathedral and into the concert hall, is significant here.[26]

Benjamin Britten (1913–76) may be compared with Tippett, not only because of his pacifism, or for the way he wished to communicate political and social concerns through his music (the 1961 *War Requiem*, with its combination of the Latin Mass with war poetry, is an obvious example), but also for his revival of older musical genres. In his case, this was notably English opera, exemplified by *Peter Grimes* in 1945 which he combined with more contemporary non-Western (usually Asian) forms. Of three of his settings on the psalms, *Psalm 100*, composed for Winchester Cathedral Choir in 1984, was, like Tippett's version of this psalm, unpublished, and *Psalm 95* was composed for Morning Prayer at Westminster Abbey in 1961. But it is his *Psalm 150* which is most noteworthy. Commissioned in 1962 to mark the centenary of his old school in Lowestoft, its popularity is due to

---

[25] For a setting of Psalms 81 and 137, as well as 100, 23 and 131, and psalm compositions by Bernstein, to be discussed shortly, see *Bernstein: Chichester Psalms and Missa Brevis* and *Walton: Belshazzar's Feast* (conductor R. Shaw) Telarc (1989), ASIN B000003CV7.

[26] For a setting of Tippett's *A Child of Our Time*, along with Stravinsky's *Symphony of Psalms* (to be discussed shortly), see *The Sixteen Edition À la Gloire de Dieu* (conductor H. Christophers) Cor 16013 (1995).

the way Britten chose to perform it through a children's choir (it had its first performance by children from Northgate School, Ipswich, at Aldeburgh's Jubilee Hall in 1963). Music for children was vitally important for Britten, and the score of Psalm 100 allows children the chance to improvise in instrumentation – blowing, scraping and hitting whatever they can find – and the lively march followed by a chromatic section and a choral hymn of praise collectively allows 'everything that hath breath' to 'praise the Lord': the cymbals at the end are used against the litany of other instruments to celebrate God's glory. Yet again, therefore, like Walton and Tippett, Britten's Psalm 100 offers another example of the transference of the psalms from the sacred to the secular.[27]

Brief mention must be made of other innovative English composers. *John Harvey* (b. 1939), who studied for some time with Britten, used his experience in electronic composition to experiment with liturgical choral works for Winchester Cathedral, where his son was a chorister. The fusion of the traditional forms of Anglican chant with dissonant chords which overlap with each other recalls both electronic musical effects and the echoing spaces in cathedral architecture. His anthem *I Love the Lord* from Ps. 116:1–4,7–9 (1976) is a fine example of this, with its gentle and haunting start, its anguished middle section and final resolution, imitating the moods of the psalm, all brought together by the G major chord as a symbol of faith which sounds through most of the anthem.[28]

John Rutter (b. 1945), follows the British choral tradition exemplified by Vaughan Williams and Howells, although he also draws from a European tradition much broader than this. He has produced works in many genres, including a piano concerto, children's operas, and music for television, but he is best known for his choral works, many of which were compositions for his 'Cambridge Singers' to perform. Of his choral compositions, the anthems and Christmas music are the best known; his *Psalmfest* (1993) is the most relevant example here, bringing together nine psalms in nine distinct representations of human experience: Psalm 27 ('The Lord is my Light and Salvation') for example, is a composition for sufferers of AIDS; here the prominence of the clarinet part echoes the psalmist's search for consolation. Psalm 146, by contrast, is a celebration of the two hundred and fiftieth birthday of a Lutheran Church in the USA: here the timpani, brass and organ bring the work to life.[29]

One could add many more Christian composers to this list. Zoltán Kodály (1882–1967), for example, composed *Psalmus Hungaricus* in 1923, using Psalm 55 to mark the fiftieth anniversary of the union of Buda and Pest. In England, examples include *James MacMillan* (b. 1959) for his version of Psalm 96 (*A New* Song: 1997),

---

[27] On Britten's *Psalm 150,* see *BBC Proms Programme, 12 August 2000,* p. 5. A recording of Psalm 150, by the New London Children's Choir, is *Christ's Nativity, St Nicolas, Psalm 150* (conductor S. Bedford), Naxos (2003), ASIN B0000DJEM4.

[28] On Harvey's adaptation of Psalm 116, see *BBC Proms Programme, Monday 17 July,* pp. 23–5.

[29] For an arrangement of *Psalmfest,* as well as Requiems which include psalms such as 130 and 23, see *John Rutter: Requiem* (conductor S. Cleobury), Hyperion (1997) 66947.

and *Kenneth Leighton* (1929–88) for his composition *Fantasy No. 6: 'Toccata on Hanover'* (1975) on Psalm 104. From the United States, one important composer is *Charles Ives* (1874–1954) whose works on *The Sixty-Seventh Psalm* in 1888–9, on *Psalm 54: for Unaccompanied Voices* in about 1894, on *Psalm 100* in about 1902 and *Psalm 90: for Mixed Chorus, Organ and Bells* in 1923–4 are noteworthy. Each of Ives' works reveals experimentation with new techniques; the most kaleidoscopic (and the only one which really pleased the composer) is Psalm 90 ('Lord, thou hast been our dwelling place ...'), with its constant low C on the organ with another, an octave lower, pulsating constantly, each to symbolize the eternal presence of God – the subject of the psalm. Another contrasting American example is the wide-ranging *Milton Babbit* (b. 1916) whose *From the Psalter* (2002) uses a jazz medium, combining parts of Psalm 13 with two stanzas from Psalms 40 and 41 which were taken from Philip Sydney's Psalter because of their precise rhythm and rhyme. Similarly *Jon Magnussen* (b. 1967) composed the evocative *Psalm* in 2004, using verses from Jerome's Psalter to develop an idea taken from a ballet score for a choreography by José Limón concerning people faced with annihilation of their race.[30]

One composer who has had an enormous influence on different presentations of psalmody is the Estonian-born Russian Orthodox *Arvo Pärt* (b. 1935). Although he moved to Vienna and from there in the 1980s to Berlin, Pärt's Eastern European background is evident in his orchestral, chamber, organ and piano music, but most especially in his choral works, from which there are several examples from the psalms. Sometimes this is heard in the lingering *melismatic focus on just one verse of a psalm; but more especially it is Pärt's ability to create what has been termed a 'floating silence' which takes the listener from the words and music of the psalm into the mysterious and silent presence of God. *De Profundis*, composed between 1977 and 1980, is a wistful and nostalgic work; *Two Slavonic Psalms*, written between 1984 and 1987, using two short psalms, 117 and 131, evokes a real sense of the numinous, with its contrasts of unison and harmony, of high and deep voices, working towards a point where the psalms seem to finally disappear into a sacred, silent space. *Miserere* (1989–92) interprets Psalm 51 as much in relation to the fearful majesty of God as to the grateful acceptance of forgiveness of sins; the use of timpani and the insertion of 'Dies Irae' and the final gradual evaporation into silence evoke again a sense of awesome distance between the psalmist and his God. Representative works include *Ein Wahlfahrtslied: Psalm 121* (1984 and 1996), *Cantate Domino* (1977) and another version of this (Psalm 96 in the NRSV), *Psalm 95* (1995).[31]

Born in the nineteenth century, but really an early-twentieth-century composer, *Igor Stravinsky* (1882–1971) is difficult to categorize, in that he was inspired

---

[30] For a recording and notes on Magnussen's *Psalm*, see people.ias.edu/~jonm/Dance.htm.
[31] See www.musicolog.com/part.asp. For a recording of Psalm 130, see *De Profundis* (conductor P. Hillier) Harmonia Mundi (1997), ASIN B0000007FC; for Psalm 51, see *Miserere* (conductor D.R. Davies), ECM (2000), ASIN B000024ZBC.

by *Romanticism at the beginning of his musical career, but moved some way beyond it by the end. As far as psalmody is concerned, Stravinsky also took the psalms away from the sacred and into the profane. Born in Russia, he spent time in France and finally found home on the west coast of America. Although probably better known for his later works which were as much part of neo-Classicism as they were of Romanticism, such as *The Firebird* (1910), *Apollo* (1928), *Orphée* (1948) and *Oedipus Rex* (1948), it is his earlier *Symphony of Psalms*, an orchestral and choral work of some twenty-three minutes, begun at Christmas 1926 but not completed until 1930, which was inspired, somewhat anachronistically, by the Romantic movement. Stravinsky actually imagined a church congregation (he had by 1926 reaffirmed his Orthodox faith) rather than a theatre audience, but he nevertheless wanted the work to stand on its own merits, not in a category of 'religious music'. The three movements, which originally used Church Slavonic, but later settled on the Vulgate, nevertheless form an experimental type of liturgy: the work moves from prayer ('Exaudi orationem meam, Domine', from Ps. 38:13–14, which returns repeatedly to an E minor key), to promise ('Expectans expectavi Dominum', from Ps. 39:2–4, with its double fugue, first for instruments, then for voices) and finally to praise ('Laudate Dominum', from Psalm 150, which moves from a slow introduction of both instruments and voices to a faster and ebullient middle section, subsiding to a slower apotheosis at the end). The Latin medium allowed further experimentation in musical plays on words, creating what have been termed 'sound colours', and as full a meaning as possible is drawn out from the most important words: this is seen best in the great finale, Psalm 150, where Stravinsky uses every syllable of each word to full effect (for example Do-mi-num and All-el-u-ia).[32]

By contrast, it is mainly American composers who have interpreted the psalms in particular western ways – through jazz, through blues, through *a capella*, and through reggae rhythms. The use of 'reggae psalms' is particularly extraordinary because of the ways in which Rastafarians disassociate themselves from both the Jewish and Christian faiths, yet take the psalms (as well as other parts of the Bible) and 'Africanize' them to express a particular Caribbean identity. The lament psalms and imprecations become songs of freedom from political domination and are particularly apt, and some twenty are frequently referred to. JAH is, after all, their hero deity (Ras Tafari, Emperor Haile Selassie I) and it is convenient that his name is found in the Psalms as an abbreviation for Yahweh (e.g. Psalm 68:4). Amongst the most frequently quoted psalms are 35:1–4 and 55:3,9,11. Also prominent is Psalm 137, as the protest song against black oppression and exile from the Caribbean: popularized by 'Bonnie (Boney) Em' in 1975, and later adapted by Peter Tosh (1977), Bob Marley (1980) and Jimmy Cliff in the reggae film *The Harder They Come* (1973), it is a well-known version even today. The following

---

[32] On Stravinsky's *Symphony of Psalms*, see *BBC Proms Programme*, 6 September 2000, pp. 5–8, and the recording listed in note 26 above.

extract reveals the political-theological reference to Haile Selassie, the Alpha and Omega:

> By the rivers of Babylon, where we sat down,
> there we wept, when we remembered Zion.
> 'Cause, the wicked carried us away in captivity,
> Required from us a song
> How can we sing King Alpha's song
> In a strange land?
> Sing it aloud, awn, awn, awn [on and on]
> Sing the song of freedom, sister, awn, awn, awn, ...

This example shows just how far the psalms have moved into secular life, even serving as songs of subversion for social change in ways quite different from the Jewish and Christian representations.[33]

Most of the Jewish musical responses to psalmody are also from America. Characteristically somewhat later than in Christian tradition, Jewish responses to psalmody in music and art began to develop by the end of the nineteenth century, only to really thrive in the twentieth. One obvious example is *Leonard Bernstein* (1918–90). The son of middle-class Russian émigrés, born in Lawrence, Massachusetts, he had to persuade his father – a son of generations of rabbis and himself a student of the Talmud – to let him take piano lessons and embrace a musical career. Yet his contribution to the musical world, as teacher, communicator, conductor, pianist and composer, shows how he lived out his own dictum that 'Life without music is unthinkable, music without life is academic. That is why my contact with music is a total embrace'. His conducting the performance of Beethoven's Ninth Symphony in Berlin at the time of German reunification (changing *Ode to Joy* to *Ode to Freedom*) illustrates this, as does his diverse and extraordinary talents exemplified in compositions as various as his jazz ballet, *Fancy Free* (1944), his opera, *Trouble in Tahiti* (1952), his film score music for *On the Waterfront* (1954), his musical, *West Side Story* (1960), his symphony, *Kaddish* (1963), dedicated to the memory of President Kennedy, and his multi-media work *Mass: A Theater Piece for Singers, Players and Dancers* (1971). Bernstein's enjoyment of the theatrical context is equally evident in his performance of *Chichester Psalms* at the 1965 Chichester Festival, and provides a striking example of Jewish and Christian collaboration where the psalms are concerned (noting Chagall's presence in that same cathedral through the presentation of Psalm 150 in stained glass some thirteen years later). Following a tradition inspired by Rossi in Venice, Bernstein's version of Psalm 150 was performed in Hebrew by a male chorus of boys and bass voices to the accompaniment of six brass, two harps and percussion and strings. It has all the echoes of Bernstein's Broadway musical experiences, and the

---

[33] On the Rastafarians' use of psalmody, especially of Psalm 137, see N.S. Murrell (2000).

sheer enthusiasm for the joy of performance shines through, despite what Bernstein described as a 'shockingly small time of rehearsal ... [but] the choirs were a delight! ... the orchestra was swimming in the open sea ... but somehow the glorious acoustics ... cushion everything so that even mistakes sound pretty'. He reflected on this experience later:

> These psalms are a simple and modest affair,
> Tonal and tuneful and somewhat square,
> Certain to sicken a stout John Cager
> With its tonics and triads in E-flat major.

The invitation to praise in the first movement (Ps. 108:2 ['Urah, hannebel V'kinnorah! : Awake, psaltery and harp!']) is followed by the hymn of praise itself – Psalm 100, which is set to a jazz-like dance rhythm accompanied by a vast amount of percussion, each contributing to the 'joyful noise' (Ps. 100:1). The second movement interprets rather poignantly Psalm 23 through a solo voice and harp, opening into a male chorus singing the first part of Psalm 2 to a more agitated, percussion-dominated beat – contrasting the uneasy relationship between music of peace and of war. The final movement starts with an elegiac introduction on the organ, leading to a full-chorus melodic interpretation of Psalm 131, ending with a haunting intonation of Psalm 133 by unaccompanied chorus, as a final vision of peace is anticipated. In brief, *Chichester Psalms* not only communicates a critical political message to a wide audience but is also a fitting example of the Jewish use of psalmody as drama and entertainment, but here, within a Christian setting.[34]

Other distinctive Jewish composers of psalmody include the following. *Charles Loeffler* (1861–1935) was born in Alsace, trained in Germany and emigrated to America in 1881; his *By the Waters of Babylon* (1901) echoes the experience of his life. *Arnold Schoenberg* (1874–1951) was born in Vienna, moved to Germany and emigrated to the United States; his *De Profundis* (1950) is a six-voice *a capella* chorus on Psalm 130, dedicated to the founding of the State of Israel in 1948. This is a stirring composition, contrasting the rhythmic pairing of voices with other parts in full unison; the climax, 'He shall redeem Israel', contrasts a sustained high soprano voice with choral chant, repeated and sustained again, fitting for the contemporary occasion. *Shulamit Ran* was born in 1949 in Israel but now lives in the United States; her composition for choir and orchestra, *Supplications* (2002), is described as 'the human quest for faith'; starting with the Shema, Ran takes up four psalms, part in English, part in Hebrew, and through the contrast of lingering harmonies and crashing symbols and choral eruptions she portrays a journey of faith: Psalm 23 is used as an expression of faith, the first part of Psalm 22 as protest,

---

[34] On Bernstein's *Chichester Psalms*, see *BBC Proms Programme, Thursday 17 August 2000*, pp. 21–6 and the recording listed at note 25 above. See also www.telarc.com/gscripts/title.asp?gsku=0181.

Psalm 115 as a vow of confidence, and the latter part of Psalm 22 as affirmation of God.[35]

The final two Jewish composers also use Hebrew, although each is more concerned with the psalms as performance than with their synagogue use. Steve Reich (b. 1937) is undoubtedly one of the most inventive and prolific American composers of his generation, from his *It's Gonna Rain* (1965) to his *You Are (Variations)* (2004). Some fifty innovative works experiment with pianos, strings, ensembles, organs, drums, choruses and even electric guitar, and take up a variety of genres. His *Tehillim* (1981), written after his Jewish faith had been rekindled in the 1970s, comes out of his earlier period of experimentation, following a period of training in Hebrew cantillation. Reich combines his intuitive appreciation of the Hebrew with hints of plainsong, resulting in rhythmic and melodic patterns which are like 'sung-speech', developing the balance between the ensemble and voices in different ways in four very different psalms. The overall effect is of four performances which are sympathetic to the sound of the Hebrew words as well as to the meaning of the passage as a whole. Reich chose four psalms (19, 34, 18 and 150) which he considered to be of interest to Jews and non-Jews alike. Psalm 19, with its solo voice introduction, opens out to a kaleidoscope of sound, reaching out to the glory of God in the heavens; Psalm 34 plays between the *melismatic and *counterpoint, making use of two-voice canons and instrumental solos, as it explores the psalmist's changing moods; Psalm 18 uses more languid chromatic changes to stress the Hebrew parallelism which dominates the psalm; and Psalm 150 focuses on the 'Hallelujah' by using strings, wind, drums, symbols and voices.[36]

Another unusual example is *John Harbison* (b. 1938), for although not Jewish, he was invited by the Chicago Symphony Orchestra to compose *The Four Psalms* (1998) in commemoration of the fiftieth anniversary of the founding of the State of Israel. Never having been to Israel, he was sent there to gain insights for the piece, only to return with insights not only about the sufferings of the Israelis but about the plights of the Palestinians and Bedouins as well. His work also takes up four psalms. Psalm 114 ('When Israel went out of Egypt ...') is an expression of the peoples' adversity; Psalm 126 ('When the Lord restored the captivity of Zion ...') symbolizes new hope; Psalm 137 ('By the waters of Babylon ...') returns to the theme of continual adversity, and Psalm 133 ('Behold how good and pleasant it is when brethren dwell together in unity ...') is used to communicate not only Jewish faith, but hope for universal peace amongst all peoples. Interspersed between the four psalms, in Hebrew, are comments and reflections, in English,

---

[35] On the psalms arrangements of Ives, Babbit, Magnussen, Ran and Harbison, with programme notes on each of their performances at the Carnegie Hall (2002), see www.americancomposers.org/rel20021103.htm. More details of Schoenberg's works, including psalms, are at www.schoenberg.at. One recording of *De Profundis* is *Arnold Schoenberg in America* (BBC Singers, director P. Boulez), Sony Classical (1995) SMK 62022.

[36] On Reich's arrangements of psalms, see www.stevereich.com/. *Steve Reich: Tehillim, Three Movements* (conductor R.de Leeuw) is on Elektra Nonesuch (1994) 7559-79295-2.

from those Harbison met in Israel. Partly choral, partly theatrical, the theme of 'from Jewish adversity to universal peace' makes this a controversial but optimistic work.[37]

We end with recent illustrations which draw together this wide variety of musical approaches from Christian and Jewish traditions. One is by Karl Jenkins: his *The Armed Man: A Mass for Peace* was commissioned by Guy Wilson, Master of The Armouries, as an interfaith reflection on the effects of war on the eve of the millennium. Jenkins combines a fifteenth-century theme tune ('The Armed Man') with Moslem prayer ('Call to Prayers') and Christian liturgy ('Kyrie', 'Sanctus' and 'Agnus Dei') and plainsong versions of Jewish psalms: 'Save me from Bloody Men' is a poignant setting to Psalms 56 and 59, whilst 'Benedictus' symbolizes the gradual turning from fear to faith, taken from Psalm 118. This is a most moving example of psalmody as the universal cry of the human heart, inspired by both Jewish and Christian traditions.

The other illustration is from a programme on Australian Radio ('Radio National Home') when in 2005 Rachael Kohn presented the music of the psalms through four great traditions – Anglican, Orthodox, Catholic and Jewish. The contributors used a variety of psalm mediums from their own traditions – psalms sung to secular hymn tunes and to Hasidic melody, and psalms using Gregorian plainchant and antiphonal chants. The programme confirms two transformations in psalmody which have been emphasized here: first, the increasing collaboration between both Jews and Christians as common ground, whereby poetic speech in musical form can communicate beyond the doctrinal and liturgical constraints of a particular culture; and secondly, the increasing (albeit still much underplayed) role of women in performing the psalms, and even occasionally composing and conducting them.[38]

Concluding Observations

This array of representations – not only in music, art, but also in devotional and academic works, and in translations and liturgical innovations – raises an important question about how we continue to use the psalms today. The advantage of the long perspective of nearly three thousand years of reception history is that it allows one to see just how many ways a single psalm can be interpreted. Taking the

---

[37] On Harbison's *Four Psalms*, see M. Holwin at www.americancomposers.org/psalms_holwin_article.htm. For recordings of the psalms in Hebrew, see musicfromisrael.com/cgi-bin/miva?Merchant2/merchant.mv+store_code=M&screen=PROD&product_code=CD-179.

[38] On Karl Jenkins, see www.karljenkins.com; *The Armed Man* is produced by Virgin Records (2001) 72438 8 11015 2 0. On the programme [24 April 2005] of Anglican, Greek Orthodox, Catholic and Jewish psalmody, see www.abc.net.au/rn/relig/**spirit**/stories/s1348911.htm.

twentieth century alone, and taking one psalm, 137, as a typical example, its varying uses are quite extraordinary. It was a psalm deemed inappropriate for some Christian liturgies because of its cursing language, yet it was a psalm used by Reform Judaism to rekindle Zionist hopes. It was used in Roger Wagner's woodcuts contrasting the 'strange land' with the London docklands; it was one of Vaughan Williams' earliest compositions when he was still at the Royal School of Music; it was an unpublished composition by Howells in 1917 lamenting the atrocities of the First World War; it was used by Walton in *Belshazzar's Feast* to illustrate the celebration of the Jews at the downfall of an abusive foreign power; it has been used as a 'reggae psalm', speaking about the exile from the Caribbean, as a protest against black oppression; and it was used by Harbison to address the ongoing adversity of the Jewish people. Each representation brings new light to bear on the familiar text, and together they make it very clear that it is impossible to invest these texts with just one meaning. However much one can know about the original purpose of these texts (and as we have seen, in most cases this is now admitted to be very little), a really important issue is what the text means for the reader today – and this, of course, may be very different from what it meant for the reader some decades ago.

This chapter has thus revealed that the many voices interpreting psalmody in the twentieth century have been a source of enrichment, not least because they have created a deeper appreciation of both the Jewish and Christian faiths. Further, in the latter part of this period at least, the perceptions of the psalms as a possession only for synagogue and church have been laid open to question and their various expressions of humanity at prayer and praise before God have been made available for a more universal purpose.

Conclusion: From Introduction to Commentary

This book has taken us through several different emphases in its survey of the reception of psalmody. The first chapter illustrated how the psalms served as prophecies, particularly for interpreters who sought to illustrate from them the superiority of the Christian faith. By the second chapter, it was seen how the psalms were valued more for their liturgical, theological and artistic worth. In the third chapter, we saw how by the Middle Ages both Jews and Christians read the psalms in increasingly refined and systematic ways, in order to demonstrate that these were texts which established the supremacy of one faith over the other. In the fourth chapter, which focused on the Reformation, the emphasis was on making the psalms more universally accessible through translation, which resulted in new liturgical, musical and literary experimentations. In the fifth chapter, we noted two often conflicting emphases – on the one hand, a more rational and detached reading of the psalms as ancient cultic poetry, and on the other, a more committed confessional approach which used them as contemporary prayers and hymns. And by the sixth chapter, it became clear that the psalms have served as a catalyst in helping different faith communities to work with greater collaboration in the face of an increasingly secular culture.

So, taken as a collection, the psalms have served very different purposes in different generations. We can also trace these changes of emphasis in another way, by looking at the ways in which the different methods used to interpret them have also altered over time. In *devotional and exegetical* works, there has been a clear progression from interpreting the psalms only in relation to David, to reading them as referring to David or Christ alone, to understanding them as about both David and Christ, to viewing them in terms of what they can reflect about universal human experience. By the twentieth century this resulted in a greater understanding and respect between the two major faiths who had argued over the psalms' worth and meaning for so long. We have also seen how, especially in *exegetical* writings, the emphasis gradually changed from reading the psalms in order to glean their historical and literal meaning, to understanding them as having a more hidden theological agenda – whether Jewish or Christian – to interpreting them in ways which have held in tension both the historical and theological approaches. By the twentieth century this had transmuted into an interest in the literary composition of the entire Psalter or of its smaller collections, rather than a focus only on the historical and theological concerns in individual psalms.

In matters of *translation*, the psalms have moved from existing mainly in a unifying language, Hebrew (although we should recognize that, particularly since the findings at Qumran, this was a limited unity, given the several different canonical collections), to wider accessibility, first in Greek and then in Latin, through to many vernacular versions – Aramaic, Syriac, Old and Middle English, Elizabethan English. Beginning with the Reformation, and especially evident in the twentieth century, the sheer plethora of new translations has made it impossible to adhere to one universally acceptable version; before the Reformation, when there were fewer 'official' translations – and in many cases, when there was one authoritative version, such as the Septuagint or the Vulgate – the Psalms provided a common discourse, offering one translation which could be quoted and memorized, whether in preaching, teaching, prayer or liturgy.

As for the *liturgical* use of the psalms, we have traced their reception in the different faith communities, through the temple to the synagogues, in cathedral and in monastic offices, and seen how the prescriptions set for the daily, weekly and monthly recitation of the entire Psalter have kept the faith of these communities alive in times of crisis and persecution. Despite various liturgical reforms in both faiths, the psalms have retained a prominent place in hymnody and prayer, in the Latin churches as well as in the churches of the East, in rabbinical writings as well as in the works of Protestant reformers, in Reform Judaism, Anglicanism and the Catholic churches. Liturgical reforms proliferated in the last part of the twentieth century, when, as with multiple translations, the many variant liturgies became a source of confusion rather than consolidation for many denominations, resulting in the marginalization of the Psalter as a whole in liturgy – or at best, the predominance of just a small number of individual psalms.

With respect to the *aesthetic* reception of psalmody, the earlier cerebral interpretations gradually gave way to more imaginative responses. In art and then in music these were initiated by Christians, but were soon taken up by Jews; whereas in poetic imitation, Jewish initiatives were later adapted by Christians. These various aesthetic types of reception have usually coexisted independently in the two faith traditions, but in the twentieth century there were several collaborative initiatives in music, art and literature, so that the psalms have moved beyond the confines of a particular faith community and have been used in more secular cultures as well.

These five strands of reception history offer both problems and possibilities when we consider the ways in which future generations might receive the psalms.

There has been perhaps too much experimentation in language and liturgy, with the result that the psalms' overall effectiveness has been fragmented and reduced; yet there have been great successes in academic, devotional and aesthetic areas, where the psalms have been able to hold together previously divided factions and communicate beyond a faith tradition to a wider culture beyond it. There are still many ways in which the use of the psalms could be explored: for example, how they might address more effectively contemporary issues – since their distinctive genre, as prayers and praises to God set in poetic form, offers a unique opportunity to address social, ecological and gender issues as they impact upon faith communities. An encouraging sign is that Jews and Christians are beginning to acknowledge together the richness of their shared heritage of psalmody, and work together to share creatively that legacy, beyond the confines of their own faiths.

But, as we noted in the introduction, this is the first of two volumes: its purpose has been to provide a cultural and historical framework within which we might make a reception-history commentary on each psalm more accessible. The introduction referred to Psalm 8 as a good example of this; here we might also include other psalms which have had a richer reception history than others. Psalm 1, for example, features frequently in this volume simply because it introduces the Psalter, and thus is given special attention in many illuminated manuscripts as well as by those who, more recently, have sought to read the Psalter from a more literary point of view. But Psalm 1 is also theologically rich for its emphasis on the law, traditionally causing friction between Jewish commentators, who affirmed it, and Christian reformers, who questioned it; further, it is a psalm that has been controversial for more recent translators because of the first words, 'blessed is the *man*'. Psalm 2 has similarly created a good deal of interest in art because of its place at the beginning of the Psalter, and has received similar attention in theological works, causing many disputatious writings between Jewish scholars, who saw the figure as pertaining to a past king (probably David) or to a coming Messiah, and Christian commentators who understood that it must be a veiled prophetic reference to Christ. But Psalm 2 is also interesting because it resonates with what we now know about the sacral role of the king as practised in the wider ancient Near East; whilst for those of a more literary persuasion, it is significant because of its several linguistic correspondences with the first psalm, suggesting that the first two psalms form a pair, with theologically contrasting themes. So a commentary on the reception history of individual psalms would have to give particular attention to these two psalms. The next psalm in the Psalter with a more abundant reception history is Psalm 8. So in the commentary as we move through the Psalter, more attention will be given to the richer psalms: an indication of which psalms will receive more treatment than others can be seen in the index at the end of this book.

The more specific commentaries in the second volume cannot be properly understood without using this volume as a kind of reference work which will make the reception history of individual psalms have a broader interpretive context. When taken together, both volumes should convince the reader that whether one looks at the reception history of psalmody from a historical, literary or theological point of view, the rich vibrancy of the psalms, and their capacity to offer such a wide variety of interpretations, will be recognized not as a hindrance to a reasonable faith but as a vital assistance to it.

Glossary

accessus: prayer of preparation made before celebration of Eucharist.

Akitu: Babylonian New Year Festival, honouring Marduk.

Alexandrian Codex: fifth-century manuscript of biblical books mainly accepted by the Greek-speaking church.

Alexandrian commentators: third–fourth-century CE school influenced by Greek thought, reading Scripture in an allegorical way.

Amidah (meaning 'standing'): Jewish prayer recited standing three times daily, using a form of prayer known as *Shemoneh Esrei*.

Analogical reading: prayerful contemplation of scripture popularized in monastic tradition.

Antiochene commentators: fourth–sixth-century school, active mainly in Syria, reading Scripture in historical and literal way.

Apologists: early church writers who defended Christianity against Jewish and Greek criticism.

Arianism: fourth-century heresy denying divinity of Christ which was condemned at the Councils of Nicea (325), Constantinople (381) and Chalcedon (451).

Asaphite collection: collection of psalms (50, 73–83), mainly communal laments, with title 'Psalms of Asaph'.

Ashkenazi Jews: Jews originally from medieval Jewish communities of Rhineland who dispersed throughout eastern Europe, united by Yiddish language.

Awakening: religious movements experienced by American colonial Protestants; one, known as the **First Great Awakening**, was experienced between the 1730s and 1740s, whilst another, known as the **Second Great Awakening**, followed some seventy years later.

Bible Moralisée: picture book dating from Middle Ages, usually with eight images a page and texts in Latin or French bringing out moral implications.

Books of Hours: medieval illuminated manuscripts with illustrated prayers and psalms to aid public and private devotion.

Breviary: medieval liturgical book, popular from eleventh century onwards, of prayers, hymns, psalms, readings and notations for daily use in *Divine Office.

Canon Criticism: study of how the whole collection of biblical writings has been received by Christian communities through the centuries.

Canticles: collection of (usually) fourteen non-psalmic hymns (seven from OT, four from NT, three from Apocrypha) first used in early Christian liturgy.

Cappodocian fathers: fourth-century monastic movement from Syria, exploring the compatibility of Christianity with Greek Philosophy.

Carolingian Renaissance: eighth- and ninth-century cultural revival during reigns of the Frankish kings Charlemagne and Louis the Pious.

Catena: daily prayer offered primarily to Virgin Mary, focusing mainly on the *Magnificat*.

'cathedral office': western short-hand referring to two offices a day (morning and evening prayer) compared with monastic offices, seven or eight times a day.

Confessing Church: Christian resistance movement in Nazi Germany whose leaders suffered imprisonment in concentration camps.

Council of Chalcedon: fourth of seven Ecumenical Councils (451 CE); repudiated *monophysitism and set out Chalcedonian Creed, which upheld that Christ had two natures, human and divine.

Council of Ephesus: third of seven Ecumenical Councils (431 CE), which repudiated *Nestorianism.

Council of Trent: response of Roman Catholic Church (1545–61) to challenges of Protestant Reformation.

Counterpoint: technique developed in the Renaissance, exploring relationship between two or more voices in terms of rhythm and harmony.

Deism: seventeenth-century movement prominent in England, France and America with emphasis on reasonable belief in a non-interventionist Creator God.

Derash (literally, 'interpretation'): search for hidden meanings in biblical text, whether for allegorical or homiletic purposes.

Diatessaron: second-century Syriac translation combining all four Gospels into one.

Diet of Worms: assembly of Estates of Holy Roman Empire in 1521 when Martin Luther was officially condemned for his theology.

Diocletian persecution: last, and most severe, episode of persecution of Christians, from 303–4, under Roman Emperor Diocletian.

Dispensationalism: belief in literal fulfilment of Biblical prophecy and imminent return of Christ.

Dissolution of the Monasteries: period between 1538 and 1541 when Henry VIII confiscated the property of monastic institutions.

Divine Office: also known as '**Divine Liturgy**' or 'Canonical Hours' or 'Cursus' – i.e. the duty to recite monastic hours of prayer.

Donatism: early fourth-century exclusivist church heresy from north Africa which believed that the effectiveness of all sacraments was dependent upon moral purity of minister.

Eisegesis: reading a subjective interpretation into a text.

Elegiac: imitating classical poetic metre of two lines, one with six basic beats to a line, the other with five.

Emancipation: abolition in the nineteenth century of discriminatory laws which failed to recognize Jews as equal citizens.

Empiricism: theory of knowledge emphasizing role of experience in formation of ideas.

Enlightenment: intellectual movement in the seventeenth and eighteenth centuries which advocated reason as a means of establishing e.g. social and ethical systems.

Enthronement psalms: group of psalms (including 93–9) which celebrate Yahweh's rule over all creation.

Eschatological: concerning events to take place before end of time.

Exegesis: attempting to establish objective reading of a text.

Fourth Lateran Council: twelfth Ecumenical Council called by Pope Innocent III in 1215, resulting in clerical reform and renewal of Dominican and Franciscan orders.

Gaonic Period: way of dating Jewish history in context of spread of Islam – from rise of Abbasids in eighth century to rise of Fatimids in the eleventh century.

Gattungsgeschichte/Gattungen (literally 'history of different forms'): study of biblical genres both in prose and poetry.

Gemarah, or Gemara (meaning 'completion'): section of Talmud containing rabbinical commentaries, especially on *Mishnah, usually referring to sixth-century CE Babylonian version (500 CE) rather than the fourth-century CE Palestinian one.

Genizah: depository in synagogue where religious manuscripts in Hebrew, containing the holy name of God, were stored before a 'ritual burial'.

Gloss: note made in margins or between lines of a book, in which meaning of the text in its original language is explained, often in another language.

Gnosticism: movement popular in the second century CE, considered heretical, which advocated the way to salvation through acquiring inner knowledge;

Gutenberg Press: first printing press, completed in 1440, with replaceable/moveable wooden or metal letters; revolutionizing availability of texts.

Haggadah (meaning 'telling' [a story]): account of liberation from slavery (as told in Exodus) especially at Passover time.

Halakah (meaning 'walking [according to the Law]'): refers to whole corpus of Jewish law – biblical, rabbinic and Talmudic.

Hallel (meaning 'praise'): includes Psalms 113–18 (praising God for exodus) and 145–50 (praising God for creation); used especially at Passover.

Hashem (meaning 'the name'): Jewish term for God whose actual name could not be uttered.

Hasidim (meaning 'separated ones'): originally denoting Jewish pietists during Maccabean times, later referring to twelfth- and thirteenth-century Jewish movement in Rhineland, and later still to nineteenth-century pietist movement from Eastern Europe.

Haskalah (from 'sekhel', meaning intellect): eighteenth-century movement among European Jews who sought to adopt *Enlightenment values and engage with secular world through intellectual discourse.

Hazzan: synagogue cantor.

Hexapla: six-columned work of various Hebrew and Greek versions of Old Testament, attempting to bring Greek into line with Hebrew 'original'.

High Church Reformers: often associated with Oxford Movement, sometimes termed *Tractarians, whose concern was to demonstrate the Church of England was the direct descendant in worship and doctrine of early Apostolic church.

Historical criticism: branch of Biblical criticism, often contrasted with *Literary criticism, determining the historical, geographical and cultural setting of a text.

History of Religions School: nineteenth-century German school of thought which studied religion as a socio-cultural phenomenon.

Humanism: Broadly denotes emphasis or study of human achievements, without necessarily denying existence of God.

Iconoclasticism/Iconoclasm: opposition to religious images, especially in Byzantine churches in the eighth and ninth centuries and in Reformation churches in the sixteenth and seventeenth centuries.

Illuminated manuscripts: medieval texts which were complemented by the addition of decorated initials, borders and miniatures, initially using gold or silver.

Introit: antiphon or liturgical text (often using psalm) at beginning of celebration of Roman Catholic Mass and Lutheran Divine Service.

Jamestown settlers: Virginia Company Explorers who landed on Jamestown Island and in 1607 established Virginia English Colony on banks of James River.

Jansenism: Flemish Catholic movement between the sixteenth and eighteenth centuries, emphasizing original sin and Calvinistic notion of predestination, eventually condemned as heretical.

Jesse Tree: decoration in Psalters depicting Jesse, father of David, asleep with his descendants growing out of him like a tree, with Christ at pinnacle.

Judengassen (literally, 'Jewish ghettos'): where during Nazi period Jews were forced to live on account of their ethnicity.

Kabbalah (literally 'receiving'): mystical Jewish sect founded upon theory of second revelation to Moses, characterized by belief in God's simultaneous immanence and transcendence.

Karaites: eighth-century Jewish sect opposed to claim that only the written Torah was authoritative, thus rejecting rabbinic tradition.

Kathismata: Orthodox liturgical tradition, dividing Psalter into twenty sections, so it could be read weekly in its entirety (and during Lent, twice a week).

*Kedushta/Kedusha (meaning 'holiness'): part of *Amidah prayer which includes blessings of God's holy name; often improvised by *piyyutim.

lectio divina (meaning 'divine reading'): method of praying Scripture, to promote deeper communion with God, particularly popular in monastic tradition.

Literary criticism: application of modern methods for analysing literature to Bible; often contrasted with *Historical criticism.

Lollards: late medieval reformers who emphasized authority of Scripture over the authority of Clergy; condemned by both religious and secular authorities.

Lübeck Bible: printed Bible from 1494, written in Low German Dialect, including some 100 woodcuts.

LXX: Roman numerals for seventy, denoting the Septuagint, the oldest known Greek version of Hebrew Bible translated between the third and first centuries BCE in Alexandria.

Maccabean: Jewish rebel movement which fought against the Seleucid rule in the second century BCE, founding Hasmonean royal dynasty in Israel until 63 BCE when Pompey conquered Jerusalem.

Mahzor (literally meaning 'cycle'): specialized version of Jewish Prayer book (*Siddur*) used especially at New Year Festival and Day of Atonement.

Mandeans: second-century *Gnostic group, often associated with the teachings of John the Baptist, believing enlightenment came through baptism and that death brought about deliverance of soul.

Manichaeans: third-century *Gnostic sect of Iranian origin believing world to have been created by a 'demon-god'; they practised strict asceticism to overcome original sin.

Marcionism: second-century *Gnostic sect from Rome, whose gospel of 'love over law' led to rejection of Old Testament in favour of New.

Massoretic Text (MT): Earliest complete text of Hebrew Bible, associated with rabbinical group of scribes in Galilee from the second to ninth centuries CE.

Melismatic technique: changing pitch of a syllable of text while it is being sung; contrasts with *syllabic* technique where each syllable is matched to a single note.

Midrash(im) (literally meaning interpretation[s]): refers to Jewish *exegesis, whether of Hebrew Bible, or of legal and homiletic commentaries on it.

Miniscule: ninth-century script in small cursive style (usually Greek), replacing uncial script (in larger disconnected letters).

Mishnah (meaning 'repetition'): first record of Rabbinic oral law from about 200 CE, transmitted later mostly in Aramaic as *Gemarah, together forming *Talmud.

Missal: liturgical book containing instructions and texts for celebration of Mass. 'The Roman Missal' was published in 1570 to replace use of different missals.

Mode: series of musical intervals which determine musical keys or pitches.

Monophysites: sectarian group who, in reaction to *Nestorianism, believed Jesus had one divine nature; considered heretical after *Council of Chalcedon.

Montanists: second-century apocalyptic movement from Phrygia which valued contemporary outpourings of the Spirit above ancient prophecy.

Moravian: early-eighteenth-century movement combining love of Scripture with revitalized hymnody.

Mudéjar: Moors and native Andalusians who remained in Iberia after the Christian *Reconquest,* yet still practised Islam, creating a particular style of architecture and decoration.

Neo-Platonism: third-century development of Platonic philosophy opposed to dualistic interpretations of Plato's thought.

Nestorianism: third- and fourth-century Syrian heresy which affirmed two distinct persons in Christ, one human, one divine, condemned at *Council of Ephesus, leading to Nestorian Schism (separation of Assyrian and Byzantine churches).

Non-conformist: term used after 1662 Act of Uniformity referring to any English subject belonging to a church other than Church of England.

Pelagianism: fourth-century heresy from Italy advocating that humans have responsibility for their own salvation, thus minimizing the redemptive role of sacraments.

Peshat (meaning 'plain' or 'simple'): literal meaning of the text, contrasted with **derash*.

Peshitta (meaning, in Aramaic, 'straight'): denotes versions of Syriac Bible in Aramaic.

Pesukei de-zimra (literally 'verses of song'): blessings and praises for Torah used at morning prayer, including parts of several psalms.

Petrarchan (also known as 'The Italian Sonnet'): Type of sonnet, dating from the thirteenth century, usually of 15 lines, in which 9th line signals change in tone or mood of poem.

Philosophes: leading philosophical, political, and social writers of eighteenth-century French **Enlightenment.

Pilgrim Fathers: group of radical Puritans who sailed from Plymouth to Cape Cod in 1620 in *Mayflower*.

Pindaric ode: Formulaic poem with a three-part structure (strophe, antistrophe and epode) corresponding to movements by chorus in a Greek drama.

Piyyutim (from Greek, meaning 'creations'): Jewish liturgical poem in Hebrew or Aramaic, often imitating style of psalms, composed to be used during religious services.

Polyglot: book containing same biblical text in more than one language.

Pontifical Biblical Commission: committee of Cardinals (1901–) commissioned to safeguard Catholic interpretation of Scripture; from 1971, a more consultative body.

Post-exilic: period after Persian period of Jewish restoration in 537 BCE.

Post-modernism: twentieth-century term indicating and approving pluralism of diverse styles throughout humanities.

Pre-exilic: period before Babylonian captivity of Jews in 586 BCE.

Proper Psalm: specific psalms appointed for use at special occasions throughout the church year.

Prymer: thirteenth–sixteenth-century book of Devotions for laity, usually comprising 'Little Office of Blessed Virgin Mary', 'Office for Dead' (for Vespers), and Matins, Lauds, Gradual Psalms (120–34), Penitential Psalms (6, 32, 38, 51, 102, 130, 143) and Litany of Saints.

Psalms of Ascents (also 'Songs of Ascents' and 'Gradual Psalms'): name given to Psalms 120–34, possibly sung by Levites on fifteen Temple steps; anthology for pilgrims going up to Jerusalem for one of three great feasts.

Puritans: sixteenth-century movement – sometimes used derogatively – rejecting both Roman Catholic theology and Laudian reform of Church of England after Elizabethan Religious Settlement.

Quakers (also Religious Society of Friends or 'peace church'): distinctive seventeenth-century English religious movement with little hierarchical structure and no creeds.

Quire (usually referred to as 'choir'): area in western part of chancel between nave and sanctuary.

Qumran: Jewish sect which lived by the shores of the Dead Sea from the second century BCE to the first century CE; produced *Dead Sea Scrolls*.

Reader Response Criticism: literary critical theory prominent in 1980s, noting the meaning given to texts by purposeful interpretations of different readers.

Reconstructionist Judaism: American-based Jewish movement, inaugurated in nineteenth century as radical branch of Conservative Judaism.

Redaction Criticism: method seeking to uncover intended theological purpose of final editor by analysing biblical text as a whole rather than in smaller parts.

Reform Judaism: originating from nineteenth-century Germany, prevalent in America, represents a more inclusivist and liberal response to Jewish faith.

Rhetorical Criticism: focus on different forms of biblical language by looking at specific points authors intended to make.

Roman Breviary: book setting out regulations for celebration of Mass or other Canonical Offices, divided according to four seasons of year, usually including Psalter.

Romanticism: eighteenth-century intellectual movement from Western Europe, reacting to 'rationalization' of nature and promoting folk art and customs.

Sacra pagina (meaning 'sacred page'): ways in which medieval interpreters brought academic skills to revered biblical texts.

Sapphic: poetic form spanning four lines, the first three of which are eleven syllables and the last line consisting of five syllables.

Sarum Rite: medieval form of Roman Rite, originally associated with Salisbury Cathedral, used especially before Reformation.

Schola cantorum: Paid schools of musicians, allow clergy to concentrate on liturgical concerns.

Scholasticism: Method of learning emphasizing dialectical reasoning, prominent between the twelfth and fourteenth centuries, aiming to reconcile ancient classical philosophy with medieval Christian theology.

Scholia: Grammatical, critical or explanatory comments inserted into margins of ancient manuscripts as *glosses.

Seder (meaning 'order'): Jewish prayer book containing set order of daily prayers. Also known as *Siddur*.

Sefirot: ten enumerations of God in *Kabbalistic Judaism through which He reveals Himself to humankind.

Sephardic Jews: Jews originally living in Spain and Portugal who in the fifteenth century fled to other parts of Europe, England, Africa and Asia Minor.

Shema' (meaning 'Hear [this]'): Jewish declaration of faith in one God, usually recited in morning and at night (Deut. 6:7).

Shemoneh Esreh (meaning 'Eighteen Blessings'): Central prayer in *Amidah, which observant Jews recite up to three times daily.

Shofar: horn used as a musical instrument for Jewish religious purposes.

Siddur: see *Seder.

Sigla: abbreviations used by ancient and medieval scribes writing in Latin.

Spenserian: form of sonnet which combines Italian and English forms, using three quatrains and a couplet, yet employing linking rhymes between the quatrains.

Talmuds (Palestinian and Babylonian): commentaries on *Mishnah edited in third–fourth and sixth centuries respectively.

te'amim: Hebrew term for 'accents' or 'notations' used in *Massoretic text, suggesting musical adaptation of psalms

terza rima: Italian verse form with rhyme scheme.

theodicy: justification of God's goodness and justice in face of existence of evil.

Tract: liturgical term referring usually to series of psalm verses used in Roman Mass instead of Alleluias during Lent.

Tractarianism: eighteenth-century High Church movement in Oxford which popularized its theology by *Tracts of the Times*.

tropological reading: pragmatic form of biblical interpretation emphasizing moral edification of Scripture.

typological reading: contrasting Old Testament events and theology with New Testament events and theology – e.g. waters of Red Sea/waters of Jordan in theology of Baptism.

Tzidduk Ha-din (meaning 'Justification of Judgement'): ninth-century burial liturgy.

Ugaritic: language used in N. Syria, evident in Ras Shamra texts (discovered c. 1928) illustrating ways in which OT writers have borrowed phrases, idioms and vocabulary from surrounding cultures.

Unitarian: belief in the oneness of God (rather than Father–Son–Holy Spirit), ultimately advocating moral authority but not divinity of Jesus.

Vatican Councils: Vatican I = nineteenth-century Ecumenical Council summoned by Pope Pius IX in1868; **Vatican II,** opened under Pope John XXIII in 1962 and closed under Pope Paul VI in 1965, was on issues of modernity in church – e.g. permitting vernacular in the celebration of Mass.

Vulgate (meaning 'common'): Jerome's fourth–fifth-century Latin version of the Bible in language of people (i.e. not in official 'Ciceronian' Latin).

Wars of Religion: series of conflicts fought between Catholics and Huguenot Protestants from middle to end of the sixteenth century.

*yeshivah: Orthodox Jewish institution for Torah and Talmudic study.

Zohar, Book of: mystical commentary on Torah, written in medieval Aramaic and Hebrew, used in *Kabbalah Judaism.

References

Abbreviations of Periodicals, Yearbooks and Reference Series not produced in full in References

ALW	*Archiv für Liturgiewissenschaft*
BASOR	*Bulletin of the American Schools of Oriental Research*
BBB	Bonner biblische Beiträge
BHT	Beiträge zur historischen Theologie
CBQ	*Catholic Biblical Quarterly*
EETS	Early English Texts Society
Est Bib	*Estudios bíblicos*
Exp	*Expositor*
FRLANT	Forschungen zur Religion und Literatur des Alten und Neuen Testaments

HeyJ	*Heythrop Journal*
HKAT	Handkommentar zum Alten Testament
HSS	Harvard Semitic Monographs
HTR	*Harvard Theological Review*
HTS	*Harvard Theological Studies*
HUCA	*Hebrew Union College Annual*
JBL	*Journal of Biblical Literature*
JQR	*Jewish Quarterly Review*
JSNTSS	Journal for the Study of the New Testament Supplement Series
JSOTSS	Journal for the Study of the Old Testament Supplement Series
JTS	*Journal of Theological Studies*
KAT	Kommentar zum Alten Testament
KHAT	Konkordanz zum Hebräischen Alten Testaements (G. Lisowsky)
NTS	New Testament Studies
PIBA	The Proceedings of the Irish Biblical Association
RevQ	Revue de Qumran
SBLDS	Society of Biblical Literature Dissertation Series
SBLMS	Society of Biblical Literature Monograph Series
SBLSCS	Society of Biblical Literature Septuagint and Cognate Studies
SNT	Schriften des Neuen Testaments
StPat	*Studia Patristica*
StTh	*Studia Theologica*
ThLZ	*Theologische Literaturzeitung*
TU	Texte und Untersuchungen zur Geschichte der altchristlichen Literatur
WUNT	Wissenschaftliche Untersuchungen zum Neuen Testament
ZAW	*Zeitschrift für die alttestamentliche Wissenschaft*

Works Cited in More than One Chapter

Ackroyd, P.R. and Evans, C.F. (eds.) 1970: *The Cambridge History of the Bible* Vol. 1. Cambridge: Cambridge University Press.

Altmann, A. (ed.) 1967: *Jewish Medieval and Renaissance Studies*. Cambridge, MA: Harvard University Press.

Attridge, H.W. and Fassler, M.E. (eds.) 2003: *Psalms in Community: Jewish and Christian Textual, Liturgical, and Artistic Traditions*. Leiden & Boston: Brill.

Backhouse, J.M. 1979: *The Illuminated Manuscript*. Oxford: Phaidon.

Bailey, M. 2000: Psalmic Music in Orthodox Liturgy as Foundation, Movement, and Ministry. *Jacob's Well*, Spring/Summer: see www.jacwell.org/spring_summer2000/psalmic_music_in_orthodox_liturg.htm.

Balla, E. 1912: *Das Ich der Psalmen*, FRLANT 16. Göttingen.

Barthélemy, D. 1996: L'appropriation juive et chrétienne du Psautier. In R.D. Weis and D.M. Carr (eds.), *Gift of God in Due Season*. Sheffield: Sheffield Academic Press, 206–18.

Bloemendaal, W. 1960: *The Headings of the Psalms in the East Syrian Church*. Leiden: Brill.
Bradshaw, P.F. and Hoffman, L.A. (eds.) 1991a: *The Making of Jewish and Christian Worship*. London: University of Notre Dame Press.
Bradshaw, P.F. and Hoffman, L.A. (eds.) 1991b: *The Changing Face of Jewish and Christian Worship in North America*. London: University of Notre Dame Press.
Braude, W.G. 1959: *The Midrash on Psalms*, Vols. 1 & 2. New Haven: Yale University Press.
Cheyne, T.K. 1904: *The Book of Psalms or the Praises of Israel*. London: Kegan Paul, Trench, Trübner & Co.
Danby, H. (tr) 1933: *The Mishnah*. Oxford: Clarendon Press.
Davison, W.T. 1893: *The Praises of Israel: An Introduction to the Study of the Psalms*. London: Charles H. Kelly.
Day, J. 1990: *Psalms*, Old Testament Guides. Sheffield: JSOT Press.
Donin, H.H. 1980: *To Pray as a Jew: A Guide to the Prayer Book and Synagogue Service*. London: Basic Books.
Eaton, J.H. 1999: Book of Psalms. In J. H. Hayes (ed.) *The Dictionary of Biblical Interpretation*, Vol. 2. Nashville, TN: Abingdon, 324–49.
Eaton, J.H. 2003: *The Psalms: a Historical and Spiritual Commentary with an Introduction and New Translation*. London, New York: T&T Clark International.
Elbogen, I. (tr) 1993: *Jewish Liturgy: A Comprehensive History*. New York: Jewish Publication Society of America.
Fleischer, P.V. (ed.) 2002: *Targum and Scripture: Studies in Aramaic Translation and Interpretation in Memory of Ernest G. Clarke*, Studies in the Aramaic Interpretation of Scripture 2. Leiden: Brill.
Flint, P.W. and Miller, P.D (eds.) 2005: *The Book of Psalms. Composition and Reception*. Leiden, Boston: Brill.
Flint, P.W. 1997: *The Dead Sea Scrolls and the Book of Psalms*. New York, Leiden & Köln: Brill.
Gillingham, S. 2007: Psalm 8 through the Centuries. In J.S. Burnett, W.H. Bellinger and W.D. Tucker (eds.), *Diachronic and Synchronic: Reading Psalms in Real Time*, Library of Hebrew Bible/Old Testament Studies. London: T & T Clark International. Forthcoming.
Grabar, A. 1969: *Christian Iconography: A Study of Its Origins*, Bollinger Series XXXV, 10. Princeton: Princeton University Press; London: Routledge & Kegan Paul.
Green, A. (ed.) 1986: *Jewish Spirituality from the Bible through the Middle Ages*. London: Routledge & Kegan Paul.
Gutmann, J. 1971: *No Graven Images: Studies in Art and the Hebrew Bible*. New York: Ktav Pub. House.
Hiebert, R.J.V., Cox, C.E. and Gentry, P.J. (eds.) 2001: *The Old Greek Psalter: Studies in Honour of Albert Pietersma*, JSOTSup 332. Sheffield: Sheffield Academic Press.
Holladay W.L. 1993: *The Psalms through Three Thousand Years*. Minneapolis: Fortress Press.
Houlden, J.L. (ed.) 1995: *The Interpretation of the Bible in the Church*. London: SCM Press.
Jones C., Wainwright G. and Yarnold E. 1978: *Study of Liturgy*. New York: Oxford University Press.
Kessler, C. 1991: Les psaumes dans la liturgie juive. *LumVie* 40, 13–24.
Kraeling, E.G.H. 1955: *The Old Testament Since the Reformation*. New York: Harper and Row.
Kugel, J.C. 1987: Topics in the History of the Spirituality of the Psalms. In A. Green (ed.), *Jewish Spirituality from the Bible through the Middle Ages*. New York: Crossroad, 113–44.
Lamb, J.A. 1962: *The Psalms in Christian Worship*. London: Faith Press.
Lampe, G.W.H. (ed.) 1969: *The Cambridge History of the Bible*, Vol. 2. *The West from the Fathers to the Reformation*. Cambridge: Cambridge University Press.

Leveen, J. 1944: *The Hebrew Bible in Art*. Oxford: Oxford University Press.

Levy, B.S. (ed.) 1992: *The Bible in the Middle Ages: its influence on literature and art*, Medieval and Renaissance Texts and Studies Series, Vol. 89. Binghampton, NY: Medieval & Renaissance Texts and Studies.

Lockhart, A. (ed.) 1994: Stained Glass. Pitkin Guide. Sussex: Ditchling.

Maher, M. 1994: The Psalms in Jewish Worship. *PIBA* 17, 19–36.

Moyise, S. and Menken, M. (eds.) 2004: *The Psalms in the New Testament*. London: Continuum.

Neale, J.M. and Littledale, R.F. 1874–79: *A Commentary on the Psalms from Primitive and Medieval Writers*, 4 Vols. London: J. Masters and Co.

Petuchowsi, J. 1968: *Prayerbook Reform in Europe: the Liturgy of the European Liberal and Reform Judaism*. New York: World Union for Progressive Judaism.

Posner, R., Kaploun, U. and Sohen, S. (eds.) 1975: *Jewish Liturgy, Prayer and Synagogue Service through the Ages*. Jerusalem: Keter Publishing House.

Prothero, R. 1903: *The Psalms in Human Life*. London and New York: T. Nelson.

Read, H. (ed.) 1960: *English Stained Glass*. London: Thames and Hudson.

Reif, S.C. 1983: Jewish Liturgical Research: Past, Present and Future. *JJS* 34, 161–70.

Reif, S.C. 1993: *Judaism and Hebrew Prayer: New Perspectives on Jewish Liturgical History*. Cambridge: Cambridge University Press.

Rosenthal, J.M. (ed.) 1967: *Studies in Texts in Jewish History, Literature and Religion*, 2 Vols. Jerusalem: Rubin Mass.

Sabourin L. 1974: *The Psalms. Their Origin and Meaning*. New York: Alba House.

Saebø, M. (ed.) 1996: *Hebrew Bible/Old Testament. The History of its Interpretation*, Vol. 1: Part I (Antiquity). Göttingen: Vandenhoeck and Ruprecht.

Saebø, M. (ed.) 2000: *Hebrew Bible/Old Testament. The History of its Interpretation*, Vol. 1: Part II (The Middle Ages). Göttingen: Vandenhoeck and Ruprecht.

Sanders, J.A. 1965: *The Psalms Scroll of Qumran Cave 11 (11 Q Psa)*. Discoveries in the Judean Desert of Jordan, 4. Oxford: Clarendon.

Spurgeon C.H. 1860–67: *The Treasury of David, containing an Original Exposition of the Book of Psalms*, 7 Vols. London.

Stec, D.M. 2005: *The Targum of the Psalms*, The Aramaic Bible, Vol. 16. Collegeville, MI: Liturgical Press.

Taft, R. 1986: *The Liturgy of the Hours in the East and the West. The Origins of the Divine Office and Its Meaning for Today*. Collegeville, MI: Liturgical Press.

Taft, R. 2004: Christian Liturgical Psalmody: Origins, Development, Decomposition, Collapse. In H.W. Attridge and M.E. Fassler (eds.), *Psalms in Community. Jewish and Christian Textual, Liturgical, and Artistic Traditions*. Leiden: Brill, 7–33.

Tournay, R.J. (tr. J.E. Crowley) 1988: *Seeing and Hearing God with the Psalms: the prophetic liturgy of the second temple in Jerusalem*. Sheffield: JSOT Press.

Van Deusen, N. (ed.) 1999: *The Place of the Psalms in the Intellectual Culture of the Middle Ages*. Albany, NY: State University of New York Press.

Wallwork, N. 1977: Psalter and the divine office. *Studia Liturgica* 12/1.

Wieder, L. (ed.) 1995: *The Poets' Book of Psalms. The Complete Psalter as Rendered by Twenty-Five Poets from the Sixteenth to the Twentieth Centuries*. Oxford: Oxford University Press.

Wilson, G.H. 1985a: *The Editing of the Hebrew Psalter*, SBLDS 76. Chico CA: Scholars Press.

Young, F., Ayres L. and Louth A. (eds.) 2004: *The Cambridge History of Early Christian Literature*. Cambridge: Cambridge University Press.

References

(Other works, mainly those not explicitly on the Psalms, but nevertheless having informed this book and thus referred to by way of italics in the footnotes, can be found at www.bbibcomm.net/)

Chapter 1

PRIMARY SOURCES

Augustine, E.T.S Hegbin and F. Corrigan 1960: *Expositions on the Psalms.* ACW 29, 30. Newman Press.
Jerome, tr. M.L. Ewald 1964, 1967: *Homilies on the Psalms.* FC 48, 57.

SECONDARY SOURCES

Alexander, D.R. 2001: *The King-Priest of Psalm 110 in* Hebrews, SBL 21.New York: Peter Lang.
Attridge, H.W. 2004: The Psalms in Hebrews. In S. Moyise and M. Menken (eds.), *The Psalms in the New Testament.* London & New York: T&T International, 197–212.
Austermann, F. 2000: Thesen zur Septuaginta-Exegese am Beispiel der Untersuchung des Septuaginta-Psalters. In A. Aejmelaeus and U. Quast (eds.), *Der Septuaginta-Psalter und seine Tochterübersetzungen* MSU 24. Göttingen: Vandenhoeck and Ruprecht, 380–6.
Auwers, J.M. 1994: L'organisation du psautier chez les Pères grecs. In J. Irigoin (ed.), *Psautier chez les Pères,* Strasbourg: Centre d'Analyse et de documentation patristiques, 37–55.
Balentine, S.E. 1984: The Royal Psalms and the New Testament: From "messiah" to "Messiah". *Theological Educator* 29, 56–62.
Bastiaensen, A. 1989: Psalmi, Hymni and Cantica in Early Jewish Tradition. In E.A. Livingstone (ed.), *Second Century: Tertullian to Nicaea in the West, Clement of Alexandria and Origen, Athanasius (Vol 3 of Papers Presented to the Tenth International Conference on Patristic Studies Held in Oxford, 1987),* St Patr. 21. Leuven: Peeters.
Beckwith, R.T. 1995: The Early History of the Psalter. *TB* 46, 1–27.
Bellinger, W.H 1990: The Psalms and Acts: reading and re-reading. In N.H. Keathley (ed.), *With Steadfast Purpose.* Texas: Baylor University.
Berder, M. 1996: "*La pierre rejetée par les bâtisseurs*": *Psaume 118.22–23 et son emploi dans les traditions juives et dans le Nouveau Testament.* Paris: Gabalda.
Bernstein, M. 2005: A Jewish Reading of the Psalms. In P.W. Flint and P.D. Miller (eds.), *The Book of Psalms. Composition and Reception.* Leiden & Boston: Brill, 476–504.
Beutler, J. 1979: Psalms 42–43 in Johannesevangelium. *NTS* 25, 33–57.
Bourke, V.J. 2001: Augustine on the Psalms. In F. van Fleteren and J.C. Schnaubelt, CSA (eds.), *Augustine: Biblical Exegete.* Collectanea Augustiniana, NY, Washington & Oxford: Peter Lang, 55–70.
Bradshaw, P.F. 1995: From Word to Action: the Changing Role of Psalmody in Early Christianity. In M.R. Dudley (ed.), *Like a Two-Edged Sword, The Word of God in Liturgy and History.* Norwich & Norfolk: Canterbury Press, 27–39.

Braulik, G.P. 2004: Psalter and Messiah: Towards a Christological Understanding of the Psalms in the Old Testament and the Church Fathers. In D.J. Human and C.J.A. Vos (eds.), *Psalms and Liturgy*. London: T & T Clark International, 15–40.
Bright, P. 1997: Singing the Psalms: Augustine and Athanasius on the integration of the self. In J. McCarthy (ed.) *The Whole and Divided Self*. New York: Crossroad, 115–29.
Brock, S. 1998: *Hymns of Paradise: St Ephraem. Introduction and Translation*. Crestwood, NY: St Vladimir's Seminary Press.
Brooke, G.J. (ed.) 1985: *Exegesis at Qumran: 4 Q Florigelium in its Jewish Context*, JSOTSup 29. Sheffield: JSOT.
Brooke, G.J. 2004: The Psalms in Early Jewish Literature in the Light of the Dead Sea Scrolls. In S. Moyise (ed.), *The Psalms in the New Testament*. Edinburgh: T & T Clark, 5–24.
Buchinger, H. 1995: Die älteste christliche Psalmenhomilie: Zu Verwendung und Verständnis des Psalters bei Hippolyt. *TThZ* 104, 125–44; 272–98.
Carleton Paget, J. 1996: The Christian Exegesis of the Old Testament in the Alexandrian Tradition. In M. Saebø (ed.), *Hebrew Bible/Old Testament. The History of its Interpretation* 1/1. (Antiquity). Göttingen: Vandenhoeck and Ruprecht, 478–542.
Carroll, T.K. tr. N. Rian 2000: Commentary of Saint Ambrose on Twelve Psalms. *Downside Review*, 118, 306–9.
Collins, A.Y. 1997: The Appropriation of the Psalms of Individual Lament by Mark. In C.M. Tuckett (ed.), *The Scriptures in the Gospels*. Louvain: Leuven University Press, 223–341.
Collins, A.Y. 2003: The Psalms and the Origins of Christology. In H.W. Attridge and M.E. Fassler (eds.), *Psalms in Community. Jewish and Christian Textual, Liturgical and Artistic Traditions*. Leiden: SBL, Brill, 101–12.
Cook, E.M. 2002: The Psalms Targum: Introduction to a New Translation, with Sample Texts. In P.V. Fleischer (ed.), *Targum and Scripture: Studies in Aramaic Translation and Interpretation in Memory of Ernest G. Clarke*. Leiden: Brill, 185–201.
Cooper, C.M. 1950: Jerome's 'Hebrew Psalter' and the new Latin version. *JBL* 69 No 3, 233–44.
Cox, C.E. 2001: Schaper's *Eschatology* meets Kraus's *Theology of the Psalms*. In R.J.V. Hiebert, C.E. Cox and P.J. Gentry (eds.), *The Old Greek Psalter: Studies in Honour of Albert Pietersma*, JSOTSup 332. Sheffield: Sheffield Academic Press, 289–311.
Croke, B. 1984: Dating Theodoret's Church History and Commentary on the Psalms. *Byzantion* 54, 59–74.
Daley, B.E. 2004: Finding the Right Key: The Aims and Strategies of Early Christian Interpretation of the Psalms. In H.W. Attridge and M.E. Fassler (eds.), *Psalms in Community. Jewish and Christian Textual, Liturgical, and Artistic Traditions*. Leiden and Boston: Brill, 189–206.
Daley, B.E. 2002: Is Patristic Exegesis still Usable? Reflections on the Early Christian Interpretation of the Psalms. *Communio* 29, 185–216.
Daly-Denton, M. 2000: *David in the Fourth Gospel: The Johannine Reception of the Psalms*. Leiden: Brill.
Daly-Denton, M. 2004: The Psalms in John's Gospel. In S. Moyise and M. Menken (eds.), *The Psalms in the New Testament*. London: T. & T. Clark International, 119–37.
Devreesse, R. 1939: *Le Commentaire de Théodore de Mopsueste sur les Psaumes I–LXXX*, Studi e Testi 93. Vatican City: Vatican City Press.
Dillon, R.J. 1987: The Psalms of the Suffering Just in the Accounts of Jesus' Passion. *Wor* 61, 230–40.
Doble, P. 2004: The Psalms in Luke-Acts. In S. Moyise and M. Menken (eds.), *The Psalms in the New Testament*. London: T. & T. Clark International, 83–117.

Dupont, J. 1962: L'interprétation des psaumes dans les Actes des Apôtres. In R. de Langhe (ed.), *Le Psautier: Ses origines, ses problèmes littéraires, son influence.* Louvain: Publications universitaires, 357–88.
Dupont, J. 1974: "Assise à la droite de Dieu". L'interprétation du Ps 110,1 dans le Nouveau Testament. In E. Dhanis (ed.) *Resurrexit: Actes du Symposium international sur la resurrection de Jésus (Rome 1970).* Rome: Libreria Editrice Vaticana, 340–422.
Dysinger, L. 2005: *Psalmody and the Practice of Prayer in the Writings of Evagrius Ponticus,* Oxford Theological Monographs. Oxford & New York: Oxford University Press.
Enns, P. 1997: The Interpretation of Psalm 95 in Hebrews 3.1–4.13. In C.E. Evans and J.A. Sanders (eds.), *Early Christian Interpretation of the Scriptures of Israel.* JSNTSS 148. Sheffield: Sheffield Academic Press, 352–63.
Eriksson, L.O. 1991: *'Come, Children, Listen to Me': Psalm 34 in the Hebrew Bible and in Early Christian Writings,* ConBot 32. Stockholm: Almquist and Wicksell.
Evans, C.A. 2005: Praise and Prophecy in the Psalter and in the New Testament. In P.W. Flint and P.D. Miller (eds.), *The Book of Psalms. Composition and Reception.* Leiden, Boston: Brill, 551–79.
Fiedler, P. 1988: Zur Herkunft des gottesdienstlichen Gebrauchs von Psalmen aus dem Frühjudentum. *ALW* 30, 229–237.
Fischer, B. 1991: Zur Relecture chrétienne des Psalters im patristischen Zeitalter: Neue Publikationen aus Frankreich: Marie-Josèphe Rondeau. In *Jahrbuch für Antike und Christentum, Jahrgang 34,* 159–63.
Flashar 1912: Exegetische Studien zum Septuagintapsalter. *ZAW* 32, 81–116, 161–89, 241–68.
Flint, P.W. 1992: The Psalms Scroll from the Judean Desert and the Septuagint Psalter. In L.J. Greenspoon (ed.), *Seventh Congress of the International Organisation for the Septuagint and Cognate Studies Paris 1992.* Atlanta: Scholars Press, 203–17.
Flint, P.W. 1994: The Psalms Scroll from the Judean Desert: Relationships and Textual Affiliations. In G.J. Brooke (ed.) *New Qumran Texts and Studies: Proceedings of the First Meeting of the International Organization for Qumran Studies.* Leiden: Brill, 31–52.
Flint, P.W. 1997: *The Dead Sea Psalms Scrolls and the Book of Psalms.* Leiden: Brill.
Flint, P.W 1998: The Book of Psalms in Light of the Dead Sea Scrolls. *Vetus Testamentum* 48, 453–72.
Füglister, N. 1988: Die Verwendung und das Verständis der Psalmen und des Psalters um die Zeitenwende. In Hg von J Schreibner, *Beiträge zur Psalmenforschung Psalm 2 und 22.* Würzburg: Echter Verlag, 319–94.
Gillingham, S. 2002: From Liturgy to Prophecy: The Use of Psalmody in Second Temple Judaism. *CBQ* 64/3, 470–89.
Guinot, J.N. 1994: L'In Psalmos de Theodorot: une relecture critique du commentaire de Diodore de Tarse. In *Le Psautier chez les Pères.* Strasbourg: Centre d'Analyse et de Documentation patristiques, 97–135.
Harman, A.M. 1969: Aspects of Paul's use of the Psalms. *Westminster Theological Journal* 32, 1–23.
Harrisville, R.A. 1985: Paul and the Psalms: a formal study. *Word & World* 5/2, 168–79.
Hay, D.M. 1973: *Glory at the Right Hand: Psalm 110 in Early Christianity,* SBLMS 18. Nashville, TN & New York: Abingdon.
Hays, R.B. 1993: Christ prays the Psalms: Paul's use of an early exegetical convention. In A. Malharbe and W. Mecks (eds.), *The Future of Christology.* Fortress: Minneapolis, 122–36.
Heine, R.E. 1995: *Gregory of Nyssa's Treatise on the Inscriptions of the Psalms: Introduction, Translation and Notes.* Oxford: Clarendon Press.

Hengel, M. 1993: "Setze dich zu meiner Rechten!" Die Inthronisation Christi zur rechten Gottes und Psalm 110,1. In M. Philonenko (ed.), *Le Trône de Dieu*, WUNT 69. Tübingen: Mohr Siebeck, 108–94. Tr 'Sit at My right Hand!' The Enthronement of Christ at the Right Hand of God and Psalm 110:1. In M. Hengel, *Studies in Early Christology*, Edinburgh: T & T Clark, 119–225.

Hiebert, R.J.V. 2001: Syriac Biblical Textual History and the Greek Psalter. In R.J.V. Hiebert, C.E. Cox and P.J. Gentry (eds.), *The Old Greek Psalter: Studies in Honour of Albert Pietersma*, JSOTSS 332. Sheffield: Sheffield Academic Press, 178–204.

Hiebert, R.J.V. 2005: The Syriac Versions. In P.W. Flint and P.D. Miller (eds.), *The Book of Psalms. Composition and Reception*. Leiden: Brill, 505–36.

Hill, R.C 1993: Psalm 45: A *locus classicus* for Patristic Thinking on Biblical Inspiration. StPat 25, 95–100.

Hill, R.C. 1997: The Spirituality of John Chrysostom's Commentary on the Psalms. *Journal of Early Christian Studies* 5, no. 4, 569–79.

Hill, R.C. 1998a: Chrysostom, Interpreter of the Psalms. *Est-Bib* 56, 61–74.

Hill, R.C. 1998b: Chrysostom's Commentary on the Psalms: Homilies or Tracts? In P. Allen, R. Canning and L. Cross (eds.), *Prayer and Spirituality in the Early Church*. Queensland: Centre for Early Christian Studies, 301–17.

Hill, R.C. 2004: His Master's Voice: Theodore of Mopsuestia on the Psalms. *HeyJ* XLV, 40–53.

Holm-Nielsen, S. 1960a: *Hodayot: Psalms from Qumran*. Aarhus: Universitatsforlaget.

Holm-Nielsen, S. 1960b: The Importance of Late Jewish Psalmody for the Understanding of Old Testament Psalmodic Tradition. *STH* 14, 1–53.

Howell, J.C. 1987: Jerome's Homilies on the Psalter in Bethlehem. In K.G. Hoglund, E.F. Huwiler, J.T. Glass and R.W. Lee (eds.), *The Listening Heart: Essays in Wisdom and the Psalms in honour of Roland E. Murphy, O. Carm.*, JSOTSup 58. Sheffield: JSOT Press, 181–97.

Irigoin, J. 1994: *Le Psautier chez les Pères*. Strasbourg: Centre d'Analyse et de Documentation patristiques, 33.

Jeffrey, P. 2004: Philo's Impact on Christian Psalmody. In H.W. Attridge and M.E. Fassler (eds.), *Psalms in Community. Jewish and Christian Textual, Liturgical, and Artistic Traditions*. Leiden: Brill, 147–87.

Jellicoe, S. 1972: The Psalter Text of St Clement of Rome. In J. Schreiner Würzburg (ed.) *Wort, Lied und Gottesspruch: Festschrift für Joseph Ziegler*, Echter Verlag: Katolisches Bibelwerk, 59–66.

Johnson, E.E. 1992: Hermeneutical Principles and the Interpretation of Psalm 110. *Bibliotheca Sacra* 149, 428–37.

Jones, D.R. 1968: Background and Character of the Lukan Psalms. *JTS* 19, 19–50.

Keesmat, S.C. 2004: The Psalms in Romans and Galatians. In S. Moyise and M. Menken (eds.), *The Psalms in the New Testament*. London: Continuum, 139–62.

Kistenmaker, S.E. 1961: *The Psalm Citations in the Epistle to the Hebrews*. Amsterdam: Soest.

Koch, D.A. 1994: Auslegung von Psalm 1 bei Justin und im Barnabasbrief. In herausg von K. Seybold und E. Zenger, *Neue Wege der Psalmenforschung*. Freiburg im Breisgau: Basel, Wien: Herder, 223–42.

Koch, D.A. 1986: *Die Scrift als Zeuge des Evangeliums: Untersuchungen zur Verwendung und zum Verständnis der Schrift bei Psalms*, BHT 69. Tübingen: Mohr-Siebeck.

Lange, H.D. 1972: Relationship between Psalm 22 and the Passion Narrative. In *Concordia Theological Monthly* 43, 610–21.

Leeb, H. 1967: *Die Psalmodie bei Ambrosius*, Wiener Beiträge zur Theologie 18. Vienna: Herder.

Leschert, D.F. 1995: *Hermeneutical Foundations of Hebrews: A Study in the Validity of the Epistle's Interpretation of Some Citations from the Psalms* (8, 45, 95). Lewiston, New York and Lampeter: Edwin Mellen Press.
Linton, O. 1969: Interpretation of the Psalms in the Early Church. *T U* LXXIX = *St Pat IV*, 143–56.
Linton, O. 1981: The Trial of Jesus and the Interpretation of Psalm CX. *NTS* 27, 656–72.
Loader, W.R.G. 1978: Christ at the right hand: Psalm 110:1 in the New Testament. *NTS* 24, 199–217.
Lohfink, N. 1994: Psalmen im Neuen Testament. Die Lieder in der Kindheitsgeschichte bei Lukas. In herausg. von K. Seybold und E. Zenger, *Neue Wege der Psalmenforschung*. Freiburg im Bresgau, Basel & Wien: Herder, 105–25.
Lund, J. 1988: *The Influence of the Septuagint on the Peshitta: A Re-evaluation of Criteria in Light of Comparative Study of the Versions in Genesis and Psalms*. Jerusalem: Hebrew University.
Lund, J. 1995: Grecisms in the Peshitta Psalms. In P.B. Dirksen and A. Van der Kooij (eds.), *The Peshitta as Translation*, Monographs of the Peshitta Institute, Leiden 8. Leiden: Brill, 85–102.
Maier, J. 1983: Zur Verwendung der Psalmen in der synagogalen Liturgie (Wochentag und Sabbat). In Hg von H-j Becker and R. Kaczynski, *Liturgie und Dichtung. Ein interdisziplinäres Kompendium 1: Historisches Präsentation*. St Ottilien, 55–91.
Maier, J. 1987: Psalm 1 im Licht antiker judischer Zeugnisse. In M. Oeming and A. Graupner (eds.), *Altes Testament und christliche Verkundigung*. Stuttgart: W Kohlhammer, 353–65.
Mansoor, M. 1961: *The Thanksgiving Hymns*. Grand Rapids, Minnesota: W.B. Eerdmans.
Martinez, F.G. 1996a: Psalms Manuscripts from Qumran Cave 11: A Preliminary Edition. *Rev Q* 65–68, 73–107.
Mays, J.L 1985: Prayer and Christology: Psalm 22 as Perspective on the Passion. *Theology Today* 42, 322–31.
McCaffrey, U.P. 1981: Psalm Quotations in the Passion Narratives of the Gospels. *Neotestamentica, Journal of the New Testament Study of South Africa* 14, 73–89.
McCarthy, D.P. 1992: Saint Jerome's Translation of the Psalms: the Question of Rabbinic Tradition. In H.J. Blumberg (ed.), *'Open thou mine eyes ...' Essays on Aggadah and Judaica presented to Rabbi William G. Braude on his eightieth birthday and dedicated to his memory*. Hoboken, NJ: KTAV, 155–91.
McKinnon, J. 1994: Desert Monasticism and the Later Fourth-Century Psalmodic Movement. *Music and Letters* 75, 505–21.
McNamara, M. 2000: *The Psalms in the Early Irish Church*, JSOTSup 165. Sheffield: Sheffield Academic, 239–301.
McVey, K.E. 1989: *Ephrem the Syrian. Hymns*. Classics of Western Spirituality. New York: Paulist Press.
Menken, M.J.J. 2004: The Psalms in Matthew's Gospel. In S. Moyise and M. Menken (eds.), *The Psalms in the New Testament*. London: Continuum, 61–82.
Menn, E.M. 2004: Sweet Singer of Israel: David and the Psalms in Early Judaism. In H.W. Attridge and M.E. Fassler (eds.), *Psalms in Community. Jewish and Christian Textual, Liturgical, and Artistic Traditions*. Leiden: Brill, 61–74.
Meredith, A. 1996: Review. Gregory of Nyssa's Treatise on the Inscriptions of the Psalms. *JTS* 47, 691–3.
Moritz, T. 2004: The Psalms in Ephesians and Colossians. In S. Moyise and M. Menken (eds.), *The Psalms in the New Testament*. London: Continuum, 181–96.

Moritz, T. 1996: *A Profound Mystery. The Use of the Old Testament in Ephesians* (Psalms 11:1 and 88:7), SNT 85. Leiden: Brill.
Moyise, S. 2004: The Psalms in the Book of Revelation. In S. Moyise and M. Menken (eds.), *The Psalms in the New Testament,* London: Continuum, 231–246.
Moyise, S. and Menken M. (eds.) 2004: *The Psalms in the New Testament.* London: Continuum.
Muhlenberg, E. 1987: Zur Uberlieferung des Psalmenkommentars von Origenes. In *Texte und Textkritik.* Berlin: Akademie-Verlag, 441–51.
Murphy R.E. 1994: The Psalms: Prayers of Israel and the Church. *TBB* 32, 133–7.
Murphy, R.E. 1992: The Psalms and Worship. *Exp* 8, 23–31.
Mussner, F. 1986: Die Psalmen im Gedankengang des Paulus in Rom 9–11. In *Freude an der Weisung des Herrn.* Stuttgart: Verlag Katholisches Bibelwerk.
Nasuti, H.P. 2005: The Interpretive Significance of Sequence and Selection. In P.W. Flint and P.D. Miller (eds.), *The Book of Psalms. Composition and Selection.* Leiden, Boston: Brill, 311–39.
Noth, M. 1930: Die fünf syrische überlieferten apokryphen Psalmen. *ZAW* 48, 1–23.
O'Keefe, J.J. 2000: 'A Letter that Killeth': towards a reassessment of Antiochene Exegesis in Diodore, Theodore, and Theoderet on the Psalms. *Journal of Early Christian Studies* 8.1, 83–104.
Olofsson, S. 1997: The *Kaige* Group and the Septuagint Book of Psalms. In B.A. Taylor (ed.), *IX Congress of the International Organization for Septuagint and Cognate Studies, Cambridge 1995,* SBLSCS 45. Atlanta, GA: Scholars Press, 189–230.
Paulien, J. 2001: Criteria and the Assessment of Allusions to the Old Testament in the Book of Revelation. In S. Moyise (ed.), *Studies in the Book of Revelation.* Edinburgh: T & T Clark, 113–30.
Pease, A.S. 1907: Notes on St. Jerome's Tractates on the Psalms. *JBL* 26, 107–31.
Pedersen, K.S. 1995: *Traditional Ethiopian Exegesis of the Book of the Psalms.* Wiesbaden: Harrassowitz.
Pietersma, A. 2000a: *A New English Translation of the Septuagint and Other Greek Translations Traditionally Included under That Title: The Psalms.* Oxford: Oxford University Press.
Pietersma, A. 2001a: Exegesis and Liturgy in the Superscriptions of the Greek Psalter. In B.A. Taylor (ed.), *X Congress of the International Organization for Septuagint and Cognate Studies, Oslo 1998,* SBLSCS 51. Atlanta: Society of Biblical Literature, 99–138.
Pietersma, A. 2001b: The Place of the Origin of the Old Greek Psalter. In P.M.M. Daviau, J. M. Wevers and M. Wiegl (eds.), *The World of the Arameans I. Biblical Studies in Honor of Paul-Eugène Dion* JSOTSup 324. Sheffield: Sheffield Academic Press, 252–74.
Pietersma, A. 2005: Septuagintal Exegesis and Superscriptions. In P.W. Flint and P.D. Miller (eds.), *The Book of Psalms. Composition and Reception.* Leiden: Brill, 443–75.
Pietersma, A. 2000b: The Present State of the Critical Text of the Greek Psalter. In A. Aejmelaeus and U. Quast (eds.), *Der Septuaginta-Psalter und seine Tochterübersetzungen.* Göttingen: Vandenhoeck & Ruprecht, 12–32.
Poque, S. 1986: Les Psaumes dans les Confessions. In A.M. la Bonnardière (ed.), *Saint Augustin et la Bible,* Bible de tous les temps 3. Paris: Editions Beauchesne, 155–66.
Price, R.M. 1985: *A History of the Monks in Syria.* E Tr by R.M. Price from Theodoret, Bishop of Cyrrhus, Kalamazzo Mich Cistercian Publications.
Reemts, C. 2000: *Schriftauslegung: Die Psalmen bei den Kirchenvatern.* Neuer Stuttgarter: Altes Testament 33:6. Stuttgart: Katholisches Bibelwerk.

Reynard, J. 1997: La magnanimité de David dans l' ln inscriptiones psalmorum de Gregoire de Nysse. *StPat 32,* 208–12.
Robins, V.K. 1992: The Reversed Contextualization of Psalm 22 in the Markan Crucifixion: a Socio-Rhetorical Analysis. In F. van Segbroeck (ed.), *The Four Gospels: Festschrift Frans Neirynck.* Bibliotheca Ephemeridum Theologicarum Lovaniensium100. Leuven: Leuven University Press, 1161–83.
Rondeau M.-J. 1982–5: *Les Commentaires Patristiques du Psautier IIIe–Vc siècles,* Vol. I Orientala Christiana Analecta 219. Rome: Pontifical Institutum Studiorum Orientalum.
Rondeau, M.-J. 1960: Le Commentaire sur les Psaumes d'Évagre le Pontique. *Orientalia Christiana Periodica* 26, 307–48.
Rondeau, M.-J. 1974: D'où vient le technique utilisée par Grégore de Nyasse dans son traité 'Sur les Titres des Psaumes'. *Mélanges des Religions offerts à H.Cl. Puech.* Paris: Presses Universitaires de France, 263 –87.
Rose, A. 1962: L'Influence des Psaumes sur les Annonces et les Récits de la Passion et de la Résurrection dans les Evangiles. In R. de Langhe (ed.), *Le Psautier: Ses Origines. Ses Problèmes Littéraires, Son Influence.* Louvain: Publications universitaires, 295–356.
Rösel, M. 2001: Die Psalmüberschriften des Septuaginta-Psalter. In E. Zenger (ed.), *Der Septuaginta Psalter,* Freiburg: Herder, 125–48.
Runia, D. 2001a: Philo's Reading of the Psalms. *Studia Philonica* 13, 102–22.
Sanders, J.A. 1962: The Scroll of Psalms (11 Q Pss) from Cave 11: A Preliminary Report. *BASOR* 165, 11–15.
Sanders, J.A. 1963: Psalm 151 in 11 Q Pss. *ZAW* 75, 73–86.
Sanders, J.A. 1964: Two non-canonical Psalms in 11 Q Ps^a. *ZAW* 76, 57–75.
Sanders, J.A. 1965a: Pre-Massoretic Psalter Texts. *CBQ* 27, 114–23.
Sanders, J.A. 1966a: The Psalter at the Time of Christ. *The Bible Today* 22, 142–69.
Sanders, J.A. 1966b: Variations in the Psalms Scroll (11 Q Ps^a). *HTR,* 83–94.
Sanders, J.A. 1967: *The Dead Sea Psalms Scroll.* Ithaca, NY: Cornell University Press.
Sanders, J.A. 1993: A Hermeneutic Fabric: Psalm 118 in Luke's Entrance Narrative. In C.A Evans and J.A. Sanders, *Luke and Scripture: The Function of Sacred Tradition in Luke-Acts.* Minneapolis: Fortress Press, 140–53.
Schaper, J. 1995: *Eschatology in the Greek Psalter,* WUNT, 2 Reihe 76. Tübingen: Mohr Siebeck.
Schröten, J. 1995: *Entstehung, Komposition und Wirkungsgeschichte des 118. Psalms.* BBB 95. Weinheim: Beltz.
Schuller, E.M. 1994–5: The Cave 4 Hodayot Manuscripts: A Preliminary Description. *JQR* 84, 137–50.
Schuller, E.M. 1996: *Non-Canonical Psalms from Qumran: A Pseudepigraphic Collection.* HSS 28, Atlanta: Scholars Press.
Sieben, H.-J. 1973: Athanasius über den Psalter: Analyse seines Briefes an Marcellium. *ThPh* 48, 157–73.
Skehan, P. 1963: The Apocryphal Psalm 151. *CBQ* 25, 407–9.
Skehan, P. 1964: A Broken Manuscript from Qumran (4 Q Ps^b). *CBQ* 26, 313–22.
Skehan, P. 1965a: The Biblical Scrolls from Qumran and the Text of the Old Testament. *BA* 28, 87–100.
Skehan, P. 1965b: A Broken Acrostic and Psalm 9. *CBQ* 27, 1–5.
Skehan, P.W. 1976: Again the Syriac Apocryphal Psalms. *CBQ* 38, 143–58.
Soffer, A. 1957: The treatment of anthropomorphisms and anthropopathisms in the Septuagint of Psalms. *HUCA* 28, 85–107.

Stead, G.C. 1985: St Athanasius on the Psalms. *Vigilae Christianae* 39 No. 1, 65–78.
Steck, O.H. 1994: Zur Rezeption des Psalters im apokryphen Baruchbuch. In Von K. Seybold und E. Zenger (eds.), *Neue Wege der Psalmenforschung*. Freiburg im Breisgau, Basel and Wien: Herder, 361–80.
Stewart, C. 2001: Imageless Prayer and the Theological Vision of Evagrius Ponticus. *Journal of Early Christian Studies* 9, 173–204.
Stewart-Sykes, A. 2001: Appendix: 'Hippolytus' Homily on the Psalms. In A. Stewart-Sykes (ed.), *Hippolytus, On The Apostolic Tradition: an English Version with Introduction and Commentary*. Crestwood, NY: St Vladimir's Seminary Press, 177–98.
Swancutt, D.M. 2004: Christian "Rock" Music at Corinth? In H.W. Attridge and M.E. Fassler (eds.), *Psalms in Community. Jewish and Christian Textual, Liturgical, and Artistic Traditions*. Leiden: Brill, 125–43.
Thoma, C. 1983: Psalmenfrömmigkeit im rabbinischen Judentum. In M. Becker and R. Kaczynski, *Liturgie und Dichtung I Band*. St. Ottilien: Eos, 91–105.
Tournay, R.J. 1988: *Voir et Entendre Dieu avec les Psaumes*. Cahiers de la Revue Biblique 24. Paris.
Van der Kooij, A. 2000: Zur Frage der Exegese im LXX-Psalter. Ein Beitrag zur Verältnissbestimmung zwischen Original und Übersetzung. In A. Aejmelaeus and U. Quast (eds.), *Der Septuaginta-Psalter und seine Tochterübersetzungen*. Göttingen: Vandenhoeck & Ruprecht, 366–79.
Van der Kooij, A. 2001: The Septuagint of Psalms and the First Book of Maccabees. In R. J. Hiebert, C.E. Cox and P.J. Gentry (eds.), *The Old Greek Psalter: Studies in Honour of Albert Pietersma*. JSOT Supplement Series 332. Sheffield: Sheffield Academic Press, 229–47.
Van der Ploeg, J.P.M. 1973: Fragments d'un psautier de Qumran. In M.A. Beel *et al* (eds.) *Symbolae biblicae et mesopotamicae Francisco Mario Theodoro de Liagre Bohl dedicatae*. Leiden: Brill, 208–9.
Van der Ploeg, J.P.M. 1992: Fragments de Psaumes de Qumran. In Z. Jan Kapera (ed.), *Intertestamental Essays in Honour of Jozef Taduesz Milik*. Krakow: Enigma Press, 233–37.
Van der Woude, A.S. 1974: Die fünf syrischen Psalmen. In E. Osswald (ed.), *Poetische Schriften*. Gutersloh.
Van Rooy, H.F. 1999: *Studies on the Syriac Apocryphal Psalms*. Journal of Semitic Studies Supplement 7. Oxford: Oxford University Press.
Van Rooy, H.F. 2005: The Psalms in Early Syriac Tradition. In P.W. Flint and P.D. Miller (eds.) *The Book of Psalms. Composition and Reception*. Leiden, Boston: Brill, 537–50.
Van Tilborg, S. 1988: Language, Meaning, Genre and Reference: Matthew's Passion Narrative and Psalm 22. *HTS* 44, 883–908.
Vogel, A. 1951: Studien zum Pesitta-Psalter. *Biblica* 32, 32–56, 198–231, 336–63, 481–502.
Wacholder, B.Z. 1988: David's Eschatological Psalter 11 Q Psalms. *HUCA* 59, 23–72.
Waddell, C. 1995: A Christological Interpretation of Psalm 1? The Psalter and Christian Prayer. *Communio* 22/3, 502–21.
Wagner, J.R. 1997: Psalm 118 in Luke-Acts: Tracing a Narrative Thread. In C.E. Evans and J.A. Sanders (eds.), *Early Christian Interpretation of the Scriptures of Israel*, JSNTSS 148. Sheffield: Sheffield Academic Press, 154–78.
Ward, B. 1975: *The Sayings of the Desert Fathers: The Alphabetical Collection* A.R. Mowbray & Co. London: Cistercian Publications.

Watts, J.W 1990: Psalm 2 in the Context of Biblical Theology. *Horizons in Biblical Theology* 12, 52, 73–91.

Watts, R. 2004: The Psalms in Mark's Gospel. In S. Moyise and M. Menken (eds.), *The Psalms in the New Testament*. London: Continuum, 25–46.

Weitzman, M.P. 1982: The Origin of the Peshitta Psalter. In J.A. Emerton and S.C. Reif (eds.), *Interpreting the Hebrew Bible: Essays in Honour of E.I.J. Rosenthal*. Cambridge: Cambridge University Press, 277–98.

Weren, W. 1989: Psalm 2 in Luke-Acts: an Intertextual Study. In S. Draisma (ed.), *Intertextuality in Biblical Writings. Essays in Honour of Bas van Iersel*. Kampen, Netherlands: J H Kok, 189–203.

Wevers, J.W. 2001: The Rendering of the Tetragram in the Psalter and Pentateuch: A Comparative Study. In R.J.V. Hiebert, C.E. Cox and P.J. Gentry (eds.), *The Old Greek Psalter: Studies in Honour of Albert Pietersma*, JSOT Sup 332. Sheffield: Sheffield Academic Press, 21–35.

Wilcox, M. 1985: The Aramaic Targum to Psalms. In *Proceedings of the Ninth World Congress in Jewish Studies*. Jerusalem: World Congress of Jewish Studies, 143–50.

Wiles, M. 1970 (a): Origen as Biblical Scholar. In P.R. Ackroyd and C.F. Evans (eds.), *The Cambridge History of the Bible* Vol. 1. Cambridge: Cambridge University Press, 454–89.

Wiles, M. 1970b: Theodore of Mopsuestia as Representative of the Antiochene School. In P.R. Ackroyd and C.F. Evans (eds.), *The Cambridge History of the Bible Volume I*. Cambridge: Cambridge University Press, 489–510.

Willems, G.F. 1990: Les Psaumes dans la liturgie juive. *Bijdragen* 51, 397–417.

Williams, H.H.D. 2004: The Psalms in 1 and 2 Corinthians. In S. Moyise and M. Menken (eds.), *The Psalms in the New Testament*. London: Continuum, 163–80.

Willis, J.T 1990: A Cry of Defiance – Psalm 2. *JSOT* 47, 35–50.

Wilson, G.H. 1983: The Qumran Psalms Manuscripts and the Consecutive Arrangement of Psalms in the Hebrew Psalter. *CBQ* 45, 377–88.

Wilson, G.H. 1985b: The Qumran Psalms Scroll Reconsidered: Analysis of the Debate. *CBQ* 47, 624–42.

Wilson, G.H. 1997: The Qumran 'Psalms Scroll' (11QPSa) and the Canonical 'Psalter': A Comparison of Editorial Shaping. *CBQ* 59, 448–64.

Woan, S. 2004: The Psalms in 1 Peter. In S. Moyise and M. Menken (eds.), *The Psalms in the New Testament*. London: Continuum, 213–30.

Wolfenden, G. 1990: The Psalms in Jewish and Early Christian Worship. *P & P* 4, 309–13.

Zenger, E. 2001: *Der Septuaginta-Psalter: Sprachliche und theologische Aspekt*, Herders biblische Studien 32. Freiburg im Bresgau: Herder.

Chapter 2

SECONDARY SOURCES

Anderson, J.C. 1983: The Date and Purpose of the Barberini Psalter. *Cahiers archéologiques* 31, 35–67.

Anderson, J.C. 1988: On the Nature of the Theodore Psalter. *Art Bulletin* 70, 55–68.

Anderson, J.C. 1998: Further Prolegomena to a Study of the Pantokrator Psalter: An Unpublished Miniature, Some Restored Losses, and Observations on the Relationship with the Chludov Psalter and Paris Fragment. *Dumbarton Oaks Papers* 52, 305–21.

Auwers, J.M. 1994: L'organisation du psautier chez les Pères grecs. In *Le Psautier chez les Pères*. Strasbourg: Centre d'Analyse et de Documentation patristiques, 97–135.

Bailey, R.N. 1983: 'Bede's text of Cassiodorus' commentary on the Psalms. *JTS 34* 189–93.

Bernstein, M. 1997: Torah and its Study in the Targum of Psalms. In J. Gurock and Y. Elman (eds.), *Hazon Nahum: Studies in Honor of Dr. Norman Lamm on the Occasion of His Seventieth Birthday*. Hoboken: Yeshiva University Press, 39–67.

Bernstein, M. 2005: A Jewish Reading of the Psalms. In P.W. Flint and P.D. Miller (eds.), *The Book of Psalms. Composition and Reception*. Leiden, Boston: Brill, 476–504.

Browne, G.M. (tr.) 2002: *The Abbreviated Psalter of the Venerable Bede*. Grand Rapids, MI: W.B. Eerdmans.

Cook, E.M. 2002: The Psalms Targum: Introduction to a New Translation, with Sample Texts. In P.V. Fleischer (ed.), *Targum and Scripture: Studies in Aramaic Translation and Interpretation in Memory of Ernest G. Clarke*. Studies in the Aramaic Interpretation of Scripture 2. Leiden: Brill, 185–201.

Corrigan, K.A. 1992: *Visual Polemics in the Ninth-Century Byzantine Psalters*. New York: Cambridge University Press.

Diez Marino, L. 1982: Haggadic Elements in the Targum of Psalms. *Proceedings of the Eighth World Congress of Jewish Studies, Division A*. Jerusalem: World Union of Jewish Studies, 131–7.

Halporn, J.W. 1987: The Modern Edition of Cassiodorus' Psalm Commentary. In J. Dummer (ed.) *Texte und Textkritik*. Berlin: Akademie-Verlag, 239–47.

Hiebert, R.J.V 1989: *The 'Syrohexaploric' Psalter*. Atlanta, GA: Scholars Press.

Hiebert, R.J.V. 2005: The Place of the Syriac Versions in the Textual History of the Psalter. In W. Flint and P.D. Miller (eds.), *The Book of Psalms. Composition and Reception*. Leiden: Brill, 505–36.

Hill, R.C. 2004: His Master's Voice: Theodore of Mopsuestia on the Psalms. *HeyJ* XLV, 40–53.

Komlosh, Y. 1964: Distinctive Features in the Targum of Psalms. In J.M. Grintz and J. Liver (eds.), *Studies in the Bible Presented to Professor M.H. Segal*. Jerusalem: Kiryat Sepher, 265–70.

Kuhn, S. 1965: *The Vespasian Psalter*. Ann Arbor: University of Michigan Press.

Maier, J. 1983: Zur Verwendung der Psalmen in der synagogalen Liturgie (Wochentag und Sabbat). In Hg von H-J Becker and R. Kaczynski, *Liturgie und Dichtung. Ein interdisziplinäres Kompendium 1: Historisches Präsentation*. St Ottilien, 55–91.

Marwick. L. 1956: *The Arabic Commentary of Salmon ben Yeruham the Karaite on the Book of the Psalms CH. 42–72*. Philadelphia: Dropsie College for Hebrew and Cognate Learning.

McNamara, M. 1999: Christology and the Interpretation of the Psalms in the Early Irish Church. In T. Finen and C. Twomey (eds.), *Studies in Patristic Christology*, Dublin: Four Courts Press, 196–223.

McNamara, M. 2000: *The Psalms in the Early Irish Church*, JSOTSup 165. Sheffield: Sheffield Academic, 239–301.

Nasuti, H.P. 1999: *Defining the Sacred Songs: Genre, Tradition and the Post-critical Interpretation of the Psalms*, JSOTSup No. 218. Sheffield: Sheffield Academic Press.

Nasuti, H.P. 2005: The Interpretive Significance of Sequence and Selection. In P.W. Flint and P.D. Miller (eds.), *The Book of Psalms. Composition and Selection*. Leiden, Boston: Brill, 311–39.

Nowacki, E. 1995: Antiphonal Psalmody in Christian Antiquity and the Early Middle Ages. In G.M. Boone (ed.), *Essays on Medieval Music in Honor of David G. Hughes*, Isham Library Papers 4, Cambridge: Harvard University Department of Music.

Ramsey, R.L. 1912: Theodore of Mopsuestia and St Columban on the Psalms / Theodore of Mopsuestia in England and Ireland. *ZCP* 8, 421–51;452–96.

Rondeau, M.-J. 1985: *Les Commentaires Patristiques du Psautier IIIe–Ve siècles*, Vol. 2 *Exégèse Prosopologique et Théologie*. Orientala Christiana Analecta 219. Rome: Pontifical Institutum Studiorum Orientalum.

Rondeau, M.-J. 1974: D'où vient le technique utilisée par Grégoire de Nyasse dans son traité 'Sur les Titres des Psaumes'. *Mélanges des Religions offerts à H.Cl. Puech*. Paris: Presses Universitaires de France, 263–87.

Schiemenz, G.P. 1996: The Painted Psalms of Athos. In A Bryer and M. Cunningham (eds.), *Mount Athos and Byzantine Monasticism, Papers from the 28th Spring Symposium of Byzantine Studies, Birmingham, March 1994, Society for the Promotion of Byzantine Studies, Publications, 4*. Aldershot, UK & Brookfield VT: Variorum, 223–36.

Schokel, L.A. 1989: Interpretation de los Salmos hasta Cassiodoro: Sinteses historica. *Est Bib* 47, 5–26.

Sed-Rajna, G. 1992: Hebrew Illuminated Manuscripts from the Iberian Peninsula. In V.B. Mann, T.F. Glick and J.D. Dodds (eds.), *Convivencia. Jews, Muslims, and Christians in Medieval Spain*. Jewish Museum, NY: George Braziller, 133–55.

Shunary, J. 1966: Avoidance of Anthropomorphism in the Targum of Psalms. *Textus* 5, 133–44.

Simon, U. 1991: *Four Approaches to the Book of Psalms from Saadiah Gaon to Abraham ibn Ezra*, Series in Judaica: Hermeneutics, Mysticism and Religion. New York: State Union of New York Press.

Sokolow, M. 1984: Saadiah Gaon's Prolegomenon to Psalms. *Proceedings of the American Academy of Jewish Research* 51, 131–74.

Taylor, D.G.K. 1998–9: The Great Psalm Commentary of Daniel of Salah. *The Harp: A Review of Oriental and Syriac Studies* XI–XII, 33–42.

Tikkanen, J.J. 1975: *Die Psalterillustration im Mittelalter*. Soest, Netherlands: Deveco Pubishers.

Toswell, M.J. 1995–6: The Late Anglo-Saxon Psalter: Ancestor of the Book of Hours. *Florilegium* 14, 1–24.

Van der Horst K., Noel W. and Wustefeld W.C.M. (eds.) 1996: *The Utrecht Psalter in Medieval Art. Picturing the Psalms of David*. London: Harvey Miller.

Van Rooy, H.F. 2005: The Psalms in Early Syriac Tradition. In P.W. Flint and P.D. Miller (eds.), *The Book of Psalms. Composition and Reception*. Leiden & Boston: Brill, 537–50.

Walsh, P.G. 1991: *Cassiodorus: Explanation of the Psalms*, Vol 1. Psalms 1–50. New York/Mahwah, NJ: Paulist Press.

Walsh, P.G. 1992: *Cassiodorus: Explanation of the Psalms*, Vol 2. New York/Mahwah, NJ: Paulist Press.

Walsh, P.G. 1993: *Cassiodorus: Explanation of the Psalms*, Vol 3. New York/Mahwah, NJ: Paulist Press.

Walsh, P.G. 1998: *Cassiodorus teaches Logic through the Psalms*. Washington, DC: Catholic University of America Press.

Ward, B. 1991, 2002[2]: *Bede and the Psalter* Jarrow Lecture 1991. The Rector of Jarrow, Jarrow-on-Tyne; Oxford: SLG Press.

Weitzmann, K. 1980: *Byzantine Liturgical Psalters and Gospels*. London: Variorum Reprints.

Wilcox, M. 1985: The Aramaic Targum to Psalms. *Proceedings of the Ninth World Congress in Jewish Studies*. Jerusalem: World Congress of Jewish Studies, 143–150.

Wiles, M. 1970 (b): Theodore of Mopsuestia as Representative of the Antiochene School. In P.R. Ackroyd and C.F. Evans (eds.), *The Cambridge History of the Bible Volume I,* Cambridge: Cambridge University Press, 489–510.
Willems, G.F. 1990: Les Psaumes dans la liturgie juive. *Bijdragen* 51, 278–92.
Wright, D.H. 1967: *The Vespasian Psalter,* Early English Manuscripts in Facsimile 14. Copenhagen: Rosenkilde and Baggar.
Wybrew, H. 1990: *The Orthodox Liturgy: The Development of the Eucharistic Liturgy in the Byzantine Rite.* Crestwood, NY: St Vladimir's Seminary Press.

Chapter 3

Primary Sources

Thomas Aquinas, 1995 tr. M. Rzeczkowski: *Commentary on the Psalms of David.* In B.M. Ashley (ed.), *Thomas Aquinas, The Gifts of the Spirit: Selected Spiritual Writings,* Hyde Park, NY: New City Press, 95–133.
The Kennicott Bible. 1957: Bodleian Library Picture Book 11, Bodleian Library.
Glossa Ordinaria. 1844–1864: Migne, P.L. CLXII. Paris: Excudebatur apud Migne, 1187–669.
Anselm of Laon. 1844–1864: *Glossa Interlinearis: Writings.* In Migne, P.L., CLXII. Paris: Excudebatur apud Migne, 1187–660.
Peter Lombard. 1988: *Prologue to the Commentary on the Psalter.* In A.J. Minnis and A.B. Scott (trs. and eds.), *Medieval Literary Theory and Criticism c. 1100–c. 1375: The Commentary-Tradition.* Oxford: Clarendon Press, 105–12.
Fairweather, E.R. 1956: *A Scholastic Miscellany: Anselm to Ockham,* London: SCM Press.
Richard Rolle 1988 tr. R. Allen: 'The English Psalter and Commentary'. In *Richard Rolle: The English Writings, The Classics of Western Spirituality.* New York: Paulist Press, 65–85.
Richard Rolle 1928 tr. G. Hodgson: *Richard Rolle's Version of the Penitential Psalms, with his Commentary, based on that of S. Augustine.* London: Faith Press.

Secondary Sources

Alford, J.A. 1995: Rolle's English psalter and Lectio Divina. *Bulletin of the John Rylands University Library of Manchester* 77, 47–59.
Anderson, A. 1993: *Bernardinao de Sahaún's Psalmodia Christiana,* Christian Psalmody. Salt Lake City: University of Utah Press.
Avalos, H. 1996: Columbus as Biblical Exegete: A Study of the *Libro de las profeciás.* In B. Le Beau (ed.), *Religion in the Age of Exploration: The Case of Spain and New Spain,* Omaha: Creighton University Press, 59–80.
Backhouse, J. 1989: *The Luttrell Psalter.* London: The British Library.
Backhouse, J. 1993: *The Isabella Breviary.* London: The British Library.
Baker, J. and Nicholson, E.W. 1973: *Commentary of Rabbi David Kimhi on Psalms CXX–CL,* University of Cambridge Oriental Publications 22. Cambridge: Cambridge University Press, 59–80.
Beit-Arié, M. (ed.) 1985: *Worms Mahzor: Introductory Volume.* Vaduz and Jerusalem: The Jewish National and University Library.

Beit-Arie, M. 1996: *The Parma Psalter. A Thirteenth Century Illuminated Manuscript*. London: Facsimile Editions.
Bennett, A. 1980: The Windmill Psalter: The Historiated E of Psalm One. *Journal of the Warburg and Courtauld Institute* 43, 52–67.
Berger, D. 1979: *The Jewish-Christian Debate in the High Middle Ages*. Philadelphia: JPS.
Bosniak, J.B. 1954: *The Commentary of David Kimchi on the Fifth Book of the Psalms CVII–CL*. New York: The Jewish Seminary of America.
Buelbring, K.D. (ed.) 1891: *The Earliest Complete English Prose Psalter*, EETS OS97. London: Published for the Early English Text Society by K. Paul, Trench, Trübner & Co. Ltd.
Burkhart, L. 1995: A Doctrine for Dancing: The Prologue to the Psalmodia Christiana. *Latin American Indian Literatures Journal* 11, 21–33.
Cahn, W. 2004: Illuminated Psalter Commentaries. In H.W. Attridge and M.E. Fassler (eds.), *Psalms in Community. Jewish and Christian Textual, Liturgical, and Artistic Traditions*. Leiden: Brill, 241–64.
Christe, Y. 2004: The Bible of Saint Louis and the Stained-Glass Windows in the Sainte-Chapelle, Paris. In R. Gonzálvez Ruiz (ed.), *The Bible of Saint Louis, II, Commentary Volume*. Barcelona: M. Moleiro, 449–91.
Cockerell, S.L. 1907: *The Gorleston Psalter*. London: Chiswick Press.
Del Rosal, J.P. 1988 tr. P.S. Sneesby 2003: *The Synagogue Decoration at Cordoba and Toledo*. Cordoba and Madrid: Ediciones El Almendro.
Deuchler, F. 1967: *Der Ingeborgpsalter*. Berlin: Walter de Gruyter & Co.
Dyer, J. 1989: The Singing Psalms in the Early Medieval Office. *Speculum* 64, 535–78.
Dyer, J. 1999: The Psalms in Monastic Prayer. In N. van Deusen (ed.) *The Place of the Psalms in the Intellectual Culture of the Middle Ages*, Albany, NY: State University of New York, 59–89.
Edmunds, S. 1983: *The Kennicott Bible and the Use of Prints in Hebrew Manuscripts*. Bologna: Universita di Bologna.
Egbert, D.D. 1932: The Tickhill Psalter. An English Illuminated Manuscript of the early Fourteenth Century. *Bulletin of the New York Public Library* 36, 663–78.
Esterson, S.I. 1935: The Commentary of Rabbi David Kimchi on Psalms 42–72. *HUCA* 10, 309–443.
Everett, D. 1922: The Middle English Prose Psalter of Richard Rolle of Hampole, *Modern Language Review* 17, 217–27; 337–50.
Everett, D. 1923: The Middle English Prose Psalter of Richard Rolle of Hampole. *Modern Language Review* 18, 381–93.
Fassler, M.E. and Baltzer, R.A. (eds.) 2000: *The Divine Office in the Middle Ages*. New York: Oxford University Press.
Fassler, M.E. 2001: Psalmody and the Medieval Cantor. In M.E. Fassler (ed.), *Musicians for the Churches: Reflections on Vocation and Formation*. New Haven, CT: Institute of Sacred Music, Yale University, 3–13.
Fassler, M.E. 2004: Hildegard and the Dawn Song of Lauds: An Introduction to Benedictine Psalmody. In H.W. Attridge and M.E. Fassler (eds.), *Psalms in Community. Jewish and Christian Textual, Liturgical, and Artistic Traditions,* Leiden: Brill 215–39.
Feuer, A.C. (tr. and ed.) 1985: *Tehillim*, Artscroll Tanach Series. New York: Mesorah.
Finch, R.G. and Box, G.H. 1919: *The Longer Commentary of R. David Kimchi on the First Book of Psalms,* Translations of Early Documents Series III, Rabinic Texts. London: SPCK.
Finkelstein, A. 1993: Changes in Christian Anti-Jewish Polemic in the Twelfth Century. In *Perceptions of Jewish History*. Berkeley, University of California Press, 172–201.
Fleming, J. 1991: Christopher Columbus as a Scriptural Exegete. *LQ* 5.2, 187–98.

Fox, J. 2000: The Tickhill Psalter. *The Nottinghamshire Historian* 65, 7–9.
Fox, J. 2001: The Tickhill Psalter. *The Nottinghamshire Historian* 66, 8–11.
Gibson, M., Heslop, T.A. and Pfaff, R.W. (eds.) 1992: *The Eadwine Psalter: Text, Image and Monastic Culture in Twelfth Century Canterbury*. London and University Park: Modern Humanities Research Association; Pennsylvania: Pennsylvania State University Press.
Goodwin, D.L. 2006: *'Take hold of the robe of a Jew': Herbert of Bosham's Christian Hebraism*. Leiden, Boston: Brill.
Gross-Diaz, T. 1996: *The Psalms Commentary of Gilbert of Poitiers: From Lectio Divina to the Lecture Room*. Leiden and Boston: Brill.
Gross-Diaz, T. 1999: From Lectio Divina to the Lecture Room: The Psalm Commentary of Gilbert of Poitiers. In N. Van Deusen (ed.), *The Place of the Psalms in the Intellectual Culture of the Middle Ages*. Albany, NY: State University of New York, 91–104.
Gross-Diaz, T. 2000: What's a good soldier to do? Nicholas of Lyra on the Psalms. In L. Smith and P. Krey (eds.), *The Biblical Commentaries of Nicholas of Lyra*, Leiden: Brill.
Grossman, A. 1996: Rashi's Commentary on Psalms and Jewish-Christian Polemics. In D. Rappel (ed.), *Studies in the Bible and Education presented to Professor Moshe Ahrend*. Jerusalem: Touro College Press, 59–74.
Gruber, M.I. 2004: *Rashi's Commentary on Psalms*. Leiden and Boston: Brill.
Hailperin, H. 1963: *Rashi and the Christian Scholars*. Pittsburgh: Princeton University Press.
Haney, K. 2002: *The St. Albans Psalter, an Anglo-Norman Song of Faith*. New York: Peter Lang Publishing.
Hoffman, L.A. 2004: Hallels, Midrash, Canon, and Loss: Psalms in Jewish Liturgy. In H.W. Attridge and M.E. Fassler (eds.), *Psalms in Community. Jewish and Christian Textual, Liturgical, and Artistic Traditions*. Leiden: Brill, 33–60.
Holladay, W.L. 1993: 'The Psalms for Christians: In the West until the Reformation, and in the East'. In *The Psalms through Three Thousand Years*. Minneapolis: Fortress Press, 161–90.
Huyck, P. 1994: *Rosary Psalms*. UK: St Paul's Publications.
James, M.R. 1922: Robert Grosseteste on the Psalms. *JTS* 23, 181–85.
Kuczynski, M.P. 1995: *Prophetic Song: The Psalms as Moral Discourse in Late Medieval England*. Philadelphia: University of Pennsylvania Press.
Kuczynski, M.P. 1997: Rolle among the Reformers: Orthodoxy and Heterodoxy in Wycliffite copies of Richard Rolle's English Psalter. In D.F Pollard and R. Boenig (eds.), *Mysticism and Spirituality in Medieval England*. Woodbridge: Boydell and Brewer, 177–202.
Kuczynski, M.P. c. 1999: The Psalms and Social Action in Late Medieval England. In N. Van Deusen (ed.), *Place of the Psalms in the Intellectual Culture of the Middle Ages*. Albany, NY: State of Union of New York, 191–214.
Lara, J. 2004: Feathered Psalms: Old World Forms in a New World Garb. In H.W. Attridge and M.E. Fassler (eds.), *Psalms in Community: Jewish and Chirstian Textual, Liturgical, and Artistic Traditions*. Leiden: Brill, 293–312.
Lingas, A. 2004: Tradition and Renewal in Contemporary Greek Orthodox Psalmody. In H.W. Attridge and M.E. Fassler (eds.), *Psalms in Community. Jewish and Christian Textual, Liturgical, and Artistic Traditions*. Leiden: Brill, 341–358.
Menn, E.M. 2001: Praying King and Sanctuary of Prayer, Part I: David and the Temple. Origins in Rabbinic Psalms Commentary (Midrash Tehillim). *Journal of Jewish Studies*, 298–323.
Menn, E.M. 2004: Sweet Singer of Israel: David and the Psalms in Early Judaism. In H.W. Attridge and M.E. Fassler (eds.), *Psalms in Community. Jewish and Christian Textual, Liturgical, and Artistic Traditions*. Leiden: Brill, 61–74.

McKinnon, J.W. 1999: The Book of Psalms, Monasticism and the Western Liturgy. In N. van Deusen (ed.), *The Place of the Psalms in the Intellectual Culture of the Middle Ages*. Albany, NY: State University of New York Press, 43–58.

Metzger, T. 1977: Les Illustrations d'un Psautier Hébreu Italien de la fin du XIIIe siècle Le MS Parm. 1870 – De Rossi 501 de la Bibliotheque Palatine de Parma. *Cahiers Archéologiques* XXVI, 145–62.

Meyer, H. 1986: Der Psalter als Gattung in der Sicht der mittelalterlichen Bibelexegese. *Frühmittelalterliche Studien* 20, 1–24.

Narkiss, B. 1985: *Worms Mahzor: MS. Jewish National and University Library Heb. 4⁰ 781/1 /*. London: Distributor Cyelar Publishing Co Ltd.

Narkiss, B. 1996: *The Golden Haggadah*. London: British Library Publishing.

Nasuti, H.P. 1999: *Defining the Sacred Songs*, JSOTSup 218. Sheffield: Sheffield Academic Press.

Newman, B. 1988: *Symphonia: A Critical Edition of the "Symphonia armoniae celestium revelationum"*. Ithaca, NY: Cornell University Press.

Noel, N.W. 1995: *The Harley Psalter*. Cambridge: Cambridge University Press.

Nordström, C.O. 1967: *The Duke of Alba's Castilian Bible*, Acta Universitatis Upsaliensis – Figura Nova Series 5. Uppsala, Sweden: Almquist and Wiksell.

Openshaw, K.M. 1992: The Symbolic Illustration of the Psalter: An Insular Tradition. *Arte Medievale* NS 6, 41–60.

Pächt, O., Dodwell, C.R. and Wormald, F. 1960: *The St Albans Psalter (Albani Psalter)*. London: Warburg Institute.

Panayotova, S. 2005: *The Macclesfield Psalter*. Cambridge: Fitzwilliam Museum.

Rabinowitz, L. 1935–6: Does Midrach Tillim Reflect the Triennal Cycle of Psalms? *JQR* 26, 349–68.

Rosenthal, E.I.J. 1960: Anti-Christian Polemic in Medieval Bible Commentaries. *JJS* XI, 115–35.

Rosenthal, J.M. 1967: Anti-Christian Polemics in the Biblical Commentaries of Rashi. In J.M. Rosenthal (ed.), *Studies in Texts in Jewish History, Literature and Religion*, 2 vols. Jerusalem: Rubin Mass, 101–16.

Ryan, T.F. 2000: *Thomas Aquinas as Reader of the Psalms*. Notre Dame: Notre Dame Press.

Rzeczkowski, M. 1995: Thomas Aquinas' Commentary on the Psalms of David. In B.M. Ashley (ed.), *Thomas Aquinas, The Gifts of the Spirit: Selected Spiritual Writings*. Hyde Park, NY: New City Press, 95–133.

Sarna, N.M. 1971: Hebrew and Bible Studies in Medieval Spain. In R.D. Barnett and W.M. Schwab (eds.), *The Sephardi Heritage: Essays on the History and Cultural Contribution of the Jews of Spain and Portugal, Vol. 1: The Jews in Spain and Portugal Before and After the Expulsion of 1492*. New York: KTAV Publishing House.

Schiemenz, G.P. 1996: The Painted Psalms of Athos. In A. Bryer and M. Cunningham (eds.), *Mount Athos and Byzantine Monasticism*. London: Variorum, 223–36.

Signer, M. 2002: *Psalmody, Prophecy or History: The Context of the Psalter in the Exegesis of Rabbi Solomon ben Isaac of Troyes*. Yale Symposium Papers 2002. Yale: Yale University Press.

Simon, U. 1991: *Four Approaches to the Book of Psalms from Saadiah Gaon to Abraham ibn Ezra*. New York: State University of New York Press.

Smalley, B. 1983: *The Study of the Bible in the Middle Ages*. Oxford: Basil Blackwell.

Soltesz, E. 1967: *Biblia Pauperum. The Estergom Blockbook of Forty Leaves*. Budapest: Corvina.

Taft, R.F. 1991: Psalmody. In A. Kazhdan (ed.), *Oxford Dictionary of Byzantium*, New York: Oxford University Press.

Talmage, F.E. 1975: *David Kimchi: The Man and the Commentaries*, Harvard Judaic Monographs I. Cambridge, MA: Harvard University Press.
Van Der Horst K., Noel, N.W. and Wustefeld, W.C.M. 1996: *The Utrecht Psalter in Medieval Art. Picturing the Psalms of David*. London: Harvey Miller.
Van Deusen, N. and Colish, M.L. 1999: Ex utroque et in utroque: Promissa mundo gaudia, Electrum and the Sequence. In N. Van Deusen (ed.), *The Place of the Psalms in the Intellectual Culture of the Middle Ages*. Albany, NY: State University of New York, 105–38.
Webber, R. 2000: *The Prymer. The Prayer Book of the Mediaeval Era adapted for Contemporary Use*. Brewster, MA: Paraclete Press.
Wormald, F. 1973: *The Winchester Psalter*. New York: Graphic Society Greenwich Conn.
Yerushalmi, Y.H. 1974: *Leaves from the Oldest Illustrated Printed Haggadah*. Philadelphia: Cambridge University.

Chapter 4

PRIMARY SOURCES

Calvin, J., Anderson, J. tr. 1843–55, 1948–9: *Calvin's Commentaries: Psalms Vols 1–V*. Edinburgh: Calvin Translation Society; Grand Rapids, MI: W.B. Eerdmans.
Dillenberger, J. 1975: The Author's Preface to the Commentary on the Book of the Psalms. In J. Dillenberger (ed.), *John Calvin. Selections From His Writings*. Missoula, MT: Scholars Press.
Donne, J. 1971: The second of my Prebend Sermons upon my five Psalmes Preached at S. Pauls, January 29. 1625. In J.M. Mueller (ed.) *Donne's Prebend Sermons*. Cambridge MA: Harvard University Press, 91–111.
Erasmus, D. 1997: *Expositions of the Psalms*, Collected Works 63. Translated and annotated by M.J. Heath and edited by D. Baker-Smith. Toronto: University of Toronto Press.
Watts, I. 1816: *Psalms of David imitated in the language of the New Testament*. Derby: Hymry Mozeley.

SECONDARY SOURCES

Baldwin, E.C. 1919: Milton and the Psalms. *Modern Philology* 17.8, 457–63.
Black, C. 1985: Unity and diversity in Luther's biblical exegesis: Psalm 51 as a test-case. *Scottish Journal of Theology* 38 No. 3, 325–45.
Boddy, M. 1966: Milton's Translations of Psalms 80–88. *Modern Philology* 64.1, 1–9.
Cabaniss, A. 1985: The background of metrical psalmody. *Calvin Theological Journal* 20, 191–206.
Cabrol, F. 1934: *The Roman Missal*. New York: Kennedy.
Carbonnier-Burkard, M. 1997: Calvin lecteur des psaumes: L'anatomie de l'âme. *Bulletin de la Société de l'Histoire du Protestantisme Français* 143, 131–4.
De Jong, J.A. 1994: 'Anatomy of all parts of the Soul': Insights into Calvin's Spirituality from his Psalms Commentary. In W.H. Neusner (ed.), *Calvinus Sacrae Scripturae Professor: Calvin as Confessor of Holy Scripture*. Grand Rapids, MI: W.B. Eerdmans.
Doelman, J. 1993: George Wither, the Stationers Company and the English Psalter. *Studies in Philology* 90, 74–82.

Dorenkamp, J.H. 1972: The Bay Psalm Book and the Ainsworth Psalter. *Early American Literature* 7, 3–16.

Dubinski, R. 1986: Donne's Holy Sonnets and the Seven Penitential Psalms. *Renaissance and reformation/Renaissance et Reforme* 10 No. 2, 201–16.

Eire, C. 2004: Calvin's Geneva and the Psalms. In W. Attridge and M.E. Fassler (eds.), *Psalms in Community. Jewish and Christian Textual, Liturgical, and Artistic Traditions*. Leiden: Brill, 285–92.

Ellinwood, L. (ed.) 1971, 1974: *Thomas Tallis. English Sacred Music II, EECM 13*. London: Stainer and Bell; London: P. Doe.

Fisken, B.W. 1985: Mary Sidney's Psalmes: education and wisdom. In M.P Hannay (ed.), *Silent but for the Word*. Kent, Ohio: Kent State University Press.

Freer, C. 1972: *Music for a King: George Herbert's Style and the Metrical Psalms*. Baltimore & London: Johns Hopkins University Press.

Greene, R. 1990: Sir Philip Sidney's Psalms, the Sixteenth Century Psalter, and the Nature of Lyric. *Studies in English Literature* 30, 19–40.

Hale, J.K. 1994: Why did Milton Translate Psalms 80–88 in April 1648? In J.N. King (ed.), *The English Renaissance and Reformation: Literature, Politics and Religion*. Manchester: Manchester University Press, 55–62.

Hale, J.K. 1995: Milton's Sonnet 18 and Psalm 137. *Milton Quarterly* 29.3: 91.

Hamlin, H. 2004: *Psalm Culture and Early Modern Literature*. Cambridge: Cambridge University Press.

Hannay, M.P. 1991: 'Wisdome the wordes': psalm translation and Elizabethan women's spirituality. *Religion and Literature* 23, 65–82.

Hannay, M.P., Kinnamon, N.J. and Brennan, M.G. (eds.) 1998: *The Collected Works of Mary Sidney Herbert Countess of Pembroke, Vol 2: The Psalmes of David*. Oxford: Clarendon Press.

Hannay, M.P. 2001: 'So May I With the *Psalmist* Truly Say': Early Modern English Women's Psalm Discourse. In B. Smith and U. Appelt (eds.), *Write or Be Written: Early Modern Women Poets and Cultural Constraints*. Aldershot and Burlington, 105–27.

Hasler, R.A. 1965: Influence of David and the Psalms upon John Calvin's life and thought. *Hartford Quarterly, Newyears*, 7–18.

Heath, M.J. 1991: Allegory, Rhetoric and Spirituality: Erasmus's Early Psalm Commentaries. In A. Dalzell, C. Fantazzi and R.J. Schoeck (eds.), *Acta Conventus Neo-Latini Torontonensis*. Binghamton, NY: Medieval & Renaissance Texts & Studies, 363–70.

Hobbs, R.G. 1990: Hebraica veritas and traditio apostolica: Saint Paul and the Interpretation of the Psalms in the Sixteenth Century. In D.C. Steinmetz (ed.), *Bible in the Sixteenth Century*. Durham, NC; London: Duke University Press, 83–99.

Hull, J.M. 2002: From Experiential Educator to Nationalist Theologian: the Hymns of Isaac Watts. *Panorama: International Journal of Comparative Religious Education and Values* 14, 91–106.

Hunter, W.B. Milton Translates the Psalms. *Philological Quarterly* 40, 484–94.

Jacobson, J. 1988: The Choral Music of Salamone Rossi. *American Choral Review* XXX 110.4, 2–70.

Johnson, S. 2000: Sing unto the Lord a New Song. In *BBC Proms: 14 July – 9 September 2000 Programme*, 15–19.

Jones, S. 2004: 'Soul Anatomy': Calvin's Commentary on the Psalms. In H.W. Attridge and M.E. Fassler (eds.), *Psalms in Community. Jewish and Christian Textual, Liturgical, and Artistic Traditions*. Leiden and Boston: Brill, 265–84.

Kinnamon, N. 1981: Notes on the Psalms in Herbert's *The Temple*. *George Herbert Journal* 4/2, I, 10–29.

Knighton, T. 2005: Thomas Tallis c.1505–85: Nine Tunes for Archbishop Parker's Psalter (1567). In *BBC Proms: 15 July –10 September 2005*, 12–16.

Lara, J. 2004: Feathered Psalms: Old World Forms in a New World Garb. In H.W. Attridge and M.E. Fassler (eds.), *Psalms in Community: Jewish and Christian Textual, Liturgical, and Artistic Traditions*, Leiden: Brill, 293–312.

Mays, J.L. 1988: Calvin as an Exegete of the Psalms. *Calvin Studies IV*, 95–103.

Mays, J.L. 1990: Calvin's Commentary on the Psalms: the Preface as Introduction. In T. George, *John Calvin and the Church*. Louisville: Westminster, John Knox Press.

Meyer, U. 1997: *Biblical Quotation and Allusion in the Cantata Libretti of Johann Sebastian Bach*. Studies in Liturgical Musicology 5. London: Scarecrow Press.

Millar, P. 1949: *Four Centuries of Scottish Psalmody*. London & New York: Oxford University Press.

Pitkin, B. 1993: Imitation of David: David as a Paradigm for Faith in Calvin's Exegesis of the Psalms. *16th Century Journal* 24, 843–64.

Pratt, W.S. 1933: *The Significance of the Old French Psalter*. New York: The Hymn Society.

Pritchard, R.E. (ed.) 1992: *The Sidney Psalms*. Manchester: Carcanet Press.

Quinn, D.B. 1958: John Donne's Sermons on the Psalms and the Tradition of Biblical Exegesis. *DAI* 8/6, 21–31.

Radzinowicz, M.A. 1989: *Milton's Epics and the Book of Psalms*. Princeton: Princeton University Press.

Rathmell, J.C.A. (ed.) 1963: *The Psalms of Sir Philip Sidney and the Countess of Pembroke*. New York: New York University Press.

Reid, W.S. 1971: The Battle Hymns of the Lord: Calvinist Psalmody of the Sixteenth Century. In Carl S. Meyer (ed.), *Sixteenth Century Essays and Studies* Vol. 2. St Louis: The Foundation of Reformation Research, 36–54.

Rummel, E. (ed.) 1990: *The Erasmus Reader*. Toronto: University of Toronto Press.

Rupprecht, O.C. 1983: Timeless Treasure: Luther's Psalm Hymns. *Concordia Theological Quarterly* 47, 131–46.

Russell, S.H. 1968: Calvin and the messianic interpretation of the Psalms. *Scottish Journal of Theology* 21, 37–47.

Sessions, W.A. 1996: Surrey's Psalms in the Tower. In H. Wilcox, R. Todd and A. MacDonald (eds.), *Sacred and Profane: Secular and Devotional Interplay in Early Modern British Literature*. Amsterdam: VU University Press, 17–31.

Shaheen, N. 1999: *Biblical References in Shakespeare's Plays*. Newark, DE: University of Delaware Press.

Shepherd Jr., M.H. 1976: *The Psalms in Christian Worship: A Practical Guide*. Minneapolis: Aysbury.

Stackhouse, R.A. 1997: *The Language of the Psalms in Worship: American Revisions of Watt's Psalter*. London: Scarecrow Press.

Stallings, L.R. 1978: The Unpolished Altar: The Place of the Bay Psalm Book in American Culture. *DAI* 38, 6730A–31A.

Steinberg, T.L. 1995: The Sidneys and the Psalms. *Studies in Philology* 92, 1–17.

Steinmetz, D.C. 1980: Luther as an Interpreter of the Psalms. In D.C. Steinmetz, *Luther and Staupitz: An essay in the Intellectual Origins of the Protestant Reformation*. Durham, NC: Duke University Press, 50–67.

Swain, K.M. 1999: Contextualising Mary Sidney's Psalms. *Christianity and Literature* 48, 253–60.

Todd, R. 1987: 'So Well Attyr'd Abroad': A Background to the Sidney-Pembroke Psalter and Its Implications for the Seventeenth-Century Religious Lyric. *Texas Studies in Literature and Language* 29, 74–93.

Trill S. 1996a: 'Speaking to God in his phrase and word': Women's use of the Psalms in early modern England. In S.E. Porter (ed.), *Nature of Religious Language*. Sheffield: Sheffield Academic Press, 269–83.

Trill, S. 1996b: Sixteenth Century Women's Writing: Mary Sidney's *Psalmes* and the 'Femininity' of Translation. In W. Zunder and S. Trill (eds.), *Writing and the English Renaissance*. London: Longman, 140–58.

VanderWilt, J.T. 1995: John Calvin's Theology of Liturgical Song. *Christian Scholars Review* 25, no 1, 24–25.

Witvliet, J.D. 1997: The Spirituality of the Psalter: Metrical Psalms in Liturgy and Life in Calvin's Geneva. *Calvin Theological Journal 32*, 273–97.

Zim, R. 1981: *English Metrical Psalms: Poetry as Prose and Prayer 1535–1601*. Cambridge: Cambridge University Press.

Chapter 5

PRIMARY SOURCES

1655: John Eliot's *Indian Bible (Up-Biblum God)*. Cambridge, MA.

1903–11: *The Historical Catalogue of Printed Editions of Holy Scriptures in the Library of the British and Foreign Bible Society*. London: British and Foreign Bible Society.

SECONDARY SOURCES

Baethgen, F. 1892: *Die Psalmen*. Göttingen: HKAT.

Balla, E. 1912: *Das Ich der Psalmen*, FRLANT 16. Göttingen: Vandenhoeck & Ruprecht.

Barmann, L.F. 1964: Newman on the Psalms as Christian prayer. *Worship* 38, 207–14.

Benson, R.M. 1901: *The War Songs of the Prince of Peace*. London: John Murray.

Briggs, C.A. and E.G. 1906: *A Critical and Exegetical Commentary on The Book of Psalms*, Vol. I. Edinburgh: T. & T. Clark.

Briggs, C.A. & E.G. 1907: *A Critical and Exegetical Commentary on The Book of Psalms*, Vol. II. Edinburgh: T. & T. Clark.

Cheyne, T.K. 1891: *The Origin and Religious Contents of the Psalter in the Light of Old Testament Criticism and the History of Religions*, Bampton Lectures 1889. London: Kegan Paul, Trench Trübner & Co Ltd.

Davison, W.T. 1893: *The Praises of Israel: An Introduction to the Study of the Psalms*. London: Charles H. Kelly.

De Wette, W.M.L. 1811, 1823: *Commentar über die Psalmen*. Heidelberg.

Delitzsch, F. 1859–60: *Biblischer Commentar über die Psalmen*. Leipzig:Dörffling & Franke.

Delitzsch, F.(tr. F. Bolton) 1952, 1986: *Biblical Commentary on the Psalms*. Grand Rapids, MI: W.D. Eerdmans.

Dimmock, H. 1791: *Notes Critical and Explanatory on the Books of Psalms and Proverbs, intended to correct the grammatical errors of the text from the collations of the Mss. By Dr. Kennicott on the Psalms*. Gloucester: R. Raikes.

Driver, S. 1891, 2005: *Introduction to the Literature of the Old Testament*. Montana: Kessinger Publishing.
Duhm, B. 1899, 1922: *Die Psalmen*, KHAT XIV. Freiburg: J.C.B. Mohr.
Fischer, B. 1986: Eine Predigt Johann Henry Newmans aus dem Jahre 1840 zur Frage des christlichen Psalmenverständnisses. In Ernst Haag and Frank-Lothar Hossfeld (eds.), *Freude an der Weisung des Herrn*. Stuttgart: Verlag Katholisches Bibelwerk, 69–79.
Furness, H.W. 1898: *The Book of Psalms: A New English Translation (with explanatory notes and appendix by J. Wellhausen)*, The Polychrome Bible, 14. London: James Clark & Co.
Gunkel, H. 1904: *Ausgewählte Psalmen*. Göttingen.
Gunkel, H. 1913: Psalmen. In *Die Religion in Geschichte und Gegenwart*. Band IV, cols. 1927–49.
Hengstenberg, E.W. 1842–1849: *Commentar über die Psalmen*. Berlin: Ludwig Oehmigke.
Hengstenberg, E.W., tr. P. Fairbairn 1851: *A Commentary of the Psalms*. Edinburgh: T & T Clark.
Hupfeld, H. 1888: *Die Psalmen übersetzt und ausgelegt*. Bearbeitet von W. Nowack. Gotha: F.A. Perthes.
Keble, J. 1827: *The Christian Year*. Oxford: W. Baxter.
Keble, J. 1839: *The Psalter in English Verse*. London: Gresham Publishing Company.
Kirkpatrick, A.F. 1902: *The Book of Psalms*. Cambridge.
Kitto, J. 1845: *The Pictorial Sunday Book*. London.
Kitto, J. 1850: *Daily Bible Illustrations Vol V, Job and the Poetical Books,* Edinburgh.
Levi, D. 1789–93: *The Translation of the Hebrew Prayers and Services into English*. London.
Lowth, R. 1753: *De sacra poesi Hebraeorum* Oxford: Clarendon; E Tr by G. Gregory, *Lectures on the Sacred Poetry of the Hebrews,* J. Johnson, London, 1787; republished London: Routledge and Thoemmes Press 1995.
Meyer, F.B. 1910: *David – Shepherd, Psalmist, King*. London: Morgan and Scott.
Montgomery, J. 1822: *Songs of Zion, being Imitations of the Psalms*. London: Longman, Hurst, Rees, Orme and Brown.
Montgomery, J. 1828: *The Christian Psalmist*. Glasgow: Griffin.
Musgrave, M. 1996: *Brahms, A German Requiem*. Cambridge: Cambridge University Press.
Newman, J.H. 1865: *Dream of Gerontius*. London: Burns and Oates.
Olshausen, J. 1853: *Die Psalmen* (KHAT). Leipzig: S. Hirzel.
Payne, B. 1709, 1731: *The Parish Clerk's Guide*. London: John Marsh.
Rahlfs, A. 1892: *'Ani und 'Anau in den Psalmen*. Göttingen: Vandenhoeck & Ruprecht.
Rechter, D. 2002: Western and Central European Jewry in the Modern Period: 1750–1933. In M. Goodman (ed.), *The Oxford Handbook of Jewish* Studies. Oxford and New York: Oxford University Press, 376–411.
Ruskin, J: 1886–9: *Praeterita*, 3 vols. Orpington: G. Allen.
Smend, R. 1888: Über das Ich der Psalmen. *ZATW* 18, 49–147.
Spurgeon, C.H. 1860–67: *The Treasury of David, Containing an Original Exposition of the Book of Psalms,* 7 vols. London.
Spurgeon, C.H. 1887: *The Golden Alphabet ... being a Devotional Commentary upon the One Hundred and Nineteenth Psalm*. London.
Street, S. 1790: *A New Literary Version of the Book of Psalms of Dr. Kennicott 1772*. London: B. White & Son.
Wallace, T.H.S. (ed.) 2003: *Quakerpsalms – A Book of Devotions*. Malden, MA: New Foundation Fellowship.
Weintraub, Rabbi Simcha (ed.) 1994: *Healing of Soul, Healing of Body: Spiritual Leaders Unfold Strength and Solace in Psalms*. Woodstock, VT: Jewish Lights Publishing.

Chapter 6

PRIMARY SOURCES

(Full details of Bibles, Psalters and Hymn Books and Service Books are given on the website)
1943 *Divino afflante Spiritu* Encyclical Letter of His Holiness Pius XII on Biblical Studies and opportune ways of promoting them. [Dated: 30 Sept 1943] (Trans. Canon G.D. Smith). London: Catholic Truth Society.
1972: *Thesaurus:* Abbotts' Congress.

SECONDARY SOURCES

(Full details of the authors and titles referred to in the text of this chapter are included in the website)
Aejmelaeus, A. and Quast, U. (eds.) 2000: *Der Septuaginta-Psalter und seine Tochterübersetzungen*. Göttingen:Vandenhoeck & Ruprecht.
Allen, L. 1983, 2002: *Psalms 101–150*, Word Biblical Commentary 21. Nashville, TN: Thomas Nelson Publishers.
Alter, R. 1985, 1990: *The Art of Biblical Poetry*. New York; Basic Books; Edinburgh: T & T Clark.
Anderson, A.A. 1972: *The New Century Bible Commentary, Psalms 1–72*. Grand Rapids, MI: W.B. Eerdmans; London: Marshall, Morgan and Scott.
Auffret, P. 1979–81: Structure littéraire de l'Hymne à Sion de 11QPs^a XXII, 1–15. *RevQ* 10, 203–11.
Auffret, P. 1982: *La Sagesse a bâti sa maison: Études de structures littéraires dans l'Ancien Testament et spécialement dans les psaumes*. Göttingen: Vandenhoeck & Ruprecht.
Auffret, P. 1995: *Merveilles à nos yeux: étude structurelle de vingt psaumes dont celui de 1Ch 16, 8–36*. Berlin: Walter de Gruyter.
Balla, E. 1912: *Das Ich der Psalmen* (FRLANT 16). Göttingen: Vandenhoeck & Ruprecht.
Begrich, J. and Gunkel, H. 1933: *Introduction to the Psalms: the Genres of the Religious Lyric of Israel*, tr. J.D. Nogalski in 1988. Macon, GA: Mercer University Press.
Berlin, A. 1985: *The Dynamics of Biblical Parallelism*. Bloomington, IN: Indiana University Press.
Birkeland, H. 1955: *The Evildoers in the Book of Psalms*. Oslo: I kommisjon hos J. Dybwad.
Bonhoeffer, D., tr. J.W. Doberstein 1954: The Secret of the Psalter. In *Life Together*. San Francisco: Harper & Row, 45–7.
Bonhoeffer, D. 1970: *The Psalms. Prayer Book of the Bible*. Minneapolis: Augsburg Publishing House.
Bonnard, P. 1960: *Le Psautier selon Jérémie: influence littéraire et spirituelle de Jérémie sur trente-trois psaumes*. Paris: Éditions du Cerf.
Bratcher, R.G. and Reyburn, W.D. (eds.) 1991: *A Translator's Handbook on the Psalms*. New York: United Bible Society.
Brook, J. 2001: *Arthur Wragg, Twentieth-Century Artist, Prophet and Jester*. Bristol: Sansom and Company.
Brooke, G.J 1989–90: Psalms 105 and 106 at Qumran. *Rev Q* 14, 267–92.

Brueggemann, W. and Miller, P.D. (eds.) 1995: *The Psalms and the Life of Faith*. Minneapolis: Fortress Press.
Buttenweiser, M. 1938, 1969: *The Psalms. Chronologically Arranged with a New Translation.* New York: KTAV.
Carmignac, J. 1961: Interprétation du Psaume 37 (4 Q Ps 37). In J. Carmignac (ed.), *Les Textes de Qumran traduits et annotés*. Paris: Lerouzay et Ane W11, 119–26.
Casey, M. 1994: The Prayer of Psalmody. In *The Undivided Heart: The Western Monastic Approach to Contemplation*. Petersham, MA: St Bedes Publications, 79–94.
Childs, B. 1971: Psalm Titles and Midrashic Exegesis. *Journal of Semitic Studies* XVI, 137–50.
Church, J.R. 1990: *Hidden Prophecies in the Psalms*. West Jefferson, NC: Cliffside Publishing House.
Clements, R.E. 1983: Interpreting the Psalms. In R.E. Clements (ed.) *A Century of Old Testament Study*. Guildford: Lutterworth Press, 76–98.
Clifford, R.J. 2005: What Kind of Psalter do we want in the New Lectionary? *Worship* 79, 258–62.
Clifford, R.J. 2002: *Psalms 1–72*. Nashville, TN: Abingdon Press; Edinburgh: Alban Press.
Clifford, R.J. 2003: *Psalms 73–150*. Nashville, TN: Abingdon Press; Edinburgh: Alban Press.
Clifford, R.J. 2004: Texts and Translations in Tension. In H.W. Attridge and M.E. Fassler (eds.) *Psalms and Community. Jewish and Christian Textual, Liturgical, and Artistic Traditions*. Leiden and Boston: Brill, 359–64.
Coggan, D. 1998: *Psalms 1–71*. Oxford: Bible Reading Fellowship.
Coggan, D. 1999: *Psalms 73–150*. Oxford: Bible Reading Fellowship.
Craigie, P.C. 1983: *Psalms 1–50*, Word Biblical Commentary 19. Waco, TX: Word Books.
Crenshaw, J.L. 2001: *The Psalms. An Introduction*. Grand Rapids, MI: W.B. Eerdmans.
Dahmen, U. (ed.) 2003: *Psalmen- und Psalter-Rezeption im Frühjudentum: Rekonstruktion, Textbestand, Struktur und Pragmatik der Psalmenrolleb 11Qpsa aus Qumran*. Leiden: Brill.
Dahood, M. 1966: *Psalms I: 1–50. Introduction, Translation, and Notes*. The Anchor Bible 16. New York: Doubleday.
Dahood, M. 1968: *Psalms II: 51–100. Introduction, Translation, and Notes*. The Anchor Bible 17. New York: Doubleday.
Dahood, M. 1970: *Psalms III: 101–150. Introduction, Translation, and Notes*. The Anchor Bible 17A. New York: Doubleday.
Davison, W.T. 1893: *The Praises of Israel: An Introduction to the Study of the Psalms*. London: Charles H. Kelly.
Drillock, D. 1997: Liturgical Song in the Worship of the Church. *St. Vladimir's Theological Quarterly* 41, 183–218.
Driver, S.R. 1915: *Studies in the Psalms*. London and New York: Hodder and Stoughton.
Eaton, J.H. 1995: *Psalms of the Way and the Kingdom: a Conference with the Commentators*. Sheffield: Sheffield Academic Press.
Endres, J.C. 2002: Psalms and Spirituality in the 21st Century. *Interpretation* 56, 143–54.
Field, A.M. (ed.) 2001: *The Monastic Hours. Directory for the Celebration of the Work of God and Directive Norms for the Celebration of the Monastic Liturgy of Hours*. Collegeville, MN: The Liturgical Press.
Fischer, N. 2003: *Opening to You: Zen-Inspired Translations of the Psalms*. London: Penguin Books.
Flint, P.W. 1997: *The Dead Sea Scrolls and the Book of Psalms*. New York, Leiden & Köln: Brill.

Flint, P.W. and Miller, P.D. (eds.) 2005: *The Book of Psalms. Composition and Reception* (SVT XCIX/IV). Leiden and Boston: Brill.

Foray, J.M. and Rossini-Paquet, F. 2000: *Message Biblique Marc Chagall*. Paris: Éditions de la Réunion des musées nationaux.

Foster, P. (ed.) 2002: *Chagall Glass at Chichester and Tudeley*. Otter Memorial Paper 14, University College, Chichester.

Freedman, N. 1980: *Pottery, Poetry, Prophecy: Studies in early Hebrew Poetry*. Winona Lake: Eisenbrauns.

Frost, D. 1981: *Making the Liturgical Psalter*, The Morpeth Lectures 1980, Grove Liturgical Study 25. Bramcote, Notts: Grove Books.

Gelston, A. 1975: Psalms at the Daily Services. *Churchman* 89, 267–75.

Gerstenberger, E.S. 1988: *Psalms. Part 1, with an Introduction to Cultic Poetry*. Grand Rapids, MI and Cambridge: W.B. Eerdmans.

Gerstenberger, E.S. 2001: *Psalms, Part 2, and Lamentations*. Grand Rapids, MI and Cambridge: W.B. Eerdmans.

Gillingham, S. 1994: *The Poems and Psalms of the Hebrew Bible*. Oxford: Oxford University Press.

Gillingham, S. 2005: The Zion Tradition and the Editing of the Hebrew Psalter. In J. Day (ed.), *Temple and Worship in Biblical Israel*, London: T&T Clark, 308–41.

Gillingham, S. 2006: Power and Powerlessness in the Psalms. In P.McCosker (ed.), *What is it that Scripture Says? Essays in Biblical Interpretation, Translation and Reception in Honour of Henry Wansborough*. London: T&T Clark, 25–49.

Girard, M. 1994–6: *Les Psaumes redécouverts: de la structure au sens*, 2e éd. rev et corr. Saint-Laurent, Québec: Bellarmin.

Girard, M. 1984: *Les Psaumes: Analyse structurelle et interprétation. 1–50*, Recherches Nouvelle Série, 2. Montreal: Éditions Bellarmin; Paris: Cerf.

Griffiths, B. and Roper, R. (eds.) 1996: *Psalms for Christian Prayer*. London: Harper Collins/Fount.

Hawkins, P.S. 2004: Singing a New Song: The Poetic Afterlife of the Psalms. In H.W. Attridge and M.E. Fassler (eds.) *Psalms in Community: Jewish and Christian Textual, Liturgical. And Artistic Traditions*. Leiden & Boston: Brill, 381–94.

Hiebert, R.J.V., Cox, C.E. and Gentry, P.J. (eds.) 2001: *The Old Greek Psalter: Studies in Honour of Albert Pietersma*, JSOT Sup 332. Sheffield: Sheffield Academic Press.

Hossfeld, F.L. and Zenger, E. 1993: *Die Psalmen 1–50*, NEB. Würzburg: Echter and HThKAT; Freiburg, Basel & Wien: Herder.

Hossfeld, F.L. and Zenger, E. 2000: *Die Psalmen 51–100*, NEB. Würzburg: Echter and HThKAT; Freiburg, Basel & Wien: Herder.

Hossfeld, F.L. and Zenger, E. 1998: *Der Psalter in Judentum und Christentum*, HBS 18. Freiburg, New York: Herder.

Hossfeld, F.L. and Zenger, E. 2005: *Psalms 2: Hermeneia – A Critical and Historical Commentary on the Bible*. Minneapolis: Augsburg Fortress.

Hunter, A.G. 1999: *Psalms, Old Testament Readings*. London and New York: Routledge.

Jackson, G. 1997: *The Lincoln Psalter*. Manchester: Carcanet.

Jasper, R.C.D. 1968: *The Daily Office*. London: SPCK & Epworth Press.

Jessing, M. 2001: *The Book of Psalms*. Peebles: published by author.

Johnson P. and Firth D. (eds.) 2005: *Interpreting the Psalms. Issues and Approaches*. Leicester: IVP.

Johnson, A.R. 1955: *Sacral Kingship in ancient Israel*. Cardiff: University of Wales.

Johnson, M.E. (ed.) 2005: *Benedictine Daily Prayer. A Short Breviary.* Collegeville, MN: Liturgical Press.
Keel, O. tr. T. J. Hallett 1978: *The Symbolism of the Biblical World.* London: SPCK.
Kittel, R. 1905: *Die Psalmen übersetzt und erklärt*, KAT XIII. Leipzig: A. Deichert.
Kraus, H.-J. 1986: *Theology of the Psalms.* Minneapolis: Augsburg Publishing House and London: SPCK.
Kraus, H.-J., tr. H.C. Oswald 1988: *Psalms 1–59: A Commentary.* Minneapolis: Augsburg.
Kraus, H.-J., tr. H.C. Oswald 1989: *Psalms 60–150: A Commentary.* Minneapolis: Augsburg.
Kugel, J. 1981: *The Idea of Biblical Poetry.* Yale: Yale University Press.
Lathrop, G. 2004: Texts in Tension: Translations for Contemporary Worship. In H.W. Attridge and M.E. Fassler (eds.), *Psalms in Community. Jewish and Christian Textual, Liturgical, and Artistic Traditions.* Leiden: Brill, 373–8.
Leaver, R. (ed.) 1984: *Ways of Singing the Psalms.* London: Collins.
Lewis, C.S. 1958: *Reflections on the Psalms.* London: G. Bles.
Lingas, A. 2004: Tradition and Renewal in Contemporary Greek Orthodox Psalmody. In H.W. Attridge and M.E. Fassler (eds.), *Psalms in Community. Jewish and Christian Textual, Liturgical, and Artistic Traditions.* Leiden: Brill, 341–56.
Lohfink, N.1992: Psalmengebet und Psalterredaktion. *ALW* 34, 1–22.
Löhr, M. 1922: *Psalmenstudien.* Berlin: W. Kohlhammer.
Martin, R. 1995: Roger Wagner's Visionary Landscapes. *Image* 10.
Mays, J. 1994: *Psalms.* Louisville: John Knox Press.
Merton, T. 1956: *Praying the Psalms.* London: Sheldon Press.
Miller, P.D. 1994: 'Dietrich Bonhoeffer and the Psalms'. *Princeton Seminary Bulletin*, ns 15, no. 3, 135–37.
Mowinckel, S. 1951 (tr. A.P. Thomas 1962, 1982): *The Psalms in Israel's Worship.* Oxford: Basil Blackwell.
Mulder, M.J. and Dirksen, P.B. (eds.) 1988: *The Peshitta: its Early Text and History: Papers read at the Peshitta Symposium held at Leiden 30–31 August 1985.* Leiden: Brill.
Murray, A.G. 1966: Gelineau Psalmody. In *The Psalms: A New Translation arranged for Singing.* London: Collins.
Murrell, N.S. 2000: Tuning Hebrew Psalms to Reggae Rhythms: Rastas' Revolutionary Lamentations for Social Change. *Cross Currents* 50, 252–40.
Nowell, I. 1993: *Sing a New Song: The Psalms in the Sunday Lectionary.* Collegeville, MN: Liturgical Press.
Oesterley, W.O.E. 1939: *The Psalms.* London: SPCK.
Osherow, J. 1999: *Dead Men's Praise.* New York: Grove Press.
Pietersma, A. 2000: *The New Translation of the Septuagint: The Psalms.* Oxford: Oxford University Press.
Podechard, E. 1949: *Le Psautier: traduction littérale et explication historique.* Lyon: Facultés Catholiques.
Ramshaw, G. and Lathrop, G. (eds.) 1993: *Psalter for the Christian People: An Inclusive Revision of the Psalter of the Book of Common Prayer 1979.* Collegeville, MN: Liturgical Press.
Rienstra, M.V. 1992: *Swallow's Nest: A Feminine Reading of the Psalms.* Grand Rapids, MI: W.B. Eerdmans.
Ringgren, H. 1963: *The Faith of the Psalmists.* London: SCM Press.
Rodd, C. 1963: *Psalms 1–72.* London: Epworth Press.
Rodd, C. 1964: *Psalms 73–150.* London: Epworth Press.

Rosenberg, D. 1976: *Blues of the Sky*. New York: Harper and Row.
Schokel, A. 1988: *A Manual of Hebrew Poetics*. Roma: Pontificio Istituto Biblico.
Shepherd, Jr. M.H. 1976: *The Psalms in Christian Worship: A Practical Guide*. Minneapolis: Aysbury.
Skehan, P. 1975: 'Jubilees' and the Qumran Psalter. *CBQ* 37, 343–47.
Stuhlmueller, C. 1983: *Psalms 1. Psalms 1–72*. Wilmington: Michael Glazier.
Stuhlmueller, C. 1983: *Psalms 1. Psalms 73–150*. Wilmington: Michael Glazier.
Talmon, S. 1989: Extra-Canonical Psalms from Qumran – Psalm 151. In *The World of Qumran from Within. Collected Studies*. Jerusalem-Leiden, 244–72.
Tate, M. 1990: *Psalms 51–100*, Word Biblical Commentary 20. Dallas, TX: Word Books.
Terrien, S. 2003: *The Psalms: Strophic Structure and Theological Commentary*. Grand Rapids, MI: William B. Eerdmans.
Tov, E. 1996: Special Layout of Poetical Units in the Texts from the Judean Desert. In J. Dyk (ed.), *Give Ear to my Words. Psalms and Poetry in and around the Hebrew Bible, Festschrift N.A. van Uchelen*. Amsterdam, 115–28.
Wagner, R. 1988: *In a Strange Land*. Oxford: The Besalel Press.
Wagner, R. 1994: *The Book of Praises*, Vol. I (Psalms 1–41). Oxford: The Besalel Press.
Weiser, A. (tr. H. Hartwell) 1962: *The Psalms: A Commentary*. London: SCM.
Whybray, N. 1996: *Reading the Psalms as a Book*, JSOTSup, 222. Sheffield: Sheffield Academic Press.
Widengren, G. 1937: *Hebrew and Accadian Psalms of Lamentations as Religious Documents*. Stockholm: Aktiebolaget Thule.
Willems, G.F. 1990: Les Psaumes dans la liturgie juive. *Bijdragen* 51 394–417.
Wragg, A. 1934: *The Psalms for Modern Life*. New York: Claude Kendall.
Yadin, Y. 1966: Another Fragment (E) of the Psalms Scroll from Qumran Cave 11 (11 Q Ps[a]). *Textus* 5, 1–10.
Zenger, E. 1994: New Approaches to the Study of the Psalms. *PIBA* 17, 37–54.

Index of Psalms

1	7, 9, 24, 26, 27, 30, 34, 36, 37, 40, 50, 52, 54, 56, 63, 64, 65, 67, 82, 86, 90, 92, 95, 97, 98, 99, 116, 117, 133, 134, 137, 138, 148, 152, 154, 179, 180, 182, 184, 200, 218, 229, 248, 252, 261, 265, 276, 277, 278, 281, 283, 286, 293, 295, 311	2	5, 7, 12, 16, 17, 18, 22, 23, 24, 27, 29, 32, 33, 40, 44, 53, 56, 57, 82, 84, 86, 86, 90, 95, 133, 134, 139, 145, 154, 169, 179, 182, 198, 200, 201, 211, 222, 255, 270, 278, 281, 283, 305, 311
		2:1	10, 20, 23, 188, 249
		2:2	20, 23, 188, 249
		2:3	188, 249
1:1	10, 16, 99, 116, 124, 125, 126, 248, 252, 261	2:4	188
		2:6	134
1:2	10, 116, 126	2:7	14, 15, 17, 18, 20, 22, 23, 31, 84, 86, 129
1:3	65, 176		

Index of Psalms

2:8	23, 39, 116, 123, 129, 157, 173		258, 261, 268, 270, 281, 293, 295, 311
2:9	23, 157, 188	8:1	60, 128, 232
2:10–12	12, 60	8:2	17, 128
		8:4	248, 249, 250, 251
3	7, 29, 30, 52, 53, 71, 133, 139, 142, 179, 189, 200, 264, 278, 292	8:5	253, 254
		8:6	22, 253
		8:7	21, 253
3:3	60, 118	8:8	253
3:4	116	8:9	253
3:5	26		
3:7	60	9	8, 184, 253
		9:1	118
4	53, 71, 117, 133, 134, 179, 183, 200, 212, 270, 293	9:2	60
		9:3	118
4:1	60, 177	9:10	116
4:2	60	9:14	122
4:3	60	9:21	115
4:7	116		
4:9–10	148	10	8, 222
		10:1	115
5	9, 52, 71, 179, 182, 200, 222, 255	10:7	20
		10:12	116
5:2	177		
5:3	116	11	29, 57, 116, 255
5:5	118	11:3	175
5:7	70, 109	11:7	60
5:8	60		
5:9	20	12	29, 38, 44, 57, 171, 195
		12:1	60
6	39, 55, 57, 62, 103, 113, 114, 138, 154, 169, 179, 187, 200, 209, 222, 255	12:6	173
		13	62, 103, 186, 302
6:1–4	60	13:2–6	60
6:3	116	13:3	177
6:10	17	13:5–6	109
7	7, 44, 71, 169, 179, 236, 255	14	187, 255
7:1	177	14:1–2	20
7:1–2	60		
7:3	116	15	7, 30, 52, 53, 65, 134, 154, 182, 200, 202, 278
7:7–9	10		
7:8	116	15:1	30, 126
		15:2	126
8	3, 4, 8, 21, 22, 24, 32, 33, 40, 44, 53, 57, 68, 90, 92, 103, 118, 154, 179, 180, 184, 189, 210, 223, 224, 238, 252, 253,	15:5	65
		16	55, 87, 222, 237, 264
		16:8	249

Index of Psalms

16:8–11	20	22:17–18	18
16:10	20, 29, 31, 64, 188	22:18	19
16:11	18, 249	22:19	17
		22:20	145
17	62, 255, 290	22:27	109
17:1	109, 110	22:28	109
17:8	173		
17:13	119, 136	23	1, 26, 27, 44, 55, 134, 144, 150, 153, 169, 173, 177, 187, 224, 227, 376, 264, 266, 295, 298, 299, 305
17:15	227		
18	7, 70, 145, 169, 255, 269, 270, 277, 281, 292, 306		
		23:1–2	231
18:3	109, 110	23:4	126
18:35–38	145	23:5	72
18:43	36		
18:49	21	24	26, 27, 29, 45, 103, 154, 156, 182, 200, 202, 215, 222, 227, 236, 239, 240, 264
19	38, 44, 70, 86, 87, 90, 103, 143, 154, 161, 169, 206, 210, 211, 236, 269, 270, 277, 306		
		24:3	119
		24:7–8	25
		24:7–10	49, 178, 188
19:1–6	203		
19:2	118	25	62, 114, 142, 181, 222, 270, 293
19:4	21, 26, 129, 161		
19:8	216	25:1–6	67, 68
19:14	70	25:5	118, 119
		25:14	119
20	144, 145, 201, 269	25:16	262
21	52, 116, 154, 162, 201, 269, 255	26	31, 44, 49, 53, 63, 97
		26:5–8	221
21:5	25	26:8	70, 71, 109
22	10, 14, 16, 17, 19, 24, 25, 26, 29, 32, 33, 39, 44, 53, 55, 57, 62, 84, 87, 90, 101, 102, 103, 115, 154, 184, 211, 222, 290, 298, 305, 306	27	64, 97, 189, 257, 264, 291, 301
		27:1	115, 151
		27:4	109, 118
22:1	11, 16, 17, 18, 19, 288	28	49, 255
22:4–9	14	28:2	109, 110
22:6	16, 248		
22:7	16, 188	29	5, 32, 33, 134, 264, 270, 273
22:8	16, 188	29:2	109
22:9	17	29:3	30
22:14–15	10	29:9	175
22:15	173		
22:15–17	14	30	7, 33, 44, 54, 57, 62, 169, 236, 264
22:16–18	19, 25, 65		

354 Index of Psalms

30:1	109	38	55, 57, 62, 97, 103, 113, 114, 138, 154
30:3	31	38:13–14	303
31	55, 63, 116, 181, 222, 293	38:15	177
31:1–5	103	39	64, 97, 134, 227, 264, 290
31:2	119	39:2–4	303
31:3	119	39:4–7	223
31:5	18, 212, 224	39:5	173
31:6	119		
31:10	216	40	154, 302
31:13–15	288	40:3	207
31:19	13	40:4	248
31:22–24	221	40:6	8
		40:7	269
32	55, 57, 62, 103, 113, 114, 138, 143, 154, 237, 283	40:7–9	22
32:1–2	20	41	16, 17, 116, 237, 302
32:2	248	41:9	10, 16, 19
32:10	136	41:12–16	221
33	33, 38, 44, 70, 236, 238, 270, 298	42	7, 16, 17, 62, 82, 99, 182, 188, 207, 222, 237, 257, 278, 282, 285, 297, 299
34	7, 24, 25, 26, 49, 52, 53, 62, 70, 71, 134, 153, 184, 205, 207, 236, 248, 252, 253, 261, 299, 306	42:3	127
		42:5	16, 18
		42:11	16, 136
34:1–6	25, 285	43	17, 52, 103, 207, 222
34:3	44	43:5	16
34:6	247, 250, 251		
34:7	254	44	62, 169, 255, 288, 299
34:8	22, 247, 251, 298	44:1–4	273
34:10	216	44:23	65
34:12–16	22		
34:13	22, 70	45	10, 24, 25, 26, 28, 29, 32, 33, 40, 44, 57, 86, 154, 189, 198, 201, 203, 207, 210, 211, 253, 269, 281, 284
34:20	22		
35	57, 90, 115, 255		
35:1–4	303	45:6	22, 25, 30, 86
		45:6–9	19
36	52, 142	45:7	22, 26
36:1	20	45:8	30
36:7–10	44		
		46	5, 82, 140, 142, 143, 156, 173, 186, 218, 227, 229, 259, 281
37	10, 269, 289		
37:11	11	46:1	173
37:12	157	46:5	187
37:25	289	46:11	173

47	7, 29, 44, 82, 154, 160, 161, 181, 182, 184, 186, 264, 270, 271, 281, 298, 299	56	29, 307
		56:4	182
47:8–9	273	56:11	182
		57	29, 52, 62, 154, 176, 184, 227, 292
48	5, 45, 154, 212, 225, 236, 238, 264, 281, 290	57:1–11	277
48:2	288	57:2	184
48:2–3	173	57:4	119
		57:7–10	176
49	68, 269		
		58	255
50	39, 97, 270	58:1	157
50:1–6	221		
		59	237, 255, 292, 307
51	7, 11, 29, 31, 40, 41, 44, 51, 52, 53, 54, 55, 57, 62, 64, 65, 71, 103, 113, 114, 116, 126, 138, 139, 142, 170, 181, 184, 187, 213, 214, 222, 223, 272, 272, 276, 284, 286, 292, 302	59:16–17	176
		60	10, 102, 160, 255
		60:5–12	277
		61	116
		61:2	109, 184
		61:6–8	221
51:3	114	61:8	176
51:4	20		
51:7	173	62:1	110
51:15	154, 175	62:13	16, 20
51:18	288		
51:18–19	82, 269	63	40, 50, 52, 53, 62, 71, 103, 255, 263
51:33–34	170		
		63:5	41
52	63, 97, 118, 182, 292		
52:8	109, 110, 176	64	40, 52, 62
53	36	65	52, 171, 189
53:1	20, 118	65:5–13	109
53:2	20		
53:6	288	66	183, 222
		66:4	109
54	29, 62, 154, 182, 184, 255, 292, 302		
		67	52, 53, 62, 71, 103, 109, 122, 160, 182, 187, 229, 255
55	57, 62, 68, 182, 184, 222, 255, 284, 301	67:5	58
55:3	303	68	5, 10, 26, 44, 53, 57, 97, 154, 156, 182, 186, 200, 212, 224, 255, 299
55:5–6	184		
55:9	303		
55:11	92, 303	68:1	157

Index of Psalms

68:4	303	78	19, 69, 72, 82, 101, 188, 200, 255, 270, 294, 295
68:5	249		
68:7–10	273	78:1–2	28
68:18	22, 29, 188	78:2	17
68:19	11	78:2–3	12
68:20	175	78:16	19
68:31	135	78:20	19
68:35	109	78:23–24	72
		78:24–25	19
69	9, 14, 16, 17, 19, 24, 26, 29, 44, 53, 54, 62, 69, 154, 211, 255	79	5, 82, 91, 97, 111, 255, 270
		79:2	12
69:1–2	174	79:2–3	12
69:8	19	79:8–10	181
69:9	19, 21		
69:13	70, 71, 109	80	5, 97, 99, 166, 178, 179, 180
69:13–17	221	80:3	118
69:21	10, 16, 18, 19, 67, 188	80:8–9	179
69:25	20	80:15	248
69:31	269		
		81	8, 44, 45, 64, 82, 97, 116, 200, 236, 238, 264, 270, 283, 299, 300
70	53, 62, 255, 270		
70:1	154, 190		
70:21	52		
		82	5, 19, 44, 53, 236, 238, 264, 270, 281
71	62, 116		
		82:1	26, 202
72	5, 29, 40, 44, 63, 85, 87, 100, 145, 159, 189, 198, 201, 203, 211, 218, 229, 262, 269, 278, 281	82:1–2	10
		82:6	19
72:8–11	85	83	55, 255
		83:11–18	157
73	269, 278		
73:4–5	174	84	8, 62, 82, 109, 134, 166, 172, 182, 223, 229, 236, 298
73:17	109, 110		
		84:1–3	109
74	5, 270, 281, 289	84:4	70, 71
74:8–11	283	84:9–10	299
74:12	65	84:10	299
74:13–14	202, 273	84:12	248
		85	126, 154
75	154, 161, 162, 255	85:21–22	170
76	52, 82, 170	86	62, 134, 187, 189, 222
		86:6	109, 110
77	5, 237	86:7	177

86:8–10	23	94	45, 91, 236, 238, 264
86:9	19	94:11	21
86:16	248	94:12	248
		94:15	136
87	29, 200, 208, 209, 212, 283		
87:2	288	95	7, 52, 53, 71, 103, 137, 182, 222, 224, 236, 239, 255, 256, 260, 264, 270, 271, 281, 300, 302
87:3	38		
87:6	118		
88	29, 52, 55, 154, 222	95:1	23, 109, 175, 299
88:2	109, 110	95:2	21
88:4–13	18	95:3	21
88:13	109	95:4	291
		95:5	21
89	5, 12, 44, 53, 82, 84, 87, 154, 198, 203, 208, 255, 269, 270, 277, 278, 281	95:6	70, 109
		95:7–11	21
		95:11	21
89:2	262		
89:4–5	20, 21	96	7, 26, 186, 205, 227, 237, 270, 271, 281, 301, 302
89:6–7	202		
89:10–11	273	96:9	109
89:16	249	96:12	291
89:19	36		
89:21	20	97	7, 97, 189, 270, 271, 281, 300
89:49	278		
		97:7	22
90	7, 40, 44, 52, 70, 159, 171, 195, 212, 223, 224, 229, 236, 237, 257, 272, 277, 278, 281, 298, 302	98	7, 44, 64, 97, 159, 185, 222, 255, 270, 271, 281
90:13	118	99	7, 270, 271, 281
		99:1	109
91	44, 53, 70, 71, 116, 156, 222, 236, 278	99:2	288
		99:5	109
91:11	26		
91:11–12	29	100	44, 49, 70, 97, 103, 109, 122, 149, 160, 170, 182, 185, 206, 222, 229, 236, 239, 240, 255, 256, 270, 298, 299, 300, 301, 302, 305
92	44, 45, 52, 70, 166, 170, 224, 236, 238, 239, 240, 264		
92:9	274	100:1	64, 175, 299, 305
92:12	176	100:1–2	109
		100:3	181
93	7, 44, 45, 50, 70, 103, 122, 222, 236, 238, 239, 240, 270, 271, 273, 278, 281	100:4	215
		101	9, 38, 54, 65, 116, 255, 279
93:1–2	273	101:1–8	9

102	11, 55, 57, 62, 44, 82, 97, 101, 103, 113, 114, 138, 154, 184, 189	110:2	82
		110:4	22
102:1–2	9	111	109, 116, 154, 205, 225, 239, 270
102:2	109, 110		
102:6	102		
102:7	101	112	44, 70, 71, 99, 111, 190, 225, 269
102:12–13	109		
102:16	288	112:1	248
102:21	288	112:9	21, 99
102:25–27	22		
		113	49, 112, 154, 184, 188, 225
103	44, 62, 101, 142, 187, 205, 236	113:1	113
		113:9	221
103:13	249		
103:15–17	239	114	8, 112, 142, 154, 168, 170, 178, 179, 182, 190, 222, 293, 306
104	44, 95, 101, 154, 171, 176, 203, 206, 215, 222, 238, 270, 281, 302	114:1	113
		115	8, 161, 222, 236, 277, 306
104:4	22	115:4–7	12
104:6	176		
104:12	17	116	8, 55, 257,
104:17	101	116:1–4	301
		116:3	65
105	69, 188, 189, 200, 237, 255	116:7–9	301
105:1–5	70, 270	116:8	65, 119
		116:10	21
106	69, 82, 99, 101, 188, 255, 270	116:13	65
		116:19	189
107	154, 161, 271, 278, 297	117	158, 170, 187, 190, 225, 302
107:7	209	117:1	21, 103, 262
108	72, 154, 222, 277, 291	118	15, 16, 17, 18, 19, 22, 24, 40, 44, 52, 53, 71, 103, 154, 156, 257, 307
108:2	305		
109	9, 57, 97, 115, 255, 284	118:1	14, 157
109:18	20	118:6	123
		118:15	14
110	5, 15, 16, 17, 18, 19, 22, 24, 25, 27, 28, 29, 32, 33, 40, 44, 45, 53, 57, 64, 86, 97, 99, 154, 184, 188, 190, 203, 210, 211, 218, 225, 268, 270, 278, 281	118:16	14
		118:19–24	212
		118:20	14, 163
		118:22	18, 19, 20
		118:22–23	17, 22
		118:24	186, 188
110:1	16, 17, 18, 20, 21, 22, 25, 86	118:25–26	15
		118:26	14, 17, 18, 19

118:27	14	129	103
118:41	19	129:7–8	10
119	26, 37, 38, 40, 52, 53, 54, 55, 60, 61, 62, 82, 86, 103, 108, 117, 139, 144, 154, 182, 184, 185, 211, 214, 228, 255, 269, 283	130	36, 44, 55, 57, 62, 103, 109, 113, 114, 138, 142, 154, 171, 181, 183, 207, 215, 227, 264, 302, 305
119:9	181	131	103, 116, 117, 305
119:12a	44		
119:49–64	181	132	5, 12, 26, 44, 49, 53, 109, 154, 200, 269, 278
119:54	186		
119:153–154	70	132:7	109
119:158	208	132:11	20
119:164	41	132:13–14	288
		132:17	26
120	7, 44, 53, 55, 103, 129, 255, 281		
		133	109, 305, 306
		133:1	110
121	44, 103, 109, 116, 166, 171, 187, 222, 228, 257, 299, 302	134	44, 53, 71, 201, 236, 239, 240, 255
121:1	110		
122	103, 184, 189, 227, 288, 299	135	44, 69, 70, 71, 161, 184, 201, 236, 255, 277
122:2–7	288		
122:3–5	109	135:19	162
122:6–9	109	135:21	288
123	103, 117	136	44, 69, 70, 176, 178, 179, 187, 206, 236, 255
123:3	262		
124	103, 156, 187, 229	137	5, 36, 60, 74, 82, 106, 107, 115, 142, 162, 165, 171, 187, 198, 221, 237, 255, 288, 296, 298, 299, 300, 303, 306, 308
124:1	117, 157		
125	103, 170, 283		
125:1	288		
		137:2	173
126	103, 171, 195, 238, 306	137:5–7	288
126:2	215		
126:3	215	138	29
126:5–6	223	138:1	109
		138:2	109
127	14, 103, 184, 187, 188, 190, 229, 269		
		139	38, 55, 154, 189, 255, 257, 262, 264, 269
128	103, 127, 166, 184, 222, 229, 257, 269		
		140	40, 255
128:5–6	288	140:3	20

Index of Psalms

141	40, 116, 170, 236, 255, 263, 270	146:10	288
141:2	40	147	8, 44, 184, 187, 205, 212, 224, 227, 270, 278
142	29, 293–4	147:2	288
143	52, 53, 55, 57, 62, 71, 103, 113, 114, 138, 142, 154, 255, 270	148	40, 41, 44, 45, 50, 52, 53, 71, 122, 103, 229, 270, 278, 295, 296
143:2	21	148:13	19
144	117, 236, 269, 277, 278	149	40, 41, 44, 53, 101, 103, 122, 171, 181, 187, 227, 255, 278
144:3	248		
144:9	176	149:2	122
144:15	70, 71	149:7–9	157
145	44, 70, 97, 154, 236, 264, 278, 283	150	40, 41, 44, 53, 57, 103, 117, 122, 136, 170, 182, 186, 187, 212, 223, 224, 227, 236, 237, 239, 240, 277, 278, 281, 292, 293, 300, 303, 304, 306
145:14–20	178		
146	18, 44, 70, 71, 129, 166, 205, 278, 301		
		150:6	175, 299
146:6	20		

Index of Names

Further references to authors can be found in the bibliography on pp. 322–50 and also on www.bbibcomm.net.

Abraham ibn Ezra   82–3, 105, 236
Abraham ben Jacob   164
Ackroyd, Peter   276, 286
Adam, David   287
Adamo, David Tuesday   284
Adhelm of Sherborne   60
Ainsworth, Henry   158
Albertz, Reiner   272
Albright, William   274
Alcuin of York   61–2, 113, 114
Alexander, Cecil Frances   215
Alexander, J.A.   278
Allegri, Gregario   184
Allen, Leslie   276
Alter, Robert   280, 289
Ambrose of Milan   37–8, 40
Anderson, Arthur   276
Andrew St. Victor   88–9, 94, 118
Anselm of Leon   88
Aquinas, Thomas   58, 92, 94, 118
Arno of Salzburg, Bishop   61
Arundel, Archbishop   125
Athanasius   28, 29, 31, 56
Attridge, Harold   279
Auffret, Pierre   279
Augustine of Canterbury   53, 59, 124

Augustine of Hippo   38–9, 56, 57, 58, 62, 76, 93, 95, 99, 113, 114
Auwers, J.-M.   267
Avrohom Chaim Feuer, Rabbi   254

Babbit, Milton   302
Bach, Johann Sebastian   186–7
Bacon, Francis   171, 195, 196
Baethgen, Friedrich   200
Bail, Ulrike   284
Bailey, Mark   264
Balla, Emile   219
Barclay, William   286
Barth, C.   278
Barton, John   258
Basil of Caesarea   30, 41, 45, 50, 52
Baur, Ferdinand Christian   199
Beauchamp, Emile   279
Becket, Thomas à   89
Bede   54, 58, 59–61, 113
Beethoven, Ludwig van   220, 221–2, 239
Begrich, Joachim   268
Bekhor Shor, Joseph   85
Benedict of Nursia   51–2, 56, 59
Benson, Richard Meux, Fr.   214
Berlin, Adele   253, 280
Bernstein, Leonard   304–5
Bernstein, Moshe   244, 280
Beyerlin, Walter   273
Billings, William   161
Bird, William   182–3
Biscop, Benedict   63
Blake, William   217
Blitheman, William (John)   183
Bonhoeffer, Dietrich   282–3, 285
Bourgeois, Louis   142
Brady, Nicholas   153
Braga, Don Solomon di   108
Brahms, Johannes   220, 223–4
Bratcher, Robert G.   252
Braun, Joahim   280
Brettler, Marc   253
Breck Reid, Stephen   280
Briggs, C.A.   198, 203, 267
Briggs, E.G.   198, 203
Britten, Benjanim   300–1
Brown, Francis   203
Brown, William   280
Brueggemann, Walter   272, 275, 277, 278, 280
Bucer, Martin   142
Bunyan, John   173
Burns, Robert   218
Butterfield, William   228

Calvin, John   141–6
Carey, William   234
Carter, Philippe   284
Cassian, John   40, 41, 60
Cassiodorus   56–7, 58, 61, 63, 90, 93, 113, 114, 201
Celestine I, Pope   54
Ceolfrith, Abbot   60, 63
Chagall, Marc   291–3
Challoner, Richard   231
Charlemagne, Emperor   61
Charles I, King   152, 154
Charles II, King   158, 189
Charles V, King   155
Chaucer, Geoffrey   126, 127
Cheyne, Thomas Kelly   198, 202
Childs, Brevard   275, 277
Chrysostom, John   31, 32–3, 40, 45, 50, 51, 55, 257
Cisneros, Cardinal Francisco Xaménez de   129
Claissé-Walford, Nancy de   278, 280
Clement VII, Pope   155
Clement, Bishop of Rome   24–5, 28, 40
Cliff, Jimmy   303
Clifford, Richard   276, 280
Coggan, Donald   286
Cohen, Abraham   253
Cole, Robert   278
Coleridge, Samuel Taylor   218
Columbanus   54
Columbus, Christopher   129
Constantine   43
Coppens, Joseph   274
Cotter, Jim   286
Cotterill, Thomas   229
Cotton, John   158
Coverdale, Miles   135–6, 147, 149, 150, 154
Cowper, William   204, 208–9

Cox, Dermot   286
Cox, Richard   181
Craigie, Peter   276
Cranmer, Thomas   137, 155, 266
Creach, Jerome   276, 287
Crenshaw, James   277
Cromwell, Oliver   156, 189
Crowley, Robert   146

Dahmen, Ulrich   282
Dahood, Mitchell   274, 276
Dale, Ronald   287
Daniel of Salah   56
Davidson, Robert   286
Davies, Irwin   293
Davison, William   219
Day, John   274, 276
Daye, John   150, 151
Decius   43
Delekat, Lienhard   273
Delitzsch, Franz   219–20, 278
Delitzsch, Friedrich   282
Dimmock, Rev H.   199
Diocletian   43
Diodore of Tarsus   31–2, 37
Doddridge, Philip   204, 208
Dombkowski Hopkins, Denise   287
Dominic of Castile, St.   116
Donne, John   174
Drillock, David   264
Driver, Samuel R.   198, 203
Duhm, Bernhard   219

Eaton, John   258, 267, 271, 275, 276, 279
Ebbo, Archbishop of Rheims   64
Edmund of Abingdon   94
Edwards, Jonathan   161
Egeria   42
Eichrodt, Walter   275
Elgar, Edward   224–5
Eliot, John   231–4
Eliot, T.S.   256
Elizabeth I, Queen,   146
Elliott, Charlotte   204, 215
Ephraim the Syrian   34
Erasmus Roterdamus, Desiderius   133–4, 140

Eusebius, Bishop of Caesarea   31, 32, 40, 60
Evagrius Ponticus   34–5, 41

Farmer, Kathleen A.   284
Fassler, Margot   279
Ferdinand III   109
Firth, David   277
Flint, Peter   279, 280
Fokkelman, Jan   280
Formstecher, Solomon   239
Fox, George   204, 205
Foxe, John   147
Freedman, Noel   280
Friedländer, David   235
Frost, David   257
Fry, Elizabeth   205

Gabrieli, Giovanni   183
Galloway, Alec   291
Gascoigne, George   171
Geiger, Abraham   239
Gelineau, Joseph   258, 259, 261
Geller, Stephen   280
Gelston, Anthony   258
Germain of Auxerre   54
Gerstenberger, Erhard   272, 280
Gesenius, Wilhelm   201
Gibbons, Christopher   186
Gibbons, Orlando   186
Gilbert of Poitiers   90, 95, 201
Gillingham, Susan   277, 279
Girard, Marc   279, 283
Goethe, Johan Wolfgang von   217
Gold, Victor   249
Golding, Arthur   146
Gorham, Geoffrey, Abbot   99
Goudimel, Claude,   143
Goulder, Michael   271, 280
Gregory II, Pope   59, 66
Gregory III, Pope   66
Gregory XI, Pope   125
Gregory the Great, Pope   51–2, 53, 56, 58–9, 113, 259
Gregory the Illuminator   49
Gregory of Narek, St.   49, 50
Gregory of Nyssa   30, 32, 36
Grieg, Edvard   226

Grønbech, Vilhelm 269
Grosseteste, Robert 91
Guadalajara, Moses Arragel de 104–5
Gunkel, Hermann 201–2, 268–71, 272, 273, 279
Guzman, Don Luis de 104

Haïk-Vantoura, Suzanne 280
Handel, G.F. 187–8
Harbison, John 306–7
Hargreaves, John 283
Harvey, John 301
Hassell Bullock, C. 277
Haydn, Joseph 221
Haye, John de la 146
Hengstenberg, Ernst 220
Henry I, King 65
Henry V, King 115
Henry VIII, King 156, 168
Herbert of Bosham 89, 95, 118
Herbert, George 174–7
Hertz, Chief Rabbi 244
Hesychius of Jerusalem 35
Hetland, David 291
Hilary of Poitiers 36
Hildegard of Bingen 121–3
Hill, Edmund 283
Hippolytus of Rome 26–7, 40
Holladay, W.L. 1, 279
Homer 32
Hopkins, John 149, 151, 152
Hossfeld, Frank-Lothar 279
Howard, David 267, 278
Howard, Henry 156
Howells, Herbert 298–9
Hugh St. Victor 88, 89
Hunter, Alisdair 279
Hupfeld, Hermann 200
Hussey, Walter 292
Hyde, Edward 158

Inglesby, Paul 287
Irenaeus 25–6, 45
Isabella of Castile 129

Jackson, Gordon 252, 265
Jacob ben Ashur 164

Jacob, Edmond 275
Jacobson, Israel 238
Jaki, Stanley L. 286
James I, King 147, 156
Jasper, R.C.D. 255
Jenkins, Karl 307
Jerome 28, 36–7, 45, 54, 56, 60, 63, 76, 86, 91, 96, 99, 133, 260
Jessing, Michael 295
John XXIII, Pope 260
John Paul II, Pope 288
Johnson, Aubrey R. 267, 271
Johnson, Philip 277
Joseph ibn Hayyim 108
Judah ha-Levi 69
Julian the Apostate 43
Justin Martyr 25, 28

Kant, Immanuel 194–5, 217
Karan, Joseph 85
Keats, John 218
Keble, John 204, 213–14, 215
Keel, Othmar 273
Kennicott, Benjamin 107, 199, 236
Kempis, Thomas à 208
Kethe, William 149
Kimchi, David 85, 86–7, 107–8
Kimchi, Joseph 85
Kimchi, Moses 85
King, Henry, Bishop of Chichester 152
Kirkpatrick, Alexander F. 219
Kitto, John 230
Knight, George 286
Knox, John 153
Knox, Ronald 259
Kodály, Zoltán 301
Kohn, Rachael 307
Kraus, Hans-Joachim 270–1, 275, 276
Kugel, James 280
Kuntz, J. Kenneth 267, 280

Lamb, Charles 218
Langland, William 125–6, 127
Langton, Stephen 91
Laud, Archbishop 154
Law, William 205
Leeser, Isaac 237

Leighton, Kenneth   302
Leo III, Pope,   61, 66
Leon Modena, Rabbi   165
Levi, David   236
Levine, Herbert   290
Lewandowski, Louis   239
Lewis C.S.   256, 285–6
Littledale, R.F.   212
Loeffler, Charles   305
Lohfink, Norbert   279
Lombard, Peter   91, 95
Louis IX, King   97–8
Lowth, Robert   215–16, 217, 236
Loyola, Ignatius   128
Luther, Martin   137–141, 147
Luttrell, Sir Geoffrey   97
Lydgate, John   115

MacMillan, James   301
Madolfo, Carleen   278
Magnussen, Jon   302
Magonet, Jonathan   290
Marbeck, John   146
Marcus Aurelius   43
Marley, Bob   303
Marot, Clément   142
Mary Tudor, Queen   147, 149
Mays, James   276, 27
Matthew, Thomas *see* Rogers, John
McCann, J. Clinton   275, 280
Meer, William van der   280
Meir ben Yitzhak, Rabbi   69
Mendelssohn, Felix   222, 236
Mendelssohn, Moses   224, 235, 239
Merton, Thomas   285
Michaelis, Johann David   199
Mikhail of Smolensk, Bishop   101
Millard, Mattius   276
Miller, Patrick   276, 278, 279, 280
Milton, John   174, 177–80
Misere, Arnold   305
Mitchell, David   275
Monteverdi, Claudio   184
Montgomery, James   218, 229
Moor, Johannes C. de   280
Morley, Thomas   183
Moses ibn Ezra   83

Moses ibn Giqatilah   82, 236
Moses ibn Zabara   108
Mowinckel, Sigmund   269–71, 279
Mozart, Wolfgang Amadeus   225–6
Murphy, Roland   286

Nachman of Breslov, Rabbi   237–8
Naumberg, Samuel   239
Neale, John Mason   204, 212
Newman, John Henry   211–12
Newton, Isaac   196, 234
Newton, John   204, 208–9
Nicholas de Herford   125
Nicholas of Lyra   94, 118
Nogalski, James   268

Olivetan, Peter   141
Olshausen, Justus   198
Origen of Alexandria   24, 28–9, 31,
    36, 45, 56, 76
Osherow, Jacqueline   288–9

Pachelbel, Johann   186
Palestrina, Giovanni
    Pierluigi da   183
Parker Matthew,
    Archbishop   147, 151
Parry, Hubert   229–7
Pärt, Arvo   302
Payne, Benjamin   229
Peter I of Castile, King   109
Peter the Chanter   91
Peterson, Eugene   287
Philip the Chancellor   94
Philo of Alexandria   13, 22,
    25, 28
Pickett, Brian   287
Pious, Emperor Louis   64
Pius V, Pope   155, 166
Pius IX, Pope   259
Pius X, Pope   155
Pius XII, Pope   259
Pleins, J. David   283
Prez, Josquin des   180
Priestley, Joseph   236
Proclus Diadochus   30
Prothero, Roland   1, 219

Index of Names

Purcell, Henry   189
Purvey, John   125
Pusey, Edward   204, 213, 214

Raabe, Paul   280
Rad, Gerhard von   275
Radnoti, Miklos   289
Raikes, Gwynneth M.N.   284
Ran, Shulamit   305
Rashbam   85, 86
Rashi   84, 86, 87, 163
Ravenscroft, Thomas   159, 175
Reich, Steve   305
Reinstra, Marchiene, Vroon   284–5, 294
Reyburn, William D.   252
Richard St. Victor   89
Ricoeur, Paul   272
Robertson Smith, William   198
Rodd, Cyril   276
Rodger, Patrick   286
Rolle, Richard   114, 124
Rogers, John   136
Rogerson, John   258, 287
Rosenberg, David   265
Rossi, Salamone   165, 184, 239
Rous, Francis   153
Rowley, Harold Henry   275
Ruffinelli of Mantua   164
Ruskin, John   204, 210–11
Rutter, John   301

Saadiah Gaon   73–4, 82, 117
Sabourin, Leopold   276
Salmon ben Yeruham   74
Samuel Ben Meir, Rabbi *see* Rashbam
Samuel Halevi Abulafia   109
Sandys, George   152
Schaefer, Konrad   286
Schiller, F. von   217
Schmemann, Alexander   264
Schmidt, Hans   273
Schökel, Alonso   280
Schubert, Franz   220, 224, 239
Schumann, Robert   220, 223
Schütz, Heinrich   184, 185–6
Schutz, Roger   262

Seerveld, Calvin   287
Seybold, Klaus   273, 275, 276, 278
Shakespeare, William   172
Shelley, P.B.   218
Shlomo Yitzhaki, Rabbi *see* Rashi
Sidney, Mary   169
Sidney, Philip   169
Smend, Rudolph   198
Smith, Mark   286
Snaith, Norman   275
Solomon ha-Kohen   164
Solomon ibn Gabirol   69
Spinoza, Baruch   234
Spurgeon, Charles   209–10, 212, 214
Spyridon, Archdeacon   101
Stancliffe, David   258
Stanford, Charles   227
Sternhold, Thomas   149, 150, 151, 152
Strabo, Walafrid   88
Strauss, David Friedrich   199
Stravinski, Igor   302–3
Street, Stephen   199
Stuhlmueller, Carroll   276
Sulzer, Solomom   239

Tallis, Thomas   151, 181–2
Tanner, Beth   284
Tate, Marvin   276
Tate, Nahum   153
Taylor, Kenneth   249
Temple, Archbishop   244
Terrien, Samuel   276
Tertullian of Carthage   26, 27, 40, 45
Théodore de Bèze   143
Theodore of Caesarea   67
Theodore of Mopsuestia   31, 45, 54, 55, 66
Theodoret of Cyrrhus   33, 37, 41, 45
Tickhill, John de   97
Tippett, Michael   300
Tosh, Peter   303
Trajan   43
Tye, Christopher   181
Tyndale, William   134–5, 139, 147

Valentinus   27
Valerian   43
Vallotton, Annie   250

Vaughan, Henry   171
Vaughan Lock, Anne   170
Vaughan Williams, Ralph   298
Vivaldi, Antonio   185, 189–90
Voltaire   196

Wagner, Roger   295–7
Walton, William   299–300
Watson, Wilfred   280
Watts, Isaac   159–61, 206
Weiser, Artur   270–1, 276
Wellhausen, Julius   198, 200
Wesley, Charles   204, 206, 207, 208
Wesley, John   161, 204, 206, 207, 208
Westermann, Claus   272, 277
Wette, W.M.L de   200–1
Whitefield, George   161
Whitney, Isabella   170
Whybray, Norman   279
William of Shoreham   124
Willson, David   205
Wilmot, John   152
Wilson, Gerald   277, 278, 280, 284
Wilson, Guy   307
Winkworth, Catherine   215
Wither, George   151
Wittingham, William   147, 149, 150
Wittstruck, Thorne   267
Woodford, Samuel   171
Wordsworth, William   218
Wragg, Arthur   293, 294
Wright, G. Ernest   275
Wyatt, Thomas   168
Wycliffe, John   125

Xavier, Frances   128

Yannai   69
Yared of Aksum   50
Yefet ben 'Ali Helivi   74

Zenger, Erich   267, 278, 279, 280
Zevit, Ziony   273
Zwingli, Ulrich   141, 147

Subject Index

A History of the Monks in Syria 41
A New Metrical Psalter 262
A Serious Call to a Devout and Holy Life 205
A Translator's Handbook on the Psalms 252
Aachen 61
Abbreviated Psalter (Bede) 60–1, 63
accent 34
accessus 90, 92
acrostic forms 34, 118
Act for the Advancement of True Religion 136

Act of Uniformity 137
Acts of the Apostles 14, 18, 20, 37, 75
Adon Olam 69
Africa
 Africanize psalms 303
 North 37, 38, 43, 49, 73
 South 258
 voyages of discovery 128
 West 234
Against Heresies 25
Against the Jews 26
Against Marcion 26
Against Praxeas 26

akolouthia 30
Aleppo 120
Alexandria 8, 12, 13, 28–9, 30, 36, 39, 46, 50, 72
Alexandrian Codex 29, 31
Alexandrian commentators 28–9, 30, 32, 33, 34, 35, 45, 55–6
Algonquin Indians 231–2
alliteration 171
Alternative Service Book 258
Amazing Grace 208
Ambrosian Rite 38, 42
America 158–62, 203–4, 206
   and Enlightenment 197
   voyages of discovery 128
   War of Independence 161
Amidah 44, 69, 236, 240
Amiens 79
Ampleforth 263
Amsterdam Haggadah 164
Andalusia 83, 85, 111
Anglo-Norman 80, 87, 96
Anglo-Saxon 87
Animadversions 179
Answer to the Jews 26
anti-Semitism 134, 138, 140, 145, 163, 222, 224, 282, 287
Antioch 24, 31, 36, 37, 39, 45, 46, 50, 252
Antiochene commentators 31–3, 35
antiphons 41, 42, 51, 52, 59, 121, 122, 181, 184, 260, 263, 264, 298
Apocalypse of Abraham 13
Apocrypha, the 12, 17, 231, 250, 251
Apologists 24–7, 28, 30, 45
Apostolic Constitutions 40, 55
Apostrophe to Zion 9, 13, 14
Arabic 50, 66, 67, 73, 74, 75, 76, 81, 82, 83, 104, 109, 110, 129, 164
Arabs 73, 82
Aragon 111
Aramaic 11, 16, 34, 35, 43, 56, 68, 69, 71–2, 73, 76, 81, 84, 123, 129, 310
Aramaic Targums on the Psalms 71–2
Arianism 29, 34, 35, 36, 38
archaeology 202, 268
architecture
   cathedral 79, 12–3, 108, 299, 301
   synagogue 108–10

Armenian churches 49–50
   rites of burial 55
art
   Christian 166–8, 293–7
   early development of 76
   illuminated psalters 62–8
   Jewish 75, 163–6, 291–3
   Jewish response to Christian 79
   see also architecture, calligraphy, manuscript illumination, stained glass, woodcuts
Asia 128
assonance 34
Assyrians 32
Athanasian Creed 124
Athens 30, 264
Australian Prayer Book 258
Austria 197, 222, 235

Babylon 5, 11, 32, 36, 46, 71, 72, 73, 74, 107, 111, 115, 119, 270, 273
Babylonian Talmud 69, 72, 164
Baghdad 73
baptism, of Jesus 15, 17, 18, 30, 57
Barcelona 79, 96, 111, 123
Baruch, book of 13
Basel 141
Basra 74
Bay Psalm Book 158, 161
Beatitudes 16
Belgium 197
Belles Heures 104
Benedictine Rule/Benedictines 52–4, 58, 59, 60, 63, 64, 66, 87, 92, 98, 99, 114, 115, 122, 155, 263, 297
Berlin 220, 222, 235, 239, 302, 304
Bethlehem 36, 37, 41
bible translations
   American Standard Version 231
   Authorized Version *see* King James Bible
   Bishops' Bible 147
   Common Bible 251
   Contemporary English Version 251
   Coverdale Bible 135–7, 170, 175, 246, 249, 254, 256
   Douai Rheims Bible 148–9, 155, 231, 247
   English Revised Version 231

bible translations (*cont'd*)
   English Standard Version 251
   Geneva Bible 147–8, 150, 151, 156, 157,
      172, 175, 246
   Great Bible 136, 147, 155
   Gutenberg Bible 167
   Indian Bible 231
   King James Bible 147–9, 172–3, 175,
      231, 234, 236, 246, 247, 248, 249, 25,
      253, 254
   Lübeck Bible 295
   Matthew's Bible 136
   Mozarabic Bible 66, 104
   New English Bible 251
   New International Version 250
   New King James Version 250
   New Living Translation 249
   New Revised Standard Version 250
   Revised English Bible 251
   Revised Standard Version 250
   The Alba Bible 104–5
   The Good News Bible 250, 251
   The Jerusalem Bible 247
   *The Jewish Society Publication
      Bible* 253
   The Jewish Study Bible 253, 254
   The Kennicott Bible 105, 107–8
   The Living Bible 249, 251
   The New Jerusalem Bible 247–8, 260
   The New Jewish Version 253
   *The New Testament and Psalms: An
      Inclusive Version* 249
   Visigothic-Mozarabic Bible 66
Birdshead Haggadah 111
Black Death 124
Blues of the Sky 252, 265
Bobbio monastery 54
Bodleian Library 53, 65, 107
Bologna 163
Book of Common Order 153
Book of Common Prayer 137, 146, 154,
   166, 258
Book of Divine Works 122
Book of Psalms Ainsworth) 158
Books of Hours 103–4, 110, 113, 116,
   121, 166, 167, 204
Booths, festival of 111
Breviaries 70, 103, 110, 120, 121, 166

British and Foreign Bible Society 234
British Council of Churches 255
British Library 63, 67
Buddhism 285
Burford Priory 263
Burgundy 63, 262
Byzantine Empire 50, 263
Byzantine Rite 50–1
Byzantium 46, 49, 66, 68, 101–2, 120
   fall of 79

Cadiz 73
Caesarea 24, 28, 31, 34, 36, 37, 46, 50
Cairo 69, 82
Calligraphy 76, 105, 240
Cambridge 89, 98, 114, 133, 148, 174,
   181, 212, 227, 257, 301
Canada 258
canon-criticism 277
Canonical Hours of Prayer 50, 104, 137
Canonical Hymns and Spiritual Songs 151
cantatorii 42, 121
Canterbury 53–4, 59, 63, 80, 95–6, 102
Canterbury Tales 126, 127–8
canticles 12, 42, 51, 64, 97, 104, 124, 128,
   153, 181, 184, 211, 227, 261, 262
Cappodocia 41, 49
Cappodocian Fathers 30–1, 34, 35, 36, 45
Carolingian Renaissance 61, 62
carpet pages 67, 105, 108
Castille 104–5
Catalonia 96, 111
Cathach of St. Columba 54
Catholic church 55, 79, 114, 124, 135
   artistic representation 166–7
   Calvin and 141
   reform of liturgy 154–5
   version of scripture 231, 247
Carthage 38, 46
catena 10, 20, 22, 91
cathedral
   art and architecture 79
   decline of liturgy 120
   offices 42, 45, 47, 49, 53, 59, 70, 75, 77
   schools 59, 61, 87
   stained glass 12, 108
Chalcedon, Council of 24
Chanson of Alexis 99

Chapel Royal 152, 181, 182, 183, 186, 189
Chartres 79, 80, 87, 90, 92, 102
Chichester 244, 292, 293, 304, 305
choirs 34, 121, 142, 183, 184, 185, 223, 238, 239, 260, 299
choirmaster 8
Christ
   anti-Christian polemic 85–7
   baptism of 30
   bridegroom 207, 210
   and the church 39
   corner stone 22
   the creator 34
   and David 145, 309, 311
   David as type of 211, 280
   David points to 119
   David as prophet of 91
   David superceded by 14, 23, 25, 26
   divine nature 22, 24, 26, 27, 34
   fifth monarchy 179
   goal of all scripture 29
   greater than David 21
   Grieg and 226
   hidden presence in psalms 57, 89–90, 274
   ideal figure 37
   inclusive language and 248
   in Jesse Tree 97, 98, 99, 102
   light of the world 42
   in manuscript illumination 65, 67, 68
   matter of psalms 92, 93
   messiah 20, 26, 56, 81, 86, 311
   moral life of 113
   moral teachings 25
   new David 24
   no mention in Brahms Requiem 223
   not in psalms 84
   passion of 62
   in Piers Plowman 126
   logos 28
   psalms witnesses to 28
   psalms not about 31–2
   relation to gospels 200
   relationship to church 21
   resurrection and ascension 29
   righteous sufferer 21, 24
   Romantics contrast with David 218
   sufferings of 10, 42, 211, 282, 283
   superiority over angels 22
   superior to Moses 23, 86
   two natures 33, 34, 57, 89
   types from life of 35
   voices of 39, 54, 138, 139
   as Word of God 25
Christians
   address Jesus as God 26
   and divergent beliefs 24
   exchange of learning with Jews 80, 239
   as Jews 13–14, 25
   as *minim* 84
   poetic imitation adapted by 310
   shared heritage 311
   tensions of Zionism 288
   under Constantine 43
   use of sacred space 109
Chronicon 88
church attendance 196, 266
Church Fathers
   eastern 24–35
   western 36–9
Church Missionary Society 234
Church of Ireland Hymnal 215
Cistercians 53
Civil War
   English 151, 157–8, 174, 179
   Scottish 156
Cluniacs 53
Codex Amiatinus 60, 63
Codex Brucianus 27
Codex Grandior 63
Codex Vaticanus 8
Cologne 92
Columban Office 54
commentaries 24, 75–6, 219–20
   Calvin 144
   change of emphasis 199–203
   Commentarii in Psalmos (Diodore) 32
   decline of 191
   eclipsed by Calvin's 146
   Qumran 9, 11
Commentarioli (Jerome) 37
Commentary on the Psalms (Eusebius) 31
Commentary on the Psalms from the Primitive and Mediaeval Writers 212 commentators
   Christian 87–94

Commentary on the Psalms from the Primitive and Mediaeval Writers (cont'd)
  decrease in number 131–3
  eastern church 28–34
  Jewish 82–7
  scholastic 90
  western church 35–9
Common Worship 258–9, 260, 261
communication, speed of 230, 246
Compline 41, 53, 229, 260
concert hall 221, 222, 224, 240, 298, 300
Confessing Church 282
Confessions 38
congregation 38, 69, 140, 141, 142, 143–4, 154, 155, 180, 205, 208, 209, 238, 239, 256, 260, 261, 264 *see also* laity
Constantinople 32–3, 34, 36, 46, 50, 52, 57, 58, 61, 67, 72, 79, 11, 163, 252
  fall of 120
Constantinople Midrash 117
Coptic church 50, 55, 67, 252
Cordoba 73, 79, 82, 108
Corinthians, epistles to the 21, 22
Council of Christians and Jews 244
Counter Reformation 148, 168
Coutras, Battle of 157
crusades 79, 84, 85, 98, 120

daily offices 45, 51, 52, 59, 113, 121, 122, 154–5, 229, 255–8, 259, 260, 263
Danes 63
dark ages 63
David – Shepherd, Psalmist, King 210
Day of Atonement 44, 68, 111, 236, 264
De Bello Turcico 134
De Metris et Tropis 60
De Psalmorum Usu Liber 61
Dead Sea Scrolls 9 *see also* Qumran
Declarations of Human Rights 197
Dedication of the Temple, feast of 44
Defence of the Holy Church 115
Deism 195, 220–1, 223, 225
derash 81, 84, 85, 86
Desert Fathers 34, 41
devil, the 16, 26, 29, 163
Dialogue with Trypho 25
Diatessaron 33

Didascalicon 88, 89
Diet of Worms 140
dissenters 149
Disibodenburg 121
disputation and dialogue, Jewish-Christian 80, 86, 15, 123, 131–3, 242
Distinctiones super psalterium 94
Divine Comedy 168
Divine Liturgy/Office 49–50, 54, 59, 104, 120, 264
Doctrine, psalms to support 21, 27, 28, 36
Dominican Order 116
Donatism 39
Dorchester Abbey 103
doxologies 41, 51, 121
Dunbar, Battle of 158

Ecclesiastical History of the English People 60
Ecclesiasticus, book of 13, 215
ecumenism 229, 254–9, 262, 266
Edessa 33, 34, 46, 120
Edinburgh 153, 158, 254
Edomites 82, 84
Egypt 5, 19, 27, 34, 36, 41, 46, 69, 73, 74, 200, 202, 273
Ein' Feste Burg ist unser Gott 140–1
El Libro de las Profecías 129
Elohim 7
Ely 181
empiricism 195
Enarratio in Primum Psalmum 133
Enarrationes in Psalmos 38, 39, 95
England 49, 53, 59–62, 79, 80, 90, 91, 135
  commentators on Psalms 59–62
  cultural language 96
  illustrated manuscripts 95–9
  and Italy 63
English Baptist Society 234
Enlightenment, the 192, 194–7, 199, 201, 204, 206, 211, 217, 219, 220, 230, 242, 266
  Jewish 234–6, 237
engraving 167
Ephesians, epistle to the 22–3
Ephesus, Council of 55

Epistles, Pauline   21–3
Erfurt   186
Ethiopia   42
Ethiopic church
   Jewish influence   50
Eucharist   38, 55, 229, 263
evensong   137, 181
exiles   5–6, 12, 107
exodus   19, 179
Expositio Psalmi   37
Expositio Psalmorum   57, 113
Expositiones in Psalmos (Chrysostom)   33

Faith and Order Movement   255
Feast of Weeks   23
feminist writing   284–5, 244, 294
Ferrara   163, 165
First Lateran Council   123
First Vatican Council   259
Fitzwilliam College, Cambridge   98
Florence   63, 163, 188, 197
florilegium   10, 27, 76
folk culture   217
folk melodies   49
form-criticism   200–1, 272
Four Psalms (Grieg)   226
Fourth Lateran Council   106
Fragmenta in Psalmos   35
France   49, 53, 59, 61, 62, 79, 80, 82, 82, 83, 84, 88–90, 91, 97, 98, 99, 102, 103, 115, 123, 133, 142, 143, 146, 156, 197, 279
French Revolution   217, 238

Galatians, epistle to the   21
Gaonic period   68, 117
Gates of Prayer   265
Gaul   43, 46
Gemara   72
gender-inclusive language   247–9, 250, 251, 254, 261
Geneva   141–4, 147, 149, 153
Genizah   82
Gentiles   21, 26, 39, 45, 84, 119, 139, 238, 239
Gethsemane   16, 102
ghettos   133
Girdle Books   104

Gittith   8, 93, 118–19, 210
glorias   52
Gloria Patri   41
Gloss(es)   31, 35, 47, 54, 56, 61, 63, 64, 65, 66, 67, 72, 76, 83, 84, 85, 87, 88, 89, 90, 91, 93, 94, 95, 96, 99, 105, 113, 114, 115, 118, 119, 124, 126, 130, 136, 137, 140, 146, 147, 156, 199
   musical   123
Glossa Interlinearis   88
Glossa Ordinaria   88
glossaria   61
Gnosticism   26, 27, 28
Golden Haggadah   111–12
Goostly Psalmes and Spirituall Songs   149
Gospels
   historical value   199–200
   John   18–20, 38
   Luke   17–18
   Mark   15–16
   Matthew   16–17, 28, 41
Goths   47
Graeco-Roman setting   24, 34
grammar, Hebrew   73
Granada   73
Grand Tour   197
Great Awakening
   First   161, 204, 206
   Second   204
Great Schism   79
Greece   24, 46, 49, 79, 120, 197, 263, 264
Greek   3, 11, 43, 51
   philosophy   24, 28, 83
   psalm singing in   40
   translation of Psalms into   8–9, 310, 254
   version used in Ephesians   22
Greeks   12, 82
   Origen's concern   28–9
Gregorian Rite   42
Güttenberg Press   103

Haggadah-de-Tehillim   117
Haggadoth   111, 163, 164
Hagia Sophia   120
Hail Mary   116
Halle   188, 200
Hallel   44, 71, 111, 164, 236, 293

Hamlet 173
Hanukkah 264
harmony, four-part 146, 162, 175
Hasideans 12
Hasidim 12, 198, 237–8
Haskalah 192, 235
hazzan 164
Hebrew 3, 9, 22, 28, 37, 43, 51, 214
　in music 303
　word and number meanings 118
Hebrews, epistle to the 15, 21–2
Hellenistic exegesis 22
heresy 24, 30, 34, 36, 38, 115, 135, 203, 259
Hexapla 28, 37, 56
high church reformers 204
Hildesheim 101
Hippo 38
historical criticism 247, 268–71, 277
History of Religions School 201
Hodayot 10
Holocaust 244, 287, 288, 289, 290
Holy Week 42, 184
homilies 24, 28, 30, 32–3, 36, 42, 55, 57, 58, 75–6, 113, 117, 119, 156
Homily on the Psalms 40
hours of prayer 40, 41, 42, 50, 52, 55, 104, 137, 155
Huguenots 157
humanism 194–5, 196
Humiliati 121
Hundred Years War 124
Hungary 197
Hymn of the Three Young Men 12
hymns 37–8, 42, 50–1, 140–1, 142
　ancient 211–12
　of Isaac Watts 159–61
　Jewish 238
　Wesley's 207
Hymns Ancient and Modern 212, 229

Icones biblicae 164
iconoclasticism 62, 66, 75
Imitation of Christ 208
impressionist painters 228
In Inscriptiones Psalmorum 30
In Psalmos Davidicos Commentarii 91

Incarnation, the 29
inclusive language 247–51, 256, 258, 259, 260, 265, 284
India 128
indulgences 114, 138, 142
industrial revolution 196, 207
Institutes of Christian Religion 141, 144
interlinear translation 64
Ireland 46, 49, 53, 54, 56, 116
Irish Psalters 32, 66, 97
Ishmaelites 82
Islam 49, 50, 53, 55, 66, 67, 72, 73, 83, 105, 120
Israel 305, 306
Italy 46, 49, 53, 59, 63, 69, 105, 107, 111, 163, 197, 239
ivory plaques 68

Jansenism 204
Jarrow 59–60, 63
Jerusalem 7, 8, 11–12, 14, 15, 17, 18, 19, 24, 30, 34, 35, 36, 37, 42, 43, 46, 69, 73, 74, 102, 105, 109, 111, 114, 120, 128, 129, 247, 271, 287, 290, 291
Jesuits 128
Jesse Tree 79, 96, 97, 98–9
　in stained glass and architecture 102–3
Jesus *see* Christ
Jewish-Christian discourse/dialogue 45, 89, 94, 239, 242–6, 274, 281–2, 290, 304, 307
Jews
　Ashkenazi 69, 70, 110, 164
　Emancipation of 165, 235
　exchange of learning with Christians 80
　fundamentalist iconoclasm 66, 67, 75
　Hellenistic 8
　interpretation of OT 26
　in Italy 106–7
　persecution of 43, 106–7
　reconciling differences 3
　reconstructionist 265
　resistance to Gospel 20
　Sephardic 69, 70, 110, 164, 165, 236
Joint Liturgical Group 255, 257
Judaism

churches' relationship with 2
Hebrew preserving identity 163
Origen's concern 28
Reform 163, 238–9, 264, 288, 308
Talmudic period 68
Judengassen 133

Kabbalah 81, 237
Karaites 73–4, 75, 76, 82, 83, 84, 105, 117
kathismata 50–1, 263
Keble College 228
Kedushta 69, 70
King Richard II 173
King Richard III 173
Kristallnacht 283, 300

laity 103–4, 116, 121, 125, 140, 142, 143, 144, 190, 210
Lantern of Lizt 115
Laodicaea, Synod of 27, 34
Laon 79, 80, 87, 88, 90, 91, 92, 93, 102
Latin 3, 51, 56, 59, 60, 259
    Bibles and Psalters the norm 125
    psalm singing in 40
    use at Taize 262
Lauds 40, 50, 52, 53, 55, 104, 122, 229, 260, 263
laypersons 60
Le Mans 79
lectio divina 56, 87, 89
lectionaries 256–7
Leipzig Mahzor 111
Lent 50, 13, 175
Letter to Marcellinus 29, 31
Lincoln 182
literary imitation 131, 168–80
Lithuania 237
Little Office of the Blessed Virgin 104
Liturgical Psalter 51, 258
liturgy 1
    Catholic revisions 154–5, 259
    Christian 40–2
    denominational differences 228–30
    Eastern churches 49–51
    experimentation 258
    Jewish 43–6, 236, 264, 265
    Luther's reforming 140

Orthodox 263–4
Western churches 51–5
Livorno 165, 166
Logos 28
Lollards 114–5, 125, 130, 156
Lombardy 49, 121
London Missionary Society 234
Lord's Prayer 116
Luxemburg 79
LXX (see Septuagint)
Lyons 46, 121
Lyra Germanica 215

Macbeth 173
Maccabees, book of 11, 13
Madrid 105
madrigals 165, 182, 183, 185
Magi 26, 11, 104
Magnificat 153, 183, 184, 186, 225, 226
Magyars 63
Mahzor 70, 111, 113, 164
Mainz 84, 167, 292, 293
Malaga 73
Mandeans 27
Manicheans 27, 38
Mantua 163, 164, 165, 184, 239
manuscript illumination 2, 54, 63, 65–8, 76, 95–102, 104–8, 297
    Byzantine influence 101
    Christocentric emphasis 97
    decline of 124, 131, 166–7
    difference of Christian and Jewish 113
    lack of Jewish 75
    reflect social concerns 96, 97, 98, 101
    two styles 64
Marcionism 26, 27
Margaretting 103
Marston Moor, Battle of 157
martyrs 12, 93, 119
Masada 9
Mass, the 59, 121, 122, 128, 140, 155, 181, 182, 184, 190, 260
    Tridentine 183
masses, musical settings to 184
Massachusetts 158, 161
matins 41, 50, 54, 97, 98, 104, 122, 175, 181, 229

376 Subject Index

Messiah   7, 84, 87, 119
  Christ as   20, 26, 81, 86–7, 311
Massoretic Text (MT)   9, 85, 253, 274
Merchant of Venice   173
Mercia   63
Methodists/Methodism   204, 208, 256–7
metre   69, 136, 143, 149, 151–3, 159, 162, 168, 169, 170, 172, 178, 179, 262
Mexico   128
Middle English   2, 114, 124, 125, 127, 128
Midnight Vigil   41
Midrash Tehillim   45, 117, 119, 123, 130
midrashic exegesis   22, 25, 45
Midsummer Night's Dream   173
Milan   37, 38, 46, 121
Miserere Mei Deus   126, 184–5
Mishnah   43–4, 68, 72, 83, 110, 236
Missals   70
mission(s)   230, 231–4, 266
modes, musical   151, 182
monastic communities   41–2, 62, 263
  decline of liturgy in east   120
  founding of new   52
  Rules   52–4
  schools   87
  singing of psalms   58
monks   41, 52, 53
Monkwearmouth   60, 63
monophysites   56
monotheism   82–3, 202, 275
Montanists   27
Monte Amiata   63
Monte Cassino   52
Moralitates super psalterium   94
Moravians   204, 206
Moses, song of   12
motets   180–1, 182, 183, 184, 185, 187, 223, 227, 298
Mount Athos   67, 264
Mount Sabos   120
Mount Studious   120
Mudéjar stuccowork   109
music   3, 59, 69–70, 76, 121, 131, 140–1, 142, 180–90, 220–8, 244, 280, 298–307
  Baroque style   184
  blues   262, 303
  English composers   297–301

  experimentation   185, 190
  jazz   262, 300, 302, 303, 305
  Jewish   164–6, 239–40, 304–7
  as performance   300
  reggae   262, 303, 308
  trio sonata   165
Music for Common Worship I   261
myths   199, 200, 202, 267, 268, 269, 270, 271, 273, 281

Naassenes   27
Nahal Heber   9
Nahal Seelim   9, 14
Naples   92, 197
Narbonne   85
national identity   197, 198
Navarre   82
neo-Platonic philosophy   24, 25, 30, 32, 35, 37
Nestorianism   33, 35, 57
Netherlands   104, 143, 146
New Hymns for all Seasons   261
New Moon, feast of   44
New Year Festival   44, 68
New Zealand   258
nocturn   41
nonconformists   149
None   53, 104, 260
North Africa   37, 43, 49
Norwich   183
Notulae et Expositiones super Psalmos   88
Nova Vulgata   260
numbers   39, 118, 237–8
Nunc Dimittis   153

Office of the Dead   55, 104, 113
Old English   60, 64, 66, 76, 124
Olney Hymns   209
Ordo Monasterii   40
Orléans   141, 157
Othello   173
Oxford   80, 207, 213, 216
  University   125, 148, 203
Oxford Movement   215, 229

Padua   163, 239
pagans   43, 234
papacy   125

parables   17
Paradise Lost   129, 177–8
paraphrase   144, 149, 249
Paraphrase upon the Psalmes of David   152
Paris
    Notre Dame   79
    Sainte-Chapelle   102
    university of   88
Passover   17, 44, 68, 69, 71, 111
Peace of Constantine   42
Peasants' Revolt   124
Pelagianism   33, 35, 38, 39
penance   114
Pentateuch, the   13, 25, 28, 71, 135
    second   73, 117
Pentecost   23, 44
persecution   43
    Diocletion   31
    Jewish   79, 123
    Lollards   114
Persian culture   34
pesher   10, 15, 21, 76, 80, 81
Peshitta   33, 34, 56
pesukei de zimra   70, 236, 240
Peter, first epistle of   22
philology, Hebrew   73, 83
philosophes   196
Phrygia   27
Piers Plowman   126–7, 128, 130
Pilgrim's Progress   173–4, 298
Pindaric odes   172
piyyutim   68, 69, 76, 82, 111, 123, 164, 288
plainsong/chant   42, 50, 59, 69, 122–3, 136, 146, 164, 184, 259, 261
    Ambrosian   38, 59, 76, 262
    Anglican   154, 216, 261
    Fellasha   50
    Gregorian   59, 69, 76, 146, 164, 183, 226, 259, 262, 283, 307
Platonic philosophy   22, 28
Plea for Deliverance   9, 14
pluralism   242, 262, 263, 266
poetry   60, 68–9, 82–3, 168–80, 213, 274, 280
    Hebrew   136, 216, 217, 236
pogroms   282, 288
Poitiers   90
Poland   133, 197, 237, 288

Polychrome Bible on the Psalms   198
Pontifical Bible Commission   259
Portugal   79, 105, 128, 133, 146, 197
Postilla super Psalmos   92, 94
Postilla super Psalterium et Cantica Canticorum   94
postillae   93, 94
Postillae Perpetuae in universam S. Scripturam   94
post-modernism   242
postulants   41, 54
Prato Haggadah   111–13
prayer books   103–4
    Jewish   2, 70, 110–13
    see also Books of Hours
pre-Raphaelite school   228
Prime   52, 53, 55, 104, 229, 260
printing   135, 167
    Jewish presses   163
private devotion   54, 68, 95, 205
    Ruskin's   210–11
proof-texting   28, 30, 53
prophecy   4, 17, 19, 24, 27, 31, 72, 82, 92, 115, 119, 138, 220
prophetic bias   2, 9–11
prosopological exegesis   29, 31, 36, 39, 54
Prymers   103, 104, 113, 121, 137
Psalm Book in Metre   151
Psalm Praise   261, 262
Psalmes of David From the New Translation of the Bible Turned into Meter   152
Psalmodia Christiana   128
psalmoi idiotikoi   27, 38
Psalms
    allegorical use   28, 30, 35, 36, 37, 38, 56, 57, 68, 81
    Alleluia   62
    analogical reading   81
    Aristotelian prologue   92
    of Ascents   7, 61
    Augustine and   38–9
    authoritative use for Jewish Christians   25
    authorship   82, 89, 197–8, 220
    bridge between OT & NT   26
    Christocentric reading   35, 39
    Christological categories   57

Psalms (cont'd)
  Christological interpretation 32, 64–5, 209, 210
  controversial 40, 44
  for critical occasions 229
  cursing 255, 258
  dating of 198, 200, 201, 202, 203, 219, 268
  of David 7
  democratization of 190
  didactic use of 22
    Christian 113–16
    Jewish 117–19
  funeral 55
  gradual 59, 154
  grammatical reading 133
  historical approach to 31–3, 35, 64–5, 68
  imitations of 11–13, 14, 27, 34, 42, 68–9, 161–2, 174, 178, 208
  interfaith human experience 244–5
  introductions to 276–7
  introit 59
  John's use of 18–20
  lament 14, 17, 113, 177
  literal reading 56, 64–5, 81
  literary-critical studies 280
  literary structure 278
  liturgical use 18, 34, 37–8, 40–6, 56, 59, 75
  Luke's use of 17–18
  main types 200–2
  marginalization of 194–7
  Mark's theological use of 16
  Matthew's didactic use of 16
  memorized from liturgy 40
  Messianic 44–5
  metrical 140–1, 142, 149–54
  midrashic use of 20
  moral prophesies 115
  Near Eastern setting 273–5
  number of 9
  overshadowed by Torah 117
  penitential 61, 62, 113, 138, 142
  personal devotion of Bach 188, 189
  philological reading 133
  and political aspirations 129, 156–62, 174, 179
  practical and theological use 283–4, 285
  as prayer 34–5, 82
  prayer book of all denominations 255
  preaching of 141
  private devotional use 61–2, 194
  'proper' 44, 68, 176
  as prophecies 13, 18, 19, 25, 28, 74
    in New Testament 14–23
  and Protestant theology 139
  for public occasions 188, 189
  royal 5, 18, 189
  sacramental discourse 37
  speakers in 31, 36, 39, 54
  theological message of 275–6
  titles 30, 32
  tropological 81
  typological reading 81
  use in monastic rules 52
  utopian imagery from 129
  Zion 5
Psalms and Hymns 215
Psalms for General Healing 237
Psalms for Today 262
Psalms in English Verse 104
Psalms of David Imitated 159, 161, 206
Psalms of Solomon 12
Psalms of the Festival of Bema 27
Psalms to Jesus 27
Psalter(s)
  Amesbury 98
  Anglo-Geneva 150
  Augustine's revision of 38
  Barberini 67
  Becker 185
  biblical 51
  Blanche of Castille 97–8
  compilation of 5–9
  Coverdale's 137, 146, 150, 158, 216, 258
  Douce 65
  Eadwine 96, 124
  Ecusa 258
  Gallican 38, 54, 60, 64, 65, 155
  Genevan 143
  Gorleston 98
  Grail 260
  Great Canterbury 96
  Greek 8, 10

Harley 95, 102
Hebrew 8, 9
ICEL 261
Illuminated 62–8, 79, 102
Imola 98
Ingeborg 97, 102
Irish 54, 66, 97
Khludov 67–8, 101
Kiev 101–2
Lincoln 252
liturgical 51, 258
Luttrell 96–7, 98
Macclesfield 98
Munich 98
New Cathedral 261
New England Psalm Book 159
Old Latin 53
Oxford 213, 261
Pantokrator 67
Paris 32, 66, 76, 124
Parma 105–7, 108, 111, 163
Quincuplex 137
as reading primer 53
Revised 256, 257
Richard Rolle 114, 124
Sidney 169, 170, 172, 174–5, 179
St. Albans 99
St. Louis 98
Sternhold and Hopkins 150–3
Stuttgart 65
Syrohexaplaric 56
Theodore 67–8, 101, 120
Tiberius 98
Tickhill 96–7
Troyes 65
Utrecht 64, 65, 66, 67, 95, 96
Verona 65
Vespasian 63–4, 76, 124
West Midlands 124
Westminster 98
Winchester 98
Windmill 96–7
Psalter in English Verse 213, 214
Psalterium Feriale 51, 60, 64, 70
Psalterium Gallicanum 37, 60, 64, 89
Psalterium Hebraicum 37, 57, 60, 61, 63, 89
Psalterium Romanum 37

Psalterium Vetus 37
pseudo-Bede 91
Purim, feast of 44, 236
Puritans 147, 158–9, 204

quaestio 61
Quakers 204, 205, 251
Qumran 9–13, 14, 15, 16, 17, 22, 74, 274, 277, 280, 310

rabbinic literary traditions 43
Ras Shamra 273–4
Rastafarians 303
reader-response criticism 277
redaction-criticism 277
Reflections on the Psalms 285–6
refrains 34, 274, 280
rejected stone 17, 22
remez 81
Revelation, book of 23
revivalist movements 204–15
Rheims 64, 79, 291, 292
rhyme 34, 69, 140, 149, 151, 153, 168, 179, 187, 213, 214, 262, 290, 302
righteous sufferer 16, 18, 19, 21, 24
Roman Breviary 155
Roman Rite 42
Romans, book of 20–1, 26
Romanticism 217–19, 220–1, 228, 303
Rome 61, 72, 133
  church at 26, 36
  Gregory at 58
  imperial 15, 23, 24, 46, 56
  persecution at 43
  republican model 197
  sack of 155
rosary 116
Rotterdam 133
Rules, monastic
  Rule of Ailbe 54
  Benedictine 52–4, 58, 59
  Masters' Rule 52
  The Monks Rule 54
  The Rule of the Monastery of Tallaght 54

Sabaïtic rites 120
Sabbath liturgy, Jewish 44–5, 123

Salisbury   174, 175
Sapphic model   169, 170
Saracens   63
Saragossa   82
Sardinia   49
Sarum Rite   137
Scetis   41
schola cantorum   38, 59
Scholasticism   61, 89, 90, 95, 124, 125, 133, 146, 199
Scholia (Evagrius)   34
Sci vias Domini   122
Scotland   49, 53, 146, 147, 153, 156
scribes   7, 95, 96
Second Vatican Council   229, 255, 257, 260, 281
secularization   192, 226, 228, 230, 234, 239
Seder   111, 236
Sefirot   237
sensus Judaicus   80
Septuagint   8, 9, 19, 22, 43, 44, 72, 76, 242, 252, 282, 310
seven deadly sins   114, 126
Seville   73, 79
sharakans   49
Shema'   70
Shirburn Castle   98
Shoah   288
Sicily   49, 59
Siddur(im)   70, 264, 265
sigla   69–70
Silex Scintillans   171
singing   69, 142, 161–2, 205–6, 229, 257, 261, 259–60
  a capella   239, 299, 300, 303, 305
  antiphonal   37
  congregational   180
  Sistine Chapel   184–5
  in unison   153, 158, 164
slave trade   208
Society for the Proclamation of the Gospel   232
Society for the Promotion of Culture among the Jews   235
Society for the Propagation of the Gospel   232
sod   81

Song of Deborah   12
Song of Moses   12
Songs of Ascents   9, 55, 129, 277
Songs of the Sabbath Sacrifice   13
Songs of Zion, being Imitations of the Psalms   218
sonnets   168, 170, 175, 179
South Africa   258
Spain   46, 49, 66, 68, 69, 70, 73, 75, 79, 80, 81, 82, 83, 96, 104, 105, 107, 108, 110, 111, 123, 128, 129, 133, 146, 157, 197, 204, 236
St. Albans   101, 114
St. Catherine's monastery   120
St. Denis   79
St. Paul's Cathedral Library   89
St. Victor, Abbey of   87, 88–90
stained glass   79, 102–3, 108, 228, 291–2, 293, 304
stasis   50
state occasions   184, 227
Strasbourg   79, 142
Stromata   28
strophes   34
Studious   67–8, 120
Subiaco   52
Summa de bono   94
Summa Theologica   92
superscriptions   7, 8, 62, 117, 253, 277, 280, 292
Switzerland   141–2, 282
Syria   33, 40, 41, 50, 55, 68, 72, 79, 120, 263, 273
Syriac   2, 9, 11, 32, 33, 51, 54, 55–6, 310
  psalm singing in   40
Syro-Palestine   5, 46, 73

Tabernacles, feast of   44, 272
Taize   262
Talmud   45, 69, 71, 72, 73, 75, 76, 83, 84, 86, 105, 123, 164, 253, 304
Targums   11, 33, 43, 45, 71, 75, 76, 84, 85
taxis   30
Tempest   128
Temple   5, 7, 10, 15, 17, 19, 25, 32, 43, 44, 69, 70, 71, 72, 82, 105, 109, 110, 111, 119, 129, 163–4, 197, 200, 201, 219, 264, 271, 272, 275, 290

temptations   16–17, 176
Terce   52, 104, 260
terza rima   168–9, 289
tetrachord   49
The Book of the Covenant   85
The Book of Psalms or the Praises of Israel   198
The Christian Psalmist   229
The Christian Year   213
The City of God   38
The Collection of Psalms and Hymns   206
The Common Worship Psalter pointed for Anglican Chant   261
The Complete Artscroll Siddur   265
The Daily Office   255, 256, 258, 260
The Dream of Gerontius   224–5
The Faerie Queene   128
The First Epistle of Clement   24–5
The Harder They Come   303
The Laon Gloss   91, 93
The Liturgy of the Hours   260
The Pictorial Sunday Book   230
The Proof of Apostolic Preaching   25
The Psalms: A New Translation for Liturgy   258
The Psalms: Hebrew Text and English Translation   252
The Psalms in Human Life   1, 219
The Psalms: Prayer Book of the Bible   282
The Psalms through Three Thousand Years   1
The Psalter Newly Pointed   261
The Sacramentory   260
The Sayings of the Desert Fathers   41
The Scottish Psalter   149, 153–4, 157, 158, 178
The Seven Penitential Psalms   114
The Seven Psalms   114
The Translation of the Hebrew Prayers and Services into English   236
The War Songs of the Prince of Peace   214
The Way of Holiness   214
The Whole Book of Psalms (Sternhold & Hopkins)   149, 150
The Whole Booke of Psalmes (Ravenscroft)   175
theatre   221, 240, 304–5
Thirty Years War   185

Tobit, book of   12, 13
Toledo   73, 80, 105, 109, 123
Torah   7, 13, 43, 44, 70, 71, 72, 73, 81, 86, 87, 108, 113, 117, 118, 235, 237, 264, 274, 275, 276, 282
Tractarians   211, 214
Tractatus (Jerome)   37
Tractatus super Psalmum   36
transfiguration   15, 17, 18, 35
Translation of Certain Psalms into English Verse   171
transubstantiation   125
Treasury of David   209–10
Trent, Council of   155, 163, 166, 183, 259, 260
Trés Riches Heures   104
Tridentine Mass   183
Trinity, the   26, 83
Trinity College, Cambridge   89
Troyes   79, 84, 85
Tübingen School   199–201
Turkey   49, 79
Turks   120, 134
typology   32, 33, 35, 85, 102–3, 248
Tyre   50

Ugarit   273, 274, 280, 281
Ukraine   237
Uncial script   8, 63, 64
Union Prayer Book   265
university schools   80, 87, 80, 125
usury   30, 65
Utopia   129

Vatican Museum   67
veneration of saints   125
Venice   133, 163, 165, 183–4, 185, 189–90, 197, 304
vernacular
  Jewish liturgy   265
  translation   124–9, 131, 230
verse units/divisions   64, 147
Vespers   41, 50, 53, 55, 97, 98, 104, 120, 190, 229, 260, 263
  Mozart and   225–6
Vespers (Monteverdi)   184
Vetus Itola   37
Victorine School   88–90, 94

vigils 52, 55, 260
Vilvorde 135
Visigoth conquests 49
voyages of discovery 128–9
Vulgate 37, 63, 85, 87, 88, 92, 124, 125, 127, 133, 134, 135, 139–40, 146, 148, 155, 231, 247, 250, 259, 303, 310

Waldenses 121
Wars of Religion 156–7
Wartburg 139
Ways of Singing the Psalms 262
Weeks, festival of 23, 111
Westminster Assembly 178
Whitby, Synod of 60
Wigmore 89
Wisdom of Solomon 12, 14
Wittenberg 137, 138, 139

women 100–1, 143, 144, 169–71, 204, 205, 215, 238, 284–5, 307
woodcuts 295–7
words, importance of 174, 185, 191
Worksop 97
World Council of Churches 255
World Wide Web 246
Worms 69, 84
Worms Mahzor 111, 163–4
worship, public 42

Yahweh 7, 8, 197, 247, 303
yeshivah 84, 89
Yom Layabasheh 69
York 61, 103

Zemirot 123
Zion/ism 5, 134, 238, 287–8, 308
Zohar, Book of 81, 105